Pain Neuroscience Education

Teaching People About Pain

2nd Edition

Adriaan Louw
PT, PhD

Emilio Puentedura
PT, DPT, PhD, OCS, GDMT, FAAOMPT

Stephen Schmidt
PT, MPhysio, OCS, FAAOMPT

Kory Zimney
PT, DPT

The procedures and practices described in this book should be implemented in a manner consistent with professional standards set for the circumstances that apply in each situation. Every effort has been made to confirm accuracy of the information presented and to correctly relate generally accepted practices.

The authors, editor and publisher cannot accept responsibility for errors or exclusions or for the outcome of the application of the material presented herein. There is no expressed or implied warranty of this book or information imparted by it.

Designed and published by OPTP.
3800 Annapolis Lane N #165
Minneapolis, MN 55447
800.367.7393 | OPTP.com
Copy edited by OPTP.
All images from Adriaan Louw, unless otherwise noted.

ISBN # 978-1-942798-11-8

Foreword

By **Mark A. Jones** Cert PT, BS (Psych), Grad Dip Advan Manip Ther, MAppSc (Manip Physio), Program Director, Master of Advanced Clinical Physiotherapy, School of Health Sciences, University of South Australia

It is a privilege to write the foreword to the second edition of *Pain Neuroscience Education*. I have known the authors for many years and am inspired by their dedication and contribution to physical therapy through their teaching, research and publications. I will provide a brief biography of myself to enable readers to appreciate the context from which my views developed, followed by my opinion on the importance of critical thinking and reasoning to the integration of pain science into physical therapy practice as promoted in this book.

I initially studied psychology at the University of Florida with an emphasis on behavioral science and therapy. Torn between continuing this direction to qualify as a psychologist versus pursuing my competing interest in physical therapy related to my father (physical therapist and head of physical therapy schools, University of Iowa then Florida International University), I chose physical therapy and completed my training at the University of Iowa. I was fortunate to begin my physical therapy career surrounded by experienced and highly skilled clinicians who had completed postgraduate manual therapy programs, including Tom Holland, Joe Farrell, Bob Johnson and Terry Olson. Their mentoring and a presentation on "Neural Tension" by the late Bob Elvey inspired me to travel to Australia to undertake my own postgraduate study under Geoff Maitland. That proved to be a year that would significantly shape my thinking, my practice and, eventually, my teaching. At a time when Universities were less of a business requiring large classes to operate, we had a class of nine students. This enabled greater time for developing clinical skill and knowledge alongside current biomedical theory. My classmates included Louis Gifford and David Butler who, like me, survived an intensive year trying to master the thorough examination, manual skills and way of thinking inherent in the "Maitland Concept."

It is easy in hindsight to critique limitations in previous practice and teaching based on contemporary understandings. While our learning that year was biased to joints and neural tension (over soft tissue, motor control/strength, pain science and psychosocial factors) it was Maitland's insistence on a systematic and comprehensive patient examination, with a balance in clinical judgments being informed by physical signs and symptoms and patho-anatomical research evidence, that sparked my interest in clinical reasoning.

Louis and David collectively and individually went on to make significant contributions through their professional development courses and publications to the translation of pain science to physical therapy practice. Louis' courses, lectures and his *Topical Issues in Pain* books 1-5, and later his *Aches and Pains* books, facilitated a change in physical therapists' thinking around the world to see their patients' pain and disability as more than symptomatic tissues associated with pathology, pathomechanics and physical dysfunction.

David promoted the same shift in thinking in his teaching and his books *Mobilisation of the Nervous System, The Sensitive Nervous System* and his two *Explain Pain* texts. Louis and David (and others, for example the late Max Zusman from Perth, Western Australia) inspired physical therapy academics worldwide to revise their curricula to include pain science within a biopsychosocial framework. David in particular was singlehandedly responsible for this shift in thinking and teaching in our University of South Australia postgraduate program. Following Maitland's and then Patricia Trott's retirements I had taken over as Program Director and David developed and taught what was likely one of the first postgraduate manual therapy program subjects on Pain Mechanisms. Louis' and David's pioneering contributions were far from just a passing fad with numerous academics and researchers, for example Paul Watson, Mick Thacker, Lorimer Moseley, Jo Nijs, Adriaan Louw and Emilio Puentedura, to name a few, echoing and extending their teaching.

Evolution in physical therapy thinking and practice has occurred throughout the history of our profession, underpinned by a combination of open-mindedness and critical thinking. Critical thinking is inherent in evidence-based practice but also in the skilled clinical reasoning required to apply evidence and theory to practice and the exploration in practice that precedes research validation. The importance of clinical reasoning to professional competency and capability is evident in the errors in human judgment that have been shown to mostly be linked to assumptions leading to premature, biased conclusions with incomplete analytical deliberation and incomplete consideration/testing of alternatives.[2,4] Assumptions are enmeshed in beliefs and practice biasing our (and our patients') perceptions, analysis and actions. Early manual therapy training was biased by the biomedical model and assumptions regarding pathology, tissue dysfunction, biomechanics and physical explanations for pain, disability and how manual therapy worked. These beliefs are now recognized as incomplete.

Incomplete beliefs unfortunately led some to totally discard prior understandings and practice in favor of new beliefs and practice. This is evident in those physical therapists who completely abandon prior physical/manual therapy rather than integrating new theory and practice with revised understanding of the mechanisms by which pain, disability and effective therapeutic interventions operate. Using new understandings to revise, not simply discard, prior beliefs leads to transformative learning and revised practice.[5] Tensions evident in physical therapy forums debating the ascendance of psychosocial, education, hands-off focused therapy over physical, education, hands-on focused therapy seem to reflect this dichotomy between the biological and the psychosocial and between pain science and biomedical science. Interestingly, despite critique of Maitland's bias to manual therapy and joint treatment, his original "brick wall" concept explicitly acknowledged the limitation of knowledge, including research-based knowledge,[3] and I am confident he would applaud the biopsychosocial and pain science shift in thinking Louis, David and this book promote.

The biopsychosocial philosophy of health highlights the multifactorial nature of pain and disability reflecting the scope of knowledge, assessment, clinical reasoning and management physical therapists require. While practice must be informed by research generated theory and clinical guidelines, application of theory and research to practice requires thorough assessment and analysis of all potential physical, psychological, environmental and social factors comprised in patients' individual presentations. The importance of skilled biopsychosocially driven clinical reasoning to evidence-based practice is well captured in the following quote:

> "Scientific method focuses on one variable at a time across a hundred identical subjects to extract a single, generalisable 'proof.' Clinical practice deals with a hundred variables at a time within one subject in order to optimize a mix of outcomes intended to satisfy the particular subject's current needs and desires."[1]

The authors' *Pain Neuroscience Education* text is a wonderful example of integrating new knowledge into practice without completely discarding all prior knowledge and practice. Their significantly updated chapters on "Cognition and Pain," "The Neuroscience of Pain," and "The Bigger Picture of Pain" provide excellent contemporary overviews of pain theory essential to inform patient assessment, reasoning and management. Their chapters on "Patient Education," "Teaching People about Pain," "Clinical Implementation of PNE" and "Putting it All Together" combine research evidence with their own vast personal, experience-based evidence to applying pain science theory in practice. One of the greatest challenges in education is facilitating the translation and application of theory to practice. Theory alone is insufficient to change practice as learners need help in seeing what it actually looks like when applied in patient assessments; help in using integrated theory when making clinical judgments and help in using theory to inform management. This is exactly what these chapters and the book as a whole provides; an extremely useful bridge between theory and practice that equips readers with pain neuroscience education strategies they can use in their own practice.

Reference

1. Cox, K (1999) *Doctor and patient: Exploring critical thinking*, University of New South Wales Press, Sydney.
2. Jones, MA (in press for 2018) Clinical Reasoning: Fast and Slow Thinking in Musculoskeletal Practice, In: Jones MA and Rivett DA (eds) *Clinical Reasoning in Musculoskeletal Practice*, 2nd edn. Elsevier.
3. Jones MA 2014 Clinical reasoning: from the Maitland Concept and beyond. In: Hengeveld E, Banks K (eds), *Maitland's Vertebral Manipulation, Management of Neuromusculoskeletal Disorders – Volume One*, 8th edn Churchill Livingstone/ Elsevier, Edinburgh, p 14-82.
4. Kahneman, D (2011) *Thinking, Fast and Slow*. Allen Lane, London.
5. Mezirow J (2009) Transformative learning theory. In: Mezirow J, Taylor EW, and Associates. *Transformative Learning in Practice: Insights from Community, Workplace, and Higher Education*. San Francisco, CA: Jossey-Bass Wiley: 18-31.

Foreword

By **Louis Gifford**
FCSP Chartered Physiotherapist

I'm honored to have been asked to write the foreword for this book. The authors were interested in my "pain journey," and both have kindly acknowledged the influence of my "Mature Organism Model" on their clinical practice in the 1990s and their subsequent teaching. This book, *Pain Neuroscience Education*, gives me a strong sense of personal satisfaction. Let me tell you why.

After completing my physiotherapy training, I always knew I wanted to specialize in the treatment of musculoskeletal pain. My father was a big influence – a physiotherapist, a natural communicator and a manual therapist who'd learned his trade from osteopaths and bone setters in the late 1940s and 50s. He was an impressive operator and my observations of him in work mode as a youngster left me in awe. I came to realize that he was way ahead of his time – not only for his exceptional hands and people skills but also for his diagnostic brilliance combined with his ability to instill physical confidence in his patients.

My father's influence led me to get immersed in manual therapy, and within four years of qualifying as a Chartered Physiotherapist, Philippa Tindle and I moved to Adelaide, Australia to study and complete our Graduate Diploma in Manipulative Therapy. This was 1985. Being taught by Geoff Maitland was a dream come true and I learned a great deal in the program and afterward working in Geoff's practice for a couple of years. One of the greatest things I learned from Geoff Maitland was his incredible ability to listen and communicate with his patients. However, manual therapy wasn't all I thought it was, and I felt a quietly growing skepticism and desire for rational explanations. I wasn't seeing the results I expected, especially with the large population of patients with chronic whiplash-associated disorders and repetitive strain injuries that frequented Geoff's practice. Due to the very nature of manual therapy, their problems were effectively reduced to some spinal joint "comparable sign," their range of movement to pain was observed, a very specific mobilization technique was performed and the range was reassessed. The range to pain invariably improved and the technique was repeated a few times during the session, and then the process was repeated. Patients were often seen three times a week, week in and week out, month in and month out. I cannot ever recall exercise of any relevance being given to the patient. The treatment was entirely passive, and there was no patient responsibility in the whole process. The brunt of all therapist-patient interactions was in communicating the symptom behavior during the range of movement assessment. To me, the symptoms were very cleverly "played with," but the patient never moved on.

Remember, to provide a little fairness and balance, we didn't know then what we know now. Reflecting, I now realize that I'd stumbled on a significant truth that would hugely influence my future. This was that chronic pain, or maybe even all pain, lacked an adequate explanation. The tissue- and biomechanical-centered explanations and the biomedical model that we were taught just didn't explain the broken lives and madly complicated body charts I continually witnessed!

Thanks to the course and Geoff, what I was learning and getting much better at was skilled physical examination of musculoskeletal tissues and the ability to think, reason and communicate at the level of knowledge we had back then.

In the early 1980s in the UK, and while in the course in Adelaide in 1985, we were all learning the latest "neural provocation" tests pioneered by the late Bob Elvey for the upper limb, and the slump test pioneered by the late Geoff Maitland. What contemporary therapists now call an "upper limb neurodynamic test" was called the "Brachial Plexus Tension test of Elvey" and many of the students in the Adelaide manipulative therapy program studied normal responses of these tests for their research projects. I'm mentioning this because it was probably the start of a wider, bigger and better integration of science into manual therapy. David Butler, in particular, stands out and, as most now know, made a massive contribution by researching and integrating nerve biology, physiology, mechanics and many "new" neural tests and treatment techniques in the later 1980s and early 1990s. David, along with Mark Jones, whose work on clinical reasoning is well known, were both classmates of mine on the 1985 course.

During the few years that followed the course, there was a heightened atmosphere of "new direction" with the Adverse Mechanical Tension (AMT) analysis of chronic arm symptoms in patients with repetitive strain injuries and whiplash. David was responsible for a plethora of new AMT tests (since called neurodynamic tests) and later went on to publish his first book, *Mobilisation of the Nervous System*. Here, at last, was a scientific and rationally based attempt to try and make better sense of those complex patients.

I have to say I enjoyed the fresh look at nerves as a "moving" tissue, but in all honesty, I was never entirely convinced that adverse nerve mechanics and abnormal nerve movement was enough to account for the chronic pain symptom pictures I continued to puzzle over. My experience with these new techniques for repetitive strain injury and whiplash, while exciting to start with, still seemed to amount to "playing with the symptom responses." It was still passive manual therapy but applied to a "new" tissue.

Philippa Tindle and I headed back to the UK in early 1988 where we both took over the family practice in Cornwall. I remained in contact with David, who by the early 1990s was travelling far and wide teaching AMT courses and bringing an exciting new era to physiotherapy. I occasionally assisted him on his courses when he was in Europe and the UK, and it was during one of these in Holland that I started reading a chapter by the late and famous pain scientist, Dr. Patrick Wall. The chapter title was "Neuropathic pain and injured nerve: central mechanisms."[1] It changed my professional life because it explained how the central nervous system could plastically change if it was given enough of an incoming "afferent barrage" from an injured nerve or from inflamed and damaged tissues. These plastic changes could result in impulse barrages being self-generated from within the CNS, which then could result in massive spreads of inappropriate sensitivity and a massive enlargement of receptive fields.

This was a far better explanation for chronic whiplash and repetitive strain injury related pain! Pain and spread of pain not coming from the tissues but being generated in a maladaptive fashion from within the CNS! Wow! The pain meant nothing, it was useless, and this revelation meant that I suddenly lost my clinical fear of it. This was what I was going to tell my patients! No need to fear the pain. You're not broken; your pain processing system has gone mad!

These passive treatments that I'd rather denigrated as mere "playing with pain," I realized now were merely "playing with processing!" I immersed myself in the literature, firstly of central mechanisms and then later, seeing the biological similarities, in the biology of memory. I actually met with Patrick Wall and we both agreed that the central pain mechanisms and the biology of memory were vastly similar, something he hadn't really thought about! I also enjoyed much discussion with the memory biologist Steven Rose, whose book *The Making of Memory* was hugely influential. Memory involved synaptic plasticity in representational neural networks and increasing efficiency of those synapses – in effect, the formation of a memory was the formation of new neural circuit – and so was pain.

For me, chronic pain was like an "annoying tune" playing in your head, and this became very easy to explain to receptive patients. It also dawned on me that once something was committed to memory it was very hard to get rid of, and the same applied to ongoing chronic pain. Doing pain-focused passive manual therapy techniques to patients in 20-minute time slots was hardly enough to erase a pain memory! An exciting voyage of understanding and implementing had started. Those chronic pain presentations were beginning to make sense and a massive shift in my treatment and management strategies was clearly required.

Over the next two to three years, I obsessively reveled in the pain, memory, phantom-limb, placebo, and stress literature and started to integrate what I was learning into clinical practice. I started teaching the "Clinical Biology of Aches and Pains" courses and so began my shift away from the purist manual therapy and passive dominated approach to pain problems. I sensed freedom and was excited by what I was discovering.

Clinically, one of the big things I started to do was spend plenty of time with the chronic pain patients, not only listening but also getting them to try and see their problem from a different perspective. Without really knowing it I was getting patients to shift their thinking about their problem from one of "there's something seriously wrong with me... nobody's found the cause yet... when they do...they'll be able to fix what's wrong and I'll be better...." to one of "there's a flaw in my processing system.... the tissues have healed.... they're safe to start loading...the pain has remained on when it shouldn't have."

A few patients changed massively. They lost their concern and fear, and with guidance started to unlearn all the bad overprotective movement patterns and get active and fitter. They got their lives back together. Some got fitter than they had ever been. I was starting to change a few lives, and my confidence was growing. Pain mechanisms made it all make sense, yet in a passive therapy dominated world I felt very alone. In my "Aches and Pains" lectures, I introduced the pain science and meshed it with the ways I was explaining things to patients. I tried to get my audience of professionals to shift their thinking – which, for the most part, proved to be harder than shifting it with my patients!

The key was to demonstrate using real patients. Information doesn't change many people's hardened beliefs, but witnessing change certainly can. I think it was around 1994 or 1995 when David Butler and I decided to start teaching a five-day course together using patients. The course was called "The Dynamic Nervous System" and attracted a great many physiotherapists who were really expecting, at least in those early days, an "advanced" Butler AMT mobilization course with Louis Gifford assisting. Well, what they got from me was pain mechanisms, the integration of pain into clinical reasoning and me out in front with a live patient with chronic pain. I delved deeply into all the dimensions of their problem, examining them and then spending a great deal of time explaining their pain problem with the aim of shifting their thinking from "my problem means I'm damaged in some way, I cannot move on..." to "my body has healed but my pain processing system is at fault..."

I saw the patients over three days of the course and spent a great deal of time with them. Many of the patients made massive changes and, thankfully, helped many of the entrenched manual therapists to grasp what I was about. I still hear from course participants that the course and the patients I grappled with were clinical life-changers.

Pleasingly, David saw what I was up to and came along. Those early courses in a way were a mismatch. I was emphasizing "hands-off and start talking" – or at least top-down (get the head right/accepting) before bottom-up (doing any form of physical treatment). David was still emphasizing hands-on, teaching the tension tests and all the neural mobilizing sliders and tensioners that were all the rage then. Over the few years we taught the course, David also immersed himself in the pain literature and the course became more balanced with the passive mobilizing being placed much more comfortably and with less emphasis. Pain mechanisms were integrated into clinical reasoning. Time and again the course feedback indicated that it was the live patients and David's "Pain, art and politics" lecture that left a deep impression, hugely challenged their beliefs and shifted them to see a much bigger picture.

By 1997 or 1998, we were taking the course all over Europe but also to South Africa and back to Adelaide! I can remember Lorimer Moseley in the Adelaide audience as well as a great many of the well-established manual therapy heavies there. As many of you will know, and will read about in this book, Lorimer went on to do a great deal of impressive research on pain education and also co-authored the *Explain Pain* book with David. UK-based physiotherapist Mick Thacker added a massive amount of key declarative knowledge and was a great supporter of our exciting and revolutionary mission!

The integration of psychosocial factors into clinical practice forged ahead in the UK with the formation of the Physiotherapy Pain Association, the publication of its work in the "Topical Issues in Pain" series and later university-run courses headed by physiotherapists who were awarding Masters in Pain Science and Pain Management. The integration of Cognitive Behavioral Therapy (CBT) into mainstream physiotherapy has become significant.

In the last 15-18 years, there has been a pain revolution in physiotherapy, which I feel honored to have played a small part in. *Pain Neuroscience Education* is an excellent place to begin the journey of learning and change that started back in the early 1990s for physiotherapy and physical therapy. I hope this book sells worldwide and is soon considered as essential reading – not only for the naive and budding undergraduate but also for those who teach and educate and those whose role is to deal with the difficult and stubborn problem that is acute and chronic musculoskeletal pain.

For me this book represents something special. I worked very hard trying to understand pain in those early days. I worked hard trying to explain it to my colleagues and I worked very hard in explaining it to my patients. It is with a great sense of personal satisfaction that a very big part of my professional life – explaining and teaching about pain – has now gotten such excellent support from the research and clinical community. The authors have distilled and presented a great deal of this and their own research, and provided a first class guide to starting out on the "explaining" voyage that is such an important part of good pain management.

I would like to finish with a simple appeal. When I first started teaching the "Clinical Biology of Aches and Pains" courses in 1993, I used to put a slide up with this on it:

"When I go to my doctor, I have four questions that I'd like answered...

- 'Doc, what's wrong with me?'
- 'Doc, how long's it going to take to get better?'
- 'Doc, is there anything I can do to help myself?'
- 'Doc, is there anything that you can do to help me?'"

Louis Gifford writing the foreword to *Pain Neuroscience Education* – May 3, 2013: Fowey Cornwall. Image from Phillipa Tindle.

If your treatment approach embraces these four questions and gives understandable answers that are based on rational medicine, science, and biology, then you're doing a great service to the patient. Remember, every pain problem, acute or chronic, has a thinking, reasoning and emotional brain attached to it. Enjoy and study this book; it will help you hugely.

Louis Gifford
FCSP Chartered Physiotherapist
May 5, 2013

Reference

1. Wall, P. (1991). Neuropathic pain and injured nerve: Central mechanisms. *Br Med Bull*, 47(3): 631-643.

Preface

A Day in the Clinic with Louis Gifford

Philippa Tindle, BSc, BA, MCSP, HPC
Chartered Physiotherapist

Firstly, congratulations to the authors for the second edition of *Pain Neuroscience Education* and secondly, thank you for inviting me to add to Louis' original foreword. I was lucky enough to meet and train with Louis in 1978 and then live with him from 1981. We worked together in our clinic from 1988 to 2013, until he stopped clinical work in May 2013 to write his *Aches and Pains* books. Louis died in February, 2014.

Adriaan asked me, "What was a clinic day like with Louis?" Great fun, but also a challenge and hard work because Louis always strived to learn something new each day! This could range from a better way to explain the patient's pain (in their words and framework) to working through a movement that was impossible in one starting position to finding a solution that was more functionally relevant and easier to achieve (a lot of dancing went on in our clinic!).

So here are some of Louis' "tips from the coal face":

Be prepared

Louis' day started early. It was important to him to read through each of his patient's notes, however long it took, so that he was fully prepared for the patient encounter. He wanted to be confident with the details of each individual and he strived to fully understand the patient's beliefs and understanding of their problem and how he was going to help them.

Listen and hear

I now have the privilege of being able to read 25 years of Louis' past patient notes. I can look at the body chart, read his hand-written notes (with shorthand!), visualize the patient, fully understand their problem and the direction Louis took their treatment and the reasoning why – remarkable note-taking with the nuances of the patients' language and pain descriptions in full. There are no wasted words – everything notated was significant and could be referred back to. He used a pen and paper for this (although he could type very quickly) as it allowed him to run with the patient's narrative easily, flipping from body chart to notes while still listening and keeping eye contact with the patient. He sat on a stool with the notes resting on the plinth, and the patient was alongside, safe and secure. Everybody was treated with equal care and consideration.

Get the patient on your side – empathy and understanding

Louis always said that the initial consult was the key encounter; listen and hear the patient's story, put the patient at ease and show them that you understand their problem and what they want. I love to talk and Louis would often say to me, "Let the patient talk!" Even now when I'm assessing a new patient I can still hear his words! (In my defense, and if I was quiet with a patient, he would also ask, "What was wrong with you today?"). After the first interview Louis would be pretty confident that he could answer What's wrong? How long? What can I do for myself? What can you do for me? The subjective led to a relevant but thorough physical examination (you might be the first clinician to do this well) and then give simple, non-threatening explanations of findings. I do remember way back in the early days of "explaining pain" Louis gave out handouts that were probably too complicated, and in later years he definitely simplified these explanations (think input, processing and output). Confidence that hurt doesn't mean harm was a real game changer too.

Thanks to Louise Nicholettos, a chartered physiotherapist who has worked with us since 2009, who recently wrote these words about Louis.

> "For me Louis' magic ingredient was genuinely caring about his patients. His enthusiasm for his job was infectious. As a clinician, his subjective interview skills were something that really stood out. He would put the patient so completely at ease, such that they told him everything, including the real cause and the solution to their problem."

"Make it easy" and "little and often" – (Graded activity)

Louis also had the skills and enthusiasm to "sell" exercises and movements to patients. He made them relevant to the problem. He negotiated dosage, achievable goals and then made them fun. He got on the floor and did exercises with patients. He even ran and walked with others. And when the patient re-visited he checked the exercises out and changed them, giving them even more value and relevance. There are many individually designed "stick men" exercise and movement sheets drawn by Louis that patients tell me they still do daily because they "make a difference." Louis would always be inventive with exercises and help patients prove their use.

Belief and optimism – "BO"

> A day in our clinic with Louis could bring both tears and laughter, not everybody was "fixed" but everybody was heard and cared for, everybody was given the time they needed and the starting tools to help them recover and rehabilitate.

Sometimes they weren't ready for change and went away to return later when they were. Some only needed one consult to diagnose, re-assure and give permission to get going again with confidence and the knowledge of the normal timeframe of recovery. Louis had all the clinical skills to adapt to anybody's needs. And as our great friend Dr. Mick Thacker said, "Patients are better treated the world over because of Louis' influence on the physiotherapy profession." We all miss him.

Phillipa Tindle
January, 2018

From the Authors

Our original goal for writing this text was to create a single, user-friendly resource for clinicians and students learning to apply pain neuroscience education (PNE) in the treatment of patients with chronic musculoskeletal pain complaints. We have taught seminars and presented at professional conferences on this topic for several years. In the last 10 years, we have conducted and published dozens of research papers on various issues pertaining to PNE. Our research, clinical and teaching experiences told us that this information needed to be shared not only within our particular profession, but with all clinicians and personnel involved in patient care. Ultimately, we wanted to make PNE accessible and relevant for clinicians to be able to implement it in their clinical practice. Of course, once we began the process of writing this textbook, we realized it was easier said than done. We hope this final product achieves our original goal.

PNE contains chapters that provide sufficient information about the neurobiology and neurophysiology of pain to allow all clinicians engaged in patient care to understand and apply the concepts within the framework of movement-based treatments. The "biopsychosocial approach" in the treatment of persistent musculoskeletal pain complaints has gained much deserved prominence in clinical practice, but we fear that most clinicians may be wary of becoming de-facto psychologists in the process. This textbook emphasizes the value of adding PNE to your regular clinical practice, not replacing it with an education-only approach.

In Chapter 1, we point out that clinicians are seeing more and more patients with chronic pain problems and how the current models of evaluation and treatment have been ineffective and insufficient. We stress the impact of cognitions on pain and, conversely, how chronic pain can adversely affect cognitions, beliefs, emotions and behaviors. Changing faulty patient cognitions regarding their pain is imperative for movement-based treatment to be effective, and we argue that therapists are capable and ideally situated to address faulty cognitions.

Chapter 2 provides all the details you need to know about PNE, including its evolution and the evidence for its effectiveness. We also report the latest evidence for PNE addressing pain, disability, fear-avoidance, pain catastrophization, movement and healthcare utilization. Additionally, in line with the new systematic review of PNE, the chapter showcases significant insight into the content, delivery methods, duration, frequency, and other aspects of its provision. In this chapter, we point out that our traditional biomedical education models have not been found to be helpful and might, in fact, make pain worse. We also note that the compelling evidence for a PNE approach gives us some direction and guidance regarding its clinical application.

In Chapter 3, we demonstrate how learning and understanding pain neuroscience and neurophysiology can be readily achieved through the analysis of the questions posed in the Neurophysiology of Pain Questionnaire (NPQ), the revised NPQ (rNPQ) and Louis Gifford's Mature Organism Model (M.O.M). In this second edition we use the M.O.M and the various biological and physiological processes and systematically update the reader's knowledge of pain science. Additionally, each section showcases the various NPQ and rNPQ questions and answers, further helping clinicians develop a deeper and richer understanding of how pain works. We make the point that pain is not a simple matter of input. Pain is much more complex but our ever-increasing knowledge of how pain works can help us transfer a deeper understanding to our patients.

In Chapter 4, we argue explaining how pain works to a patient in pain can be made easier through the use of patient-friendly language, images, stories and metaphors. This chapter features an extensive rewrite of the original textbook, adding numerous new metaphors, examples and stories to explain pain to patients. The chapter uses patient language and teaches clinicians step-by-step how to explain complex pain issues such as central sensitization, spreading pain, pain neuromatrix, immune responses, neuroplasticity and more. All stories and metaphors are accompanied with new drawings to facilitate the learning process. This is our "how do you actually do it (PNE)" chapter.

Chapter 5 covers important clinical application guidelines to ensure success with a PNE approach. The new textbook features an extensive rewrite and addition of various new clinical application sections, including the screening of patients appropriate for PNE, telehealth, group PNE, billing, documentation, etc. We discuss the importance of time to ensure that the education can be provided but also the cost-effectiveness aspects of providing that time. Also covered are billing issues, training of clinical staff, development of tools and props to enhance the education and the various outcome measures available to measure progress with the approach. The importance of combining PNE with other therapeutic modalities is emphasized, especially exercise or movement-based therapies. We also briefly discuss the importance of "deep learning" and some of the strategies currently available to promote it. Chapter 5 also explores the world of behavioral medicine in light of PNE, including stages of change models, motivational interviewing principles, etc.

In Chapter 6, we present the bigger picture of pain and emphasize the various biological body systems that are engaged to protect during a pain experience. We feel this topic is extremely important for the patient with chronic pain to learn, as it can provide insight into why they might feel, act and behave in the manner that they do. It can be truly liberating for a patient in chronic pain to receive biological explanations for the various experiences associated with their persistent pain. The chapter provides guidelines for treating patients with chronic pain by addressing those biological body system changes and makes the point that understanding why a patient might have persistent pain can open so many avenues for treatment options. Clinicians need not be stumped and left wondering what they can do when confronted with a patient with chronic pain. PNE opens many doors for treatment options and leaves clinicians realizing they can offer so much more to their patients than just exercise and simple reassurance. The outflow of the current research and the mainstay of Chapter 6 is the PNE+ program. PNE is effective, but when combined with other therapeutic treatments (the behavioral part), its efficacy is increased. Chapter 6 shows how more than 20 therapeutic treatments, part of the PNE+ program, can naturally start and enhance the endogenous mechanisms as a means to build an anti-opioid program.

Finally, in Chapter 7, we provide a conclusion, summary and some thoughts on the future direction of PNE, specifically focused on preemptive PNE. With the growing evidence for PNE treating chronic pain, new emerging research is showing its benefit as a preemptive treatment for surgery, acute pain, general population, etc. We showcase the exciting research in this area pertaining to lumbar surgery, knee replacement surgery, shoulder surgery, acute low back pain and middle school children.

None of us knew about how pain actually works until we attended a few seminars and presentations from leaders in this field. Until we had heard the messages from Louis Gifford, David Butler and Lorimer Moseley, our practice was stuck in the manual/mechanical therapy paradigm. We had our share of successful outcomes, but equally, we were left distressed by those more complex patients with pain that couldn't be explained by mechanical dysfunctions. Learning about the neuroscience and neurophysiology of pain was an eye-opening experience and required of us a significant paradigm shift. We found it truly liberating. Our hope is that, with this second-edition textbook, you will experience a similar sense of excitement and discover that there is so much we can offer to our more difficult patients – those with chronic pain.

Acknowledgements

Writing a book might appear to be solitary work. Nothing could be further from the truth. It requires unlimited amounts of support and collaboration. This can be as intense and exhausting to those supportive, collaborative people as it is to the writers. We'd like to thank the following people and let them know, or at least be reminded of, how vital they have been in completing this project.

Thank you to the many influential supervisors, advisors, peers and authority figures within our profession. Not only have you provided wisdom, insight, vision and passion, but were nice enough to stop, listen, speak a kind word and spend time with us. This includes the late Geoff Maitland, the late Bob Elvey, Peter Rice, David Butler, Lorimer Moseley, Michael Shacklock, the late Louis Gifford, Ina Diener, Lance Twomey, Tim Flynn, Josh Cleland, Paul Mintken, Lynette Crous, Marietta Uys, Merrill Landers and many more. Special thanks to all the instructors at the International Spine and Pain Institute for their guidance, support and insight into various aspects contained in this book.

To every physical therapist, physician and patient who participated in our research, thank you for your willingness to be involved in these projects, your collegiality, your trust in us and your interest in being a part of the future of pain science.

To the International Spine and Pain Institute, thank you for your financial support of our research work.

To OPTP, thank you for your support in editing, designing, publishing and distributing this book. Also, thank you to Rod Bohner for your artwork.

To our parents and siblings, thank you for your steadfast support and encouragement and for providing us with our first examples of hard work and dedication.

To our children, Hailey and Samuel Louw; Benjamin, Georgina and Alexander Puentedura; Ella and Jackson; and Tyler, Ella and Lanie, thank you for being patient with fathers who were too often tired and absent while in pursuit of projects like this book. You've never doubted how much we love each of you.

Lastly, but most importantly, we dedicate this book to our wives, Colleen Louw, Danielle Puentedura, Tina Zimney and Janet Schmidt. Their continued support, enthusiasm and love made this book possible. Without it, there would be no book. Those countless days you spent being both a father and a mother to our children have grounded our families with your love and support.

Adriaan Louw
Emilio "Louie" Puentedura
Kory Zimney
Steve Schmidt

Table of Contents

Education is Therapy

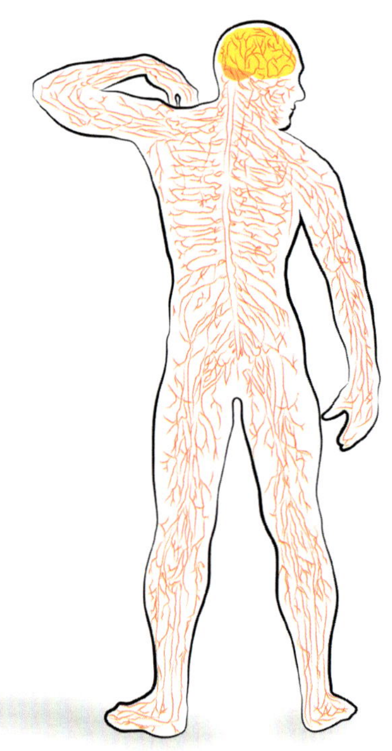

Chapter 1

Cognitions and Pain

1.1: The Pain Epidemic

The world is in pain.[1] Epidemiological data from all over the world show a global struggle with pain, especially chronic pain. The United Nations and World Health Organization have recognized chronic pain as a global burden in need of significant attention.[2] Chronic pain is often defined as pain that persists beyond normal tissue healing time, which is generally thought to be between three and six months.[3,4] Current research suggests that approximately 56 percent of people globally suffer from regular body pain on a weekly basis (Figure 1.1).[5-10]

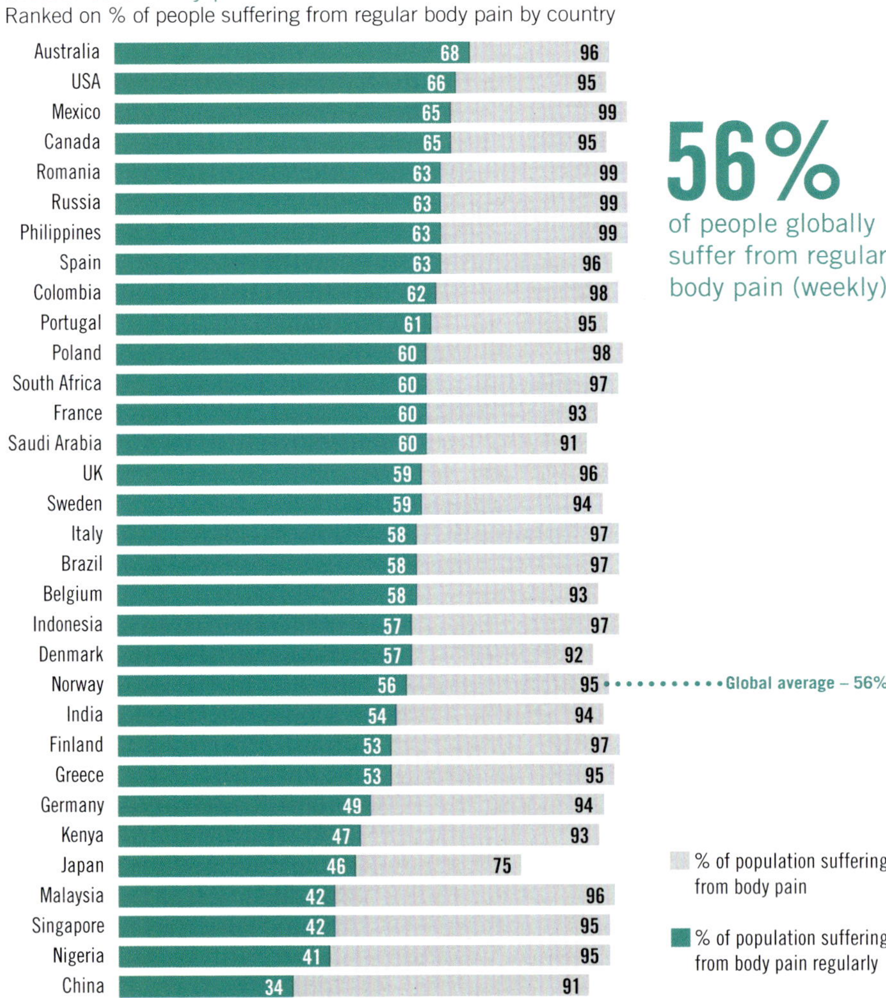

Figure 1.1: Global pain epidemic (Recreated from dailytelegraph.com/au).

In the United States (US), the Institute of Medicine (IOM) estimates 126.1 million adults experience pain over a three-month period, with 25.3 million suffering from daily chronic pain.[11,12] More alarming is the fact that the chronic pain epidemic seems to be increasing. Epidemiological data from the early 1990s show one in seven people were struggling with chronic pain, whereas the recent data indicate that it is now more like one in four.[2,3,11] Within these staggering numbers is the associated cost of chronic pain; for example, in the US it is estimated $560-635 billion dollars are spent on an annual basis in the management of chronic pain.[11,13]

Even though pain is a global epidemic, the US has a very unique and troubling issue: The opioid epidemic. Americans, accounting for five percent of the world's population, consume 80 percent of the opioids, and 99 percent of the hydrocodone globally.[14] The Centers for Disease Control (CDC) reports that prescription opioids are causing three times more fatalities than heroin and cocaine combined,[15] with 259 million prescriptions written in the US in 2012 (Figure 1.2).[16] It is currently estimated nearly 100 people die in America every day from prescription pain medication (Figure 1.3 on the following page).

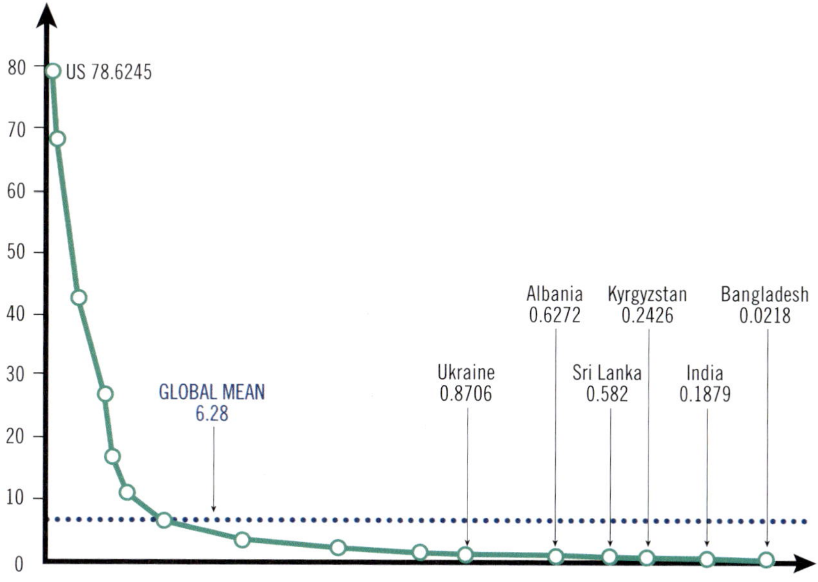

Figure 1.2: The United States opioid epidemic (image recreated from the CDC).

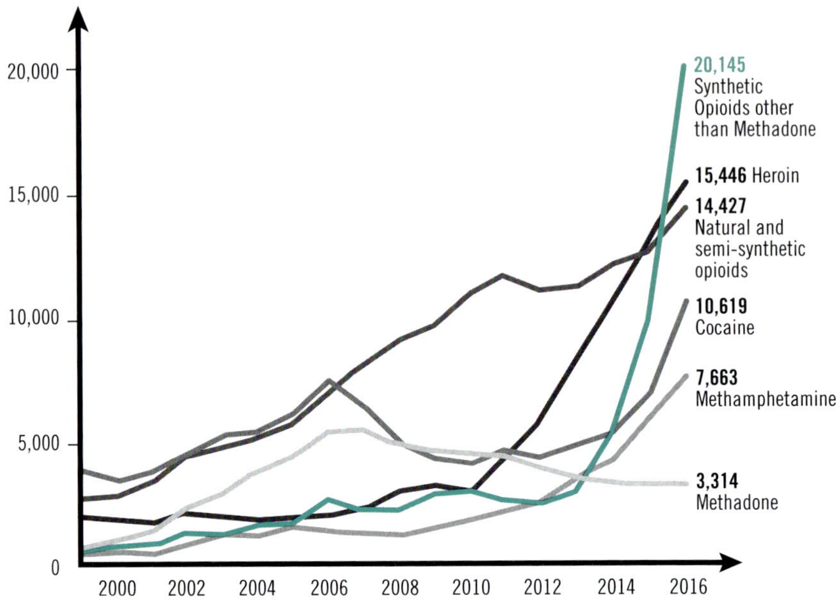

Figure 1.3: Drugs involved in US overdose deaths from 2000 – 2016 (image recreated from the CDC).

The pain epidemic is taking a toll. Apart from the financial burden and suffering of patients, there is also a psychological cost to clinicians. Treating people with chronic pain is difficult and poses significant challenges for clinicians. For example, there is evidence that physical therapists (PT) struggle when treating patients with chronic pain.[17,18] Although it is likely that many factors are involved, it is believed that a significant contribution to this clinical struggle is the lack of training and preparedness for treating chronic pain.[17,19] Not only are clinicians under-prepared to treat this challenging population, but the pain models they follow are outdated and treatment options that flow out of these models are often ineffective, leading to additional frustration. PT, especially orthopedic PT, is traditionally rooted in a biomedical model that focuses on tissues and tissue injury.[20-22] To address this pain epidemic, clinicians should have fundamental knowledge of modern pain science, which has made significant advances in recent years;[23-25] yet old theories still prevail.[26-28] For example, in 1965 the Gate Control theory explained how an interaction of thin and large diameter nerve fibers can impede signal transmission in the dorsal horn, changing processing and influencing an individual's pain experience.[25,29] This revolutionary theory was in almost every textbook in the biological and medical sciences by the mid-1970s.[25] More than 50 years later, the Gate Control theory is still used to teach pain in medical schools and health sciences,[26,30,31] despite the original author (Melzack) asking clinicians and scientists to expand their pain knowledge and to move beyond the Gate Control theory.[26,27] With advances in brain scanning, neuroimmunology, and our understanding of psychosocial contributors, it is reasonable to question if the current clinician is equipped to deal with the pain epidemic, given the limited pain neuroscience in their curriculum.[24,32]

The traditional biomedical model suggests that every disease process (dysfunction) can be explained in terms of an underlying deviation from normal function, such as faulty biomechanics, a pathogen or injury. The model implies that pathology and symptoms are correlated such that a greater expression of symptoms in patients would indicate greater underlying pathology (Figure 1.4a). The model proposes that correction of the underlying pathology with treatment (for example, injection, surgery, manipulation or exercise) should result in elimination of the symptoms and subsequent restoration of normal function in the patient (Figure 1.4b).[33] Clinical experience and pain science research tell us otherwise. Many patients will demonstrate physical and diagnostic signs that they have recovered from injury, yet they will continue to report symptoms/pain (Figure 1.4c).[33,34]

Conversely, it has been well documented that many healthy asymptomatic people and patients often have significant tissue pathology (age changes to the spine, "bulging" discs, etc.), yet experience little to no pain (Figure 1.4d).[33,35,36] The time has come for clinicians to take on the more comprehensive biopsychosocial model.[37,38] The biopsychosocial model encompasses more than just the biological factors (anatomy, physiology, and patho-anatomy) in human functioning by addressing the psychological (thoughts, emotions, and behaviors) and social (work, culture, and religion) factors, which are known to play a significant role in the patient's pain experience. A true biopsychosocial model includes a greater understanding of how the nervous system processes injury, disease, pain, threat, and emotions.[39,40]

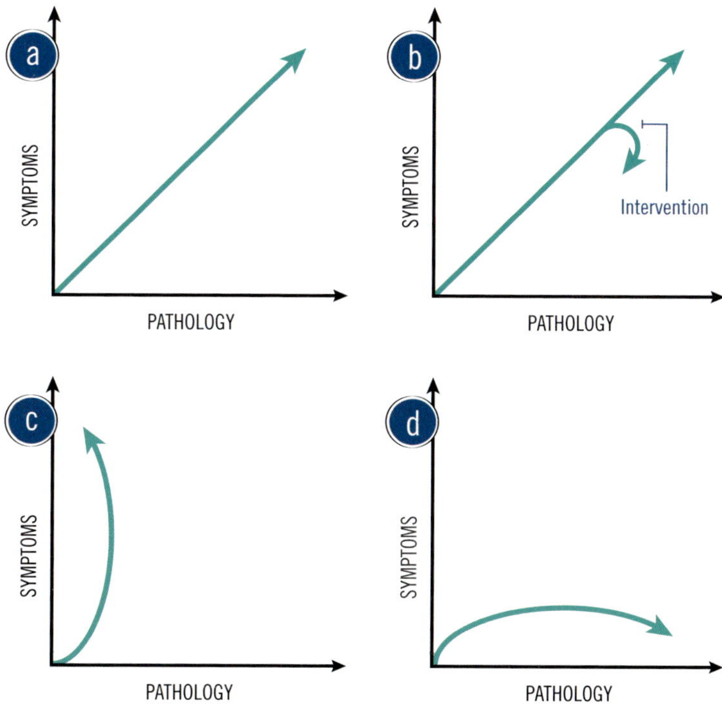

Figure 1.4: The failure of the biomedical model to predict pain (Haldeman, 1990).

1.2: Cognitions and Pain

There is significant debate about what constitutes a true biopsychosocial approach[22,40] and it could be argued that the list would vary, depending on each patient and his/her specific clinical presentation (Figure 1.5).[41]

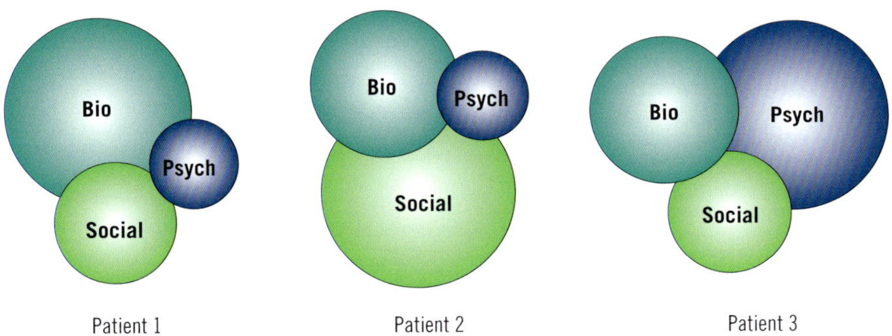

Figure 1.5: Variability of biopsychosocial presentations. Image from Jull.[41]

At the heart of a true biopsychosocial approach is cognition. What a patient thinks, feels, and believes about his or her condition will significantly impact their examination, treatment, and prognosis.[42] Many clinicians attempting to practice a biopsychosocial approach may experience trepidation and concerns that they may be inappropriately entering the realm of psychotherapy. We should certainly acknowledge that serious debilitating psychological issues such as depression, abuse, and various other psychological disorders, when noted in our examination, need referral to a professional for psychological counseling. However, clinicians need to carefully rethink their role in helping these severely affected patients and not simply default to a "for referral only" approach.

For example, PT can be seen as treating faulty human movement and function. Consider the following scenarios:

- A patient presents with pain and disability. After a skilled subjective and objective examination, the PT determines a stiff joint or movement is associated with the pain and disability. Treatment incorporating manual therapy would be considered appropriate according to established clinical guidelines. It is hypothesized that manual therapy or passive joint movement may restore normal movement and this will then be associated with the observed clinical improvement.

- A patient presents with pain and disability. After a skilled subjective and objective examination, the PT determines that altered muscle recruitment is associated with the pain and disability. In this case, a motor control strategy may be considered appropriate to alter motor control issues and, thereby, alleviate pain and disability.

- A patient presents with pain and disability. After a skilled subjective and objective examination, the PT determines that there is a soft tissue problem, e.g., trigger point, which may be preventing optimal function and movement. Physical treatment of the trigger point via ischemic compression or mechanical disruption through the use of dry needling may be considered appropriate avenues to restore normal movement and function.

- A patient presents with pain and disability. After a skilled subjective and objective examination, the physical therapist determines that the main reason for their limited function and mobility is altered/inappropriate beliefs about their pain, such as fear-avoidance. Where are the clinical guidelines to cover such a clinical presentation and whose job is it to treat their altered beliefs?

It has been well established that cognitions such as fear, anxiety and pain catastrophization are strongly correlated to pain and disability.[42-44]

This suggests that clinicians working on restoring human movement should address these altered cognitions for patients to feel, move, and function better. Furthermore, the notion that physical and psychological issues are separate and somewhat unrelated issues represents a classic flaw in medicine, based on the Cartesian model of pain that emphasizes the mind-body split (Chapter 3).[45] Clinicians should readily agree that treatment interactions can alter faulty cognitions. How can you treat any patient without providing education? Education is therapy. Education is medicine. Such education may seem benign and informal, yet recent research has shown its powerful impact on patient pain and disability. A major theme of this textbook, which follows nearly 20 years of scientific and clinical research on pain neuroscience education (PNE), is the concept of altering patients' beliefs to alter their pain experiences.

1.3: A Clinical Example

Here is a clinical example to illustrate the connection between cognitions and pain. This patient was referred to PT with chronic pain:[46]

> *"Suzy" is a doctor's wife with three years of low back pain (LBP) and recently diagnosed with fibromyalgia. She has seen numerous healthcare providers and her most recent treatment involves epidural steroid injections, radio-frequency nerve ablation and spinal stabilization exercises. She is now once again referred to PT for additional treatment. She has "good" and "bad" days with her pain, but more "bad" days than "good" days. Her pain is in the low back and starting to spread down the legs (Figure 1.6). Her pain comes and goes and "seems to have a mind of its own." Stress increases her pain considerably. She does not sleep well. She has had to stop cooking meals, as standing > 20 minutes increases the pain, which will then last one to two days. She is unable to sit > 60 minutes in a car during a road trip. She comes to PT for help. Her Oswestry Disability Index (ODI) and Fear Avoidance Beliefs Questionnaire (FABQ) scores are extremely high.*

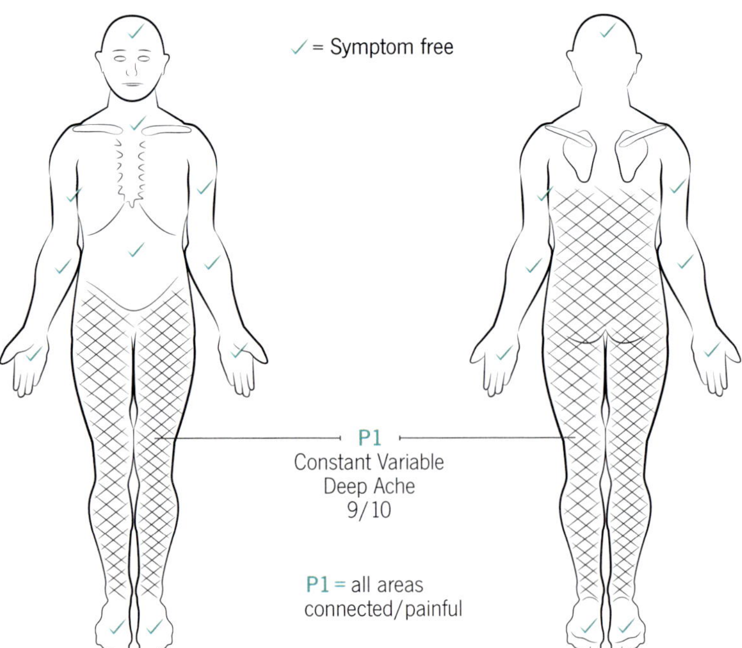

Figure 1.6: Chronic Pain Body Chart (from the authors).

Additional information:

- Her general health is good
- She "used to" work out a lot, mainly Pilates and yoga
- She denies any significant joint problems
- She reported a family history of LBP
- She is unable to work as a part-time office manager due to her pain

Her physical tests reveal the following:

- Forward flexion: 10 degrees = pain (Figure 1.7)
- Extension: 10 degrees = pain
- Straight leg raise (SLR): sensitive at 45 degrees (L = R)
- Slump test: leg pain increases when neck flexion is added
- Palpation:
    - Tender L1 – L5 spinous processes
    - Tender sacroiliac joint (SIJ)/Posterior superior iliac spine (PSIS)
    - Tender – bilateral hips
- Spinal stabilization: Unable to perform a coordinated deep corset contraction

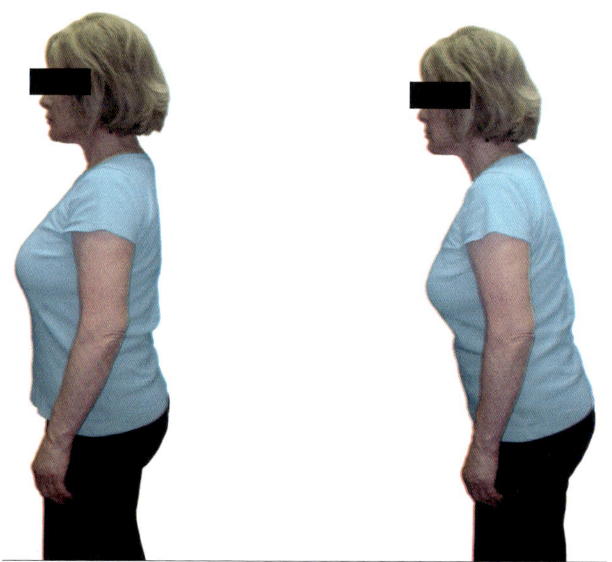

Figure 1.7: Patient with chronic pain ("Suzy") at rest/neutral and maximum forward flexion.

In Figure 1.7, it is obvious that forward flexion is limited. The patient encountered increased pain and stopped further motion into forward flexion. When she was questioned about why she stopped, the patient answered, *"I don't want the pain to get worse."* Further exploration of her thought processes and reasoning for stopping the movement elicited the following statement: *"If I bend more, the pain will increase; I have a 'bulging' disc and it will get worse!"*

It should be clear from this case example that thoughts and beliefs can impact movement and function. The patient believes her "bulging" disc will get worse, may "bulge" even more, and there is a real risk in bending. This voluntary restriction, based upon beliefs related to her back, is likely to impact physical treatments, which are the mainstay of movement-based professions such as PT, occupational therapy (OT), chiropractic, etc. How willing will this patient be to let a clinician apply passive (manual therapy) or active (exercise) movement to her spine to alleviate the pain, restricted range of motion (ROM) and disability? How willing would she be if she believes that provocation of pain is an indicator of increased damage?

Recent PT classification-based approaches to the treatment of LBP may be considered for this patient.[47-49] Is there a possibility that she may fit into a specific sub-group that might statistically predict her probability for success? A quick scan of clinical prediction rules for various patients with LBP reveals that, in this case, it is unlikely she will benefit from spinal manipulation,[50,51] spinal stabilization,[52,53] lumbar traction,[54] or directional preference.[55] Again, even if the patient met the requirements of a sub-group, the PT would still need to convince her to participate in the proposed treatment. Furthermore, the PT would likely be making the false assumption that there was a predominately mechanical origin for the cause of the widespread pain. Pain is far more complex as will be discussed in Chapter 3.

Clearly, a deeper biopsychosocial approach is needed. What does Suzy know about her pain? What does Suzy want to know about her pain? What do you, the clinician, want Suzy to know? Evidence-based medicine has driven quantitative research to the forefront of clinical practice and care decisions.[56] Quantitative research, with systematic reviews, randomized controlled trials and meta-analyses, has led to experimentally designed, tested and "proven" treatment approaches for patients by delivering treatment protocols. Even though a particular treatment intervention may have high-level evidence to support it, and its use has been shown to statistically improve pain and function in appropriately selected patients, the clinician will still need to address the patient's fear and faulty cognitions. A part of evidence which is often forgotten is provided by qualitative research, especially when seeking what the patient wants and expects. It is now widely accepted that evidence-based medicine involves the best of the available scientific research and the clinical experience of the clinician, but also, powerfully, patient expectations and beliefs.[57-59] Qualitative studies and sound clinical reasoning, intuition and experience (see Foreword by Louis Gifford) show that patients want answers to the following:[60,61]

1. What is wrong with me?
2. How long will it take?
3. What can I (the patient) do for it?
4. What can you (the clinician) do for it?
5. (We added another; a US-specific question):

   How much will it cost?

These questions are consciously (and unconsciously) dealt with every day in clinical practice by patients and clinicians. To illustrate (i) the use of these questions and (ii) the complexity of pain, two examples are shown:

Example 1: Acute ankle sprain

A young football player presents to PT with an acute, grade one ankle sprain. By following the simple algorithm of questions above, clinicians should easily be able to explain an ankle sprain to the player. It's a fundamental part of treatment. As for *"how long it will take,"* it is reasonable in an orthopedic model to assure the athlete and parents *"it's going to be OK"* and he will be better in no time.[62] The patient and his parents are given simple instructions on self-care to perform at home and the clinician can easily explain the intended plan of care as he attends therapy for a few sessions. In all, an acute grade one ankle sprain from a cost perspective will be relatively inexpensive and short-lived.

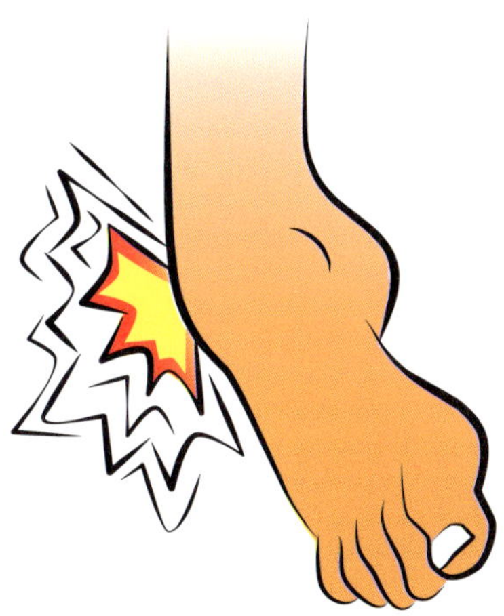

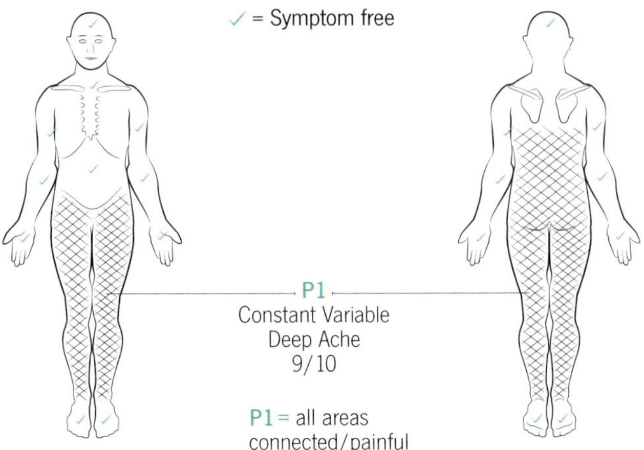

Example 2: Suzy's case of chronic LBP

If Suzy was the next new patient, the clinician would be confronted with the same clinical questions. Let's try it. *"What is wrong with me?"* Can you, as with the acute ankle sprain, provide a clear and concise explanation for her pain? What about prognosis? *"How long will it take?"* Are you brave enough to say *"you're going to be OK?"* Will she also be much better in a week or two? What do you want her to do at home? What will your treatment plan look like? The cost? According to the IOM over $31,000 is spent per patient (such as Suzy) per year in the US.[11] This is a perfect example of why chronic pain is so difficult to treat. We cannot use the same model that seemingly works well for acute, sub-acute and perioperative pain for people like Suzy. Actually, two key questions for people with chronic pain should likely be modified:

- *What is wrong with me?* should be: *Why do I hurt, or why do I still hurt?*
- *How long will it take?* should be: *Is there any hope? Can this get better?*

These questions (and answers) are complicated. How would you answer these questions for this patient? How confident are you in your answers? To treat patients with chronic pain, we need to change cognitions and understanding about pain before a movement-based program can be successful.[24,63] Two particular cognitions have been powerfully linked to poor outcomes and are a major focus in PNE:

- Fear and fear-avoidance[64-66]
- Catastrophization, especially pain catastrophization[63,67]

In order to help patients such as Suzy, fear-avoidance and pain catastrophization should not only be assessed at the time of the initial consultation, but addressed by a PT before and while engaging in a movement-based approach of therapeutic exercise, manual therapy, pacing and graded exposure.

1.4: Fear and Fear-Avoidance

Fear is best defined as a distressing negative experience induced by a perceived threat. Fear and its impact on pain have been discussed extensively, yet many clinicians do not readily understand the debilitating effect of fear on movement and recovery.[68-72] In the now famous quote by the late Dr. Gordon Waddell:

> "The fear of pain is worse than pain itself."[69]

This statement is underscored by the fact that numerous studies evaluating LBP include the use of scales addressing fear, such as the FABQ and Tampa Scale of Kinesiophobia (TSK).[70,73-75] Fear within the chronic pain population is often associated with the belief that increased activity, movement or exercise will not only increase pain, but further damage tissues. Patients with pain deal with the unknown, including diagnosis, how long the injury will take to heal, how long before they return to function, how the pain might or might not influence their return to employment, financial wellbeing, etc. The clinical manifestation of these unknowns may present itself as increased fear.

It is clear that clinicians need to not only take the patient's fear into consideration, but also find a way to quantify it. The most commonly used measure is the FABQ (See Table 1.1 on the following page). The FABQ is a 16-item questionnaire that was designed to quantify fear and avoidance beliefs in individuals with chronic LBP.[72] The FABQ has two subscales: 1) a four-item scale to measure fear avoidance beliefs about physical activity (FABQ-PA) and 2) a seven-item scale to measure fear-avoidance beliefs about work (FABQ-W). Each item is scored from 0 to 6 with possible scores ranging between 0 and 24 and 0 and 42 for the physical activity and work subscales, respectively, with higher scores representing an increase in fear-avoidance beliefs. A high FABQ score has been associated with chronic disability secondary to LBP.[72,73]

Table 1.1: The Fear Avoidance Beliefs Questionnaire (FABQ).

Name: ______________________________ Date: _____/_____/_____
mm dd yy

Here are some of the things other patients have told us about their pain. For each statement, please circle the number from 0 to 6 to indicate how much physical activities such as bending, lifting, walking or driving affect or would affect your back pain.

	Completely Disagree			Unsure			Completely Agree
1. My pain was caused by physical activity.	0	1	2	3	4	5	6
2. Physical activity makes my pain worse.	0	1	2	3	4	5	6
3. Physical activity might harm my back.	0	1	2	3	4	5	6
4. I should not do physical activities which (might) make my pain worse.	0	1	2	3	4	5	6
5. I cannot do physical activities which (might) make my pain worse.	0	1	2	3	4	5	6

FABQPA (2,3,4,5): ________ /24

The following statements are about how your normal work affects or would affect your back pain.

	Completely Disagree			Unsure			Completely Agree
6. My pain was caused by my work or by an accident at work.	0	1	2	3	4	5	6
7. My work aggravated my pain.	0	1	2	3	4	5	6
8. I have a claim for compensation for my pain.	0	1	2	3	4	5	6
9. My work is too heavy for me.	0	1	2	3	4	5	6
10. My work makes or would make my pain worse.	0	1	2	3	4	5	6
11. My work might harm my back.	0	1	2	3	4	5	6
12. I should not do my regular work with my present pain.	0	1	2	3	4	5	6
13. I cannot do my normal work with my present pain.	0	1	2	3	4	5	6
14. I cannot do my normal work until my pain is treated.	0	1	2	3	4	5	6
15. I do not think that I will be back to my normal work within 3 months.	0	1	2	3	4	5	6
16. I do not think that I will ever be able to go back to that work.	0	1	2	3	4	5	6

FABQW (6,7,9,10,11,12,15): ________ /42

The FABQ is often used to screen patients with LBP to assess their potential risk for prolonged disability. It has been suggested that a FABQ-PA sub-scale score > 15 and a FABQ-W sub-scale score > 34 is associated with a high risk for prolonged disability from LBP.[73,76] In line with these elevated scores, it is then suggested these patients be treated with a more comprehensive biopsychosocial or multi-disciplinary approach.[73] In Chapter 5 we will delve further into the FABQ's clinical use; screening use and other "fear of movement" scales such as the TSK (Table 1.2). Both the FABQ and TSK have been adapted and used for patients with pain conditions other than LBP.[71] It is important to realize there are various shortcomings of the FABQ, including its relevance for people who do not work, i.e., retired, students, etc. In regard to fear-avoidance, it is furthermore important to distinguish between fear and phobia. The relationship between fear and pain was first described by Lethem et al. 1983.[77] Almost a decade later, Kori et al. presented their thoughts about kinesiophobia.[78] It is believed that persistent fear of an object or situation that exceeds natural and normal fears is considered a phobia and the exaggerated fear (phobia) of movement is thus kinesiophobia.[78] Kinesiophobia is often measured with the TSK.[79] Each of the 17 items is scored on a four-point Likert-type scale that ranges from strongly disagree [1] to strongly agree [4]. Total scores range from 17 to 68, and higher scores indicate more fear of movement and/or (re)injury.[79]

For PTs who are not formally using the FABQ or TSK for various reasons, the authors feel it is imperative to assess and develop a working knowledge of the patient's level of fear as it impacts their rehabilitation significantly. For example, clinicians might ask simple fear-related questions such as: What are you afraid of? Are you afraid the pain will get worse and/or are you afraid treatment will increase your pain? A skilled, thorough subjective examination should include listening for statements from patients regarding their fears. As you work your way through the book, and the overall concept of "digging deeper," you may realize that the beauty of questionnaires such as the FABQ is not only in the scores, but the questions. We argue that the individual FABQ questions can be used not only as assessment tools, but also as an easy way to teach a patient about pain. Depending on how a patient answers a question, the clinician can review and discuss the question and its answer. This may help them reconceptualize their pain, which is the cornerstone of PNE.[80]

Table 1.2: The Tampa Scale of Kinesiophobia.

Below are statements about some beliefs regarding your pain and function. Read each statement and rate how much you agree with the statement.

	Strongly Disagree	Disagree	Agree	Strongly Agree
1. I'm afraid that I might injure myself if I exercise	1	2	3	4
2. If I were to try to overcome it, my pain would increase	1	2	3	4
3. My body is telling me I have something dangerously wrong	1	2	3	4
4. My pain would probably be relieved if I were to exercise	1	2	3	4
5. People aren't taking my medical condition seriously enough	1	2	3	4
6. My accident has put my body at risk for the rest of my life	1	2	3	4
7. Pain always means I have injured my body	1	2	3	4
8. Just because something aggravates my pain does not mean it is dangerous	1	2	3	4
9. I am afraid that I might injure myself accidentally	1	2	3	4

Table 1.2: The Tampa Scale of Kinesiophobia *(continued)*.

	Strongly Disagree	Disagree	Agree	Strongly Agree
10. Simply being careful that I do not make any unnecessary movements is the safest thing I can do to prevent my pain from worsening	1	2	3	4
11. I wouldn't have this much pain if there weren't something potentially dangerous going on in my body	1	2	3	4
12. Although my condition is painful, I would be better off if I were physically active	1	2	3	4
13. Pain lets me know when to stop exercising so that I don't injure myself	1	2	3	4
14. It's really not safe for a person with a condition like mine to be physically active	1	2	3	4
15. I can't do all the things normal people do because it's too easy for me to get injured	1	2	3	4
16. Even though something is causing me a lot of pain, I don't think it's actually dangerous	1	2	3	4
17. No one should have to exercise when he/she is in pain	1	2	3	4

In regard to fear and fear-avoidance, an iconic behavioral model was developed by behavioral psychologists Vlaeyen and Linton, the Fear-Avoidance (FA) Model, to describe how pain, disability, affective distress and physical disuse develop as a result of persistent avoidance behaviors motivated by fear.[64] (See Figure 1.8). It is interesting to note that after injury and the resulting pain experience, two very different pathways, or choices, lead to two very different outcomes.

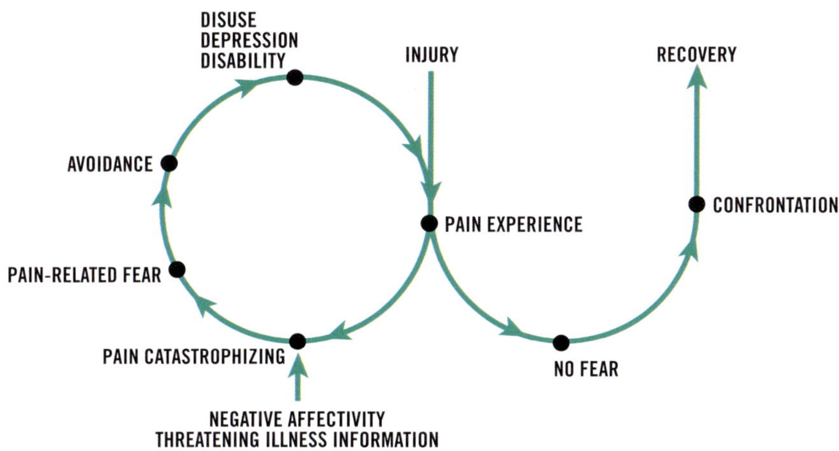

Figure 1.8: The Fear-Avoidance Model. Image adapted from Vlaeyen & Linton (2000).

In Figure 1.9 as seen on the following page, we extrapolate on the FA Model. Clinicians working with patients with chronic pain will likely see several features that may appear to be quite familiar from the clinical point of view:

7a Threat: In the FA model, injury is set as an initiating event for the pain experience. Although injury may cause the start of the pain experience, many patients develop chronic pain in the absence of injury.[24,80] Furthermore, injury and pain are not synonymous as we will discuss later in Chapter 3. Pain is an output of the brain based on the brain's evaluation of perceived threat.[24,80] Patients facing emotional issues related to work, family and life may have those stressful issues as the initiation of their pain experience and clinicians should be aware of this. The International Association on the Study of Pain (IASP) states pain can be from an emotional or physical issue and warrants inclusion in the FA model.[3] Even more than emotional overload, if we believe pain is an evaluation of threat, the FA model (7a) should be further expanded, as threats come in a variety of forms. The traditional FA model showcases injury, while we propose the addition of emotional overload. Surely diseases or health of a person's tissues, potentially even their perception of the health of their tissues,

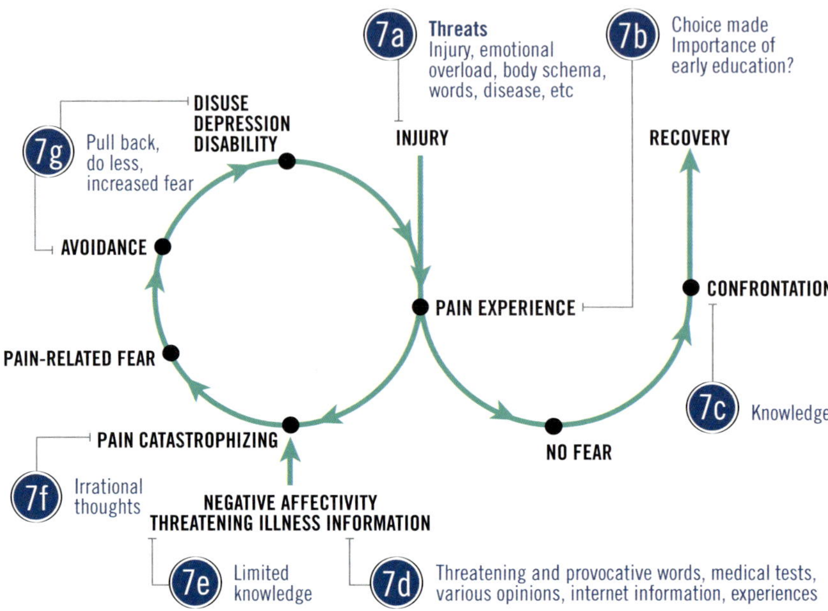

Figure 1.9: Clinical application of the Fear-Avoidance (FA) model.

should be added as potential initiating events for a pain experience. Furthermore, emerging neuroplasticity research has shown that structural changes in the brain, especially the somatosensory maps, i.e., smudging, may trigger a pain experience (Chapter 3).[81] Threats may indeed also include provocative medical terms or information (misinformation), which may trigger a pain experience. We therefore suggest "injury" in the original FA model be replaced with "threat" to account for the various known and even unknown stressors the brain has to analyze in the development of a pain experience.

7b Early decision: A person's experience and subsequent response to a threat, such as an injury, disease or even emotional overload, is very interesting. Some people may endure seemingly similar injuries, yet some develop no lasting pain experience, while others start a life of persistent pain. There are likely many factors impacting this "development" of pain (Chapter 3) and these could include genetic coding, environmental issues, peer pressure, social or cultural issues, upbringing, knowledge, anxiety, coping skills and more. It is, therefore, clear that several factors will impact the development of a pain experience.[63,82-85] More compelling is the fact that early intervention, especially education, may have a significant impact on whether an individual moves toward a successful recovery or begins a cycle of fear-avoidance.[86-88] It is important, however, to realize that a pain experience is normal and this calls into question the premise of interventions aiming to "prevent pain." Based on the FA model and neuroscience, pain is normal and serves a biological function in the acute stage, but what we do about it (disability) may be far more important. Can we really prevent pain? If we could prevent pain, should we? Surely we can agree that we should aim to prevent disability or even chronic pain.

7c Knowledge: It is widely known that chronic pain is more prevalent in patients with lower educational levels.[89,90] Conversely, it has been shown that healthcare providers who experience a similar injury to non-medically trained persons will report significantly less pain and disability.[91,92] Knowledge, in this case, may be seen as allaying any possible fears such that events may be confronted head-on with an expectation that recovery will follow. This premise of knowledge being a potential factor in patients moving toward the path of recovery should be seen as a significant target for preemptive educational strategies, i.e., pre-operative PNE (see Chapter 7).[93-95]

7d Medical threats: Patients in pain invariably attend medical appointments, undergo tests and experience a variety of healthcare providers and their corresponding treatment interventions. During this medical journey, threatening and provocative terminology is likely to induce some level of fear and thereby increase the pain experience.[96-98]

7e Limited knowledge: Pain and knowledge are intricately intertwined. Whereas having appropriate knowledge (7c) may allay fears and allow confrontation/dealing with the situation, limited or incorrect knowledge can have a powerful and negative effect on the pain experience.[89,90]

7f Irrational thoughts: With limited or incorrect knowledge, poor decisions are likely to be made. This limited or incorrect information may lead to an inability to foresee anything other than the worst possible outcome. This is defined as pain catastrophizing. As discussed in subsequent chapters, this is very important as "cup half-empty" scenarios are very challenging to shift to the positive [99] and have a significant impact on increasing a pain experience.[100] It is now well established that increased pain catastrophization (cup half-empty) results in an anti-opioid and anti-cannaboid action, decreasing endogenous mechanisms which ultimately increases a pain experience.[100]

7g Pull back: With persistent pain and limited help, patients may start a social withdrawal process. The social withdrawal is likely due to pain, lack of energy, limited mobility, family issues, lack of goals and more. This withdrawal process can further reinforce the notion of how badly they are affected and can propel the pain experience into a downward spiral. Additionally, apart from pain, loneliness and social isolation have been correlated with an increased risk for various serious illnesses including stroke and coronary heart disease.[101]

A recent version of the FA model was recently presented by the behavioral team of Vlaeyen, Linton and Crombez (Figure 1.10).[102] The updated model provides some additions worth discussing:

- The authors removed injury from the original model, replacing it with nociception. This is encouraging as injury and pain are not synonymous and it opens the inclusion of other stimuli such as thermal, mechanical or chemical, including inflammation from a progressive osteoarthritic knee. On the downside, it still does not open the gateway to emotional triggers to pain, or even neuroplasticity changes associated with a pain experience.[81]

- Pain is closely linked to threat and thus in line with the current belief that pain is an output of the brain based on perception of threat, thus warranting a threat appraisal in this process.

- The path to recovery includes various additional patient attributes which may powerfully drive them toward recovery, including priorities, goals, optimism (cup half-full) and positive affect. This is important as we need to develop a better understanding of what it takes to move in this direction.

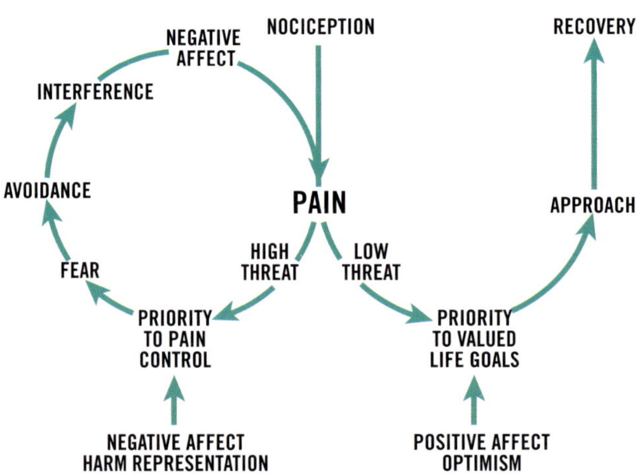

Figure 1.10: Expanded version of the FA model (Adapted from Vlaeyen, Linton and Crombez).

From a clinical perspective, it is important for clinicians to have an idea of where a patient may be on the FA model when they present for treatment. Even though tools such as the FABQ, TSK or the Pain Catastrophization Scale (PCS) give us an idea of where patients are, their clinical comments may give us further clues if they're on the road to recovery (Figure 1.11) or in the proverbial pain roundabout (Figure 1.12):

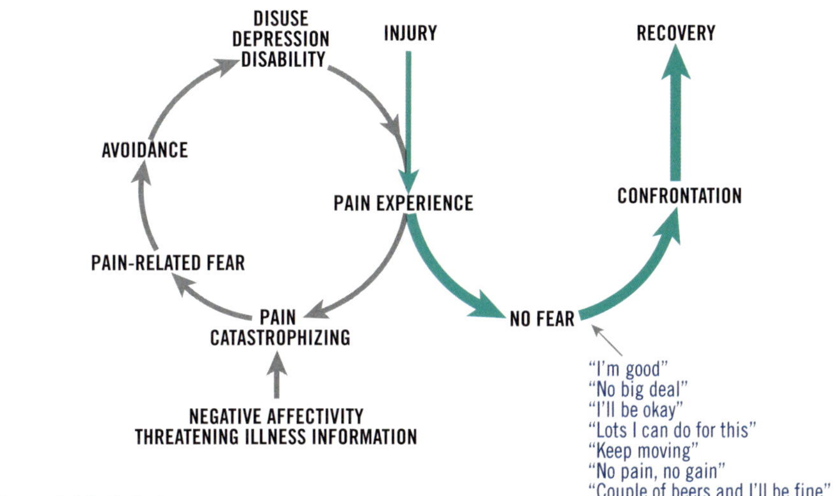

Figure 1.11: Path to recovery.

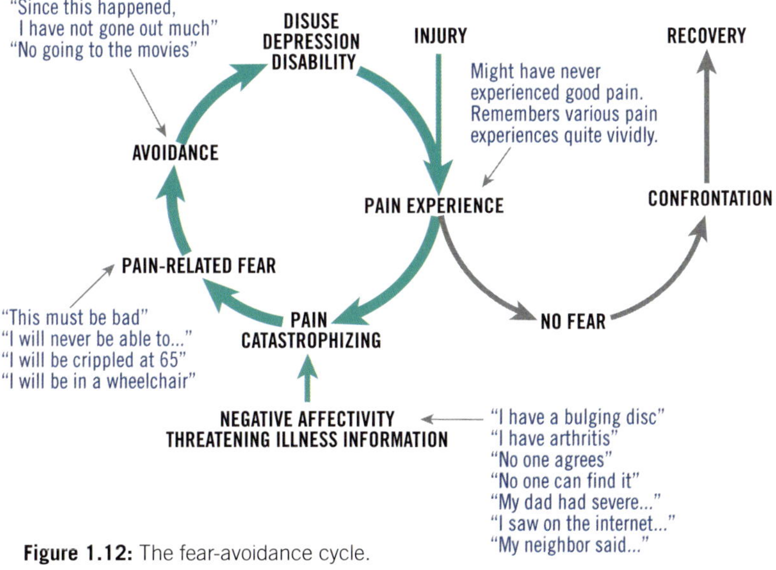

Figure 1.12: The fear-avoidance cycle.

1.5: Pain Catastrophizing

Catastrophizing is defined as the inability to foresee anything other than the worst possible outcome, however unlikely, or experiencing a situation as unbearable or impossible when it is just uncomfortable. Catastrophizing due to pain is often associated with chronic pain and referred to as pain catastrophization.[63,103]

The most commonly used tool for measuring catastrophization is the PCS (Table 1.3). The PCS is a self-report questionnaire that assesses inappropriate coping strategies and catastrophic thinking about pain and injury. The PCS has been used in previous PNE studies and has been shown to have strong construct validity, reliability, and stability.[67,104] The PCS utilizes a 13-item, five-point Likert scale with higher scores indicating elevated levels of catastrophizing. Previous studies utilizing the PCS have shown a median score of 18 for healthy individuals and in patients with pain, the PCS is generally higher.[104]

As with fear, clinicians should train themselves to listen for catastrophizing phrases, which may include: "*That's it…life is over, might as well bury me now…*"; "*Now that I have a bulging disc, I will never walk again*"; "*Because of my arthritis, I will be in a wheelchair soon*" or "*I've got arthritis. I will never run again.*"

Table 1.3: Pain Catastrophizing Scale.

Instructions: We are interested in the types of thoughts and feelings that you have when you are in pain. Listed below are thirteen statements describing different thoughts and feelings that may be associated with pain. Using the following scale, please indicate the degree to which you have these thoughts and feelings when you are experiencing pain.

	Not At All	To a Slight Degree	To a Moderate Degree	To a Great Degree	All The Time
1. I worry all the time about whether the pain will end	0	1	2	3	4
2. I feel I can't go on	0	1	2	3	4
3. It's terrible and I think it's never going to get any better	0	1	2	3	4

	Not At All	To a Slight Degree	To a Moderate Degree	To a Great Degree	All The Time
4. It's awful and I feel that it overwhelms me	0	1	2	3	4
5. I feel I can't stand it anymore	0	1	2	3	4
6. I become afraid that the pain will get worse	0	1	2	3	4
7. I keep thinking of other painful events	0	1	2	3	4
8. I anxiously want the pain to go away	0	1	2	3	4
9. I can't seem to keep it out of my mind	0	1	2	3	4
10. I keep thinking about how much it hurts	0	1	2	3	4
11. I keep thinking about how badly I want the pain to stop	0	1	2	3	4
12. There's nothing I can do to reduce the intensity of the pain	0	1	2	3	4
13. I wonder whether something serious may happen	0	1	2	3	4

1.6: Beliefs

Apart from fear and pain catastrophizing, various other maladaptive beliefs may be in need of change to allow for normal movement, exercise and function, let alone participation in rehabilitation.[97,105] Impaired beliefs include the following:

- Belief that pain is always bad
- Belief that all pain must be gone before engaging in normal activity, movement and therapy
- Belief that passive treatment is the answer
- Belief that pain will increase with any/all activity
- Belief that work is potentially harmful

Along with altered cognitions such as fear, beliefs, and pain catastrophizing, several other impaired psychosocial issues have been found to correlate to pain, development of chronicity, healthcare expense and compliance with treatment.[82,106] These factors are often referred to as "Yellow Flags."[106]

1.7: Yellow Flags

LBP is the most widely reported musculoskeletal disorder in western civilization and estimated to be second only to the common cold in reasons for seeking medical care.[107,108] Epidemiological data indicates approximately 80 percent of people will develop LBP in their life.[107-109] What is truly remarkable is that LBP is currently as prevalent as it was 100 years ago and most likely will be the same 50 years from now (Figure 1.13).[108,110] What has increased, however, is disability due to LBP. The most alarming epidemiological data:

Ten percent of patients with LBP account for nearly 90 percent of the cost.[111-113]

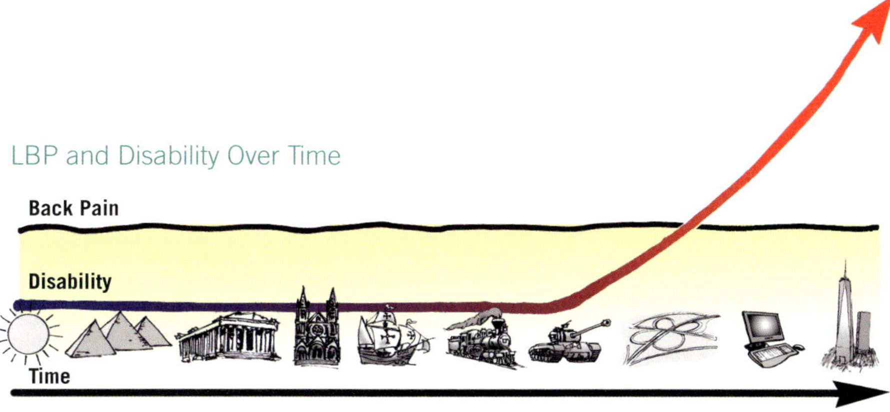

Figure 1.13: The prevalence of low back pain has remained the same over time, while disability has increased (image from Louw, et al.).[114]

With the huge financial impact of a small sub-group, scientists set out the determine if there were psychosocial issues that may have been predictive of persistent LBP and if subsequent tailored treatment may lessen the burden of LBP.[106] Although yellow flags have evolved considerably, it is worth spending some time outlining them. Yellow flags are psychosocial factors that have been shown to correlate to the development of chronic pain (Figure 1.14). The subsequent use of the FABQ, TSK and PCS is an extension of the original "yellow flags" research.

Figure 1.14: Psychosocial yellow flags. Image from Louw.[115]

Apart from the previously discussed issues of fear, pain catastrophizing, and beliefs, yellow flags like various emotions, behaviors, family, and work issues, as well as medical examinations and treatment issues, were also identified in regard to pain and recovery.[106] These factors are listed in Table 1.4 on the following page.

Table 1.4: Additional psychosocial yellow flags.

Behaviors	**Work**
• Extended rest • Withdrawal from social life, daily life and people • Compliance issues with therapy • Report of extremely high intensity of pain, e.g., 15 on a 0-10 Visual Analog Scale • Excessive reliance on use of aids or appliances • Problems sleeping • High intake of alcohol and medication • Smoking	• History of manual work • Job dissatisfaction • Problems with peers and supervisors • Low educational background • Low socioeconomic status • High physical demand • Working shifts – especially at night • Negative experience of workplace management of pain or injury
Compensation issues	**Emotions**
• Lack of financial incentive to return to work • History of claims due to other injuries or pain problems	• Fear of increased pain with activity, work or therapy • Depression • Irritability • Anxiety
Diagnosis and treatment	**Family**
• Health professional sanctioning disability • Conflicting diagnoses • Diagnostic language leading to catastrophization and fear • Number of healthcare providers visited • Expectation of a "techno-fix" • Lack of satisfaction with treatment	• Overprotective spouse • Punitive responses from spouse

As stated before, yellow flags have evolved. Some factors, e.g., fear and catastrophizing, have been studied in greater depth. Additional flags have also been identified (Figure 1.15).

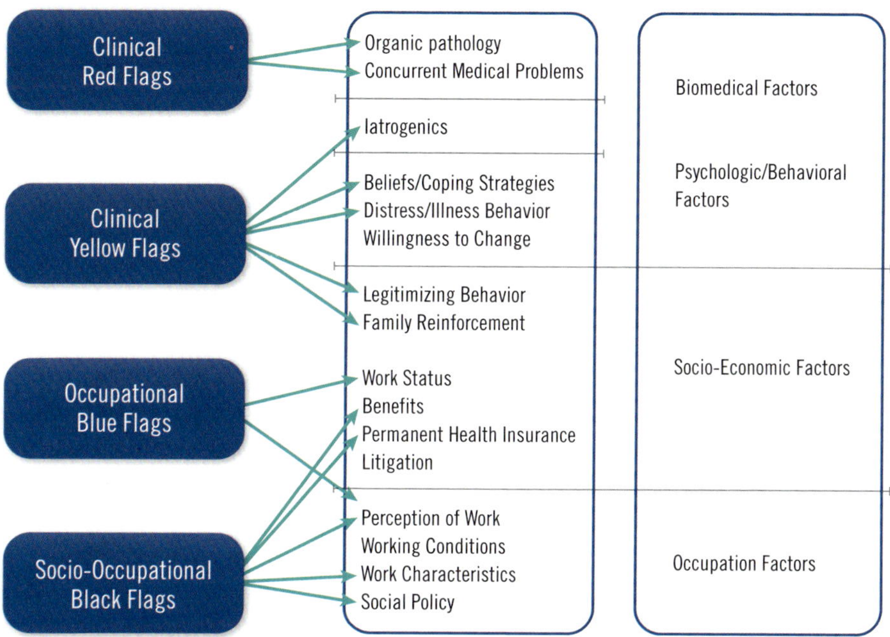

Figure 1.15: Additional flags identified as representing barriers to recovery (from Mark Jones).

- **Red Flags:** There are many different "flags" clinicians need to consider. Probably the most well-known flags are "red flags,"[116,117] keeping to the fundamental first rule of medicine: Do No Harm.

- **Blue Flags:** These are specific occupational issues and involved perceived features of work that are often associated with higher rates of symptoms, ill health and work loss. High physical or emotional (stress) demands of the job, low ability to control the work environment, problems with management, poor social support from colleagues, perceived time pressure, and lack of job satisfaction are examples of blue flags.

- **Black Flags:** These are considered socio-occupational issues, such as national healthcare policy, rates of pay, negotiated entitlements, employer policy, sickness policy, restricted duties policy, management style, organization size and structure, trade union support, content-specific aspects of work, ergonomics, hours and shift work.

It should be noted that there is considerable overlap between the yellow, blue and black flags.

1.8: Returning to the Patient

Considering the discussion thus far, let's revisit our case example. It could easily be argued that this patient may have various cognitive issues that are limiting her ability and willingness to bend forward. They are also likely to limit her ability/willingness to fully participate in treatment. These issues include fear, pain catastrophizing, different explanations for her pain, failed treatments, social withdrawal and, perhaps, the effect of provocative language used to describe why she has her pain ("bulging disc").

Clinicians should not label her as a "difficult" patient or a "malingerer." Because of the issues she has faced, this patient believes there is significant danger in bending forward. It might even be more correct to suggest that her brain believes it is dangerous. This belief is based on all the available information the brain has regarding the "bulging disc." In this case, the brain uses pain to protect (Figure 1.16). Other systems are used to protect as well, e.g., muscle guarding, possibly some increased levels of adrenaline, faster and shallower breathing and even a linguistic response of "oooooooh" as she flexes forward. Therefore, when considering potential intervention strategies, it is critical to consider how to change her knowledge and understanding about her pain problem before a movement-based program can be successful.

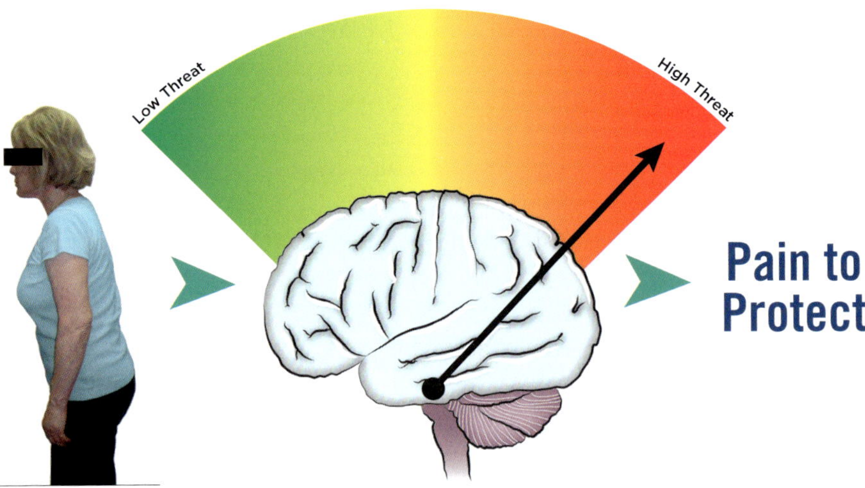

Figure 1.16: "Suzy's" brain believes there is danger in bending forward, and produces pain to protect her.

This interpretation of her forward flexion is in line with the current neuroscience definition of pain:

> Pain is a multiple system output activated by the brain based on perceived threat.[24]

1.9: Key Points from Chapter 1

- Clinicians have seen and will continue to see many patients with chronic pain
- Current models of evaluation and treatment are insufficient
- Cognitions impact pain
- Chronic pain affects cognitions, beliefs, emotions, and behaviors
- Changing cognitions must occur to allow movement-based approaches to be effective
- Therapy should address faulty cognitions

Chapter 1 References

1. Global Burden of Disease Study C. Global, regional, and national incidence, prevalence, and years lived with disability for 301 acute and chronic diseases and injuries in 188 countries, 1990-2013: a systematic analysis for the Global Burden of Disease Study 2013. *Lancet.* Aug 22 2015;386(9995):743-800.
2. Woolf AD, Pfleger B. Burden of major musculoskeletal conditions. *Bull World Health Organ.* 2003;81(9):646-656.
3. Merskey H, Bogduk N. *Classification of Chronic Pain.* 2nd ed. Seattle: IASP Press; 1994.
4. Wall PD, Melzack R. *Textbook of Pain.* 5th ed. London: Elsevier; 2005.
5. Raftery MN, Sarma K, Murphy AW, De la Harpe D, Normand C, McGuire BE. Chronic pain in the Republic of Ireland-Community prevalence, psychosocial profile and predictors of pain-related disability: Results from the Prevalence, Impact and Cost of Chronic Pain (PRIME) study, Part 1. *Pain.* May 2011;152(5):1096-1103.
6. Johannes CB, Le TK, Zhou X, Johnston JA, Dworkin RH. The prevalence of chronic pain in United States adults: results of an Internet-based survey. *The journal of pain: official journal of the American Pain Society.* Nov 2010;11(11):1230-1239.
7. Parthan A, Evans CJ, Le K. Chronic low back pain: epidemiology, economic burden and patient-reported outcomes in the USA. *Expert review of pharmacoeconomics & outcomes research.* Jun 2006;6(3): 359-369.
8. Azevedo LF, Costa-Pereira A, Mendonca L, Dias CC, Castro-Lopes JM. Epidemiology of chronic pain: a population-based nationwide study on its prevalence, characteristics and associated disability in Portugal. *The journal of pain: official journal of the American Pain Society.* Aug 2012;13(8):773-783.
9. Bekkering GE, Bala MM, Reid K, et al. Epidemiology of chronic pain and its treatment in The Netherlands. *The Netherlands journal of medicine.* Mar 2011;69(3):141-153.
10. Jakobsson U. The epidemiology of chronic pain in a general population: results of a survey in southern Sweden. *Scand J Rheumatol.* 2010;39(5):421-429.
11. Medicine I-lo. *Relieving Pain in America: A Blueprint for Transforming Prevention, Care, Education, and Research.* Washington, DC: The National Academies Press; 2011.
12. Nahin RL. Estimates of pain prevalence and severity in adults: United States, 2012. *J Pain.* Aug 2015;16(8):769-780.
13. Nahin RL. Estimates of pain prevalence and severity in adults: United States, 2012. *The journal of pain: official journal of the American Pain Society.* Aug 2015;16(8):769-780.
14. Manchikanti L, Fellows B, Ailinani H, Pampati V. Therapeutic use, abuse, and nonmedical use of opioids: a ten-year perspective. *Pain Physician.* Sep-Oct 2010;13(5):401-435.
15. Patrick SW, Fry CE, Jones TF, Buntin MB. Implementation Of Prescription Drug Monitoring Programs Associated With Reductions In Opioid-Related Death Rates. *Health Aff* (Millwood). Jul 01 2016;35(7):1324-1332.
16. Paulozzi LJ. Prescription drug overdoses: a review. *J Safety Res.* Sep 2012;43(4): 283-289.
17. Latimer J, Maher C, Refshauge K. The attitudes and beliefs of physiotherapy students to chronic back pain. *The Clinical journal of pain.* Jan-Feb 2004;20(1): 45-50.
18. Nijs J, Roussel N, Paul van Wilgen C, Koke A, Smeets R. Thinking beyond muscles and joints: therapists' and patients' attitudes and beliefs regarding chronic musculoskeletal pain are key to applying effective treatment. *Manual therapy.* Apr 2013;18(2):96-102.
19. Cox T, Puentedura E, Louw A. An Abbreviated Therapeutic Neuroscience Education Session Improves Pain Knowledge in First Year Physical Therapy Students But Does Not Change Attitudes or Beliefs *Journal of Manual & Manipulative Therapy.* 2017;25(1):11-21.
20. Henrotin YE, Cedraschi C, Duplan B, Bazin T, Duquesnoy B. Information and low back pain management: a systematic review. *Spine.* May 15 2006;31(11): E326-334.
21. Houben RM, Vlaeyen JW, Peters M, Ostelo RW, Wolters PM, Stomp-van den Berg SG. Health care providers' attitudes and beliefs towards common low back pain: factor structure and psychometric properties of the HC-PAIRS. *Clinical Journal of Pain.* Jan-Feb 2004;20(1):37-44.
22. Weiner BK. Spine update: the biopsychosocial model and spine care. *Spine.* Jan 15 2008;33(2):219-223.

23. Moseley GL. Reconceptualising pain according to modern pain science. *Physical Therapy Reviews.* 2007;12: 169-178.
24. Moseley L. Unraveling the barriers to reconceptualization of the problem in chronic pain: the actual and perceived ability of patients and health professionals to understand the neurophysiology. *The journal of pain: official journal of the American Pain Society.* May 2003;4(4):184-189.
25. Melzack R. From the gate to the neuromatrix. *Pain.* Aug 1999;Suppl 6:S121-126.
26. Hoeger Bement MK, Sluka KA. The Current State of Physical Therapy Pain Curriculum in the USA: A Faculty Survey. *The journal of pain: official journal of the American Pain Society.* Nov 12 2015.
27. Cox T, Louw A, Puentedura E. An abbreviated therapeutic neuroscience eduation session improves pain knowledge in first-year physical therapy students but does not change attitudes or beliefs. *Journal of Manual & Manipulative Therapy.* 2016.
28. Louw A, Schmidt SG. Chronic pain and the thoracic spine. *J Man Manip Ther.* Jul 2015;23(3):162-168.
29. Melzack R, Wall PD. Pain mechanisms: a new theory. *Science.* Nov 19 1965;150(3699):971-979.
30. Mezei L, Murinson BB, Johns Hopkins Pain Curriculum Development T. Pain education in North American medical schools. *The journal of pain: official journal of the American Pain Society.* Dec 2011;12(12):1199-1208.
31. Scudds R, Solomon P. Pain, and its managment: a new pain curriculum for occupational therapists and physical therapists. *Physiother Can.* 1995;47(2):77-84.
32. Louw A, Puentedura EJ, Zimney K, Cox T, Rico D. The clinical implementation of pain neuroscience education: A survey study. *Physiother Theory Pract.* Nov 2017;33(11):869-879.
33. Haldeman S. Presidential address, North American Spine Society: failure of the pathology model to predict back pain. *Spine.* 1990;15(7):718-724.
34. Iwamoto J, Takeda T, Wakano K. Returning athletes with severe low back pain and spondylolysis to original sporting activities with conservative treatment. *Scandinavian journal of medicine & science in sports.* Dec 2004;14(6):346-351.
35. Alyas F, Turner M, Connell D. MRI findings in the lumbar spines of asymptomatic, adolescent, elite tennis players. *British journal of sports medicine.* Nov 2007;41(11):836-841; discussion 841.
36. Waris E, Eskelin M, Hermunen H, Kiviluoto O, Paajanen H. Disc degeneration in low back pain: a 17-year follow-up study using magnetic resonance imaging. *Spine.* Mar 15 2007;32(6):681-684.
37. Foster NE, Delitto A. Embedding psychosocial perspectives within clinical management of low back pain: integration of psychosocially informed management principles into physical therapist practice–challenges and opportunities. *Physical therapy.* May 2011;91(5):790-803.
38. Linton SJ, Shaw WS. Impact of psychological factors in the experience of pain. *Physical therapy.* May 2011;91(5):700-711.
39. Louw A, Butler DS. Chronic Pain. In: S.B. B, Manske R, eds. *Clinical Orthopaedic Rehabilitation. 3rd Edition* ed. Philadelphia, PA: Elsevier; 2011.
40. Jull G, Sterling M. Bring back the biopsychosocial model for neck pain disorders. *Manual therapy.* Apr 2009;14(2):117-118.
41. Jull G. Biopsychosocial model of disease: 40 years on. Which way is the pendulum swinging? *British journal of sports medicine.* Aug 2017;51(16):1187-1188.
42. Vlaeyen JW, Kole-Snijders AM, Boeren RG, van Eek H. Fear of movement/(re) injury in chronic low back pain and its relation to behavioral performance. *Pain.* Sep 1995;62(3):363-372.
43. Meeus M, Nijs J, Van Oosterwijck J, Van Alsenoy V, Truijen S. Pain Physiology Education Improves Pain Beliefs in Patients With Chronic Fatigue Syndrome Compared With Pacing and Self-Management Education: A Double-Blind Randomized Controlled Trial. *Arch Phys Med Rehabil.* Aug 2010;91(8): 1153-1159.
44. Moseley GL. Evidence for a direct relationship between cognitive and physical change during an education intervention in people with chronic low back pain. *European Journal of Pain.* 2004;8:39-45.
45. Goldberg JS. Revisiting the Cartesian model of pain. *Medical hypotheses.* 2008;70(5):1029-1033.
46. Louw A, Puentedura EL, Mintken P. Use of an abbreviated neuroscience education approach in the treatment of chronic low back pain: a case report. *Physiotherapy theory and practice.* Jan 2012;28(1): 50-62.

47. Fritz JM, Cleland JA, Childs JD. Subgrouping patients with low back pain: evolution of a classification approach to physical therapy. *J Orthop Sports Phys Ther.* Jun 2007;37(6):290-302.
48. Nee RJ, Coppieters MW. Interpreting research on clinical prediction rules for physiotherapy treatments. *Manual therapy.* Apr 2011;16(2):105-108.
49. Haskins R, Rivett DA, Osmotherly PG. Clinical prediction rules in the physiotherapy management of low back pain: a systematic review. *Manual therapy.* Feb 2012;17(1):9-21.
50. Flynn T, Fritz J, Whitman J, et al. A clinical prediction rule for classifying patients with low back pain who demonstrate short-term improvement with spinal manipulation. *Spine.* Dec 15 2002;27(24):2835-2843.
51. Childs JD, Fritz JM, Flynn TW, et al. A clinical prediction rule to identify patients with low back pain most likely to benefit from spinal manipulation: a validation study. *Ann Intern Med.* Dec 21 2004;141(12):920-928.
52. Hicks GE, Fritz JM, Delitto A, McGill SM. Preliminary development of a clinical prediction rule for determining which patients with low back pain will respond to a stabilization exercise program. *Arch Phys Med Rehabil.* Sep 2005;86(9): 1753-1762.
53. Rabin A, Shashua A, Pizem K, Dickstein R, Dar G. A clinical prediction rule to identify patients with low back pain who are likely to experience short-term success following lumbar stabilization exercises: a randomized controlled validation study. *J Orthop Sports Phys Ther.* Jan 2014;44(1):6-B13.
54. Fritz JM, Lindsay W, Matheson JW, et al. Is there a subgroup of patients with low back pain likely to benefit from mechanical traction? Results of a randomized clinical trial and subgrouping analysis. *Spine.* Dec 15 2007;32(26):E793-800.
55. Hefford C. McKenzie classification of mechanical spinal pain: profile of syndromes and directions of preference. *Manual therapy.* Feb 2008;13(1):75-81.
56. Sackett DL. Evidence-based medicine. *Spine.* May 15 1998;23(10):1085-1086.
57. Silagy C. Evidence vs experience. *Australian Doctor.* 1999;April.
58. Puentedura EJ, Cleland JA, Landers MR, Mintken PE, Louw A, Fernandez-de-Las-Penas C. Development of a clinical prediction rule to identify patients with neck pain likely to benefit from thrust joint manipulation to the cervical spine. *The Journal of orthopaedic and sports physical therapy.* 2012;42(7):577-592.
59. Benedetti F. Placebo and the new physiology of the doctor-patient relationship. *Physiol Rev.* Jul 2013;93(3):1207-1246.
60. Verbeek J, Sengers MJ, Riemens L, Haafkens J. Patient expectations of treatment for back pain: a systematic review of qualitative and quantitative studies. *Spine.* Oct 15 2004;29(20): 2309-2318.
61. Gifford L. *Aches and Pain.* Cornwall: Wordpress; 2014.
62. Thomas KB. General practice consultations: is there any point in being positive? *British medical journal.* May 9 1987;294(6581):1200-1202.
63. Kovacs FM, Seco J, Royuela A, Pena A, Muriel A. The correlation between pain, catastrophizing, and disability in subacute and chronic low back pain: a study in the routine clinical practice of the Spanish National Health Service. *Spine.* Feb 15 2011;36(4):339-345.
64. Vlaeyen JWS, Linton SJ. Fear-avoidance and its consequences in chronic musculoskeletal pain: a state of the art. *Pain.* 2000;85:317-322.
65. Vlaeyen JW, Linton SJ. Fear-avoidance model of chronic musculoskeletal pain: 12 years on. *Pain.* Jun 2012;153(6): 1144-1147.
66. Waddell G, Newton M, Henderson I, al. e. A fear-avoidance beliefs questionnaire (FABQ) and the role of fear avoidance beliefs in chronic low back pain and disability. *Pain.* 1993;52:157-168.
67. Nijs J, Meeus M, Heins M, Knoop H, Moorkens G, Bleijenberg G. Kinesiophobia, catastrophizing and anticipated symptoms before stair climbing in chronic fatigue syndrome: an experimental study. *Disabil Rehabil.* 2012;34(15):1299-1305.
68. Cleland JA, Fritz JM, Childs JD. Psychometric properties of the Fear-Avoidance Beliefs Questionnaire and Tampa Scale of Kinesiophobia in patients with neck pain. *Am J Phys Med Rehabil.* Feb 2008;87(2):109-117.
69. Crombez G, Vlaeyen JW, Heuts PH, Lysens R. Pain-related fear is more disabling than pain itself: evidence on the role of pain-related fear in chronic back pain disability. *Pain.* 1999;80(1):329-339.
70. George SZ, Dannecker EA, Robinson ME. Fear of pain, not pain catastrophizing, predicts acute pain intensity, but neither factor predicts tolerance or blood pressure reactivity: an experimental investigation in pain-free individuals. *European journal of pain (London, England).* Jul 2006;10(5):457-465.

71. Mintken PE, Cleland JA, Whitman JM, George SZ. Psychometric properties of the Fear-Avoidance Beliefs Questionnaire and Tampa Scale of Kinesiophobia in patients with shoulder pain. *Archives of physical medicine and rehabilitation*. Jul 2010;91(7):1128-1136.
72. Waddell G, Newton M, Henderson I, Somerville D, Main CJ. A Fear-Avoidance Beliefs Questionnaire (FABQ) and the role of fear-avoidance beliefs in chronic low back pain and disability. *Pain*. Feb 1993;52(2):157-168.
73. Fritz JM, George SZ. Identifying psychosocial variables in patients with acute work-related low back pain: the importance of fear-avoidance beliefs. *Physical therapy*. Oct 2002;82(10): 973-983.
74. Fritz JM, George SZ, Delitto A. The role of fear-avoidance beliefs in acute low back pain: relationships with current and future disability and work status. *Pain*. Oct 2001;94(1):7-15.
75. George SZ, Fritz JM, Bialosky JE, Donald DA. The effect of a fear-avoidance-based physical therapy intervention for patients with acute low back pain: results of a randomized clinical trial. *Spine*. Dec 1 2003;28(23):2551-2560.
76. Williamson E. Fear Avoidance Beliefs Questionnaire (FABQ). *The Australian journal of physiotherapy*. 2006;52(2):149.
77. Lethem J, Slade PD, Troup JD, Bentley G. Outline of a Fear-Avoidance Model of exaggerated pain perception – I. *Behaviour research and therapy*. 1983;21(4): 401-408.
78. Kori SH, Miller RP, Todd DD. Kinesophobia: a new view of chronic pain behaviour. *Pain Management*. 1990;Jan/Feb:35-43.
79. Hapidou EG, O'Brien MA, Pierrynowski MR, de Las Heras E, Patel M, Patla T. Fear and Avoidance of Movement in People with Chronic Pain: Psychometric Properties of the 11-Item Tampa Scale for Kinesiophobia (TSK-11). *Physiother Can*. Summer 2012;64(3):235-241.
80. Moseley GL. Reconceptualising pain acording to modern pain sciences. *Physical Therapy Reviews*. 2007;12: 169-178.
81. Marinus J, Moseley GL, Birklein F, et al. Clinical features and pathophysiology of complex regional pain syndrome. *Lancet Neurol*. Jul 2011;10(7):637-648.
82. Grotle M, Vollestad NK, Brox JI. Screening for yellow flags in first-time acute low back pain: reliability and validity of a Norwegian version of the Acute Low Back Pain Screening Questionnaire. *The Clinical journal of pain*. Jun 2006;22(5):458-467.
83. Raudenbush B, Canter RJ, Corley N, et al. Pain threshold and tolerance differences among intercollegiate athletes: implication of past sports injuries and willingness to compete among sports teams. *North American Journal of Psychology Publisher*. March 2012 2012;14(1).
84. Shah VS, Taddio A, Bennett S, Speidel BD. Neonatal pain response to heel stick vs venepuncture for routine blood sampling. *Archives of disease in childhood. Fetal and neonatal edition*. Sep 1997;77(2): F143-144.
85. Horsley R. Factors that affect the occurrence and chronicity of occupation-related musculoskeletal disorders. *Best Pract Res Clin Rheumatol*. Feb 2011;25(1):103-115.
86. Buchbinder R, Jolley D. Effects of a media campaign on back beliefs is sustained 3 years after its cessation. *Spine*. Jun 1 2005;30(11):1323-1330.
87. Buchbinder R, Jolley D, Wyatt M. 2001 Volvo Award Winner in Clinical Studies: Effects of a media campaign on back pain beliefs and its potential influence on management of low back pain in general practice. *Spine*. Dec 1 2001;26(23): 2535-2542.
88. Oliveira VC, Ferreira PH, Maher CG, Pinto RZ, Refshauge KM, Ferreira ML. Effectiveness of self-management of low back pain: systematic review with meta-analysis. *Arthritis care & research*. Nov 2012;64(11):1739-1748.
89. Holm LW, Carroll LJ, Cassidy JD, Ahlbom A. Factors influencing neck pain intensity in whiplash-associated disorders. *Spine*. Feb 15 2006;31(4):E98-104.
90. Schmidt CO, Raspe H, Pfingsten M, et al. Back pain in the German adult population: prevalence, severity, and sociodemographic correlates in a multiregional survey. *Spine (Phila Pa 1976)*. Aug 15 2007;32(18):2005-2011.
91. Virani SN, Ferrari R, Russell AS. Physician resistance to the late whiplash syndrome. *J Rheumatol*. Sep 2001;28(9): 2096-2099.
92. Louw A, Puentedura EJ, Zimney K. A clinical contrast: physical therapists with low back pain treating patients with low back pain. *Physiotherapy theory and practice*. Nov 2015;31(8):562-567.
93. Louw A, Diener I, Landers MR, Zimney K, Puentedura EJ. Three-year follow-up of a randomized controlled trial comparing preoperative neuroscience education for patients undergoing surgery for lumbar radiculopathy. *Journal of spine surgery*. Dec 2016;2(4):289-298.

94. Louw A, Diener I, Landers MR, Puentedura EJ. Preoperative pain neuroscience education for lumbar radiculopathy: a multicenter randomized controlled trial with 1-year follow-up. *Spine.* Aug 15 2014;39(18):1449-1457.
95. Louw A, Podolak J, Zimney K, Schmidt S, Puentedura E. Can Pain Beliefs Change in Middle School Students? A Study of the Effectiveness of Pain Neuroscience Education. *Physiother Theory Pract.* 2017 – Accepted for publication.
96. Morr S, Shanti N, Carrer A, Kubeck J, Gerling MC. Quality of information concerning cervical disc herniation on the Internet. *The spine journal: official journal of the North American Spine Society.* Apr 2010;10(4):350-354.
97. Sloan TJ, Walsh DA. Explanatory and diagnostic labels and perceived prognosis in chronic low back pain. *Spine.* Oct 1 2010;35(21):E1120-1125.
98. Wilson D, Williams M, Butler D. Language and the pain experience. *Physiotherapy research international: the journal for researchers and clinicians in physical therapy.* Mar 2009;14(1):56-65.
99. Ledgerwood A, Boydstun AE. Sticky prospects: loss frames are cognitively stickier than gain frames. *Journal of experimental psychology.* General. Feb 2014;143(1):376-385.
100. Benedetti F, Thoen W, Blanchard C, Vighetti S, Arduino C. Pain as a reward: changing the meaning of pain from negative to positive co-activates opioid and cannabinoid systems. *Pain.* Mar 2013;154(3):361-367.
101. Valtorta NK, Kanaan M, Gilbody S, Ronzi S, Hanratty B. Loneliness and social isolation as risk factors for coronary heart disease and stroke: systematic review and meta-analysis of longitudinal observational studies. *Heart.* Jul 01 2016;102(13):1009-1016.
102. Vlaeyen JW, Crombez G, Linton SJ. The fear-avoidance model of pain. *Pain.* Aug 2016;157(8):1588-1589.
103. Garcia-Campayo J, Serrano-Blanco A, Rodero B, et al. Effectiveness of the psychological and pharmacological treatment of catastrophization in patients with fibromyalgia: a randomized controlled trial. *Trials.* 2009;10:24.
104. Sullivan MJL, Bishop SR, Pivak J. The pain catastrophizing scale: Development and validation. *Psychological Assessment.* 1995;7:524-532.
105. Mutsaers JH, Peters R, Pool-Goudzwaard AL, Koes BW, Verhagen AP. Psychometric properties of the Pain Attitudes and Beliefs Scale for Physiotherapists: A systematic review. *Manual therapy.* Jan 23 2012.
106. Kendall NAS, Linton SJ, Main CJ. "Guide to assessing psychosocial yellow flags in acute low back pain: risk factors for long term disability and work loss." Wellington: Accident Rehabilitation & Compensation Insurance Corporation of New Zealand and the National Health Committee; 1997.
107. Cherkin DC. Primary care research on low back pain. The state of the science. *Spine.* Sep 15 1998;23(18):1997-2002.
108. Deyo RA, Mirza SK, Martin BI. Back pain prevalence and visit rates: estimates from U.S. national surveys, 2002. *Spine.* Nov 1 2006;31(23):2724-2727.
109. Lurie JD, Birkmeyer NJ, Weinstein JN. Rates of advanced spinal imaging and spine surgery. *Spine.* Mar 15 2003;28(6):616-620.
110. Waddell G. *The Back Pain Revolution.* Second ed. Edinburgh: Elsevier; 2004.
111. Linton SJ, Hellsing AL, Hallden K. A population-based study of spinal pain among 35-45-year-old individuals. Prevalence, sick leave, and health care use. *Spine.* Jul 01 1998;23(13): 1457-1463.
112. Linton SJ, Nordin E. A 5-year follow-up evaluation of the health and economic consequences of an early cognitive behavioral intervention for back pain: a randomized, controlled trial. *Spine.* Apr 15 2006;31(8):853-858.
113. Hashemi L, Webster BS, Clancy EA, Volinn E. Length of disability and cost of workers' compensation low back pain claims. *Journal of occupational and environmental medicine / American College of Occupational and Environmental Medicine.* Oct 1997;39(10):937-945.
114. Louw A, Flynn TW, Puentedura E. *Everyone Has Back Pain.* Minneapolis, MN: OPTP; 2015.
115. Louw A. *Why You Hurt: A Neuroscience Approach to Pain.* Minneapolis: OPTP; 2013.
116. Leerar PJ, Boissonnault W, Domholdt E, Roddey T. Documentation of red flags by physical therapists for patients with low back pain. *The Journal of manual & manipulative therapy.* 2007;15(1):42-49.
117. Ross MD, Boissonnault WG. Red flags: to screen or not to screen? *J Orthop Sports Phys Ther.* Nov 2010;40(11):682-684.

Notes

Chapter 2

Patient Education

2.1: Education

Education is therapy. Knowledge is therapy. Chapter 1 clearly indicates that patients need education. The question now arises as to what type of education is needed; this includes content and educational delivery methods. Patient education is defined as any set of planned educational activities designed to improve a patient's health behaviors, health status or both. Such activities are aimed at facilitating the patient's knowledge base.[1,2] In all healthcare educational strategies, i.e., smoking cessation, weight loss, etc., the "holy grail" is true behavior change after receiving an educational intervention.[3] In order for a patient to change behavior, three key elements are necessary: knowledge, motivation and opportunity. Education as a means of imparting knowledge would thus be a foundational component of treating chronic pain. Additionally, as will be argued throughout this book, the content and delivery methods can be highly motivational, further enhancing behavior change. Patient education has always had a strong history in nursing, and in PT it has always been seen as a non-specific intervention. Table 2.1 highlights some common styles of education, including their reported benefits and pitfalls. The list is by no means an authoritative review of patient education, but likely an introductory listing for most clinicians. After reviewing Table 2.1, most clinicians will likely identify styles of education they commonly encounter and utilize in clinical practice. Do they work? In general, there is a lack of convincing evidence for the usefulness of education in musculoskeletal conditions as a standalone intervention.[2,4-6] This should not be surprising considering education-only strategies are rarely successful. As an example, education for smoking cessation ("smoking kills"), despite costing billions of dollars, results in only a 20 percent success rate.[7-9]

Common provocative injury pictures (adapted from the internet).

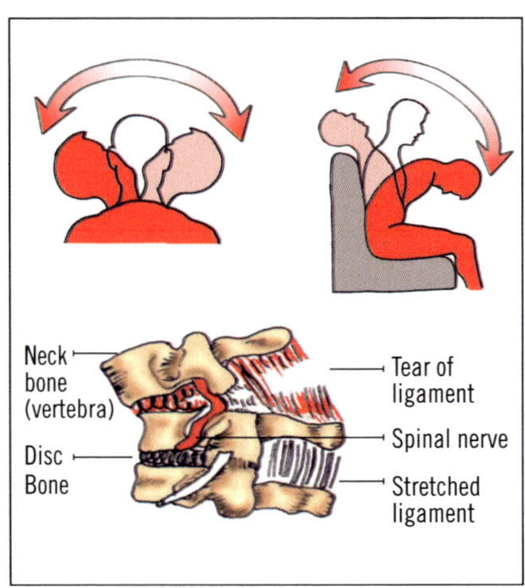

Figure 2.1: Whiplash-associated disorder.

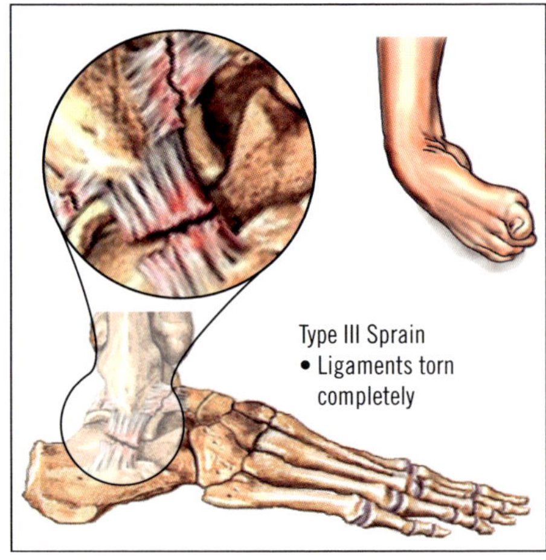

Figure 2.2: Ankle sprain.

The question all healthcare providers should ask is: why isn't education more effective? Review Table 2.1 again, and then view Figures 2.1 and 2.2. These images, adapted from the internet, display two commonly encountered injuries: Motor vehicle collision with a whiplash-associated disorder, and an ankle sprain. Would viewing these images help a patient recover faster or even help ease pain, fear or anxiety? Although the answer might seem to be quite simple, it is not readily understood by clinicians that viewing images like this do not only "not help," but may in fact have a negative effect on a patient.[10,11]

Table 2.1: Summary of common patient education styles.

Education Style	Positives	Negatives
1. Verbal one-on-one[12-14]	• Personal • Patient and condition specific • Ability to answer patient questions	• Expensive financially and in terms of manpower • Limited efficacy for mass communication • Time consuming • Limited recall
2. Video/DVD[15-17]	• Cheap and easy to produce • Mass education • Standard message	• Impersonal • Limited ability to answer patient questions • Inability to modify for specific conditions or circumstances
3. Websites[18,19]	• Standardized message • Ability to make it interactive • Accessibility • Mass education • Ability to make it affordable for the consumer • Engaging current/future learning platforms	• Impersonal • Costly to design and maintain • Telehealth limitations with billing and licensure for PTs • Content not always reflective of latest evidence

Table 2.1: Summary of common patient education styles *(continued).*

Education Style	Positives	Negatives
4. Booklets/ Pamphlets[20-22]	• Cheap and easy to produce • Mass education • Standardized message	• Impersonal • Low compliance • Monotone and boring • Inability to answer individualized specific patient questions
5. TV Advertising[23,24]	• Mass education • Visual and auditory • Ability to change behavior • Standardized message	• Expensive • Due to short exposures (i.e. 30 seconds), repeated messages are needed • Inability to answer individualized specific patient questions
6. Email[25,26]	• Quick, fast • Keeping up with technology • Personal	• Can be time consuming • Patient technological limitations • Privacy issues • Billing issues
7. Joint Models[27]	• Visual • Realistic • Accompanies verbal education	• Can induce fear • Biomedical in nature • Fear-inducing focus on negatives, i.e., "bulging discs," red color indicating bleeding and inflammation, etc.
8. Back School[28-30]	• Standardized training • Deliver content in group format	• May induce fear • Limited efficacy • Biomedical content • Often not individualized

PT is deeply rooted in a biomedical model focusing on tissues and tissue injury.[11,31-33] The biomedical model seeks to find and correct a presumed anatomical or biomechanical fault. Once the identified fault is "fixed" it is expected that pain and disability will be resolved (Figure 1.4).[34] Not only have these models shown limited efficacy in decreasing pain and disability, they may increase fear in patients. This increased fear may in turn increase their pain.[35,36] Although healthcare professionals intended to provide helpful information, biomedical education may have inadvertently encouraged inaccurate or unhealthy beliefs related to the nature of pain. A truly wonderful illustration of this can been seen in the classic experiment where patients underwent lumbar discectomy. Patients who were shown their "damaged disc" material that was removed in the surgery recovered significantly better than those who were not shown their excised disc material.[37] What's intriguing is that the positive results included not only subjective pain ratings, but also neurological findings such as weakness and paresthesia.

- Leg pain (91.5 vs. 80.4%; $p<0.05$)
- Back pain (86.1 vs. 75.0%; $p<0.05$)
- Limb weakness (90.5 vs. 56.3%; $p<0.02$)
- Paresthesia (88 vs. 61.9%; $p<0.05$)
- Reduced analgesic use (92.1 vs. 69.4%; $p<0.02$)

Patients who were given their "disc material" kept it for weeks and months after the surgery as a means to have "proof" that the disc material (which they likely believed was the root of their pain) was gone. This may seem far-fetched, but the clinical reality is that patients often carry with them old, well-aged and origami-like folded imaging and medical tests results, which are readily pulled out when a new healthcare provider is encountered. The new version? Have you seen the screen saver of an MRI on a patient's cell phone? This all reiterates the notion that we have indoctrinated patients so much that they become fascinated with the information and/or they feel the need to "prove" they have something really wrong with them because nobody believes them. It is hard to get well when you have to prove you are ill. It is argued that the educational strategies employed in Table 2.1 are likely limited partly due to the content of their message.[38] These educational sessions are heavily focused on biomedical information (anatomy, biomechanics and physiology) to educate patients about their pain. Instead, this newly acquired biomedical education may reinforce the anatomical source of pain and even induce fear.[39,40] Louis Gifford noted the clinical dichotomy which arose:

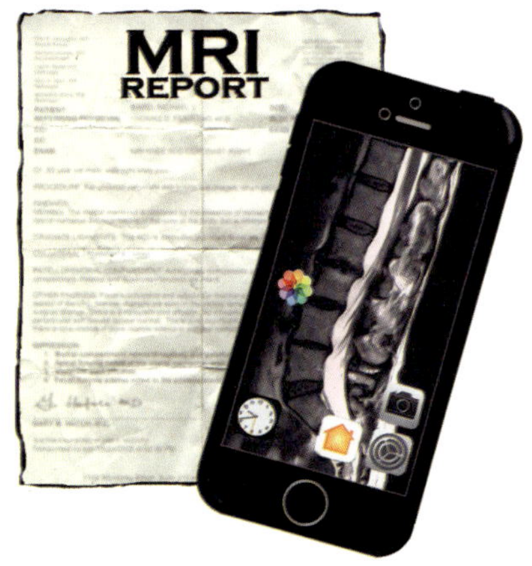

> Patients attend therapy with LBP and we spend all our time teaching them about the low back and little to nothing about the actual reason they are there...pain[41]

This is a key message. Think about it carefully: Suzy (Chapter 1) is coming to PT with LBP and we spend an enormous amount of time teaching her about the back; the age changes, the health of her discs, how she should bend, sit and pick up boxes, etc. The problem? What brings her to PT? Pain. She is taught very little, if anything, about pain – the main reason she is coming to PT. Patients in pain want to know more about pain[42] and providers underestimate patients' need for and ability to understand pain.[27,43,44]

2.2: Pain Neuroscience Education (PNE)

A new model to educate patients as a means to modulate pain and disability was needed. In the literature, PNE as we currently view it, began approximately 20 years ago thanks to the late Louis Gifford.[38,45] PNE started as a blend of basic science, clinical experience, collaboration with other professionals and PTs' newfound interest in neurodynamics, referred to as "neural tension" in the mid to late 1980s.[41,46,47] In the golden age of manual therapy, pain science sprouted from manual therapy via the development and use of neurodynamics.[47-49] The early "neural tension," however, was more likely "another tissue to mobilize," using similar manual therapy principles and vantage points.[41] To its credit, "neural tension" did move us out of the joints and muscles (biomedical model), inching us closer to the brain, the nervous system, and viewing our patients though a multisystem approach (biopsychosocial model). As our understanding of pain grew, it sprouted PNE along with other emerging pain treatments such as graded motor imagery (GMI) (Figure 2.3). This newfound interest culminated in early pain science papers,[47,50] along with the first documented presentation of PNE ("Explaining Pain to Patients") at the IASP conference in Austria in 1999 by Louis Gifford and Heather Muncey.[51] By virtue of explaining a pain experience to a patient with this newfound knowledge of pain, PNE was developed.

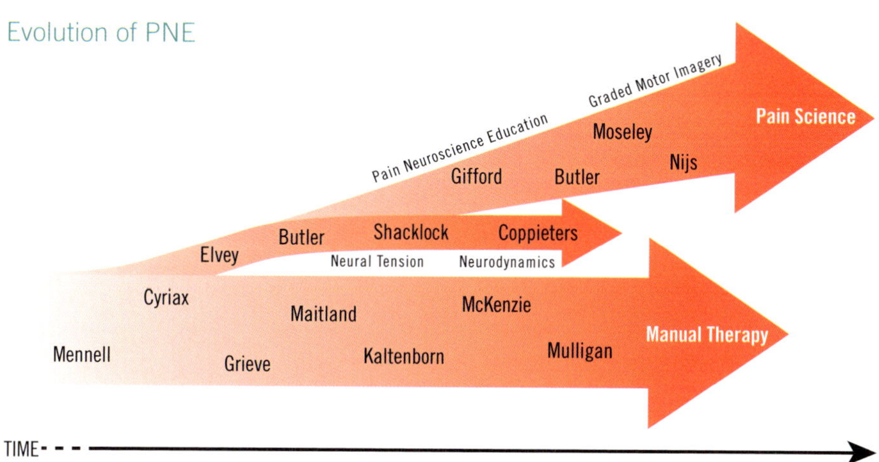

Figure 2.3: Evolution of pain science in physical therapy.

The first study involving PNE was published by Moseley in 2002.[52] By concealed randomization, 57 patients with chronic LBP were allocated to either a four-week combined PT and education program or management as directed by their general practitioners (usual care). The dependent variables of interest were pain and disability. Assessors were blind to group allocation. Outcome data from 49 subjects (86 percent) showed a significant treatment effect. The four-week combined PT and education program reduced pain and disability by a mean of 1.5/10 points on a numerical rating scale and 3.9 points on the 18-point Roland Morris Disability Questionnaire (RMDQ), respectively. The treatment effect was maintained at one-year follow-up. The findings supported the efficacy of combined PT and education program in producing symptomatic and functional change in moderately disabled patients with chronic LBP. What exactly did they do for education?

"Each subject participated in a one-hour education session, once per week for four weeks. The education session was in a one-to-one seminar format, conducted by an independent therapist, and focused on the neurophysiology of pain with no particular reference to the lumbar spine."

In other words, the PNE session educated patients about pain but at the same time de-focused anatomical issues. Since 2002, research into PNE has expanded to include published case studies, case series, randomized controlled trials and various systematic reviews. Since the original study by Moseley, subsequent activity in the field of PNE research has increased considerably, extending beyond chronic LBP and starting to explore various applications and aspects of teaching people about pain (Figure 2.4).

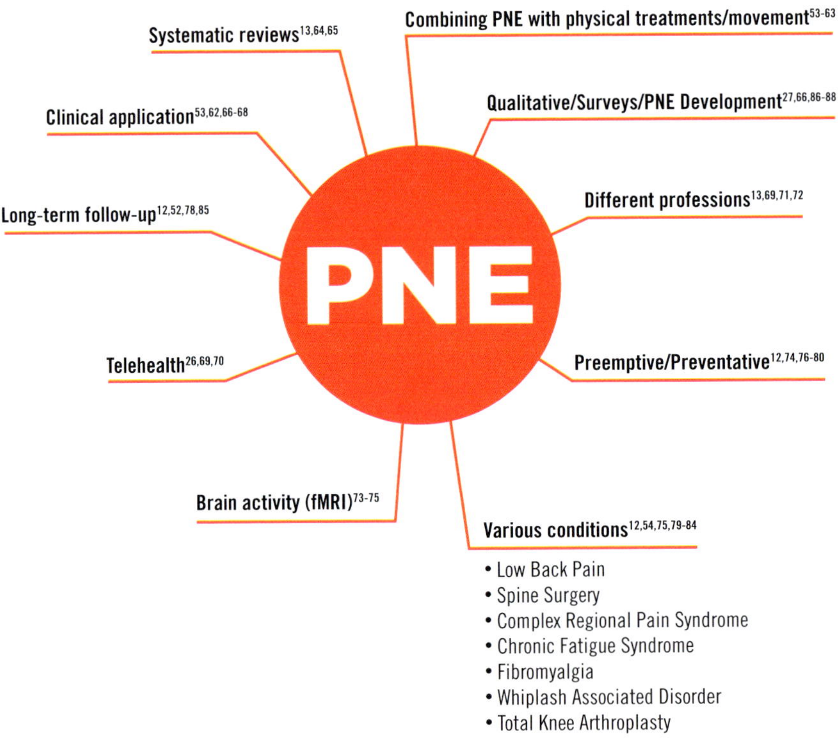

Figure 2.4: Research activity in the field of PNE.

2.3: Evidence for PNE

With all the attention surrounding PNE, the question was posed: Does it work? To answer the question, a systematic review of RCTs was warranted. In 2010, an initial systematic review of PNE was published, with inconclusive results due to the review only consisting of two published studies.[65] In 2011, another systematic review of PNE was conducted for musculoskeletal pain, this time consisting of six high-quality RCTs, one pseudo-RCT, and one comparative study involving 401 subjects.[64] This review showed that for chronic musculoskeletal pain disorders, there is compelling evidence that an educational strategy addressing neurophysiology and neurobiology of pain (PNE) can have a positive effect on pain, disability, catastrophization, and physical performance. In 2016, the same research team updated the systematic review, dropping the lower level studies (pseudo-RCT, comparative studies) and only focusing on high-level RCTs.[13] The updated review, now comprising 13 RCTs, provided strong evidence for PNE improving pain ratings, pain knowledge, disability, pain catastrophization, fear-avoidance, attitudes and behaviors regarding pain, physical movement and healthcare utilization.[12,14,52,84,85,89-96] These three systematic reviews clearly indicated the growing efficacy of PNE as well as research activity in this field.

To develop a greater clinical understanding of the potential impact of PNE, we need to look no further than the number needed to treat (NNT), as it is quite revealing. The NNT offers a measurement of the impact of an intervention by estimating the number of patients who need to be treated with that intervention to prevent one additional bad outcome. Another way of saying this is the number of patients that need to be treated for one of them to benefit compared with a control in a clinical trial. The lower the NNT, the more effective the treatment. The "perfect" NNT is 1:1, implying for every one patient who receives the intervention, one is successfully treated by that intervention. In regard to chronic LBP, Moseley showed that the NNT for PNE addressing function is 2:1 and for pain 3:1.[52] This implies that for every two patients with chronic LBP who receive PNE, one will have successful functional improvement, while one in three will have significant improvement in their pain (Figure 2.5 on the following page).

To put this into perspective, we should compare the NNT for PNE to the current "gold standards" for treating chronic pain. For most chronic pain conditions, current practice guidelines, systematic reviews and meta-analyses call for the use of membrane stabilizing medication (i.e., gabapentin) and antidepressants (i.e., selective serotonin reuptake inhibitors – SSRI). What is interesting is that the NNT for gabapentin is calculated as 6:1 and for SSRIs as 7:1.[97,98] Additionally, other calculations can also be made to look at numbers needed to harm (NNH) or numbers needed to kill (NNK). The comparison of the NNT to the NNH or NNK provides a potential assessment of the risk-benefit ratio. To date, no studies have been performed on the NNH or NNK for PNE; however, it's important to realize no systematic reviews pertaining to musculoskeletal pain have shown a fatality after patient education. In contrast to PNE, both membrane stabilizers and anti-depressants have been shown to cause serious and life-threatening side-effects.[99-101]

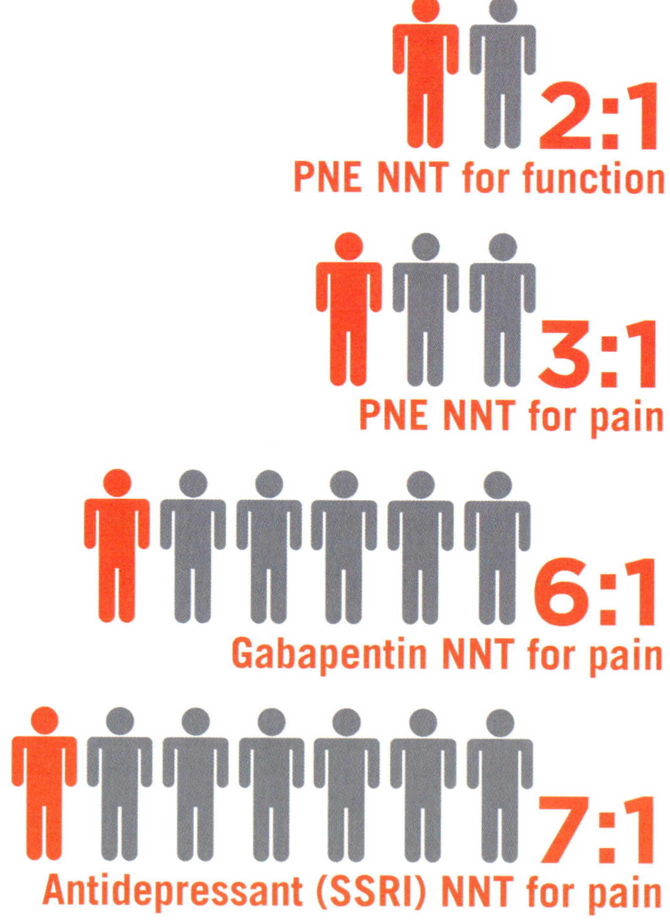

Figure 2.5: Relative efficacy of PNE as shown through number needed to treat (NNT).

Allowing for the overall efficacy of PNE, the following breakdown delves into the various specific effects of PNE on pain, disability, various psychosocial factors (fear-avoidance, pain catastrophization, etc.), movement restrictions and healthcare utilization:

PNE specifically addressing pain[13]:

Ten of the 13 studies in the most recent systematic review evaluated the effect of PNE on pain.

1. The mean improvement of pain at one month was 1.5 on the numeric pain rating scale (NPRS) (95% CI 0.7 to 2.3) for those receiving the intervention over those in the control group. This difference was shown to have a significant treatment effect ($p < 0.01$) with a NNT to gain clinical significance of 3.0 (95% CI 2 to 8). At one-year follow-up, this difference maintained in regard to improvement with pain 1.9 (95% CI 1 to 2.8) with a NNT of 2.0 (95% CI 1 to 4).[54]

2. There was a significant decrease in pain on NPRS from five-week "on-going usual treatment" to end of four-week treatment intervention and 12-month follow-up. The "individual education" group showed a treatment effect of 3.1 (95% CI 1.8-4.2) on NPRS at the conclusion of four-week intervention and the "group education" group showed a 2.7 (95% CI 1.6-3.9) reduction on NPRS. The difference between pre-treatment and post-treatment between independent and group treatment was 1.0 (95% CI .3-2.0).[56]

3. There was a significant time and group interaction from pre-test to post one-month follow-up for PNE group over control group of exercise and traditional education group with decrease in NPRS. This difference leveled off at the three-month post intervention time measurement point.[57]

4. Pressure pain threshold decreased in both groups over time but no between-group differences were found at the end of the intervention. There was a significant difference in pain neuroscience knowledge in experimental group over control group ($p<0.001$).[59]

5. Both treatment groups showed a significant improvement with respect to improved pain ratings with the PNE group showing statistically ($p< 0.001$) superior outcomes compared to the traditional therapy group at three-month and 12-month follow-up. The mean differences between groups for three months and 12 months respectively for NPRS were 2.1 (95% CI 2.7 to 1.4) and 1.3 (95% CI 2.1 to 0.5).[58]

6. Analysis showed that both groups improved over time in NPRS but there was no significant effect between groups in regard to pain with reading either the PNE book or control book. Increased knowledge about pain biology in the experimental group over advice group (p<0.01) with an effect size Cohen d=1.7.[71]

7. A spatial summation procedure showed no significant differences at two weeks post-intervention with PNE compared to control, but there was a significant difference at three months (p=0.041). There was no significant difference in pressure pain threshold or Pain Vigilance and Awareness Questionnaire between groups over assessment periods. The Neurophysiology of Pain Questionnaire showed a significant increase in response with experimental group (p<0.001) but not control group (p=0.150).[102]

8. There was no significant effect for low back or leg pain between the PNE group and the control group over the 12 months. Overall, time effects for decreased pain for both groups were significant (p<0.002). There was short term (one-month follow-up) effect with significant decrease in pain for low back and leg (p<0.046) but it plateaued over the three, six and 12-month follow-up.[103]

9. No group interaction for pain intensity was found between the trigger point dry needling group with PNE (-3.6 (95% CI -6.0 to -1.1)) or without PNE (-4.2 (95% CI -6.6 to -1.7)), but time interaction was significant for both groups (p<0.002). There was no group interaction differences for pressure pain threshold measurements but there was a significant time interaction post-treatment at all three measurement points.[60]

10. Statistical differences were found for overall group interaction by time and also between group interaction at three-month follow-up favoring the PNE group but none at six-week follow-up on the visual analogue scale. Visual analogue change at three months for education group compared to control group was -25.4±26.7 and -6.6±30.7, respectively.[61]

PNE specifically addressing dysfunction[13]:

Twelve of the 13 studies addressed function through various functional measurement tools. Six studies looked at general functional improvement scores through use of Roland Morris Disability Questionnaire (RMDQ)[54,56,57,60,104] or Short Form 36 Health Status Survey (SF-36)[102]. Eight of the studies used more specific questionnaires based on diagnostic or functional status. The diagnostic or specific functional measurement tools used were Oswestry Disability Index (ODI)[58,60,103], Neck Disability Index (NDI)[55], Patient Specific Functional Scale (PSFS)[71], Fibromyalgia Impact Questionnaire (FIQ)[82,102], Revised Illness Perception Questionnaire for Fibromyalgia (IPQ-R_FM)[82], and Quebec Back Pain Disability Scale[61].

1. Both groups improved in regard to disability with mean improvement of the intervention group over control of 3.9 points on the RMDQ (95% CI 2.0 to 5.8). With number needed to treat of 2.0 (95% CI 2 to 5) for the RMDQ.[54]

2. Between-group change favored the intervention group with a mean effect of 2.4 (95% CI 0.8 to 4.2) on the RMDQ.[56]

3. Experimental group improved in RMDQ by 2.0 points (95% CI 0.4 to 3.6) compared to control group post treatment.[104]

4. There was a non-significant trend toward a more favorable outcome with experimental group in improvement of RMDQ (p=0.127).[57]

5. Both groups showed significant improvement over time with treatment for ODI scores. The group receiving PNE had a significant (p<0.001) mean difference improvement of -9.7 (95% CI -12.7 to -6.7) at three months and -8.2 (95% CI -12.6 to -3.8) at 12 months compared to the other group ODI score. The group receiving PNE showed an overall ODI improvement over 12 months of 13.7 (95% CI 11.4 to 16.1; p<0.001)[58]

6. Both groups improved over time in regard to disability as measure through PSFS, but no differential effect between groups was found (p=0.07).[71]

7. Significant between-group differences were found in favor of experimental group for SF-36 physical functioning (p=0.046), general health perceptions (p<0.001) and vitality (p=0.047) sub scores. A large effect size (Cohen's *d*) was found for the SF-36 health perceptions scale (d=-0.98). The remaining SF-36 sub scores and FIQ did not show significant effects for between-group differences.[102]

8. No significant effects were found between groups for FIQ and all effect sizes for FIQ domains were small. Illness perception as measured through IPQ-R_FM did not show any statistically different effects between groups.[82]

9. There were no significant between-group interactions found ($p>0.167$), both groups showed improvement over time in regard to function as measured with ODI ($p<0.002$).[103]

10. ODI scores showed no significant group interaction changes for ODI ($p=0.542$) or RMDQ ($p=0.111$). There was an effect for time for both groups for ODI ($p<0.001$) and RMDQ ($p<0.001$).[60]

11. NDI showed significant improvement ($p<0.01$) for both experimental groups compared to control group at the four, eight and 16-week follow-ups.[55]

12. Functional disability showed significant ($p<0.05$) group by time interaction but was not statistically significant between groups at six weeks ($p= 0.83$) or three months ($p=0.09$). A greater percent of participants in PNE reported benefits from treatment for functional disability at both measurement points with only the three-month follow-up showing significant ($p=0.034$) findings.[61]

PNE specifically addressing psychosocial factors[13]:

Outcomes related to psychosocial factors were measured in 11 of the 13 studies. Researchers chose a mixture of validated tests consisting of Pain Catastrophizing Scale (PCS)[59,71,82,102,104], Pain Coping Index (PCI)[59,102], Tampa Scale of Kinesiophobia (TSK)[55,57,59-61,102], Pain Self Efficacy Questionnaire (PSEQ)[57], Fear Avoidance Beliefs Questionnaire (FABQ)[55,58], Survey of Pain Attitudes (revised) (SOPA(R))[104], Hopkins Symptoms Checklist (HSCL-25)[58], and Beliefs about surgery questionnaire[103].

1. Both SOPA(R) and PCS were better in the experimental group compared to control group ($p<0.001$ for both). Effect size for SOPA(R) total was 9.0 (95% CI 6.5-11.5) and PCS 6.0 (95% CI 3.8-8.2).[104]

2. No statistically significant effect for PSEQ or TSK-13.[57]

3. Significant reduction ($p=0.009$) in PCS for ruminating scale in the PNE group compared to control, coping strategies (PCI) trended toward significance with "distraction" ($p=.021$) and worrying ($p=0.011$). The TSK did not reach a level of significance when comparing groups.[59]

4. FABQ for physical subscales showed significant changes favoring the experimental group at three months -3.6 (95%CI -5.3 to -1.9; p<0.001) and 12 months -4.7 (95% CI -6.5 to -3.0; p<0.001). The work subscale of the FABQ also showed favorable results toward the experimental group at both time measurement intervals -5.7 (95% CI -7.8 to -3.6; p<0.001) and -5.6 (95% CI -8.7 to -2.5, p<0.001), respectively. The HSCL-25 also showed significant results at three months -0.12 (95% CI -0.19 to -0.04) and 12 months -0.13 (95% CI -0.22 to -0.04) in favor of the experimental group.[58]

5. A large significant shift (p<0.01) in PCS scores were found in the pain metaphor group compared to the control advice group initially and at three-month follow-up, with large effect size at three-month follow-up (Cohen *d*=0.7). When the control group was crossed over to metaphor group, it also showed significant (p<0.01) improvements in PCS.[71]

6. Mean scores of PCI and TSK decreased with treatment; however, they did not reach a level of significance for between-group differences.[102]

7. In regard to PCS there were no between-group or within-group changes found.[82]

8. Main effect for more favorable postoperative opinion in experimental group over control group on three questions: "fully prepared for surgery" (p=0.01), "pre-operative education prepared well" (p=0.001), and "met expectations" (p=0.042).[103]

9. Treatment with PNE had a greater reduction (p=0.008) of kinesiophobia than those treated without PNE. Between-group change in favor of PNE on the TSK was -12.7 (95% CI -21.3 to -4.0).[60]

10. With the TSK, significant (p<0.05) improvements were demonstrated immediately post-treatment, at eight weeks and at 16 weeks favoring experimental group one to control. Similar significant effects were also shown in the TSK favoring experimental group two versus control at eight weeks and 16 weeks. There were no differences in TSK when comparing the two experimental groups. Effect size of experimental group one for TSK was (d=1.22) and (d=1.02) for experimental group two. Significance (p<0.5) for FABQ was similarly in favor of experimental group one and two over control with difference between the two experimental groups. Effect size for experimental 1 (d=0.78) and experimental 2 (d=1.13).[55]

11. No statistical interaction was found with TSK.[61]

PNE specifically addressing impaired movement[13]:

Four of the studies looked specifically at an impairment in movement. All three studies chose different physical performance tasks to study.

1. Forward bending and straight leg raise were improved greater in the experimental group over the control group ($p<0.001$ for both). Abdominal "drawing-in" task did not show between group differences.[104]

2. Physical performance measurements of repeated sit-to-stand test, fifty-foot walk test and five-minute walk test did not show any significant changes between the experimental and control group.[57]

3. No significant changes between the experimental and control group at three months.[58]

4. Visual Analog Fatigue Scale (VAFS) and Neck Flexor Muscle Endurance Test (NFME) were significant ($p<0.05$) at eight and 16-week follow-ups. Experimental group one was significant ($p<0.01$) for VAFS and NFME. In experimental group two the NFME test was significant ($p<0.01$) but not for VAFS.[55]

PNE specifically addressing healthcare utilization[13]:

Three studies explored changes in healthcare utilization following PNE. Each study utilized different outcomes measurements for their study design.

1. At one-year follow-up, the experimental group had a mean of ± SD 3.6±2 healthcare visits for low back pain, which was statistically less ($p<0.001$) than the control group who made a mean ± SD 13.2±5 visits.[54]

2. Reduction of sick leave days extracted from the Orebro Screening Questionnaire was significant ($p<0.01$) in the experimental group ($z=2.95$). There was also a significant ($p<0.001$) reduction in care-seeking after intervention ($z=4.79$).[58]

3. Overall reduction in healthcare costs for medical treatment at one-year follow-up was less for experimental group (mean=$22,678.57, SD=$3,135.30) compared to control group (mean=$4,833.48, SD=$3,256.00) ($z=-2.700$, $p=0.007$).[103]

Pain Knowledge[13]:

The systematic reviews showed that educating people about their pain may be a more advantageous approach than traditional biomedical education for improving pain, psychosocial factors, functional ability, movement impairments and healthcare utilization. In addition to the positive effects of PNE described in the literature, interest also shifted to the ability to measure increased pain knowledge after a PNE lecture – for patients and healthcare providers. In 2003, Moseley conducted the first study to measure the pre- and post PNE knowledge of 276 patients with chronic pain and 288 healthcare providers after a PNE lecture. In order to measure "pain knowledge," a pain knowledge questionnaire used for medical students was adapted to be aligned with modern pain biology information.[43] The neurophysiology of pain questionnaire (NPQ) consisted of 19 questions in a true-false format. In that study, it was shown that patients and healthcare providers could indeed increase their knowledge of pain following a PNE lecture. To date, various studies have used the NPQ to explore PNE's ability to increase knowledge (Table 2.2 on the following page).

Table 2.2: Increased knowledge of pain utilizing the NPQ.

Author	Audience	PNE Lecture	NPQ Before PNE	NPQ After PNE	NPQ Increase
Moseley[43]	Patients with chronic pain (unspecified)	3-hour large group format lecture	29%	61%	32%
Moseley[43]	Healthcare providers	3-hour large group format lecture	55%	78%	23%
Meeus, et.al[84]	Patients with chronic fatigue syndrome	Individualized session with each patient (unspecified duration)	34%	72%	38%
Gallagher, et.al[71]	Patients with chronic pain (unspecified)	Book of pain metaphors	63%	89%	26%
Van Oosterwijk, et.al[92]	Patients with fibromyalgia	Two one-on-one individualized PNE sessions (unspecified duration)	29%	59%	30%
Louw, et.al[77]	Middle school kids	30-minute PNE lecture	29%	61%	32%
Louw, et.al[76]	Middle school kids	30-minute PNE lecture	32%	56%	24%
Louw, et.al[105]	Patients with chronic pain (unspecified)	2-hour large group format lecture	47%	68%	21%
Louw, et.al[106]	Pre-operative lumbar surgery	30-minute individualized PNE session	68%	75%	7%
Cox, et.al[72]	Physical therapy students	3-hour PNE lecture	41%	77%	36%

From Table 2.2 it can be seen that, following a variety of PNE lecture formats and durations on patients, healthy individuals and healthcare providers, there is in an increase in pain knowledge (mean 27 percent). Furthermore, various studies utilizing the NPQ have shown this increase in knowledge, for the most part, to be sustained at three and six months post PNE.[72,91,92,105] Recently, due to its popularity in research, the NPQ itself came under scrutiny with the analysis of its psychometric properties.[107] Rasch analysis was undertaken on NPQ data from a convenience sample of 300 patients with spinal pain, and test-retest reliability was assessed in a sample of 45 patients with low back pain. This study showed that, although the NPQ has some limitations, it is a useful tool to assess a patient's conceptualization of pain biology and to evaluate a change in pain cognitions for use in clinical practice and research. The end result was a revised NPQ consisting of 12 questions (rNPQ) instead of the original 19-point NPQ (Table 2.3).

Table 2.3: Revised Neurophysiology of Pain Questionnaire (rNPQ).

#	Statement	True	False	Unsure
1.	It is possible to have pain and not know about it.		X	
2.	When part of your body is injured, special pain receptors convey the pain message to your brain.		X	
3.	Pain only occurs when you are injured or at risk of being injured.		X	
4.	When you are injured, special receptors convey the danger message to your spinal cord.	X		
5.	Special nerves in your spinal cord convey "danger" messages to your brain.	X		
6.	Nerves adapt by increasing their resting level of excitement.	X		
7.	Chronic pain means that an injury hasn't healed properly.		X	
8.	Worse injuries always result in worse pain.		X	
9.	Descending neurons are always inhibitory.		X	
10.	Pain occurs whenever you are injured.		X	
11	When you injure yourself, the environment that you are in will not affect the amount of pain you experience, as long as the injury is exactly the same.		X	
12	The brain decides when you will experience pain.	X		

It is also interesting to note that the NPQ and rNPQ not only have been used to measure knowledge of pain but as a teaching tool.[84] By reading the NPQ questions and discussing the answers with patients, the NPQ can be used as a "script" for a PNE curriculum.

The content and educational delivery methods of PNE[13]:

With the focus on establishing the evidence for PNE and the increasing amount of research into it, a fundamental clinical issue arose: What exactly is PNE and how is it delivered? In the 2011 systematic review of PNE, apart from the evidence, the authors included a section on the content and educational delivery methods of PNE, with the intent to shed light on its clinical application.[64] The updated review, published in a special issue on "Perspectives of pain neuroscience education," further explored the practical application of PNE in clinical settings.[13, 52]

Naming the intervention[13]:

The original systematic review[64] reported on the various names given to the educational intervention of explaining the biology of the pain experience to the patient with the aim of reducing pain and disability. The variation in the interventional name used by the various authors continues.

- Pain neurophysiology education[61]
- Therapeutic patient education[55]
- Neuroscience education[60]
- Pain physiology education[56,59,102]
- Pain neuroscience education[82,103]
- Neurophysiology education[104]
- Pain biology education[57]
- Neurophysiology of pain education[54]

Two studies did not directly call the educational intervention a specific name but were a part of a book of metaphors and stories to help understand the biology of pain[71] and the cognitive component of the education intervention.[58] With the numerous descriptions this educational approach has gathered, a recent special issue featuring various experts in this field asked scientists, teachers and clinicians to unify around one singular term: pain neuroscience education (PNE).[108] This call for a singular name was to help dispel misconceptions and provide a universal language and should be seen similar to the nomenclature issues in manual therapy with the words "mobilization," "manual therapy" and "manipulation."[109]

Patient characteristics[13]:

The latest systematic review reported on 734 subjects, with 398 of them receiving PNE (70 percent female). The mean age of subjects receiving educational intervention was 41.7 years old. The youngest cohort had a mean age of 24±10[104] and the oldest cohort was 50.9±6.2[61]. In the systematic review, PNE was utilized for multiple pain conditions: LBP, chronic fatigue syndrome, fibromyalgia, lumbar radiculopathy awaiting lumbar surgery, and chronic neck pain. Figure 2.4 showcases various additional diagnoses in which PNE was administered, including Complex Regional Pain Syndrome, whiplash associated disorders and total knee arthroplasty.[75,79-81]

Content of PNE[13]:

Specific content of each of the educational sessions can be found in the published systematic review. A summary of the PNE content reveals the likely curriculum for PNE:

- Neurophysiology of pain[54-61,71,82,102-104]
- No reference of anatomic or patho-anatomic models[54,56,60,104]
- No discussion of the emotional or behavioral aspects of pain[56,104]
- Nociception and nociceptive pathways[56,60,61,71,82,102-104]
- Synapses[56,104]
- Action potentials[103]
- Spinal inhibition and facilitation[56,58,71,102,104]
- Peripheral sensitization[56,58,71,82,102-104]
- Central sensitization[56,58,61,71,82,102-104]
- Plasticity of the nervous system[56,71,102-104]
- Psychosocial factors and beliefs contributing to pain[55,58,60,61,71,82]

The book *Explain Pain*[110] by Butler and Moseley was directly referenced in six of the studies.[57,59-61,82,102]

Professionals performing PNE[13]:

PTs have been the delivery professional of PNE in all of the studies found in the review. In one study utilizing booklets, the lead author was an OT, but no direct education (other than the book, authored by a PT) was provided.[91] Even though PNE has its roots in PT, it is imperative to understand that this does not imply only physical therapists can deliver PNE. In fact, as PNE evolves, a specific line of study related to PNE is its interdisciplinary reach. In a recent study, researchers trained professions other than PT, showing an ability to increase NPQ scores in physicians, social workers, psychologists, pharmacists and nurses.[69] Given the enormity of the pain epidemic, it's imperative that PNE be taught to multiple professions so they can provide it to their patients.

Duration and frequency of PNE[13]:

The time and frequency of delivery has varied with a shift toward shorter durations in the more recent studies. Longest duration of the documented sessions was four hours[56] in one session, with shortest duration being around 30 minutes.[59,60,102,103] The shortest frequency was a one-time educational session[61,103,104] with other studies utilizing education spread out over multiple episodes during the course of treatment.

Educational format and tools[13]:

The primary format for delivery of PNE was verbal one-on-one between the patient and provider. Two studies in the recent review utilized group sessions[56,61] and one study did not have any face-to-face contact, only the information from an educational booklet [71]. The one-on-one sessions were typically not presented in a lecture format, but more often designed in a conversational format to encourage subjects to ask questions so material could be individualized. Various teaching aids were used during the delivery of the education, including prepared pictures, PowerPoint, drawings, examples, metaphors and books complementing the in-person education information. The systematic review and subsequent "how to" papers described the use of metaphors and examples for the delivery of PNE, along with images.[53,67,88] The delivery of PNE via stories are consistent with the notion that people remember stories better than factual information, and is in line with mankind's transition of information over time.

Adjunct treatment to PNE[13]:

Different methodologies were used in the designs for each of the studies showcased in the systematic review. PNE was used in conjunction with other active movement-based therapy interventions that consisted of:

- Mobilization and manipulation[54]
- Soft tissue massage[54]
- Muscle and neural mobilization[54,55]
- Trunk stabilization[54,56,57]
- Circuit-based aerobic exercise[57]
- Movement exercises[58]
- Paced/graded exposure with activities of daily living[58,59]
- Trigger point dry needling[60]
- Neck stabilization exercises[55]
- Aquatic exercise program[61]
- None (PNE only)[71,82,102-104]

The combination of PNE with a physical treatment is very important. It is well established that education-alone strategies are often very limited to facilitate true behavior change. In fact, a review of the aforementioned "physical" treatments combined with PNE reveals an important aspect of PNE: In all but one of the studies that combined PNE with a physical treatment, pain was statistically significantly improved ($p<0.05$), while none of the PNE-only studies were able to reduce pain (Figure 2.6).

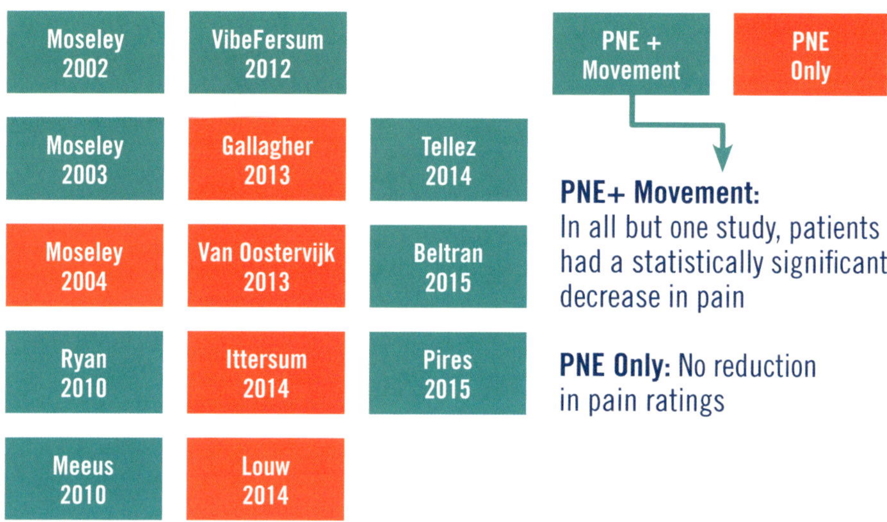

Figure 2.6: Relative effectiveness of PNE plus physical treatment versus PNE only.

Summary of PNE content and delivery methods[13]:

Considering the evidence for PNE and following the extensive review of content and delivery methods, PNE can be best applied as follows:

> *Clinicians should educate patients in a one-on-one session using various examples, metaphors and images explaining the neurobiology and neurophysiology of their pain experience while simultaneously defocusing anatomical tissues. Additionally, patients attending such a one-on-one session should be provided with homework to reflect on their learning experience, and return to therapy to answer questions and progress. This educational approach should include physical movement, especially aerobic exercise.*

2.4: Managing Pain

Based on the current evidence for PNE, we believe we can *treat* chronic pain, not merely *manage* chronic pain. "Manage" infers a maintenance of the status quo or, at least, making sure it does not get any worse. If a patient starts with an average pain rating of eight out of 10 on a visual analog scale (VAS) and six months later it is five, and one year later at three, is it purely managing pain? We believe not. Various six, 12 and now 36-month studies show a positive and downward trend in regard to pain ratings after the utilization of PNE:

- PNE for chronic LBP:[52] One year later, pain improved by almost three points on a 10-point scale (Figure 2.7)
- Individual versus group PNE:[85] Average reduction in pain was 3.1 (1.8-4.2) for the individual education group versus 2.7 (1.6-3.9) in the group education session at one year

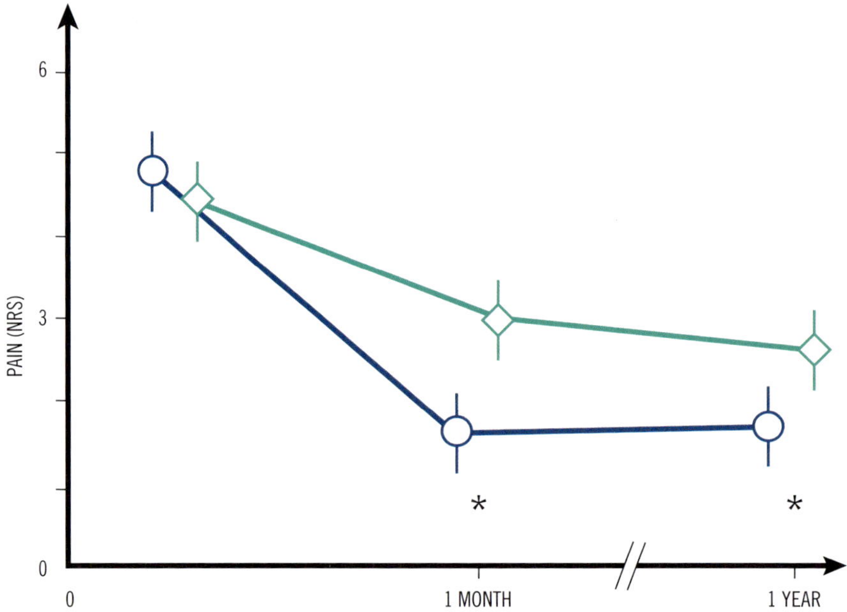

Figure 2.7: Pain rating changes in one year after PNE. The PNE plus physical therapy group (circles) demonstrated statistically significant differences in pain ratings compared to a control group (diamonds). Asterisks denote statistical significance ($p<0.025$). Graph adapted from Moseley (2002).

2.5: Key Points from Chapter 2

- Biomedical education models are not effective in altering pain
- Biomedical education may actually make pain worse by increasing pain-related fear and pain catastrophization
- There is compelling and growing evidence for the PNE approach
- There is growing direction and guidance for clinical application of PNE

Chapter 2 References

1. Gross A, Forget M, St George K, et al. Patient education for neck pain. *Cochrane Database Syst Rev.* 2012;3:CD005106.
2. Haines T, Gross A, Goldsmith CH, Perry L. Patient education for neck pain with or without radiculopathy. *Cochrane Database Syst Rev.* 2008(4):CD005106.
3. Prochaska JO, DiClemente CC. Stages of change in the modification of problem behaviors. *Progress in Behavioral Modification.* 1992;28:183-218.
4. Engers A, Jellema P, Wensing M, van der Windt DA, Grol R, van Tulder MW. Individual patient education for low back pain. *Cochrane Database Syst Rev.* 2008(1):CD004057.
5. Gross AR, Aker PD, Goldsmith CH, Peloso P. Patient education for mechanical neck disorders. *Cochrane Database Syst Rev.* 2000(2):CD000962.
6. McDonald S, Hetrick SE, Green S. Pre-operative education for hip or knee replacement. *Cochrane Database Syst Rev.* 2008(4).
7. Gilpin EA, Pierce JP, Farkas AJ. Duration of smoking abstinence and success in quitting. *Journal of the National Cancer Institute.* Apr 16 1997;89(8):572-576.
8. Raherison C, Marjary A, Valpromy B, Prevot S, Fossoux H, Taytard A. Evaluation of smoking cessation success in adults. *Respiratory Medicine.* Oct 2005;99(10):1303-1310.
9. Oztuna F, Can G, Ozlu T. Five-year outcomes for a smoking cessation clinic. *Respirology.* Nov 2007;12(6):911-915.
10. Sloan TJ, Walsh DA. Explanatory and diagnostic labels and perceived prognosis in chronic low back pain. *Spine* (Phila Pa 1976). Oct 1 2010;35(21):E1120-1125.
11. Nijs J, Roussel N, Paul van Wilgen C, Koke A, Smeets R. Thinking beyond muscles and joints: therapists' and patients' attitudes and beliefs regarding chronic musculoskeletal pain are key to applying effective treatment. *Manual Therapy.* Apr 2013;18(2):96-102.
12. Louw A, Diener I, Landers MR, Puentedura EJ. Preoperative pain neuroscience education for lumbar radiculopathy: a multicenter randomized controlled trial with 1-year follow-up. *Spine.* Aug 15 2014;39(18):1449-1457.
13. Louw A, Zimney K, Puentedura EJ, Diener I. The Efficacy of Therapeutic Neuroscience Education on Musculoskeletal Pain – A Systematic Review of the Literature. *Physiother Theory Pract.* 2016;32(5):332-355.
14. Moseley GL, Hodges PW, Nicholas MK. A randomized controlled trial of intensive neurophysiology education in chronic low back pain. *Clinical Journal of Pain.* 2004;20:324-330.
15. Brison RJ, Hartling L, Dostaler S, et al. A randomized controlled trial of an educational intervention to prevent the chronic pain of whiplash associated disorders following rear-end motor vehicle collisions. *Spine.* Aug 15 2005;30(16):1799-1807.
16. Oliveira A, Gevirtz R, Hubbard D. A psycho-educational video used in the emergency department provides effective treatment for whiplash injuries. *Spine.* Jul 1 2006;31(15):1652-1657.
17. Lin PC, Lin LC, Lin JJ. Comparing the effectiveness of different educational programs for patients with total knee arthroplasty. *Orthop Nurs.* Sep-Oct 1997;16(5):43-49.
18. Hering K, Harvan J, Dangelo M, Jasinski D. The use of a computer website prior to scheduled surgery (a pilot study): impact on patient information, acquisition, anxiety level, and overall satisfaction with anesthesia care. *AANA J.* Feb 2005;73(1):29-33.
19. Saryeddine T, Levy C, Davis A, et al. Patient education as a strategy for provider education and engagement: a case study using myJointReplacement.ca. *Healthc Q.* 2008;11(1):84-90.
20. Burton AK, Waddell G, Tillotson KM, Summerton N. Information and advice to patients with back pain can have a positive effect. A randomized controlled trial of a novel educational booklet in primary care. *Spine.* Dec 1 1999;24(23):2484-2491.
21. McGregor AH, Burton AK, Sell P, Waddell G. The development of an evidence-based patient booklet for patients undergoing lumbar discectomy and un-instrumented decompression. *Eur Spine J.* Mar 2007;16(3):339-346.

22. Louw A, Diener I, Puentedura E. Comparison of Terminology in Patient Education Booklets for Lumbar Surgery. *International Journal of Health Sciences.* 2014;2(3):47-56.
23. Buchbinder R, Jolley D. Effects of a media campaign on back beliefs is sustained 3 years after its cessation. *Spine.* Jun 1 2005;30(11):1323-1330.
24. Buchbinder R, Jolley D, Wyatt M. 2001 Volvo Award Winner in Clinical Studies: Effects of a media campaign on back pain beliefs and its potential influence on management of low back pain in general practice. *Spine.* Dec 1 2001;26(23): 2535-2542.
25. Lorig KR, Laurent DD, Dcyo RA, Marnell ME, Minor MA, Ritter PL. Can a Back Pain E-mail Discussion Group improve health status and lower health care costs?: A randomized study. *Arch Intern Med.* Apr 8 2002;162(7):792-796.
26. Louw A. Therapeutic neuroscience education via e-mail: a case report. *Physiother Theory Pract.* Nov 2014;30(8): 588-596.
27. Louw A, Butler DS, Diener I, Puentedura EJ. Preoperative education for lumbar radiculopathy: A Survey of US Spine Surgeons. *International Journal of Spine Surgery.* 2012;6:130-139.
28. Brox JI, Storheim K, Grotle M, Tveito TH, Indahl A, Eriksen HR. Systematic review of back schools, brief education, and fear-avoidance training for chronic low back pain. *The Spine Journal: Official Journal of the North American Spine Society.* Nov-Dec 2008;8(6):948-958.
29. Maier-Riehle B, Harter M. The effects of back schools—a meta-analysis. *Int J Rehabil Res.* Sep 2001;24(3):199-206.
30. Straube S, Harden M, Schroder H, et al. Back schools for the treatment of chronic low back pain: possibility of benefit but no convincing evidence after 47 years of research-systematic review and meta-analysis. *Pain.* Oct 2016;157(10):2160-2172.
31. Houben RM, Ostelo RW, Vlaeyen JW, Wolters PM, Peters M, Stomp-van den Berg SG. Health care providers' orientations towards common low back pain predict perceived harmfulness of physical activities and recommendations regarding return to normal activity. *European Journal of Pain* (London, England). Apr 2005;9(2):173-183.
32. Henrotin YE, Cedraschi C, Duplan B, Bazin T, Duquesnoy B. Information and low back pain management: a systematic review. *Spine.* May 15 2006;31(11): E326-334.
33. Weiner BK. Spine update: the biopsychosocial model and spine care. *Spine.* Jan 15 2008;33(2):219-223.
34. Haldeman S. Presidential address, North American Spine Society: failure of the pathology model to predict back pain. *Spine.* 1990;15(7):718-724.
35. Greene DL, Appel AJ, Reinert SE, Palumbo MA. Lumbar disc herniation: evaluation of information on the internet. *Spine* (Phila Pa 1976). Apr 1 2005;30(7):826-829.
36. Morr S, Shanti N, Carrer A, Kubeck J, Gerling MC. Quality of information concerning cervical disc herniation on the Internet. *The Spine Journal: Official Journal of the North American Spine Society.* Apr 2010;10(4):350-354.
37. Tait MJ, Levy J, Nowell M, et al. Improved outcome after lumbar microdiscectomy in patients shown their excised disc fragments: a prospective, double blind, randomised, controlled trial. *J Neurol Neurosurg Psychiatry.* Sep 2009;80(9):1044-1046.
38. Louw A, Puentedura EJ, Zimney K, Schmidt S. Know Pain, Know Gain? A Perspective on Pain Neuroscience Education in Physical Therapy. *J Orthop Sports Phys Ther.* Mar 2016;46(3):131-134.
39. Vlaeyen JW, Crombez G, Linton SJ. The fear-avoidance model of pain. *Pain.* Aug 2016;157(8):1588-1589.
40. Vlaeyen JWS, Linton SJ. Fear-avoidance and its consequences in chronic musculoskeletal pain: a state of the art. *Pain.* 2000;85:317-322.
41. Gifford L. *Aches and Pains.* Cornwall: Wordpress; 2014.
42. Louw A, Louw Q, Crous L. Preoperative education for lumbar surgery for radiculopathy. *SA Journal of Physiotherapy.* 2009;65(2):3-8.
43. Moseley GL. Unravelling the barriers to reconceptualisation of the problem in chronic pain: the actual and perceived ability of patients and health professionals to understand the neurophysiology. *The Journal of Pain: Official Journal of the American Pain Society.* 2003;4(4): 184-189.

44. Ronnberg K, Lind B, Zoega B, Halldin K, Gellerstedt M, Brisby H. Patients' satisfaction with provided care/information and expectations on clinical outcome after lumbar disc herniation surgery. *Spine*. Jan 15 2007;32(2):256-261.
45. Louw A, Puentedura E. *Therapeutic Neuroscience Education: Teaching patients about pain*. Minneapolis, MN: OPTP; 2013.
46. Moseley GL, Butler DS. Fifteen Years of Explaining Pain: The Past, Present, and Future. *The Journal of Pain: Official Journal of the American Pain Society*. Jun 5 2015.
47. Gifford L, Butler D. The integration of pain sciences into clinical practice. *The Journal of Hand Therapy*. 1997;10:86-95.
48. Butler DS. Adverse mechanical tension in the nervous system: a model for assessment and treatment. *Australian Journal of Physiotherapy*. 1989;35: 227-238.
49. Elvey R. Brachial plexus tension test and the pathoanatomical origin of arm pain. In: Glasgow E, Twomey L, eds. *Aspects of Manipulative Therapy*: Lincoln Institute of Health Sciences; 1979:105-110.
50. Gifford LS. Pain, the tissues and the nervous system. *Physiotherapy*. 1998;84:27-33.
51. Gifford L, Muncey H. "Explaining Pain to Patients." Paper presented at: International Association on the Study of Pain 1999; Vienna, Austria.
52. Moseley L. Combined physiotherapy and education is efficacious for chronic low back pain. *The Australian Journal of Physiotherapy*. 2002;48(4):297-302.
53. Louw A, Zimney K, O'Hotto C, Hilton S. The clinical application of teaching people about pain. *Physiother Theory Pract*. Jul 2016;32(5):385-395.
54. Moseley G. Combined physiotherapy and education is efficacious for chronic low back pain. *Aust J Physio*. 2002;48: 297-302.
55. Beltran-Alacreu H, López-de-Uralde-Villanueva I, Fernández-Carnero J, La Touche R. Manual Therapy, Therapeutic Patient Education, and Therapeutic Exercise, an Effective Multimodal Treatment of Nonspecific Chronic Neck Pain: A Randomized Controlled Trial. *American Journal of Physical Medicine & Rehabilitation/Association of Academic Physiatrists*. 2015.
56. Moseley GL. Joining Forces - Combining Cognitiion - Targeted Motor Control Training with Group or Individual Pain Physiology Education: A Successful Tretment For Chronic Low Back Pain. *Journal of Manual & Manipulative Therapy*. 2003;11(2):88-94.
57. Ryan CG, Gray HG, Newton M, Granat MH. Pain biology education and exercise classes compared to pain biology education alone for individuals with chronic low back pain: a pilot randomised controlled trial. *Manual Therapy*. 2010;15(4):382-387.
58. Vibe Fersum K, O'Sullivan P, Skouen J, Smith A, Kvåle A. Efficacy of classification- based cognitive functional therapy in patients with non-specific chronic low back pain: A randomized controlled trial. *European Journal of Pain*. 2013;17(6):916-928.
59. Meeus M, Nijs J, Van Oosterwijck J, Van Alsenoy V, Truijen S. Pain physiology education improves pain beliefs in patients with chronic fatigue syndrome compared with pacing and self-management education: a double-blind randomized controlled trial. *Archives of Physical Medicine and Rehabilitation*. 2010;91(8):1153-1159.
60. Téllez-García M, de-la-Llave-Rincón AI, Salom-Moreno J, Palacios-Ceña M, Ortega-Santiago R, Fernández-de-las-Peñas C. Neuroscience education in addition to trigger point dry needling for the management of patients with mechanical chronic low back pain: A preliminary clinical trial. *J Bodyw Mov Ther*. 2014;19(3):464-472.
61. Pires D, Cruz EB, Caeiro C. Aquatic exercise and pain neurophysiology education versus aquatic exercise alone for patients with chronic low back pain: a randomized controlled trial. *Clinical Rehabilitation*. 2015;29(6):538-547.
62. Louw A, Puentedura E, Nijs J. A Clinical Perspective on a Pain Neuroscience Education Approach to Manual Therapy. *Journal of Manual & Manipulative Therapy*. 2017.
63. Louw A, Farrell K, Landers M, et al. The effect of manual therapy and neuroplasticity education on chronic low back pain: a randomized clinical trial. *Journal of Manual & Manipulative Therapy*. 2016:1-8.

64. Louw A, Diener I, Butler D, Puentedura E. The effect of neuroscience education on pain, disability, anxiety, and stress in chronic musculoskeletal pain. *Arch Phys Med Rehabil.* 2011;92:2041-2056.
65. Clarke CL, Ryan CG, Martin DJ. Pain neurophysiology education for the management of individuals with chronic low back pain: systematic review and meta-analysis. *Manual Therapy.* Dec 2011;16(6):544-549.
66. Louw A, Puentedura EJ, Zimney K, Cox T, Rico D. The clinical implementation of pain neuroscience education: A survey study. *Physiother Theory Pract.* Nov 2017;33(11):869-879.
67. Nijs J, Paul van Wilgen C, Van Oosterwijck J, van Ittersum M, Meeus M. How to explain central sensitization to patients with 'unexplained' chronic musculoskeletal pain: practice guidelines. *Manual Therapy.* Oct 2011;16(5):413-418.
68. King R RV, Ryan CG, Martin D. . A Novel Interactive Diagram to Explain Pain Neurophysiology to Patients with Chronic Musculoskeletal Pain (CMP): A Practical Guide. *Pain and Rehabilitation.* 2017;42(Winter):22-30.
69. Louw A, Vogsland R, Marth L, Marshall P, Landers M, Cox T. Pain Neuroscience Education across Healthcare Disciplines. Submitted for publication. 2017.
70. Reis FJJ, Bengaly AGC, Valentim JCP, et al. An E-Pain intervention to spread modern pain education in Brazil. *Braz J Phys Ther.* Sep - Oct 2017;21(5): 305-306.
71. Gallagher L, McAuley JH, Moseley GL. A Randomized-controlled Trial of Using a Book of Metaphors to Reconceptualize pain and Decreass Catastrophizing in people with Chronic Pain. *The Clinical Journal of Pain.* 2013;29:20-25.
72. Cox T, Puentedura E, Louw A. An Abbreviated Therapeutic Neuroscience Education Session Improves Pain Knowledge in First Year Physical Therapy Students But Does Not Change Attitudes or Beliefs *Journal of Manual & Manipulative Therapy.* 2017;25(1):11-21.
73. Moseley GL. Widespread brain activity during an abdominal task markedly reduced after pain physiology education: fMRI evaluation of a single patient with chronic low back pain. *The Australian Journal of Physiotherapy.* 2005;51(1): 49-52.
74. Louw A, Puentedura EJ, Diener I, Peoples RR. Preoperative therapeutic neuroscience education for lumbar radiculopathy: a single-case fMRI report. *Physiother Theory Pract.* Oct 2015;31(7):496-508.
75. Fercho KA, Baugh LA, Louw A, Zimney K. Pain Neuroscience Education Effect on Pain Matrix Processing in an Individual with Complex Regional Pain Syndrome: A Single Subject Research Design. *European Pain Journal.* 2017 - Submitted for publication.
76. Louw A, Benz P, Podolak J, Zimney K, Wassinger CA. Pain Neuroscience Education for Middle School Kids and Fear of Physical Activity. *Physiotherapy* 2017 - Submitted for Publication.
77. Louw A, Podolak J, Zimney K, Schmidt S, Puentedura E. Can Pain Beliefs Change in Middle School Students? A Study of the Effectiveness of Pain Neuroscience Education. *Physiother Theory Pract.* 2017 - Accepted for publication.
78. Louw A, Diener I, Landers MR, Zimney K, Puentedura EJ. Three-year follow-up of a randomized controlled trial comparing preoperative neuroscience education for patients undergoing surgery for lumbar radiculopathy. *J Spine Surg.* Dec 2016;2(4):289-298.
79. Louw A, Zimney K, Puentedura E, Reed J. Immediate Effects of Preoperative Pain Neuroscience Education for Patients Undergoing Total Knee Arthroplasty: A Case Series *Physiother Theory Pract.* 2017;Accepted for publication.
80. Louw A, Reed J, Zimney K, Puentedura E, Grimm D, Landers M. A Randomized Clinical Trial of Preoperative Pain Neuroscience Education for Total Knee Arthroplasty. 2018; Submitted for publication.
81. Van Oosterwijck J, Nijs J, Meeus M, et al. Pain neurophysiology education improves cognitions, pain thresholds, and movement performance in people with chronic whiplash: a pilot study. *Journal of Rehabilitation Research and Development.* 2011;48(1):43-58.
82. Ittersum MW, Wilgen CP, Schans CP, Lambrecht L, Groothoff JW, Nijs J. Written pain neuroscience education in fibromyalgia: a multicenter randomized controlled trial. *Pain Practice.* 2014;14(8): 689-700.

83. Louw A, Puentedura E. Therapeutic Neuroscience Education, Pain, Physiotherapy and the Pain Neuromatrix. *International Journal of Health Sciences.* 2014;2(3):33-45.
84. Meeus M, Nijs J, Van Oosterwijck J, Van Alsenoy V, Truijen S. Pain Physiology Education Improves Pain Beliefs in Patients With Chronic Fatigue Syndrome Compared With Pacing and Self-Management Education: A Double-Blind Randomized Controlled Trial. *Arch Phys Med Rehabil.* Aug 2010;91(8):1153-1159.
85. Moseley GL. Joining forces - combining cognition-targeted motor control training with group or individual pain physiology education: a successful treatment for chronic low back pain. *J Man Manip Therap.* 2003;11(2):88-94.
86. Louw A, Zimney K, Cox T, O'Hotto C, Wassinger CA. The experiences and beliefs of patients with complex regional pain syndrome: An exploratory survey study. *Chronic Illness.* Jan 01 2017:1742395317709329.
87. Landers MR, Puentedura E, Louw A, McCauley A, Rasmussen Z, Bungum T. A population-based survey of lumbar surgery beliefs in the United States. *Orthopedic Nursing.* Jul-Aug 2014;33(4):207-216.
88. Louw A, Butler DS, Diener I, Puentedura EJ. Development of a preoperative neuroscience educational program for patients with lumbar radiculopathy. *American Journal of Physical Medicine & Rehabilitation/Association of Academic Physiatrists.* May 2013;92(5):446-452.
89. Ryan CG, Gray HG, Newton M, Granat MH. Pain biology education and exercise classes compared to pain biology education alone for individuals with chronic low back pain: a pilot randomised controlled trial. *Manual Therapy.* Aug 2010;15(4):382-387.
90. Vibe Fersum K, O'Sullivan P, Skouen JS, Smith A, Kvale A. Efficacy of classification-based cognitive functional therapy in patients with non-specific chronic low back pain: a randomized controlled trial. *European Journal of Pain.* Jul 2013;17(6):916-928.
91. Gallagher L, McAuley J, Moseley GL. A randomized-controlled trial of using a book of metaphors to reconceptualize pain and decrease catastrophizing in people with chronic pain. *The Clinical Journal of Pain.* Jan 2013;29(1):20-25.
92. Van Oosterwijck J, Meeus M, Paul L, et al. Pain physiology education improves health status and endogenous pain inhibition in fibromyalgia: a double-blind randomized controlled trial. *The Clinical Journal of Pain.* Oct 2013;29(10):873-882.
93. van Ittersum MW, van Wilgen CP, van der Schans CP, Lambrecht L, Groothoff JW, Nijs J. Written pain neuroscience education in fibromyalgia: a multicenter randomized controlled trial. Pain Practice: *The Official Journal of World Institute of Pain.* Nov 2014;14(8):689-700.
94. Tellez-Garcia M, de-la-Llave-Rincon AI, Salom-Moreno J, Palacios-Cena M, Ortega-Santiago R, Fernandez-de-Las-Penas C. Neuroscience education in addition to trigger point dry needling for the management of patients with mechanical chronic low back pain: A preliminary clinical trial. *Journal of Bodywork and Movement Therapies.* Jul 2015;19(3):464-472.
95. Beltran-Alacreu H, Lopez-de-Uralde-Villanueva I, Fernandez-Carnero J, La Touche R. Manual Therapy, Therapeutic Patient Education, and Therapeutic Exercise, an Effective Multimodal Treatment of Nonspecific Chronic Neck Pain: A Randomized Controlled Trial. *American Journal of Physical Medicine & Rehabilitation/Association of Academic Physiatrists.* Apr 16 2015.
96. Pires D, Cruz EB, Caeiro C. Aquatic exercise and pain neurophysiology education versus aquatic exercise alone for patients with chronic low back pain: a randomized controlled trial. *Clin Rehabil.* Jun 2015;29(6):538-547.
97. Moore RA, Derry S, Aldington D, Cole P, Wiffen PJ. Amitriptyline for fibromyalgia in adults. *The Cochrane Database of Systematic Reviews.* 2015;7:CD011824.
98. Moore RA, Wiffen PJ, Derry S, McQuay HJ. Gabapentin for chronic neuropathic pain and fibromyalgia in adults. *The Cochrane Database of Systematic Reviews.* 2011(3):CD007938.
99. Riediger C, Schuster T, Barlinn K, Maier S, Weitz J, Siepmann T. Adverse Effects of Antidepressants for Chronic Pain: A Systematic Review and Meta-analysis. *Frontiers in Neurology.* 2017;8:307.

100. Wiffen PJ, Derry S, Bell RF, et al. Gabapentin for chronic neuropathic pain in adults. *Cochrane Database Syst Rev.* Jun 09 2017;6:CD007938.
101. Cheeta S, Schifano F, Oyefeso A, Webb L, Ghodse AH. Antidepressant-related deaths and antidepressant prescriptions in England and Wales, 1998-2000. *The British Journal of Psychiatry: The Journal of Mental Science.* Jan 2004;184:41-47.
102. Van Oosterwijck J, Meeus M, Paul L, et al. Pain physiology education improves health status and endogenous pain inhibition in fibromyalgia: a double-blind randomized controlled trial. *The Clinical Journal of Pain.* 2013;29(10):873-882.
103. Louw A, Diener I, Landers MR, Puentedura EJ. Preoperative Pain Neuroscience Education for Lumbar Radiculopathy: A Multicenter Randomized Controlled Trial With 1-Year Follow-up. *Spine.* Aug 15 2014;39(18):1449-1457.
104. Moseley GL, Nicholas MK, Hodges PW. A randomized controlled trial of intensive neurophysiology education in chronic low back pain. *The Clinical Journal of Pain.* 2004;20(5):324-330.
105. Louw A, Zimney K, Puentedura E. Retention of pain neuroscience knowledge: a multi-centre trial. *New Zealand Journal of Physiotherapy.* 2016;44(2):91-96.
106. Louw A, Diener I, Puentedura EJ. The short term effects of preoperative neuroscience education for lumbar radiculopathy: A case series. *International Journal of Spine Surgery.* 2015;9:11.
107. Catley MJ, O'Connell NE, Moseley GL. How good is the neurophysiology of pain questionnaire? A Rasch analysis of psychometric properties. *The Journal of Pain: Official Journal of the American Pain Society.* Aug 2013;14(8):818-827.
108. Louw A, Puentedura EL, Zimney K. Teaching patients about pain: It works, but what should we call it? *Physiother Theory Pract.* Jul 2016;32(5):328-331.
109. Mintken PE, Derosa C, Little T, Smith B. Moving past sleight of hand. *J Orthop Sports Phys Ther.* May 2010;40(5):253-255.
110. Butler DS, Moseley GL, Sunyata. *Explain Pain.* Noigroup Publications Adelaide; 2003.

Chapter 3

The Neuroscience of Pain

3.1: What you Need to Know about the Neuroscience of Pain

Chapter 2 and current evidence for PNE indicates clinicians need to be able to explain various aspects of neuroscience.[1,2] The NPQ probably left you dazed and unsure of your clinical future. Can you remember (from school) the basic concepts of central sensitization, peripheral sensitization, inhibition and facilitation of the nervous system, nociception and pain, neurons and synapses, etc.? How about explaining a disc injury to a patient with LBP, without using provocative terms such as "herniation," "rupture" or "bulge?"

The iceberg-effect: Being smarter than your patient

To explain complex neuroscience to patients specific to their pain experience, plan of care and prognosis, you need to know a lot about a lot of "stuff." This is often referred to as the iceberg effect (personal communication – Moseley). Picture an iceberg – we only see about 10 percent sticking out the water with the remaining 90 percent below the waterline. The premise is the 10 percent of the visible iceberg represents information the patient needs to better understand about their pain experience. The 90 percent that remains under the waterline represents the knowledge and experience of the clinician which informs the PNE message (e.g. anatomy, biomechanics, tissue healing, neurobiology, neurophysiology, kinesiology, ethics, evidence-based practice, etc.). Given the complexity and individual nature of any human's pain experience, this implies that the modern clinician utilizing PNE must truly become a life-long learner.

3.2: Traditional and Old Pain Models

The early history of pain is strongly associated with religious beliefs, often with pain being some type of "punishment" or test from a deity.[3,4] Various early descriptions of pain can be found in the historical perspective of pain:[3,4]

- Aristotle: "Passion of the soul"
- Hippocrates: "Fluid imbalance"
- Prior to Renaissance: "Punishment or test from God"
- Chinese Medicine (3000 years ago): "Ying and yang"

A major shift in how we, as humans, view pain occurred around the Renaissance period, which has left a significant imprint on society.[3,4]

Cartesian model of pain (René Descartes 1596-1650)

René Descartes was a French philosopher, mathematician, and scientist who was considered to be the father of modern western philosophy. One specific aspect of Cartesian philosophy which continues to impact modern thinking was his conceptualization of pain. In his 1664 Treatise of Man, Descartes theorized that the body was more like a machine, and that pain was a disturbance that passed down along nerve fibers until the disturbance reached the brain (Figure 3.1):

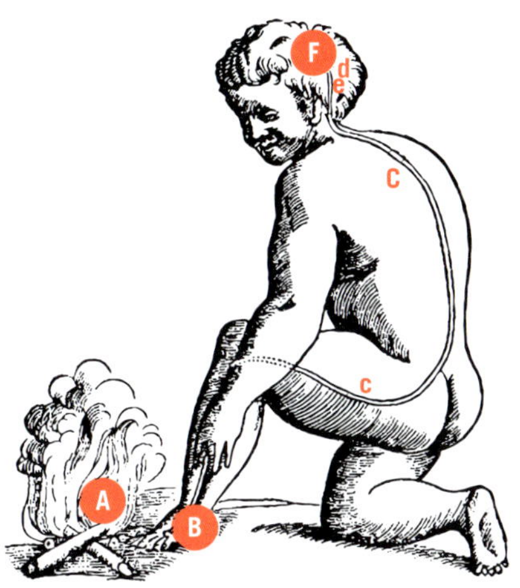

Figure 3.1: Cartesian model of pain.

"Particles of heat" (**A**) activate a spot of skin (**B**) attached by a fine thread (**cc**) to a valve in the brain (**de**) where this activity opens the valve, allowing the animal spirits to flow from a cavity (**F**) into the muscles causing them to flinch from the stimulus, turn the head and eyes toward the affected body part, and move the hand and turn the body protectively.

Prior to Descartes' philosophy, pain was often thought to reside in the "heart." In lieu of our modern neuroscience interest in the brain's role in a human's pain experience, it is important to point out that Descartes' journey to the brain was revolutionary and worth mentioning. Unfortunately, Descartes' model is likely to blame for many of the misconceptions of pain and is a driving force in the thought processes underlying the treatment of pain, even now in the 21st century.[5,6] If we follow the Cartesian model of pain and consider how to "treat" pain, we are left with several options:

1. Take your foot out of the fire; avoid the fire

Even though this makes sense, avoidance is not a long-term solution, especially when we consider behavioral medicine. The modern-day analogy is to avoid movement, activities or even social interaction and human contact. Although avoidance has a place in an acute or postoperative setting, it might become maladaptive if perpetuated. For example, following a severe ankle sprain using crutches and avoiding weight bearing on ankle seems logical, but if continued for longer than necessary, it might have detrimental effects including bone loss, muscle wasting, and loss of proprioceptive function. Specific to chronic pain, avoidance of physical activity and movement is powerfully associated with disuse and disability. Avoidance of social contact and human exposure is also maladaptive and linked to depression. Disuse, depression, and disability in turn increase a pain experience, which in turn might increase catastrophization and fear avoidance, thus starting a viscous cycle (Figure 3.2).

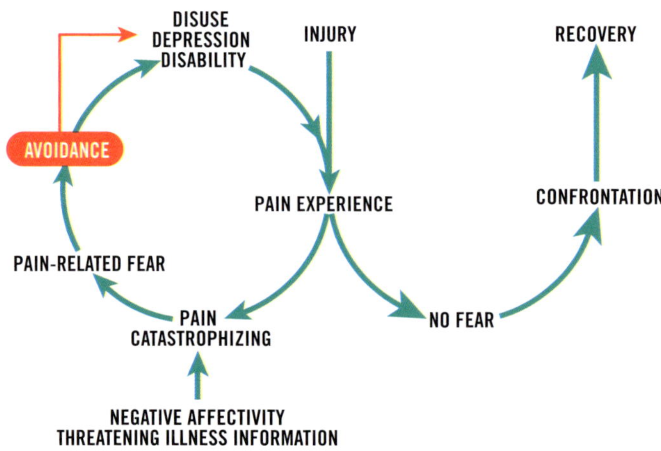

Figure 3.2: Avoidance fueling disuse, depression and disability and, ultimately, more pain.

2. Put the fire out

A logical way to ease "pain" in the Cartesian model would be to put the fire out. By dousing the fire, the stimulus is taken away and the message is not sent onto the brain. The modern-day analogy of "putting the fire out" is dousing the "pain generator" (fire) with medications, injections, etc. The current pain epidemic and resultant opioid epidemic is a good example how this approach is not working. The use of medication and injections are increasing rapidly, yet pain rates are going up. During a five-year period, Medicare expenditures in the US increased by 629 percent for epidural steroid injections and expenditures for opioid prescriptions for Medicare increased by 423 percent (Figure 3.3).[7]

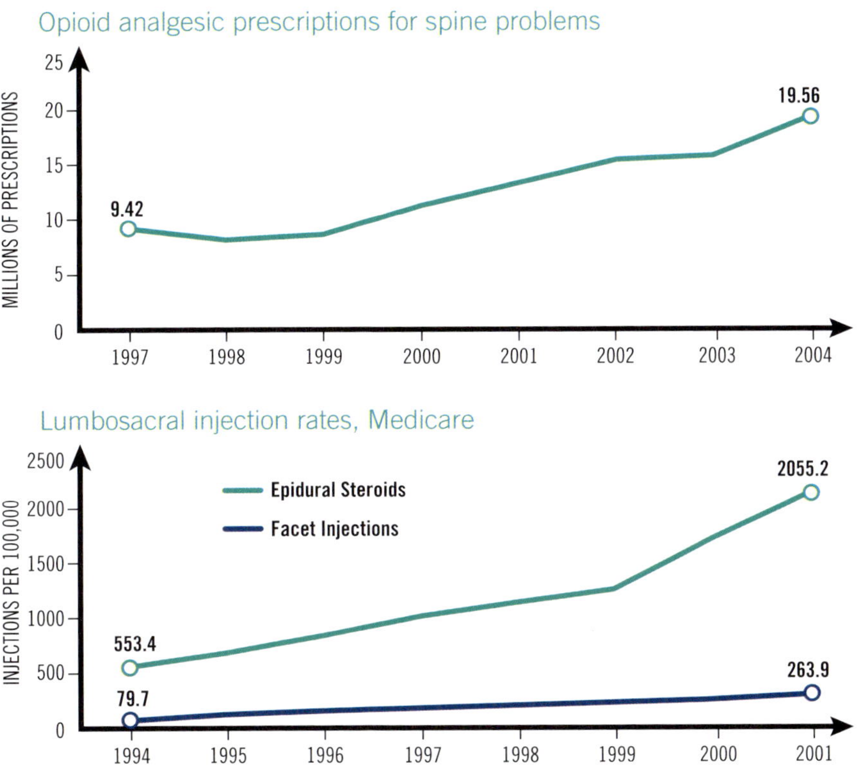

Figure 3.3: Opioid and lumbosacral injection rates for Medicare in the mid-1990s to early 2000s (Image from Deyo, et. al 2009).

Clinicians will also often try to "find the pain generator" or "put the fire out." In manual therapy approaches, such as the Maitland approach, they may use meticulous palpation, constant patient-questioning and feedback along with clinical reasoning to "zoom in" and find the exact, singular most painful spinal segment responsible for the person's pain.[8] As for "putting fires out" by slowing or eliminating the message to reach the brain, therapists may utilize Gate Control.[9]

Gate Control (Melzack and Wall 1965)[9]

Following the Renaissance period, scientific efforts focused heavily on increasing the understanding of the neurophysiology of the nervous system. This included work on receptors and nerve fibers, with Pacini (1831) discovering "pressure and vibration" receptors; Meissner and Wagner (1852) "light touch" receptors and Von Frey (1896) "heat and cold" receptors.[3,4,9] Along with the Descartes model and the discovery and focus on receptors and nerve fibers, pain was primarily seen as an overstimulation of these various receptors.[3,4,9] This thought process was the predominant model for treating pain until 1965 following the introduction of Gate Control by Melzack and Wall.[9] Apart from the Cartesian model of pain, it could be argued that the Gate Control theory (Pain Gate), remains the predominant mechanism clinicians use to understand pain and develop treatments to modulate a patient's pain experience. With the interest and focus on various nerve fibers, including classifications based on speed of conduction and size ($A\alpha$, $A\beta$, C, etc.), Gate Control provided a theory on the interplay of these various fibers in the spinal cord. Melzack and Wall proposed that a gating mechanism exists in the dorsal horn of the spinal cord. Small nerve fibers ("pain receptors") and large nerve fibers ("normal receptors") synapse on projection cells, which travel up the spinothalamic tract to the brain, and inhibitory interneurons within the dorsal horn. The interplay among these connections was thought to determine when "painful" stimuli would proceed to the brain (Figure 3.4).

Many PT and OT treatments such as large amplitude passive range of motion, transcutaneous electrical neuromuscular stimulation (TENS) or massage are thought to control pain, in part, by activating low-threshold, large-diameter, non-nociceptive sensory nerve fibers dealing with touch, pressure and vibration, which inhibit "pain transmission" by closing the gate to "pain transmission" at the spinal cord level. Anecdotally, this may explain why people rub an injury site or even "walk it off," stimulating nerve fibers that might override the "pain signals." Although the Gate Control theory explains many observations regarding pain and modulation, it has various shortcomings, in lieu of the new, updated research in regard to pain:[10-12]

- Gate Control cannot account for phantom limb pain in patients with amputation.
- Gate Control does not explain pain below the level of injury in complete spinal cord injury.
- Gate Control cannot account for the complex immune and inflammatory processes (i.e., homoncular smudging), which have now been shown to be key components in a pain experience.
- Gate Control does not explain emotional or psychological issues pertaining to the development and maintenance of a pain experience. Where does abuse fit into the development and/or maintenance of a pain experience?
- Gate Control does not account for various social aspects of pain
- Gate Control is often drawn showing only "information up to the brain." What about the inhibitory "downward" messaging associated with endogenous mechanisms?

Gate Control

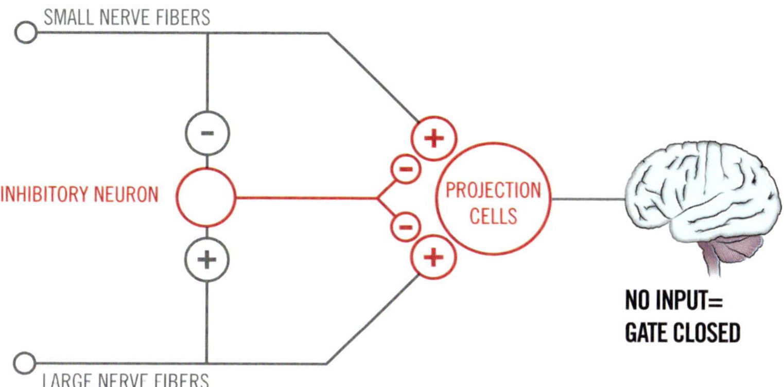

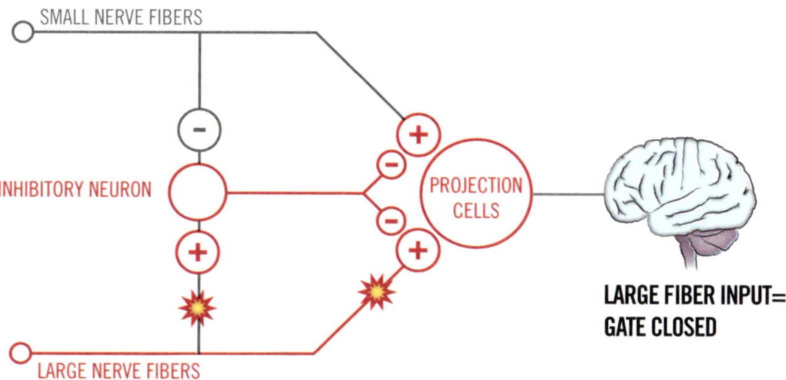

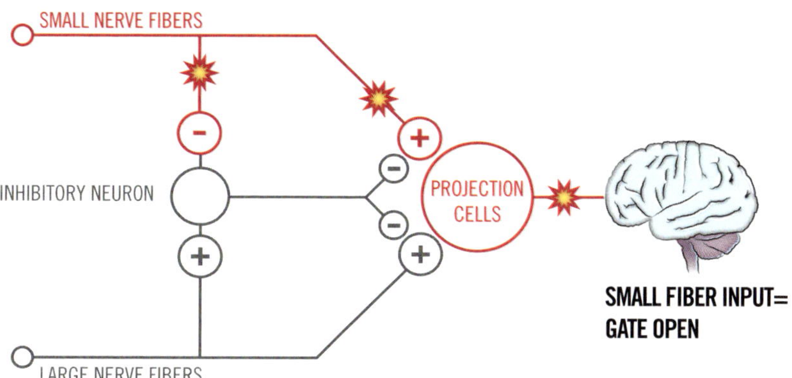

Figure 3.4: The interplay among these connections was thought to determine when "painful" stimuli would proceed to the brain.

The longevity and dominance of Gate Control and the emergence of new research, i.e., pain neuromatrix, has seemingly resulted in a standoff: Should clinicians leave Gate Control behind and move onto the new "wonders" of pain science or blend Gate Control with modern theories? Melzack, one of the original authors of Gate Control, urged clinicians to move "beyond the Gate" but surely there are aspects that are still valid?[10] Gate Control concepts are still relevant and as we further explore a human's pain experience in Chapter 3, we will show why nociception and especially the amount and duration of nociception may be a key element in the development of central sensitization. Therefore, we argue it is imperative to push the envelope and new frontiers, but be able to ponder the place and importance of older theories such as Gate Control. Altering nociception can indeed alter a human's pain experience, but by combining this "bottom up" approach with powerfully emerging "top down" approaches such as PNE, a more powerful model emerges to help a patient with their pain experience.[13]

3. Cut the wire (or remove the painful part)

By cutting the wire, the message is stopped from reaching the brain. The modern-day analogy is surgery and nerve ablations, or even amputations. If the Cartesian model worked, then surgery should be 100 percent successful; so should nerve ablation and even amputations. It is now well established that nearly 40 percent of people experience the same, if not worse, pain after spine surgery.[14-20] Following knee or hip joint replacement, it is estimated one in five patients still experience significant pain and disability.[21,22] Even though Descartes' pain theory is over 350 years old, the model still drives modern-day decisions, including surgery. Consider this abstract, published in a high-ranking journal, showcasing the Cartesian model at its finest in 2007.[23]

Pain 131 (2007) 214-218

Relief of post-herpetic neuralgia by surgical removal of painful skin: 5 years later

Karin Lottrup Petersen, Michael C. Rowbotham
UCSF Pain Clinical Research Center, Department of Neurology, University of California, San Francisco, CA 94115, USA

Received 25 August 2006; received in revised form 24 January 2007; accepted 6 March 2007

Abstract

Surgical removal of painful skin was first attempted as a treatment for chronic intractable post-herpetic neuralgia (PHN) more than a century ago, but long-term follow-up has rarely been reported. A patient who underwent surgical excision of 294 cm^2 of thoracic skin comprising the entire area of pain and allodynia in October 2000 has been followed for 5.5 years post-surgery. Our initial report presented evidence of benefit in the form of reduced pain, elimination of allodynia, and reduced medication consumption during the first post-operative year. Unfortunately, pain steadily increased and now exceeds pre-surgery levels despite increased medication use. Pain topography and characteristics are different from pre-surgery and may relate to the pathophysiology of PHN. Skin resection cannot be recommended as a treatment for PHN.

© 2007 International Association for the Study of Pain. Published by Elsevier B.V. All rights reserved.

Descartes' model of pain continues to exert influence on how people view pain:

- Assumption that there is a direct link between the amount of tissue damage and the level of pain experienced. Patients, and many clinicians, truly believe this.
- All pain is caused by injury and increased pain means more damage.
- Division of mind and body, where pain is either physical or psychological (physical versus mental). This may have fueled the social stigma of psychological issues or even psychological pain.
- In chronic pain, according to the Cartesian model, tissues are not healing and therefore damage is ongoing.
- Nociception and pain are synonymous
- Pain is an input driven system
- Nervous system function is simplistic, such as a wire

If you review Chapter 1, specifically the chronic pain and opioid epidemic, you're left to wonder why the world struggles so much with chronic pain. There are likely numerous reasons but we believe that the way both clinicians and the public have viewed pain is likely one of the big reasons. There is a pressing need to update medical practitioners' and society's view of pain.

3.3: Changing Beliefs about Pain

Through the evolution of various nerve fibers and receptors, and the Gate Control Theory in 1965, it was thought that the brain played little to no role in a human's pain experience. For example, around World War I, it was shown that soldiers with extensive cerebral cortex injuries still experienced pain, suggesting that the brain played only a limited role in pain.[24] Similarly, in 1937, Penfield showed that electrical stimulation of the exposed cortex during surgery caused little pain, once again fueling the notion that pain was sub-cortical and strengthening the belief that overstimulation of nerve fibers was associated with pain.[25] Everything was primed for the revolutionary Gate Control Theory in 1965.[9] There were, however, some glimpses of hope along the way leading us towards the brain, which we now know plays a pivotal role in a human's pain experience.[11] In 1962, it was shown that lesions in the anterior cingulate reduced chronic pain distress, and in 1969 it was demonstrated that lesions to the primary (S1) and secondary (S2) somatosensory cortex reduced a pain experience.[26] The field of neuroscience, specifically pain neuroscience, took a major leap forward in the early 1990s with the development of various brain imaging capabilities. Research using positron emission tomography (PET) and single photon emission computed tomography (SPECT) scans showed that the application of painful, superficial cutaneous heat activated multiple cortical and subcortical brain areas.[27,28] This technology shifted a lot of attention towards the human brain and its role in a human's pain experience, ultimately culminating in the shift to the pain neuromatrix.[10,11]

The question which now arises: How do we learn, or relearn pain science, especially from a clinical perspective? The good news is there is an easy, clinical answer. In the first edition of this textbook,[29] the NPQ was used as the curriculum. By reviewing the questions of the NPQ or rNPQ[30] and providing evidence to substantiate why an answer should be true or false, readers themselves also learned the latest pain neuroscience, a technique used in some PNE studies.[31] Additionally, in the world of PT, an iconic pain model emerged in the mid-1990s as pain science emerged from the world of manual therapy. Published in 1998, the Mature Organism Model (M.O.M) was revolutionary, showcasing the many complexities surrounding a human pain experience.[32,33] The model (Figure 3.5) combines many of the critical elements for understanding pain:

- Tissue (nociceptive) contributions to a pain experience.
- The modulating influence (positive and negative) of the environment on a pain experience.
- Peripheral nervous system inputs into the spinal cord (peripheral neurogenic mechanisms) including ion channel activation, demyelination, development of abnormal impulse generating sites, adequate blood supply to the nervous system, etc.

- Peripheral inputs entering into the spinal cord with gating and transmission to second-order neurons with the intent to pass information onto the brain (modes of operation in the dorsal horn).[34]
- The brain's processing of information (pain neuromatrix) along with various contextual influences, including environment, experiences, memory, beliefs, culture, etc. (true biopsychosocial approach).
- Output mechanisms in response to threat appraisal, heavily driven by various biological and physiological processes, which in turn heavily influences the brain, plasticity, immune function, the neuroendocrine system, health of tissues and the overall pain experience.

It is highly recommended that clinicians develop a working knowledge of the various neurobiological and neurophysiological processes in the M.O.M, thus reconceptualizing pain according to modern neuroscience.

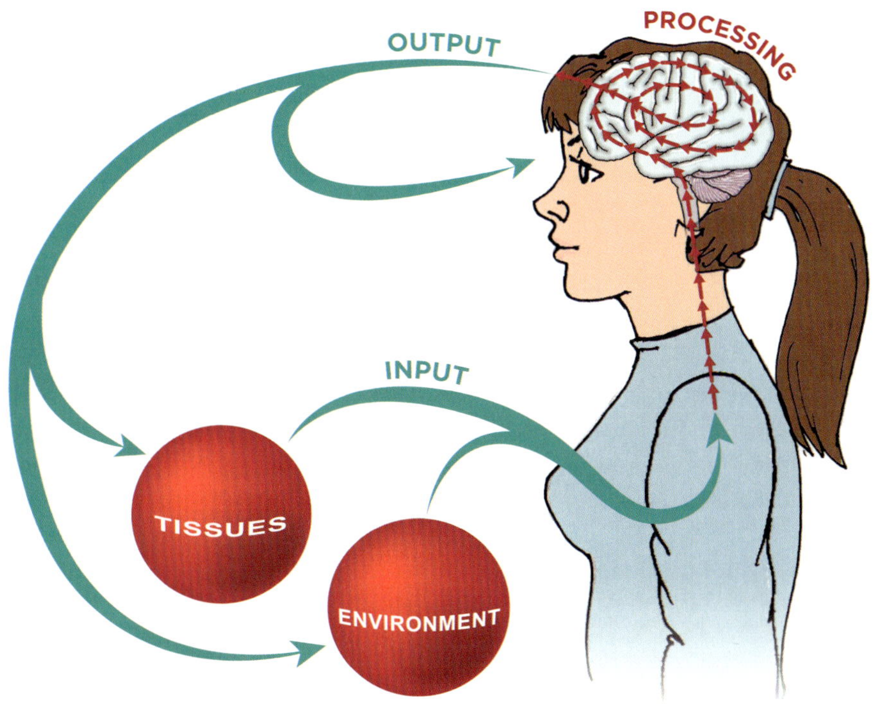

Figure 3.5: The Mature Organism Model – Adapted from Gifford.[32]

When Louis Gifford was questioned in 2013 about the M.O.M and how he would change it, some 15 years later, given all the advances in pain science, his answer was quite simple: "I would not change it; it's just plain biology" – indicating the overall relative simplicity of this model (Gifford – personal communication). In its simplest form, the M.O.M features three key elements:

- **Input mechanisms:** Input mechanisms refer to the various forms of information sent into the spinal cord and brain for processing. This includes information from the tissues (nociception), environmental influences and the peripheral nervous system, outside the dorsal horn.

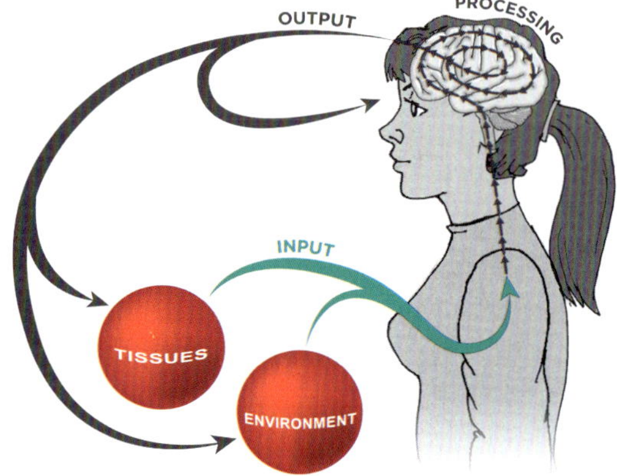

- **Processing mechanisms:** The processing mechanisms refer to the structures and processes inside the central nervous system (CNS) and brain processing the information sent by the various input systems. The processing mechanisms include processing sensory, cognitive and emotional aspects of the experience, ultimately putting a value on the information and coming to some form of conclusion.

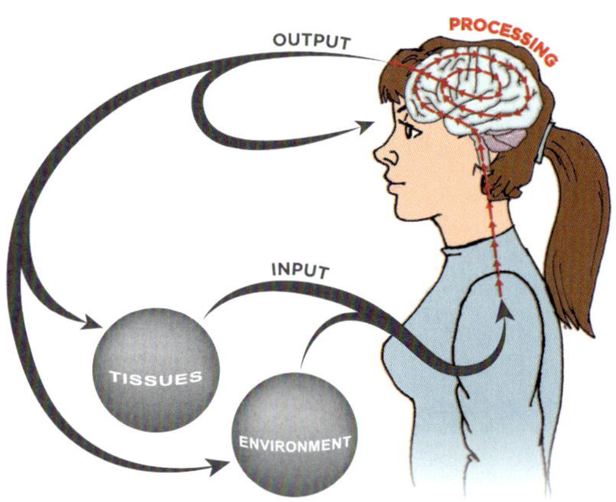

- **Output mechanisms:** Biologically, there is a response to the input and the brain's interpretation of the experience. The output mechanisms include various biological systems and are strongly driven by survival instincts in lieu of a pain experience.

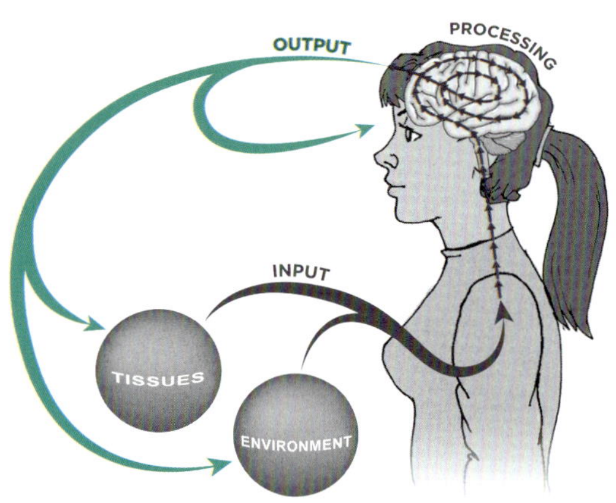

3.4: Input Mechanism: Tissues

NPQ and rNPQ statements:	NPQ/rNPQ #
When part of your body is injured, special pain receptors convey the pain message to your brain	NPQ 1; rNPQ 2
Pain only occurs when you are injured	NPQ 2
Pain only occurs when you are injured or at risk of being injured	rNPQ 3
When you are injured, special receptors convey the danger message to your spinal cord	rNPQ 4
The body tells the brain when it is in pain	NPQ 6
Chronic pain means an injury hasn't healed properly	NPQ 9; rNPQ 7
The brain decides when you will be experiencing pain	NPQ 11; rNPQ 12
Worse injuries result in worse pain	NPQ 12; rNPQ 8
Pain occurs whenever you are injured	rNPQ 10
When you are injured, chemicals in your tissue can make nerves more sensitive	NPQ 18
In chronic pain, chemicals associated with stress can directly activate danger messenger nerves	NPQ 19

In school, clinicians are taught about various nerve fiber types, based upon size and speed of conduction – A, B and C fibers.[35,36] These nerve fibers are also typically categorized as being responsible for things such as pain, light touch or pressure.[37]

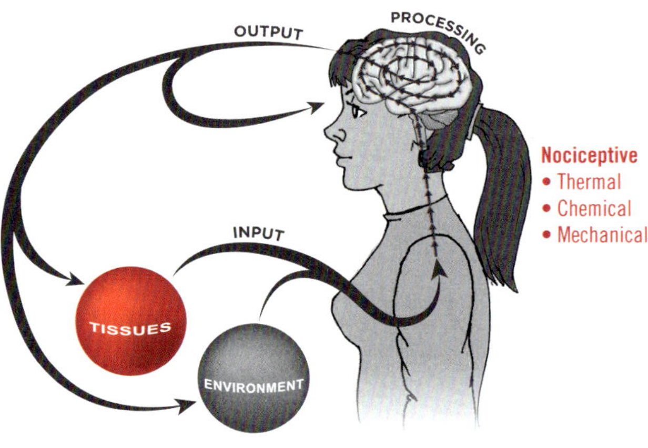

Type A fibers are the thickest and fastest conducting. They are myelinated, have a diameter of between 1.5-2.0 microns and their speed of conduction varies from 4-120 meters per second (m/sec), which indicates they are exhibit fast conduction of impulses. Examples of type A fibers are motor (efferent) fibers and afferent fibers from the skin.

Type B fibers are medium in size, i.e., they are smaller than type A fibers but larger than type C. They are myelinated, have a diameter of 1.5-3.5 microns and their speed of conduction is 3-15 m/sec, which indicates they are slower than type A fibers. Examples of type B fibers are preganglionic autonomic efferent fibers.

Type C fibers are the smallest and thinnest. They are traditionally described as non-myelinated, have a diameter of 0.1-2 microns and their speed of conduction is 0.5-4 m/sec, which indicates they have the slowest conduction speed. Examples of type C fibers are postganglionic autonomic efferent fibers and afferent fibers from the skin. Many clinicians are taught C fibers are "pain fibers" and responsible, along with A-delta fibers, for "conducting pain."

If C and A-delta fibers do "conduct pain," then all injuries would hurt and it could potentially endanger your life. For example, if you were to walk and sprained your ankle, it would likely cause pain (Figure 3.6). This is easy to understand and makes sense: tissue injury causes activation of the A-delta and C fibers that send "pain messages" via sensory afferent nerves to the dorsal horn of the spinal cord. The "pain messages" are passed from the dorsal horn via second-order neurons to the brain to call upon action, such as an antalgic gait, seeking medical help, canceling plans to run the local marathon this weekend and more.

Now imagine that same ankle sprain but it occurs while crossing a busy street. As you walk across the street, you sprain your ankle, but out of the corner of your eye you see a speeding bus heading your way. Everyone will agree that, in this case, the ankle will not hurt, and you'll get out the way of the speeding bus to the sidewalk on the other side. Once on the other side, the ankle may start to hurt. What happened? If the injured ankle had sent "pain messages" to the brain, the pain could potentially have been so debilitating it would have caused you to fall, grab the ankle and be run over by the bus. Why did it not hurt, then? The only thing the ankle can send the brain is a "danger message." The ankle contains various nociceptors, easily activated by inflammatory chemicals, temperature changes and mechanical input from the tissues. This nociceptive message will be passed onto the spinal cord and, ultimately, the brain via second-order neurons. Pain is, therefore, a brain construct. It is important that therapists designate these fibers as 'nociceptive fibers,' rather than 'pain fibers.'

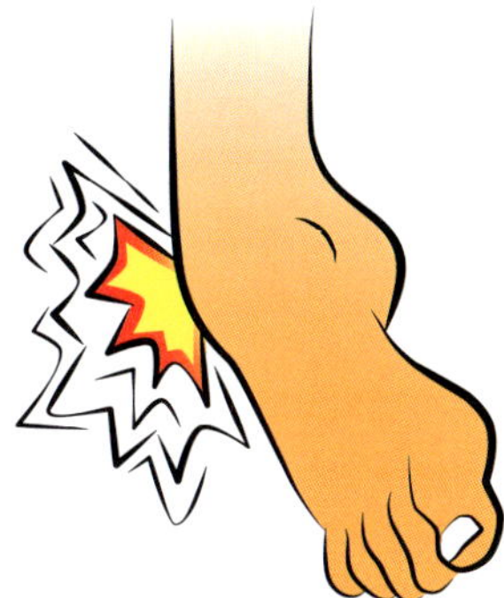

Figure 3.6: Based on traditional teaching, an ankle sprain stimulates nerve fibers "conducting pain," thus resulting in a pain experience.

Consider the following:

- The ear contains various 'vibration' and 'sound receptors.' Messages from these receptors are processed into 'hearing' by the brain.
- The eye contains 'light receptors' that send messages to the brain, which are processed by the brain to produce 'vision.'
- Joints, muscles, tendons, ligaments, skin, etc., contain 'nociceptors' and the brain may process these nociceptive messages into 'pain.'

This redefinition is not merely a play on words or semantics, but rather, an important shift in the language and concept of PNE. Why did the ankle not hurt with the speeding bus bearing down on you? In that situation, the brain determined that the bus was a larger threat to survival and, therefore, no pain was produced to protect the ankle, allowing the person to get out of the way. Once out of danger and on the sidewalk, the brain might produce pain in the ankle. Pain is a decision by the brain based on perception of threat.[11,12] The brain constantly receives information from the environment, as well as the body, and determines the most appropriate response based on survival, experience, and threat. There are numerous examples where people have significant injury, yet experience little to no pain. Tissues contain nociceptive or danger fibers, but it is the brain that decides if pain is needed to protect or not. In reality, there are no such things as pain fibers in the human body; only nociceptive fibers.

Many patients (and even some clinicians) believe that pain and injury are synonymous. Injury and disease states may or may not be experienced as pain. Many normative studies on asymptomatic subjects show the poor correlation between the health of the tissues and a pain experience:

- **Low back:**
  - It is estimated that 40 percent of asymptomatic people have a "bulging disc" on magnetic resonance imaging (MRI).[38,39]
  - Disc "bulges" reabsorb in a matter of weeks and months.[40-44]
  - In 40-year-old asymptomatic males and females, between 25-50 percent will demonstrate disc degeneration and signs of injury, endplate changes, foraminal stenosis and facet joint degeneration on spinal imaging.[45]
  - Lumbar spine degeneration starts in a person's early 20s and there is little correlation between arthritis and LBP in later life.[45-48]
  - In asymptomatic elite tennis players 33 percent had a spondylolisthesis when scanned, with several showcasing pars fractures, stress fractures, etc., yet no pain.[39]
  - Despite presenting with the same LBP, patients receive completely different MRI results when visiting different imaging centers and have different radiologists interpret the findings.[49]

- **Neck:**
  - Among people with significant degeneration visible in their imaging, only 10 percent experience pain.[50]
  - Ninety percent of asymptomatic people undergoing cervical MRI scan have a "bulging" disc (including people in their early 20s).[51]
  - Demolition derby drivers crash over 1500 times during their career; averaging over 24 miles per hour, and yet almost all report no chronic whiplash-associated neck pain.[52]

- **Shoulder Joint:**
  - One in three people over the age of 30 and two out of three people over the age of 70 have abnormal MRI findings related to their shoulder, including complete rotator cuff tears.[53-55]
  - After successful rotator cuff surgery and postoperative rehabilitation to regain full range of motion, strength and function, 90 percent of patients' MRI reports reveal "abnormal findings" and 20 percent still have a complete rotator cuff tear.[56]

- **Knee Joint:**
  - In asymptomatic individuals, 25-50 percent of MRIs reveal significant "degenerative" changes, highlighting the poor correlation between knee osteoarthritis, pain and disability.[57,58]
  - In active collegiate basketball players with no knee pain, 35 percent of the MRI scans show significant abnormalities.[59]
  - It is currently estimated that one in three knee replacements are unnecessary.[60]

- **Hip Joint:**
  - MRI of asymptomatic people show abnormalities in 73 percent of hips and labral tears in 69 percent of the asymptomatic group.[61]
  - Hip MRI studies show that femoroacetabular impingement and labral injuries are common in asymptomatic individuals.[62]
  - In hockey players with no hip pain, two out of three have scans that show significant degenerative changes.[63]

Therefore, injury and/or degenerative processes can be present, yet people may experience little to no pain. Furthermore, it is important to remember tissue injuries heal. Even tissues with slow rates of healing, such as intervertebral discs, have been shown to heal over time.[40,42,64] In the acute and sub-acute phase of injury and subsequent healing, it may be quite reasonable to think that pain and tissue injury are correlated. Even taking into consideration variables such as tissue type, general health, occupation, etc., tissues will undergo relatively predictable stages of healing as time progresses (Figure 3.7). In contrast, the pain experience is poorly correlated to these stages of healing.[65]

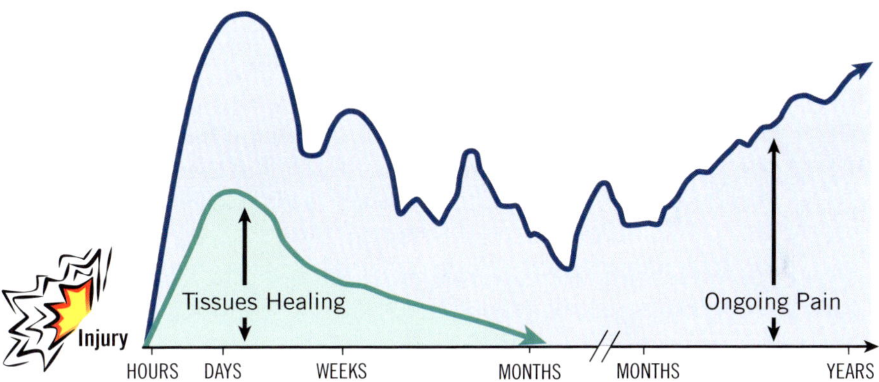

Figure 3.7: As time progresses, tissues demonstrate predictable stages of healing.

The opposite is also true. Many people suffer from significant pain, yet no injury has occurred and no disease process can be identified. The IASP defines pain as a sensory and emotional experience.[66] In line with this definition and reflecting back on material covered in Chapter 1 where we discussed the fear avoidance model, there is compelling evidence that some patients develop pain due to life stressors such as an emotional overload.[67,68] Many clinicians can attest to the fact that patients may present for treatment with significant pain yet recall no injury or accident. It is important to emphasize that this is not a psychosomatic issue. If we were to follow the classic Cartesian thinking, it would be easy to classify this pain as psychological. However, this form of Cartesian thinking is outdated and wrong when applied to patients with pain. It is now recognized that these patients experience pain and disability similar to patients who have had an injury event.[69,70] In these cases, the public perception is that pain is not real or 'in their head' if it is not physical and this is outdated and incorrect.

Another Cartesian artifact and misbelief related to tissues and pain is that worse injuries always result in worse pain. This belief that worse injuries result in worse pain might seem rational, but it's amazing how often the opposite occurs. Many unfortunate souls have arrived in hospital emergency departments impaled or severely injured following some gruesome accident, yet they may report experiencing little or no pain.[71-73] So many examples exist where injury is apparent and there is little to no pain reported. Examples include soldiers being shot and not being aware of it, or athletes competing despite significant tissue damage or injury. Conversely, small and seemingly insignificant injuries, such as paper cuts or cutting a nail too close to the nail bed, may result in marked pain experiences.

If there are no "pain receptors" in the human body, but technically only nociceptive receptors, it is important to develop a working knowledge of nociception. This knowledge, along with your growing knowledge of the M.O.M, will showcase how various systems are intertwined and heavily influence a pain experience. It is well documented in neuroscience that nociceptors are stimulated either mechanically, thermally or chemically.[35,36] These various stimuli instigate an action potential in order to send information to the CNS. In Figure 3.8 we showcase the stimuli, but also expand the categories:

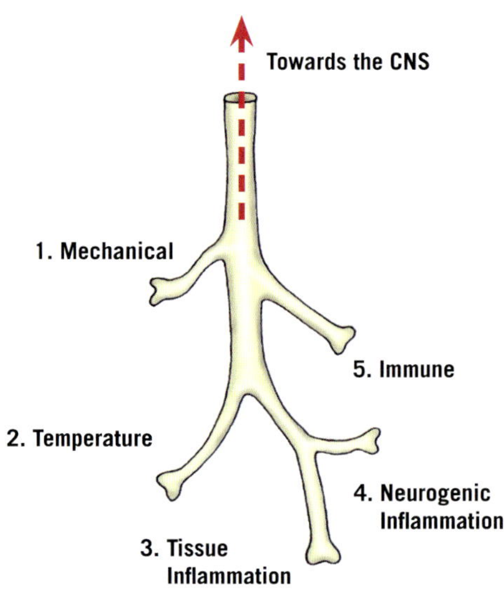

Figure 3.8: Various stimuli associated with nociceptive activation.

- **Mechanical:** Mechanical deformation of nerve fibers; activation of A-delta and C fibers may activate nociceptive receptors. This may be due to "mechanical" issues such as fractures, sprains, strains, surgery, etc. Exposed axons with no myelin can be mechanically stimulated causing an action potential. In double crush, a phenomenon where axons are compressed at both ends with mechanical compression, the resultant chemically induced inflammation in the nerve has been shown to increase the development of mechanosensitivity.[74] Mechanosensitive ion channels can be activated via pressure/palpation (Section 3.3).[75,76]

- **Temperature:** Extreme ends of the spectrum – cold or heat – can activate nociceptors.[77] Think of frost-bite or burns. Activation of an action potential can also occur via temperature-sensitive ion channels, i.e., activated by cold or heat.[76]

- **Tissue inflammation:** When tissues are injured, there is a release of various chemicals in/around the tissues by the damaged cell membranes: bradykinin, prostaglandin, serotonin, leukotrienes, etc.[78,79] The immune cells also release macrophages, cytokines and histamine via mast cells. Collectively, these chemical agents have become known as part of the inflammatory "soup."[80]

- **Neurogenic inflammation:** Axons fire bi-directionally. When an axon is stimulated, it fires into the CNS (orthodromic impulses) and passes information onto the brain. However, axons also fire "backward" toward the terminal ending and peripheral tissues, which is referred to as antidromic impulse or retrograde depolarization.[81,82] For example, when you sprain your ankle, axons fire toward the CNS, but impulses also fire toward the ankle.[83] This retrograde depolarization facilitates increased release of substance P, noradrenaline, neurokines, calcitonin-gene-related peptides, nerve growth factor, etc. Substance P is vasoactive and contributes to mast cell degranulation, which releases histamine. This in turn signals release of macrophages and enzymes.[84] These chemical releases infuse the "soup" with more inflammatory cells, and activate nociceptors, thus increasing CNS barrage.

- **Immune:** Albeit slower, the immune system activates to help deal with impending threat. Inflammatory activity facilitates the release of cytokines and macrophages. Increased activity of interleukins and tumor-necrosis factor alpha increase the inflammatory response, and activate nociceptors. Various ion channels are activated by the increased immune cells.[85] Future immune responses can activate/re-activate nociceptors in the affected area. A good example is "feeling" the old elbow injury when you have the flu. Circulating cytokines, due to the flu, activate nociceptors in/around the elbow.[76]

The fact that nociceptors are activated by a variety of various stimuli, including various circulating chemicals in the human body, is important in understanding a pain experience. Anything that alters immune responses (coping skills, illness, chronic stress, sleep deprivation, etc.), levels of adrenaline or epinephrine (stress, fear, anxiety, pain, etc.) or inflammation (estrogen, testosterone, foods, sleep, exercise, etc.) may indeed help develop an extra sensitive nervous system.

NPQ and rNPQ statements:	NPQ/rNPQ #	Answer
When part of your body is injured, special pain receptors convey the pain message to your brain	NPQ 1; rNPQ 2	False
Pain only occurs when you are injured	NPQ 2	False
Pain only occurs when you are injured or at risk of being injured	rNPQ 3	False
When you are injured, special receptors convey the danger message to your spinal cord	rNPQ 4	True
The body tells the brain when it is in pain	NPQ 6	False
Chronic pain means an injury hasn't healed properly	NPQ 9; rNPQ 7	False
The brain decides when you will be experiencing pain	NPQ 11; rNPQ 12	True
Worse injuries result in worse pain	NPQ 12; rNPQ 8	False
Pain occurs whenever you are injured	rNPQ 10	False
When you are injured, chemicals in your tissue can make nerves more sensitive	NPQ 18	True
In chronic pain, chemicals associated with stress can directly activate danger messenger nerves	NPQ 19	True

3.5: Input Mechanism: Environment

NPQ and rNPQ statements:	NPQ/rNPQ #
When you are injured, the environment that you are in will not have an effect on the amount of pain that you experience	NPQ 13
When you injure yourself, the environment that you are in will not affect the amount of pain you experience, as long as the injury is exactly the same	rNPQ 11

All injuries occur in some kind of environment. Ankle sprains, motor vehicle collisions, and back pain do not occur without some influence from the environment. Environmental issues such as work, stress and anxiety, financial concerns, beliefs, and fears can significantly impact how a patient may experience the injury.[86] The environmental influences can be seen as having either a positive (lessening the pain experience) or negative (increasing the pain experience) influence.

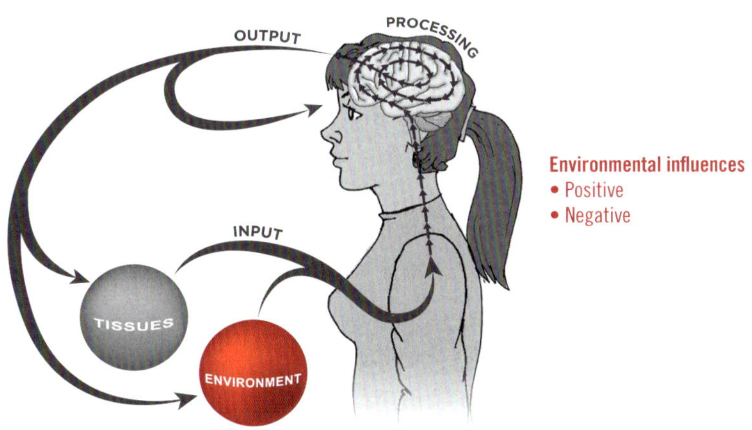

Negative:

- It has been shown that injuries occurring in high-stress environments, such as car accidents, injury at a stressful job, etc., have a much higher chance of producing persistent pain.[87,88]

- It is reported that injuries sustained in high-stress environments are seven to eight times more likely to result in chronic pain.[89]

- When the medico-legal environment allows litigation for pain and suffering, recovery following motor vehicle collision slows.[90]

- Some cultures that tend to have a more expressive communication style may be more likely to be just as expressive when describing their pain experience.[91-93] However, it is likely that this will be highly variable among individuals and it is important not to assume a person will communicate in such a manner based on their cultural upbringing.

- Circumcised boys develop more pain sensitivity later in life[94-96] and it's thought to be linked to post traumatic stress disorder (PTSD), depression, anger, low self-esteem and problems with intimacy.[97]

- When babies are exposed to repetitive needle pricks in neonatal intensive care units, plasticity within the nervous system may lead to increased pain sensitivity later in life.[98,99]

- High local unemployment rates are strong predictors of chronic pain and disability.[100]

- In the classic Boeing aircraft company study, it was shown that job satisfaction was the biggest predictor of back pain, regardless what type of job the workers were physically doing.[101]

- The term socioeconomic disadvantage (SED) has been defined in many ways. However, regardless of definition, a large volume of literature has shown SED to be correlated with increased morbidity, decreased life expectancy, and higher infant mortality.[102,103]

Positive:

- Kids that play contact sports early in life may have a lower chance of developing chronic pain.[104]
- Demolition derby drivers experience an average of 1500+ motor vehicle collisions during their career, yet less than five percent develop chronic whiplash-associated neck pain. Compare this to the general population involved in motor vehicle accidents where 33 percent will develop chronic whiplash-associated pain.[52]
- Cultures that are considered to be more stoic (e.g. North American, Northern European, Asian) and are less expressive in their communication style are less likely to complain about pain.[91-93]

NPQ and rNPQ statements:	NPQ/rNPQ #	Answer
When you are injured, the environment that you are in will not have an effect on the amount of pain that you experience	NPQ 13	False
When you injure yourself, the environment that you are in will not affect the amount of pain you experience, as long as the injury is exactly the same	rNPQ 11	False

3.6: Input Mechanism: Peripheral Neurogenic

NPQ and rNPQ statements:	NPQ/rNPQ #
Nerves can adapt by increasing their resting level of excitement	NPQ 8; rNPQ 6
Receptors on nerves work by opening ion channels (sensors) in the wall of the nerve	NPQ 10
Nerves can adapt by making more ion channels (sensors)	NPQ 15
Nerves adapt by making ion channels (sensors) stay open longer	NPQ 17
In chronic pain, chemicals associated with stress can directly activate danger messenger nerves	NPQ 19

Various biological and physiological processes of the peripheral nervous system are important elements in the development of a pain experience. In this section, we will delve into three key processes: (1) ion channel expression; (2) double-crush and axoplasmic flow; and (3) blood supply to the nervous system. It is important to note that none of these processes occur in isolation. These and other processes may have interactions across multiple areas of the nervous system. For example, nerve compression and resultant immune changes in the spinal cord and brain[105] (Section 3.7).

3.6.1: Ion channels

Chemicals in the body are "electrically-charged" (ions), the most important including sodium, potassium, calcium, and chloride. Neurons contain semi-permeable membranes that regulate ions. When a neuron is not sending a signal, it is "at rest." When a neuron is at rest, the inside of the neuron is negative relative to the outside. Although the concentrations of the different ions attempt to balance out on both sides of the membrane, they cannot. When all these forces balance out and the difference in the voltage between the inside and outside of the neuron is measured, you have the resting potential. The resting membrane potential of a neuron is about -70 mV, which means that the inside of the neuron is 70 mV less than the outside. At rest, there are relatively more sodium ions outside the neuron and more potassium ions inside that neuron.

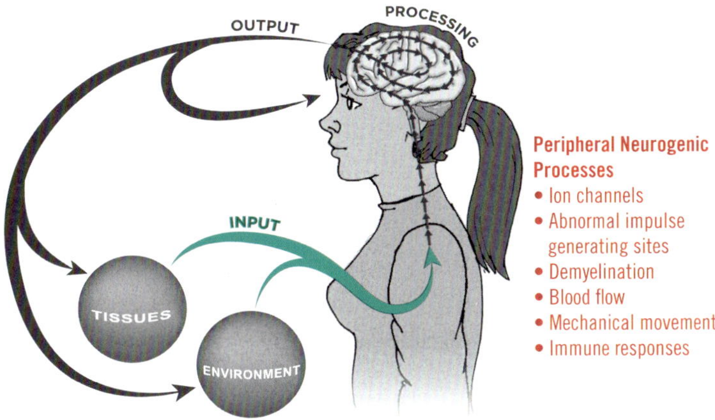

When an action potential occurs, the neuron sends information down an axon and away from the cell body. The action potential is like an explosion of electrical activity that is created by a depolarizing current. This means that some event, a stimulus, causes the resting potential to move toward 0 mV. When the depolarization reaches a threshold of about -55 mV, a neuron will fire an action potential (Figure 3.9). If the neuron does not reach this critical threshold level, then no action potential will fire. Also, when the threshold level is reached, an action potential of a fixed size will always fire. For any given neuron, the size of the action potential is always the same. There are no big or small action potentials in one nerve cell; all action potentials are the same size. Therefore, the neuron either does or does not reach the threshold required to initiate a full action potential. This is the "ALL OR NONE" principle.

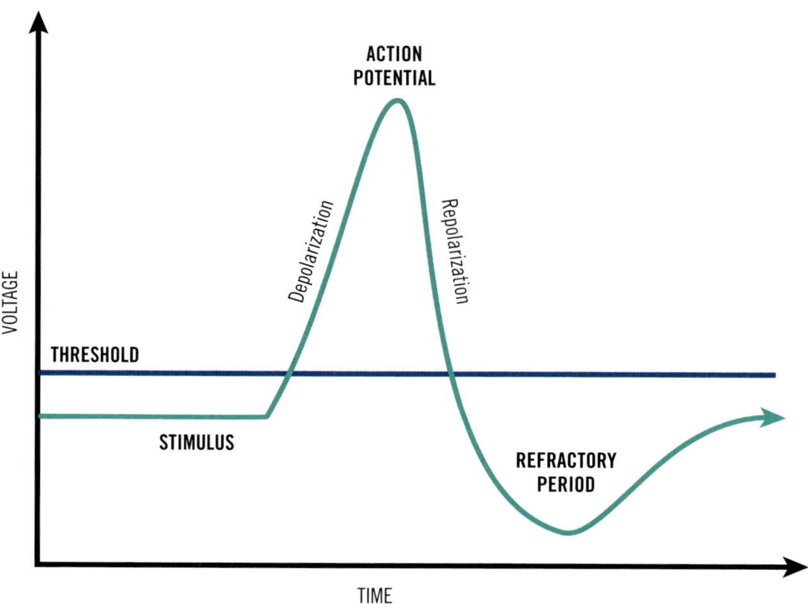

Figure 3.9: An action potential occurs when depolarization of the axon cell membrane reaches the critical threshold level.

The previous section described how a nerve has a resting membrane potential of -70 mV. It is also important to realize a nerve can have a resting membrane potential of -60 mV.[106] There is, however, a very definite threshold of -55 mV. Once -55 mV is reached, the action potential occurs. The gateway between the "outside" and "inside" of a nerve is an ion channel (Figure 3.10). Ion channels are proteins, clumped together to form a passage in the membrane of the nerve that allows ions to move in or out.[76,107]

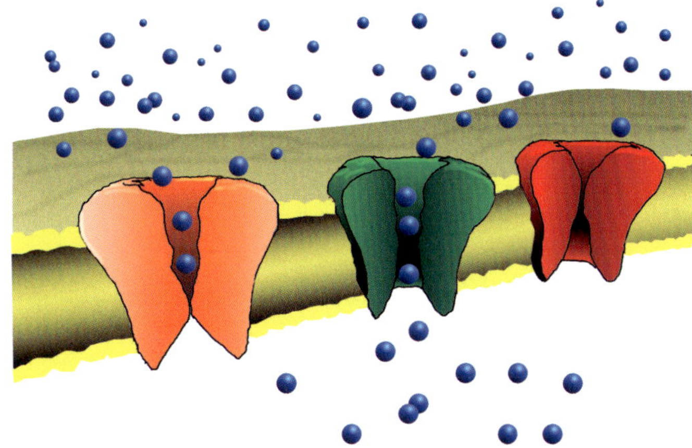

Figure 3.10: Ion channels in the axon cell membrane (axolemma) are gates that can open in response to various stimuli and allow passage of ions from outside the axon to alter the voltage across the axolemma. They could also be described as "sensors" for a more patient-friendly description.

Ion channels regulate the flow of ions across the membrane in all cells, and the opening and closing of the ion channels are governed by various signals (Figure 3.11):

- **Voltage channels** – Mainly open/close due to electrical activity of the ions
- **Chemical channels** – Open the channel with circulating fluid in the area, such as adrenaline
- **Temperature channels** – Open and close with changes in temperature
- **Mechanical channels** – Open due to mechanical stimuli, such as pressure or tension
- **Immune channels** – Open due to immune molecules, such as cytokines
- **Spontaneous channels** – Some transient receptor potential channels seem to open for no reason
- **Hydrogen channels** – Voltage-gated proton channels open with depolarization, but in a strongly pH-sensitive manner
- **Light-gated channels** – Open with changes in light

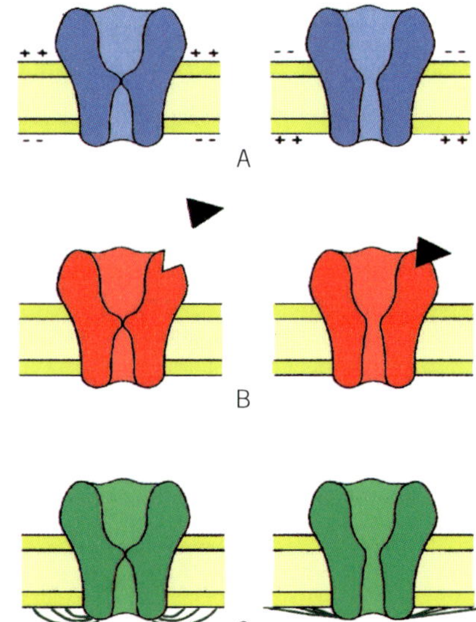

Figure 3.11: Example of various ion channels: A Voltage channels pre- and post-opening; B Chemical channels, showcasing as an example adrenaline docking into the ion channel, acting as a key and opening the ion channel; C Mechanical channel with a cytoskeleton of collagen that is mechanically acted upon (i.e., pull) and opening the channel. (Image adapted from Devor).[76]

There are a variety of types of ion channels in axons and, to date, several hundred have been identified. From a survival perspective, it is logical to consider ion channel expression from a homeostatic perspective. When all is well, and the organism is facing no threat, there is likely a need for a relatively equal expression of each type of ion channel. This relative "balance" of sensors is just enough to sense normal environmental stimuli, such as changes in temperature, changes in circulating immune molecules in the body, levels of circulating stress chemicals, etc. Within this homeostatic view of ion channel expression exists a very important neuroplastic event, which is important to consider in patients experiencing pain (Figure 3.12). Ion channel expression continually changes. It has been reported that the half-life of a typical ion channel is approximately 48 hours, thus allowing for a continued neuroplastic change in the sensitivity of the nervous system.[107,108]

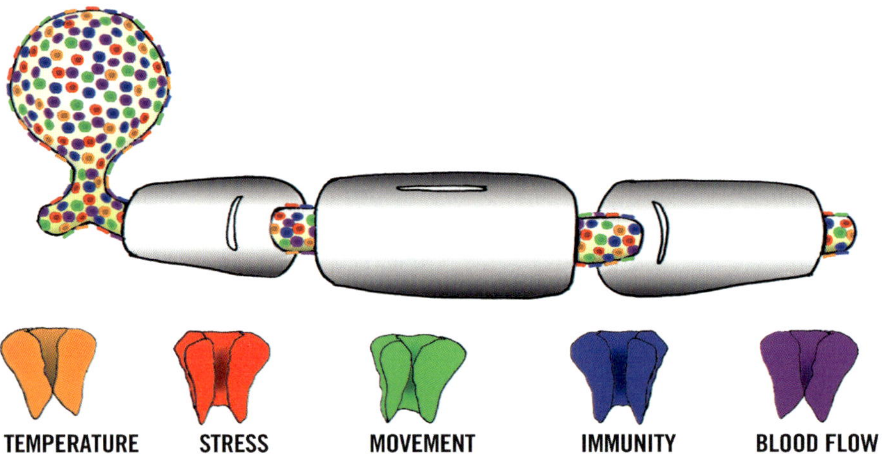

Figure 3.12: Theoretical distribution on ion channels throughout the axolemma in a homeostatic state.

Ion channel production does have a genetic/biological premise based on DNA coding. DNA provides the script for the development of proteins and, since DNA cannot escape the cell nucleus, messenger RNA (mRNA) transcribes the message and instructs the cell to build certain proteins. Depending on the type of proteins clumped together, different kinds of channels are fabricated according to genetic instructions.[76,107] This inherent genetic coding does ensure some predetermined ion channel expression, but it is believed that the more potent influences on ion channel expression may be from the brain's interpretation of the environment. When facing a specific threat, ion channels, acting as sensors, will be needed for that threat. For example, it is now well established that following a motor vehicle collision (MVC), patients develop immediate hypersensitivity of the nervous system.[87] Given the high levels of stress and anxiety in and around the MVC and the uncertainty of the future in regards to recovery, pain, and movement; higher numbers of movement-sensitive ion channels may be produced.[109] This may cause a widespread sensitization of movement of the nervous system after the accident.[109-111] This increase of mechanosensitive ion channels in response to the threat of movement in the face of high levels of pain may well explain a patient with whiplash-associated disorders demonstrating increased sensitivity and decreased movement with neurodynamic tests, such as the upper limb neurodynamic tests and slump test.[112,113] This continual change in ion channel expression (Figure 3.13) is important:

1. It provides a biological plausible explanation for "odd" pains reported by patients during treatment, e.g., pain when a weather-related cold front nears or when faced with increased stress and adrenaline levels during a preoperative period.

2. Understanding that ion channel expression is plastic provides hope for patients with chronic pain. The fact that sensitivity is continually changing implies that with proper treatment, sensitivity can be reduced to allow for decreased pain and disability.

Figure 3.13: Neuroplastic remodeling of the axolemma's ion channel expression allows for altered sensitization of the peripheral nervous system.

Even though significantly more complicated, clinically it is important to understand the concept of ion channel deposition. It is estimated that a single axon contains approximately 1 million ion channels, thus the human body has trillions upon trillions of ion channels. The typical half-life of an ion channel is estimated to be around 48 hours. Therefore (and the important clinical part), if we could freeze time and count the number of ion channels and the distribution (ratios) of the various ion channels in a person at any given time, it would be a representation of:

1. **Genetic coding** – based on genetic coding each person would have a different expression of ion channels. For example, in any large gathering, i.e., a seminar, there are some people who are "cold" and need to wear a sweater or coat, yet the person next to them are fine with only a shirt. The genetic coding behind ion channels imply some level of difference between people, at least to a small extent. Furthermore, given epigenetics (environmental influence of gene expression), differences will also ensue as we adapt to our environments, i.e., move and live in a much colder environment.

2. **What the brain thinks we need for survival** – If we consider ion channels play a significant role in protection and survival, and humans face various stressors (cold front coming into town; looming medical test or surgery, etc.), ion channels adapt accordingly to "monitor and inform" the brain of impending threats. It would make sense as weather change and temperatures plummet, we become aware of it (beyond regular senses), so we can protect ourselves – put on a coat. Similarly, if we do not monitor our stress (levels of circulating adrenaline and cortisol), we may be susceptible to a stroke or cardiac event. In this model, the brain uses its available information and adapts the sensitivity of the nervous system via ion channel expression for survival purposes.

The non-uniform distribution of ion channels warrants further investigation. Considering that ion channels are gateways between the inside of the axon and the outside, they need to be placed in the membrane of an axon. Myelinated nerves, however, have a natural barrier to ion channel insertion with the presence of the myelin sheath. Therefore, it is well documented that ion channels typically are found in higher concentrations in areas where there is less myelin (Figure 3.14).[76,107] One such area is the dorsal root ganglion (DRG). The DRG is non-myelinated and is an ideal locus for ion channel insertion. As well as being an easy target for ion channel expression, the DRG is also reported to have a specific affinity for adrenaline and mechanical ion channels.[114-116] A second target area for ion channel insertion can be found at the Nodes of Ranvier. The Nodes of Ranvier are normal, non-myelinated sections of the axons between the myelin sheets. These nodes also have high concentrations of ion channels, which is important in the electrochemical conduction of impulses. The third target area for ion channel insertion is any area along the nerve fiber where injury or a disease state has resulted in a loss of myelin.[117,118] Wherever the myelin sheath is removed from the axon, ion channels will insert into the newly exposed axolemma. Myelin can be removed from a nerve by:

- **Mechanical force:** Myelin can be physically “peeled” away from an axon. For example, during an injury, such as an inversion ankle sprain, axons (sural nerve) may have myelin removed via the sudden inversion sprain.

- **Immune processes:** There are several immune-based disease states that demyelinate axons, such as multiple sclerosis, human immunodeficiency virus (HIV), etc.[119]

- **Chemical stripping:** Inflammatory substances released at the time of an injury may dissolve the myelin surrounding the axon. Various inflammatory and immune cells are known to be part of this “chemical stripping” of the axon. For example, phospholipase-A2 in a disc herniation is a chemical released by the disc, which can denervate the adjacent axon.[120-123] This category of chemical peeling includes chemotherapy and its ability to remove myelin and potential heightened pain responses.[124,125]

It is now well established that when an abnormal concentration of ion channels is found in the axolemma, the axon develops an ability to generate its own impulses and thus not merely impulse conducting. These areas are referred to as ectopic nerve pacemakers or abnormal impulse generating sites (AIGS). Depending on the concentration of the specific type of ion channels in the area, the axon can depolarize in response to opening of those ion channels and an action potential can ensue with higher levels of adrenaline (fear, anxiety, stress or anger), movement and/or mechanical pressure, temperature shifts in the environment, etc. (Figure 3.14).

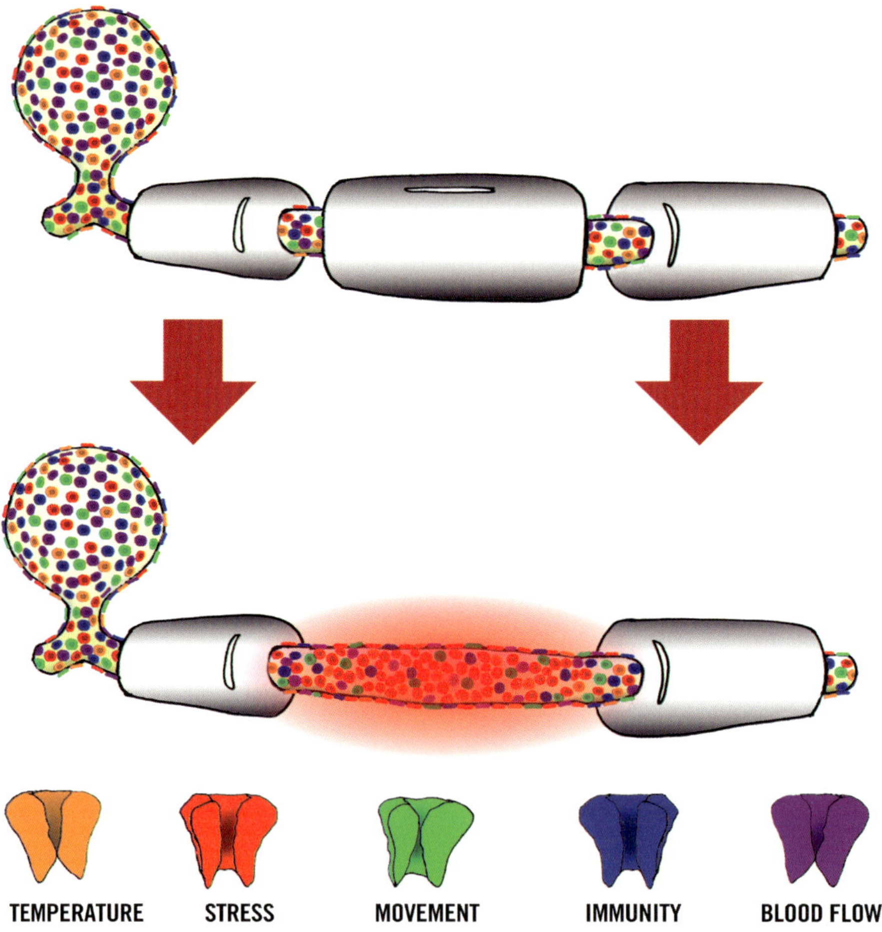

Figure 3.14: Development of an abnormal impulse generating site.

The demyelination of axons and resultant upregulation of ion channels into the bare axolemma can help clinicians explain some of the pain that patients may experience after surgery or injury. Three orthopedic examples will be familiar to most clinicians:

- **Knee arthroscopy:** It is now well documented that in a knee arthroscopy, the surgical ports inserted into the medial aspect of a patient's knee may damage the infrapatellar branches of the saphenous nerve.[126] This mechanical invasion is not only likely to sever the small nerve fibers but also remove myelin. The resultant nerve sprouting, as the nerve regenerates to reconnect with its distal segments, leaves a series of un-myelinated axons with a resulting upregulation of ion channels.[127-130] Clinically, if a patient experiences disproportionate pain following a knee arthroscopy, even though range of motion or stability appears to be unaffected, it may be more to do with nerve sensitivity than actual structural issues in and around the knee.

- **Lumbar disc herniation and radiculopathy:** There is growing evidence that lumbar radiculopathy is associated with a chemical activation of the DRG and adjacent axons. Following a disc herniation, powerful chemicals, i.e., phospholipase A2, thrombaxin, interleukins, etc., leak from the disc and not only chemically stimulate the DRG, but start a demyelination process in the proximal nerve root.[120-123] With demyelination, there is increased availability for upregulation of ion channel deposition, development of AIGS and persistent and high-level pain, despite the original disc injury healing.[124,125]

- **Medial scapular border pain mimicking Cloward referral patterns:** It is now well established that the cervical discs, as well as cervical zygapophyseal joints, are known to refer pain to the upper thoracic spine.[131,132] Cervical disc lesions, as an example, are quite common and associated with a MVC.[133-135] During the hyperextension phases of a MVC, annulus bruising, annulus tears and the resultant bleeding and inflammation have been well documented.[133-136] During the hyperflexion phase of the MVC, injured annulus fibers are often distracted, increasing annular damage and sustaining avulsion from the subchondral bone.[133-136] In lieu of the fact that mechanical compression on a healthy nerve is only associated with neurological symptoms (numbness, weakness and paresthesia),[137] a lot of focus has shifted to the inflammatory processes of the injured disc affecting the local neural tissue, especially the DRG.[136,138] With the chemical activation of the DRG, referred pain is often felt in the upper thoracic spine, clinically known as Cloward areas.[131,132] Following injection studies on the cervical discs and more recent studies using discography, cervical disc injuries can render the cervical spine rather symptom-free, but produce high levels of thoracic pain (Figure 3.15 on the following page).[139] Additionally, the cervical spine zygapophyseal joints have been shown to be a common source of pain following degenerative changes or trauma, such as a MVC.[136,140,141]

As with cervical discs, the cervical zygapophyseal joints are known to refer pain in and around the upper thoracic spine (Figure 3.15).[142,143] From a pain science perspective, though, clinicians are also urged to consider another possible pain pattern which may mimic Cloward and zygapophyseal pain referral: posterior primary rami nerves. Anatomically, the posterior primary rami of the spinal nerves arise in T2 spinal level through T6 spinal level and pursue a right-angled course through the multifidus muscle and local fascia.[144] It is proposed that with sudden hyperflexion of the neck, upper thoracic spine and ribs during a MVC, the sudden movement and mechanical stretch may cause local demyelination, resulting in a bare axolemma. The bare axolemma will in turn allow for an abnormal upregulation of ion channels locally, which may become a major source of persistent thoracic pain.

Cervical Injury Pain Referral Patterns

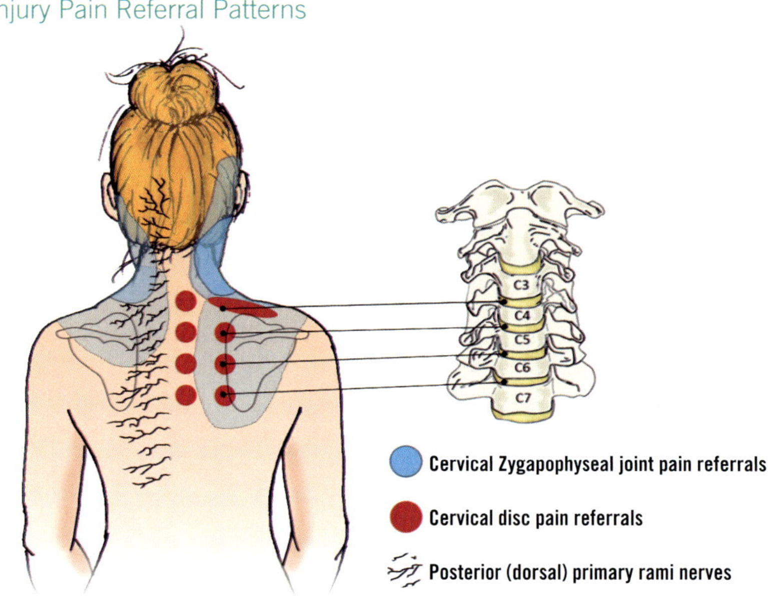

Figure 3.15: Composite image showcasing the overlap of cervical disc and cervical zygapophyseal pain referral patterns over the superficial posterior primary rami nerves. (Adapted from Louw & Schmidt).[109]

Another very important aspect in chronic pain, specific to ion channels is important: the duration of ion channel opening to allow ions in and out of the axon. Most ion channels open for milliseconds, allowing ions to polarize or depolarize the membrane.[76,107] Some channels, such as G-protein channels, can remain open for several minutes. With persistent pain, especially in the dorsal horn, second-order neurons may have higher concentrations of G-proteins.[145,146] From an evolutionary biological perspective, these higher G-protein concentrations would seem logical as the pathways would then be able to enhance nociceptive information to the brain, such as action potential windup (Section 3.4).

3.6.2: Double crush and axoplasmic flow

Originally described in 1973 by Upton and McComas, double crush refers to the phenomenon whereby an axon being compressed at one site leads to the axon becoming susceptible to damage/dysfunction at another site along the axon.[147] For example, it has been shown that a high percentage of patients with cervical radiculopathy develop carpal tunnel syndrome.[148] The double crush phenomenon is very controversial depending on who is surveyed, with the majority of PTs (85 percent) agreeing with the existence of the double crush hypothesis, half of hand surgeons (51 percent) and a minority of neurologists (24 percent).[149] One of the main reasons for the skepticism surrounding double crush is the failure of tests such as nerve conduction tests to showcase this phenomenon, therefore (in medicine) it "does not exist."[150] It is important to realize that nerve conduction tests are not fascicle-specific; cannot pick up multiple neuropathies; cannot assess the movement capabilities of the nervous system; are unable to test for central sensitization; etc. The various shortcomings from nerve conduction tests should be weighed against the clinical evidence for double crush as well as the experimental and basic science research showcasing its existence.[151]

The clinical importance of double crush, and especially compression on axons, is the fact that it leads to a cascade of events associated with increased peripheral and central sensitization, far-reaching immune responses with glial cell activation, neuroinflammation, changes in circulation and blood flow to the nervous system, etc.[151] Various studies have shown axonal compression to be associated with demyelination, which creates an opportunity for increased ion channel expression, development of an AIGS and potential barrage into the CNS (Section 3.4). To test the clinical development of entrapment and compression neuropathy, scientists developed an experiment whereby they inserted a plastic tube around the sciatic nerve of a young rat and as the rat and its sciatic nerve grew, pressure was thus steadily increased around the nerve, like a scenario often encountered in the clinic with radiculopathy. Three months later, with progressive compression, scientists showed the development of neural edema, demyelination, Wallerian degeneration and small fiber loss on the DRG and axonal damage.[152] Axonal compression thus led to a cascade of events which plays a significant role in the development of local (peripheral) sensitization, ongoing nociceptive barrage into the CNS (central sensitization) as well as immune responses which relate to altered plasticity and persistent pain.[151-153]

On a more local and cellular level, axonal compression has shown to lead to alterations in intraneural microcirculation as well as axon transport.[154,155] Axoplasmic transport refers to the movement of materials within the axon of a nerve, or intracellular transport in neurons.[74] Axonal proteins, membranes and organelles occur in the cell body of the neuron and are transported to their destination. Axoplasmic flow is bi-directional with both an antegrade and retrograde flow:

- **Antegrade** – descending away from the neuronal cell body, transporting mitochondria, vesicles, receptors and neurotransmitters.
- **Retrograde** – towards the cell body. Approximately 50 percent of the anterograde proteins are recycled via retrograde transport to the cell body. It is also believed retrograde flow serves a signaling function between axon and cell body.

In contemplating the potential effect of a double crush, it is important to realize that only minor compression (20-30mm Hg) is needed to alter axoplasmic flow. Additionally, axomplasm consistency is thought to be three to four times more viscous than water, and its ability to function optimally is dependent on adequate blood flow.[74,156] It is postulated that altered axoplasmic flow may play a significant role in the development and maintenance of the various pathological issues associated with entrapment neuropathies including the development of an AIGS, demyelination, increased mechanosensitivity, and other processes which induces peripheral neuropathic pain.[74,157,158]

When a nerve depolarizes, it fires a message toward the spinal cord to send information to the brain. This firing direction is called orthodromic (the orthodox way). Many clinicians, however, are not familiar with the notion that nerves also fire "the other way" i.e., down the nerve. This firing direction is called antidromic firing or retrograde depolarization.[159] Activation of cutaneous nociceptors can induce retrograde depolarization of small-diameter primary afferents (axon reflex), causing the release of neuropeptides such as substance P and calcitonin-gene-related peptide (CGRP).[82,159] With the release of substance P, which is vasoactive, capillaries open in the target tissues resulting in increased redness, warmth and swelling. This would imply an increase of swelling and temperature in the target tissues. Additionally, substance P causes mast cells to release histamine, resulting in an increased inflammatory response as well as sensitization of the peripheral nervous system, which may result in an actual increased pain experience. Histamine, in turn, attracts immune molecules such as enzymes and macrophages to the area. This process is referred to as neurogenic inflammation. A physically unhealthy nervous system (axonal compression, demyelination, AIGS, etc.) may result in increased retrograde depolarization, which may result in prolonged swelling and inflammation in tissues along with increased enzyme activity with potential weakening of the tissues.[83,159] It is also important to realize that thoughts also involve nerve impulses. Therefore, increased thoughts or rumination about a pain experience (i.e., anxiety, fear, etc.,) may in fact drive more antidromic impulses to target tissues, resulting in increased swelling, inflammation, etc.

3.6.3: Blood flow

It has been estimated the brain, spinal cord, and peripheral nervous system only accounts for two to three percent of the total body mass, yet it consumes approximately 25 percent of the available oxygen in the circulating blood.[160,161] Additionally, it has been shown that if an axon is lengthened six to eight percent, blood flow slows; 15 percent results in blood flow stopping; a 20 percent "axonal stretch" is associated with cell death in the dorsal horn and demyelination.[162-165] For nerves to function properly, they need adequate blood supply and oxygen. The pressures in and around tissues affect the delivery of blood supply as well as various other factors (health of the patient, movement, etc.). It is estimated only 30 mmHg pressure in an area is needed to stop blood flow.[162-165] The sensitivity of the nervous system is closely linked to blood flow; when blood flow is decreased, there is a sensitization of the peripheral nervous system and when blood flow is increased (i.e., aerobic exercise), there is a desensitization of the nervous system.[166-168] The exact mechanism as to how blood flow changes increase and decrease neuropathic pain is widely discussed, including hydrogen ion channels (ischemia)[76], immune responses,[167,169] alterations in inflammation,[168,170] dispersion of intraneural edema associated with mechanical hyperalgesia[171] and more.

The Dorsal Root Ganglion (DRG)

The DRG, being "outside the dorsal horn" of the spinal cord, constitutes another part of the peripheral nervous system and plays a significant role in a human's pain experience. The DRG is a cluster of cell bodies of the sensory (afferent) neurons. The DRG is non-myelinated, thus contains a very high number of ion channels. This high concentration of ion channels in and around the DRG leads to a heightened sensitivity of the DRG to various stimuli associated with ion channel activation.[116,172,173] The DRG is extremely mechanosensitive and it's postulated that it additionally has a high affinity for adrenaline channels, making it more susceptible to circulating adrenaline.[116] The DRG has been reported as "the most sensitive structure in the human body" and clinically it's associated with extreme pain.[116] Clinically, it's also important to realize that the DRG may display periods of extreme latency after injury, with reported after-discharge occurring two to three weeks after insult.

For example, mechanical stimulus of the DRG in a MVC[174] may "compress" the DRG, but the axon may not fire for two to three weeks. It is believed that this after-discharge may be due to a delayed immune and stress response.[175,176] In recent years, with the increased activity in research associated with complex regional pain syndrome (CRPS), a lot of attention has shifted to the DRG. Following injury it has been shown that post-ganglionic sympathetic fibers grow toward the DRG basket, weaving it around the DRG.[177] This is important, as the sympathetic nervous system, an efferent system, releases adrenaline around the already-heavily-ion-channel-populated DRG and may easily cause the firing of an action potential with the release of adrenaline (fear, anxiety, stress, etc.).[159,177] This resultant action potential fires bi-directionally. With orthodromic impulses, there is a barrage into the CNS which may result in the development of central sensitization (Section 3.4). Antidromic or retrograde depolarization in turn may fire action potentials towards the target tissues resulting in release of substance P, histamine and other vasoactive substances. This results in the target tissue redness, warmth and swelling with spreading pain and additional changes within the central nervous system (Section 3.9).[178]

NPQ and rNPQ statements:	NPQ/rNPQ #	Answer
Nerves can adapt by increasing their resting level of excitement	NPQ 8; rNPQ 6	True
Receptors on nerves work by opening ion channels (sensors) in the wall of the nerve	NPQ 10	True
Nerves can adapt by making more ion channels (sensors)	NPQ 15	True
Nerves adapt by making ion channels (sensors) stay open longer	NPQ 17	True
In chronic pain, chemicals associated with stress can directly activate danger messenger nerves	NPQ 19	True

3.7: Processing Mechanism: Spinal Cord, Dorsal Horn and Second-order Neurons

NPQ and rNPQ statements:	NPQ/rNPQ #
The timing and intensity of pain matches the timing and number of signals in danger messages	NPQ 3
In chronic pain, the central nervous system becomes more sensitive to danger messages from tissues	NPQ 5
The brain can send messages down your spinal cord that can increase the danger messages going up the spinal cord	NPQ 7
Second-order messenger nerves post-synaptic membrane potential (excitement) is dependent on descending modulation	NPQ 16
Special nerves in your spinal cord convey 'danger' messages to your brain	rNPQ 5
Descending neurons are always inhibitory	rNPQ 9

In mathematics, one plus one equals two. In pain neuroscience, one plus one may end up being five, five thousand or even five million. For a clinician to develop a working knowledge of central sensitization, a basic knowledge of the dorsal horn and the various processes are needed. In its simplest form, the dorsal horn receives nociceptive information from the target tissue via a variety of nociceptive fibers (Figure 3.16).[34] The incoming electrochemical communication of the various nociceptors are met by interneurons, which can either block the information or allow the information to be passed onto second-order neurons. The second-order neurons then take the information from spinal level to the brain for interpretation and potential action.[34,179,180] Various second-order neurons exist, with the majority of current pain research focusing on two: wide dynamic ranging (WDR) neurons and nociceptive specific (NS) neurons. It is believed that most "day-to-day" information is passed onto the brain via the WDR neurons. However, NS neurons require a certain threshold to activate and are often more associated with "if needed in case of severe threat."[34,179,180] However, at each spinal level it's far more complicated with adjacent spinal levels trying to send information in (convergence theory), sympathetic actions, immune processes, motor neurons, information from the other side of the body, etc. In a healthy, normal individual, gating via various processes only allows for selected information (exact location; side of the body; type of nociceptive information, etc.,) to enter the dorsal horn, get passed onto the brain and processed accordingly. In this case, the patient knows exactly where the information came from (i.e., dermatome), what type of stimulus (light touch versus danger) and what side of the body.[34,179,180] This ability to "feature-extract" showcases a healthy nociceptive system, able to provide accurate information to the CNS and brain. In people with chronic pain, this is not the case, thus warranting a deeper understanding of these biological and physiological processes. Additionally, when the information is sent to the brain for processing and interpretation, it has endogenous mechanisms to increase incoming information (facilitation) or suppress incoming information (inhibition).[181]

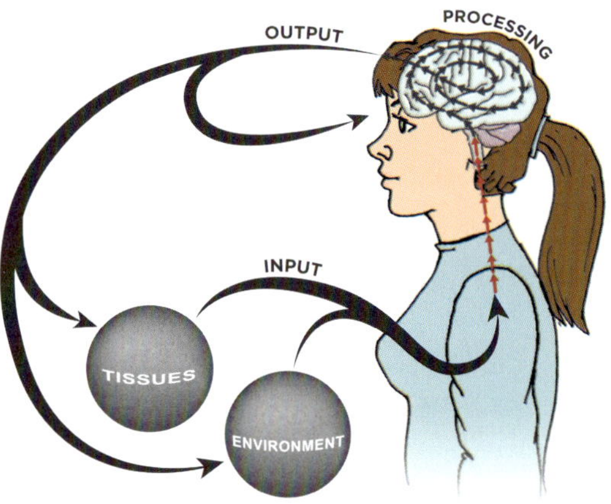

Dorsal Horn
- C-fiber barrages the dorsal horn
- Action potential windup
- Interneuron activity
- Interneuron death
- Expansion of receptor fields
- Allodynia and Hyperalgesia
- Modes of operation
  - normal mode
  - suppressed mode
  - sensitized mode
- Activation of second order neurons
- Endogenous mechanisms
- Ascending and descending control (placebo/nocebo)

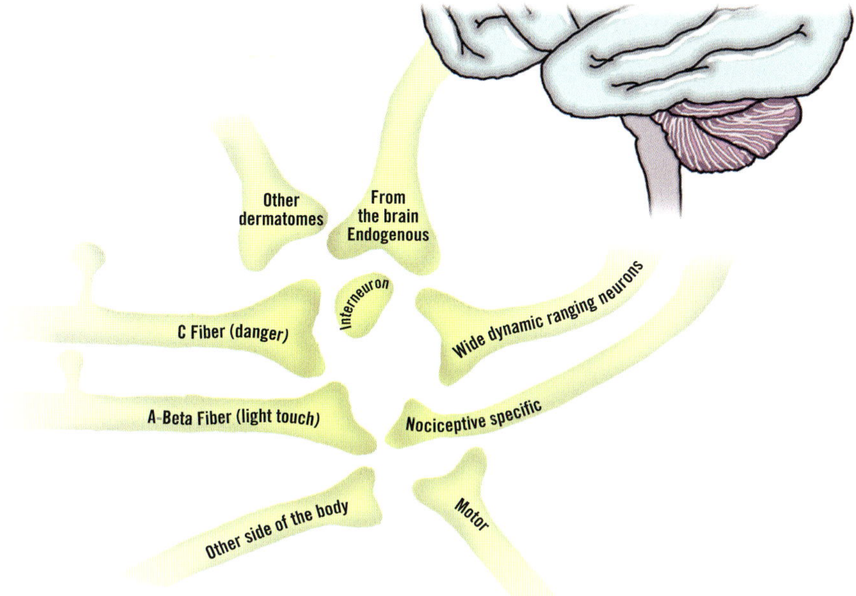

Figure 3.16: The various "players" in the dorsal horn involved in processing of nociceptive information and ultimately, a pain experience.

Following is an example to illustrate the process of suppressing (inhibiting) incoming information which occurs on a daily basis. The medial aspect of the knee contains various sensory receptors and fibers. A-beta fibers constantly send sensory information to the spinal cord for interpretation in the form of light touch. As your pants touch the medial aspect of the knee, this sensory information is passed through the spinal cord via the L3 dorsal horn, hoping to inform the brain of the pants touching the medial aspect of the knee (Figure 3.17).

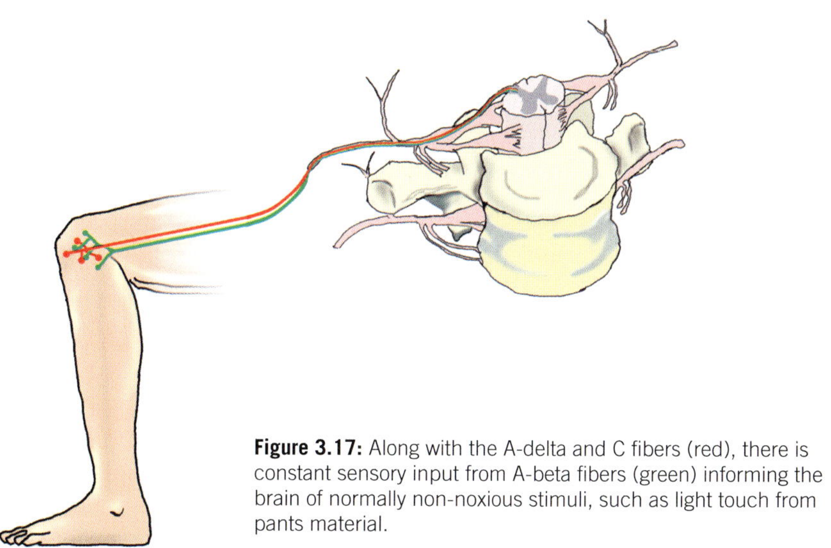

Figure 3.17: Along with the A-delta and C fibers (red), there is constant sensory input from A-beta fibers (green) informing the brain of normally non-noxious stimuli, such as light touch from pants material.

In this case, the sensory information is blocked at the spinal cord level, partly due to actions of the interneuron (Figure 3.18). These interneurons are sometimes referred to as relay neurons, association neurons, connector neurons or local circuit neurons, and are best defined as a neuron that forms a connection between other neurons. Interneurons are neither motor nor sensory. The term is also applied to brain and spinal cord neurons whose axons connect only with nearby neurons, distinguishing them from "projection" neurons, whose axons project to more distant regions of the brain or spinal cord. In the central nervous system, the term interneuron is used for small, locally acting neurons, in contrast to larger projection neurons with long-distance connections. Central nervous system interneurons are typically inhibitory and use the neurotransmitter gamma-Aminobutyric Acid (GABA) or glycine. However, excitatory interneurons using glutamate also exist, as do interneurons that release neuromodulators like acetylcholine. Following input from A-beta fibers, the interneuron may block the message with a release of GABA. In this case, the message terminates and the sensation of light touch from the pants is not registered cortically and you are, thus, not aware of the pants rubbing your leg (Figure 3.18).[34]

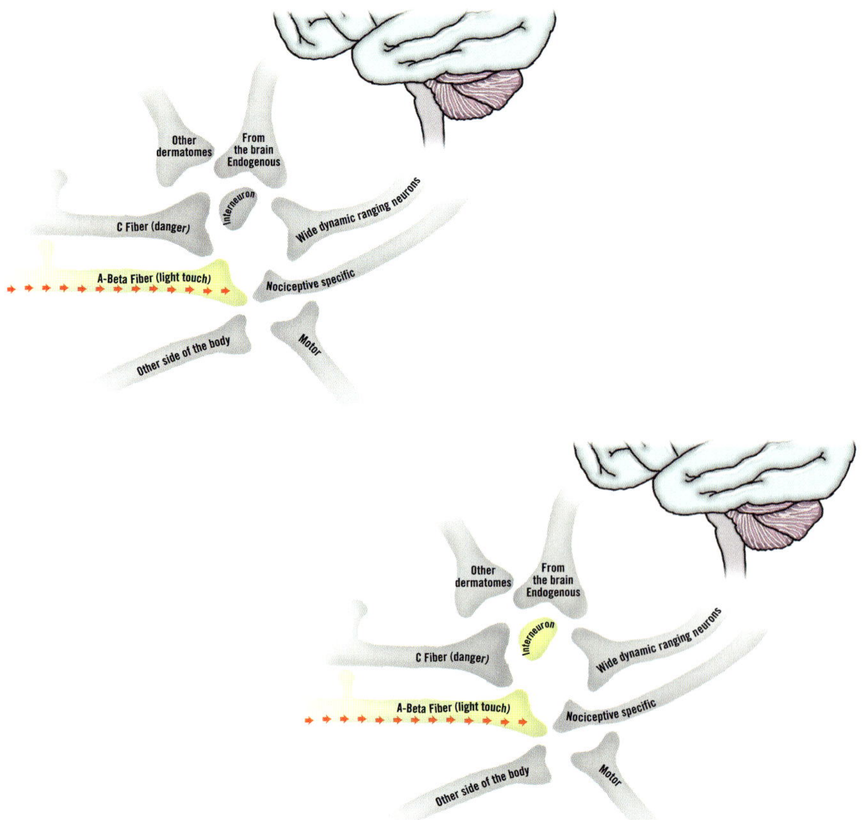

Figure 3.18: Control mode - light touch: A-beta (light touch) information is sent into the dorsal horn and the interneuron blocks the information from the second-order neurons and brain, thus rendering light touch as innocuous.

Following an acute injury, A-delta and C fibers send nociceptive information to the spinal cord with the intent to pass the message to the brain for interpretation and action. For an injury to the medial aspect of the knee, the sensory afferent input will be received into the dorsal horn of the spinal cord (L3) from the affected side (i.e., right side) (Figure 3.18). The nociceptive messages from the A-delta fibers chemically activate α-amino-3-hydroxy-5-methyl-4-isoxazolepropionic acid (AMPA) receptors on the second-order neurons via glutamate.[34,179,180,182] Second-order neurons will then relay messages from the spinal cord to the brain. The nociceptive information is passed onto the brain for interpretation and action. Although intense, pain will not usually last in this acute stage. Some of this is due to inhibition via the endogenous mechanisms of the brain, spinal cord, and descending pathways. Descending pathways, usually from the periaqueductal gray (PAG) area, produce serotonin, endorphins, opioids and enkephalins, which inhibit the nociception and, ultimately, the pain experience (Figure 3.19).[181] If stimulation of the medial knee persists (e.g., excessive valgus with prolonged walking, or sensitive nerves around the knee after surgery or injury) then nociceptive fibers will continue firing, in this case longer lasting C fibers play a greater role.

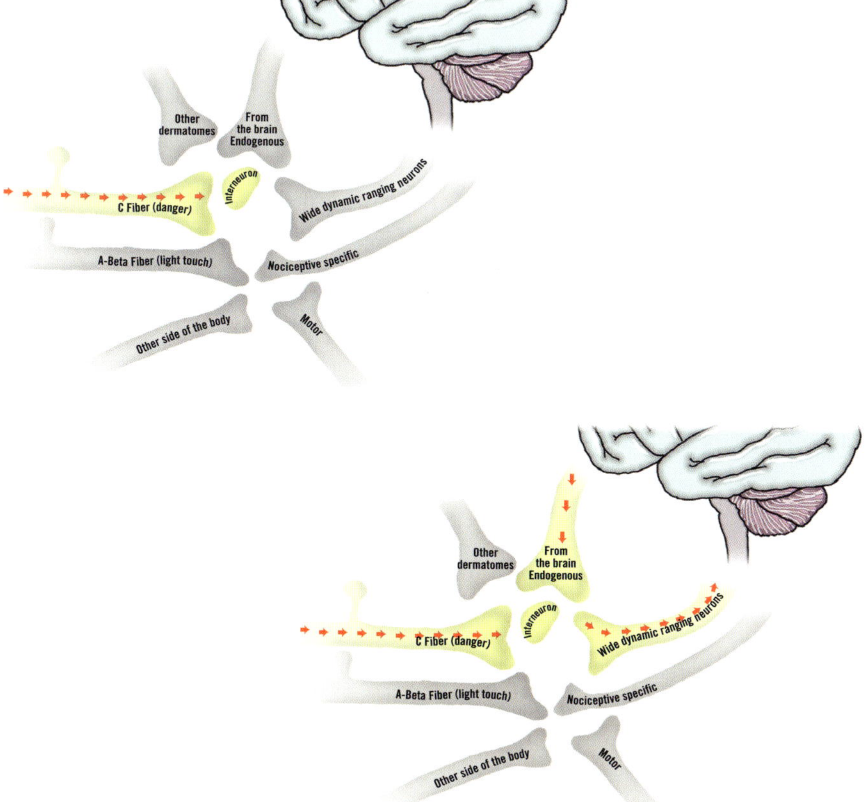

Figure 3.19: Control mode - danger. C fiber (danger – temperature, mechanical or chemical) information is sent into the dorsal horn and the interneuron allows the information to pass to the second-order neurons and brain, with a resulting activation of the descending endogenous mechanisms to modulate the pain experience.

Nociceptive input that passes the interneuron blockade needs to be sent onto the brain via second-order neurons. Basic neuroscience dictates that for a nerve impulse to continue, specific receptors are needed for specific neurotransmitters. If A-delta fibers release glutamate and there are no AMPA receptors available on the second-order neurons, the electrochemical message stops. This availability of receptors is part of the plasticity of the nervous system and may therefore modulate a pain experience. Receptors are continually replaced and the expression of receptor types is variable. The ability to feel the pants touch the medial part of the knee or threatening stimulus from the knee, is modulated by receptors on the second-order neurons and neurotransmitters. Although centrally mediated endogenous processes are important and well described in severe and acute injuries, the descending fibers from the brain are likely active in day-to-day stimuli, as well.[181]

In an injury or degenerative process, nociceptive fibers send repeated messages to the dorsal horn of the spinal cord. In the spinal cord, repeated stimulation at constant strength of dorsal root afferents, including nociceptive C fibers, can elicit a progressive increase in the number of action potentials generated by motoneurons and interneurons.[183,184] This process, referred to as "action potential windup," is the consequence of a cumulative membrane depolarization, resulting from the temporal summation of slow synaptic potentials. Simply stated, with persistent input from the periphery, changes to the spinal cord second-order neurons and, ultimately, brain pathways, lead to a heightened sensitization.[176,177] With persistent nociception via C fibers from the knee, permanent neuroplastic changes may occur. It is now well established that after a constant barrage from the C fibers, some of the interneurons may die due to high levels of amino acids.[34,182,185,186] With a persistent toxic environment, it is unlikely the interneuron will regenerate. The result is a decreased ability to modulate nociception and ultimately a pain experience (Figure 3.19). With less ability to modulate the incoming information, thresholds are easily met for nociceptive specific second-order neurons, increasing firing to the brain. Notice (Figure 3.20) how "one impulse" results in "two impulses" being sent to the brain. This amplification of input is an essential part of the development of central sensitization, hence the idea that in neuroscience one plus one is not necessarily two.

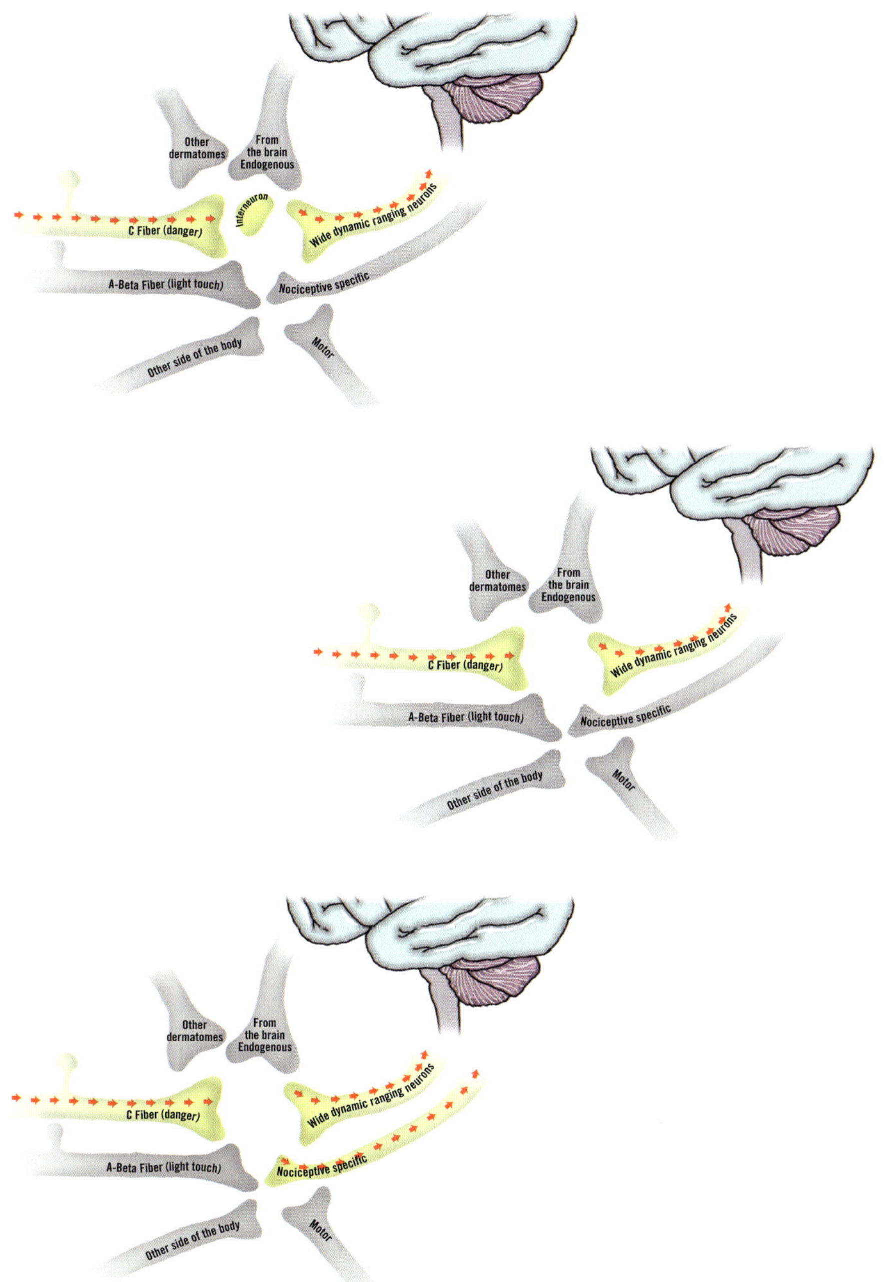

Figure 3.20: Interneuronal death with resulting upregulation of the CNS.

Second-order receptors change, as well. From a primitive survival viewpoint, the brain will want to know about danger to protect. Pain is there for protection. To facilitate this process, receptors in the second-order neurons are replaced with receptors that will facilitate an increase of danger messages to the brain for analysis. During day-to-day normal activity, receptors open and close in milliseconds.[76] In response to this threat, receptors which usually open and close fast can be replaced with receptors that stay open longer, up to several minutes, such as the G-protein receptors, which are commonly found in the central nervous system (Section 3.3.1). The end result is an "open gate." The second-order neuron is therefore more easily stimulated and fires faster, creating increased sensitivity. In the spinal cord, repeated stimulation (at constant strength) of dorsal root afferents including nociceptive C fibers can elicit a progressive increase in the number of action potentials generated by afferents and interneurons.[183,184]

This description of what happens in the central nervous system is extremely simplified; one nerve fiber brings a message to the dorsal horn of the spinal cord, which interacts with the interneuron, followed by the second-order neuron, and the message is sent to the brain. Obviously, the reality is a lot more complex (Figure 3.19):[34,179,180,185]

- A-delta, A-beta, C fibers and many more enter the dorsal horn.
- There are numerous interneurons.
- Each neuron connects with upwards of 5,000-10,000 other neurons, so there is convergence of multiple neurons onto a single neuron and divergence of that neuron onto multiple neurons.
- There are descending fibers from the brain supplying endogenous chemicals such as opioids, enkephalins, endorphins and serotonin, which allows for a cortical modulation of nociception and the pain experience.
- Convergence of adjacent spinal levels (for example, L2 and L4) also accesses the L3 spinal level.
- Other fibers are also present – motor, sympathetic, etc.
- There are many immune processes, i.e., glial cell activation, etc.
- Input to the dorsal horn is also received from the other side of the body.
- There are numerous second-order neurons from the L3 spinal level aimed at relaying the nociceptive information to the brain for interpretation.

With the loss of the interneuron, and thus a primary gating property, various spinal levels, other neurons, neurons from the other side of the body, etc., have access to second-order neurons, ultimately increasing the information the brain receives. However, the information is no longer as precise (ability to feature extract) because the brain now receives both C fiber and A-beta fiber information; information from various levels; information from the other side of the body, etc. Collectively, these processes will likely increase the threat level of the brain. Additionally, in these advanced stages, there is a reduction (or possible inability) of the brain to engage to descending endogenous mechanisms to alter the pain experience, thus in essence allowing for an increased pain experience (see Figure 3.21 on this page and Table 3.1 on the following page).

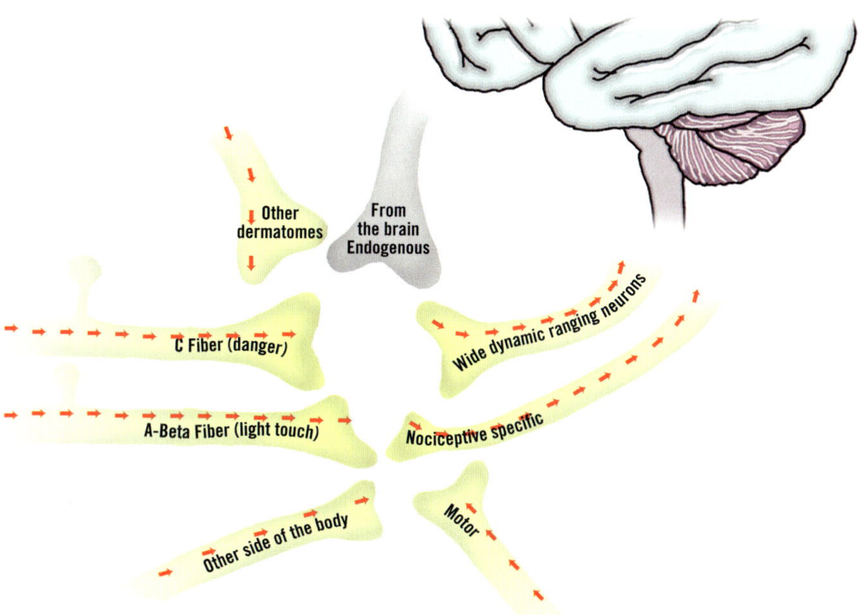

Figure 3.21: Expansion of receptor fields and increased ability of information to be sent onto the CNS and brain.

Another consequence of the constant barrage into the spinal cord is a plastic shift in the organization of neurons within dorsal horn laminae. In neuroscience, it is well understood that various nociceptors (A-beta; C, etc.) enter the dorsal horn in various layers or lamina. With the constant barrage into the CNS C fibers actually "pull back" out of certain lamina and A-beta grows in (Figure 3.22). This allows normally innocuous light touch information to access the nociceptive system, which clinically may result in light touch allodynia.[179,180]

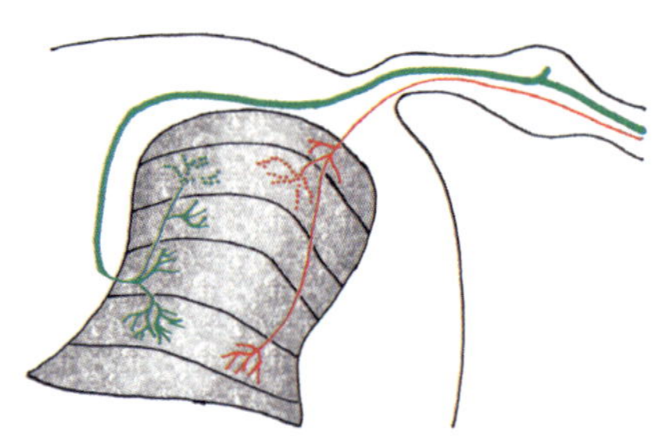

Even though very basic, this description clearly shows that many of the clinical features are real and not psychosomatic. Spreading pain, bilateral pain, pain due to light touch, etc., are biological and a consequence of the various processes described in this section.

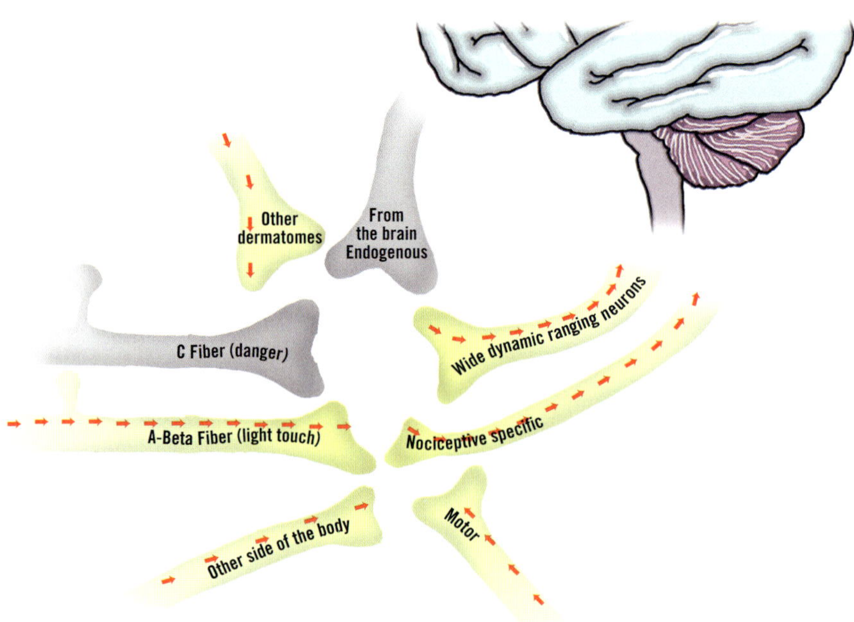

Figure 3.22: Easier access of A-beta fibers into the CNS in chronic pain.

Table 3.1: Clinical consequences of C fiber barrage into the CNS.

Process	Clinical consequence
Death of the inhibitory neurons	Decreased ability to inhibit peripheral nociception
C fibers pull back; Aβ-fibers grow in	Allodynia
Upregulation of second-order neurons	Increased firing towards the brain
Upregulation of second-order neurons	Functional shifts in the brain – pain neuromatrix
Inappropriate synapsing – other levels	Spreading pain
Inappropriate synapsing – other fibers	Sympathetic, immune, motor contributions
Inappropriate synapsing – other side	Bilateral "mirror" pains
Decreased endogenous mechanisms	Allodynia and hyperalgesia
Altered information from the periphery	Structural shifts in the brain – homuncular smudging
Alterations of immune function – glial cells	Opening of the spinal-cord-blood-barrier

Even when considering the simplistic description of central sensitization, there are some key elements that may go unnoticed:

- Acute pain predicts chronic pain. There is a growing body of evidence that the intensity and duration of acute pain predicts chronic pain.[34,110,179,180,185] With a constant barrage into the CNS, especially C fibers, there is increased chance of interneuronal death, receptor field changes, loss of inhibitory gating, etc. For example, it has been shown that patients who report a pain score of five or more (out of 10) in the first week after a wrist fracture have a significantly higher chance of developing CRPS.[187]

- In all people, the dorsal horn is quite resilient and deals with nociceptive bombardment on a regular basis. If you mildly sprain your ankle, there will be a short-term barrage increase to the CNS, but as the endogenous inhibitory mechanisms help and nociception eases from the periphery, the various systems and processes return to normal, ready for the next assault. It is the prolonged barrage and intensity of the barrage that likely predicts interneuronal death. It is also important to realize that it is only nociception and the brain's interpretation and the value it places on the information likely also plays a role in the plasticity changes in the dorsal horn, thus brining the environmental factors in again.

- With the loss of the interneuron, expansion of receptors fields and decrease in endogenous mechanisms, the clinical question will usually arise: If the interneuron does not grow back, what do we do now?

    - If you review the various images related to this section, what is the most powerful tool you can turn on? The brain. The essence of PNE is to activate the brain, improve knowledge and understanding about the pain experience. PNE has been shown to have a significant positive impact on pain catastrophization, and this in turn has been shown to have a significant ability to activate the naturally occurring opioids and cannabinoids in the brain, which can powerfully alter a pain experience.[188] This activation and the ability of getting the brain to downregulate the incoming nociception is referred to as a "top down" approach (Figure 3.23).[13]

    - Clinicians should also consider "bottom up." Even though the world of pain science has moved heavily toward the pain neuromatrix (plasticity changes, glial cell activation, PNE etc.), it is imperative to understand that various traditional approaches can also help modulate the pain experience. Gate control is still relevant, and using any and all possible means to alter input to the CNS (especially C fiber activity), it can help modulate the threat appraisal of the brain. For example:

- Cryotherapy has been shown to slow C fiber activity down, thus decreasing the nociception being sent into the dorsal horn of the spinal cord and ultimately decreasing the threat appraisal of the brain.[189] Additionally, via its vasoactive properties, ice has been shown to decrease pro-inflammatory chemicals in injured and diseased tissues, which further decreases nociception.

- Electrical stimulation, including transcutaneous electrical stimulation (TENS), has been shown to be effective in altering pain experiences via Gate Control.[190] By altering the amount and duration of peripheral input to the central nervous system, it alters information passed onto the brain and the threat appraisal of the brain.

- A foundational part of PNE, however, is the PNE+ concept of teaching a patient about pain while "doing something physical" as well.[2] The clinical manifestation, per Gifford, is "top down while bottom up" – educating while doing physical treatment.[13]

- Additionally, it is well understood that many times cognitions (i.e., fear avoidance) need to be addressed prior to physical treatment as a means to get some endogenous mechanisms to start – "top down before bottom up."[13]

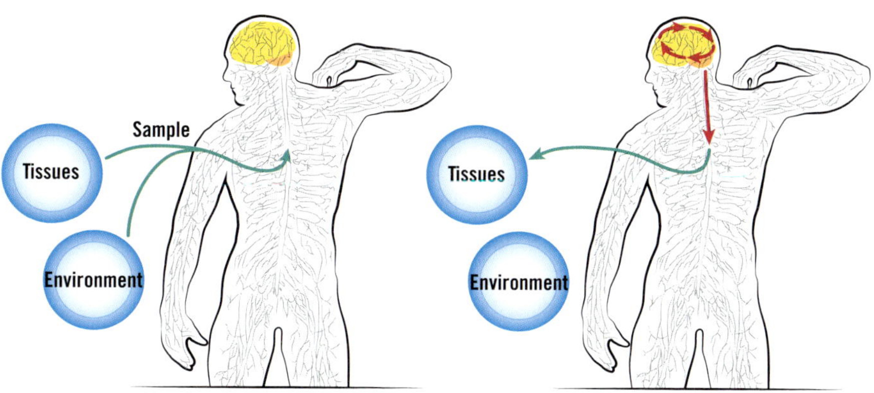

Figure 3.23: The various clinical potentials to modulate a pain experience: Top down; bottom up; top down before bottom up and/or top down while bottom up. From Gifford.[13]

With persistent input from the periphery, there is likely to be a change in the descending modulation of the brain and the endogenous chemical release of opioids, enkephalins, endorphins and serotonin.[191,192] This endogenous process is very powerful and essential for survival.[193,194] Endogenous chemicals, which are needed to modulate the incoming nociception and ultimately the pain experience, are reduced in chronic pain states (Figure 3.24).[191,192,195] In chronic pain, from an evolutionary survival perspective, the brain needs more information from the tissues (nociception) to best determine the most appropriate course of action. By reducing the normal endogenous chemicals, the brain allows more information to ascend for further interpretation.

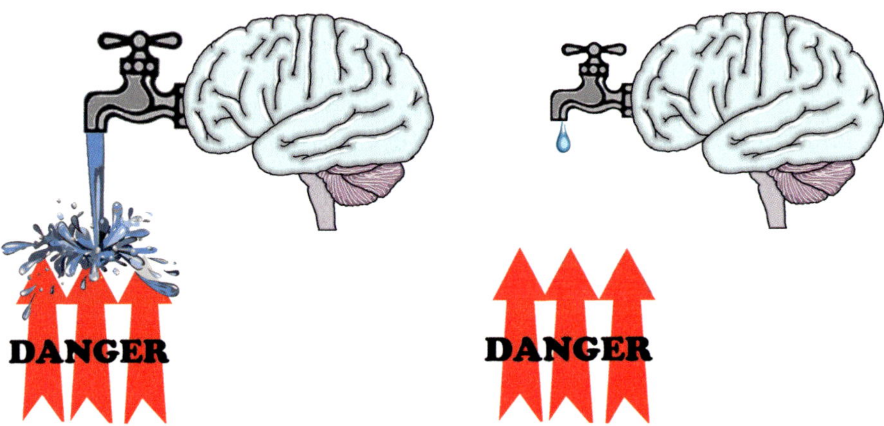

Figure 3.24: Endogenous chemicals, which are needed to modulate the incoming nociception and ultimately the pain experience, are reduced in chronic pain states. This drying up of the flow of descending modulation is sometimes referred to as a "dry brain."

The belief that "worse injuries result in worse pain" might appear to make sense, but it is amazing how often the opposite occurs. Many unfortunate individuals have arrived in hospital emergency departments impaled or severely injured following some gruesome accident, yet sometimes report experiencing little or no pain.[71-73] Many examples exist where injury is apparent and there is little to no resultant pain. Examples include soldiers being shot and not being aware of it, or athletes competing despite significant tissue damage or injury. These examples demonstrate the ability of the various endogenous mechanisms to powerfully modulate a pain experience. This descending modulation highlights a common misbelief regarding a common therapeutic effect called "placebo."[194]

Webster's Dictionary defines "placebo" as "a pharmacologically inert preparation prescribed more for the mental relief of the patient than for its actual effect on a disorder." Obviously, placebo does not only pertain to medications, but also therapeutic interventions. Unfortunately, placebo is often viewed as a "fake" or sham treatment. However, the word placebo originated from the Latin phrase for I shall please. Placebo should be seen more as the endogenous mechanisms of pain experience modulation. Beliefs and expectations are at the heart of this. Believing and expecting a treatment will work allows for an enhanced endogenous mechanism and, even if the actual, physical treatment is supposed to "do nothing," it is hard to consider the treatment fake.[196] Patients attending therapy carry expectation and beliefs in them, which can modulate their pain experiences.[197-199]

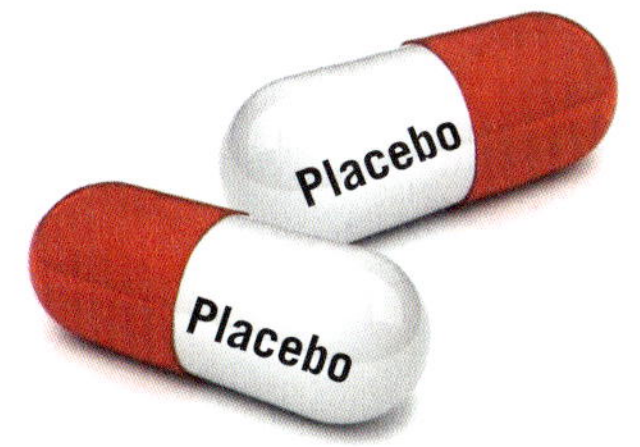

It is also noteworthy to consider the power of placebo. Placebo, or enhancing the brain's ability to modulate pain through beliefs and expectations, is likely a significant future source of treatment for patients with chronic pain. To showcase the power of placebo, consider a recent systematic review of sham surgery in orthopedics.[200] The review included six randomized controlled trials involving 277 subjects, concluding that sham surgery in orthopedics to be just as effective as actual surgery in reducing pain and disability.[201-206] As an example of the power of placebo, consider the two included studies in the systematic review pertaining to vertebroplasty for compression fractures:[202,203]

- Patients with compression fractures of the vertebral bodies were randomized to receive either the actual vertebroplasty or a sham vertebroplasty.

- Patients assigned to the actual procedure were given sedatives (not put under anesthesia, thus somewhat awake), a local anesthetic at the fracture site and a small incision. A hole was punched into the affected vertebral body through the incision and bone cement (methyl methacrylate) injected into the vertebral body under high temperature and, as it solidified, it stabilized the fracture. Instruments were removed, the incision was closed and the patient was sent to recovery.

- In the sham surgery, patients were also given a sedative, a local anesthetic and a similar incision at the fracture site. In this case, however, surgeons through the incision take a metal rod and tap on the fracture site several times without entering the vertebral body or injecting bone cement into the fracture. At the same time, scientists play a pre-recorded sound of the surgeons performing such an operation and the smell of methyl methacrylate was produced in the operating room. After the fractured vertebral body has been tapped several times, the metal rod was removed, the incision closed and the patient sent to recovery.

The fascinating part, of course, is that both groups demonstrated similar recovery levels for pain, length of hospital stay and re-fracture rates at the six-month follow-up. Does this mean surgery is not important? No, it merely showcases how powerful the brain can be. Given all the information the patient's brain had available to it (attending surgery; incision; feeling the bone being tapped; smelling methyl methacrylate; hearing the "normal" operation chatter), the brain was convinced the fracture was solidified, and thus pain was reduced by the brain.

NPQ and rNPQ statements:	NPQ/rNPQ #	Answer
The timing and intensity of pain matches the timing and number of signals in danger messages	NPQ 3	False
In chronic pain, the central nervous system becomes more sensitive to danger messages from tissues	NPQ 5	True
The brain can send messages down your spinal cord that can increase the danger messages going up the spinal cord	NPQ 7	True
Second-order messenger nerves post-synaptic membrane potential (excitement) is dependent on descending modulation	NPQ 16	True
Special nerves in your spinal cord convey "danger" messages to your brain	rNPQ 5	True
Descending neurons are always inhibitory	rNPQ 9	False

3.8: Processing Mechanism: Brain, The Pain Neuromatrix and Functional Changes in the Brain

NPQ and rNPQ statements:	NPQ/rNPQ #
Pain only occurs when you are injured	NPQ 2; rNPQ 10
The body tells the brain when it is in pain	NPQ 6
The brain can send messages down your spinal cord that can increase the danger messages going up the spinal cord	NPQ 7
The brain decides when you will be experiencing pain	NPQ 11; rNPQ 12
It is possible to have pain and not know about it	NPQ 14; rNPQ 1
Descending neurons are always inhibitory	rNPQ 9
Pain only occurs when you are injured or at risk of being injured	rNPQ 3

Nociception and pain are not synonymous. For nociception to be part of a human pain experience, the information has to be received, distributed, and interpreted by the brain. The history of pain, for the most part, is the history of nociception: overstimulation of receptors and influencing nociception.[3,4,9] Not until the early 1990s did the brain really feature in discussions about pain, but advanced scanning technology has catapulted the brain to the foreground when it comes to thinking about a human's pain experience,[27,28] culminating in the pain neuromatrix.[10,11] To understand the concept of a pain neuromatrix it is important to ask this question: How does the brain work, especially when processing danger? The simplest way to develop an immediate, easy-to-understand working knowledge of the brain is to bring up a memory. If you close your eyes and think about your grandmother or even favorite past vacation, what happens in the brain? For years it was thought a single area, the "grandma area" or "vacation area" would activate in the brain and we remember grandma or the vacation (Figure 3.25). Many people though, when thinking of grandma, remember grandma or the vacation, which means the areas in the brain associated with memory (i.e., hippocampus) must be activated. Additionally, many can "see" their grandma or vacation when they think of it, thus activating the visual areas of the brain. Additionally, many other areas would likely be activated in thinking about grandma or vacation, including smell, autonomic, auditory, movement, emotions, etc. A more realistic way to represent grandma or your vacation is the activation of various brain areas; these areas communicate and develop a "grandma map" or "vacation map" (Figure 3.25 on the following page). This is exactly how nociception and ultimately pain is processed in the brain. Various areas light up during a pain experience, communicate with each other and develop a pain map, referred to as the pain neuromatrix (Figure 3.26).[10,11]

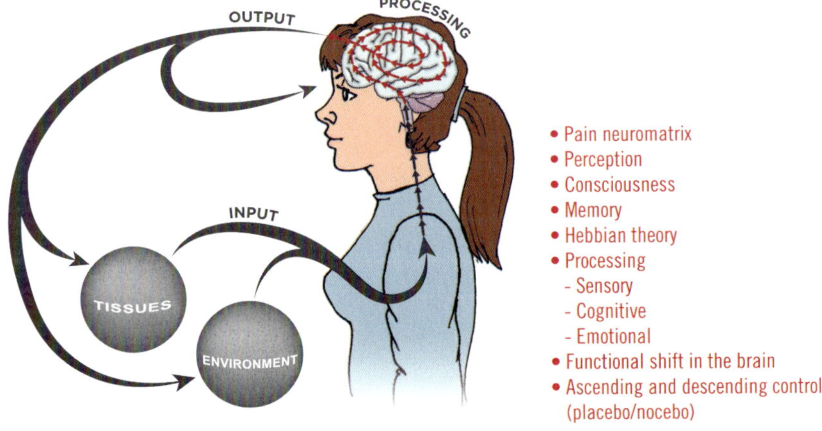

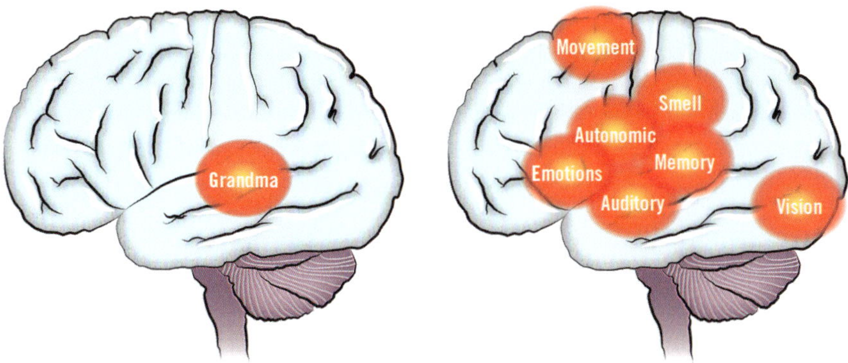

Figure 3.25: Brain activation during a memory.

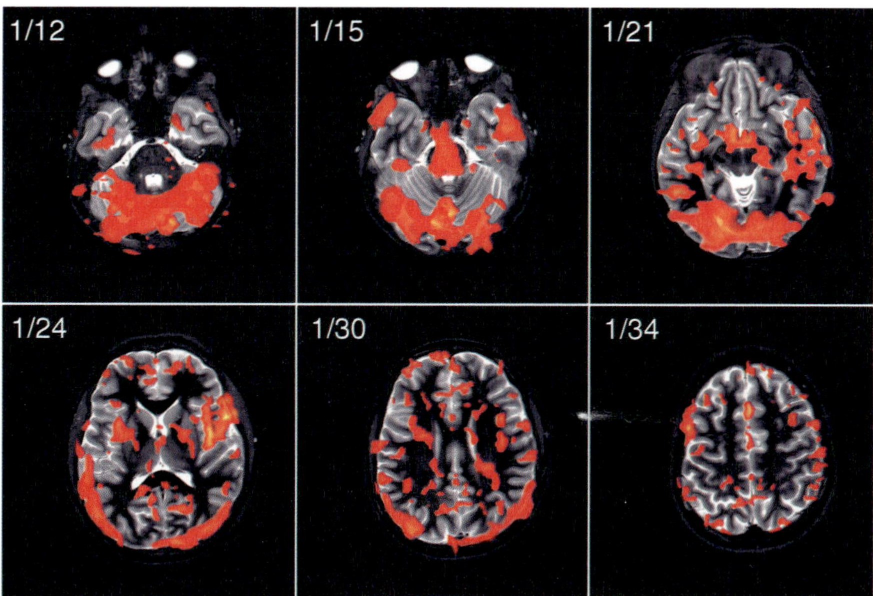

Figure 3.26: Example of widespread brain activity during spinal extension movements and associated pain experience in a patient with LBP. (Image from the authors.)

Nociception from the tissues is mainly received by the thalamus.[207,208] In acute, immediate injury states, the lower centers of the brain usually activate, process the threat and produce immediate, protective responses such as reflexive movement, adrenaline response, etc.[207,208] Once the immediate threat is processed, the information about the threat is passed onto higher cognitive areas that deal more with thoughts, planning, memory, etc.[209] Additionally, it is now also understood that in a person with chronic pain, a third layer of processing becomes more ingrained, whereby the primary circuits now activate and use the various emotional areas of the brain.[210,211] Garcia-Larrea and Peyron describe a first-order "nociceptive" cortical matrix, a second-order "perceptive-attentional" pain matrix, and a third-order "reappraisal-emotional" matrix network.[211] It is believed that the more chronic pain becomes, the more the brain's circuitry is shifted from nociceptive circuits to emotional circuits.[211,212] This shift to emotional circuits poses increased challenges in treatment. For example, increased activation of the amygdala has been correlated to more untrustworthy judgements toward healthcare providers.[213]

To determine which areas of the brain are used, scientist developed a series of different brain scanning technologies in the early 1990s.[214,215] Scientists using PET and SPECT scans showed that, with the application of painful superficial cutaneous heat stimulation, multiple cortical and subcortical brain areas activated.[27,28] This technology shifted a lot of attention toward the human brain and its role in a human's pain experience, ultimately culminating in the shift to the pain neuromatrix.[10,11] In recent years, functional magnetic resonance imaging (fMRI) has seemingly superseded both PET and SPECT scans as a means to study brain activity.[214,215] In fact, much of our current understanding of the neuromatrix is largely derived from the results of studies utilizing fMRI techniques.[214,215] MRI uses a very strong magnetic field to align our body's molecules and then uses a second magnetic pulse to invert (or "flip") them.[216,217] Because each type of molecule has a unique rate at which it reverts or "relaxes" back to the magnetically imposed alignment, it is possible to "tune" a radio frequency receiver within the MRI machine to detect particular types of molecules. The molecules to which the MRI are "tuned" determines, after

Area	Functions	Location
5. Primary Motor Cortex	• Works in association with other motor cortex areas including premotor cortex, the supplementary motor area, posterior parietal cortex and several subcortical brain regions to plan and execute movements	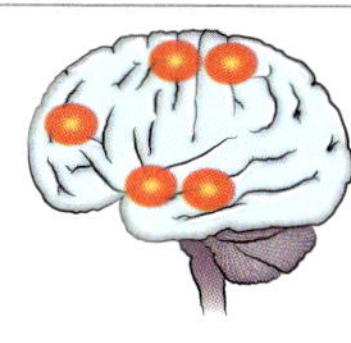

6. Hypothalamus and Thalamus	• Below the thalamus and above the brain stem
	• Links to the nervous system via the endocrine system via the pituitary gland
	• Autonomic nervous system
	• Controls:
	  ○ Body temperature
	  ○ Hunger and thirst
	  ○ Fatigue and sleep
	• Relaying sensory and motor signals to the cerebral cortex
	  ○ Consciousness
	  ○ Sleep
	  ○ Alertness
		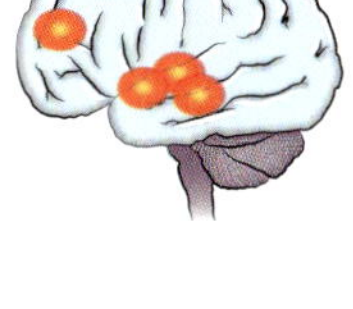

7. Prefrontal Cortex	• Planning complex cognitive behavior • Personality expression • Decision making • Moderating social behavior	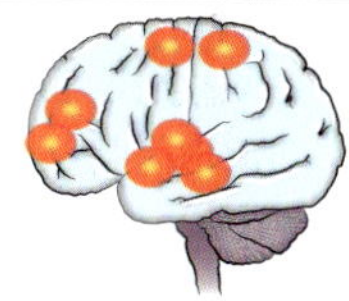
8. Cerebellum	• Movement • Balance, proprioception • Fear • Coordination	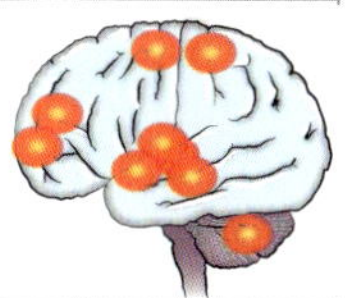
9. Spinal cord	• Gating from the periphery	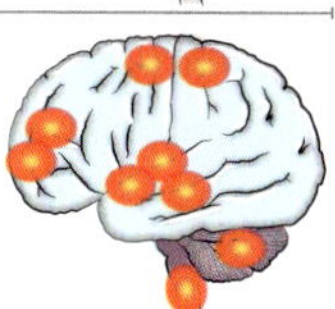

The most common areas associated with the pain neuromatrix are the anterior cingulate cortex (ACC), primary sensory cortex (S1), thalamus, anterior insula, prefrontal and posterior parietal cortices.[12,214,220] During a painful task, it is believed that these increasingly active brain areas communicate with each other, developing in essence a pain map (Figure 3.28).[221]

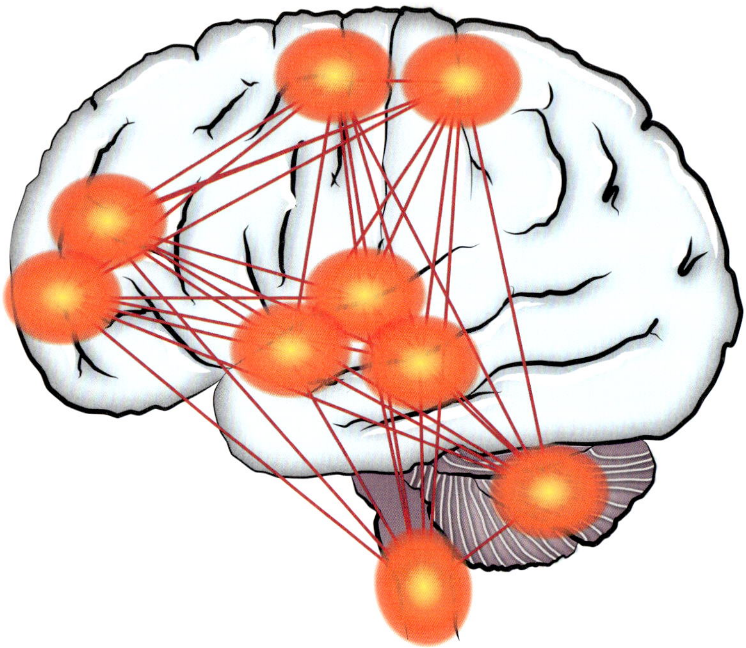

Figure 3.28: Example of a pain neuromatrix. Adapted from Puentedura and Louw.

The pain neuromatrix provides an immediate clinically important feature. There are no specific pain areas in the brain and during a pain experience, pain uses several areas. In chronic pain these areas are likely "enslaved" by pain (Table 3.3).[221,222] For example, a patient engaging in motor control exercises such as a co-contraction of transversus abdominus and multifidus (spinal stabilization exercises)[223] may have difficulty executing the precise motor control activities prescribed by this approach, since the motor cortex is being utilized as part of the pain neuromatrix.[224] From a clinical point of view, this statement is profound. For too long, patients unable to perform these precise and intriquite exercises have been accused of malingering, being lazy or not motivated. Yet from a neuroscience perspective, there is a justified reason for their difficulty with these exercises. Similarly, the concept of a pain neuromatrix using other brain areas explains many of the issues commonly seen in patients with chronic pain such as problems for focus and concentration, regulating body temperature, sleep disturbance, short-term memory issues and more.[225,226] More importantly, undertsanding these issues and being able to explain this to patients with chronic pain is the cornerstone of PNE.[227]

Table 3.3: Potential clinical consequences of the pain neuromatrix.

Area	Function	Potential Clinical Consequence
1. Amygdala	• Fear • Addictive behaviors	• Altered perception of fear with possible increased fear avoidance • Entrenched brain maps
2. Primary Somatosensory Cortex	• Somatic sensation • Visual stimuli • Movement planning	• Altered body charts • Spreading pain • Decreased tactile acuity • Visual distortion of body parts • Diminished laterality
3. Hippocampus	• Short-term and long-term memory • Spatial navigation	• Short-term memory loss
4. Anterior Cingulate Cortex	• Variety of autonomic functions • Blood pressure • Heart rate • Cognitive functions • Reward anticipation • Decision making • Empathy • Emotion • Concentration • Focus	• Inability to regulate blood pressure and heart rate • Mental "fog" • Mental fatigue • Difficulty reading • Increased indecisiveness
5. Primary Motor Cortex	• Plan movements • Execute movements	• Difficulty planning and executing movements, especially fine motor control

Table 3.3: Potential clinical consequences of the pain neuromatrix *(continued)*.

Area	Function	Potential Clinical Consequence
6. Hypothalamus and Thalamus	• Autonomic nervous system • Body temperature • Hunger and thirst • Fatigue and sleep • Consciousness • Sleep • Alertness	• Inability to regulate body temperature • Changes in eating habits • Increased fatigue • Difficulty with sleep • Mental "fog"
7. Prefrontal Cortex	• Planning complex cognitive behavior • Personality expression • Decision making • Moderating social behavior	• Problems with analytical tasks, numbers, etc. • Indecisiveness
8. Cerebellum	• Movement • Balance and proprioception • Fear • Coordination	• Decreased balance and proprioception • Decreased fine motor control
9. Spinal cord	• Gating from the periphery	• Facilitation

With the increased use and interest in brains scans, more questions have developed, along with an increase in the technological abilities of the scanning devices. For example, new fMRI technology called diffusion tensor imaging (DTI) can reveal abnormalities in white matter fiber structure and provide models of brain connectivity. It is suggested that with fMRI images of neuronal activation in the brain, a pain signature can be visualized (Figure 3.29).[209,228]

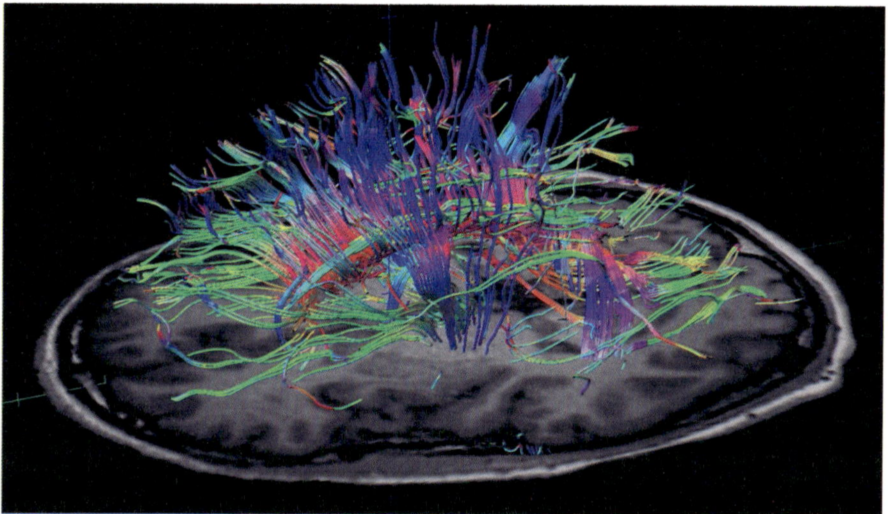

Figure 3.29: Diffusion tensor imaging scan of a patient during a pain experience. (Image from the authors.)

One area that has gained a lot of interest is the fact that when a brain area is "activated" on an fMRI it is unsure if the area is being "downregulated" or "upregulated." This analysis would make sense as even though there is activity all over the brain, some areas should be downregulated and others upregulated. In a recent systematic review of brain scans for people with LBP, scientists could showcase this exact phenomenon and showed:[229]

- Higher activation in the primary (S1) and secondary (S2) somatosensory cortices, posterior cingulate cortex, insula and medial prefrontal cortex
    - Important to note that S1, S2, the insula and medial prefrontal cortex are part of the pain neuromatrix
- Lower activation in periaqueductal gray (PAG) area
    - The PAG plays a significant role in endogenous analgesia

Adding to the complexity of the neuromatrix is the Hebbian Theory, which proposes that "neurons that fire together, wire together."[230] This is a scientific theory in biological neuroscience that explains the adaptation of neurons in the brain during the learning process. It describes a basic mechanism for synaptic plasticity wherein an increase in synaptic efficacy arises from the presynaptic cell's repeated and persistent stimulation of the postsynaptic cell. The theory suggests that "when an axon of cell A is near enough to excite a cell B and repeatedly or persistently takes part in firing it, some growth process or metabolic change takes place in one or both cells such that A's efficiency, as one of the cells firing B, is increased."[231] It is believed that the neurotransmitter dopamine, which plays a major role in reward-driven learning, may play a significant role in wiring pathways together. Every type of reward that has been studied increases the level of dopamine transmission in the brain. A variety of highly addictive drugs, including the stimulants cocaine and methamphetamine, act directly on the dopamine system. Put simply, dopamine "seals" pathways allowing for faster, more efficient neuronal pathways. The clinical importance of this kind of plasticity may be appreciated in the case where a patient suffering from shoulder pain might try to do a simple task such as raising her arm (Table 3.4).[232]

Another potential neuroplastic change that may occur in some individuals is the concept of the imprecision hypothesis of chronic pain proposed by Moseley and Vlaeyen.[233] We know that pain and fear can follow along the lines of classic conditioned response.[234] This learned response to pain can strengthen pathways in the brain as our example in Table 3.4 demonstrates. An example of a classical conditioned response is an individual that has been bitten by a dog will often times be afraid when they encounter that dog again and have physiological responses to that fear. Taking our example (Table 3.4) of having shoulder pain, an individual with an acute injury may very well develop some fear with raising her arm overhead because of the nociceptive pain associated with irritating acutely injured tissues. It has been shown that some people will then overgeneralize this fear of reaching overhead to fear with moving just partially overhead.[235] Overgeneralization is the term used for when the person that is fearful of the dog that bit them overgeneralizes it to fear of all dogs. In our example of the individual raising their arm up, the pain can be overgeneralized to any movement of the arm. This fear of pain can alter the individual's movement patterns and motor control.[236,237] Also, this learned response can be maintained after the tissues have healed. While it has been shown that this classical conditioning can amplify pain, it is not yet been shown if this conditioned response can actually elicit pain,[238] but this may explain many clinical situations that we see. The person that has pain with bending forward can be related back to lifting a heavy box, but five years later this person has been building up overgeneralizations and bending forward to put on their shoes brings on a pain experience.

Table 3.4: Hebbian Theory and pain during shoulder flexion.

Stimulus	Experienced	Brain Activation
Raising the arm to full flexion 	After sufficient nociception and brain activation, the pain neuromatrix is activated and pain is produced to protect. The patient thus experiences pain with end-range-of-motion flexion and this movement is associated with pain.	The "flexion" map is activated, communicates with adjacent maps; the full circuit is run with an end-result of pain. 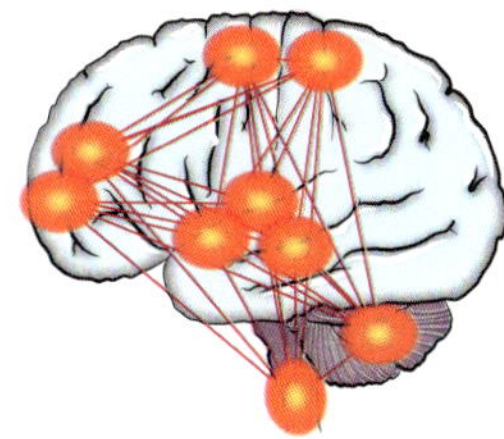
Attempting to raise the arm to full flexion again 	With repeated activation of the flexion map, dopamine seals pathways together (nerves that fire together wire together) and less flexion is required to run the complete map resulting in a pain experience. Now, only raising the arm to 90 degrees flexion results in pain.	Nerves that fire together wire together, and with dopamine become more efficient. In essence, the brain becomes better trained at producing pain with shoulder flexion. 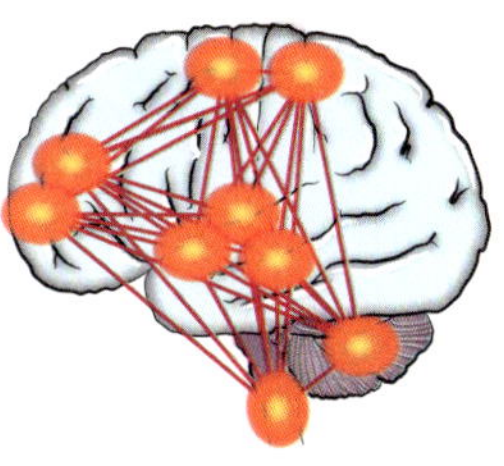
Thinking about flexing the arm 	As the circuitry that ties shoulder flexion to pain become more and more refined, less of a stimulus is needed to activate a pain experience. In this extreme case just thinking about flexion now results in pain.	Patients may think they are getting worse (from a tissue perspective), yet they're getting better, but at the wrong thing: living their pain.

Remember that tissues only contain nociceptors, not pain receptors; tissues can only inform the brain of danger. Pain must; therefore, be a brain construct based on whatever information the brain has available. It would also be timely to consider the definition of pain. The traditional and most used definition of pain is that of the IASP:[66]

> Pain is an unpleasant sensory and emotional experience associated with actual or potential tissue damage, or described in terms of such damage.

Our answers to the NPQ and rNPQ so far have highlighted the fact that the brain must process and evaluate the information. It provides us with an opportunity to also consider a more updated view of pain, from a brain processing perspective. The following definition is paraphrasing the material we have covered thus far:[12,239]

> Pain is produced by the brain after a person's neural signature (pain neuromatrix) has been activated and it is concluded that the body is in danger and action is required.

This definition of pain provides us with a view of the brain's processing of information, but it would seem to be logical from the survival perspective. Upon receiving a message about a threat, the brain processes the information regarding that threat. If the conclusion is that there is danger and action is required, pain will be produced to protect. This decision will increase activity along facilitatory pathways in the central nervous system to send additional information to the brain (Figure 3.30). If the result of the neuronal circuitry is that there is no real threat, pain will not be produced to protect and descending pathways will modulate the threat messages.[12,239]

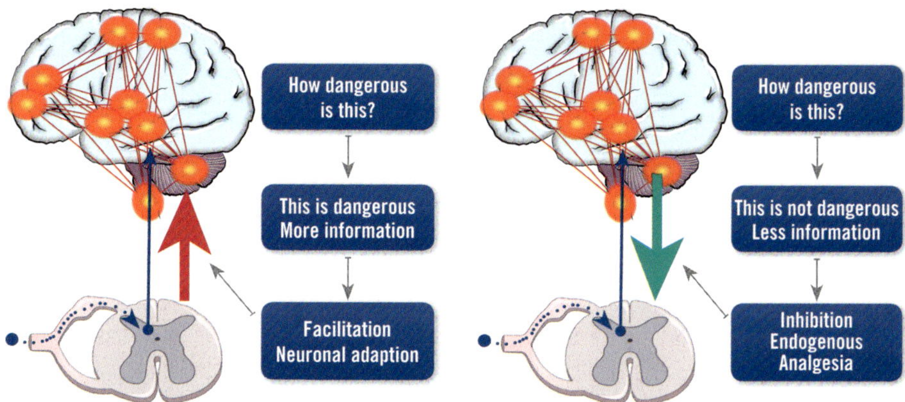

Figure 3.30: Danger messages from the body are received by the brain. A: If the brain concludes that the danger is real, facilitation will be unregulated to provide more information about the threat. B: If the brain concludes that there is no danger, inhibitory activity will modulate the danger messages.

Pain is a response by the brain based on threat. Webster's Dictionary defines "threat" as an "expression of intention to inflict evil, injury, or damage." As it pertains to pain, it could be argued that people may have different threats, based on various factors. For example, in a study comparing individuals with whiplash-associated disorders, illness and care-seeking behaviors were significantly different between medical doctors and non-medically trained individuals.[240] Both groups sustained similar injuries; however, the perception of the injury and recovery was seen as a major difference in the ensuing care-seeking behaviors between the groups. In a different study, 90 percent of PTs experience LBP while treating patients with LBP yet seek little to no treatment themselves.[241] Collectively, these studies suggest that because healthcare professionals have more understanding about the nature of an injury, the pain experience and recovery, there is less perceived threat than non-medically trained individuals. In other words, pain is based on perception of threat.[12,239]

This inclusion of "perception of threat" can easily be understood by clinicians. Patients exposed to provocative medical terminology proposed to be associated with pain, such as "degenerative disc disease," "bulging discs" and "wear and tear," show heightened levels of fear and anxiety.[242] How patients perceive the health of their tissues (correctly or incorrectly) will determine to what extent the brain will produce pain to protect.[239] It is also interesting to note how fast the brain can make such decisions, even when it is presented with limited information. A simple way to examine how the brain makes decisions is a study of visual illusions. The following illusion (Figure 3.31) from scientist Edward Adelson asks, "Which block is darker: A or B?"

If we could place two gray lines across the image, block A and block B are actually the exact same shade of gray. When the brain is confronted with a visual illusion, the brain makes the most logical choice. This is based on everything the brain knows about colors, lighting, shades, experience, logic and so forth. The brain decides block A is darker than block B. It is the most logical choice, even though it is factually incorrect. When observing the blocks, it is unlikely that you made an active choice that the blocks appeared to have a different shade... they were just different. Likewise, the brain makes the same decisions when it comes to interpreting threats to the health of body tissues. An individual is not "choosing" to have pain, the brain produces pain based on everything it knows about the injury, the body, past experiences, knowledge, etc.

Figure 3.31: Image with permission from Edward H. Adelson (1995).

Another simple example is the illusion below: Which line is longer – line ‘a’ or line ‘b’ (Figure 3.32)? Again, it may seem that line b is longer than line a, but they are actually of equal length.

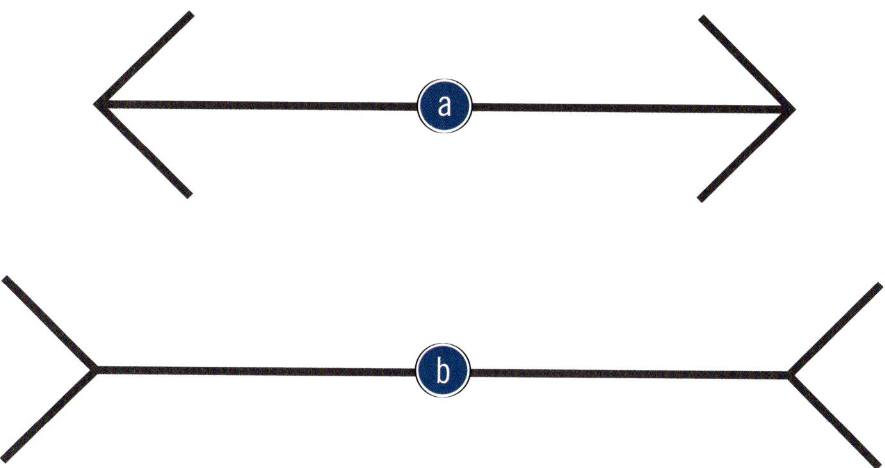

Figure 3.32: Visual illusion where arrowheads give the impression that line b is longer than line a.

This refinement of the definition of pain (perception of threat) is a key point in the treatment of pain. It is believed that PNE directly targets the perception of threat, and the cortical reorganization of perception of threat is likely a significant contributor to the effectiveness of PNE.[227] Pain is a brain construct. Since discussing the brain and its complex processing of nociception, how it utilizes various brain areas, and how changes in chemicals within the brain and activation patterns in the brain will occur with injury, it would be appropriate to reflect on the amazing brain:[37,231,243,244]

- The weight of the human brain is about three pounds.
- The cerebrum is the largest part of the brain and makes up 85 percent of the brain's weight.
- The brain is made up of about 75 percent water.
- Your brain consists of about 100 billion neurons.
- There is a network of approximately 125,000 miles of neurons in the brain.
- There are anywhere from 1,000 to 10,000 synapses for each neuron.
- There are no "pain receptors" in the brain, so the brain can feel no pain. (Note: We left the term "pain receptors" intentionally, but as per our neuroscience education, there are no "pain receptors" in the body or brain.)
- The human brain is two percent of total body weight.
- There are 100,000 miles of blood vessels in the brain.
- The human brain is the fattiest organ in the body and consists of at least 60 percent fat.
- Neurons develop at the rate of 250,000 neurons per minute during early pregnancy.
- A newborn baby's brain grows about three times its size in the first year.
- Humans continue to make new neurons throughout life in response to mental activity.
- Your brain uses 20 percent of the total oxygen in your body.
- As with oxygen, your brain uses 20 percent of the blood circulating in your body.
- If your brain loses blood for eight to 10 seconds, you will lose consciousness.
- While awake, your brain generates between 10 and 23 watts of power – or enough energy to power a lightbulb.
- The brain can live for four to six minutes without oxygen, and then it begins to die. No oxygen for five to 10 minutes will result in permanent brain damage.
- Laughing at a joke is no simple task as it requires activity in five different areas of the brain.
- The average number of thoughts that humans are believed to experience each day is 70,000.

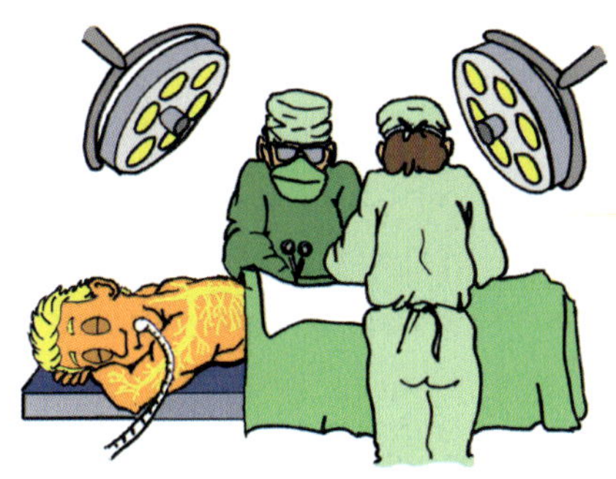

It is currently believed that it is impossible to have pain and not know about it. Pain is proposed to be a conscious decision by the brain. In contrast, it is possible to have an injury and not be aware of it, i.e., noticing a bruise a few days later and having no idea where it came from. At the heart of this issue is the understanding of consciousness, which in itself is a very complicated construct, especially when we intertwine conscious, unconscious, and subconscious states of the brain. This current view of a conscious decision of the brain producing pain helps us to understand how general anesthesia works. It is believed that anesthesia given during surgery removes the conscious experience associated with the surgery.[37] Surely there would still be nociceptive bombardment of the central nervous system during the surgical intervention, yet no pain will be experienced.[34] Anesthetics can be categorized into two classes: general anesthetics, which cause a reversible loss of consciousness; and local anesthetics, which cause a reversible loss of sensation for a limited region of the body while maintaining consciousness. Combinations of anesthetics are sometimes used for their synergistic and additive therapeutic effects. It is postulated that anesthetic agents act on neurons in the reticular activating system, suppressing alertness and awareness. Additionally, neurons in the hippocampus are affected by temporarily wiping out memory, and nuclei in the thalamus are affected to alter sensory information from the tissues.

NPQ and rNPQ statements:	NPQ/rNPQ #	Answer
Pain only occurs when you are injured	NPQ 2; rNPQ 10	False
The body tells the brain when it is in pain	NPQ 6	False
The brain can send messages down your spinal cord that can increase the danger messages going up the spinal cord	NPQ 7	True
The brain decides when you will be experiencing pain	NPQ 11; rNPQ 12	True
It is possible to have pain and not know about it	NPQ 14; rNPQ 1	False
Descending neurons are always inhibitory	rNPQ 9	False
Pain only occurs when you are injured or at risk of being injured	rNPQ 3	False

3.9: Processing Mechanism: The Pain Neuromatrix, Yellow Flags and "Personalization" of the Pain Experience

NPQ and rNPQ statements:	NPQ/rNPQ #
The body tells the brain when it is in pain	NPQ 6
The brain decides when you will be experiencing pain	NPQ 11; rNPQ 12
When you are injured, the environment that you are in will not have an effect on the amount of pain that you experience	NPQ 13
Descending neurons are always inhibitory	rNPQ 9
When you injure yourself, the environment that you are in will not affect the amount of pain you experience, as long as the injury is exactly the same	rNPQ 11

In section 3.8, brain activation is described using the example of thinking about your grandmother or a favorite vacation. This analogy was used to showcase that the whole brain is engaged during an experience, including pain. It is also interesting and important to note that each person and their representation of their grandmother or vacation is unique. Even for siblings, their grandmother or a shared vacation destination will have significant differences, hence personalizing the representation of their grandmother and vacation. This also applies to pain. Pain is a unique, individualized experience. This statement, however, should be seen in the context (section 3.8) where it's stated that it's now well established that nine key areas are found to be activated in every human's pain experience (Table 3.2). How do we reconcile these two ideas? It is important to realize that the pain neuromatrix is only one map in the brain.[245] Given the enormous complexity of neuronal activation, synaptic activity, neurotransmitters and modulators, the primary pain map can also be influenced by neighboring neural circuits, which will likely influence the individual pain experience (Figure 3.33 on the following page)[222].

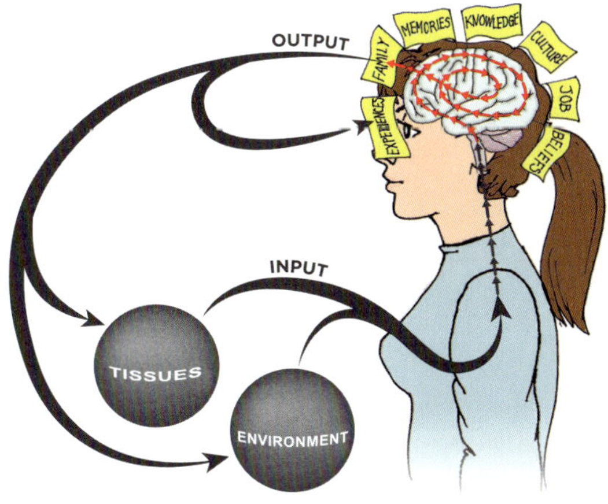

- Influences on the processing via yellow flags
- Pain neuromatrix communication with adjacent maps
- "Personalization" of the pain experience

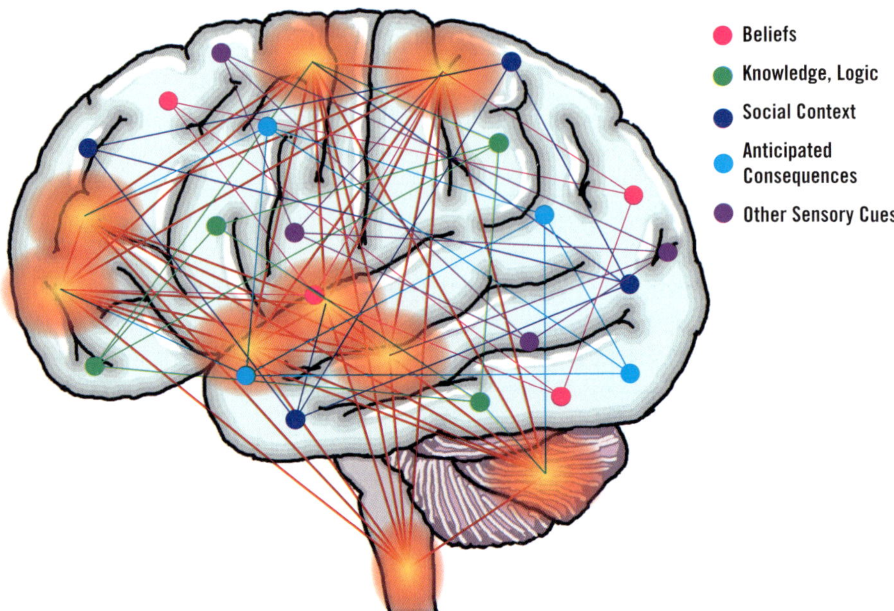

Figure 3.33: The primary pain map can also be influenced by neighboring neural circuits. Adapted from Puentedura and Louw.[222]

Each adjacent map can influence the pain neuromatrix. Experiences, beliefs, knowledge, culture, etc., can either increase or decrease the threat value of the original pain neuromatrix. This interplay between the pain neruomatrix and the various personal issues demonstrate how pain becomes individualized and how, in seemingly similar injuries, different people have different pain experiences and outcomes related to treatment.[246,247] Even though it's unlikely a true anwer exists as to which and how many adjacent maps are activated, it is likely very individualized. From a scientific perspective and even pure anecdote, certain adjacent maps must exist to account for cultural differences, personal beliefs about pain, previous experiences regarding pain, environmental influences (section 3.2), influences of the media, knowledge, social structure, coping skills, etc. In Chapter 1, various yellow flags were showcased that are powerfully associated with prolonged recovery and increased disability, including behaviors, work issues, compensation, emotions, issues pertaining to diagnosis and treatment and family issues. As a means to further elaborate how important these factors are in terms of having someone experience pain or not, consider the following list and realize how these issues may increase or decrease activation of the pain neuromatrix and ultimately the brain's assessment of threat:

- **Gender:** Even though far more complex and involving various other aspects, females experience far more muscuoskeletal pain[248] and various brain scan studies have shown different activation in men and women.[249-251] Socially agreed upon gender roles must influence the overall pain experience with norms dictating increased tolerance to pain by males and acceptance of pain as a normal part of life in females.[252-254]

- **Culture:** Responses to pain are often divided into one of two cultural categories: stoic or emotive.[91-93,255] Stoic patients are less expressive, "grin and bear it" and tend to socially withdraw. Emotive patients are more likely to verbalize their pain expressions and expect others to react. These cultural differences may influence the pain neuromatrix.

- **Work:** Various work factors have been associated with increased or decreased pain experiences and disability including time off work, work satisfaction, availability for light duty, working shifts – especially at night, etc.[100,101,256]

- **Media:** Information from media (television; websites, etc.) can influence the pain neuromatrix.[257,258]

- **Personality:** Various studies have shown that personality is closely linked to the development of pain.[259-261]

- **Socioeconomic status:** Various studies have shown that regardless of the definiton of socioeconomic disadvantage, it's strongly linked to increased pain experiences.[102,103,262]

- **Social support:** The quality and quantity of interpersonal relationships correlate to pain experience.[103,263,264]

This list can go on and on, but the overall concept is quite clear: When the nine common areas engage in the pain neuromatrix, the pain neuromatrix then engages with a variety of maps related to various issues to ultimately put meaning to the information being processed. The end result is the brain's appraisal of threat. Once again, if the brain perceives threat, pain is produced to protect and seek help. If threat is not perceived, pain is not produced (Figure 3.30). This personalization of the pain experience showcases how complex an individual's pain experience is. Furthermore, all pain is real and a conglomirate of these various processes, thus making it extremely difficult, if not impossible to consider the notion of "fake pain." This is underscored by various studies showcasing traditional "non-organic" tests or battery of tests, i.e., Waddell signs to have poor validity. Even Gordon Waddell has requested that healthcare providers stop using Waddell's signs as a measure of "faking."[265] Various studies have shown:[266,267]

- Waddell signs do not correlate with psychological distress
- Waddell signs do not discriminate organic from nonorganic problems
- Waddell signs may represent an organic phenomenon
- Waddell signs are not associated with secondary gain

The personalization of the pain experience underscores the clinical notion that treatment should be individualized for the patient and may be a reason why one-on-one PNE produces superior results to group PNE.[2,268] Additionally, the fact that so many factors ultimately determine if a person will experience pain provides an avenue whereby non-nociceptive processes can be targeted to help patients recover. The presence of abundant yellow flags may also contribute to high levels of pain catastrophization and a reduction in endogenous inhibitory mechanisms, thus directly increasing the pain experience.[188] By targeting these various yellow (danger) flags and influencing them positively (i.e., non-threatening explanations for pain; positive experiences with healthcare providers; PNE; goal setting, etc.) it is possible to shift the perspective of the patient and ultimately their pain experience.[13] A visual illustration of this clinical principle could be to paint the yellow flags green. Furthermore, the wide variety of issues that may or may not influence the pain neuromatrix underscores the need for multidisciplinary and interdisciplinary care, especially the more complex a patient's pain experience is.[269,270]

NPQ and rNPQ statements:	NPQ/rNPQ #	Answer
The body tells the brain when it is in pain	NPQ 6	False
The brain decides when you will be experiencing pain	NPQ 11; rNPQ 12	True
When you are injured, the environment that you are in will not have an effect on the amount of pain that you experience	NPQ 13	False
Descending neurons are always inhibitory	rNPQ 9	False
When you injure yourself, the environment that you are in will not affect the amount of pain you experience, as long as the injury is exactly the same	rNPQ 11	False

3.10: Output Mechanisms: The Stress Response, Endocrine System and Immune System

NPQ and rNPQ statements:	NPQ/rNPQ #
Nerves can adapt by increasing their resting level of excitement	NPQ 8; rNPQ 6
Receptors on nerves work by opening ion channels (sensors) in the wall of the nerve	NPQ 10
When you are injured, chemicals in your tissue can make nerves more sensitive	NPQ 18
In chronic pain, chemicals associated with stress can directly activate danger messenger nerves	NPQ 19

Pain is an output of the brain, when the person's individual pain neuromatrix is activated and concluded there is a threat.[12,239] Pain is thus a biological response, but only one of many. To better understand how various biological systems react to protect, a greater understanding is needed of a typical stress response.[271]

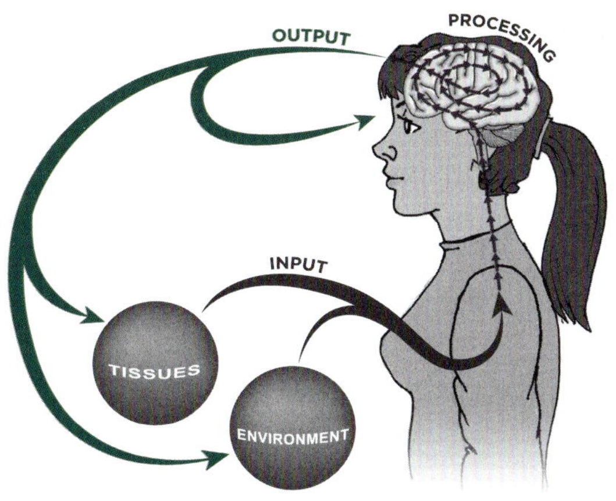

Stress Response
Homeostasis
Endocrine System
Immune System
Effects on Brain

- Memory
- Focus and concentration
- Immune with blood-brain barrier changes and plasticity changes, structural shifts in the brain

Effects on Tissues

3.10.1: Stress Response

The basic threat response, often assigned to the sympathetic nervous system, is the fight, flight, or freeze response. The stress response during an immediate threat, however, is significantly more complex and involves various other bodily systems. An example is the stress response associated with the figurative scenario of a big, roaring African lion entering the room (Figure 3.34). To deal with this immediate threat, the body reacts with various systems (Figure 3.35):

Figure 3.34: Immediate threat response.

- **Adrenaline:** Adrenaline is a centrally acting excitatory neurotransmitter and a hormone that affects just about all body tissues, but it is best known to regulate heart rate, blood vessel and air passage diameters, and metabolic shifts.[271] The action varies depending on the tissues and adrenergic receptors, for example, high levels of adrenaline cause smooth muscle relaxation in the airways but cause contraction of the smooth muscle that lines most arterioles. Adrenaline works via the sympathetic nervous system. In response to perceived threat, heart rate increases rapidly to pump blood though the body to areas needing blood and oxygen. Adrenaline causes hyper-vigilance. If a lion enters the room, it is not time for a nap.[272]

- **Muscles:** In an immediate threat response, large muscles capable of evading or facing the threat are needed. Big, strong leg muscles activate to run away. Arm muscles might activate to punch the lion and leg muscles to flee. Smaller muscles are not needed, such as postural muscles or even stabilizing muscles.[273-275] Deactivating these muscles for the immediate threat seems like a good strategy, and they should be switched back on when the threat has been removed.

- **Language:** When startled with a threat such as the lion, you will likely say a few choice words in a loud, short, sharp and abrasive voice.[276]

- **Breathing:** With the impending threat, breathing becomes faster and shallower.[277]

- **Gastrointestinal (GI) System:** Digestion of food is slowed down or even put on hold, allowing for all possible energy and blood flow to be allocated to the immediate, much needed other systems.[278]

- **Pain:** In an acute stress response, pain is often suppressed as a means of survival.[71-73]

- **Sleep:** The interest and ability to fall asleep is shifted, along with adrenal response, to stay awake and alert, with pupils dilated.

- **Reproduction:** During the acute stress response reproductive interest and function is suppressed.

- **Immune:** In the acute stress situation, albeit a very slow reacting system, immune health is of little immediate benefit, thus is in the process of being shut down.

- **Other:** There are other responses such as motivation, memory, etc.

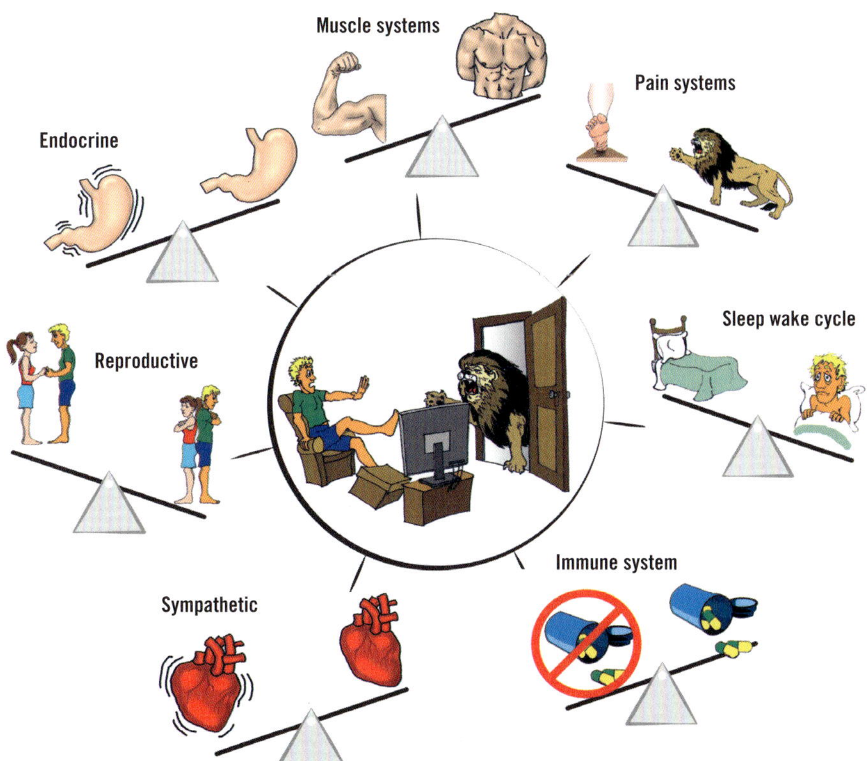

Figure 3.35: The stress response and the various bodily systems reacting to the impending threat.

Once the lion is captured by an animal control officer, the stress response dissipates and homeostatic systems help to normalize the stress reaction through the parasympathetic response and await the next stress response.[271] This process occurs daily as people are faced with minor stressors but is also capable of facing a large threat such as a lion. The system, however, is designed to elevate and then calm down, not continue running at elevated levels for prolonged periods.

Pain is a reaction to threat. Apart from the daily pain, various psychosocial issues have been correlated to a persistent pain experience.[246,247] Chapter 1 described various yellow flags and it is believed that the presence of these biopsychosocial yellow flags will, over time, result in a stress response. Put together, the lion is a metaphorical description of these yellow flags along with the daily pain.[29] Pain is normal; living and suffering in pain is not. By adding all the various stressors, along with the struggles with chronic pain, a proverbial lion enters a patient's life, which in turn activates the various stress responses (Figure 3.36).[279]

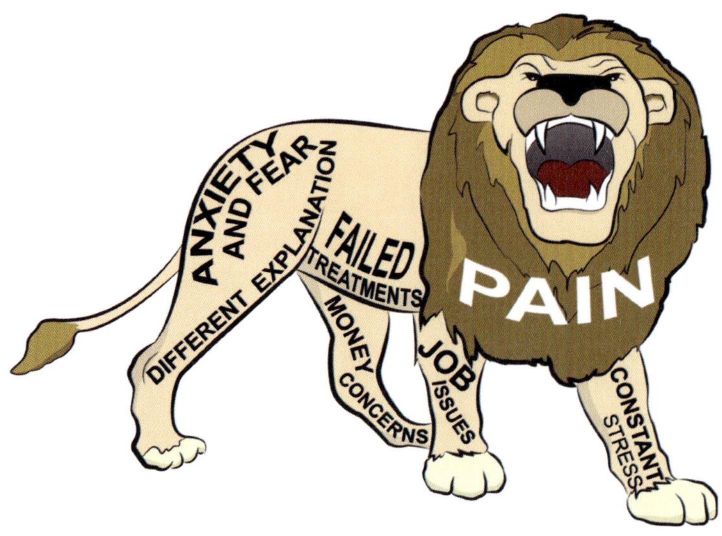

Figure 3.36: The lion as a metaphor for stressors associated with a persistent pain state.

During this acute stress response, adrenaline levels are increased. It is thought that adrenosensitive ion channels open, allowing for an easier depolarization of the nervous system and resultant pain response.[76,107] Clinically, the patient may experience pain due to stress, anxiety or fear, not just injured or damaged tissues. This pain response may explain increased pain experiences reported during high stress scenarios, such as spinal surgery, combat, litigation or motor vehicle collisions. In chronic pain, the stress response is protracted.

If the stressors and biopsychosocial factors (lion) remain in place for months, or years, the resultant chemical activation will have significant repercussions for the nervous system, body tissues and brain. The stress biology analogy would be the lion following a patient for months. The initial stress response is initially executed by adrenaline, then followed by the release of another potent hormone known as cortisol.

Adrenaline is a fast-acting neurotransmitter and likely very effective in the immediate stress response, which should last no longer than several minutes. Cortisol is a more potent and longer-lasting chemical, similar in effect to adrenaline but produced to deal with longer lasting threats.[271] Cortisol is a glucocorticoid steroid hormone produced by the adrenal gland.[16] Cortisol's primary function is to increase blood sugar, suppress the immune system and aid in fat, protein and carbohydrate metabolism.[272,280] The release of cortisol from the adrenal gland is controlled by the hypothalamus (Figure 3.37). The secretion of corticotropin-releasing hormone (CRH) by the hypothalamus triggers anterior pituitary secretion of adrenocorticotropic hormone (ACTH). ACTH is carried by the cells to the vascular cortex, where it triggers blood secretion.[281-283]

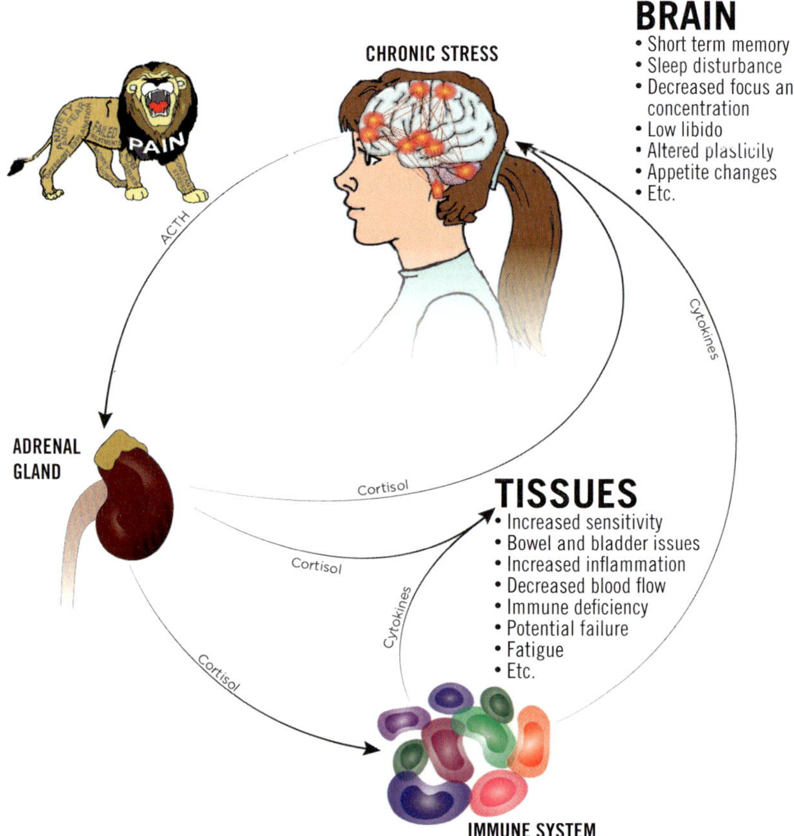

Figure 3.37: Release of cortisol from the adrenal gland in response to threat is controlled by the hypothalamus via corticotropin-releasing hormone (CRH), which triggers secretion of adrenocorticotropic hormone (ACTH) from the anterior pituitary gland. The ACTH triggers release of cortisol into the blood stream.

Cortisol prevents the release of substances in the body that cause inflammation. This is why cortisol is used to treat conditions resulting from over activity of the B-cell mediated antibody response, such as inflammatory and rheumatoid diseases and allergies. Low-potency hydrocortisone is used to treat skin problems, such as rashes, eczema and others. Elevated levels of cortisol, if prolonged, can lead to proteolysis and muscle wasting. Cortisol has a diurnal pattern, typically peaking around 8am and reaching its low point between midnight and 4am, or 3-5 hours after sleep initiation.[284,285] Cortisol levels are affected by changes in ACTH, depression, psychological stress and physiological stressors, such as illness, surgery, fear, injury and pain. Change in cortisol levels have been linked to a reduction in bone formation and thought to be responsible for the mechanism behind stress dwarfism.[286] Cortisol works along with adrenaline to create short-term memories. Long-term exposure to cortisol damages hippocampus cells, limiting learning and altering memory.[287] Cortisol dysregulation increases blood pressure, shuts down the reproductive system, and is associated with weight gain, appetite changes, and obesity.[271]

A more significant effect of cortisol change is on the immune system, specifically pro-inflammatory cytokines. Cytokines are immune molecules, and they impact tissue healing significantly.[288] During infections or trauma/injury, cytokines such as interleukin 6 (IL-6) increase 1,000-fold, thus allowing for more ion channels specific to cytokines to open up, potentially resulting in increased sensitivity. This is part of the process which occurs during a bout of the flu. When you have a flu, the immune system, partially due to the action of cytokines, produces effects upon multiple body systems including symptoms of generalized malaise, fatigue, widespread body aches, etc. A major stimulus for the production of cytokines is cortisol. With increased cytokines, there is further possibility to increase inflammatory processes all over the body, including keeping tissues inflamed.[271,288]

Inflammation is a normal biological process aimed at protecting the body tissues and signaling the start of the healing and repair process. During an injury, tissues cause the release of inflammatory substances, such as prostaglandins and bradykinins. Local C fibers, via retrograde depolarization (nerves firing the other way), will also contribute to the inflammatory process by releasing substance P, which results in a vasodilatation and mast cell release of histamine.[81,159] During a painful experience filled with many stressors (fear and anxiety), cortisol levels will be increased, resulting in increased cytokines, which may keep an injured body part swollen for a longer period.

3.10.2: Clinical manifestation of the output systems

It is proposed that patients struggling with chronic pain live under constant threat from the various issues they face and the ambiguity of an uncertain diagnosis.[289] The threat is real and, more importantly, never goes away. With a constant threat (lion), the pain neuromatrix is activated and various systems (i.e., pain, immune, sympathetic, endocrine, etc.) react and alter their function, but due to the chronicity of the situation, never allow the systems to restore to normal levels.[222,289,290] This altered output response of the multiple systems futher impacts the clinical presentation of the patient culminating in immune deficiency, sensitized GI system, altered motor control, etc. (Figure 3.37).[289,290] There is now emerging evidence that during this biological response, one system is affected more than others. Depending on which system is affected the most, it can manifest itself as a different label. Some examples could include fibromyalgia (FM); chronic fatigue syndrome (CFS); chronic lyme disease (CLD); irritable bowel syndrome (IBS); or non-celiac gluten sensitivity (NCGS), albeit some of the underlying biology is realtively the same.[289-291] For example, during a pain experience, with the addition of the various comorbid psychosocial factors, if the immune system is affected, the patient may end up with the clinical diagnosis of FM.[292] Similarly, if the endocrine system is affected, the label of CFS or CLD may ensue.[293,294] While the GI system may manifest as IBS or even NCGS (Figure 3.38).[295] This theory is fueled by a growing body of literature supporting this notion of various biological systems being activated and manifesting as different labels, yet having an underlying commonality in biology and being reponsible for the various overlapping issues in clinical presentation, medical tests and treatment approaches.[289,290]

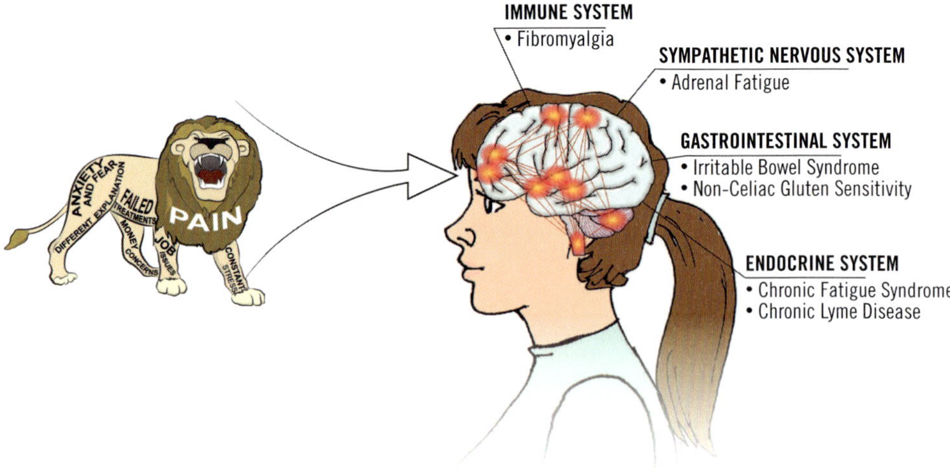

Figure 3.38: The various affected biological systems presenting as different labels.

If we were to entertain the idea that, biologically, with some small nuance differnces, FM, CFS, CLD, IBS and NCGS represent similar pertubations in various body systems, one must consider why ceratin biological systems are affected more than others? Why, for example, did the immune system become affected more in patient A, while the GI system was affected more in patient B? The precise mechanism is unknown, complex and likely multifactorial. Some authors have implicated genetic predispositions, biological "memory" of previous episodes of stress and the "weak link" theory.[289-291,296] These seem plausable and warrant further investigation. However, another possible consideration: The specialist a patient is scheduled to see may predispose to a particular diagnosis. When a patient presents at their primary healthcare provider with a constellation of signs and symptoms, they will very likely be referred to a specialist that best matches the constellation of symptoms, be it a rheumatologist, endocrinologist, immunologist, etc. It is argued that each discipline, with its narrow focus on a particular system, may indeed be a potential source for classifying patients into the various labels depending on the system they explore. This assumption concurs with the current evidence investigating the immune system in FM;[292] endocrine system in CFS[296] and CLD,[294] and GI system in IBS.[297] The concept of the various diagnostic labels we face as being biologically the same for the most part is not that far-fetched when considering the overlap between the common clinical signs and symptoms for the various conditions (Table 3.5 on the following page).[292,294,296-298]

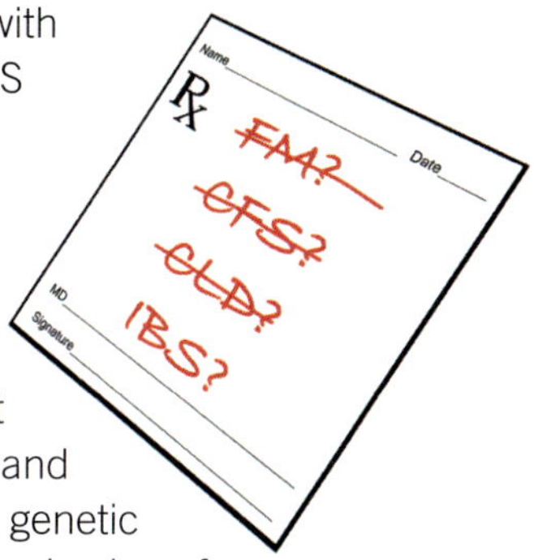

Table 3.5 Documented symptoms, diagnosis and best-evidence treatment associated with FM, CFS, IBS and CLD.

Symptoms	**FM**[292,298-300]	**CFS**[76,296,301]	**IBS**[302,303]	**CLD**[294,295,304]
Widespread pain	✔	✔	✔	✔
Joint stiffness	✔	✔		✔
Fatigue	✔	✔	✔	✔
Sleep disturbance	✔	✔	✔	✔
Depression	✔	✔	✔	
Mental fatigue	✔	✔	✔	✔
Short-term memory loss	✔	✔		✔
Sensitivity to foods	✔		✔	✔
Anxiety	✔		✔	✔
Social and functional impact	✔	✔	✔	✔
Headaches	✔	✔	✔	✔
Sexual dysfunction	✔	✔	✔	✔
Diagnosis	**FM**[292,299]	**CFS**[296,298]	**IBS**[8,39]	**CLD**[294,295,304]
Process of elimination	✔	✔	✔	✔
Current best-evidence treatment	**FM**[305-307]	**CFS**[308,309]	**IBS**[310,311]	**CLD**[294]
Cognitive therapy	✔	✔	✔	✔
Movement/exercise	✔	✔	✔	✔
Membrane stabilizers	✔	✔	✔	✔
Antidepressants	✔	✔	✔	✔

When viewing the significant overlap of the most common symptoms, it is understandable why the medical community has such trouble in specifically diagnosing any one of these conditions and why many patients suffering from chronic pain might end up with multiple labels. The addition of the various labels, along with the search for much-needed information (i.e., Internet), must surely be viewed from the vantage point of ever-increasing threat. This ongoing and increasing threat in turn fuels the pain experience and leads to additional healthcare seeking behaviors, etc., thus starting a viscous cycle. If we were to take this underlying biological systems approach one step further, it is interesting to note that many of the common symptoms listed in Table 3.5 can be found in hyperthyroidism and hypothyroidism, including fatigue, constipation, muscle weakness, muscle aches and tenderness, joint stiffness, depression, impaired memory, appetite changes, nervousness, anxiety and irritability, difficulty sleeping, etc.[299,301] By no means is it implied that patients with FM or CFS suffer from hyper or hypothyroidism, but when viewing the underlying changes associated with these labels (Table 3.6; Figure 3.37), it involves significant changes in cortisol and the hypothalamic-pituitary-adrenal (HPA) axis, which is implicated in thyroid function.[289,299] It is important to realize that FM authors have stated "hypothyroidism can mimic the symptoms of FM."[299]

Table 3.6 The various biological processes present in FM, CFS, IBS and CLD.

Biological system involved	FM[292,299,312]	CFS[293,296,313]	IBS[295,302,314]	CLD[294,304]
HPA Axis	✔	✔	✔	✔
Altered levels of cortisol	✔	✔	✔	✔
Altered immune profile via cytokines	✔	✔	✔	✔
Increased pro-inflammatory processes	✔	✔	✔	✔

To further complicate the situation for patients, it is now well established that many of these labels can only truly be diagnosed by a process of elimination (Table 3.5 on the previous page). With the absence concrete, objectifiable data (i.e., imaging or blood tests), the diagnostic process is likely to add even more uncertainty and further speculates the notion of a commonality of the various labels. In most cases blood tests are of little to no value since some biomarkers, such as cytokines, are small molecules with a short half-life, making its use in diagnosis very challenging with accuracy being questioned.[292,299,312] Even if we move past the common symptoms and diagnostic tests of these various labels and onto the current best-evidence treatment for FM, CFS, IBS and CLD, the overlap becomes even more apparent. In line with a "big-picture" view, the current best-evidence treatment for FM, CFS, IBS and CLD includes a combination of cognitive therapy, movement/exercise and medication aimed at calming the central nervous system, i.e., antidepressants and/or membrane stabilizers.

NPQ and rNPQ statements:	NPQ/rNPQ #	Answer
Nerves can adapt by increasing their resting level of excitement	NPQ 8; rNPQ 6	True
Receptors on nerves work by opening ion channels (sensors) in the wall of the nerve	NPQ 10	True
When you are injured, chemicals in your tissue can make nerves more sensitive	NPQ 18	True
In chronic pain, chemicals associated with stress can directly activate danger messenger nerves	NPQ 19	True

3.11: Plasticity and Merging of Systems

NPQ and rNPQ statements:	NPQ/rNPQ #
Pain only occurs when you are injured	NPQ 2; rNPQ 10
Nerves have to connect a body part to the brain in order for that part to be in pain	NPQ 4
The body tells the brain when it is in pain	NPQ 6
Chronic pain means an injury hasn't healed properly	NPQ 9; rNPQ 7
The brain decides when you will be experiencing pain	NPQ 11; rNPQ 12
Pain only occurs when you are injured or at risk of being injured	rNPQ 3

Chapter 3 clearly shows the critical part the brain plays in a human pain experience; no brain, no pain. Additionally, it is also now well established that pain and injury are not always correlated; many people experience pain, yet their tissues are healthy, and many people with injuries, aging, etc., experience little to no pain. The premise of these discoveries is the fact that the brain produces pain whenever it concludes there is danger and action is required.[12,239] It would thus be important to recognize threats. It is well established that threats include injury, disease states (health of the tissues), visual cues, environmental factors, trauma, surgery and more. Threats come in a variety of forms, be it as singular threats or in combination. In recent years, however, the world of neuroscience has explored an intriguing additional "threat" as it pertains to the health of the cortical maps of the human body.[214,215,220]

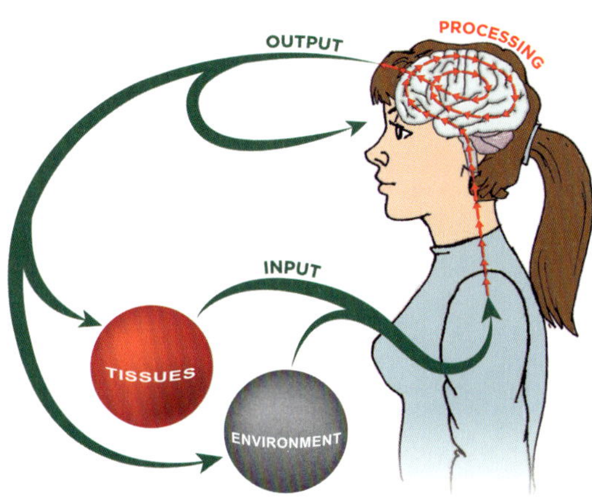

Tissues
- Inflammation
- Immune response
- Peripheral neurogenic

Spinal Cord
- Glial cell activation
- Spinal cord blood barrier open

Brain and Stress Response
- Immune responses
- Blood brain barrier changes
- Homoncular smudging and structural changes in the brain
- Central sensitization

The physical body of a person is represented in the brain by a network of neurons, often referred to as a representation of that particular body part in the brain.[25,214,315,316] This representation refers to the pattern of activity that is evoked when a particular body part is stimulated. The most famous area of the brain associated with representation is the primary somatosensory cortex (S1) known as the homunculus (Figure 3.39).[25,214,315,316]

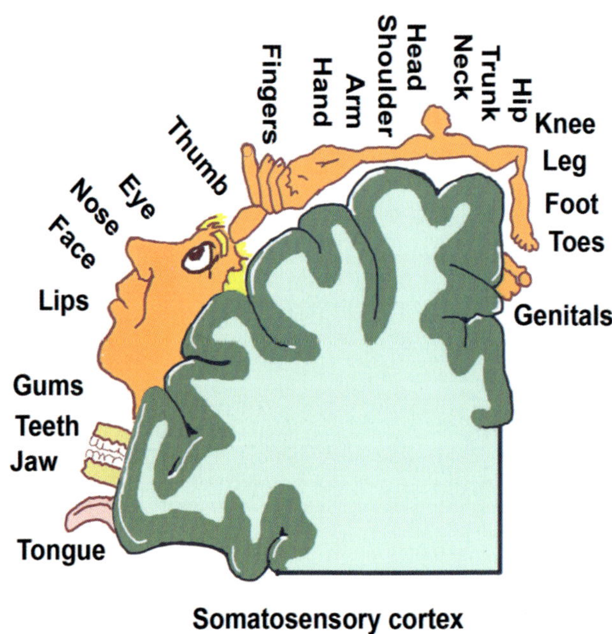

Figure 3.39: Somatosensory homunculus.

These neuronal representations of body parts are initially determined genitally but are then dynamically maintained, and change throughout life based on functional use.[317-322] It has been shown that patients with chronic pain display different S1 representations than people with no pain.[317-322] The interesting phenomenon associated with cortical restructuring is the fact that the body maps expand or contract, in essence increasing or decreasing the body map representation in the brain. Several studies have examined the brain structure (volume of gray and white matter) between healthy individuals and those suffering from chronic pain.[323-325] It has been shown that in people with chronic pain, various areas of the brain undergo volume changes, including the dorsolateral prefrontal cortex, right anterior thalamus, brainstem, somatosensory cortex and the posterior parietal cortex.[324,325] Several key issues are raised that impact treatment of patients with chronic pain:

- First, it is interesting to note that the extent of brain density changes has been correlated to pain intensity.[326] This finding correlates with a growing body of research that acute pain, especially pain intensity, may indeed be a big predictor in the development of chronic pain.[34,179,327] There is substantial evidence that persistent and high-intensity nociceptive bombardment of the CNS leads to significant long-lasting neuroplastic changes that may be irreversible (section 3.4).[34,179,180,183] The more interesting phenomenon of structural changes to the brain is the ability to restore gray matter. Gray matter changes found in chronic pain patients may not reflect true brain damage but rather a reversible consequence of the pain experience.[328] Treatments aimed at altering information to the brain (affecting nociception, education, etc.) have shown the ability to restore gray matter to the brain in chronic pain states.[328-332] It is also interesting to note that, apart from the increased gray matter in the brain, a positive effect on pain, pain catastrophization and disability was also achieved in these studies.[328-332] Although care should be taken to interpret these results and their correlation, these studies, along with a growing body of evidence, suggest strategies aimed at structurally reorganizing the brain as a means to treat chronic pain.[315,323-325,328-332]

- These changes in shape and size of body maps seem to correlate to increased pain and disability.[317,333] Although various factors have been linked to the development of this altered cortical representation of body maps in S1 such as neglect and decreased use of the painful body part,[159] it is believed that altered immune activity may be a significant source of the smudging of body maps.[105,215] An astounding fact of this reorganization of body maps is the fact that it occurs fast. It has been shown that when four fingers are webbed together for 30 minutes, cortical maps change associated with the fingers.[316] This finding has significant clinical importance as it underscores the importance of strategies such as movement, tactile, and visual stimulation of the CNS and brain early in a pain experience to help maintain S1 representation. Furthermore, it has also been shown that patients with chronic pain struggle when identifying left and right body parts (left-right discrimination).[334,335]

The clinical importance is that plasticity changes may in fact add increased threat to the brain and initiate and help maintain a pain experience.[214,215,220,318,321] The maps are biologically encoded and every human being is born with the maps intact. The maps, however, are environmentally sculpted and it is this sculpting ("use it or lose it") that may be playing a significant role in the development of pain. It is argued that when the maps are cortically healthy (sharp), the brain's threat level is likely low. The body part is easily recognized; appears to be normal size and the ability to recognize left and right (laterality) is highly accurate and fast.[178,321,336] When the body part is not moved or moved in a different manner, due to pain, being in a cast or brace, high levels of fear or does not exist (amputation), the cortical map is not "exercised" leading to various changes that impact a pain experience (Figure 3.40). Emerging neuroscience research has shown that in the absence of use of the body part there are several "neuroplastic consequences," including:[178,214,215,220,318,321,336]

- Cortical "smudging" whereby the ability to clearly identify the body part is decreased by the patient experiencing pain. It is argued that clinical tests such as two-point discrimination may in fact give clues as to the health of the cortical map in people with pain.[319,337,338]

- Difficulty with left-right discrimination. A series of studies have shown that pain and even the anticipation of pain lead to decreased ability to accurately identify left and right body parts as well as left and right movements of the spine and even facial expression in patients with headaches. Additionally, along with the decreased accuracy, patients with pain also decrease their speed in being able to identify left or right, often significantly beyond normal healthy volunteers.[334,335,339-341]

- Size changes: The cortical maps have the capacity to expand or contract, thus impacting the perceived size of the body part, which in turn significantly influences the pain experience.[178,318]

It is thought that these various alterations in body recognition increase fear, resulting in an increased pain experience. Furthermore, it is important to realize that pain can be initiated when a cortical map is altered, thus pain can be initiated due to immobilization, fear of movement, limited movement, etc.[342-344]

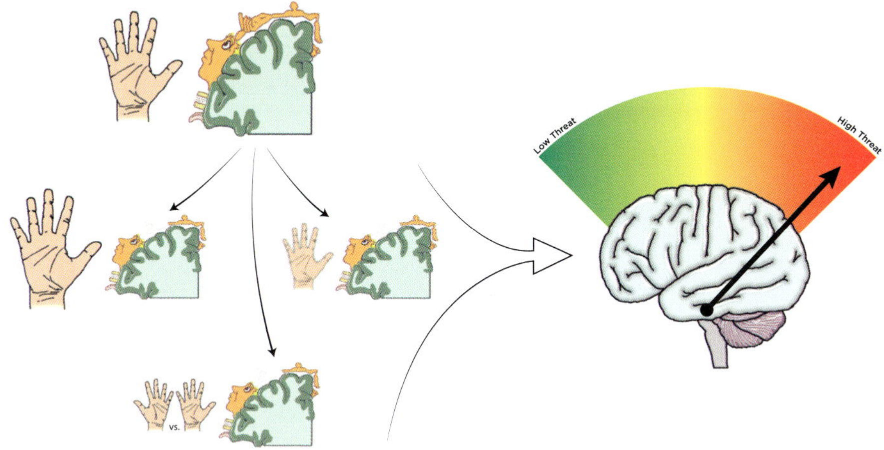

Figure 3.40 Proposed neuroplastic sequences inducing threat and, ultimately, an increased pain experience.

It is currently believed that the threat appraisal of the brain in regard to the neuroplastic changes is triggered by various immune responses. It is believed that alterations in body recognition initiate an immune response in order to protect the individual. The altered body part is a threat as it's not readily perceived as part of the person's normal body. It has even been proposed (Butler – personal communication) that the brain struggles to identify "self" from "non-self." This idea of not recognizing the body part is underscored by studies implying people with advanced pain states develop a form of "neglect."[319,345,346]

It is argued that there are likely numerous biological and physiological causes behind the alterations in body maps.[175,211,212,217,308,311,326] One area of particular interest that is very important for clinicians is emerging research regarding neuroimmune responses and tying the health of the peripheral nervous system to cortical maps and pain (section 3.3). In recent years, there has been increased interest in the interplay between the nervous system and immune system, specifically via glial cell activation.[105] Glial cells outnumber neurons 10 to one and play a critical part in immune function.[347] Scientists have shown that both injury to peripheral nerve and electrical stimulation of C fibers (barrage into the CNS) cause an increase in the permeability of the blood-spinal cord barrier as well as the blood-brain barriers.[105] Both of these barriers are critical in the CNS's ability to extract and receive correct information from the periphery, including location, side of the body, etc. These studies have shown heightened microglial activity in the dorsal horn of the spinal cord, on the affected side, which in turn triggers a cascade of immune changes.[105,153]

The importance of these aggressive immune responses to nerve compression and peripheral input into the CNS by C fibers should show therapists that peripheral processes have significant consequences not only at the triggering site, but along the axon, DRG, dorsal horn, spinal cord blood-barrier, second-order neuron activation, pain neuromatrix, blood-brain barrier and plasticity. What is even more intriguing and likely clinically relevant is the fact that the blood-spinal cord and blood-brain changes occur after only a few hours of nerve compression,[105,153] whereas clinicians often see patients with peripheral neurogenic contributions (i.e., radiculopathy) that have been present for weeks, months and even years. This connection of the various bodily systems underscores that many pain states seen in clinical practice are complex, intertwined and more widespread than what was previously believed.

NPQ and rNPQ statements:	NPQ/rNPQ #	Answer
Pain only occurs when you are injured	NPQ 2; rNPQ 10	False
Nerves have to connect a body part to the brain in order for that part to be in pain	NPQ 4	False
The body tells the brain when it is in pain	NPQ 6	False
Chronic pain means an injury hasn't healed properly	NPQ 9; rNPQ 7	False
The brain decides when you will be experiencing pain	NPQ 11; rNPQ 12	True
Pain only occurs when you are injured or at risk of being injured	rNPQ 3	False

At the heart of Chapter 3 is an updated knowledge of pain. The NPQ and rNPQ questions were discussed with the use of Gifford's M.O.M, delving into complexities of nociception, biopsychosocial risk factors, peripheral neurpathic pain, processing of information by the CNS, the pain neuromatrix, personalization of a pain experience, various biological responses and neuroplasticity. This comprehesive, clinical, layout of pain aims to provide clincians with the necessary knowledge to teach patients more about pain (PNE). Given the vast amount of clinical information covered, Moseley's definition of pain includes the various aspects covered in this chapter:

> Pain is a multiple system output activated by an individual's specific pain neuromatrix. The neuromatrix is activated whenever the brain concludes that body tissues are in danger and action is required.

It would thus be fitting to review the M.O.M of Gifford[32] and recognize its significance in representing the various contributions to pain even though it was conceived more than 20 years ago!

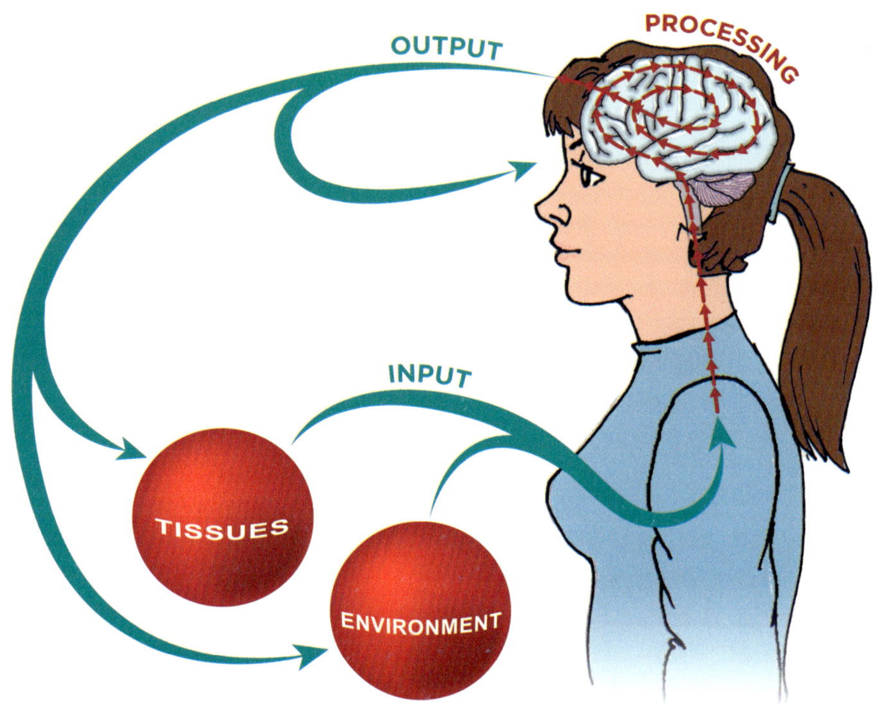

3.12: Key Points from Chapter 3

- Pain is complex
- Pain is an individual experience
- Many pain models are outdated and there is a big need for updated pain knowledge in medicine to reflect modern pain science
- There is ever-increasing knowledge of how pain works, encompassing various biological, psychological and social systems
- Pain is produced by the brain when the brain concludes there is danger
- Pain is only one of the powerful defenders

Chapter 3 References

1. Moseley GL, Hodges PW, Nicholas MK. A randomized controlled trial of intensive neurophysiology education in chronic low back pain. *Clinical Journal of Pain.* 2004;20:324-330.
2. Louw A, Zimney K, Puentedura EJ, Diener I. The Efficacy of Therapeutic Neuroscience Education on Musculoskeletal Pain – A Systematic Review of the Literature. *Physiother Theory Pract.* 2016;32(5): 332-355.
3. Chen J. History of pain theories. *Neuroscience bulletin.* 2011;27(5):343-350.
4. Jensen TS, Finnerup NB. A brief history of pain. *The Lancet Neurology.* 2014;13(9):872.
5. Wade D. Why physical medicine, physical disability and physical rehabilitation? We should abandon Cartesian dualism. *Clin Rehab.* 2006;20:85-90.
6. Goldberg JS. Revisiting the Cartesian model of pain. *Med Hypotheses.* 2008;70(5):1029-1033.
7. Deyo RA, Mirza SK, Turner JA, Martin BI. Overtreating chronic back pain: time to back off? *J Am Board Fam Med.* 2009;22(1):62-68.
8. Maitland GD. *Vertebral Manipulation.* 6th ed. London: Butterworths; 1986.
9. Melzack R, Wall PD. Pain mechanisms: a new theory. *Science.* 1965;150:971-979.
10. Melzack R. From the gate to the neuromatrix. *Pain.* 1999;Suppl 6: S121-126.
11. Melzack R. Pain and the neuromatrix in the brain *Journal of Dental Education.* 2001;65:1378-1382.
12. Moseley GL. A pain neuromatrix approach to patients with chronic pain. *Man Ther.* 2003;8(3):130-140.
13. Gifford L. *Aches and Pains.* Cornwall: Wordpress; 2014.
14. Oertel MF, Ryang YM, Korinth MC, Gilsbach JM, Rohde V. Long-term results of microsurgical treatment of lumbar spinal stenosis by unilateral laminotomy for bilateral decompression. *Neurosurgery.* 2006;59(6):1264-1269; discussion 1269-1270.
15. Loupasis GA, Stamos K, Katonis PG, Sapkas G, Korres DS, Hartofilakidis G. Seven- to 20-year outcome of lumbar discectomy. *Spine.* 1999;24(22): 2313-2317.
16. Button G, Gupta M, Barrett C, Cammack P, Benson D. Three- to six-year follow-up of stand-alone BAK cages implanted by a single surgeon. *The spine journal: official journal of the North American Spine Society.* 2005;5(2):155-160.
17. Deyo RA, Nachemson A, Mirza SK. Spinal-fusion surgery - the case for restraint. *N Engl J Med.* 2004;350(7):722-726.
18. Lipson SJ. Spinal-fusion surgery—advances and concerns. *N Engl J Med.* 2004;350(7):643-644.
19. Berg S, Tullberg T, Branth B, Olerud C, Tropp H. Total disc replacement compared to lumbar fusion: a randomised controlled trial with 2-year follow-up. *Eur Spine J.* 2009;18(10):1512-1519.
20. Oosterhuis T, Costa LO, Maher CG, de Vet HC, van Tulder MW, Ostelo RW. Rehabilitation after lumbar disc surgery. *The Cochrane database of systematic reviews.* 2014;3:CD003007.
21. Baker PN, van der Meulen JH, Lewsey J, Gregg PJ, National Joint Registry for E, Wales. The role of pain and function in determining patient satisfaction after total knee replacement. Data from the National Joint Registry for England and Wales. *The Journal of Bone and Joint Surgery: British Volume.* 2007;89(7):893-900.
22. Kennedy DM, Hanna SE, Stratford PW, Wessel J, Gollish JD. Preoperative function and gender predict pattern of functional recovery after hip and knee arthroplasty. *Journal of Arthroplasty.* 2006;21(4): 559-566.
23. Petersen KL, Rowbotham MC. Relief of post-herpetic neuralgia by surgical removal of painful skin: 5 years later. *Pain.* 2007;131(1-2):214-218.
24. Head H, Holmes G. Sensory disturbances from central lesions. *Brain: a journal of neurology.* 1911(34):102-254.
25. Penfield W, Boldrey E. Somatic, motor and sensory representation in the cerebral cortex of man as studied by electrical stimulation. *Brain: a journal of neurology.* 1937;60:389-448.
26. White JC, Sweet WH. *Pain and the Neurosurgeon.* Springfield IL: Charles C. Thomas; 1969.
27. Talbot JD, Marrett S, Evans AC, Meyer E, Bushnell MC, Duncan GH. Multiple representations of pain in human cerebral cortex. *Science.* 1991;251:1355-1358.

28. Apkarian AV, Stea RA, Manglos SH, Szeverenyi NM, King RB, Thomas FD. Persistent pain inhibits contralateral somatosensory cortical activity in humans. *Neuroscience letters.* 1992;140(2): 141-147.
29. Louw A, Puentedura E. *Therapeutic Neuroscience Education: Teaching patients about pain.* Minneapolis, MN: OPTP; 2013.
30. Catley MJ, O'Connell NE, Moseley GL. How good is the neurophysiology of pain questionnaire? A Rasch analysis of psychometric properties. *The journal of pain: official journal of the American Pain Society.* 2013;14(8):818-827.
31. Meeus M, Nijs J, Van Oosterwijck J, Van Alsenoy V, Truijen S. Pain Physiology Education Improves Pain Beliefs in Patients With Chronic Fatigue Syndrome Compared With Pacing and Self-Management Education: A Double-Blind Randomized Controlled Trial. *Arch Phys Med Rehabil.* 2010;91(8):1153-1159.
32. Gifford LS. Pain, the tissues and the nervous system. *Physiotherapy.* 1998;84:27-33.
33. Gifford LS, Butler DS. The integration of pain sciences into clinical practice. *J Hand Ther.* 1997;10(2):86-95.
34. Woolf CJ. Central sensitization: uncovering the relation between pain and plasticity. *Anesthesiology.* 2007;106(4):864-867.
35. Delcomyn F. *Foundations of Neurobiology.* New York: W.H. Freeman; 1998.
36. Barker RA, Barasi S. *Neuroscience at a Glance.* Oxford: Blackwell; 1999.
37. Carter R. *The Human Brain Book.* Firts ed. New York: Dorling Kindersley Limited; 2009.
38. Videman T, Battie MC, Ripatti S, Gill K, Manninen H, Kaprio J. Determinants of the progression in lumbar degeneration: a 5-year follow-up study of adult male monozygotic twins. *Spine.* 2006;31(6):671-678.
39. Alyas F, Turner M, Connell D. MRI findings in the lumbar spines of asymptomatic, adolescent, elite tennis players. *Br J Sports Med.* 2007;41(11):836-841; discussion 841.
40. Yukawa Y, Kato F, Matsubara Y, Kajino G, Nakamura S, Nitta H. Serial magnetic resonance imaging follow-up study of lumbar disc herniation conservatively treated for average 30 months: relation between reduction of herniation and degeneration of disc. *J Spinal Disord.* 1996;9(3):251-256.
41. Masui T, Yukawa Y, Nakamura S, et al. Natural history of patients with lumbar disc herniation observed by magnetic resonance imaging for minimum 7 years. *J Spinal Disord Tech.* 2005;18(2): 121-126.
42. Komori H, Shinomiya K, Nakai O, Yamaura I, Takeda S, Furuya K. The natural history of herniated nucleus pulposus with radiculopathy. *Spine.* 1996;21(2): 225-229.
43. Matsubara Y, Kato F, Mimatsu K, Kajino G, Nakamura S, Nitta H. Serial changes on MRI in lumbar disc herniations treated conservatively. *Neuroradiology.* 1995;37(5):378-383.
44. Zhong M, Liu JT, Jiang H, et al. Incidence of Spontaneous Resorption of Lumbar Disc Herniation: A Meta-Analysis. *Pain Physician.* 2017;20(1):E45-E52.
45. Kjaer P, Leboeuf-Yde C, Korsholm L, Sorensen JS, Bendix T. Magnetic resonance imaging and low back pain in adults: a diagnostic imaging study of 40-year-old men and women. *Spine.* 2005;30(10):1173-1180.
46. Gignac MA, Davis AM, Hawker G, et al. "What do you expect? You're just getting older": A comparison of perceived osteoarthritis-related and aging-related health experiences in middle- and older-age adults. *Arthritis and rheumatism.* 2006;55(6):905-912.
47. Thielke S, Sale J, Reid MC. Aging: are these 4 pain myths complicating care? *J Fam Pract.* 2012;61(11):666-670.
48. DePalma MJ, Ketchum JM, Saullo T. What is the source of chronic low back pain and does age play a role? *Pain medicine.* 2011;12(2):224-233.
49. Herzog R, Elgort DR, Flanders AE, Moley PJ. Variability in diagnostic error rates of 10 MRI centers performing lumbar spine MRI examinations on the same patient within a 3-week period. *The spine journal: official journal of the North American Spine Society.* 2017;17(4):554-561.
50. Okada E, Matsumoto M, Fujiwara H, Toyama Y. Disc degeneration of cervical spine on MRI in patients with lumbar disc herniation: comparison study with asymptomatic volunteers. *Eur Spine J.* 2011;20(4):585-591.
51. Nakashima H, Yukawa Y, Suda K, Yamagata M, Ueta T, Kato F. Abnormal findings on magnetic resonance images of the cervical spines in 1211 asymptomatic subjects. *Spine* (Phila Pa 1976). 2015;40(6):392-398.
52. Simotas AC, Shen T. Neck pain in demolition derby drivers. *Arch Phys Med Rehabil.* 2005;86(4):693-696.

53. Sher JS, Uribe JW, Posada A, Murphy BJ, Zlatkin MB. Abnormal findings on magnetic resonance images of asymptomatic shoulders. *The Journal of bone and joint surgery American volume.* 1995;77(1):10-15.
54. Reilly P, Macleod I, Macfarlane R, Windley J, Emery RJ. Dead men and radiologists don't lie: a review of cadaveric and radiological studies of rotator cuff tear prevalence. *Annals of the Royal College of Surgeons of England.* 2006;88(2):116-121.
55. Milgrom C, Schaffler M, Gilbert S, van Holsbeeck M. Rotator-cuff changes in asymptomatic adults. The effect of age, hand dominance and gender. *J Bone Joint Surg Br.* 1995;77(2):296-298.
56. Spielmann AL, Forster BB, Kokan P, Hawkins RH, Janzen DL. Shoulder after rotator cuff repair: MR imaging findings in asymptomatic individuals--initial experience. *Radiology.* 1999;213(3):705-708.
57. Munk B, Lundorf E, Jensen J. Long-term outcome of meniscal degeneration in the knee: poor association between MRI and symptoms in 45 patients followed more than 4 years. *Acta Orthop Scand.* 2004;75(1):89-92.
58. Bedson J, Croft PR. The discordance between clinical and radiographic knee osteoarthritis: a systematic search and summary of the literature. *BMC musculoskeletal disorders.* 2008;9:116.
59. Major NM, Helms CA. MR imaging of the knee: findings in asymptomatic collegiate basketball players. *AJR Am J Roentgenol.* 2002;179(3):641-644.
60. Riddle DL, Jiranek WA, Hayes CW. Use of a validated algorithm to judge the appropriateness of total knee arthroplasty in the United States: a multicenter longitudinal cohort study. *Arthritis Rheumatol.* 2014;66(8):2134-2143.
61. Register B, Pennock AT, Ho CP, Strickland CD, Lawand A, Philippon MJ. Prevalence of abnormal hip findings in asymptomatic participants: a prospective, blinded study. *Am J Sports Med.* 2012;40(12):2720-2724.
62. Frank JM, Harris JD, Erickson BJ, et al. Prevalence of Femoroacetabular Impingement Imaging Findings in Asymptomatic Volunteers: A Systematic Review. *Arthroscopy.* 2015;31(6):1199-1204.
63. Silvis ML, Mosher TJ, Smetana BS, et al. High prevalence of pelvic and hip magnetic resonance imaging findings in asymptomatic collegiate and professional hockey players. *Am J Sports Med.* 2011;39(4):715-721.
64. Mochida K, Komori H, Okawa A, Muneta T, Haro H, Shinomiya K. Regression of cervical disc herniation observed on magnetic resonance images. *Spine.* 1998; 23(9):990-995; discussion 996-997.
65. Haldeman S. Presidential address, North American Spine Society: failure of the pathology model to predict back pain. *Spine.* 1990;15(7):718-724.
66. Merskey H, Bogduk N., International Association for the Study of Pain. Task Force on Taxonomy. *Classification of chronic pain: descriptions of chronic pain syndromes and definitions of pain terms.* 2 ed. the University of Michigan: IASP Press; 1994.
67. Knotkova H, Crawford Clark W, Mokrejs P, Padour F, Kuhl J. What do ratings on unidimensional pain and emotion scales really mean? A Multidimensional Affect and Pain Survey (MAPS) analysis of cancer patient responses. *Journal of pain and symptom management.* 2004;28(1):19-27.
68. Huber A, Suman AL, Rendo CA, Biasi G, Marcolongo R, Carli G. Dimensions of "unidimensional" ratings of pain and emotions in patients with chronic musculoskeletal pain. *Pain.* 2007;130(3):216-224.
69. Meeus M, Nijs J. Central sensitization: a biopsychosocial explanation for chronic widespread pain in patients with fibromyalgia and chronic fatigue syndrome. *Clin Rheumatol.* 2007;26(4):465-473.
70. Nijs J, Van Houdenhove B. From acute musculoskeletal pain to chronic widespread pain and fibromyalgia: application of pain neurophysiology in manual therapy practice. *Manual therapy.* 2009;14(1):3-12.
71. Ahmad N, Busuttil A. Impaling-type head injury in a road traffic incident. *Medicine, science, and the law.* 1993;33(3):261-263.
72. Guneren E, Birinci H, Uysal OA, Eroglu L, Geary PM. Facial impaling on a scythe. *British journal of plastic surgery.* 2000;53(3):267-268.
73. Nicolaisen N, Ahmed A, Hancock T, Ogren R. Field airway management of a construction worker with an impaling rebar injury to the neck and brain. *Prehospital emergency care: official journal of the National Association of EMS Physicians and the National Association of State EMS Directors.* 2012;16(4):548-552.
74. Dilley A, Bove GM. Disruption of axoplasmic transport induces mechanical sensitivity in intact rat C-fibre nociceptor axons. *The Journal of physiology.* 2008;586(2):593-604.

75. Monsivais JJ, Sun Y. Tinel's sign or percussion test? Developing a better method of evoking a Tinel's sign. *Journal of the Southern Orthopedic Association.* 1997;6:186-189.
76. Devor M. Sodium channels and mechanisms of neuropathic pain. *The journal of pain: official journal of the American Pain Society.* 2006;7(1 Suppl 1):S3-S12.
77. Raja SN, Meyer RA, Ringkamp M, Campbell JN. Peripheral neural mechanisms of nociception. In: Wall PD, Melzack R, eds. *Textboook of Pain.* 4th ed. Edinburgh: Churchill Livingstone; 1999.
78. Drummond PD. Inflammatory consequences of cutaneous stimulation. *Experimental neurology.* 2010;222(2): 181-183.
79. Drummond PD. Inflammation contributes to axon reflex vasodilatation evoked by iontophoresis of an alpha-1 adrenoceptor agonist. *Autonomic neuroscience: basic & clinical.* 2011;159(1-2):90-97.
80. Dickerson C, Undem B, Bullock B, Winchurch RA. Neuropeptide regulation of proinflammatory cytokine responses. *Journal of Leukocyte Biology.* 1998;63:602-605.
81. Ikawa M, Atsuta Y, Tsunekawa H. Ectopic firing due to artificial venous stasis in rat lumbar spinal canal stenosis model: a possible pathogenesis of neurogenic intermittent claudication. *Spine.* 2005; 30(21):2393-2397.
82. Amir R, Devor M. Ongoing activity in neuroma afferents bearing retrograde sprouts. *Brain Research.* 1993;630: 283-288.
83. Alshami AM, Souvlis T, Coppieters MW. A review of plantar heel pain of neural origin: differential diagnosis and management. *Manual therapy.* 2008;13(2):103-111.
84. Nordin M, Nystrom B, Wallin U, Hagbarth KE. Ectopic sensory discharges and paresthesiae in patients with disorders of peripheral nerves, dorsal roots and dorsal columns. *Pain.* 1984;20(3):231-245.
85. Thacker MA, Clark AK, Marchand F, McMahon SB. Pathophysiology of peripheral neuropathic pain: immune cells and molecules. *Anesth Analg.* 2007;105:838-847.
86. Watson P, Kendall N. *Assessing psychosocial yellow flags.* In: Gifford LS, ed. Topical Issues in Pain 2. Falmouth: CNS Press; 2000.
87. Sterling M, Jull G, Kenardy J. Physical and psychological factors maintain long-term predictive capacity post-whiplash injury. *Pain.* 2006;122(1-2):102-108.
88. Walton DM, Pretty J, MacDermid JC, Teasell RW. Risk factors for persistent problems following whiplash injury: results of a systematic review and meta-analysis. *J Orthop Sports Phys Ther.* 2009;39(5):334-350.
89. Hellsing A, Linton SJ, Kalvemark M. A prospective study of patients with acute back and neck pain in Sweden. *Physical therapy.* 1994;74:116-128.
90. Cassidy JD, Carroll LJ, Cote P, Lemstra M, Berglund A, Nygren A. Effect of eliminating compensation for pain and suffering on the outcome of insurance claims for whiplash injury. *N Engl J Med.* 2000;342(16):1179-1186.
91. Fortier MA, Anderson CT, Kain ZN. Ethnicity matters in the assessment and treatment of children's pain. *Pediatrics.* 2009;124(1):378-380.
92. Bates MS, Edwards WT. Ethnic variations in the chronic pain experience. *Ethnicity & disease.* 1992;2(1):63-83.
93. Bonham VL. Race, ethnicity, and pain treatment: striving to understand the causes and solutions to the disparities in pain treatment. *The Journal of law, medicine & ethics: a journal of the American Society of Law, Medicine & Ethics.* 2001;29(1):52-68.
94. Taddio A, Katz J, Ilersich AL, Koren G. Effect of neonatal circumcision on pain response during subsequent routine vaccination. *Lancet.* 1997;349(9052):599-603.
95. Anand KJ. Effects of perinatal pain and stress. *Progress in brain research.* 2000;122:117-129.
96. Warnock F, Sandrin D. Comprehensive description of newborn distress behavior in response to acute pain (newborn male circumcision). *Pain.* 2004;107(3): 242-255.
97. Boyle GJ, Goldman R, Svoboda JS, Fernandez E. Male circumcision: pain, trauma and psychosexual sequelae. *Journal of health psychology.* 2002;7(3):329-343.
98. Shah VS, Taddio A, Bennett S, Speidel BD. Neonatal pain response to heel stick vs venepuncture for routine blood sampling. *Arch Dis Child Fetal Neonatal Ed.* 1997;77(2):F143-144.
99. Knaepen L, Patijn J, van Kleef M, Mulder M, Tibboel D, Joosten EA. Neonatal repetitive needle pricking: plasticity of the spinal nociceptive circuit and extended postoperative pain in later life. *Developmental neurobiology.* 2013;73(1):85-97.

100. Horsley R. Factors that affect the occurrence and chronicity of occupation-related musculoskeletal disorders. *Best Pract Res Clin Rheumatol.* 2011;25(1): 103-115.
101. Bigos SJ, Battie MC, Spengler DM, et al. A prospective study of work perceptions and psychosocial factors affecting the report of back injury. *Spine.* 1991;16(1):1-6.
102. Link BG, Phelan J. Social conditions as fundamental causes of disease. *Journal of health and social behavior.* 1995;Spec No:80-94.
103. Poleshuck EL, Green CR. Socioeconomic disadvantage and pain. *Pain.* 2008;136(3): 235-238.
104. Raudenbush B, Canter RJ, Corley N, et al. Pain threshold and tolerance differences among intercollegiate athletes: implication of past sports injuries and willingness to compete among sports teams. *North American Journal of Psychology Publisher.* 2012;14(1).
105. Beggs S, Liu XJ, Kwan C, Salter MW. Peripheral nerve injury and TRPV1-expressing primary afferent C fibers cause opening of the blood-brain barrier. *Molecular pain.* 2010;6:74.
106. Lewis R, Asplin KE, Bruce G, Dart C, Mobasheri A, Barrett-Jolley R. The role of the membrane potential in chondrocyte volume regulation. *J Cell Physiol.* 2011;226(11):2979-2986.
107. Devor M. Response of nerves to injury in relation to neuropathic pain. In: McMahon S, Koltzenburg M, eds. *Melzack and wall's Textbook of Pain.* Edinburgh: Elsevier; 2005.
108. Devor M, Govrin-Lippmann R, Angelides K. Na+ channel immunolocalization in peripheral mammalian axons and changes following nerve injury and neuroma formation. *Journal of Neuroscience.* 1993;13:1976-1992.
109. Louw A, Schmidt SG. Chronic pain and the thoracic spine. *The Journal of manual & manipulative therapy.* 2015;23(3): 162-168.
110. Sterling M, Jull G, Vicenzino B, Kenardy J. Sensory hypersensitivity occurs soon after whiplash injury and is associated with poor recovery. *Pain.* 2003;104(3): 509-517.
111. Sterling M, Kenardy J. Physical and psychological aspects of whiplash. Important considerations for primary care asessment *Manual therapy.* 2008; 13:93-102.
112. Yeung E, Jones M, Hall B. The response to the slump test in a group of female whiplash patients. *The Australian journal of physiotherapy.* 1997;43(4):245-252.
113. Sterling M, Treleaven J, Jull G. Responses to a clinical test of mechanical provocation of nerve tissue in whiplash associated disorder. *Manual therapy.* 2002;7(2): 89-94.
114. Howe JF, Loeser JD, Calvin WH. Mechanosensitivity of dorsal root ganglia and chronically injured axons: a physiological basis for radicular pain of nerve root compression. *Pain.* 1977;3:25-41.
115. Amir M, Michaelis M, Devor M. Membrane potential oscillations in dorsal root ganglion neurons: role in normal electrogenesis and neuropathic pain. *Journal of Neuroscience.* 1999;19: 8589-8596.
116. Devor M. Unexplained peculiarities of the dorsal root ganglion. *Pain.* 1999;Supplement 6:S27-S36.
117. Black JA, Felts P, Smith KJ, Knocsis JD, Waxman SG. Distribution of sodium channels in chronically demyelinated spinal cord axons: Immuno-ultrastructural localization and electrophysiological observations. *Brain Research.* 1991;544:59-70.
118. Redford EJ, Hall SM, Smith KJ. Vascular changes and demyelination induced by intraneural injection of tumour necrosis factor. *Brain: a journal of neurology.* 1995;118:869-878.
119. Louw J, Peltzer K, Naidoo P, Matseke G, McHunu G, Tutshana B. Quality of life among tuberculosis (TB), TB retreatment and/or TB-HIV co-infected primary public healthcare patients in three districts in South Africa. *Health Qual Life Outcomes.* 2012;10(1):77.
120. Franson RC, Saal JS, J.A. S. Human disc phospholipase A2 is inflammatory. *Spine.* 1992;17 (Suppl):S129-S132.
121. Saal JS, Franson RC, Dobrow R, al. e. High levels of inflammatory phospholipase A2 activity in lumbar disc herniation. *Spine.* 1990;15:674-678.
122. Chen C, Cavanaugh JM, Song Z, Takebayashi T, Kallakuri S, Wooley PH. Effects of nucleus pulposus on nerve root neural activity, mechanosensitivity, axonal morphology, and sodium channel expression. *Spine.* 2004;29(1):17-25.

123. Miyamoto H, Doita M, Nishida K, Yamamoto T, Sumi M, Kurosaka M. Effects of cyclic mechanical stress on the production of inflammatory agents by nucleus pulposus and anulus fibrosus derived cells in vitro. *Spine*. 2006;31(1):4-9.
124. Kautio AL, Haanpaa M, Kautiainen H, Kalso E, Saarto T. Burden of chemotherapy-induced neuropathy--a cross-sectional study. *Supportive care in cancer: official journal of the Multinational Association of Supportive Care in Cancer.* 2011;19(12):1991-1996.
125. Alizadeh A, Dyck SM, Karimi-Abdolrezaee S. Myelin damage and repair in pathologic CNS: challenges and prospects. *Frontiers in molecular neuroscience.* 2015;8:35.
126. Wijdicks CA, Westerhaus BD, Brand EJ, Johansen S, Engebretsen L, Laprade RF. Sartorial branch of the saphenous nerve in relation to a medial knee ligament repair or reconstruction. *Knee Surg Sports Traumatol Arthrosc.* 2009.
127. Portland GH, Martin D, Keene G, Menz T. Injury to the infrapatellar branch of the saphenous nerve in anterior cruciate ligament reconstruction: comparison of horizontal versus vertical harvest site incisions. *Arthroscopy.* 2005;21(3): 281-285.
128. Papastergiou SG, Voulgaropoulos H, Mikalef P, Ziogas E, Pappis G, Giannakopoulos I. Injuries to the infrapatellar branch(es) of the saphenous nerve in anterior cruciate ligament reconstruction with four-strand hamstring tendon autograft: vertical versus horizontal incision for harvest. *Knee Surg Sports Traumatol Arthrosc.* 2006;14(8): 789-793.
129. Luo H, Yu JK, Ao YF, et al. Relationship between different skin incisions and the injury of the infrapatellar branch of the saphenous nerve during anterior cruciate ligament reconstruction. *Chin Med J (Engl).* 2007;120(13):1127-1130.
130. Figueroa D, Calvo R, Vaisman A, Campero M, Moraga C. Injury to the infrapatellar branch of the saphenous nerve in ACL reconstruction with the hamstrings technique: clinical and electrophysiological study. *Knee.* 2008; 15(5):360-363.
131. Grubb SA, Kelly CK. Cervical discography: clinical implications from 12 years of experience. *Spine.* 2000; 25(11):1382-1389.
132. Cloward RB. Cervical Discography. *Acta radiologica: diagnosis.* 1963;1:675-688.
133. Demircan MN, Asir A, Cetinkal A, et al. Is there any relationship between proinflammatory mediator levels in disc material and myelopathy with cervical disc herniation and spondylosis? A non-randomized, prospective clinical study. *Eur Spine J.* 2007;16(7):983-986.
134. Taylor JR, Twomey LT. Acute injuries to cervical joints. An autopsy study of neck sprain. *Spine.* 1993;18(9):1115-1122.
135. Taylor JR, Twomey LT. Disc injuries in cervical trauma. *Lancet.* 1990;336(8726):1318.
136. Taylor JR, Twomey LT. Acute injuries to cervical joints. An autopsy study of neck sprain. *Spine (Phila Pa 1976).* 1993;18(9):1115-1122.
137. Rempel DM, Diao E. Entrapment neuropathies: pathophysiology and pathogenesis. *J Electromyogr Kinesiol.* 2004;14(1):71-75.
138. Scott JE, Bosworth TR, Cribb AM, Taylor JR. The chemical morphology of age-related changes in human intervertebral disc glycosaminoglycans from cervical, thoracic and lumbar nucleus pulposus and annulus fibrosus. *J Anat.* 1994;184 (Pt 1):73-82.
139. Tanaka Y, Kokubun S, Sato T, Ozawa H. Cervical roots as origin of pain in the neck or scapular regions. *Spine.* 2006;31(17):E568-573.
140. Bogduk N. The neck and headaches. *Neurol Clin.* 2004;22(1):151-171, vii.
141. Bogduk N. Whiplash can have lesions. *Pain Res Manag.* 2006;11(3):155.
142. Cooper G, Bailey B, Bogduk N. Cervical zygapophysial joint pain maps. *Pain medicine.* 2007;8(4):344-353.
143. Bogduk N. Role of anesthesiologic blockade in headache management. *Curr Pain Headache Rep.* 2004;8(5): 399-403.
144. Vallières E. The Costovertebral Angle. *Thoracic Surgery Clinics.* 2007;17(4): 503-510.
145. Louwette S, Labarque V, Wittevrongel C, et al. Regulator of G-protein signaling 18 controls megakaryopoiesis and the cilia-mediated vertebrate mechanosensory system. *FASEB journal: official publication of the Federation of American Societies for Experimental Biology.* 2012;26(5):2125-2136.
146. Foster AC, Kemp JA. Glutamate- and GABA-based CNS therapeutics. *Current opinion in pharmacology.* 2006;6(1): 7-17.

147. Upton ARM, McComas AJ. The double crush in nerve entrapment syndromes. *The Lancet.* 1973;August 18:359-361.
148. Radhakrishnan K, Litchy WJ, O'Fallon WM, Kurland LT. Epidemiology of cervical radiculopathy: a population-based study from Rochester, Minnesota, 1976 through 1990. *Brain.* Vol 1171994:325-335.
149. Schmid AB, Coppieters MW. The double crush syndrome revisited--a Delphi study to reveal current expert views on mechanisms underlying dual nerve disorders. *Manual therapy.* 2011;16(6):557-562.
150. Richardson JK, Forman GM, Riley B. An electrophysiological exploration of the double crush hypothesis. *Muscle & Nerve.* 1999;22:71-77.
151. Schmid AB, Nee RJ, Coppieters MW. Reappraising entrapment neuropathies--mechanisms, diagnosis and management. *Manual therapy.* 2013;18(6):449-457.
152. Schmid AB, Coppieters MW, Ruitenberg MJ, McLachlan EM. Local and remote immune-mediated inflammation after mild peripheral nerve compression in rats. *Journal of neuropathology and experimental neurology.* 2013;72(7):662-680.
153. Hu P, McLachlan EM. Macrophage and lymphocyte invasion of dorsal root ganglia after peripheral nerve lesions in the rat. *Neuroscience.* 2002;112(1):23-38.
154. Lundborg G, Myers R, Powell H. Nerve compression injury and increased endoneurial fluid pressure: a "miniature compartment syndrome". *Journal of Neurology, Neurosurgery and Psychiatry.* 1983;46:1119-1124.
155. Dahlin LB, Archer DR, McLean WG. Axonal transport and morphological changes following nerve compression. An experimental study in the rabbit vagus nerve. *J Hand Surg [Br].* 1993;18(1):106-110.
156. Mackinnon SE. Double and multiple "crush" syndromes. Double and multiple entrapment neuropathies. *Hand Clin.* 1992;8(2):369-390.
157. Dilley A, Richards N, Pulman KG, Bove GM. Disruption of fast axonal transport in the rat induces behavioral changes consistent with neuropathic pain. *The journal of pain: official journal of the American Pain Society.* 2013;14(11):1437-1449.
158. Dilley A, Bove GM. Resolution of inflammation-induced axonal mechanical sensitivity and conduction slowing in C fiber nociceptors. *The journal of pain: official journal of the American Pain Society.* 2008;9(2):185-192.
159. Marinus J, Moseley GL, Birklein F, et al. Clinical features and pathophysiology of complex regional pain syndrome. *Lancet Neurol.* 2011;10(7):637-648.
160. Dommisse GF. The blood supply of the spinal cord. *Journal of Bone and Joint Surgery.* 1974;56B(2, May):225-235.
161. Dommisse GF. The blood supply of the spinal cord and the consequences of failure. In: Boyling J, Palastanga N, eds. *Grieve's Modern Manual Therapy.* 2nd ed. Edinburgh: Churchill Livingstone; 1994.
162. Lundborg G. Intraneural microcirculation. *Orthop Clin North Am.* 1988;19(1):1-12.
163. Lundborg G, Rydevik B. Effects of stretching the tibial nerve of the rabbit. A preliminary study of the intraneural circulation and the barrier function of the perineurium. *J Bone Joint Surg Br.* 1973;55(2):390-401.
164. Rempel D, Dahlin L, Lundborg G. Pathophysiology of nerve compression syndromes: response of peripheral nerves to loading. *J Bone Joint Surg Am.* 1999;81(11):1600-1610.
165. Ogata K, Naito M. Blood flow of peripheral nerve effects of dissection, stretching and compression. *J Hand Surg [Br].* 1986;11(1):10-14.
166. Shen J, Fox LE, Cheng J. Swim therapy reduces mechanical allodynia and thermal hyperalgesia induced by chronic constriction nerve injury in rats. *Pain medicine.* 2013;14(4):516-525.
167. Chen YW, Li YT, Chen YC, Li ZY, Hung CH. Exercise training attenuates neuropathic pain and cytokine expression after chronic constriction injury of rat sciatic nerve. *Anesth Analg.* 2012;114(6): 1330-1337.
168. Kuphal KE, Fibuch EE, Taylor BK. Extended swimming exercise reduces inflammatory and peripheral neuropathic pain in rodents. *The journal of pain: official journal of the American Pain Society.* 2007;8(12):989-997.
169. Santos FM, Silva JT, Giardini AC, et al. Neural mobilization reverses behavioral and cellular changes that characterize neuropathic pain in rats. *Molecular pain.* 2012;8:57.

170. Song XJ, Gan Q, Cao JL, Wang ZB, Rupert RL. Spinal manipulation reduces pain and hyperalgesia after lumbar intervertebral foramen inflammation in the rat. *Journal of manipulative and physiological therapeutics*. 2006;29(1):5-13.
171. Schmid AB, Elliott JM, Strudwick MW, Little M, Coppieters MW. Effect of splinting and exercise on intraneural edema of the median nerve in carpal tunnel syndrome--an MRI study to reveal therapeutic mechanisms. *Journal of orthopaedic research: official publication of the Orthopaedic Research Society*. 2012;30(8):1343-1350.
172. Kras JV, Dong L, Winkelstein BA. The prostaglandin E2 receptor, EP2, is upregulated in the dorsal root ganglion after painful cervical facet joint injury in the rat. *Spine*. 2013;38(3):217-222.
173. Ozaktay AC, Kallakuri S, Cavanaugh JM. Phospholipase A2 sensitivity of the dorsal root and dorsal root ganglion. *Spine*. 1998;23(12):1297-1306.
174. Taylor JR, Twomey LT, Kakulas BA. Dorsal root ganglion injuries in 109 blunt trauma fatalities. *Injury*. 1998;29(5):335-339.
175. McLean SA. The potential contribution of stress systems to the transition to chronic whiplash-associated disorders. *Spine* (Phila Pa 1976). 2011;36(25 Suppl):S226-232.
176. Winkelstein BA. How can animal models inform on the transition to chronic symptoms in whiplash? *Spine* (Phila Pa 1976). 2011;36(25 Suppl):S218-225.
177. Ramer MS, Thompson SWN, McMahon SB. Causes and consequences of sympathetic basket formation in dorsal root ganglia. *Pain*. 1999;Suppl 6:S111-S120.
178. Moseley GL, Parsons TJ, Spence C. Visual distortion of a limb modulates the pain and swelling evoked by movement. *Current biology: CB*. 2008;18(22):R1047-1048.
179. Woolf CJ, Salter MW. Plasticity and pain: the role of the dorsal horn. In: McMahon S, Koltzenburg M, eds. *Wall and Melzack's Textbook of Pain*. 5th ed. Edinburgh: Elsevier; 2005.
180. Woolf CJ, Mannion RJ. Neuropathic pain: aetiology, symptoms, mechanisms, and management. *Lancet*. 1999;353(9168):1959-1964.
181. Villaneuva L, Fields HL. Endogenous Central mechanisms of Pain Modulation. In: Villaneuva L, Dickenson A, Ollat H, eds. *The Pain System in Normal and Pathological States*. Seattle: IASP Press; 2004.
182. Doubell TP, Mannion R, Woolf CJ. The dorsal horn: state dependent sensory processing, plasticity and the generation of pain. In: Wall PD, Melzack R, eds. *Textbook of Pain*. 4th ed. Edinburgh: Churchill Livingstone; 1999.
183. Latremoliere A, Woolf CJ. Central sensitization: a generator of pain hypersensitivity by central neural plasticity. *The journal of pain: official journal of the American Pain Society*. 2009;10(9):895-926.
184. Meeus M, Vervisch S, De Clerck LS, Moorkens G, Hans G, Nijs J. Central sensitization in patients with rheumatoid arthritis: a systematic literature review. *Seminars in arthritis and rheumatism*. 2012;41(4):556-567.
185. Woolf CJ, Doubell TP. The pathophysiology of chronic pain - increasd sensitivity to low threshold A beta fibre inputs. *Current Opinion in Neurobiology*. 1994; 4:525-534.
186. Fukuoka T, Tokunaga A, Kondo E, Miki K, Tachibana T, Noguchi K. Change in mRNAs for neuropeptides and the GABA(A) receptor in dorsal root ganglion neurons in a rat experimental neuropathic pain model. *Pain*. 1998;78(1):13-26.
187. Moseley GL, Herbert RD, Parsons T, Lucas S, Van Hilten JJ, Marinus J. Intense pain soon after wrist fracture strongly predicts who will develop complex regional pain syndrome: prospective cohort study. *The journal of pain: official journal of the American Pain Society*. 2014;15(1):16-23.
188. Benedetti F, Thoen W, Blanchard C, Vighetti S, Arduino C. Pain as a reward: changing the meaning of pain from negative to positive co-activates opioid and cannabinoid systems. *Pain*. 2013;154(3):361-367.
189. Herrera E, Sandoval MC, Camargo DM, Salvini TF. Motor and sensory nerve conduction are affected differently by ice pack, ice massage, and cold water immersion. *Physical therapy*. 2010;90(4):581-591.
190. Johnson MI, Paley CA, Howe TE, Sluka KA. Transcutaneous electrical nerve stimulation for acute pain. *Cochrane Database Syst Rev*. 2015(6):CD006142.

191. Basbaum AI, Fields HL. Endogenous pain control mechanisms. *Annals of Neurology*. 1978;4:451-462.
192. ter Riet G, de Craen AJ, de Boer A, Kessels AG. Is placebo analgesia mediated by endogenous opioids? A systematic review. *Pain*. 1998;76(3):273-275.
193. Agnati LF, Tiengo M, Ferraguti F, et al. Pain analgesia and stress: An integrated view. *Clinical Journal of Pain*. 1991;7(Suppl 1):S23-S37.
194. Benedetti F, Amanzio M. Mechanisms of the placebo response. *Pulm Pharmacol Ther*. 2013;26(5):520-523.
195. Nijs J, Kosek E, Van Oosterwijck J, Meeus M. Dysfunctional endogenous analgesia during exercise in patients with chronic pain: to exercise or not to exercise? *Pain Physician*. 2012;15(3 Suppl):ES205-213.
196. Moseley GL. *Placebo effect: Reconceptualising placebo*. Bmj. 2008;336(7653):1086.
197. Bialosky JE, Bishop MD, Cleland JA. Individual expectation: an overlooked, but pertinent, factor in the treatment of individuals experiencing musculoskeletal pain. *Physical therapy*. 2010;90(9): 1345-1355.
198. Bishop MD, Bialosky JE, Cleland JA. Patient expectations of benefit from common interventions for low back pain and effects on outcome: secondary analysis of a clinical trial of manual therapy interventions. *The Journal of manual & manipulative therapy*. 2011;19(1):20-25.
199. Puentedura EJ, Cleland JA, Landers MR, Mintken PE, Louw A, Fernandez-de-Las-Penas C. Development of a clinical prediction rule to identify patients with neck pain likely to benefit from thrust joint manipulation to the cervical spine. *The Journal of orthopaedic and sports physical therapy*. 2012;42(7):577-592.
200. Louw A, Diener I, Fernandez-de-Las-Penas C, Puentedura EJ. Sham Surgery in Orthopedics: A Systematic Review of the Literature. *Pain medicine*. 2016.
201. Moseley JB, O'Malley K, Petersen NJ, et al. A controlled trial of arthroscopic surgery for osteoarthritis of the knee. *N Engl J Med*. 2002;347(2):81-88.
202. Buchbinder R, Osborne RH, Ebeling PR, et al. A randomized trial of vertebroplasty for painful osteoporotic vertebral fractures. *N Engl J Med*. 2009;361(6):557-568.
203. Kallmes DF, Comstock BA, Heagerty PJ, et al. A randomized trial of vertebroplasty for osteoporotic spinal fractures. *N Engl J Med*. 2009;361(6):569-579.
204. Kroslak M. *Surgical treatment of lateral epicondylitis: A prospective, randomised, blinded, placebo controlled pilot study*: Faculty of Medicine, University of New South Wales; 2012.
205. Barendse GA, van Den Berg SG, Kessels AH, Weber WE, van Kleef M. Randomized controlled trial of percutaneous intradiscal radiofrequency thermocoagulation for chronic discogenic back pain: lack of effect from a 90-second 70 C lesion. *Spine*. 2001;26(3):287-292.
206. Pauza KJ, Howell S, Dreyfuss P, Peloza JH, Dawson K, Bogduk N. A randomized, placebo-controlled trial of intradiscal electrothermal therapy for the treatment of discogenic low back pain. *The spine journal: official journal of the North American Spine Society*. 2004;4(1): 27-35.
207. Dostrovsky JO. Immediate and long-term plasticity in human somatosensory thalamus and its involvement in phantom limbs. *Pain Supplement*. 1999;6:S37-S43.
208. Brisby H, Hammar I. Thalamic activation in a disc herniation model. *Spine*. 2007;32(25):2846-2852.
209. Catani M. Diffusion tensor magnetic resonance imaging tractography in cognitive disorders. *Current opinion in neurology*. 2006;19(6):599-606.
210. Fercho KA, Baugh LA, Louw A, Zimney K. Pain Neuroscience Education Effect on Pain Matrix Processing in an Individual with Complex Regional Pain Syndrome: A Single Subject Research Design. *European Pain Journal*. 2017 - Submitted for publication.
211. Garcia-Larrea L, Peyron R. Pain matrices and neuropathic pain matrices: a review. *PAIN®*. 2013;154:S29-S43.
212. Hashmi JA, Baliki MN, Huang L, et al. Shape shifting pain: chronification of back pain shifts brain representation from nociceptive to emotional circuits. *Brain : a journal of neurology*. 2013;136(Pt 9):2751-2768.
213. Benedetti F. Placebo and the new physiology of the doctor-patient relationship. *Physiol Rev*. 2013;93(3):1207-1246.
214. Flor H. The functional organization of the brain in chronic pain. In: Sandkühler J, Bromm B, Gebhart GF, eds. *Progress in Brain Research, Vol 129*. Amsterdam: Elsevier; 2000.

215. Flor H, Braun C, Elbert T, Birbaumer N. Extensive reorganization of primary somatosensory cortex in chronic back pain patients. *Neuroscience letters.* 1997;224(1):5-8.
216. Lotze M, Erb M, Flor H, Huelsman E. fMRI evaluation of somatotopic representation in human primary motor cortex. *Neuroimage.* 2000;5 Pt 1:473-481.
217. Moseley GL. Pain, brain imaging and physiotherapy--opportunity is knocking. *Manual therapy.* 2008;13(6):475-477.
218. Louw A, Puentedura EJ, Diener I, Peoples RR. Preoperative therapeutic neuroscience education for lumbar radiculopathy: a single-case fMRI report. *Physiother Theory Pract.* 2015;31(7):496-508.
219. Moseley GL. Widespread brain activity during an abdominal task markedly reduced after pain physiology education: fMRI evaluation of a single patient with chronic low back pain. *The Australian journal of physiotherapy.* 2005;51(1):49-52.
220. Flor H. *The image of pain.* Paper presented at: Annual scientific meeting of The Pain Society (Britain)2003; Glasgow, Scotland.
221. Louw A, Puentedura EJ. *Therapeutic Neuroscience Education.* Vol 1. Minneapolis, MN: OPTP; 2013.
222. Puentedura EJ, Louw A. A neuroscience approach to managing athletes with low back pain. *Physical therapy in sport: official journal of the Association of Chartered Physiotherapists in Sports Medicine.* 2012;13(3):123-133.
223. Richardson C, Hodges P, Hides J. *Therapeutic Exercise For Lumbopelvic Stabilization.* Second ed. London: Churchill Livingstone; 2004.
224. Moseley GL, Hodges PW. *Chronic pain and motor control.* In: Jull G, Boyling J, eds. Grieves Modern Manual Therapy of the Vertebral column. 4 ed. Edinburgh: Churchill-Livingstone; 2002.
225. Sapolsky RM. *Why Zebras Don't Get Ulcers.* New York: Freeman; 1994.
226. Luerding R, Weigand T, Bogdahn U, Schmidt-Wilcke T. Working memory performance is correlated with local brain morphology in the medial frontal and anterior cingulate cortex in fibromyalgia patients: structural correlates of pain-cognition interaction. *Brain: a journal of neurology.* 2008;131(Pt 12):3222-3231.
227. Louw A, Diener I, Butler DS, Puentedura EJ. The effect of neuroscience education on pain, disability, anxiety, and stress in chronic musculoskeletal pain. *Archives of physical medicine and rehabilitation.* 2011;92(12):2041-2056.
228. Catani M, Thiebaut de Schotten M. *A diffusion tensor imaging tractography atlas for virtual in vivo dissections. Cortex*; a journal devoted to the study of the nervous system and behavior. 2008;44(8):1105-1132.
229. Kregel J, Meeus M, Malfliet A, et al. Structural and functional brain abnormalities in chronic low back pain: A systematic review(). *Seminars in arthritis and rheumatism.* 2015;45(2):229-237.
230. Amit DJ, Brunel N, Tsodyks MV. Correlations of cortical Hebbian reverberations: theory versus experiment. *The Journal of neuroscience: the official journal of the Society for Neuroscience.* 1994;14(11 Pt 1):6435-6445.
231. Doidge N. *The Brain That Changes Itself.* New York: Penguin Books; 2007.
232. Girault JA, Greengard P. The neurobiology of dopamine signaling. *Arch Neurol.* 2004;61(5):641-644.
233. Moseley GL, Vlaeyen JWS. Beyond nociception: the imprecision hypothesis of chronic pain. *Pain.* 2015;156(1): 35-38.
234. Meulders A, Vansteenwegen D, Vlaeyen JW. The acquisition of fear of movement-related pain and associative learning: a novel pain-relevant human fear conditioning paradigm. *Pain.* 2011;152(11):2460-2469.
235. Meulders A, Vlaeyen JW. The acquisition and generalization of cued and contextual pain-related fear: an experimental study using a voluntary movement paradigm. *Pain.* 2013;154(2):272-282.
236. Karos K, Meulders A, Gatzounis R, Seelen HAM, Geers RPG, Vlaeyen JWS. Fear of pain changes movement: Motor behaviour following the acquisition of pain-related fear. *European journal of pain (London, England).* 2017;21(8):1432-1442.
237. Hodges PW. Pain and motor control: From the laboratory to rehabilitation. *J Electromyogr Kinesiol.* 2011;21(2):220-228.
238. Madden VJ, Harvie DS, Parker R, et al. Can Pain or Hyperalgesia Be a Classically Conditioned Response in Humans? A Systematic Review and Meta-Analysis. *Pain medicine.* 2016;17(6):1094-1111.

239. Moseley GL. Reconceptualising pain acording to modern pain sciences. *Physical Therapy Reviews.* 2007;12: 169-178.
240. Virani SN, Ferrari R, Russell AS. Physician resistance to the late whiplash syndrome. *J Rheumatol.* 2001;28(9):2096-2099.
241. Louw A, Puentedura EJ, Zimney K. A clinical contrast: physical therapists with low back pain treating patients with low back pain. *Physiotherapy theory and practice.* 2015;31(8):562-567.
242. Sloan TJ, Walsh DA. Explanatory and diagnostic labels and perceived prognosis in chronic low back pain. *Spine* (Phila Pa 1976). 2010;35(21):E1120-1125.
243. Carter R. *Mapping the Mind.* London: Weidenfeld and Nicholson; 1998.
244. Juan S. *The Odd Brain: Mysteries of our Weird & Wonderful Brains Explained.* New York: MJF Books; 2006.
245. Moseley GL. A pain neuromatrix approach to patients with chronic pain. *Manual therapy.* 2003;8(3):130-140.
246. Kendall NAS, Linton SJ, Main CJ. *Guide to assessing psychosocial yellow flags in acute low back pain: risk factors for long term disability and work loss.* Wellington: Accident Rehabilitation & Compensation Insurance Corporation of New Zealand and the National Health Committee; 1997.
247. Kendall N, Watson P. *Identifying psychosocial yellow flags and modifying management.* In: Gifford LS, ed. Topical Issues in Pain 2. Falmouth: CNS Press; 2000.
248. Tsang A, Von Korff M, Lee S, et al. Common chronic pain conditions in developed and developing countries: gender and age differences and comorbidity with depression-anxiety disorders. *The journal of pain: official journal of the American Pain Society.* 2008;9(10):883-891.
249. Paulson PE, Minoshima S, Morrow TJ, Casey KL. Gender differences in pain perception and patterns of cerebral activation during noxious heat stimulation in humans. *Pain.* 1998;76:223-229.
250. Derbyshire SW, Jones AK, Creed F, et al. Cerebral responses to noxious thermal stimulation in chronic low back pain patients and normal controls. *NeuroImage.* 2002;16(1):158-168.
251. Moulton EA, Keaser ML, Gullapalli RP, Maitra R, Greenspan JD. Sex differences in the cerebral BOLD signal response to painful heat stimuli. *American journal of physiology Regulatory, integrative and comparative physiology.* 2006;291(2):R257-267.
252. Myers CD, Riley JL, 3rd, Robinson ME. Psychosocial contributions to sex-correlated differences in pain. *The Clinical journal of pain.* 2003;19(4):225-232.
253. Myers CD, Robinson ME, Riley JL, 3rd, Sheffield D. Sex, gender, and blood pressure: contributions to experimental pain report. *Psychosomatic medicine.* 2001;63(4):545-550.
254. Sanford SD, Kersh BC, Thorn BE, Rich MA, Ward LC. Psychosocial mediators of sex differences in pain responsivity. *The journal of pain: official journal of the American Pain Society.* 2002;3(1):58-64.
255. Bates MS, Edwards TW, Anderson KO. Ethnocultural influences on variation in chronic pain perception. *Pain.* 1993;52:101-112.
256. Kapoor S, Shaw WS, Pransky G, Patterson W. Initial patient and clinician expectations of return to work after acute onset of work-related low back pain. *Journal of occupational and environmental medicine/ American College of Occupational and Environmental Medicine.* 2006;48(11): 1173-1180.
257. Buchbinder R, Jolley D. Effects of a media campaign on back beliefs is sustained 3 years after its cessation. *Spine.* 2005;30(11):1323-1330.
258. Buchbinder R, Jolley D, Wyatt M. 2001 Volvo Award Winner in Clinical Studies: Effects of a media campaign on back pain beliefs and its potential influence on management of low back pain in general practice. *Spine.* 2001;26(23):2535-2542.
259. Vossen HG, van Os J, Hermens H, Lousberg R. Evidence that trait-anxiety and trait-depression differentially moderate cortical processing of pain. *The Clinical journal of pain.* 2006;22(8): 725-729.
260. Morasco BJ, Lovejoy TI, Lu M, Turk DC, Lewis L, Dobscha SK. The relationship between PTSD and chronic pain: mediating role of coping strategies and depression. *Pain.* 2013;154(4):609-616.
261. Ledgerwood A, Boydstun AE. Sticky prospects: loss frames are cognitively stickier than gain frames. *J Exp Psychol Gen.* 2014;143(1):376-385.
262. Gran JT. The epidemiology of chronic generalized musculoskeletal pain. *Best Pract Res Clin Rheumatol.* 2003;17(4):547-561.
263. Teasell RW, Bombardier C. Employment-related factors in chronic pain and chronic pain disability. *The Clinical journal of pain.* 2001;17(4 Suppl):S39-45.

264. Murrell SA, Meeks S. Psychological, economic, and social mediators of the education-health relationship in older adults. *Journal of aging and health.* 2002;14(4):527-550.
265. Main CJ, Waddell G. Behavioral responses to examination. A reappraisal of the interpretation of "nonorganic signs". *Spine* (Phila Pa 1976). 1998;23(21):2367-2371.
266. Fishbain DA, Cole B, Cutler RB, Lewis J, Rosomoff HL, Rosomoff RS. A structured evidence-based review on the meaning of nonorganic physical signs: Waddell signs. *Pain medicine.* 2003;4(2): 141-181.
267. Fishbain DA, Cutler RB, Rosomoff HL, Rosomoff RS. Is there a relationship between nonorganic physical findings (Waddell signs) and secondary gain/ malingering? *The Clinical journal of pain.* 2004;20(6):399-408.
268. Moseley GL. Joining forces - combining cognition-targeted motor control training with group or individual pain physiology education: a successful treatment for chronic low back pain. *J Man Manip Therap.* 2003;11(2):88-94.
269. Kamper SJ, Apeldoorn AT, Chiarotto A, et al. Multidisciplinary biopsychosocial rehabilitation for chronic low back pain. *The Cochrane database of systematic reviews.* 2014;9:CD000963.
270. Nijs J, Mannerkorpi K, Descheemaeker F, Van Houdenhove B. Primary care physical therapy in people with fibromyalgia: opportunities and boundaries within a monodisciplinary setting. *Physical therapy.* 2010;90(12):1815-1822.
271. Sapolsky RM. *Why zebras don't get ulcers: an updated guide to stress, stress-related diseases, and coping.* New York: W.H. Freeman and Co; 1998.
272. Riva R, Mork PJ, Westgaard RH, Okkenhaug Johansen T, Lundberg U. Catecholamines and heart rate in female fibromyalgia patients. *Journal of psychosomatic research.* 2012;72(1): 51-57.
273. Larsson SE, Cai H, Zhang Q, Larsson R, Oberg PA. Microcirculation in the upper trapezius muscle during sustained shoulder load in healthy women--an endurance study using percutaneous laser-Doppler flowmetry and surface electromyography. *Eur J Appl Physiol Occup Physiol.* 1995;70(5):451-456.
274. Hodges PW, Richardson CA. Delayed postural contraction of transversus abdominis in low back pain associated with movement of the lower limb. *J Spinal Disord.* 1998;11(1):46-56.
275. Moseley GL. Impaired trunk muscle function in sub-acute neck pain: etiologic in the subsequent development of low back pain? *Manual therapy.* 2004;9(3):157-163.
276. Stephens R, Atkins J, Kingston A. Swearing as a response to pain. *Neuroreport.* 2009;20(12):1056-1060.
277. Koelwyn GJ, Wong LE, Kennedy MD, Eves ND. The effect of hypoxia and exercise on heart rate variability, immune response, and orthostatic stress. *Scandinavian journal of medicine & science in sports.* 2013;23(1):e1-8.
278. Bonaz BL, Bernstein CN. Brain-gut interactions in inflammatory bowel disease. *Gastroenterology.* 2013;144(1):36-49.
279. Louw A. *Why You Hurt: A Neuroscience Approach to Pain.* Minneapolis: OPTP; 2013.
280. Segal TY, Hindmarsh PC, Viner RM. Disturbed adrenal function in adolescents with chronic fatigue syndrome. *Journal of pediatric endocrinology & metabolism: JPEM.* 2005;18(3):295-301.
281. Geiss A, Rohleder N, Kirschbaum C, Steinbach K, Bauer HW, Anton F. Predicting the failure of disc surgery by a hypofunctional HPA axis: evidence from a prospective study on patients undergoing disc surgery. *Pain.* 2005;114(1-2): 104-117.
282. Van Houdenhove B, Van Den Eede F, Luyten P. Does hypothalamic-pituitary-adrenal axis hypofunction in chronic fatigue syndrome reflect a 'crash' in the stress system? *Medical hypotheses.* 2009;72(6):701-705.
283. Van Den Eede F, Moorkens G, Van Houdenhove B, Cosyns P, Claes SJ. Hypothalamic-pituitary-adrenal axis function in chronic fatigue syndrome. *Neuropsychobiology.* 2007;55(2):112-120.
284. Chervin RD, Teodorescu M, Kushwaha R, et al. Objective measures of disordered sleep in fibromyalgia. *J Rheumatol.* 2009;36(9):2009-2016.
285. Fabian LA, McGuire L, Page GG, Goodin BR, Edwards RR, Haythornthwaite J. The association of the cortisol awakening response with experimental pain ratings. *Psychoneuroendocrinology.* 2009;34(8): 1247-1251.
286. van de Ven M, Andressoo JO, Holcomb VB, et al. Adaptive stress response in segmental progeria resembles long-lived dwarfism and calorie restriction in mice. *PLoS genetics.* 2006;2(12):e192.

287. Mohs R, Mease P, Arnold LM, et al. The effect of duloxetine treatment on cognition in patients with fibromyalgia. *Psychosomatic medicine.* 2012;74(6):628-634.

288. Dinarello CA. Overview of cytokines and their role in pain. In: Watkins LR, Maier SF, eds. *Cytokines and Pain.* Basel: Birkhauser; 1999.

289. Matalka KZ. Neuroendocrine and cytokines-induced responses to minutes, hours, and days of mental stress. *Neuro endocrinology letters.* 2003;24(5):283-292.

290. Chapman CR, Tuckett RP, Song CW. Pain and stress in a systems perspective: reciprocal neural, endocrine, and immune interactions. *The journal of pain: official journal of the American Pain Society.* 2008;9(2):122-145.

291. Tada T. The immune system as a supersystem. *Annual review of immunology.* 1997;15:1-13.

292. Rodriguez-Pinto I, Agmon-Levin N, Howard A, Shoenfeld Y. Fibromyalgia and cytokines. *Immunology letters.* 2014;161(2):200-203.

293. Papadopoulos AS, Cleare AJ. Hypothalamic-pituitary-adrenal axis dysfunction in chronic fatigue syndrome. *Nature reviews Endocrinology.* 2012;8(1):22-32.

294. Halperin JJ. Chronic Lyme disease: misconceptions and challenges for patient management. *Infection and drug resistance.* 2015;8:119-128.

295. Barbara G, Stanghellini V, De Giorgio R, et al. Activated mast cells in proximity to colonic nerves correlate with abdominal pain in irritable bowel syndrome. *Gastroenterology.* 2004;126(3):693-702.

296. Holgate ST, Komaroff AL, Mangan D, Wessely S. Chronic fatigue syndrome: understanding a complex illness. *Nature reviews Neuroscience.* 2011;12(9):539-544.

297. Stasi C, Rosselli M, Bellini M, Laffi G, Milani S. Altered neuro-endocrine-immune pathways in the irritable bowel syndrome: the top-down and the bottom-up model. *Journal of gastroenterology.* 2012;47(11):1177-1185.

298. Meeus M, Ickmans K, Struyf F, et al. What is in a name? Comparing diagnostic criteria for chronic fatigue syndrome with or without fibromyalgia. *Clinical rheumatology.* 2014.

299. Millea PJ, Holloway RL. Treating fibromyalgia. *American family physician.* 2000;62(7):1575-1582, 1587.

300. Van Oosterwijck J, Meeus M, Paul L, et al. Pain physiology education improves health status and endogenous pain inhibition in fibromyalgia: a double-blind randomized controlled trial. *The Clinical journal of pain.* 2013;29(10):873-882.

301. Komaroff AL, Goldenberg D. The chronic fatigue syndrome: definition, current studies and lessons for fibromyalgia research. *The Journal of rheumatology Supplement.* 1989;19:23-27.

302. Sood R, Gracie DJ, Law GR, Ford AC. Systematic review with meta-analysis: the accuracy of diagnosing irritable bowel syndrome with symptoms, biomarkers and/or psychological markers. *Alimentary pharmacology & therapeutics.* 2015;42(5):491-503.

303. Endo Y, Shoji T, Fukudo S. Epidemiology of irritable bowel syndrome. *Annals of gastroenterology: quarterly publication of the Hellenic Society of Gastroenterology.* 2015;28(2):158-159.

304. Borgermans L, Goderis G, Vandevoorde J, Devroey D. Relevance of chronic lyme disease to family medicine as a complex multidimensional chronic disease construct: a systematic review. *International journal of family medicine.* 2014;2014:138016.

305. Bernardy K, Klose P, Busch AJ, Choy EH, Hauser W. Cognitive behavioural therapies for fibromyalgia. *The Cochrane database of systematic reviews.* 2013;9:CD009796.

306. Busch AJ, Barber KA, Overend TJ, Peloso PM, Schachter CL. Exercise for treating fibromyalgia syndrome. *The Cochrane database of systematic reviews.* 2007(4):CD003786.

307. Lunn MP, Hughes RA, Wiffen PJ. Duloxetine for treating painful neuropathy, chronic pain or fibromyalgia. *The Cochrane database of systematic reviews.* 2014;1:CD007115.

308. Larun L, Brurberg KG, Odgaard-Jensen J, Price JR. Exercise therapy for chronic fatigue syndrome. *The Cochrane database of systematic reviews.* 2015;2:CD003200.

309. Price JR, Mitchell E, Tidy E, Hunot V. Cognitive behaviour therapy for chronic fatigue syndrome in adults. *The Cochrane database of systematic reviews.* 2008(3):CD001027.

310. Huertas-Ceballos A, Logan S, Bennett C, Macarthur C. Psychosocial interventions for recurrent abdominal pain (RAP) and irritable bowel syndrome (IBS) in childhood. *The Cochrane database of systematic reviews.* 2008(1):CD003014.

311. Huertas-Ceballos A, Logan S, Bennett C, Macarthur C. Pharmacological interventions for recurrent abdominal pain (RAP) and irritable bowel syndrome (IBS) in childhood. *The Cochrane database of systematic reviews.* 2008(1):CD003017.
312. Wallace DJ. Is there a role for cytokine based therapies in fibromyalgia. *Current pharmaceutical design.* 2006;12(1): 17-22.
313. Parker AJ, Wessely S, Cleare AJ. The neuroendocrinology of chronic fatigue syndrome and fibromyalgia. *Psychological medicine.* 2001;31(8):1331-1345.
314. Bokic T, Storr M, Schicho R. Potential Causes and Present Pharmacotherapy of Irritable Bowel Syndrome: An Overview. *Pharmacology.* 2015;96(1-2):76-85.
315. Wand BM, Parkitny L, O'Connell NE, et al. Cortical changes in chronic low back pain: current state of the art and implications for clinical practice. *Manual therapy.* 2011;16(1):15-20.
316. Stavrinou ML, Della Penna S, Pizzella V, et al. Temporal dynamics of plastic changes in human primary somatosensory cortex after finger webbing. *Cerebral cortex.* 2007;17(9):2134-2142.
317. Flor H, Braun C, Elbert T, Birmbaumer N. Extensive reorganisation of primary somatosensory cortex in chronic back pain patients. *Neuroscience letters.* 1997;244:5-8.
318. Maihofner C, Handwerker HO, Neundorfer B, Birklein F. Patterns of cortical reorganization in complex regional pain syndrome. *Neurology.* 2003;61(12):1707-1715.
319. Moseley GL. I can't find it! Distorted body image and tactile dysfunction in patients with chronic back pain. *Pain.* 2008;140(1):239-243.
320. Lotze M, Moseley GL. Role of distorted body image in pain. *Curr Rheumatol Rep.* 2007;9(6):488-496.
321. Moseley GL. Distorted body image in complex regional pain syndrome. *Neurology.* 2005;65(5):773.
322. Flor H, Elbert T, Muhnickel W, Pantev C. Cortical reorganisation and phantom phenomena in congenital and traumatic upper-extremity amputees. *Experimental Brain Research.* 1998;119:205-212.
323. Schmidt-Wilcke T. Variations in brain volume and regional morphology associated with chronic pain. *Current rheumatology reports.* 2008;10(6): 467-474.
324. Schmidt-Wilcke T, Ganssbauer S, Neuner T, Bogdahn U, May A. Subtle grey matter changes between migraine patients and healthy controls. *Cephalalgia: an international journal of headache.* 2008; 28(1):1-4.
325. Apkarian AV, Sosa Y, Sonty S, et al. Chronic back pain is associated with decreased prefrontal and thalamic gray matter density. *The Journal of neuroscience: the official journal of the Society for Neuroscience.* 2004;24(46): 10410-10415.
326. Schmidt-Wilcke T, Leinisch E, Ganssbauer S, et al. Affective components and intensity of pain correlate with structural differences in gray matter in chronic back pain patients. *Pain.* 2006;125(1-2): 89-97.
327. Jull G, Sterling M, Kenardy J, Beller E. Does the presence of sensory hypersensitivity influence outcomes of physical rehabilitation for chronic whiplash?--A preliminary RCT. *Pain.* 2007;129(1-2):28-34.
328. Rodriguez-Raecke R, Niemeier A, Ihle K, Ruether W, May A. Brain gray matter decrease in chronic pain is the consequence and not the cause of pain. *The Journal of neuroscience: the official journal of the Society for Neuroscience.* 2009;29(44):13746-13750.
329. de Lange FP, Koers A, Kalkman JS, et al. Increase in prefrontal cortical volume following cognitive behavioural therapy in patients with chronic fatigue syndrome. *Brain: a journal of neurology.* 2008;131(Pt 8):2172-2180.
330. Seminowicz DA, Shpaner M, Keaser ML, et al. Cognitive-behavioral therapy increases prefrontal cortex gray matter in patients with chronic pain. *The journal of pain: official journal of the American Pain Society.* 2013;14(12):1573-1584.
331. Gwilym SE, Filippini N, Douaud G, Carr AJ, Tracey I. Thalamic atrophy associated with painful osteoarthritis of the hip is reversible after arthroplasty: a longitudinal voxel-based morphometric study. *Arthritis and rheumatism.* 2010;62(10):2930-2940.
332. Seminowicz DA, Wideman TH, Naso L, et al. Effective treatment of chronic low back pain in humans reverses abnormal brain anatomy and function. *The Journal of neuroscience: the official journal of the Society for Neuroscience.* 2011;31(20):7540-7550.

333. Lloyd D, Findlay G, Roberts N, Nurmikko T. Differences in low back pain behavior are reflected in the cerebral response to tactile stimulation of the lower back. *Spine.* 2008;33(12):1372-1377.
334. Moseley GL. Why do people with complex regional pain syndrome take longer to recognize their affected hand? *Neurology.* 2004;62(12):2182-2186.
335. Moseley GL, Sim DF, Henry ML, Souvlis T. Experimental hand pain delays recognition of the contralateral hand--evidence that acute and chronic pain have opposite effects on information processing? *Brain Res Cogn Brain Res.* 2005;25(1):188-194.
336. Moseley GF, Sim DF, Henry ML, Souvlis T. Experimental hand pain delays recognition of the contralateral hand - evidencde that acute and chronic pain have opposite effects on information processing *Cogn Brain Res.* 2005;25:188-194.
337. Catley MJ, Tabor A, Wand BM, Moseley GL. Assessing tactile acuity in rheumatology and musculoskeletal medicine--how reliable are two-point discrimination tests at the neck, hand, back and foot? *Rheumatology.* 2013;52(8):1454-1461.
338. Luomajoki H, Moseley GL. Tactile acuity and lumbopelvic motor control in patients with back pain and healthy controls. *British journal of sports medicine.* 2011;45(5):437-440.
339. Bray H, Moseley GL. Disrupted working body schema of the trunk in people with back pain. *British journal of sports medicine.* 2011;45(3):168-173.
340. von Piekartz H, Mohr G. Reduction of head and face pain by challenging lateralization and basic emotions: a proposal for future assessment and rehabilitation strategies. *The Journal of manual & manipulative therapy.* 2014;22(1):24-35.
341. von Piekartz H, Wallwork SB, Mohr G, Butler DS, Moseley GL. People with chronic facial pain perform worse than controls at a facial emotion recognition task, but it is not all about the emotion. *Journal of oral rehabilitation.* 2015;42(4):243-250.
342. Louw A. Treating the brain in chronic pain. In: C FdlP, J C, Dommerholt J, eds. *Manual Therapy for Musculoskeletal Pain Syndromes.* Vol 1. London: Churchill Livingston; 2015.
343. Meugnot A, Almecija Y, Toussaint L. The embodied nature of motor imagery processes highlighted by short-term limb immobilization. *Experimental psychology.* 2014;61(3):180-186.
344. Meugnot A, Agbangla NF, Toussaint L. Selective impairment of sensorimotor representations following short-term upper-limb immobilization. *Quarterly journal of experimental psychology.* 2016;69(9):1842-1850.
345. Moseley GL, Gallagher L, Gallace A. Neglect-like tactile dysfunction in chronic back pain. *Neurology.* 2012;79(4):327-332.
346. Moseley GL, Olthof N, Venema A, et al. *Psychologically induced cooling of a specific body part caused by the illusory ownership of an artificial counterpart.* Proceedings of the National Academy of Sciences of the United States of America. 2008;105(35):13169-13173.
347. Watkins LR, Hutchinson MR, Milligan ED, Maier SF. "Listening" and "talking" to neurons: implications of immune activation for pain control and increasing the efficacy of opioids. *Brain Res Rev.* 2007;56(1):148-169.

Chapter 4

Teaching People About Pain

4.1: Introduction

What patients think heavily impacts their pain experience as well as their recovery.[1,2] It is now well established that fear-avoidance beliefs and pain catastrophization are powerfully linked to a person's pain experience (Chapter 1).[2] The fact that beliefs impact pain drives the notion that education is a vital component of any treatment plan.[3] Education is therapy. Unfortunately, traditional education regarding pain has often centered on a biomedical explanation for pain, which has shown limited efficacy, and might even increase fear and anxiety.[4-6] In contrast to the biomedical model, emerging research has shown patients desire more education about pain, including why they hurt, why pain persists and what can be done for it.[3,7,8] All of these factors drove the evolution of PNE, a deliberate attempt to help people in pain understand the biological and physiological processes involved in their pain experience.[9,10] The emergence of the PNE concept led to increased research efforts and a rapidly expanding evidence base (Chapter 2). With a clear agenda set to teach patients more about pain, attention shifted to updating clinicians about pain first, prior to taking the knowledge to patients.[11] With various pain models outdated and emerging pain constructs such as ion channel expression, nociception versus pain, pain neuromatrix, neuroimmune responses, neuroplasticity and others becoming better understood, clinicians are becoming better equipped with pain science, in essence fulfilling the "iceberg" effect of being very knowledgeable about pain (Chapter 3). Thus, the scene is now set to take the advanced neuroscience concepts from Chapter 3 and teach patients more about pain.[12,13]

4.2: Building the Curriculum

Each person's pain experience is unique, and it is argued every patient needs an individualized plan of care.[14] Theoretically this sounds good, but in the larger scheme of more than 100 million Americans and approximately one in four people in the world experiencing some type of chronic pain,[15,16] it is critical that a pain curriculum be developed with the intent to educate the masses, and then potentially adapted as needed to specific individuals.[17] This implies a standardized approach that is accessible, affordable, easy-to-understand and able to be applied by a variety of healthcare professionals and even healthcare in general, versus a single profession. Current PNE best-evidence calls for:

- **Use of metaphors, examples and stories:**[12,13,18] Through the ages information has been passed from generation to generation via stories. The best method for teaching people about pain is to take the complex neuroscience information (Chapter 3) and use stories, metaphors and examples to convey the message to patients. This form of PNE has been shown to be very successful.

- **Pictures:**[12,13,18] As the old saying goes, "A picture is worth a thousand words." Human beings are visually oriented and pictures are extremely important when it comes to education. The negative effect of pictures has already been explored (Chapter 2), whereby pictures with provocative images and words have been shown to increase a pain experience.[6] In contrast, images also have the potential to help ease fears and pain. PNE studies use a variety of images to further explain various pain concepts, and it is believed that the combination of metaphors, examples and pictures is a powerful tool in shifting pain behaviors.

- **5th grade level:** Various learning theory studies have shown that children can be exposed to and comprehend more complex topics around 5-6th grade.[19,20] This would imply a simplification of the advanced neuroscience material, which once again is achieved with the blending of metaphors, examples, stories and images. It's interesting to note that a recent clinical survey of the use of PNE revealed it has been delivered to an age range of four to 104 years old.[12] Additionally, in a recent study, 5th through 8th grade middle school students in the US were taught PNE. Not only were 5th grade students able to comprehend PNE, but they outscored 6th, 7th and 8th grade students on the NPQ.[21] This is a key element – many clinicians believe patients might not be able to understand the "complex" neuroscience of pain, but this is not the case.[22]

- **Curriculum:** What information should be included in the pain curriculum? The good news is that this aspect of PNE is well understood:

    - Two systematic reviews of PNE that not only delved into the evidence for PNE, but explored the content and educational delivery methods of PNE, have already provided clinicians with a script as a means to develop a PNE curriculum.[23,24] By taking the list of topics showcased in the systematic reviews, clinicians should aim to address the various issues with patients.

    - The NPQ and rNPQ can be used as a guideline. In fact, this strategy has been used in previous PNE studies.[22,25]

    - It can also be argued that, for a more comprehensive curriculum, a combination of the listing by the systematic review and the content of the NPQ and rNPQ can be combined to develop what is likely the curriculum that should be used when considering PNE (Table 4.1 on the following page).

Table 4.1: PNE curriculum based on systematic reviews, the NPQ and rNPQ.

Curriculum
• Neurophysiology of pain[26-38]
• No reference of anatomic or patho-anatomic models[26-28,36]*
• No discussion of the emotional or behavioral aspects of pain[27,28]**
• Nociception and nociceptive pathways[27,28,32-36,38]
• Synapses[27,28]
• Action potentials[35]
• Spinal inhibition and facilitation[27,28,31-33]
• Peripheral sensitization[27,28,31-35]
• Central sensitization[27,28,31-35,38]
• Plasticity of the nervous system[27,28,32,33,35]

*The listing in Table 4.1 is based on original PNE research papers.[26-28,36] Given the power of the Cartesian model and its impact on the beliefs of patients struggling with pain, it is proposed that part of the PNE session should in fact educate, or de-educate patients regarding their anatomical or patho-anatomical views. This concept of de-educate to re-educate[39] is important, as a recent survey study of therapists using PNE in the clinic showed that the greatest barrier they encounter to successfully delivering PNE is a "belief that something is definitely wrong in the tissues" and the belief that "pain is due to injury or disease."[12]

**In the original description of PNE it was stated there were no discussions of the emotional and/or behavioral aspects of pain.[27,28] However, upon review of Chapter 3, it is clear that emotions and behaviors are part of the pain experience. Emotions can and do initiate and maintain a pain experience. It can be argued that if it is fundamental for a patient to understand why they hurt then an explanation is needed to showcase how emotions might not only initiate a pain experience but increase a pain experience. Additionally, it is important to appreciate the perspective that the "loss of pain" is not the ultimate goal of PNE, but rather a behavioral shift of moving and functioning "despite the pain."[11,12] If this is the case, then behavioral aspects related to rehabilitation warrant discussion in the PNE curriculum. The "plus" of PNE+, which refers to the various physical treatments that accompany PNE, is the behavioral aspect of the PNE+ program,[12,26,27,29-31,36-38,40,41] while the reconceptualization of pain refers to the cognitive restructuring. The combination of these two aspects are more powerful than either done individually, and movement and function are tied to various strategies to ease pain.[24]

4.3: Prior to PNE

It is imperative to realize there are various steps that precede the sharing of the PNE story with a patient. Chapter 5 describes in detail the clinical implementation of PNE, including important aspects such as thoroughly screening for red flags, subjective questioning and physical examinations. Obviously, in a clinical scenario, a clinician will first apply due diligence by screening for any medical etiologies and performing a review of systems.[42,43] This will be followed by a thorough interview, keeping in mind the various complexities of pain and expanding beyond the traditional interview questions.[44] The subjective examination will be followed by the physical examination as a means to further screen for red flags, confirm or negate the working hypothesis the clinician developed in the subjective examination, assess ability and willingness to move, etc.[3,45] In chronic pain, the physical examination will more than likely be quite challenging if the patient exhibits allodynia and/ or hyperalgesia.[46] Once these steps have been completed and a decision is made that PNE might be appropriate (Chapter 5),[47] a clinician will pick the appropriate story or metaphor to explain a certain aspect of their pain experience (section 4.4).[18] This screening and decision-making process prior to delivering PNE will be covered extensively in Chapter 5. Section 4.4 aims to showcase how the complex pain science material covered in Chapter 3 can be put into simple metaphors, examples and stories, accompanied by pictures.

4.4: Pain Metaphors, Examples and Images

It cannot be stressed enough that clinicians need to carefully consider the language they use with patients. Modern healthcare education has become a display of knowledge. The overwhelming evidence supports the notion of taking complex issues and making them easy to understand. What follows in this section is a series of metaphors, examples, stories and images a clinician might aim to use with a patient trying to explain a variety of "pain issues." Think of the PNE metaphors/stories as a series of available techniques. Through studying, practice and experience, clinicians will soon recognize which story works best for which situation, clinical issue and patient (Table 4.2 on the following page). This section aims to provide some guidance based on various studies where these stories have been used, expert opinion, feedback from clinicians using them on a daily basis, and patients who have been exposed to PNE. In some cases, a little knowledge of nerves, how they work and become sensitive, and how to calm them might be enough to help ease pain and fear in a patient with lumbar radiculopathy. In another case, a very detailed PNE session lasting several sessions might be needed to explain various issues the patient is complaining about, or it might even be necessary to repeat the same story for deeper comprehension. The explanations are thus not necessarily in a specific order. The education can start at any point and is determined by the patient's case as well as the clinician's experience and intuition. What follows is a PNE curriculum that has been designed and used in various studies – as a whole, or parts of it.[12,18,21,48-51]

Table 4.2: Example of matching PNE[48] to various common clinical signs and symptoms.

Signs and Symptoms	Sensitive Nerves	Nerve Sensors	Nosy Neighbors
Hyperalgesia	✔	✔	✔
Allodynia	✔	✔	✔
Spreading pain			✔
Pain sensitivity to cold and stress	✔	✔	
Immune responses		✔	✔
Inflammatory responses		✔	✔
Altered brain function responses (mental fog, depression, mental fatigue, memory loss, irritability/mood swings, weight gain, temperature regulation)			
Neuroplasticity – altered maps			
Neuroplasticity – hope for change	✔	✔	✔
Emotions and pain		✔	
Stress, anxiety and fear	✔	✔	✔
Tissue issues	✔	✔	✔
Past treatment issues	✔	✔	✔
Swelling issues			✔
Decreased function issues	✔	✔	✔
Movement, exercise, pacing and graded exposure issues	✔	✔	
Physical fatigue and sore muscle issues		✔	
Sleep issues			
Food and GI issues	✔	✔	

Calming Nerves	Pain and the Brain	Brain's Pain Map	Body Inc.'s CEO	Lions and Stress	Tissue Issues	Neurogenic Inflammation	The Brain's Body Maps	Emotions and Pain
✔	✔	✔	✔		✔	✔	✔	✔
✔	✔	✔	✔		✔	✔	✔	✔
		✔	✔			✔		✔
✔								
✔				✔		✔		✔
✔				✔	✔	✔		
	✔	✔	✔	✔			✔	✔
	✔	✔	✔	✔	✔		✔	
✔		✔	✔	✔	✔		✔	
✔	✔	✔		✔	✔	✔		✔
✔	✔	✔	✔	✔	✔	✔		✔
✔		✔	✔	✔	✔	✔	✔	✔
✔		✔	✔	✔	✔	✔	✔	✔
		✔		✔	✔	✔	✔	
✔		✔		✔	✔	✔	✔	✔
✔		✔		✔	✔	✔	✔	✔
✔				✔				
✔			✔	✔				✔
✔				✔				✔

Authors' Disclaimer

Even though the authors of this textbook have been at the forefront of PNE research, including the development of and testing of various PNE stories and metaphors, many of the stories might seem quite familiar to PNE students. Collectively, the authors have spent a significant amount of time studying, teaching and being exposed to many PNE stories by well-known therapists including Louis Gifford, David Butler and Lorimer Moseley. The versions of the stories might be different; original stories adapted for certain clinical scenarios or regions of the world, etc. It is not the intent to misrepresent the various stories or imply they are unique to the authors of this book. By virtue of the years of collaboration, some stories might sound familiar. For example, Butler, Moseley[52] and Gifford[53] have mentioned the "Toblerone®" story in their recent writings. Furthermore, the authors' exposure to postgraduate training in pain science (certifications, fellowships and residencies) as well as guiding PhD students have exposed them to new metaphors, examples and stories, or alternative versions of original stories. Students were asked to submit these for inclusion and the sections that follow include several of these with proper recognition of the contributors. Please note that in the sections that follow, you might see different versions of a similar story and some of it might seem redundant – this is purposefully designed in such a format. Patients are obviously very unique and by giving the clinician different versions of a similar theme, they might be more inclined to use a certain version for a man or a woman (car dashboard), military background (Pearl Harbor), or might be a certain time of the year (Christmas lights). The following stories are not meant to be an exhaustive list, but a foundational framework and beginning for a clinician to start to build their PNE repertoire to help the patient in front of them understand better how pain works.

4.4.1: Sensitive Nerves

It is well established that most tissues in the human body heal within three to six months. Therefore, persistent pain is more likely to be due to changes in the central nervous system and brain. During an injury or emotional response, the body's nervous system activates, increasing its state of alert; in some people, the nervous system remains extra sensitized despite tissue healing. The extra sensitization (peripheral and central sensitization) impacts function considerably. When pain limits movement and function, patients might think "something is wrong." Giving patients a different paradigm for pain limiting their function (sensitive nerves versus tissue injury) is a powerful way to get patients to reengage in activity, movement and exercise.

This story covers issues regarding:

- Peripheral neuropathic pain
- Peripheral nerve sensitization
- Central sensitization
- Hyperalgesia
- Allodynia

There are many different metaphors, examples and stories we can use to explain an extra sensitive nervous system to a patient. This metaphor is likely very important as a sensitized nervous system is likely present in anyone experiencing pain. We offer six examples to illustrate the concept of a sensitized nervous system:

- Stepping on a nail
- House alarm
- Sunburn
- Pearl Harbor
- Airport security and 9/11
- Christmas trees

4.4.1.A: **Sensitive nerves – stepping on a nail**

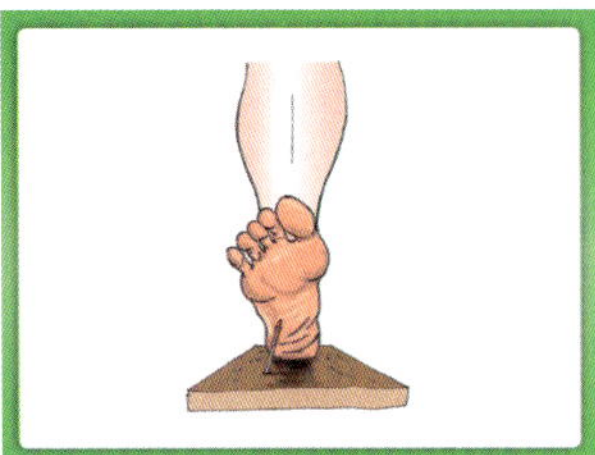

- If you step on a rusted nail, would you want to know about it?
- Why?
  - Get help
  - Get a tetanus shot
  - Take the nail out
  - Be careful of walking barefoot where there might be nails
- How do you know there is a nail in your foot?
- The message travels from the foot to the spinal cord, then on to the brain.
- The brain produces pain to grab your attention and get you to take care of the problem.

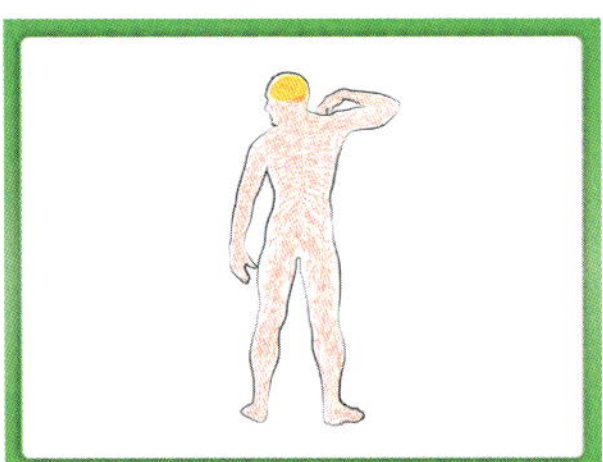

- This is the body's nervous system.
- It contains 400 individual nerves, totaling 45 miles (or 72 kilometers for the metric people).
- All the nerves are connected like an information superhighway.

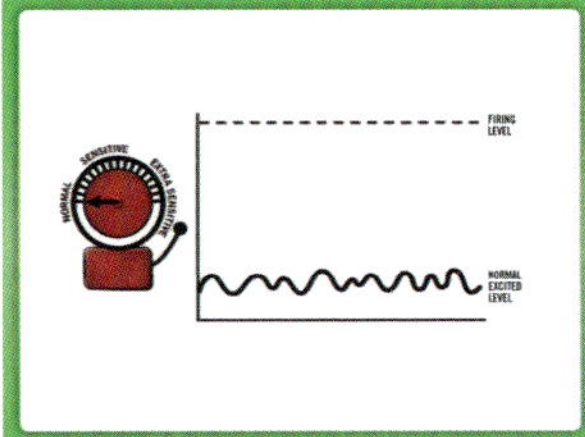

- All 400 nerves have a little bit of electricity flowing through them.
- This is normal and shows you are alive.
- Nerves are like our alarm systems, designed to send us danger messages when there is a threat, such as stepping on a rusted nail.

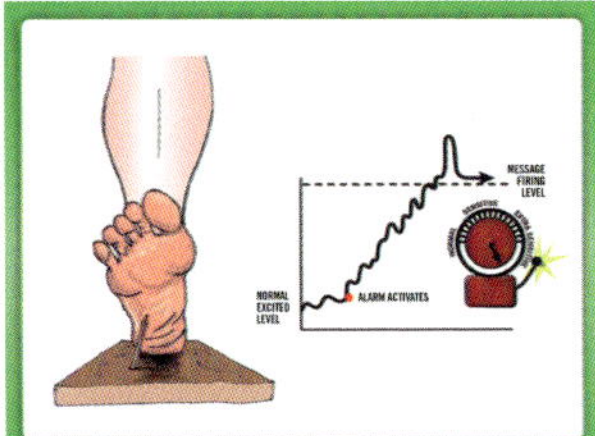

- So, when you step on a rusted nail, the alarm in your foot goes off.
- The alarm sends a "danger" message to your brain.
- The brain produces pain to grab your attention and get you to take care of the problem.

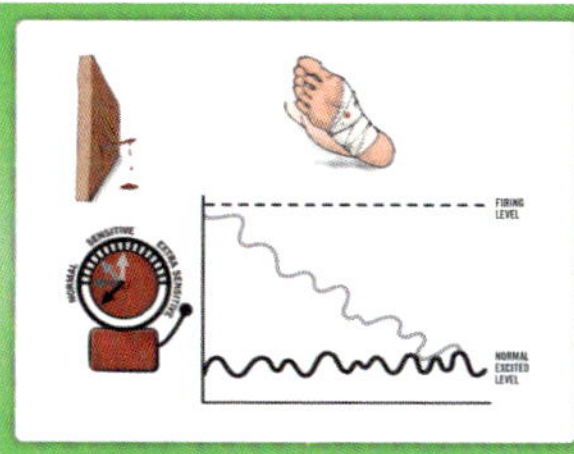

- Once you take the nail out, the alarm should go back down.
- The alarm goes down slowly.
- You will likely feel discomfort or pain in the foot for a day or two.
- This is normal.
- Once the alarm is back to its normal level, it is ready for the next danger.

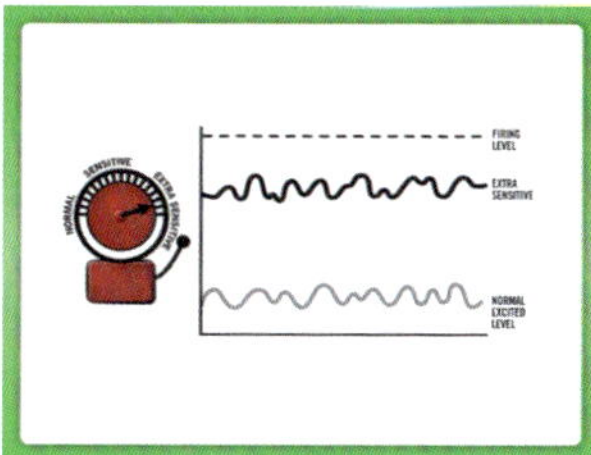

- This is key: In approximately one in four people, the alarm does not go back down.
- The alarm (nervous system) stays extra sensitive.
- If pain lasts beyond the normal healing time, it is likely due to an extra-sensitive alarm.
- Your extra-sensitive nervous system might be a big part of your pain, limited movement and sensitivity.

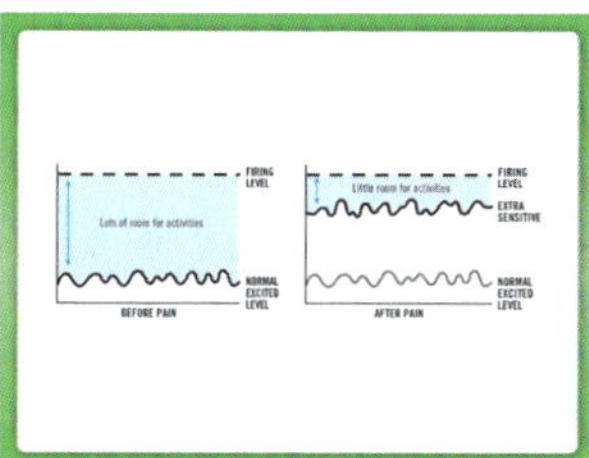

- An extra-sensitive alarm system can impact your life considerably.
- In the days before pain, you had lots of room for movement and activities without causing pain.
- Since you developed pain, it takes far less activity or movement before you experience pain.
- The limited activity and movement is not necessarily due to injury or tissue damage but an extra-sensitive alarm system.

- Why did your alarm system stay extra sensitive?
- Everything you have gone through during your pain experience can contribute to keeping the alarm system extra sensitive. For example:
  - Dealing with pain every day adds stress and can cause issues at home or work.
  - Treatments are not working; otherwise you would not be here.
  - You have been given several different explanations for your pain, which causes confusion.
- As long as you are stressed, confused, afraid, etc., your alarm is likely to remain extra sensitive.

4.4.1.B: **Sensitive nerves – house alarm**

- At your house, there is an alarm system.
- The alarm system is there to monitor anything that might threaten your safety.
- How do we set off the alarm at your house?

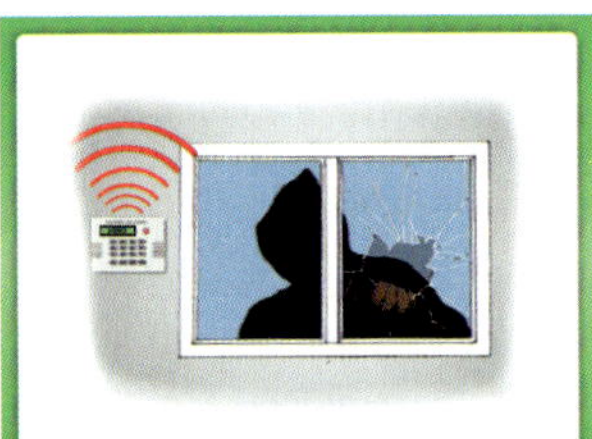

- To set off the alarm, someone must kick in the door or break the window.
- Once the door is kicked in or the window is broken, the alarm goes off.
- The main job of the alarm is to warn you of danger.

- When the alarm goes off and you wake up, what do you do?
- You likely call the police – who come and investigate.

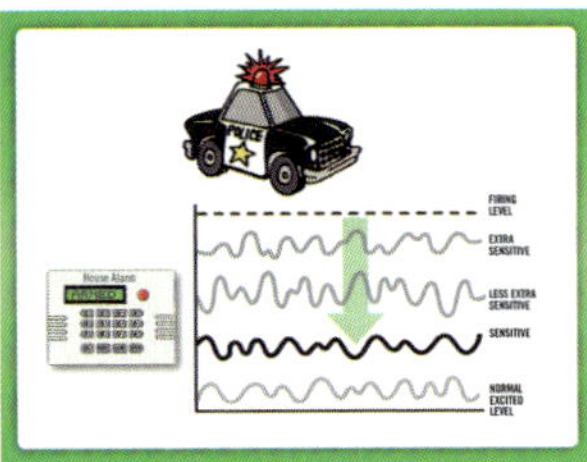

- Once the police make sure all is well (robber ran away), the alarm system is turned down, set at its normal level and ready for another potential danger – another break-in, for example.
- It is therefore a normal expectation that once danger has been assessed and eliminated, the alarm system will turn back down to its normal resting level.

- Some people, however, do not respond well to break-ins.
- The alarm woke them; there is a lot of stress and uncertainty; probably worries about insurance rates, etc.
- Additionally, it is also quite normal to be extra worried that this might happen again.

- With the increased worries, it might seem quite normal to turn the alarm down, but not all the way, thus leaving the house with an extra sensitive alarm.
- This new setting might indeed be more likely to activate if a window is broken or a door kicked in, but it might also allow the alarm to go off for unnecessary things, such as a leaf blowing by the window.
- This elevated alarm setting will likely be fine for a day or two after the break-in, but will make life difficult over time. Any time a leaf blows by...*ding-ding-ding*.... the alarm goes off.

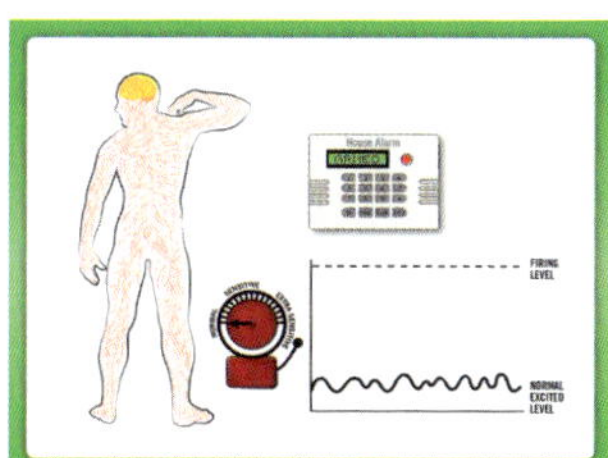

- The same issue with house alarms also occurs in human beings.
- The body has a living, breathing alarm system called the nervous system.
- It constantly monitors for threats such as an injury, stepping on a nail, surgery or even emotional stress.
- This is normal and occurs in every person.

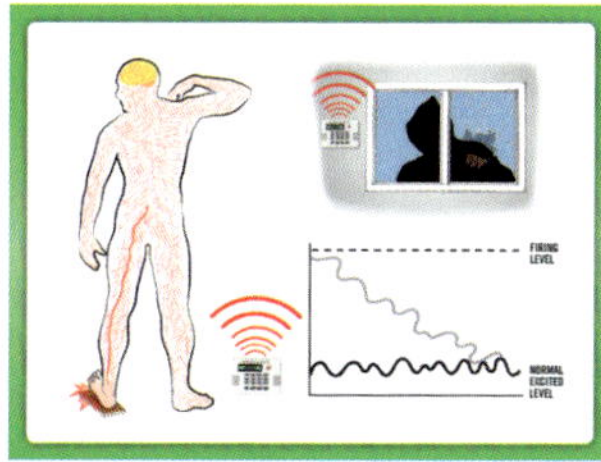

- When a threat comes along, the alarm is activated.
- Our alarm sends a message to the brain, which in turn makes us take care of the issue.
- For example, if you step on a nail, the danger message is sent to the brain so you can take action.
- This is normal and there to protect us.

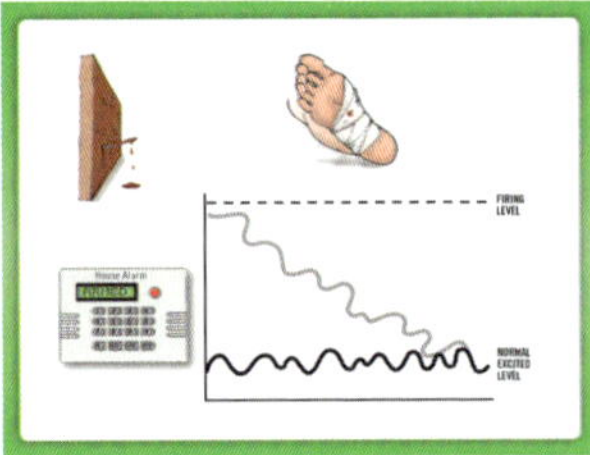

- Once the threat is eliminated, the alarm is gradually turned down and we can go on with our life.

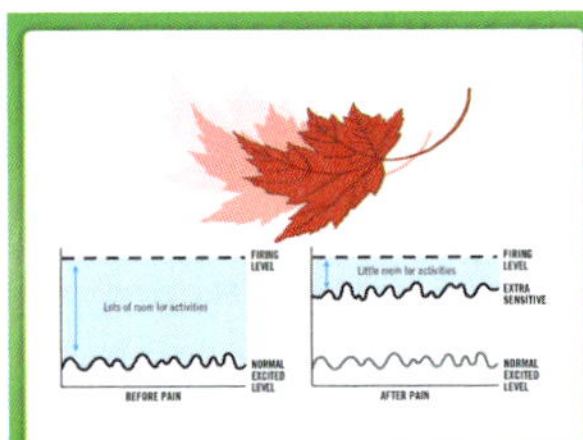

- In some people, however, the alarm is triggered by an event such as an injury, surgery, emotional time in life or irritated tissues with some inflammation, but it never calms down.
- As with the leaf example, an extra sensitive alarm system will significantly impact your ability to do things you were able to do before.
- A big reason why pain persists is an extra sensitive alarm system, even when tissues have healed.

- Why do human alarm systems stay extra sensitive?
- Everything people go through during their pain experience keeps the alarm system extra sensitive. For example:
  - Dealing with pain every day adds stress and can cause issues at home or work.
  - Treatments are not working; otherwise you would not be here.
  - You have been given several different explanations for your pain, which causes confusion.
- As long as you are stressed, confused, afraid, etc., your alarm is likely to remain extra sensitive.

4.4.1.C: **Sensitive nerves – sunburn**

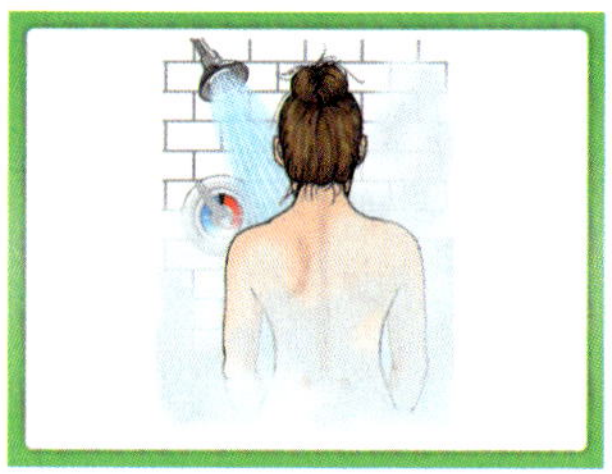

- For just a moment, imagine yourself in a "perfect" shower.
- It's a little cool outside and your muscles are a little sore and tired from a hard day's work.
- You set your shower at the perfect setting, feel the warm water flow over your body and you can feel the energy returning to your body.
- Boy, there are not many things in life as simple and yet so satisfying as a nice hot shower.

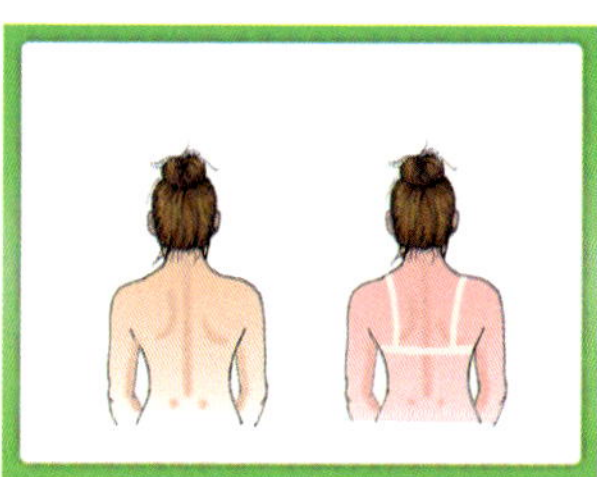

- Now imagine a sunburn.
- Just about everyone in this world has had a sunburn.
- Can you remember how you felt? Very tender and sore and likely even a little stupid since "you know better."
- By the way, the sunburn protected you, so although it's not fun, it is normal and without it's protection, we might hurt ourselves.

- With your sunburn, now imagine taking a shower.
- Without thinking, you set the shower at your normal level, expecting the same, super relaxing and rejuvenating shower.
- What happens?
- The "typical" shower setting you have become so used to is…too hot!

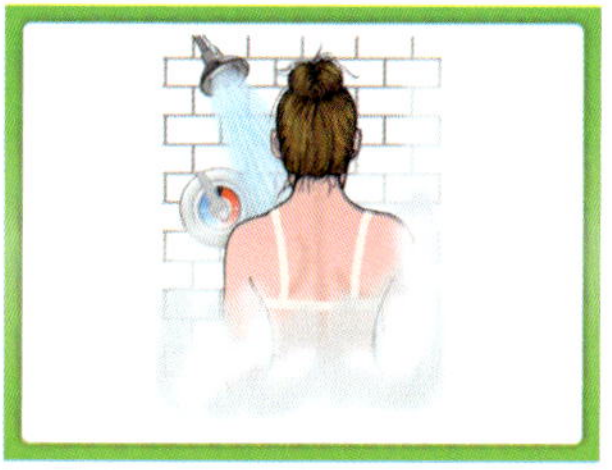

- With the sunburn, you need to turn the dial down.
- This allows you to take a shower even after a sunburn.

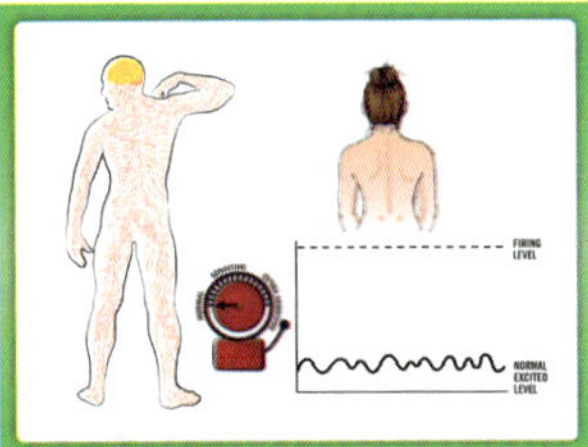

- To deal with things such as sunburn, our body needs an alarm system to protect us.
- Luckily, the body does have an alarm system – the nervous system.
- When life is good, the alarm system is relaxed and at a resting level.
- This would be the case for your skin with no sunburn.

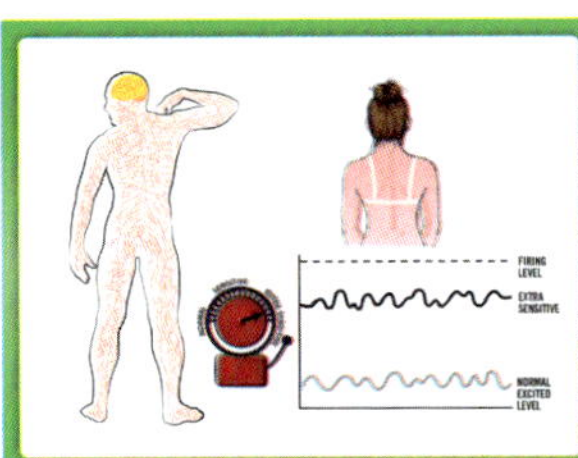

- In the case of the sunburn, the alarm system ramps up to protect you, influencing you to stay out of the sun for a while so you can recover.
- This is normal and occurs in everyone.
- With this extra sensitive alarm system, there is a much lower threshold.
- Before the sunburn you could easily handle pressure, touch or even a certain amount of warm water from the shower.
- Since the sunburn, less touch can be tolerated and water needs to be much cooler to tolerate.

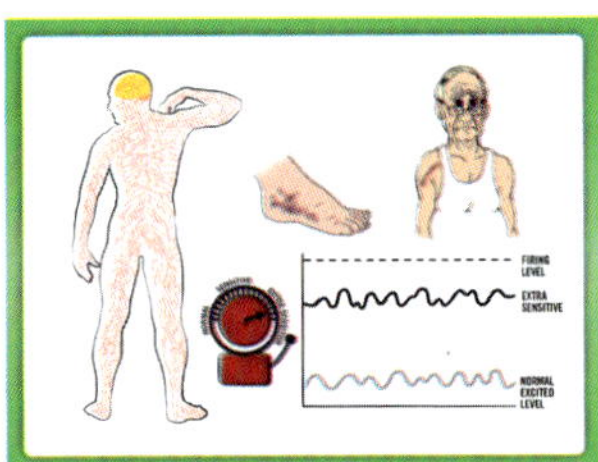

- As with the sunburn, the same situation occurs when other tissues in the body are injured, for example an ankle sprain or shoulder surgery.
- Following these events, the body's alarm system is ramped up.
- This is normal and aims to protect the area.
- For example, it's probably not a good idea to run a marathon on a sprained ankle or chop wood immediately after shoulder surgery.
- The sensitive alarm system is there to protect you.

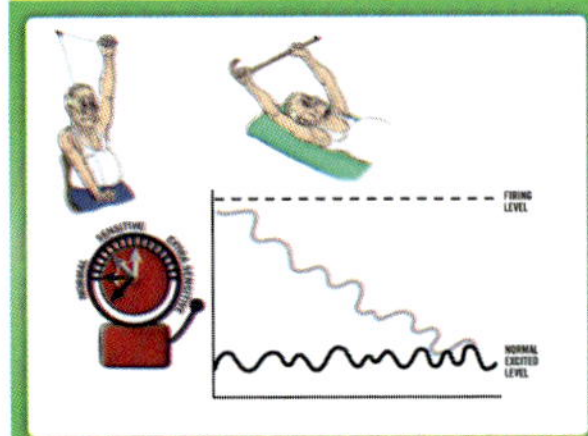

- Luckily tissues heal, just like the sunburn.
- Furthermore, "motion is lotion" and scientists have shown us movement, little and often, actually calms down the human alarm system.
- Pain felt with movement is, to a great extent, due to an extra sensitive alarm system and it's best to remind yourself:
  – Sore but safe
  – Hurt does not equal harm

4.4.1.D: **Sensitive nerves – Pearl Harbor (Timothy Benedict, PT, DPT)**

- In the military, radars are used to spot potential threats.
- Depending on the information on the screen, action might or might not be taken.

- Are you familiar with the history of the attack at Pearl Harbor?
- At 7am on December 7th, 1941, an army radar operator spotted a large group of airplanes 100 miles north of Pearl Harbor on his radar screen.
- This information was relayed to his headquarters.

- When he called his headquarters to report this, they reviewed the information about known flights in the area.
- Headquarters determined there was no threat, and the operator was told to "forget about it."
- The threat level was low.
- We all know what happened because of that decision.

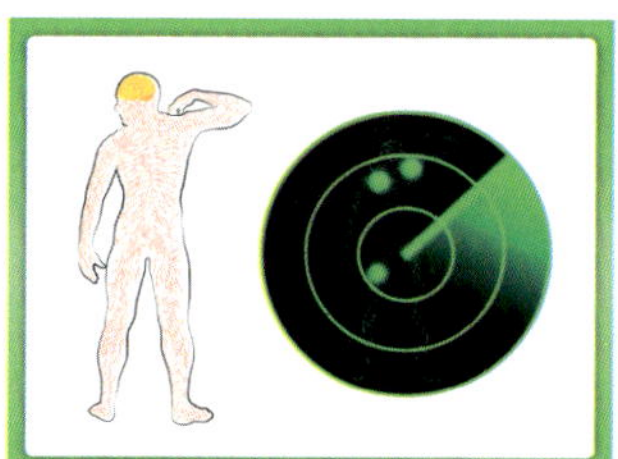

- What does that have to do with your pain?
- Just like a radar, our body has a system that scans for threats – it's called the nervous system.
- When there's a threat, it's detected and a response follows.

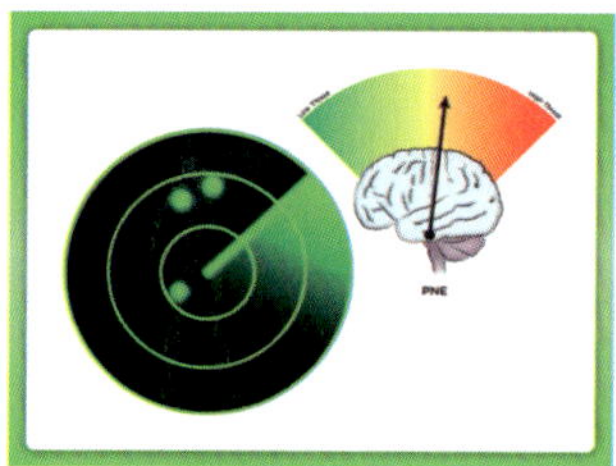

- When you have an accident, injury, surgery or even an emotional time in your life, the "living radar" – your nervous system – will detect the threat.
- Information will then be passed onto the command center – the brain – for interpretation.
- If the threat is low, little to no action is taken.
- When threat is high, action will be taken to protect you; increased pain, increased heart rate, muscle guarding, etc.

- An example might be a car accident.
- When someone hurts their neck in a car accident, the radar detects it, passes the information onto the brain, and many different responses follow:
  - Pain is produced to protect
  - Muscle guarding
  - Increased stress
  - Increased fear
  - Heart racing
  - Etc.
- This is normal and expected.

- Back to Pearl Harbor.
- Once the attack happened, what do you think happened for days, weeks and months after the attack, when a plane was detected on the radar?
- Surely both the radar operators and those at headquarters remembered what had happened, learned from it, and were more vigilant.
- Defenses went up much quicker than before.

- The same happens to people in pain.
- After an injury or surgery, the warning system will slowly but surely calm down, and the radar resumes normal function.
- The system, however, remembers and learns from the previous threat; that car accident, for example.
- Now, if any threat resembling the accident occurs (driving in similar weather conditions, or past the scene of the accident, or even just getting in the car), the system might ready itself to act rapidly.

- It's not surprising that certain triggers can initiate a pain experience, but that doesn't mean something is wrong with the tissues.
- It just means the radar, its operator, and headquarters have become very vigilant.
- Fortunately, the highly responsive system can be re-trained and re-calibrated to turn down the intensity of responses – pain, muscle guarding, etc.

4.4.1.E: **Sensitive nerves – airport security and 9/11**

- Can you remember the "good old days" of flying before 9/11?
- In those days you:
  - Could carry just about anything onto a plane
  - Get there in the nick of time to make the flight
  - Have no security checking you before the flight
  - Could have your whole family escort you to the gate and see you off
- Boy, what a time…
- This all changed after 9/11.

- After 9/11 we now have to:
  - Be at the airport at least two hours in advance
  - Limit fluids taken on board
  - Go through stringent security
  - Say goodbye to family and friends before entering security
  - Be available for additional screening
- What brought this about? Increased threat.

- Airport security monitors threats and sets threat levels all the time.
- Depending on the current threat level – be it red, orange, yellow or green – decisions are made to slacken or tighten security.
- For example, when there have been no terror attacks or threats, the threat level is lowered and, for the frequent traveler, it's quite clear.
- There is typically a lower stress level at security.
- There is less activity and security agents are more relaxed.

- What happens when there is increased risk of an attack or…. a recent attack occurred?
  - The threat level is changed from yellow to red
  - More security at the airport
  - More stringent security
  - EVERYTHING is checked
  - Security and security dogs are all over the airport sniffing around for threats
  - Everyone is more anxious and nervous

- If security continues at "super high levels" and scrutinizes and over-analyzes everything all the time, the airport will grind to a halt – people cannot make flights, pilots and flight crews cannot get to their planes, etc.
- It would thus make sense to increase threat; react, investigate and, once it's determined the threat level is not that high, to turn down the response.
- To have security ramped up every now and then seems logical, but there must be a balance throughout the year.

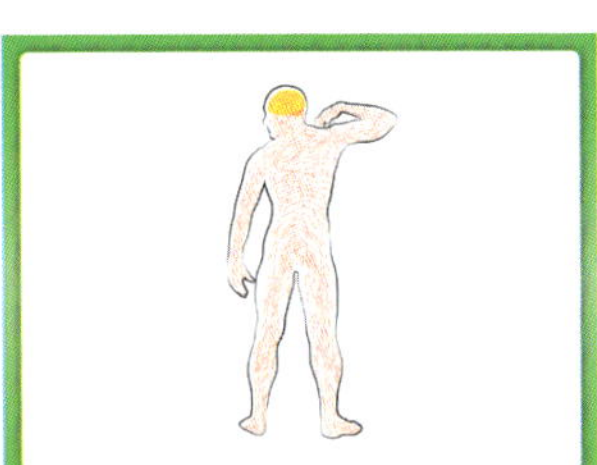

- The same airport process occurs in the human body.
- The body has a living, breathing security outfit monitoring for threats; the nervous system.
- The human body contains 400 individual nerves, totaling 45 miles or 72 kilometers for the metric people.

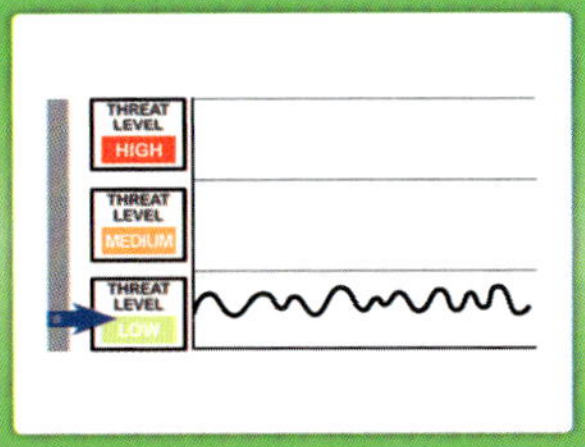

- All 400 nerves in the human body have a little bit of electricity flowing through them.
- This is normal and shows you're alive or... better yet, that there is a security team and it's doing its job.
- Nerves are like our alarm systems, designed to send us danger messages when there is a threat, such as stepping on a rusted nail.
- As long as there is no threat, the system is relaxed and all bodily systems go about their regular business.

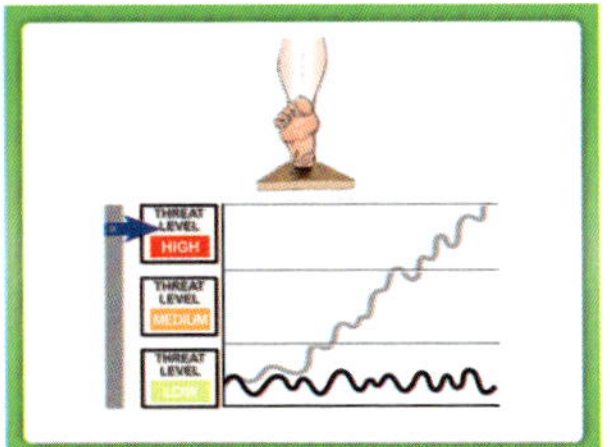

- So, when you step on a rusted nail, the alarm in your foot goes off.
- The alarm sends a danger message to your brain.
- The brain produces pain to grab your attention and get you to take care of the problem.
- In this scenario, threat level is raised and there is a response: Pain is produced to take care of the threat... the rusted nail.

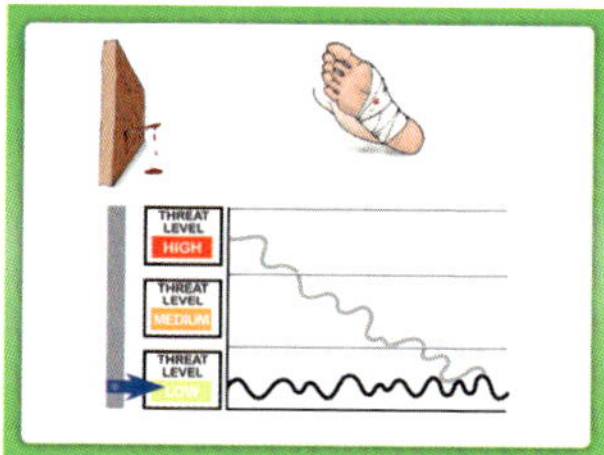

- Once you take the nail out, the alarm should go back down.
- The alarm goes down slowly.
- You will likely feel discomfort or pain in the foot for a day or two.
- This is normal.
- Once the alarm is back to its normal level, it is ready for the next danger.
- In the airport, high threat level red is lowered to low threat level yellow and things go back to "business as usual."

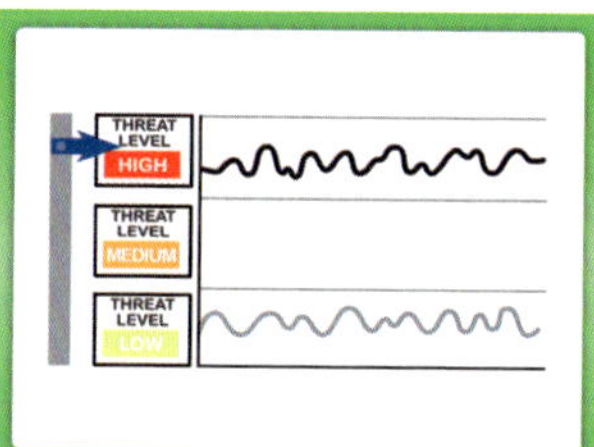

- Unfortunately, in approximately one in four people, the alarm does not go back down.
- The alarm (nervous system) stays extra sensitive.
- If pain lasts beyond the normal healing time, it is likely due to an extra-sensitive alarm.
- Your extra-sensitive nervous system might be a big part of your pain, limited movement and sensitivity.

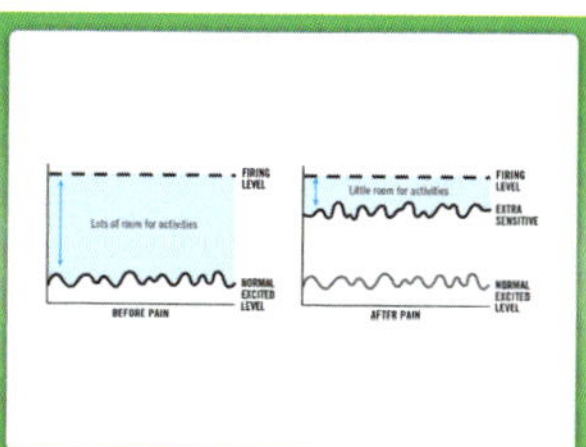

- An extra-sensitive alarm system can impact your life considerably.
- In the days before pain you had lots of room for movement and activities without causing pain.
- Since you developed pain, it takes far less activity or movement before you experience pain.
- The limited activity and movement is not necessarily due to injury or tissue damage but an extra-sensitive alarm system.

4.4.1.F: **Sensitive nerves – Christmas trees**

- Another way to think of this alarm system is Christmas season.
- When Christmas season comes, it's common to get the Christmas tree out of storage and set it up.
- Closer and closer to Christmas, the tree is filled with more and more ornaments and presents at the bottom of the tree and lots of bright lights, turned on for all to see.

- For most people, once Christmas is done, it's expected that they turn the lights off, take the decorations down and put the tree away for next year.
- In some people, however, the Christmas tree is turned on and is never turned down or put away.
- Before you know it, it's January and then February.
- Now the Christmas tree becomes a "Valentine's tree" and before you know it March's "St. Patrick's tree" and so forth…
- The tree never gets turned down or put away.

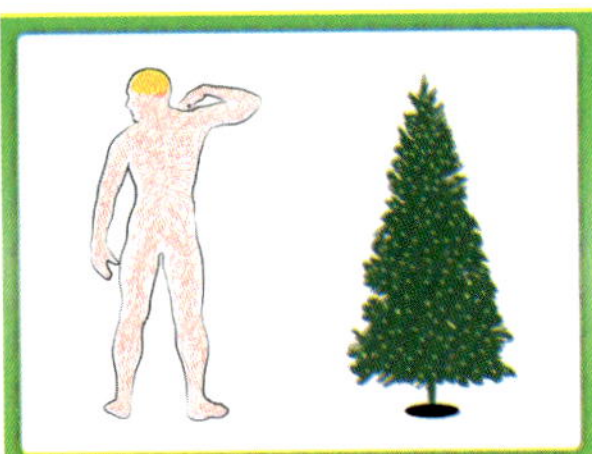

- This same process occurs when we experience pain.
- When you hurt yourself, the body's nervous system ramps up – similar to turning on the Christmas tree.
- This gets our attention and we seek help.
- Once the season is done (injury), it's expected the Christmas tree is turned down and life can return to normal.
- Unfortunately, in approximately one in four people the tree is turned on and never really turned off…

4.4.2: Nerve Sensors

Many clinicians have heard "it hurts when it's cold out" or "my pain gets worse when I am stressed." Old biomedical models of anatomy, biomechanics and patho-anatomy are ill-equipped to explain these phenomena to patients. Explaining the neuroscience of ion channel neuroplasticity and sensitivity at a patient's level allows them to develop a greater understanding of their pain. Knowing that stress chemicals in the human body and/or cold temperatures might result in increased awareness and even pain experiences, and that these experiences can be explained and changed for the better, will not only help calm patients, but provide hope. The ion channel explanations are timely, in that they merge well with the use of membrane stabilizing drugs and antidepressants for people with pain.

This story covers issues regarding:

- Ion channel expression
- Neuroplasticity
- Peripheral neuropathic pain
- Peripheral nerve sensitization
- Hyperalgesia
- Allodynia
- Membrane stabilizing drugs

Many people experience increased pain with stimuli such as cold, weather changes, stress, etc. There are different metaphors, examples and stories we can use to explain the body's alarm system sensors. We offer two examples to explain sensor plasticity:

- The alarm system's sensors
- The car dashboard

4.4.2.A: **Nerve sensors – the alarm system's sensors**

- In many cases when you encounter the front doors of a large department store or grocery store, the front doors open automatically when you approach.
- How does this happen?
- There are obviously sensors around the door sensing an eager new shopper and the doors open. Once in, the doors close behind you.

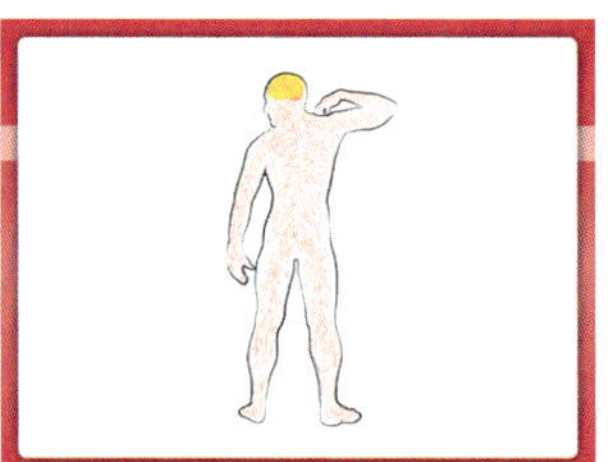

- A similar process occurs in the human body with the body's living alarm system, the nervous system.
- In our body, there are over 400 individual nerves, totaling 45 miles.
- All of these nerves are connected like highways.
- Our nerves work like an alarm system that's designed to warn us of danger, such as stepping on a rusted nail.

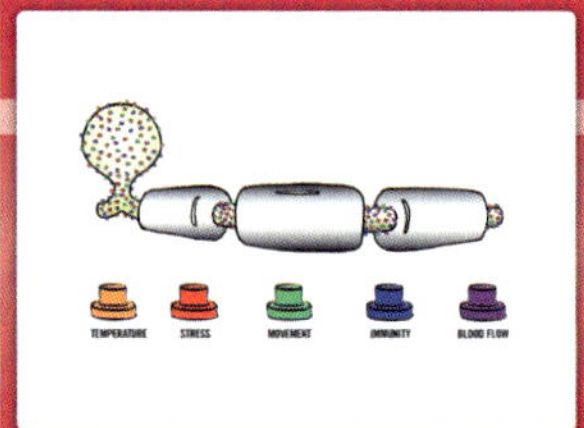

- Your alarm system is top-of-the-line.
- Apart from just telling you about dangers, such as stepping on a rusted nail, hurting your back or having surgery, your nerves also sense other changes.
- New research has shown our nerves contain sensors that will go off when:
  - It is cold outside.
  - You are stressed.
  - You move a body part or press against a body part.
  - You have the flu.
  - You sit too long.

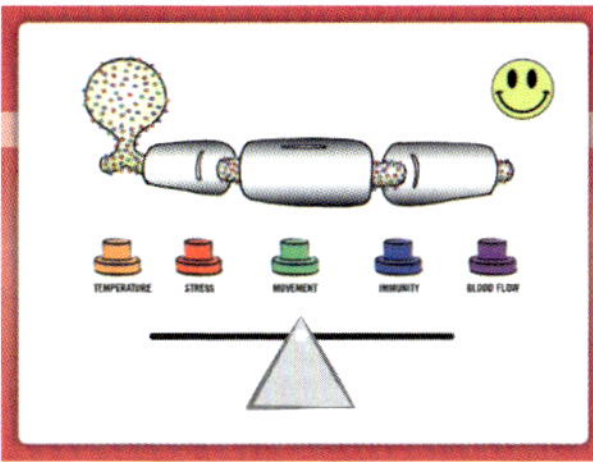

- When life is good, these sensors are balanced.
- There is just enough of each type of sensor to give us helpful information.
- For example:
  – It is cold outside; put a sweater on
  – You are a little stressed and need to calm down

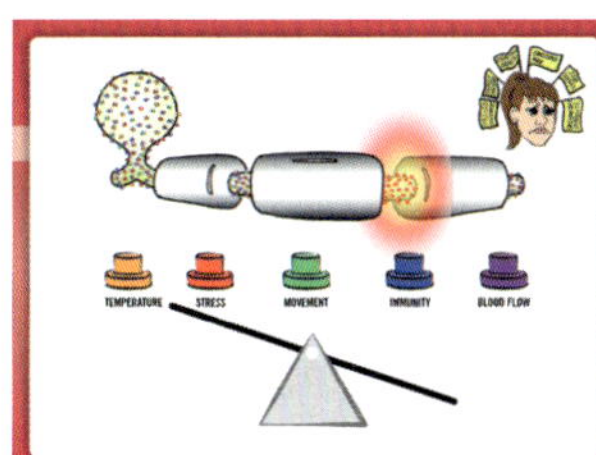

- When you develop pain, you tend to produce more sensors of a certain kind.
- This imbalance makes you more sensitive to certain stimuli. For example:
  – When you face a stressful time, such as surgery, stress might activate your alarm system.
  – When it is cold out, temperature sensors can activate the alarm system.
- What are the sensors telling you?
  – You are stressed. You need to calm down.
  – It is cold outside. Put a sweater on.
- Does an alarm message in this case mean injury? No, it just means that you are stressed, it is cold, etc.
- This is normal; it happens in all people and can be explained.

- Your nerves' sensors are constantly changing.
- The sensors are created based on what your brain thinks you need. For example:
  – If you face a stressful time, such as surgery or medical tests, you produce more stress sensors.
  – If you need to be aware of moving an arm or leg, such as after injury, you will produce more movement sensors.
- This is normal. As the threat eases or becomes understood, the sensors restore to a healthy balance.

4.4.2.B: **Nerve sensors – your car's dashboard**

- Cars have sure come a long way – from the Ford Model T to cars now even driving themselves.
- Even just the "typical" family car has become very technologically advanced with maps, Wi-Fi, built in satellite radios, etc.

- An example of how sophisticated cars have become is the dashboard and the various sensors in the modern car.
- The modern car has sensors and warning lights for:
  - Gas
  - Tire pressure
  - Seatbelts
  - Oil levels
  - Engine temperature and more
- When all is good, no sensor lights are flashing and a drive to work or visit to grandma's house is uneventful.

- Imagine you are driving down the road and your gas light comes on.
- Is this an immediate catastrophic emergency?
- Of course not – the sensor is just getting your attention so you can look for a gas station down the road.

- Once you get gas into your tank, the sensor is shut off and you are good to go.
- The sensor, however, is still there and ready to let you know when you are running low on gas again.
- In essence, the sensor does its job:
  - It gets your attention
  - You interpret the information
  - You act on the information (put gas in)
  - The sensor calms down

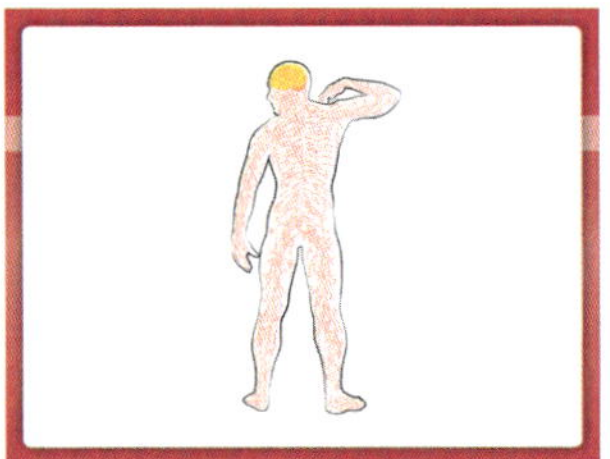

- What many people do not know is that a similar process occurs in the human body with the body's living alarm system, the nervous system.
- In our body, there are over 400 individual nerves, totaling 45 miles.
- All of these nerves are connected like highways.
- Our nerves work like an alarm system that is designed to warn us of danger, such as stepping on a rusted nail.

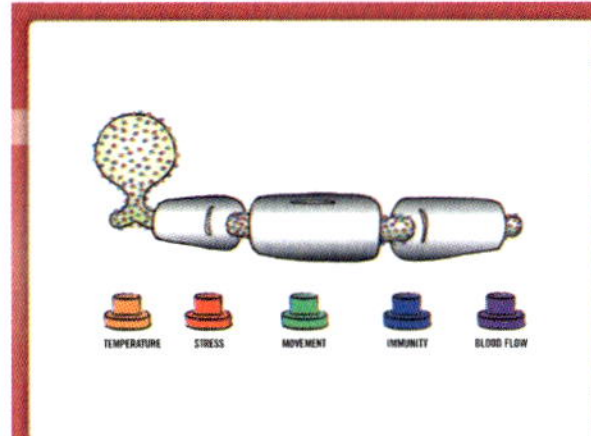

- Your alarm system is top-of-the-line.
- Apart from just telling you about dangers, such as stepping on a rusted nail, your nerves also sense other changes.
- New research has shown our nerves contain sensors that will go off when:
  - It is cold outside.
  - You are stressed.
  - You move a body part or press against a body part.
  - You have the flu.
  - You sit too long.

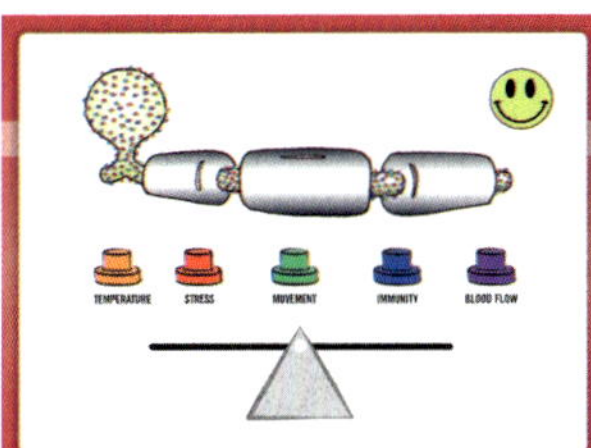

- When life is good, these sensors are balanced.
- There is just enough of each type of sensor to give us helpful information.
- For example:
  - It is cold outside; put a sweater on.
  - You are a little stressed and need to calm down.

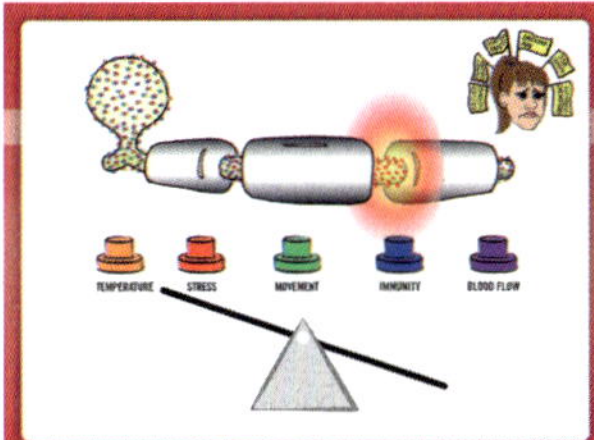

- When you develop pain, you tend to produce more sensors of a certain kind.
- This imbalance makes you more sensitive to certain stimulus. For example:
  - When you face a stressful time, such as surgery, stress might activate your alarm system.
  - When it is cold out, temperature sensors can activate the alarm system.
- What are the sensors telling you?
  - You are stressed. You need to calm down.
  - It is cold outside. Put a sweater on.
- Does an alarm message in this case mean injury? No, it just means that you are stressed, it is cold, etc.
- This is normal; it happens in all people and can be explained.

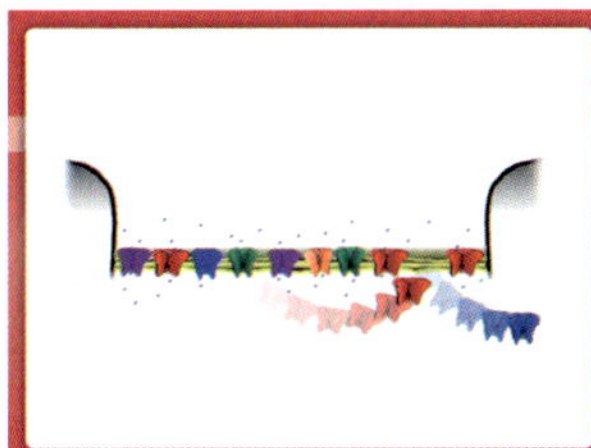

- Your nerves' sensors are constantly changing.
- The sensors are created based on what your brain thinks you need. For example:
  - If you face a stressful time, such as surgery or medical tests, you produce more stress sensors.
  - If you need to be aware of moving an arm or leg, such as after injury, you will produce more movement sensors.
- This is normal. As the threat eases or becomes understood, the sensors restore to a healthy balance.

4.4.3: Nosy Neighbors

What does it mean when pain spreads? Does it mean more injury? In people with pain, the increased peripheral and central sensitization, along with powerful changes in the brain, often leads them to experience spreading pain. Undoubtedly, this increases fear and anxiety as well as pain. Teaching patients the neurobiology of an inquisitive nervous system, along with its cousin the immune system, allows patients to see logical biological systems seeking to protect. Understanding that spreading pain is likely due to an alarm system trying to protect them allows patients to realize there is no real threat; it is normal and can be changed for the better.

This story covers issues regarding:

- Spreading pain
- Neuroplasticity
- Peripheral neuropathic pain
- Peripheral nerve sensitization
- Central sensitization
- Hyperalgesia
- Allodynia
- Immune responses

There are several ways to explain spreading pain with an underlying biological process of the nervous and immune system. We offer six examples:

- Nosy and irritated neighbor
- Car alarms
- Neighborhood break-in
- Perimeter attacks
- Party at the apartment building
- Christmas tree competition

4.4.3.A: **Nosy neighbors – nosy and irritated neighbors**

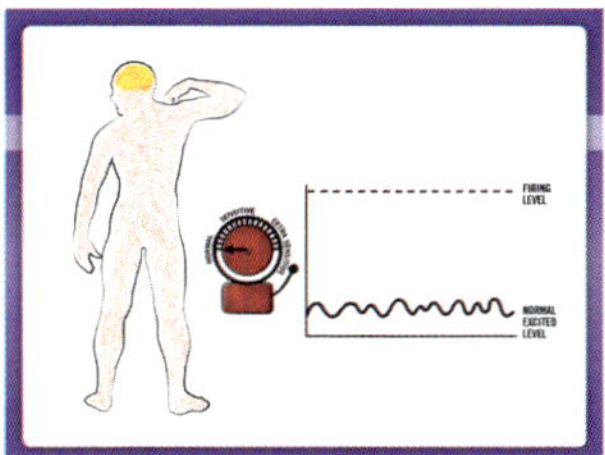

- Your body contains 400 nerves, totaling 45 miles.
- All these nerves are connected like highways.
- Our nerves work like an alarm system that is designed to warn us of danger. For example:
  - When you step on a nail, the alarm goes off and sends a message to the brain.
  - The brain produces pain to grab your attention and get you to take care of the problem.
  - After the threat is removed and action has been taken, the alarm settles down again.

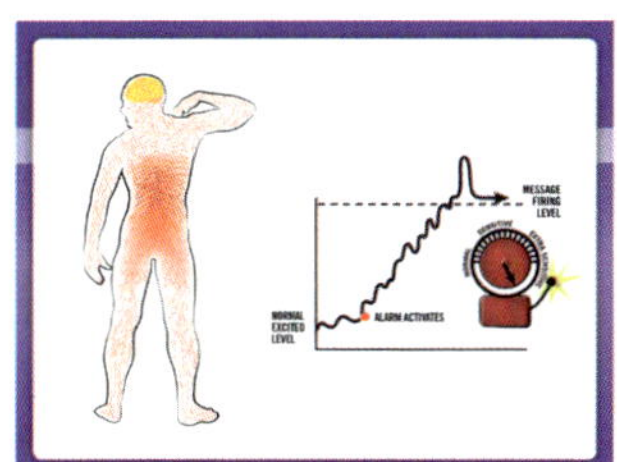

- How long have you had your pain?
- This is how long your alarm has been going off.
- It is still going off every day.

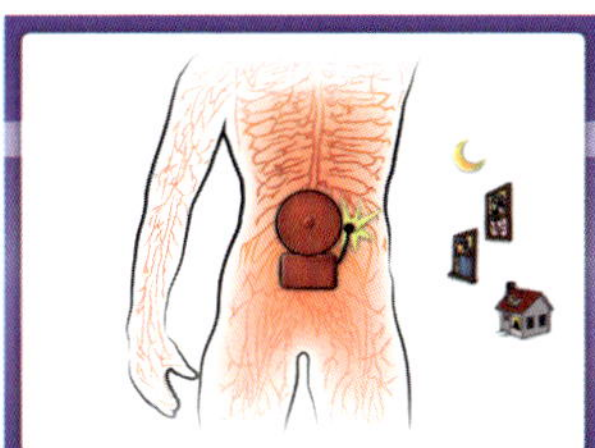

- If your home's alarm system goes off tonight at 11pm, what will your neighbors do?
- They will wake up, be a little irritable and come check on you. This is normal.
- If you shut the alarm off, they will go back to bed – all is well.
- If your alarm keeps going off for as long as you have been in pain, what would happen?
- You would have irritated and nosy neighbors.
- So, feeling pain in neighboring areas of your body does not mean there's injury; you just have irritated, nosy neighbors.
- That is why it might feel as if your pain is spreading.

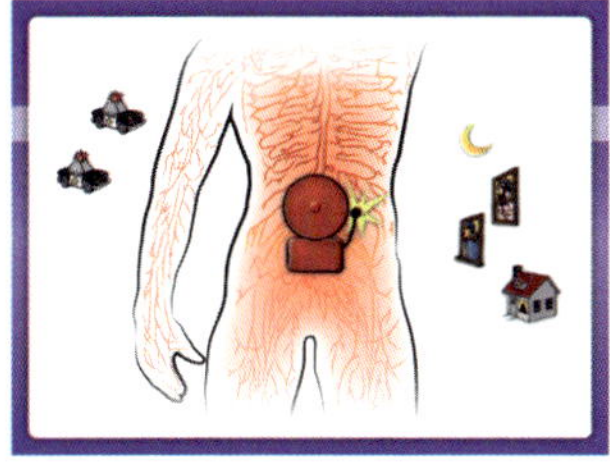

- If the alarm goes off long enough, the body's police – immune molecules – will eventually show up.
- The added immune molecules increase sensitivity and awareness of painful areas.
- It is similar to when you have the flu; you experience more pain and sensitivity due to the increased number of immune molecules.
- The police check out the alarm, the neighbors and past "crime areas" like old injury and surgery sites; you might notice increased sensitivity and awareness of these areas.
- This is completely normal and can occur anywhere in the body.

4.4.3.B: **Nosy neighbors – car alarms**

- Most modern cars are equipped with a car alarm to prevent someone stealing your car.

- Most of us also have had the unfortunate "privilege" of setting off our car alarm in the parking lot of a grocery or department store, pressing the wrong button.
- With the alarm going off, everyone stops what they are doing to look at your car.
- Embarrassed and feeling as if "the whole world is watching YOU," you point your remote to your car and disable the alarm.
- All is well and everyone goes about their business.

- In some cases, however, your alarm goes off and you are inside the department store or grocery store shopping, blissfully unaware of your alarm going off.
- What happens next?
- It is common for your car alarm, if it keeps going long enough, to set off neighboring cars, and now we have a whole bunch of car alarms going off!
- This will no doubt get everyone's attention and before long the police will even show up.

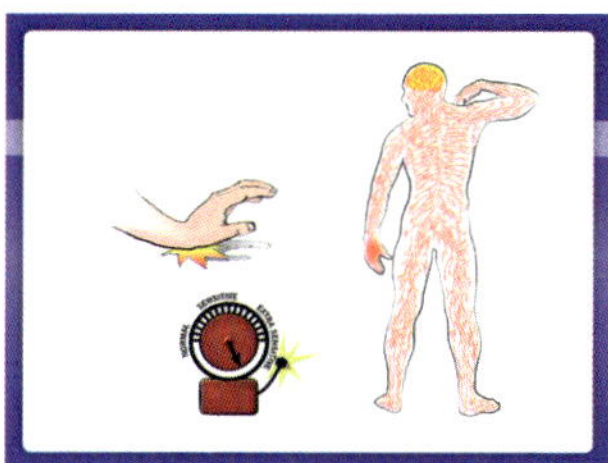

- The same "alarm" scenario also occurs in us when we experience pain.
- The body contains its own car alarm – the nervous system.
- The nervous system scans for threats and, when a threat occurs, it sets off the alarm to grab our attention and make us do something about it.
- For example, if we fall and sprain our wrist, the alarm will likely go off in the wrist telling us to go to the emergency room and have it checked out.

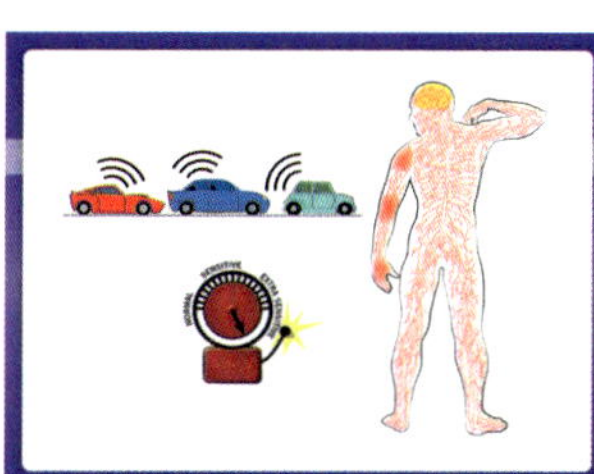

- As with the car alarm, if the alarm is not shut down and keeps going long enough, it sets off the neighboring "car" – in this case neighboring joints.
- Before we know it the "wrist car" sets off the alarm in the neighboring "elbow car" and before long… the "shoulder car."
- Now, even though you only sprained your wrist, you are aware of:
  - Your wrist
  - Your elbow
  - Your shoulder, etc.
- When pain lasts a long time, and starts "spreading," it's not necessarily an indication of more damage, but likely woken neighboring alarms.

4.4.3.C: **Nosy neighbors – neighborhood break-ins**

- Everyone can agree that few things in life are as rewarding as a good night's sleep.
- When life is all good, we nestle in, fall into a deep sleep and wake refreshed in the morning.

- Now imagine a house down the street gets broken into…
- A few days later, another one, and before you know it several break-ins have occurred in your neighborhood.

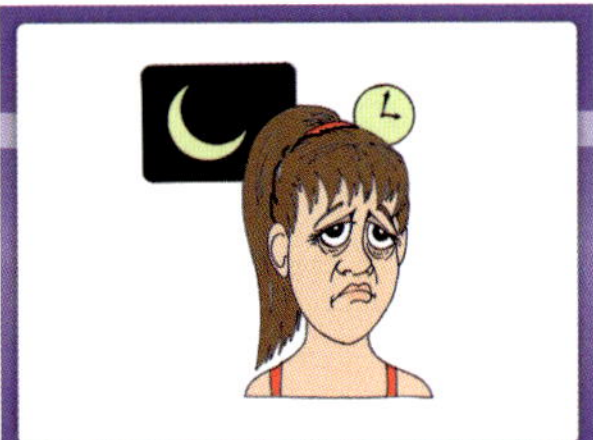

- How will this development impact your sleep?
- How about your overall wellbeing?
- Will you sleep soundly and deep or be super-alert to any and all sounds?
- So much for sleep.
- Even with this not affecting your house directly and happening several houses down the street, it surely impacts you.

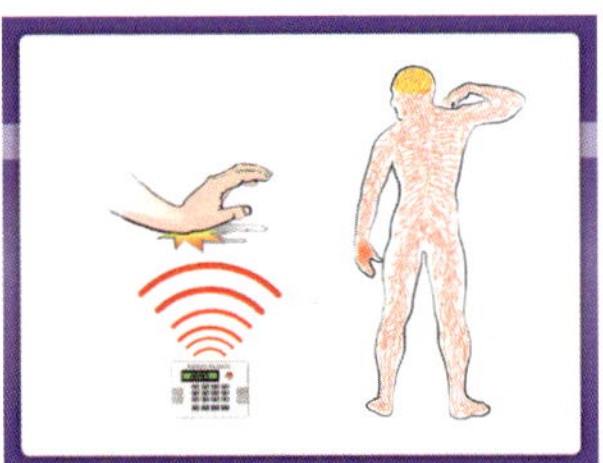

- The same process can also occur with us when we experience pain.
- When we develop pain in a body area it is similar to a break-in.

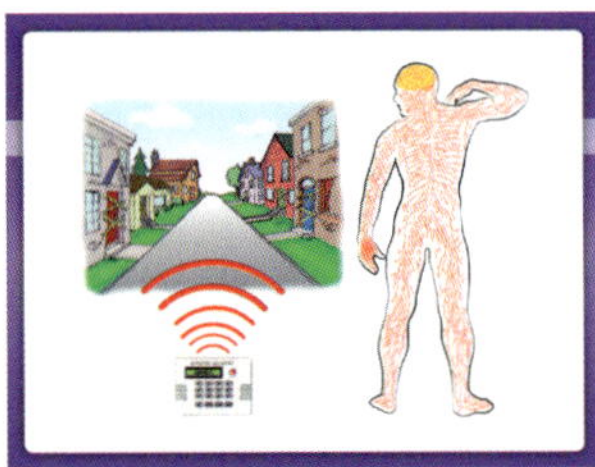

- If you develop pain in a few areas, say you have pain in your wrist and elbow, it might be similar to a neighborhood break-in spree.
- If this is the case, the whole neighborhood is more alert.
- In people with pain, the body's alarm system – the nervous system – ramps up and this has consequences:
  - Pain seems to spread.
  - Pain occurs in other sides of the body.
  - There is increased sensitivity to touch.
  - There is increased fatigue from having to deal with pain.
- Many of these symptoms are common in people with pain and are partly due to a ramped-up neighborhood, and not necessarily an indication of more injury.

4.4.3.D: **Nosy neighbors – perimeter attack (Timothy Benedict, PT, DPT)**

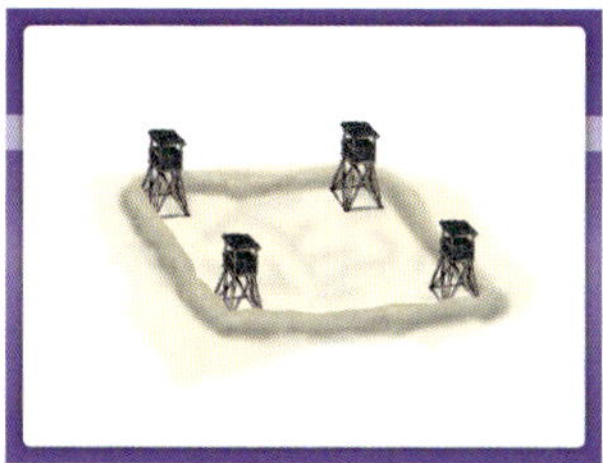

- When the military sets up a base in an occupied area, it's common to set a base camp and fortify it with a perimeter to guard against attacks.
- The perimeter typically consists of a fence, guard towers and soldiers manning the various watch towers.

- In many cases, these perimeter fences are long and the base camp quite large.
- Given the distance between various guard towers it's not uncommon when an attack occurs that a single guard tower becomes the primary response center.
- For example, a grenade is detonated close to a guard tower and the guard tower becomes active:
  - The soldiers manning the guard tower are immediately on high alert.
  - They might fire toward an enemy.
  - If the attack was in the evening, more lights are turned on

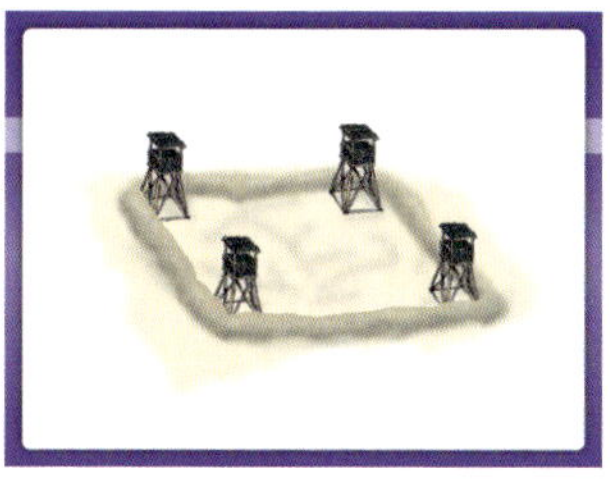

- Guard towers have significant advantages such as being fortified, more heavily armed and having great vantage points.
- Once the attack has been stopped, everything goes back to normal.
- It's not uncommon for perimeter attacks to be smaller, as a means to "test" the perimeter.
- Given these attacks are often small and short-lived, and the perimeter fences are so large, other guard towers might not even be aware of some of these attacks.

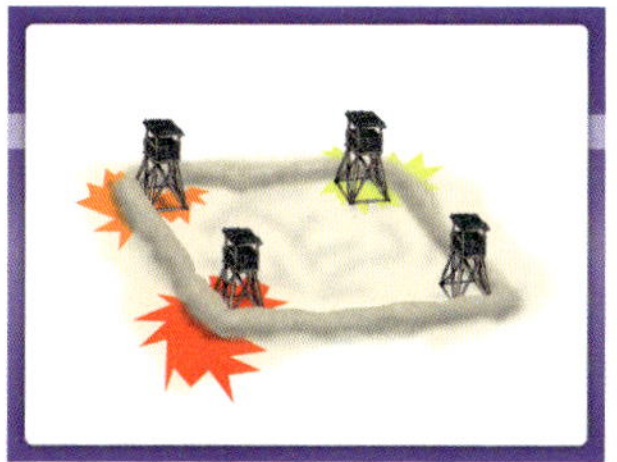

- If an attack, however, lasts longer or it is more aggressive, there is a chance that neighboring guard towers also ramp up to "full alert" with a potential threat to their area.
- The guard tower closest to the attack will likely be more alert, while one further down will be less alert, but also ramping up.
- This is normal and expected given the increased threat.

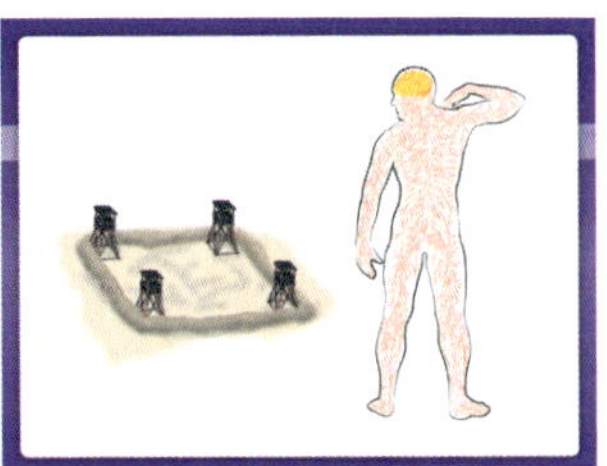

- What does this have to do with your pain?
- The same process occurs in the human body.
- Our body also has a "perimeter" fence monitoring for attacks called the nervous system.
- Your body contains 400 nerves, totaling 45 miles.
- All these nerves are connected like a perimeter fence.
- The perimeter fence is designed to warn us of danger.

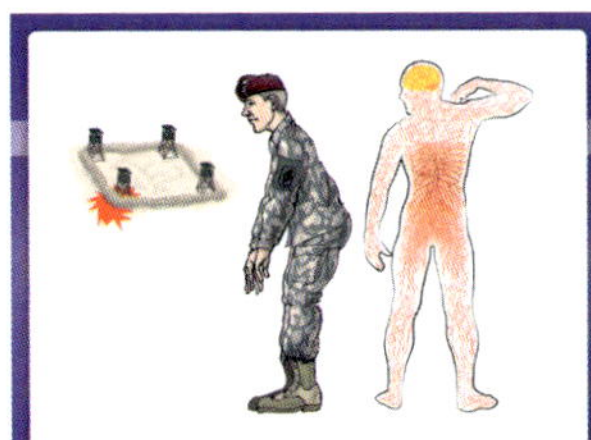

- An example of a perimeter attack might be low back pain.
- When you hurt your back, it's the equivalent of an attack whereby the one guard becomes alerted.
- This is normal and there to protect.

- In a perfect world, with proper treatment involving physical therapy, some exercise and pacing back to regular activities, pain eases.
- In this case the original attack is stopped, and everything goes back to normal.
- This, by the way, occurs in 90 percent of people with low back pain – they hurt, they seek help, get treatment, recover, and return to regular activities and the system calms down.

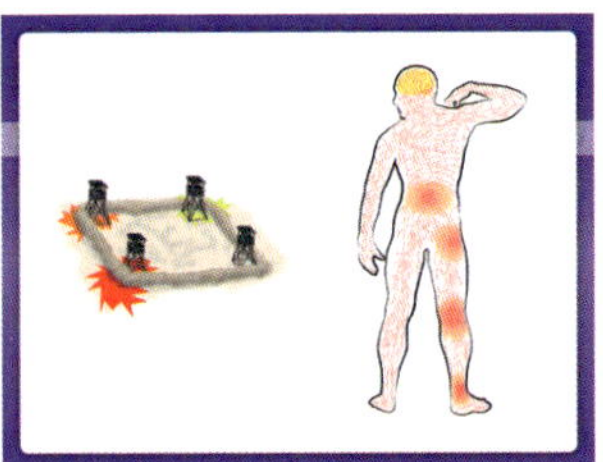

- In some people, however, when an attack occurs, the attack continues, and over time wakes the neighboring guard towers.
- For someone with low back pain, the guard towers might be located in the hip, knee and foot.
- Before long all of them are ramped up and on high alert.
- This ramp up of the nervous system results in feeling not only your original back pain, but now soreness in your back, hip, knee and ankle.

- It is therefore important to remember:
  - Tissues heal.
  - Spreading pain is not necessarily an indication of more damage but likely a system ramping up.
  - The quicker you take care of the original issue, the faster your system will calm down and prevent the ramp up of the neighboring guard towers.
  - A "sensitive" system calms down with movement – scientists have shown us that movement calms down nerves.

4.4.3.E: **Nosy neighbors – party at the apartment building (Greg Alnwick, PT, DPT, TPS, OCS)**

- Imagine you just moved into an apartment building.
- You're on the third floor and excited to start the next adventure of your life.

- Unfortunately, as you get settled in you realize the resident in the apartment right below you is a loud neighbor.
- He likes to party, plays his music very loud and stays up all night.

- What happens if he plays his music loud and all night long?
- No doubt you wake up.
- If this happens a lot you'll become an irritated neighbor.

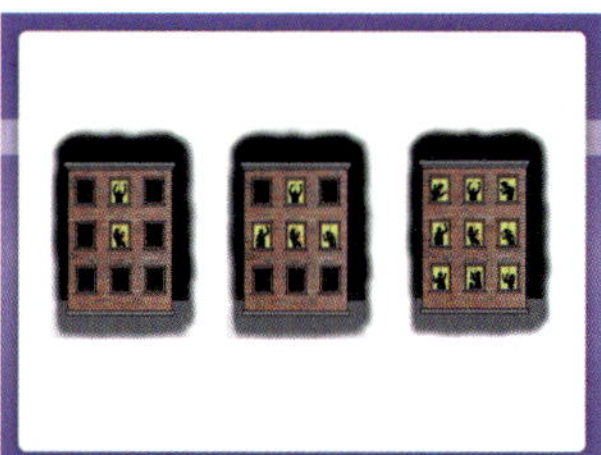

- Over time if this continues, what happens?
- The loud music and disturbance spreads throughout the apartment building and everyone in the building wakes up.
- Everyone is mad except the "party guy."

- Eventually what happens?
- The police are called to the building.
- Now with the police there and everyone all angry and upset, the whole apartment building is in an uproar and stressed.

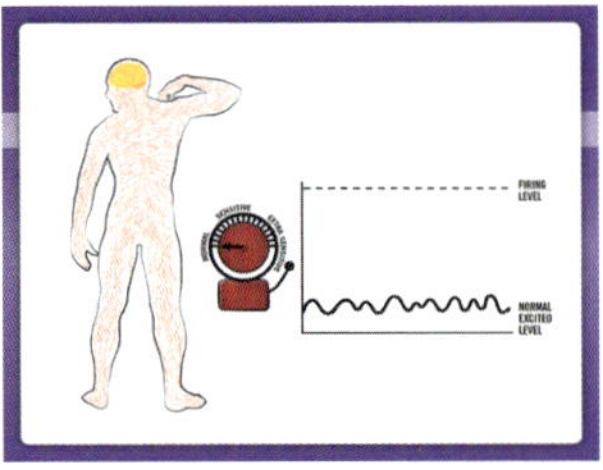

- When we experience pain, the same process occurs.
- Our nerves work like an alarm system that is designed to warn us of danger. For example:
  - When you step on a nail, the alarm goes off and sends a message to the brain.
  - The brain produces pain to grab your attention and get you to take care of the problem.
  - After the threat is removed and action has been taken, the alarm settles down again.

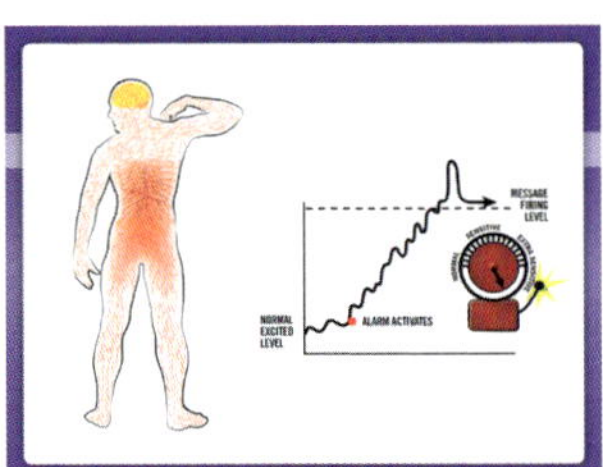

- How long have you had your pain?
- This is how long your alarm has been going off.
- It's still going off every day.

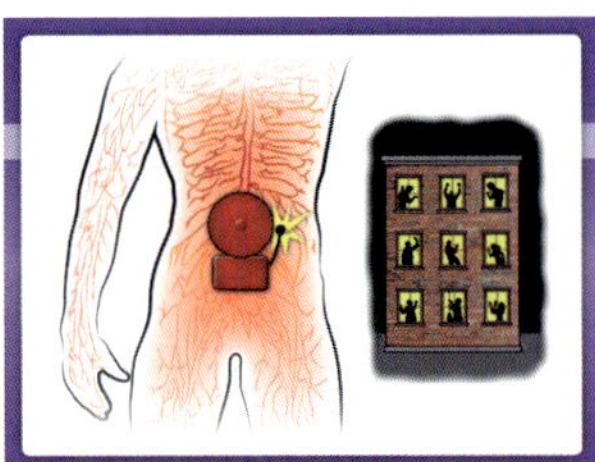

- When the alarm goes off, the same process occurs as in the apartment building.
- The loud and continuous music sets off the alarm system.
- When the alarm goes off long enough, the neighbors wake up.
- The neighbors to the low back are the hips and upper back.
- Spreading pain might not necessarily be an indication of more injury, but a system waking up more and more…

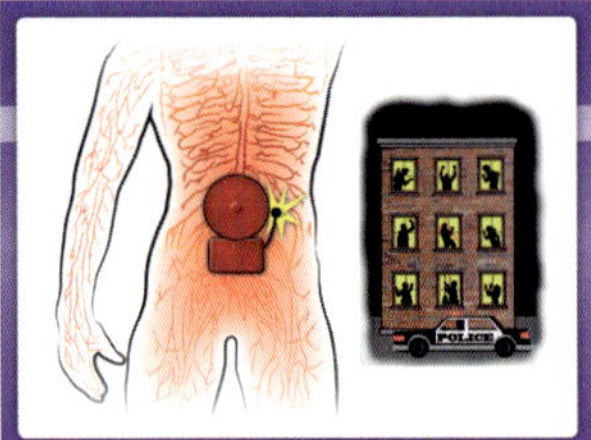

- If the noise lasts long enough, the body's police – immune molecules – will eventually show up.
- The added immune molecules increase sensitivity and awareness of painful areas.
- It is similar to when you have the flu; you experience more pain and sensitivity due to the increased number of immune molecules.
- The police check out the alarm, the neighbors and past "crime areas" like old injury and surgery sites, and you might notice increased sensitivity and awareness of these areas.
- This is completely normal and can occur anywhere in the body.

4.4.3.F: **Nosy neighbors – Christmas tree competition**

- When Christmas season comes, it's common to get the Christmas tree out of storage and set it up.
- Closer and closer to Christmas, the tree is filled with more and more ornaments and presents at the bottom of the tree and lots of bright lights, turned on for all to see.
- This year you decided to stick to a modest 5-foot Christmas tree.

- In your neighborhood, however, there is the annual "Christmas tree" competition seeing who can outdo who.
- Your neighbor looks over and thinks, "Well, I will turn mine on but bigger and brighter, so that I can win the competition this year."
- To outdo you, he decides to at least go to a 6-foot tree and add twice as many lights.

- Once you and your neighbor have your lights up and beautifully displayed for all to see, the neighbor on the other side of you chuckles and says, "You call that a Christmas tree?" and turns his 9-foot tree on, as well as the lights all over his house.
- Before you know it, the whole neighborhood's lights are on!

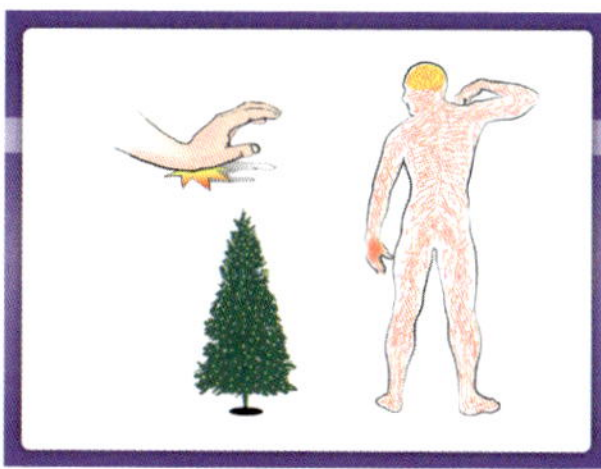

- The same process occurs to us when we are injured.
- When we fall on our wrist and hurt the wrist and there is some inflammation, it is the equivalent of turning the lights on in your wrist.
- Hopefully, as tissues heal and time goes by, the lights are turned down and all is well.

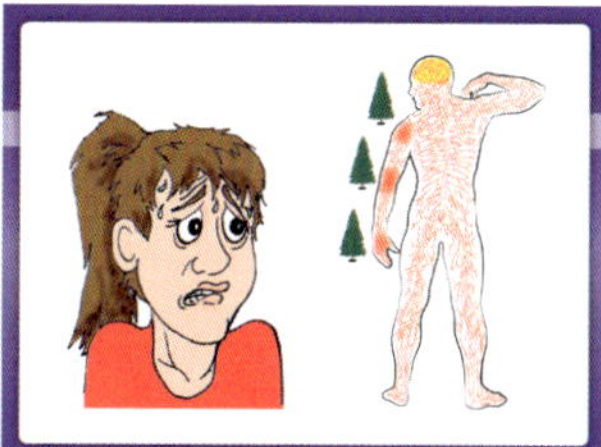

- In some people, however, when we turn on the lights in the wrist, it might cause the neighbors to also turn their lights on.
- Now the elbow lights are on, followed by the shoulder lights and… before you know it, the whole arm neighborhood is turned on.
- More than likely you will say you feel pain in your whole arm – wrist, elbow and shoulder – yet you only hurt your wrist.
- Spreading pain is not necessarily an indication of more injury but often due to a neighborhood waking up.
- It is now well understood that when we are afraid to move or afraid of pain, it might be a big reason why neighbors turn on their lights.

4.4.4: Calming Nerves

The number one question patients pose after learning about extra-sensitive nerves is, "How do I calm them down?" This is the question all clinicians want their patients to ask, because it is the right question, versus "How do we fix this?" This series of stories systematically describes various strategies healthcare providers can use to steadily help calm the nervous system, which ultimately results in decreased pain and disability. The series powerfully reframes therapy for a patient and provides hope. This exciting message of desensitization empowers the patient, offering various strategies that they can perform to further their recovery.

This story covers issues regarding:

- Peripheral neuropathic pain
- Pain neuroscience education
- Endogenous mechanisms
- Pacing
- Graded exposure
- Aerobic exercise

To illustrate the various ways of calming the sensitive alarm system, we offer several explanations:

1. Calming nerves – big picture
2. Pacing and graded exposure – spiders
3. Pacing and graded exposure – keep the fire risk low
4. Pacing: Dating pain, making popcorn and toast, and brushing teeth
5. Setting goals – grandma and Toblerone®
6. No flat tires

4.4.4.A: **Calming nerves – big picture**

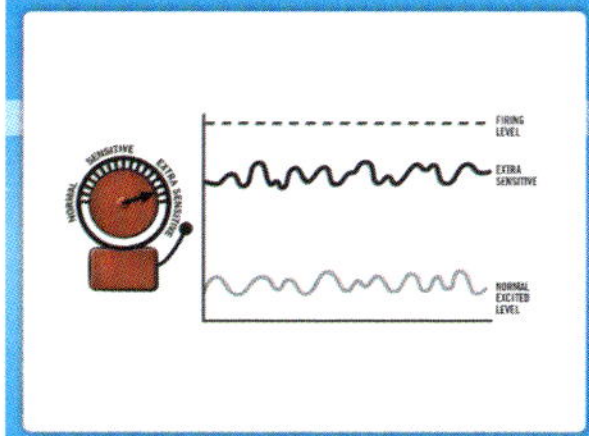

- When you have an injury or the brain thinks there is a threat, the body's alarm system (nervous system) wakes up.
- After the threat is removed, the system usually calms back down.
- In one out of four people, the alarm system does not return to the normal resting place, but remains extra sensitive. This is usually due to:
  - Fear
  - Ongoing pain
  - Failed treatments
  - Different explanations for pain
  - Various stressors
- This is not uncommon and is intended to protect you.

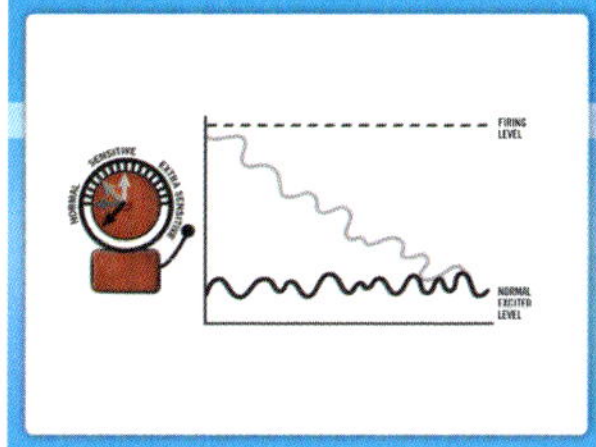

- The question now is how do we calm the nervous system?
- How do we get it back to the normal resting level?
- The answer is that you have already started the recovery process.

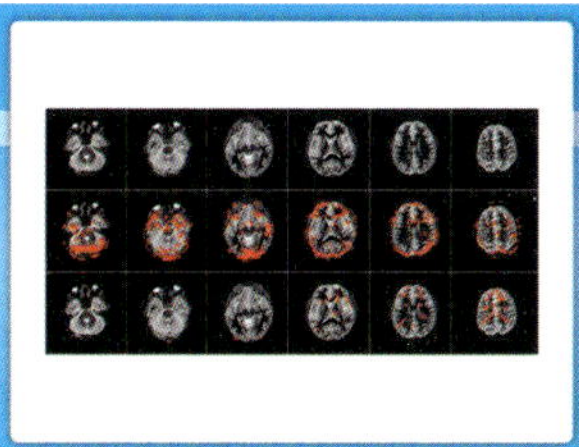

- Here is a brain scan of a patient similar to you; someone with ongoing pain who has been given various explanations for their pain, but treatments are not really helping.
  - Row 1: The patient is relaxing in the scanner, and you can see the brain is calm – no red blobs.
  - Row 2: The patient moves her painful back, and all of the red blobs show us her brain processing the pain experience.
  - Row 3: The same patient undergoes a short educational session, similar to yours, and then repeats the same back movements; this time there are significantly fewer red blobs, showing us her pain has decreased.
- By understanding more about pain and how pain works, we can actually experience less pain.

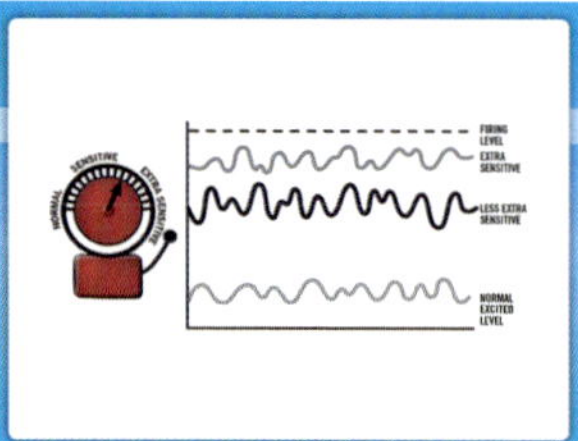

- Education is therapy.
- If you understand that a significant part of your pain is likely due to an extra-sensitive nervous system, your alarm system starts to calm down.
- As you learn about your pain today, your brain will see less of a threat and your nervous system will start to calm down.
- As the system calms down, pain actually eases.
- Remember, it will not suddenly return to normal; it is a sophisticated alarm system and will go down little by little to keep protecting you.

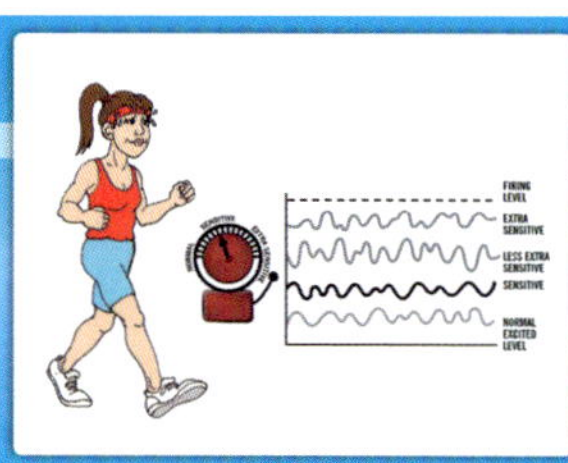

- Exercise will also help calm your nervous system.
- Remember in school when you were stressed while studying for a big test?
- What was the best thing to do? Go for a run or bike ride. After some exercise, you felt calm and more relaxed.
- Blood and oxygen calm the nerves. Easy, gentle aerobic exercise pumps blood and oxygen around the nerves, which helps calm them down.
- No need to run marathons or climb mountains: A brisk walk four to five times per week for 20-30 minutes is more than enough.

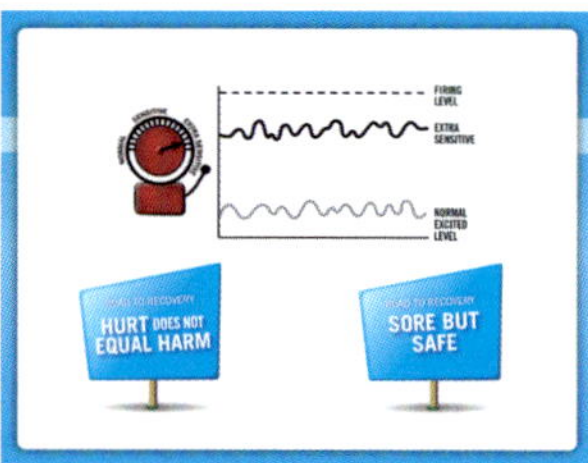

- Many people in pain are afraid of exercise because they think exercise causes pain and pain means injury.
- Let us clear up some common misconceptions:
  - Hurt does not equal harm.
  - You might be sore, but safe.
  - Understand that your alarm system is extra sensitive, and when you move or exercise, the alarm is merely telling you that your body is moving – nothing is being injured.
  - Pain that is understood and expected to some degree is not a threat and will actually decrease and eventually go away.
  - Think of the soreness you feel after a good workout.

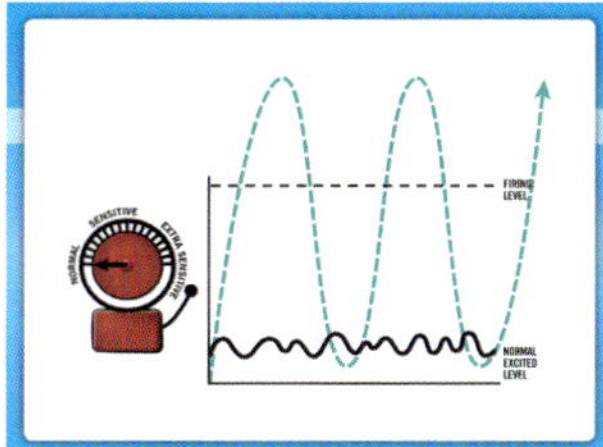

- One of the biggest reasons people in pain hurt with exercise or daily tasks is they do too much.
- Movement and activity is important, but you need to pace yourself.
- If you go too hard and crash through the pain, you might be sore for hours or days after the exercise.
- After you recover, you go at it again, paying the same price.
- After this cycle repeats several times, you will likely get frustrated and give up.
- Pace yourself. A 20-minute brisk walk that feels good with no significant soreness afterward is much better than an hour-long walk that leaves you in pain for a day or two.
- Movement and activity without significant pain will help your system calm down.

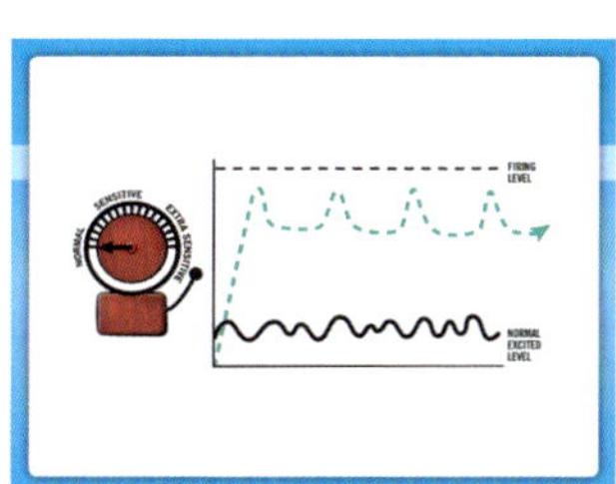

- In the opposite case, many people fear and avoid pain.
- They stop any and all activities short of pain.
- They focus on "When do I feel pain?" which actually increases their pain.
- This method hinders progress, which will leave them discouraged.
- Over time, it will take less and less activity to trigger the alarm system.

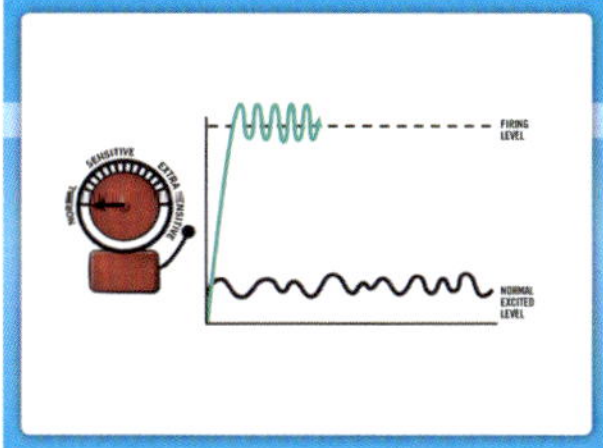

- So...what should we do?
- Tease it. Nudge it. Touch it.
- Perform a task or exercise up to the point you feel some discomfort.
- Pace yourself.
- Do not be afraid of pain, but respect it. Do not stop short, but do not crash right through.
- With your newfound knowledge of how pain works, you will not fear pain and it will start to ease.
- This allows for gradual increase in activity and exercise.

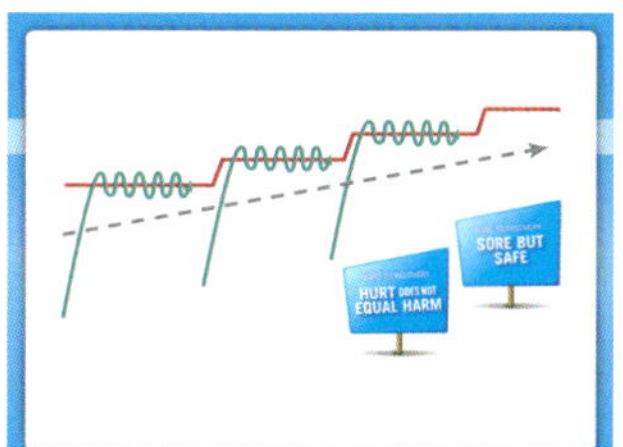

- How do you eat an elephant? One bite at a time.
- The same goes for any exercise program or task.
- Start small.
- Every other day add a small part.
- Day by day, your time, distance, duration, etc. will increase.
- A three-minute walk becomes a four-minute walk, becomes a five-minute walk, becomes a 5K and eventually becomes the Boston Marathon.

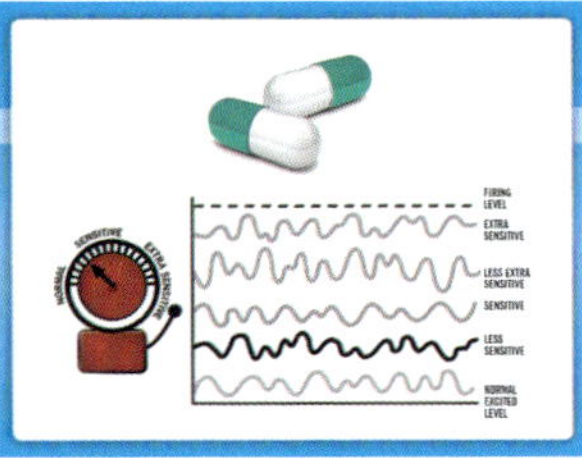

- The third way we can help calm nerves down is by using medicine.
- All questions about your medicine should be directed to your doctor.
- If your extra-sensitive alarm system limits your movement, exercise and therapy, these medications might help kick start your progress.
- Over time, medicine should be tapered and ceased with the help of your doctor.

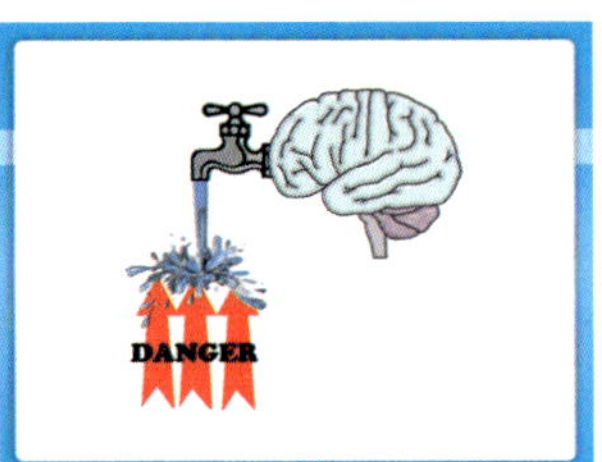

- Did you know the brain produces pain medicine as well?
- The brain has the most powerful drug cabinet in the world; we call this a wet brain.
- A wet brain is filled with lots of healthy drugs that flush down to ease incoming danger messages and the pain experience.

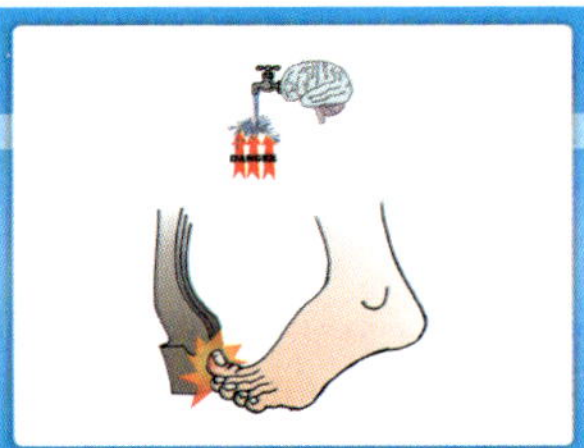

- A good example is stubbing your toe.
- When you stub your toe it really hurts, right?
- How long? Months?
- Of course not, it hurts for a few minutes.
- In this case, the brain produces pain medicine (wet brain) to dampen the danger messages and ultimately your pain experience.
- Why does your brain do it? It understands that "toe stubbing" is not a big deal and in essence tells the system, "Calm down, you're making a scene. Everyone is watching."

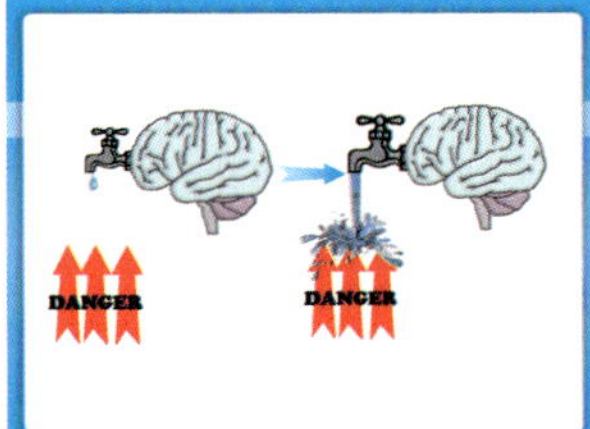

- In people with ongoing pain, the pain medicine in their brain has dried up.
- Why does this happen? To protect you. The brain takes away the pain medicine to make you more sensitive, so you will do something about it.
- How do we turn a dry brain into a wet brain?
  - Knowledge – understanding more deeply how pain works and what pain really means
  - Aerobic exercise
  - Sleep
  - Meditation and relaxation
  - Breathing
  - Manual therapy
- There are many things we can do to help you with your pain.

4.4.4.B: **Calming nerves – pacing, graded exposure and spiders (Louis Gifford)**

- Are you afraid of spiders or do you know someone who is?
- Apparently quite a few people are afraid of spiders.
- How do we go about decreasing someone's fear of spiders?

- One way might be to sign up for a TV show where people have to face their fears
- More than likely they will place you in a box and fill the box with spiders!
- More than likely this will freak you out and make you even more afraid.

- Another (more sensible) way might be a graded exposure to spiders.
- A logical starting place might be to learn more about spiders by reading a book about them.
- As with many other animals, such as sharks and snakes, scientists have shown that most people have limited and skewed knowledge that likely increases fear.
- The book in itself has little to no threat and is a relatively low level of exposure to spiders.

- The next logical step might be to look at a dead spider.
- Yes, it is a spider, but it is dead, upside down in a jar and the jar is sealed.
- This is more threatening than a book, but obviously less scary than the real thing.

- As you slowly get a handle on your fear of spiders, you will steadily increase the exposure.
- The next step might be to look at another dead spider, but it is placed on a wood block with a pin in it.
- This way the spider, even though dead, is a little more real and you are slowly exposing yourself to the threat.

- The next step is to view live spiders, but enclosed in an environment.
- This once again increases the risk.

- Next, you might actually handle a spider, but not a large hairy spider, rather a small harmless spider.

- The final phase of this graded exposure to spiders would be handling the spider you feared all along.
- You've obviously come a long way and can now move on to a life with less fear of spiders.

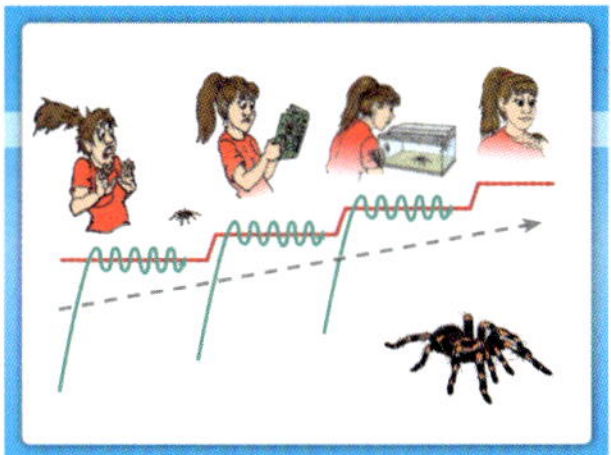

- How did you overcome your fear and move on?
- Graded exposure – slowly but surely, without massive exposure at one time, you gradually changed and now function and live at a much higher level.

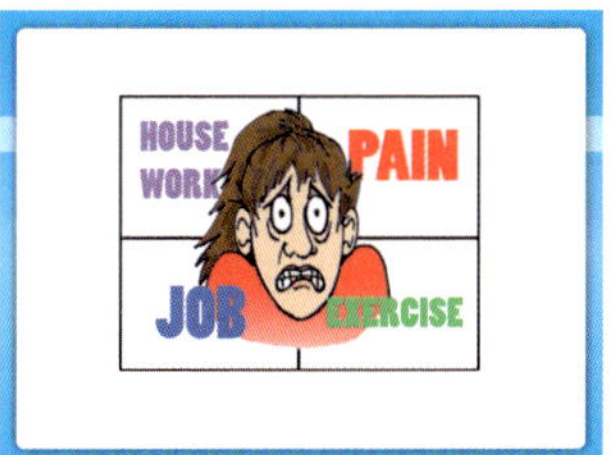

- What is really neat is that many things in life can be similarly paced, including doing work around the house, aspects of a job, exercise and even pain.

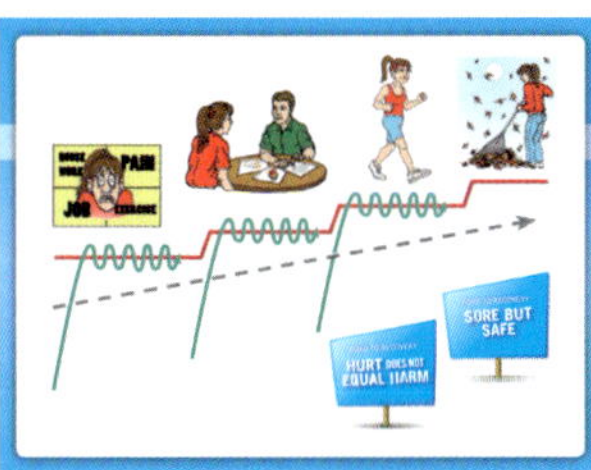

- When it comes to pain, what do we do?
- We learn about it so it becomes less scary.
- We move little and often.
- We are sore but safe; hurt does not equal harm.
- Slowly but surely we do more.
- We focus on goals, movement and daily tasks.

4.4.4.C: **Calming nerves – keep the fire risk low (Jill Lawrence, MSPT, TPS)**

- In order to alert hikers and campers about the potential for forest fires, the U.S. Forest Service often posts signs as to the relative risk for a fire given the local weather conditions and condition of the forest.

- When a forest is dry, the risk for a fire is high.
- It would therefore not take a lot of activity to start a fire – a small spark can cause a huge fire to ensue, which might take a long time to get under control.
- This might be when an area is dry or the forest is old with lots of dead, dried out trees, branches and bushes.

- The opposite is also true; when a forest is wet, the risk for a fire is low.
- If a forest is in a wet, damp area it is likely hard to get a fire to start – maybe you have seen some survival show where the hero struggles to get a fire going because it's just too wet and damp.
- It could be argued that it is less likely for a fire to start in a young, lush forest with green saplings compared to a dry forest with old, fallen down and dried up trees.

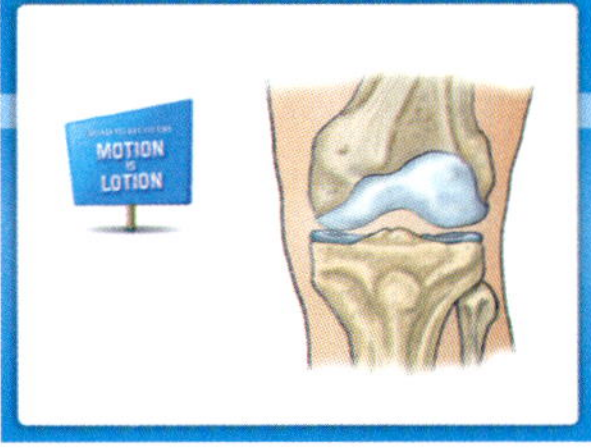

- What is interesting is that our joints also work the same way.
- As we age, our joints age. This is normal and part of being human.
- Joints need movement to keep them well-lubricated, working well, with controlled pain.

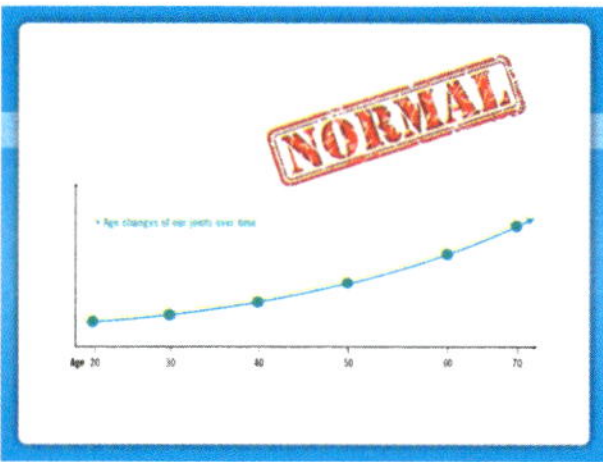

- When joints move a lot, they stay lubricated. In essence, movement keeps the forest wet.
- With this condition, the risk for a fire is low.
- With a "wet" knee you can walk and stand for hours with no major consequence.
- Scientists have shown that movement is anti-inflammatory and therefore keeps the risk for a spark and fire very low.

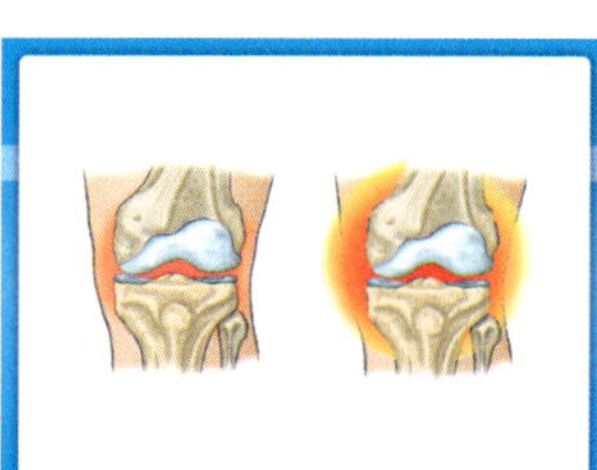

- The opposite is also true.
- As our joints age, they age like a forest.
- This now puts us in a dilemma:
  - If we do too much we might ignite a fire
  - If we do little to nothing, the forest keeps drying and the risk for future fires increases
  - With an increased risk we become afraid to move and steadily but surely move less

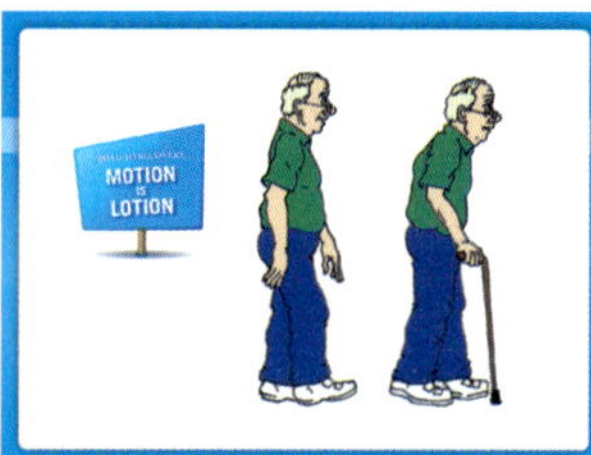

- So what do we do?
- Move – motion is lotion.
- Scientists have shown as long as we keep moving, be it little and often, we are in good shape.
- Not only do muscles and joints get a good workout and stay strong, but motion actually reduces the chance of a fire, or inflammation. Once inflammation is stirred up, it is no fun and can take a while to calm down.
- Remember: Only you can prevent forest fires.

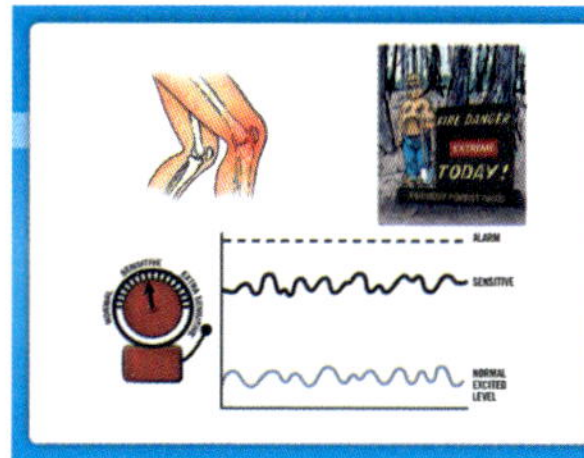

- You might be saying, "This if fine, but I hurt when I walk and feel my knee all the time."
- This is normal.
- Around all our joints there are nerves monitoring for injuries, but also for forest fires.
- As we age, the nerves, working like an alarm system, will be a little more sensitive than normal – in case there is a fire.
- This is expected and a good thing; it tells you to take a break when you have walked too much or stood too long.
- This alarm system will therefore have you be more aware of, or "feel" your knee, but it is not because of more damage – it is just monitoring your movement habits.

4.4.4.D: **Calming nerves – pacing: dating pain, making popcorn and toast and brushing teeth**

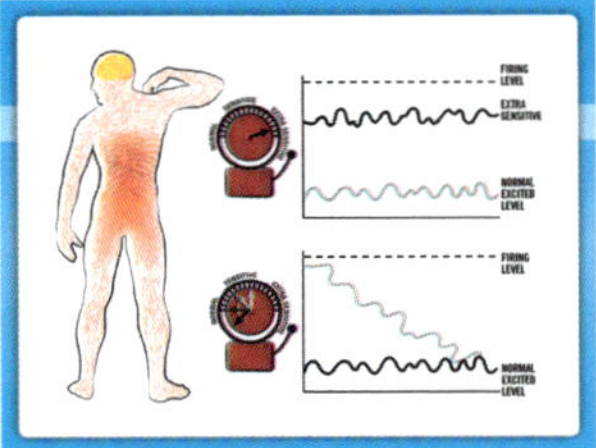

- We now know that in people who have pain lasting longer than the expected time for tissue healing, the body's alarm system – the nervous system – becomes more sensitive.
- This is normal and a way to protect you.
- In order to experience less pain and move on with your life, treatments should aim to turn down the extra sensitive alarm system.

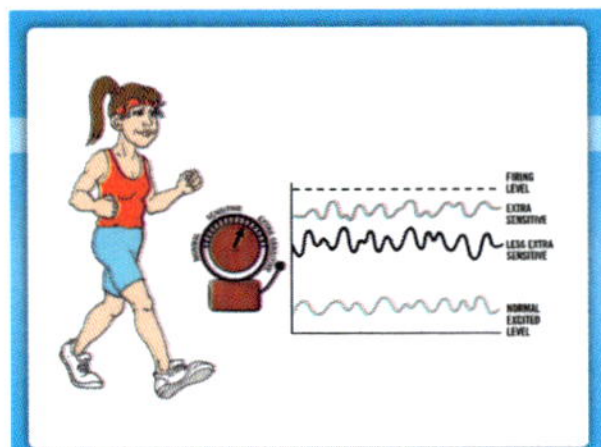

- One way to turn down an extra sensitive alarm system and experience less pain is movement
- Remember in school when you were stressed while studying for a big test?
- What was the best thing to do? Go for a run or bike ride. After some exercise, you felt calm and more relaxed.
- Blood and oxygen calm the nerves. Easy, gentle aerobic exercise pumps blood and oxygen around the nerves, which helps calm them down.

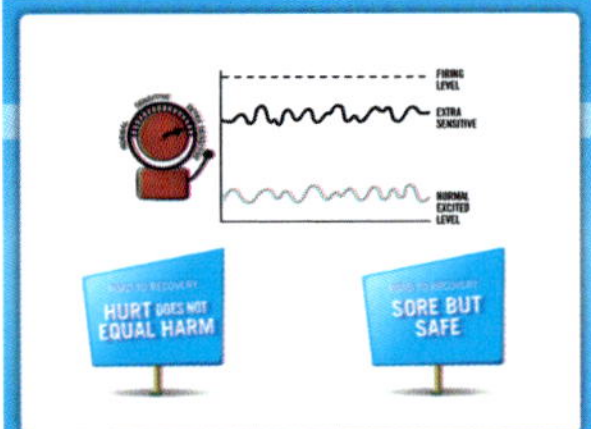

- Many people in pain are afraid of exercise because they think exercise causes pain and pain means injury.
- Let us clear up some common misconceptions.
  - Hurt does not equal harm.
  - You might be sore, but safe.
  - Understand that your alarm system is extra sensitive, and when you move or exercise, the alarm is merely telling you that your body is moving – nothing is being injured.
  - Pain that is understood and expected to some degree is not a threat and will actually decrease and eventually go away.
  - Think of the soreness you feel after a good workout.

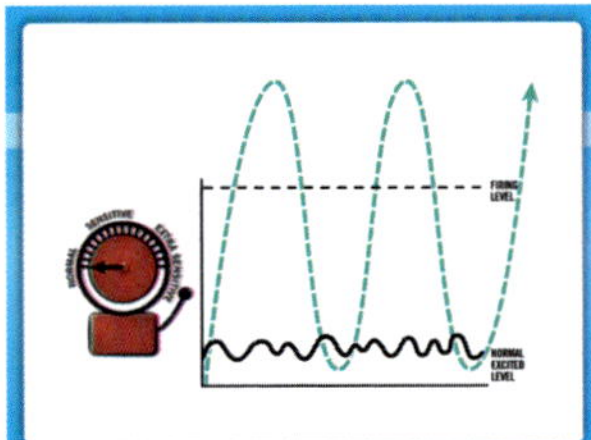

- One of the biggest reasons people in pain hurt with exercise or daily tasks is they do too much.
- Movement and activity is important, but you need to pace yourself.
- If you go too hard and crash through the pain, you might be sore for hours or days after the exercise.
- After you recover, you go at it again, paying the same price.
- After this cycle repeats several times, you will likely get frustrated and give up.
- Pace yourself. A 20-minute brisk walk that feels good with no significant soreness afterward is much better than an hour-long walk that leaves you in pain for a day or two.
- Movement and activity without significant pain will help your system calm down.

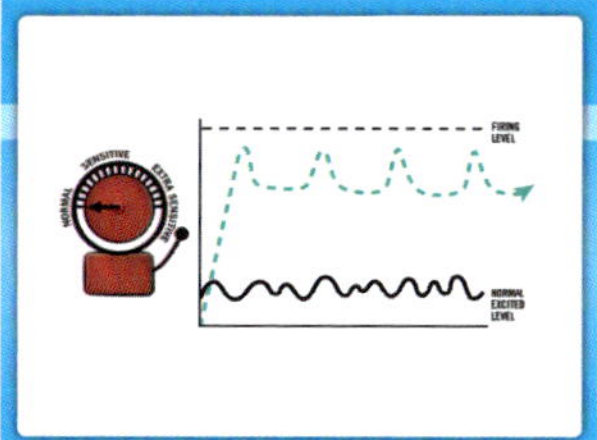

- In the opposite case, many people fear and avoid pain.
- They stop any and all activities short of pain.
- They focus on “When do I feel pain?” which actually increases their pain.
- This method hinders progress, which will leave them discouraged.
- Over time, it will take less and less activity to trigger the alarm system.

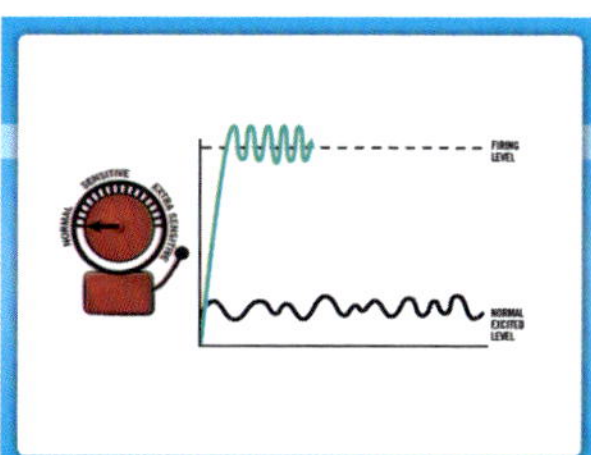

- So…what should we do?
- Tease it. Nudge it. Touch it.
- Perform a task or exercise up to the point you feel some discomfort.
- Pace yourself.
- Do not be afraid of pain, but respect it. Do not stop short, but do not crash right through.
- With your newfound knowledge of how pain works, you will not fear pain and it will start to ease.
- This allows for a gradual increase in activity and exercise.

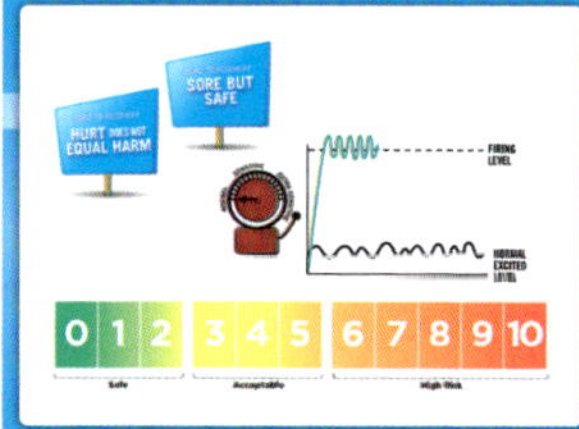

- This implies that some pain with activity and exercise is OK.
- Remember, your alarm system is a little extra sensitive, but:
  – Sore but safe
  – Hurt does not equal harm
- A good guide is the pain acknowledgement scale. Notice the name: “acknowledging pain,” not ignoring or avoiding it.
- A little bit of pain is OK.

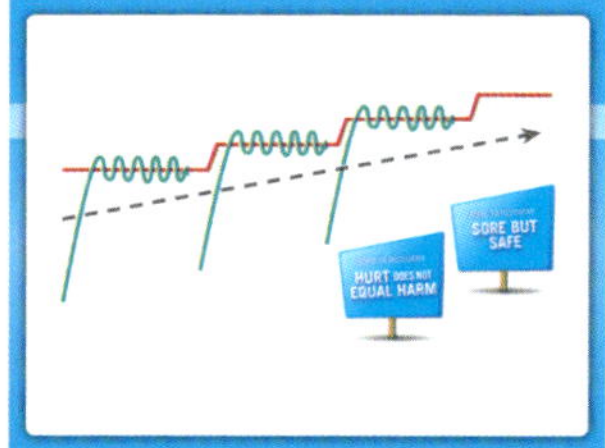

- How do you eat an elephant? One bite at a time.
- The same goes for any exercise program or task.
- Start small.
- Every other day add a small part.
- Day by day your time, distance, duration, etc. will increase.
- A three-minute walk becomes a four-minute walk, becomes a five-minute walk, becomes a 5K and eventually becomes the Boston Marathon.

(From Casey Hansen, PT, DPT, TPS)

- A nice metaphor to remember is: It is OK to take pain out to dinner, but do not date it.
- This reminds us that it is OK to "flirt" with pain – tease it, but do not get into a relationship with it. More than likely this will end up as a bad relationship.
- When you exercise and feel some discomfort, remind yourself it is OK, but tease it, and then back off.
- As you repeat this process, you do more and more and pain eases.

(From Christine Davis, OTR/L, TPS)

- A good way to remember this "healthy middle ground" is...popcorn.
- Ever made popcorn in the microwave?
- Unless you are one of those special people who have figured it out, you go through trial and error:
  - If you place it in the microwave too long...burnt popcorn, awful smell and a somewhat ruined movie night.
  - If you don't leave it in long enough it does not pop, and you have to increase the time until it's perfect.
- The best way: Start low and see what happens. If OK (not burned), we increase a little and repeat until we get the desired result.
- This is the same way we go about exercise – start easy and build slowly.

- Not a popcorn person?
- How about toast?
  - You visit a family member or friend and you're in the mood for some toast.
  - The dilemma? This is not your toaster and now the experiment starts.
  - Too long: Burnt toast.
  - Too short: Bread – not toast.
- Again, the best solution to not having burnt toast or a lingering burning smell? Start easy and build slowly...

(From Sonja McGill, PT, TPS)

- Still not convinced exercise should be paced?
- How about brushing your teeth?
- Most dentists would at minimum require you to brush your teeth twice a day – morning and evening.
- This would imply you should brush your teeth 14 times in a week.
- Does it make sense, since you are supposed to brush your teeth 14 times in a week, to wait till Sunday evening and brush your teeth 14 times?
- Sure, you have the end-result, but with a bad outcome:
  - Sore and sensitive gums
  - Likely cavities since it's not done regularly enough
- The best way? Pacing. A little bit, often...

4.4.4.E: **Calming nerves – grandma and Toblerone®**

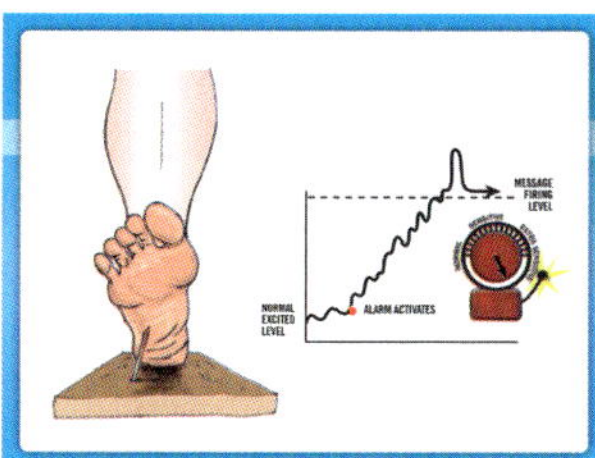

- When we step on a thumbtack or nail, the body's alarm system is triggered, letting us know there is a nail in the foot.
- Our brain produces pain to grab our attention.
- This is normal; it is to be expected and occurs to protect us.
- If we could not detect rusted nails we could get infections, which can have serious consequences.

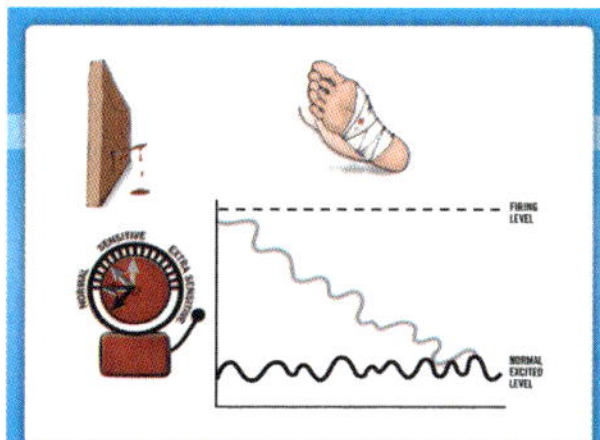

- Can you remember when you took the nail or thumbtack out? Did the pain just go away?
- No, it lingered.
- Actually, for a few days you were likely still aware of the event.
- Our alarm system is designed to let us know about threats and is not designed to "just shut off."
- It goes down, but not all the way – just in case you step on another nail or thumbtack.
- Over the course of a few days it settles and all is well.

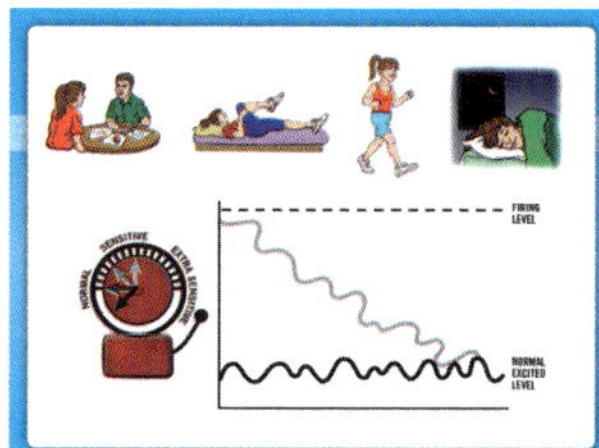

- The same process occurs in people with long-lasting pain.
- As you learn more about pain, engage in more movement, sleep better, etc., pain can and will calm down, but once again – slowly, not suddenly.
- This is again normal and expected.
- If pain protects you for months and even years, it makes no sense to "just suddenly go away."
- With patience and persistence, pain can go down.

- Pain is complex and, given that it is heavily affected by our daily activities and emotions, people with pain typically have "good" and "bad" days.
- Therefore, even as pain gets better, it still goes up and down, but overall comes down.
- A good way to think of this is Toblerone® chocolate. Imagine what this candy bar looks like if you hold it on one end and the other slopes down.
- If we charted your recovery in terms of pain, the image would look similar to Toblerone chocolate.

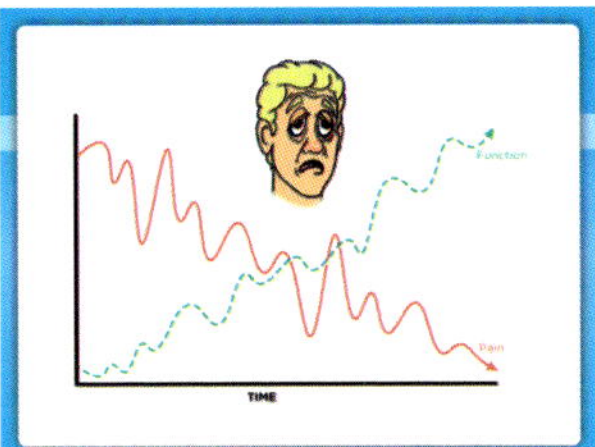

- Ever had the flu?
- When we are down we do less, but as we feel better and recover, we do more.
- The same happens with pain.
- As pain eases and you work on strategies to help your pain, you start doing more.
- Over time you are doing so many neat things you become less aware of the pain.

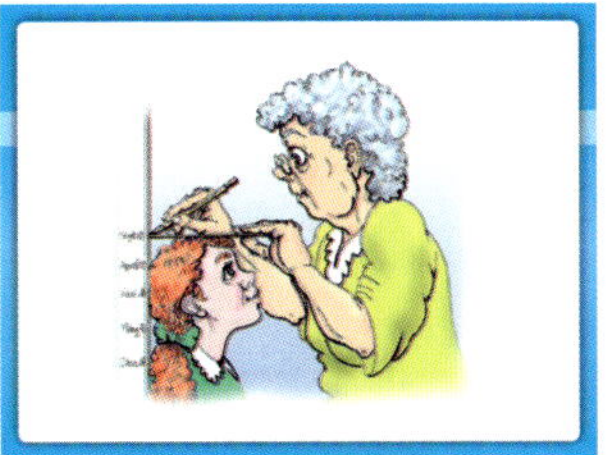

(From Colleen Louw, MPT, MEd, CSMT, TPS)

- If you have been struggling with pain for a long time, you more than likely live with it every day and are tired of it.
- This often makes recovery quite hard – if you live with it every day, it is hard to see the overall progress.
- A good example is your kids growing.
- Parents who live around their kids do not see them grow every day – it is a gradual process.
- Who sees them grow? Probably grandma.
- If grandma sees the kids every couple of months, what does she say? Boy, you are growing so fast! She might even make another mark on the wall.
- By not being here every day, grandma sees the progress.
- The same holds true for you. As you complete surveys every now and then, your therapist can see and measure your improvement, which is steady over time.

4.4.4.F: **Calming nerves – no flat tires**

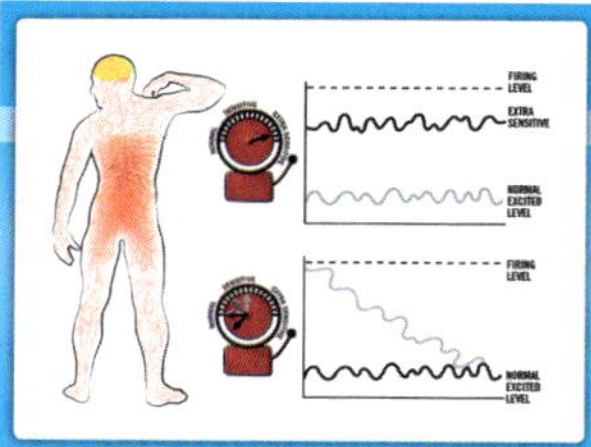

- We now know that in people whose pain lasts longer than expected, the body's alarm system – the nervous system – becomes more sensitive.
- This is quite normal and is a way to protect you.
- In order to experience less pain and move on with your life, treatments should aim to turn down the extra sensitive alarm system.

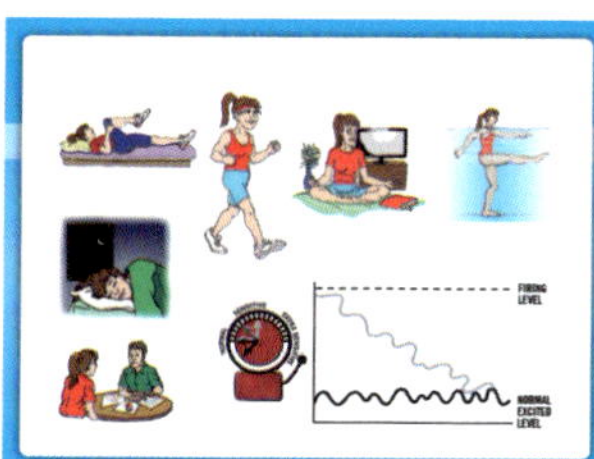

- Given the complexity of pain, there is no single approach that can "fix" pain.
- Pain can get better and does, over time, ease, but several strategies are needed to change your life.
- In recent years, scientists have looked at the various proven strategies to ease pain and found some might be more important than others.

- Scientists have shown there are four key strategies that will help you with your recovery:
  - Understanding more about your pain
  - Developing healthy sleep habits
  - Regular aerobic exercise
  - Creating goals for your future

- The important aspect is to realize you need all four key elements to truly move forward.
- If you miss one of them, it's the same as having a flat tire.
- Even though three tires are inflated and in good shape, the car cannot move with a flat tire.
- Periodically, as you work on your recovery and you feel "stuck," – check again: Am I keeping my four tires inflated or am I flat in one area?

4.4.5: Pain and the Brain

"Oh, you think it's in my head?" We hear this a lot. This mindset is based on the Cartesian model of pain, where pain is (falsely) seen as either physical or psychological (not real). The challenge for any clinician is to bridge this gap; to bring the brain into a discussion of pain without conveying the message that the patient's pain is not real. Having a patient see that tissue injury and pain are not the same and pain is a decision of the brain is powerful and has resulted in meaningful shifts in clinical practice. This series of stories bridges the tissue-brain gap.

Clinically, it is imperative to discuss the brain, but also to safeguard the message so patients don't get the idea that you think "it's in their head." Fake pain has never been scanned on any imaging studies – all pain is real. This concept is neatly described in a famous quote by David Butler:

> "The art of explaining pain
> to a patient is to tell them
> it's in their head,
> without telling them...
> it's in their head."

Louis Gifford, the pioneer in the concept of teaching people about pain, when asked how to avoid this clinical situation, had a simple answer (personal communication):

> "Try and avoid brain-talk as long as you can."

Many young energetic clinicians attend conferences and get excited about neuroplasticity, pain neuromatrix, etc., and cannot wait to tell patients about it. The clinical problem is that one needs to establish a relationship with the patient first so when we discuss the "brain," it is far less likely to illicit a visceral response. When these various stories were developed, published and used in research, a common criticism was that they were too peripheral. Up to this point, the stories, metaphors and examples centered around sensitive alarms systems, perimeter fences, etc., to explain a sensitive nervous system. This is rather deliberate and in line with Gifford's comments. It is also important to realize that many of the stories showcased to this point are also the highest ranked by patients and clinicians in clinical practice.[12]

This story covers issues regarding:

- Threat value
- Nociception versus pain
- Inhibition
- Facilitation
- Pain as an output of the brain

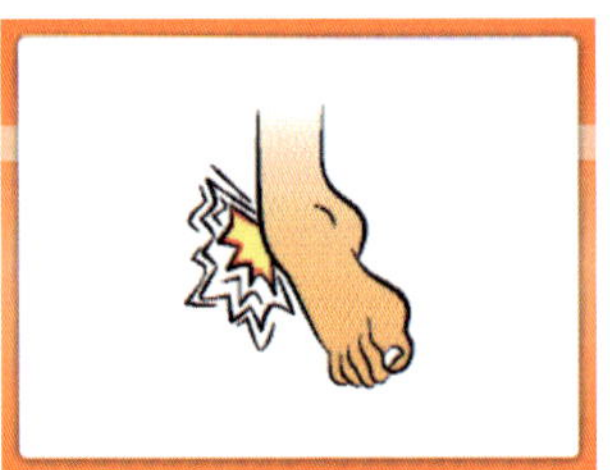

- If you sprained your ankle, would it hurt?
- Of course, ankle sprains hurt.

- Now imagine you are crossing a busy street and you sprain your ankle.
- Out of the corner of your eye you see a speeding bus heading right for you.
- Does the ankle hurt?
- Of course not. You jump out of the way.
- Once you are safely on the sidewalk, then your ankle might hurt.

- Your brain decides which one is the bigger threat. In this case, it is the bus.
- If you felt pain in your ankle, you might fall down and get hit by the bus.
- Here is the run down:
- The ONLY thing the ankle can tell the brain about is danger, not pain.
- In this case, pain would stop you or slow you down, threatening your life.
- The brain chooses not to produce pain in your ankle to protect you from the bigger threat, the bus.

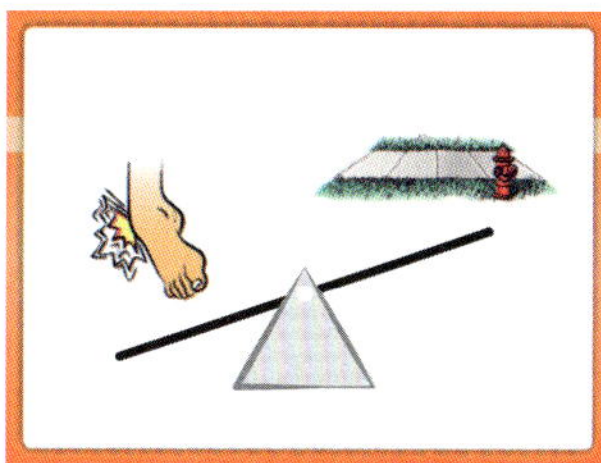

- Once you have jumped out of the way and the bus passes by, the larger threat is removed.
- Now, the brain has to choose between the threat of your sprained ankle and…the sidewalk.
- Who wins? Ankle sprain, of course.
- Now the brain might produce pain in the ankle to grab your attention and get you to seek help for your sprained ankle.
- Pain is 100 percent produced by the brain based on threat.

- Ever notice a bruise on your body and had no idea where it came from?
- In this scenario, you had a real tissue injury (bruise), but no pain.
- You cannot even remember when or how it happened.
- In this case, the brain received danger messages from your bruised tissues, but decided not to produce pain.
- Tissue injury and pain are two separate issues.
- You can have tissue injury and no pain; you can have pain and no tissue injury.
- A tissue issue might not be enough to cause pain.
- Pain is produced from your brain, not your tissues.

4.4.6: Brain's Pain Map

The general theme of PNE is making the unknowns known. Various issues with which patients struggle (memory loss, problems with focus and concentration, fine motor control difficulties, food tastes, body temperature, etc.) can be discussed using the pain neuromatrix. This teaches patients how a brain dealing with pain uses areas designated for other primary tasks, which comes at a cost. When brain areas are used for processing pain, the primary tasks often suffer. When a patient understands why they might be struggling to perform small motor control tasks, for example, they will have less fear and frustration, which can lessen their pain experience.

This story covers issues regarding:
- Pain neuromatrix
- Threat
- Neuroplasticity
- Functional MRIs
- Neuronal activation
- Pain uses in other areas
- Chronic pain enslaves those areas
- Hebbien theory: Nerves that fire together wire together

There are several different examples, stories and metaphors that can be used to showcase the increased activity of the brain during a pain experience:
- Grandma
- Battle stations
- Driving the same road every day

4.4.6.A: **Brain's pain map – grandma**

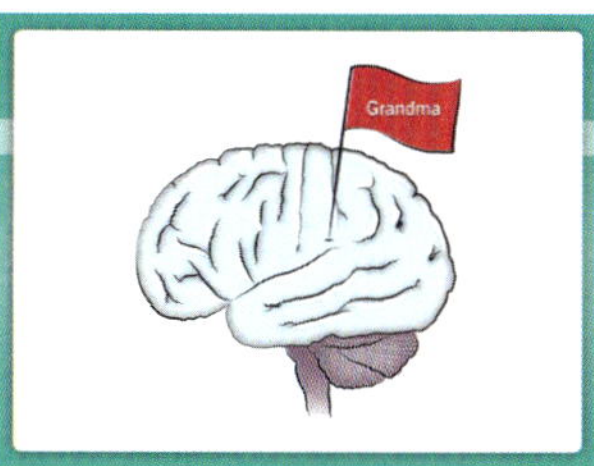

- Let's do a fun little experiment. Close your eyes and think of your grandma.
- Open your eyes.
- For years, we believed that when you think of someone, like your grandma, a little flag pops up in the grandma area and there she is...grandma.

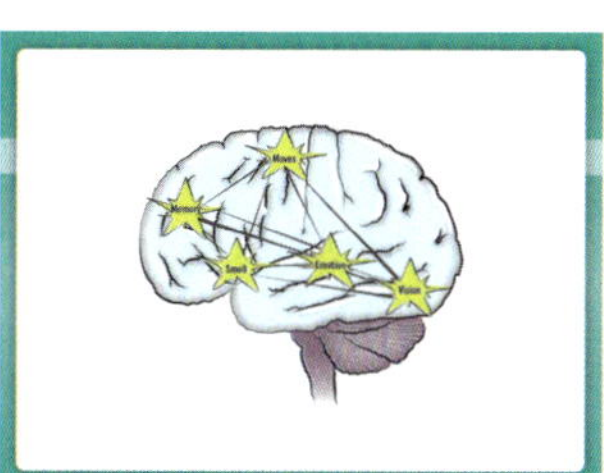

- Could you remember your grandma? That used the area of your brain that deals with memory.
- Could you see your grandma? That used the area of your brain that deals with vision, as well.
- Could you see grandma move? The movement area of your brain was used for that.
- Did you have any emotional thoughts about grandma? Did you miss her? That involved the emotional area of the brain.
- When you thought about your grandma, all of these areas talked to each other and had a "grandma meeting."
- This is your grandma map: All the areas that were used to think about grandma.
- Every grandma map is unique, just like every grandma.

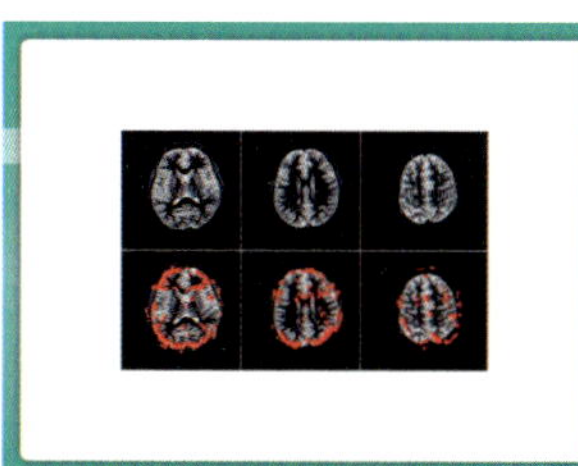

- Here is a brain scan of a patient with ongoing pain.
- In the first row, the patient is resting.
- In the second row, the patient moves her painful back, and we see a lot of red blobs.
- These blobs show the areas of the brain used to process her pain experience.
- This is a pain map, similar to your grandma map.

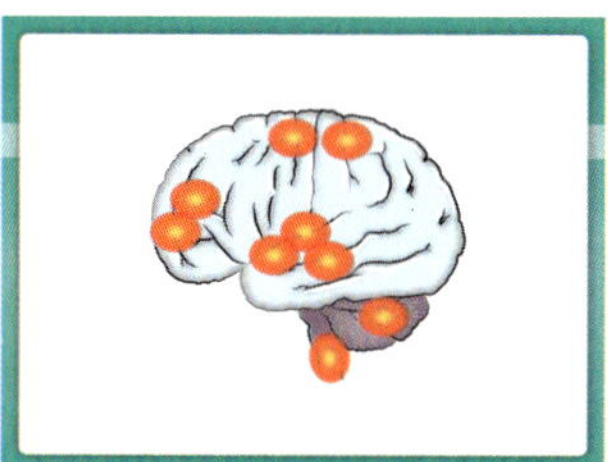

- Just like your grandma map, your pain map shows all the areas your brain uses to process danger or threat and your pain experience.
- When you experience pain, areas that usually perform other tasks are used to process pain.
- In ongoing pain, these areas are hijacked and even enslaved, affecting how they perform their usual tasks.
- Your brain is very worried about you, which keeps it very busy with pain.

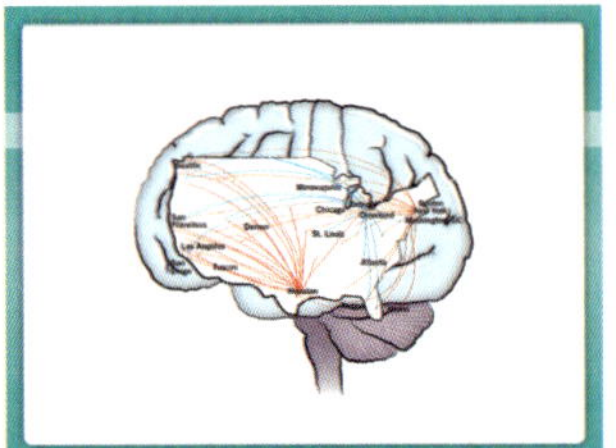

- Another way to think of it is an airline map. If you page through any airline magazine, you will notice the map showing where the airline flies.
- With all the areas in your brain processing danger messages, you have developed something similar to an airline map in the brain.
- It is important for you to know that just as in real life, people fly different airlines. Each person that experiences pain uses similar areas of the brain, but the pathways are different.
- Pain is individualized, which makes it hard to treat. You need treatment tailored to your pain.

- Many non-pain issues are due to areas of your brain being involved in a pain meeting.
- If your muscle area is in a pain meeting, you might have problems with muscle activities.
- If your focus and concentration area is in a pain meeting, you might have problems with focus and concentration.
- If your memory area is in a pain meeting, you might struggle with remembering things.
- If your area regulating body temperature is in a pain meeting, you might have hot flashes.
- If your area regulating stress chemicals is in a pain meeting, you might experience more stress and anxiety.

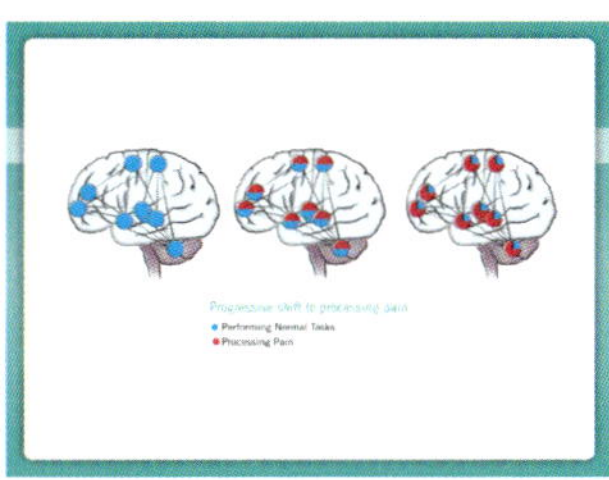

- Here is a visual way to show this shift from performing normal tasks to processing pain.
- The longer you experience pain, the busier these areas will be with pain.
- As areas spend more time processing pain, their original tasks become increasingly difficult to perform.

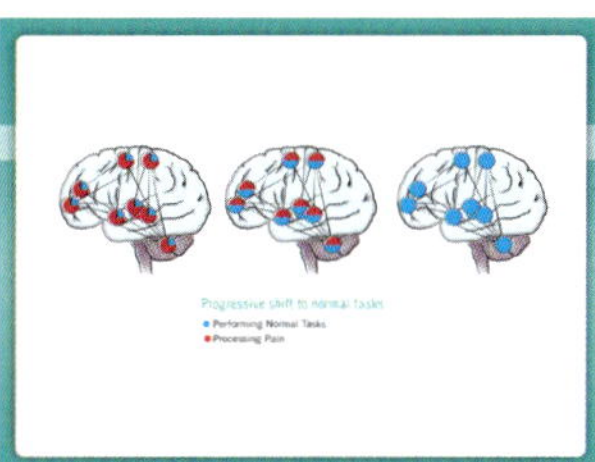

- The good news is that this process can be reversed.
- As you learn more about pain and what pain really means, your brain will become less worried.
- With less threat, the areas will slowly return to their original tasks and work less on processing pain.
- Education is therapy.
- The more you know about your pain and how it works, the better off you will be.

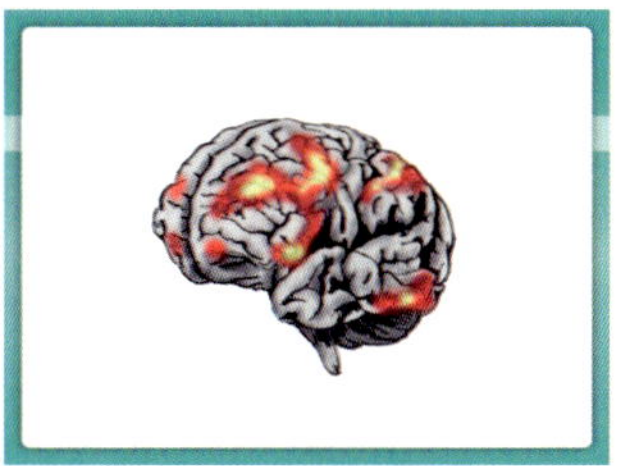

- An unfortunate saying is, "Your pain is in your head," which insinuates that the pain is not real.
- Well, your pain is produced in your head – your brain – but it is very real.
- Everyone's pain is unique; their pain maps are unique.
- Since your pain is unique, treatment needs to be tailored to your pain.
- Do not let anyone tell you how your pain should/should not be.

4.4.6.B: **Brain's pain map – battle stations (Timothy Benedict, PT, DPT)**

- For a military base to operate efficiently a variety of people are needed:
  - Soldiers to guard the perimeter and be on the lookout
  - Cooks to prepare the necessary meals
  - Medics to tend to the injured and sick
  - Engineers to work on equipment
  - Radar operators working in the communications department
  - Officers in the war room, etc.
- When all is good, everyone does their job and everything gets done.

- In a typical attack on the military base, the soldiers manning the guard towers are assigned to be the first line of defense – they're armed and ready to go.
- If the attack is brief, the assigned soldiers take care of the insurgents, repel the attack and all returns to normal.

- What if the attack lasts a long time?
- If the attack lasts longer, it likely indicates a more severe threat and EVERYONE is mobilized.
- Drop what you are doing and come help. Now cooks, engineers, etc., join in.
- There are likely more important things right now than cooking dinner.
- If this continues long enough there might be some significant consequences for the camp:
  - Meals will not get prepared
  - Equipment might not be fixed or maintained over time
  - Medical care might be limited

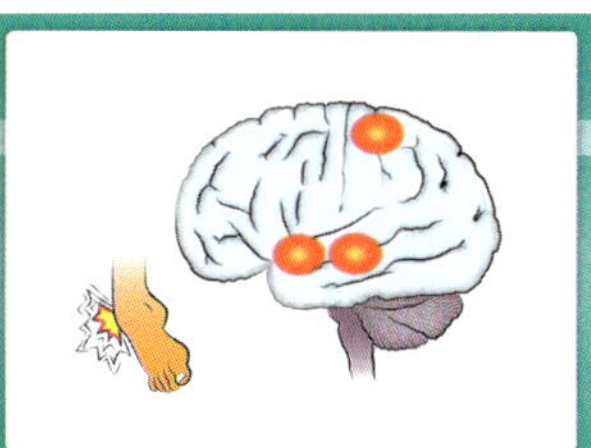

- What does this have to do with you and your pain?
- The same process occurs to us when we experience pain.
- There are many different areas in the brain that have regular jobs like focus and concentration, memory, coordinating movement, etc.
- When we experience pain, certain areas of the brain get busy, help us out, and then everyone goes back to doing their normal tasks.
- This is usually the case when we have an immediate injury and recover in a short amount of time; a simple ankle sprain, for example.

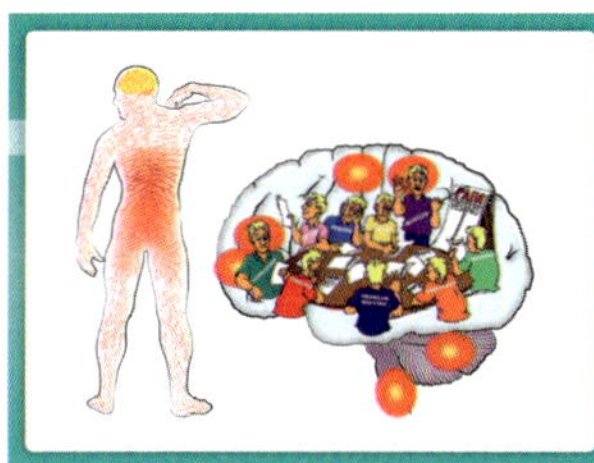

- When we experience pain for a long time and get many different opinions about our pain, treatments do not work well and there are increased worries about work and money; it is the equivalent of a full-on, long-lasting threat.
- Now, the whole base is mobilized to help.
- The same process occurs in our brain.
- Areas that have other tasks to perform are busy with pain.
- Pain is an important part of being alive and typically overrides other jobs such as focus and concentration, memory, planning movement, etc.
- If this goes on long enough, you will start noticing problems with focus and concentration, mental fatigue, short-term memory loss, etc.
- This does not mean there is something wrong with you or your brain, it is just being kept busy by pain.
- As you learn more about pain, the threat goes down and everything can shift back to normal.

4.4.6.C: **Brain's pain map – driving the same road every day**

- Imagine you're living out in thc country.
- Your daily drive into work requires you to drive a rather narrow dirt road all the way to the office.
- You do this every day, to work and back.
- You have even timed yourself and see it takes just over 42 minutes on a good day.

- You and other drivers drive this road again and again, week in and week out for months and years.
- The department of transportation notices the increased use of the road and decides to pave it.
- What happens?
- Even though you drive the same route, you end up at your destination (the office) much faster – almost 10 minutes faster!
- What changed? New car? New route? No, the road became smoother and wider allowing you to get to your destination faster.
- If this continues, the department of transportation might even widen the road to a four lane road and, guess what? It's even faster.

- How do you become good at golf?
- How do you become good at a musical instrument?
- Practice, practice, practice…
- When we perform a certain task, there is a detailed road we follow in the brain.
- By doing it again and again, we drive that road a lot and, guess what? The road changes and we can get there faster and more efficiently.
- This is how we get really good at tasks – repetition.

- This process also applies to everyday activities.
- For example, when we raise our arm there is a very detailed map we follow – let's call it the "raise your arm map" – and many areas in the brain connect to form a map.
- The end result: When you execute the map, you raise your arm.
- If you do it again and again the map changes and you can drive it faster.
- The end result is you get to your destination faster.

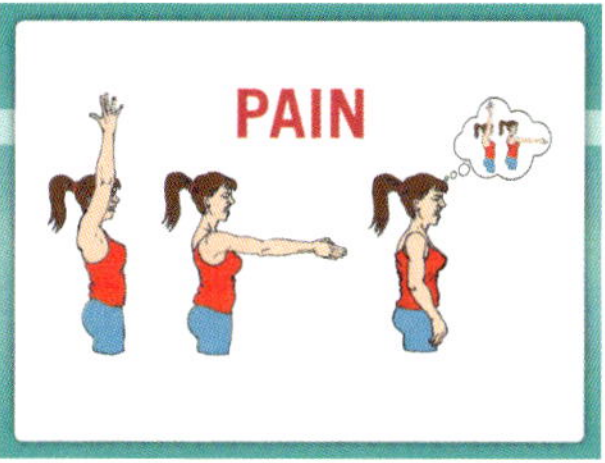

- Scientists have now shown us this process also occurs in people with pain.
- For example, after your shoulder injury it hurts to raise your arm all the way.
- After repeating this many times, the map changes and it becomes easier to activate the alarm.
- Now when you raise your arm halfway it is painful.
- With continued "practice" the map is even more efficient.
- Just thinking about raising your arm produces pain.

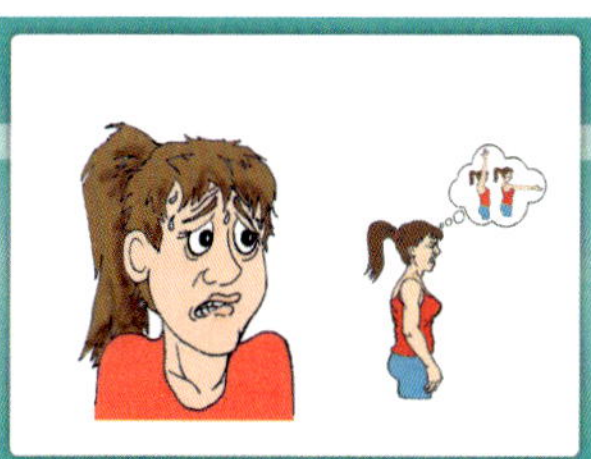

- When this happens you might be thinking:
  - I am getting worse
  - My tissues are steadily getting worse
- Actually, you are getting better…at pain.
- By doing a task again and again with the same result (pain), the map gets more and more ingrained and pain comes on faster with less movement.
- What do we do about?
  - First and foremost, know this is happening and there is nothing wrong.
  - Tissues heal and it is very unlikely your tissues are progressively getting worse.

- Another powerful way to recover is pacing.
- In pacing, we do part of a task but stop short of pain or go only a little bit into pain and then repeat the process.
- Now, the movement (for the brain) is associated with little to no pain and, by doing this again and again, the "raise the arm road" can be traveled, but the end result is different.
- By repeating this again and again, you can get better and pain-free movement, similar to getting better at golf!

4.4.7: Body Inc.'s CEO

The brain as the CEO of Body, Inc. provides another example/metaphor for explaining central sensitization as well as spreading pain. This series of stories lets you reinforce that the brain is involved in body functions, body parts "report" to the brain and pain is an output of the brain.

This story covers issues regarding:

- Inhibition
- Facilitation
- Pain neuromatrix
- Spreading pain
- Central sensitization

The main theme of the body CEO is central sensitization. Various other stories touch on this – the living alarm system, extra sensitive alarm system, radar and military response after Pearl Harbor, etc. Two additional stories might help:

1. The Chief Executive Officer (CEO) of Body Inc.
2. Processor problem with the computer

4.4.7.A: **Body Inc.'s CEO – the chief executive officer (CEO) of Body, Inc.**

- Think of a big corporate office building.
- Who is at the top? The CEO/president of the company.
- Below him or her you can find all the divisions of a company.
- In a normal company, it is common for each division to send monthly reports to the CEO.
- This allows the CEO to monitor the organization and deal with issues, should they arise.

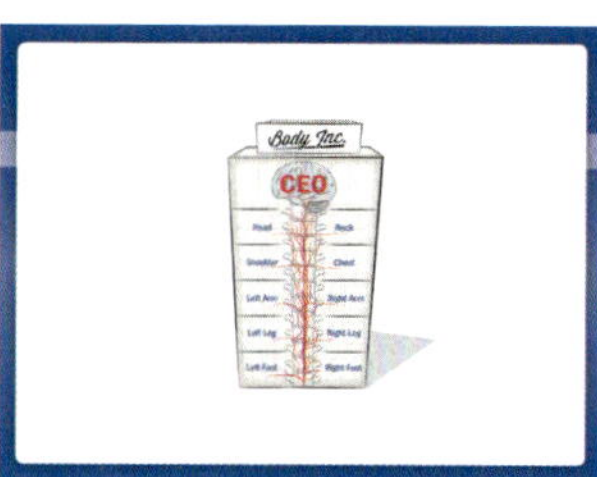

- Our body works the same way.
- The brain is the CEO of Body, Inc.
- Below the CEO is the neck division, left shoulder division, lower back division and so forth.
- As with most companies, each division sends regular reports to the CEO to let him/her know all is well.
- What happens when a division is not doing well? The CEO demands that reports are sent more often.
- Why? So they can figure out the problem and deal with the issue.

- When someone has persistent low back pain, for example, and treatments do not seem to be helping, the brain CEO gets worried about that division.
- The CEO tells the low back department to send weekly reports instead of monthly reports.
- What does this mean?
  - If you have ongoing pain, you become more "aware" of the area and might think there is something wrong. This might not be the case. You might just be more aware of the area because your brain is concerned.
  - Previous tasks that did not bother you in the past might bother you now. Again, this might not be a true indication of the health of your tissues.

- CEOs can be a bit neurotic. If one division is underperforming, the CEO might start snooping around in other divisions as well.
- Now the CEO wants all divisions to send weekly reports, so he or she can look for possible problems.
- The end result is you become more aware of other areas as well, not just the original area where pain was felt.

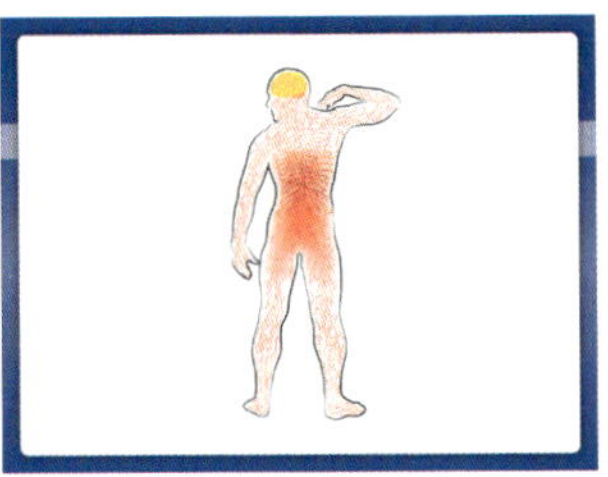

- The brain is the CEO of your body.
- When it is worried about you, it starts snooping around.
- The end result is increased awareness of other body areas.
- Thus, you feel the pain spreading further and further through your body.
- Does this mean there is new injury?
- No, it means increased sensitization. Moving these areas during exercise, for example, is perfectly fine and might actually help calm your nerves.
- Sore but safe.
- Hurt does not equal harm.

- If the CEO starts investigating the departments and finds little to no real issues, what will the CEO do?
- The CEO stops demanding weekly reports and goes back to the original monthly reports.
- If a CEO finds a department underperforming, he/she snoops around.
- The CEO finds out that a few people are on maternity leave and five others are on vacation at the same time.
- Is this a really BIG problem? No. A few changes on how many people can be gone at a time, and the problem is fixed.
- The CEO says, “Stop sending me weekly reports. I know what the issue is; it’s not a big deal.”
- The divisions go back to regular monthly reports.
- All is well at Body, Inc.

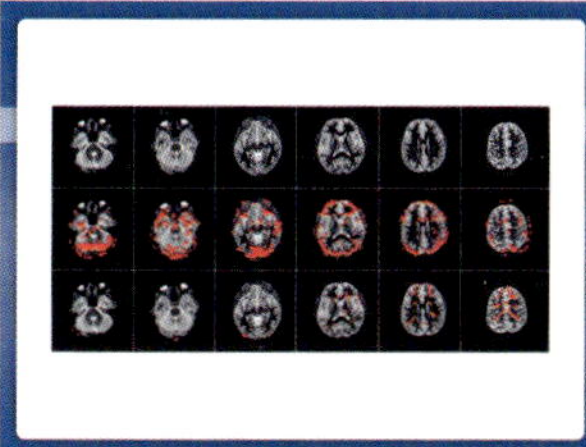

- Here is our CEO. This is a brain scan of a patient with ongoing pain.
- On the top row, the patient is resting and thus the CEO is calm.
- On the middle row, the patient moves her painful back and experiences pain. The CEO is really busy, getting a lot of reports from the back division and likely some other neighboring divisions as well.
- The last row shows the same patient, performing the same painful task after being taught more about pain, like we are doing today.
- As you can see, there are fewer red blobs.
- Since the CEO knows what is going on, the low back division does not send a lot of information, and the CEO is not that busy.
- Education is therapy.

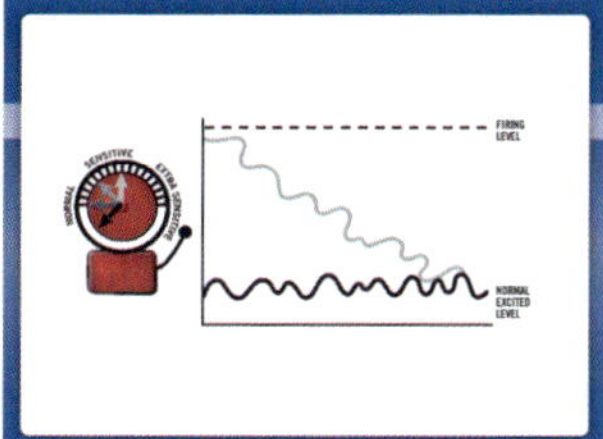

- When you understand more about pain, your body's alarm system will steadily send less and less information.
- Pain eases.
- Knowledge is therapy.

4.4.7.B: **Body Inc.'s CEO – processor problem with the computer (Louis Gifford)**

- Isn't a new flashy computer nice, especially when you have been working on an old, slow dinosaur?
- The new computer is fast – super fast.
- They keyboard is responsive, word processing is fast, etc.
- With a new computer, the processor that interprets and displays the information is brand new. When you type an "X" on the keyboard…an "X" shows up on the screen.

- What about the old computer?
- When the computer starts slowing down, letters start fading, and keys get stuck, it is no fun.
- Actually, the internal systems, such as the processor, might slow down since it is likely at its capacity to process information.
- What happens when you press an "X" now? With the slower processor you press an "X" key but nothing shows up (at least for a little while) – so you press the X again, and might be even a third time.
- Once the processor gets caught up, it over-corrects and… a whole bunch of "Xs" show up on the screen.
- What is interesting is that what you sent into the computer is not what is displayed on the screen.

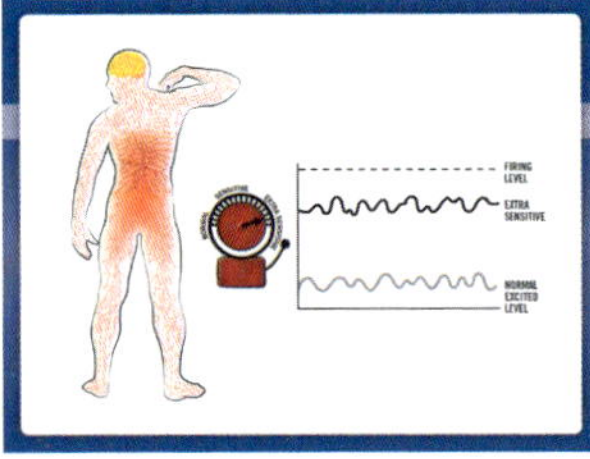

- A similar process can occur with people in pain.
- The information sent in does not match what is being displayed.
- For example, you might notice someone is barely touching your back, but it really hurts.
- The body's alarm system – the nervous system – is extra sensitive.

- Our tissues constantly send information to the spinal cord and ultimately to the brain for processing.
- When the system is overloaded, for example with lots of fear, worries about bills and work, constant pain, treatments not working, etc., the processor gets overloaded.
- Now, similar to a computer when information gets sent in (one "X"), 30 "Xs" show up on the screen.
- What does this mean? When you experience persistent pain, the pain you feel is likely not a good reflection of the health of your tissues (keyboard).
- By learning more about pain and how pain works, we speed up the processor which helps us get a more correct interpretation of the tissue information being sent.

4.4.8: Lions and Stress

Pain is only one of the outputs the brain uses to help protect. When confronted with a threat, the brain also engages various other systems. When pain persists, various systems that are helpful against short-term threats are continually engaged by the brain via stress chemicals like adrenaline and cortisol, which can have a tremendous impact. This series of stories powerfully illustrates and describes the protective mechanisms of the body and helps patients understand the various issues with which they are dealing.

This story covers issues regarding:

- Stress biology
- Fight or flight
- Sympathetic
- Adrenaline
- Cortisol
- Immune responses
- Multiple output mechanisms

Stress responses are common and many different examples can be used that ramp up the various bodily systems. We showcase two simple examples:

- Lion attacks
- Police lights

4.4.8.A: **Lions and stress – lion attacks**

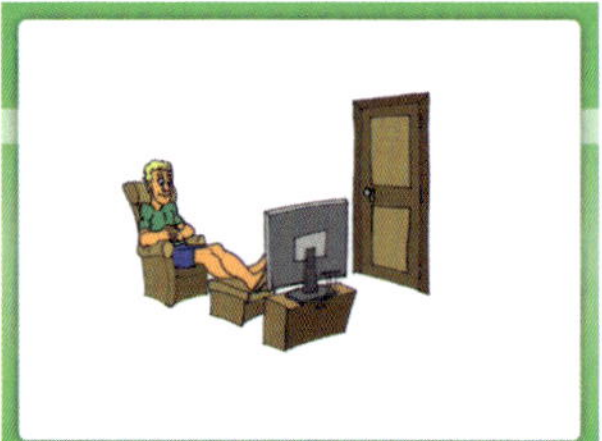

- Imagine yourself at home, relaxing and watching TV.
- Life is good.
- All of your bodily systems are relaxed.

- What would you do if a massive roaring African lion jumped into your room?
- Will you take a nap?
- Will you check your posture?
- Will you worry about the food in your stomach?
- Will you worry about healing tissues or fighting infections?
- Of course not, there's a lion in the room!

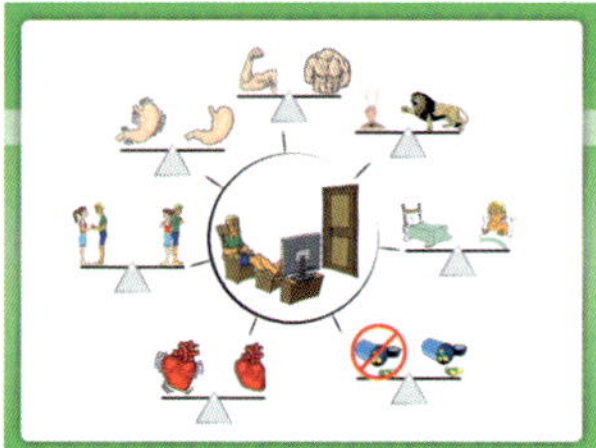

- In your body, there are various bodily systems: muscle, pain, sleep, immune, sympathetic, reproductive, digestive, etc.
- When life is good, they are evenly balanced.

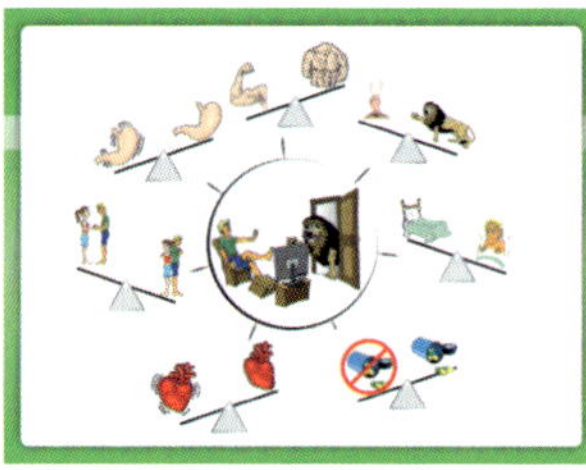

- When a big threatening lion jumps into the room, the systems shift, prioritizing tasks to help you deal with the threat.
- You are ready to run or fight, you are wide awake, etc.; restoration tasks like healing are put on hold.
- This is normal and happens to all of us.
- Think of the last time you were afraid. Might be walking in a dark alley?

- Luckily, the zookeeper comes by and removes the lion.
- The threat is gone.
- You sink into your seat. Whew!
- All of the body systems normalize again and are in balance.
- You think, "This is ridiculous! That's the third lion in my house this month!"

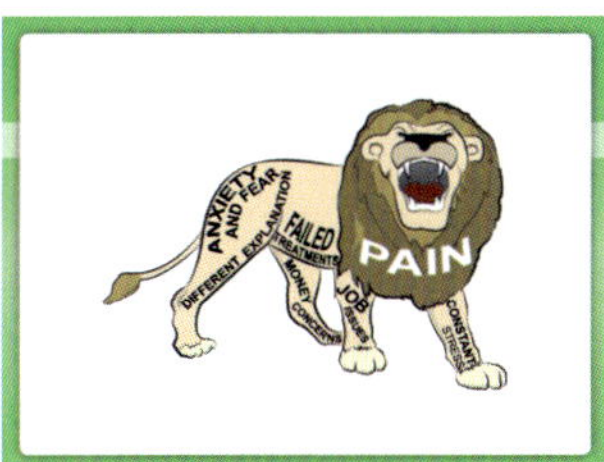

- Nice story, but what does it have to do with you?
- Ongoing pain is a big roaring African lion.
- If we add all the other issues you face, the lion gets even bigger.
- From the moment you wake up (assuming you slept), there is a big lion in your life.
- So all the bodily systems are ramped up to protect you.

- The lion has been in your life as long as you have had pain.
- Wherever you go, the lion follows you.
- The body's stress systems are thus working overtime and it affects you significantly.

- With all this stress, an increased amount of stress chemicals, and no "down time," you might start seeing some effects:
  - Mood swings
  - Problems sleeping
  - Fatigue
  - Sore and sensitive tissues
  - Memory changes
  - Low libido

- What would you do if a lion cub came into the room?
- Unless you have a major phobia of lions, you would not freak out. You might even want to pet it.
- So what does this mean?
- With a smaller threat, the stress system and stress chemicals do not need to be activated or ramped up.
- Knowing more about your pain – how it works and what it means – is the same as turning a big, roaring lion into a lion cub.
- Education is therapy.
- With increased knowledge of pain, the system can return to balance:
  - Better focus, concentration and memory
  - Less sore and sensitive tissues
  - Improved sleep

4.4.8.B: **Lions and stress – police lights (Jen DeLorenzo, PT, CFMT, MCWC, TPS)**

- Imagine you're driving down the road.
- It is a beautiful sunny afternoon and all is well.
- Suddenly, in your rearview mirror you see…the dreaded police lights flashing.
- What happens next?

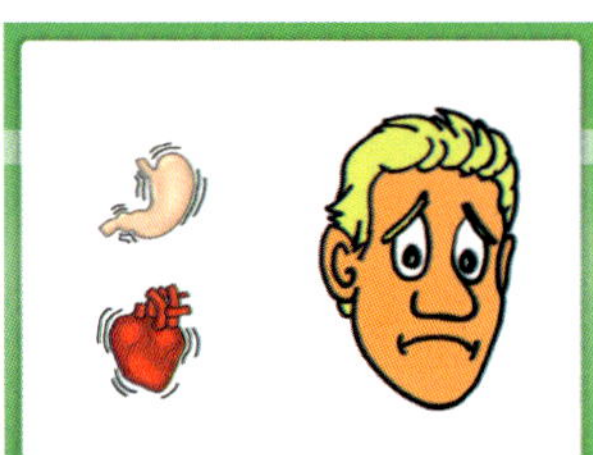

- You notice:
  - Heart rate increases
  - Muscles tighten up
  - Stomach gets upset
  - You are hypervigilant
  - You are nervous
  - You might even say a few choice words

- Then, miracle of all miracles – the police officer, with lights flashing, passes you and aims for the car ahead of you.
- Has this ever happened to you?
- What a great feeling, right?

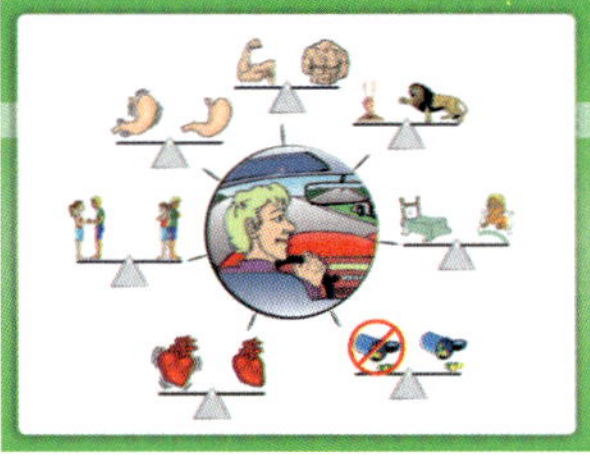

- This process of "fight and flight" is well described and understood.
- When life is good, our various bodily systems are in balance:
  - We store and use energy every day
  - We sleep when we are supposed to sleep, etc.

- When faced with stressors, such as the police flashing lights, the system shifts and:
  - Heart rate increases
  - Muscles tighten up
  - Stomach gets upset
  - You are hypervigilant
  - You are nervous
  - You might even say a few choice words

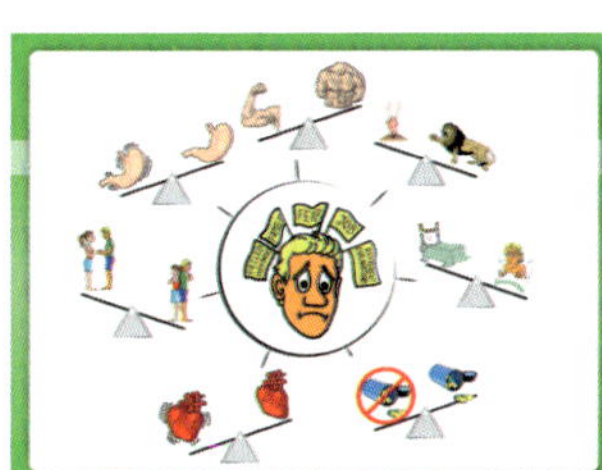

- What would happen if this happens every day, all day?
- As soon as a police car passes you, another one is spotted behind you with flashing lights?
- The various bodily systems will never have the opportunity to calm down.
- This might lead to problems with fatigue, sore muscles, upset stomach, difficulty sleeping etc.
- Unfortunately, people struggling with pain face many police lights on a regular basis, such as failed treatments, worries about money and jobs, hurting all the time, family issues, different explanations for pain, medical tests and scans, etc.
- No wonder you are tired, your muscles are sore, and you have difficulty sleeping, etc.

- How do we help this?
- Learning more about why you hurt and all the things you can do to get better reduces the threat and, in essence, eliminates the police car in the rearview mirror.
- If you now add regular exercise (little and often), have healthy sleep habits, and have some short and long-term goals, you can move further toward recovery and getting your bodily systems back to normal and balanced.

4.4.9: Tissue Issues

"This 'pain stuff' might sound good, but you don't understand, I have a…." This might be the most common phrase uttered in clinical practice when trying to change a patient's cognitions about their pain. Patients are indoctrinated in their tissues – and quite rightly so – medical people have done this for years. Of course, let us not forget the evidence of a scan! Having proper ammunition to persuade a patient to think differently about that "bulging" disc or rotator cuff injury could be just enough to open their mind to a new way of thinking about pain. This education series needs to be delivered with tact and caution. We are not aiming to make a patient think there is nothing wrong with a particular tissue, but to illustrate that "bad" tissues might not always cause pain and tissue issues are only one part of the pain experience.

This story covers issues regarding:

- Tissues heal
- Pain issue versus tissue issue
- Normal findings
- Paradigm shift
- Threat value
- Knowledge

This section is not necessarily a story but rather "ammunition." In a recent PNE clinical application survey study, clinicians utilizing PNE rated the influence of the biomedical model as the main barrier to success. Patients will challenge clinicians with information about their tissues. Unless a clinician can de-educate a patient (lessen fear, develop healthier thoughts and beliefs, etc.), the re-education (PNE) will be very challenging at best. Clinicians are advised to review section 3.1 showcasing the various "normative" data on various clinical issues such as LBP, neck pain, rotator cuff injuries, etc.

A word of caution:

Honesty without compassion is cruelty

The data from section 3.1 and what follows is scientifically correct and, if delivered without compassion and a true sense of caring, can be overly blunt. The patient needs to realize that the information you are about to share with them is done because you truly care, versus only trying to topple their "tissue-belief-pyramid."

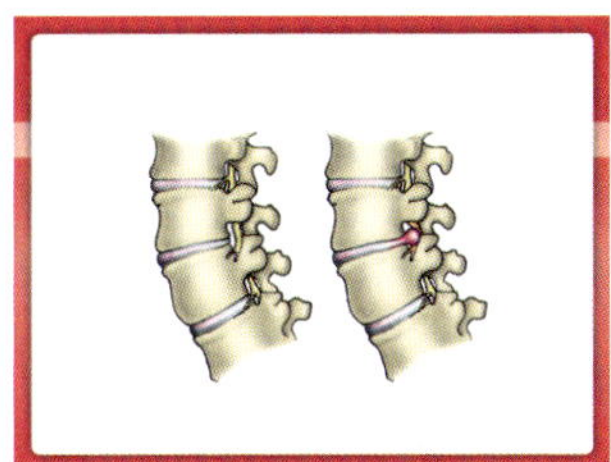

- You might be thinking, "This 'pain stuff' might sound good, but you don't understand, I have a bulging disc!"
- Sure, when you hurt your back, you might irritate some tissues, such as discs.
- Did you know?
  - If we scan the same patient with a "bulging disc" two months later, the bulge is usually 50 percent smaller and nine months later it is completely gone.
  - Discs work like a sponge, and they are 20 percent more swollen in the morning than evening. Time of day might influence what they find on the scan.
  - Scans are often done lying down, and gravity might increase the bulge. When we scan the same patient upright – the position most people function in all day – the results are much different.
  - Scans are still images and do not show what happens with movement. During movement, the swollen disc limits movement at that level to help protect you.
  - Forty percent of people with no back pain have bulging discs on scans.

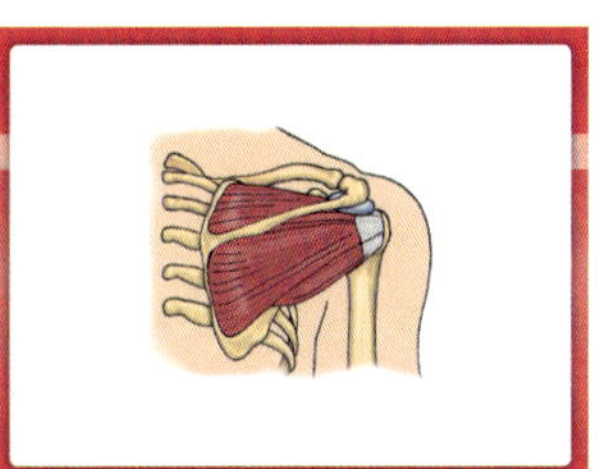

- You might be thinking, "This 'pain stuff' might sound good, but you don't understand, I have a rotator cuff injury!"
- Sure, you might have some issues with your shoulder.
- Did you know?
  - One in three people over the age of 30 have abnormal findings on scans of their rotator cuff.
  - Two in three people over the age of 70 have abnormal findings on scans of their rotator cuff.
  - Even after successful surgery for rotator cuff issues, more than two out of three people have abnormal findings on scans of their rotator cuff.

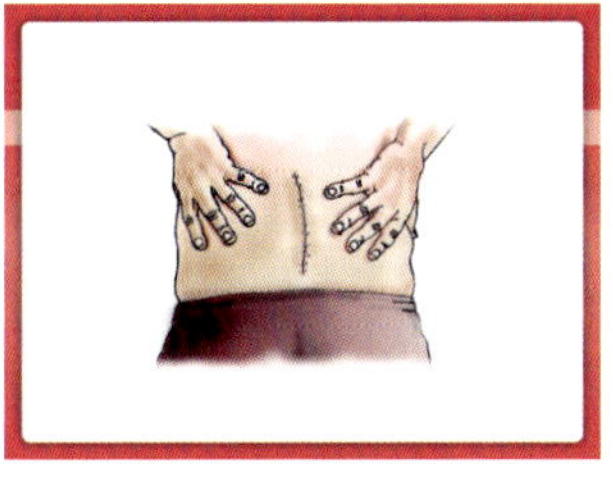

- You might be thinking, "This 'pain stuff' might sound good, but you don't understand, I had back surgery!"
- Did you know?
  - Eighty percent of NFL players who undergo the same type of back surgery return to the NFL.
  - Eighty-five percent of NBA players who undergo the same type of back surgery return to the NBA.
  - Studies have shown the vast majority of patients need not limit or restrict their activities and movements after back surgery.

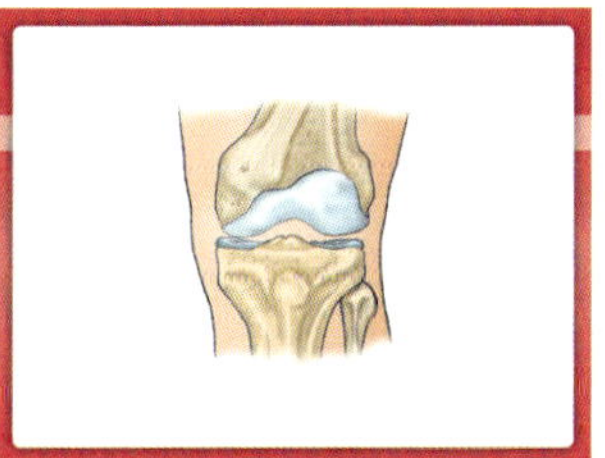

- You might be thinking, "This 'pain stuff' might sound good, but you don't understand, I have a bad knee!"
- Did you know?
  - One in three college basketball players with no knee pain show significant issues on their knee scan.
  - Only 50 percent of people with arthritis of their knee experience pain.
  - Some people have no ACL and do not even know it.

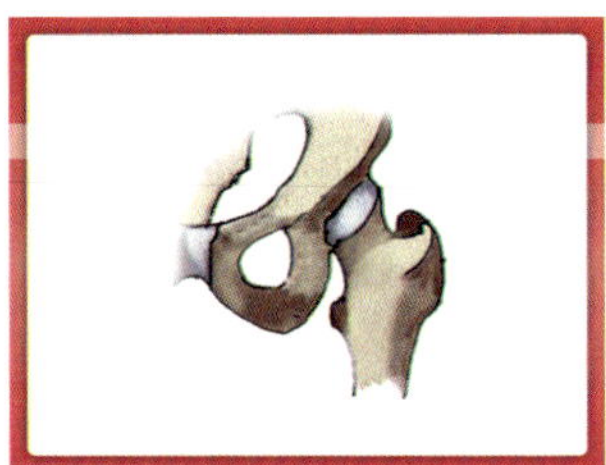

- You might be thinking, "This 'pain stuff' might sound good, but you don't understand, I have a bad hip!"
- Did you know?
  - Nearly 75 percent of people have age changes to their hip joints on a scan, yet experience no pain.
  - In hockey players with no hip pain, two out of three have scans that show significant age changes.

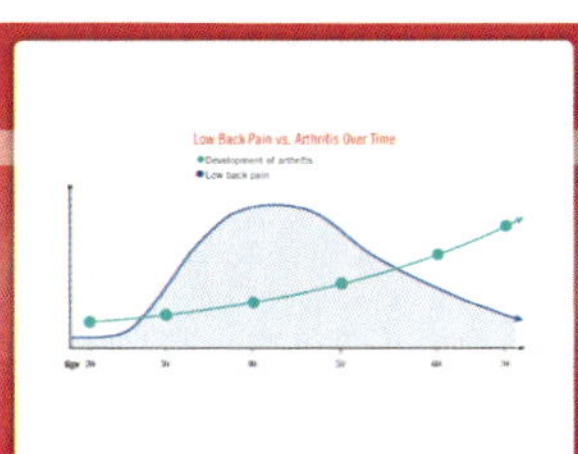

- You might be thinking, "This 'pain stuff' might sound good, but you don't understand, I have arthritis of the back!"
- Look at this graph:
- We know a human being develops a little arthritis in their spine when they are in their early 20s.
- As we age, arthritis tends to increase.
- Look at the blue curve. This curve shows when low back pain is experienced the most.
- As you can see:
  - You can have significant low back pain and only a little bit of arthritis.
  - You can have a lot of arthritis, but little to no low back pain.
- Arthritis and low back pain are two different things. You can have one or the other!

- You might be thinking, "This 'pain stuff' might sound good, but you don't understand, I was in a car accident!"
- Did you know:
  - Demolition derby drivers crash over 50 times per event.
  - Demolition derby drivers participate in an average of 30 events during their career.
  - The average speed of these collisions is 24 mph.
  - Only two to three percent of them experience long-lasting pain.
- Medically trained people (doctors, therapists, etc.) who are in similar car accidents to non-medically trained people return to work 200 times faster.

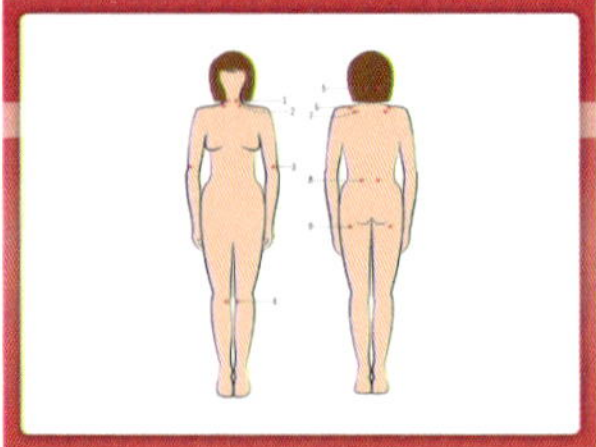

- You might be thinking, "This 'pain stuff' might sound good, but you don't understand, I have fibromyalgia!"
- There are many people with fibromyalgia who lead very productive lives, including:
  - Corporate CEOs
  - Marathon runners
  - Even physicians and therapists treating people with fibromyalgia who have fibromyalgia themselves
- A good example is Morgan Freeman. He is diagnosed with fibromyalgia and often writes about his daily struggles, yet he is a prolific actor.

This example is very important. Many times in clinical practice we encounter a pathological state, i.e., rheumatoid arthritis, multiple sclerosis, etc., and have to find a clinical way to have patients see the cup as half full. Even though it is likely very difficult, if not impossible, to even imagine what patients with these various conditions are going through, we must find a way to help them reconceptualize their situation. The reality is that there are many famous and successful people in this world that live very productive and successful lives despite having rheumatoid arthritis, multiple sclerosis, chronic low back pain, etc. Clinically, it might be helpful to share this in a tactful way with patients. By having them realize they do have a choice and their diagnosis need not be limiting, it can be a powerful shift. In Table 4.3 is a listing of some "famous" people that are productive despite various medical diagnoses.

Table 4.3: Famous and successful people with various diagnoses.

Fibromyalgia	Irritable Bowl Syndrome	Lupus
Soap Opera Actor Susan Flannery Actor Morgan Freeman Actor Michael James Hastings Artist Frida Kahlo Social Activist Florence Nightingale Singer Lady Gaga	Model Tyra Banks Actor Lynda Carter Nirvana Lead Singer Kurt Cobain Seattle Mariners Center Fielder Franklin Gutierrez President John F. Kennedy Actress Jenny McCarthy	Singer Toni Braxton Actor and TV Host Nick Cannon Pop Singer Selena Gomez

Multiple Sclerosis	CRPS	Chronic Fatigue Syndrome
TV Host Neil Cavuto NHL Hockey Player Josh Harding Country Musician Clay Walker TV Host Montel Williams	Singer and Dancer Paula Abdul American Business Man Howard Hughes Actor and Comedian Jerry Lewis	US World Cup Soccer Player Michelle Akers Singer Cher

Table 4.3: Famous and successful people with various diagnoses *(continued)*.

Stroke	Parkinson's Disease	Cancer
New England Patriots Linebacker Tedy Bruschi Editor *Elle* magazine in France Jean Dominique Bauby Wrote a book by eye-blinking the alphabet.	Evangelist Billy Graham Actor Michael J. Fox	Kansas City Chiefs Safety Eric Berry Wellness Activist Kris Carr

Rheumatoid Arthritis	Lyme Disease	Chronic Pain
Actor and Comedian Lucille Ball Actor Kathleen Turner	Actor Alec Baldwin Actor Ben Stiller	Actor Elizabeth Taylor Actor Tobey Maguire Actor George Clooney

Diabetes	Chronic Migraines	Endometriosis
Actor Halle Berry	Actor Ben Affleck	Actor, Writer, Producer, Director Lena Dunham

Celiac Disease	Psoriasis	Crohn's Disease
Reality TV Star and Talk Show Host Elisabeth Hasselbeck	Reality TV Star Kim Kardashian	Guitarist for Pearl Jam Mike McCready

Juvenile Arthritis	Psoriatic Arthritis	Sjogren's Syndrome
LPGA Golfer Kristy McPherson	PGA Golfer Phil Mickelson	International Tennis Star Venus Williams

Polysystic Ovary Syndrome	Stargardt Disease	
Fitness Instructor and TV Host Jillian Michaels	US Olympic Distance Runner Marla Runyan	

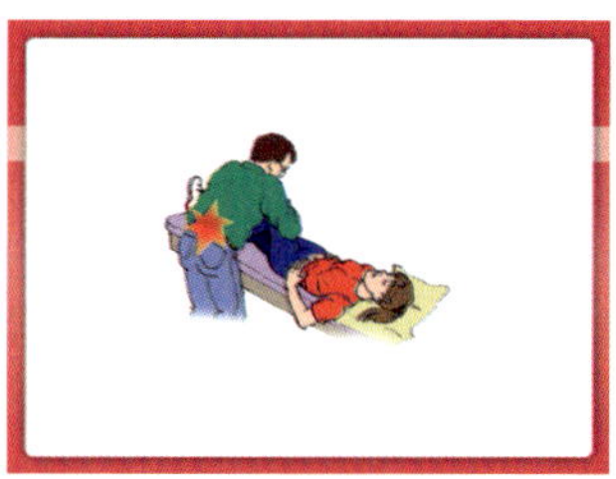

- Physical therapists have among the highest rates of low back pain.
- Often, therapists treating a patient with low back pain will be experiencing low back pain themselves.
- Even with high rates of low back pain, very few therapists take time off work.
- This is because therapists understand what pain is and how it works. They respect pain without fearing it.

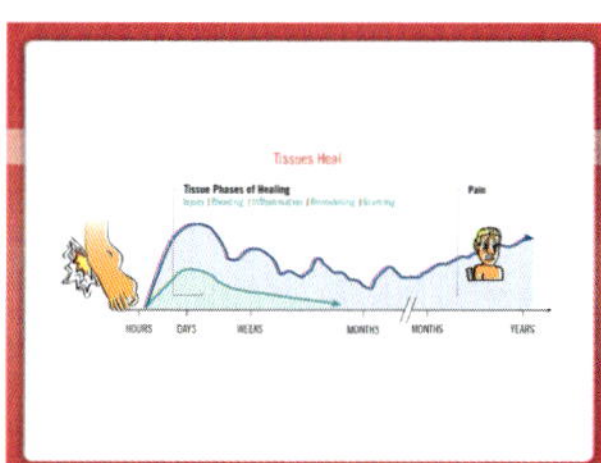

- Tissues have very predictable stages of healing.
- Most tissues in the human body heal over three to six months.
- Ongoing pain is more likely due to an extra-sensitive nervous system.

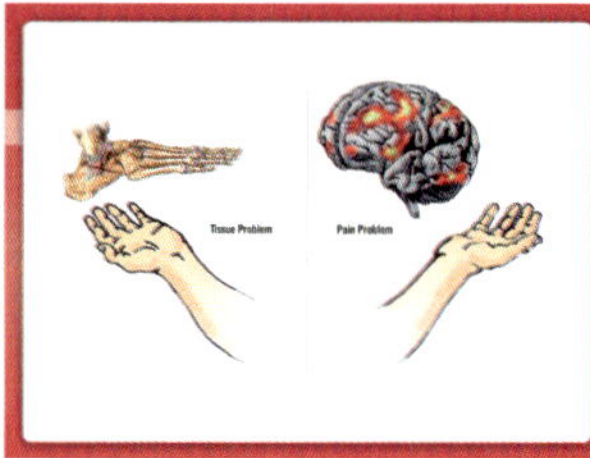

- Take a few seconds and think about the following statements.
- Yes, you are experiencing pain. We do not dispute that.
- In most people, the tissues have had adequate time to heal.
- In reality, you do not have a tissue issue, but rather a pain issue.
- Your goal should be to become an expert on pain.
- The more you know about pain, the less pain you will experience.

4.4.10: Neurogenic Inflammation

Following an injury or surgery, pain and swelling are expected. Having a joint remain swollen for months after the injury or surgery will undoubtedly cause more stress and anxiety. Teaching a patient how nerves send messages toward the spinal cord (orthodromic impulses) and toward the tissues (antidromic) helps them understand neurogenic inflammation. An unhealthy nervous system, physically and/or emotionally, can keep tissues inflamed. Armed with this information, you can then target strategies to help decrease nerve activity to help recovery.

This story covers issues regarding:

- Peripheral neuropathic pain
- Retrograde firing
- Thoughts as nerve impulses
- Immune response
- Inflammation
- Persistent swelling

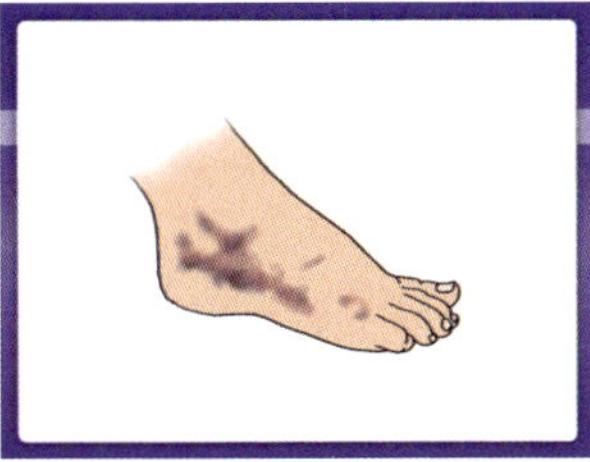

- Have you ever seen a bruise after an ankle sprain?
- When you sprain your ankle, tissues get injured.
- Tissues release chemicals that make the ankle swell and become hot and sensitive.
- This is normal; it protects you.
- The swollen, sensitive and hot ankle makes you slow down and go seek help.
- As time goes by, the ankle heals and the tissues recover.

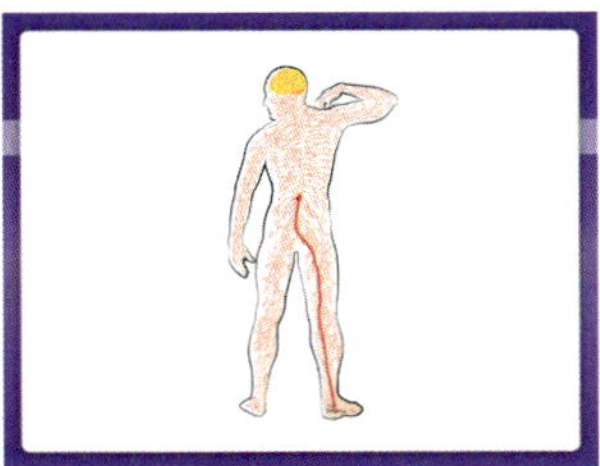

- When you sprain your ankle, the information has to travel to the brain to get your attention.
- Nerves in your ankle and foot, working like an alarm system, wake up and send danger messages to the spinal cord and then on to the brain.
- The brain might produce pain to get you to pay attention to the ankle and seek help.
- This is normal.

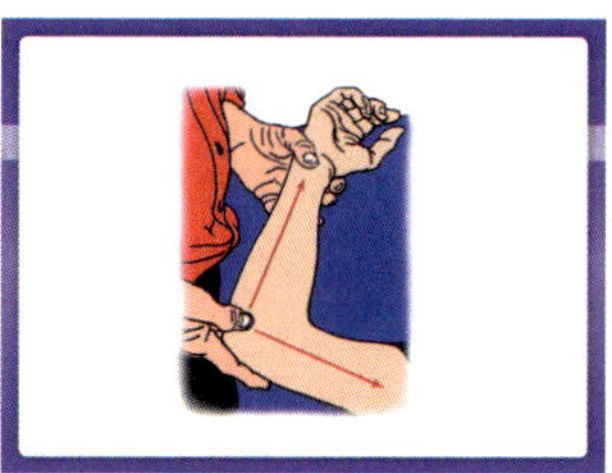

- Here's an interesting demonstration:
  - Grab your elbow and poke a little around your funny bone.
  - You will quickly find some tingling in the ring finger and pinky finger, right?
  - You will also "feel" yourself poking around the funny bone.
- Nerves fire messages both ways:
  - Down to the fingers
  - Up to the spinal cord and then onto the brain to tell you, "Stop doing that!"

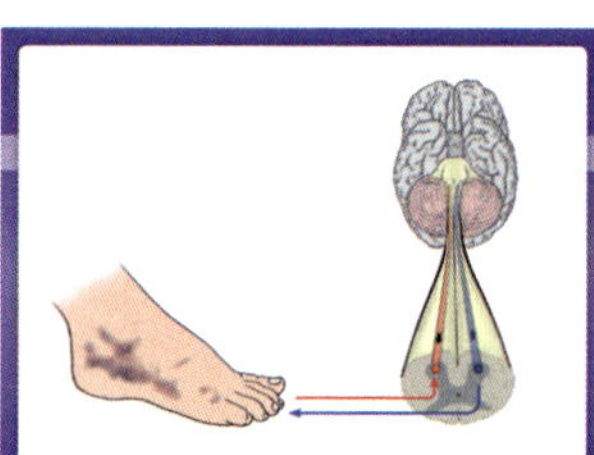

- The same "firing both ways" occurs during an ankle sprain or surgery.
- The nerves around the ankle send messages to the brain for action.
- The nerves also fire messages down to the ankle.
- The end result when nerves fire "backward" is they cause the increased release of chemicals, thus making your ankle more swollen, hot and sensitive.
- This might cause the tissues to remain swollen, hot and sensitive for long periods.

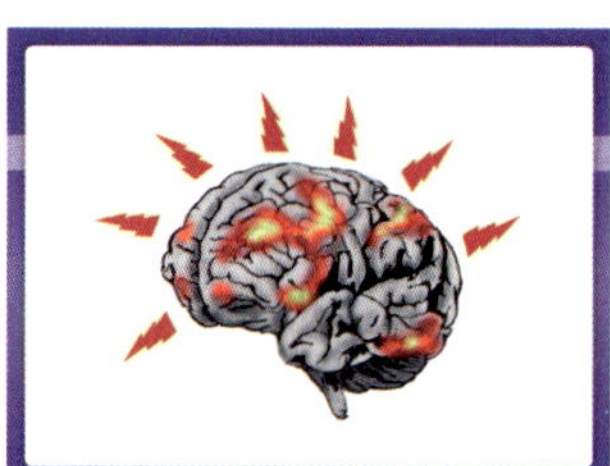

- Here's the interesting part: Thoughts are also nerve impulses.
- Worries are nerve impulses.
- When you worry a lot about your ankle or knee, it drives more nerve messages down to the tissues and can thus keep them swollen, hot and sensitive.
- What should you do?
  - Stop worrying about your "puffy ankle/knee" – it is normal and we can explain it.
    Think happy thoughts; stay calm.
    Learn more about your pain. The more you know about pain, the less often danger messages will be sent.
  - Move and exercise. Blood flow and oxygen calm the nerves.
  - Try ice to help calm nerves.

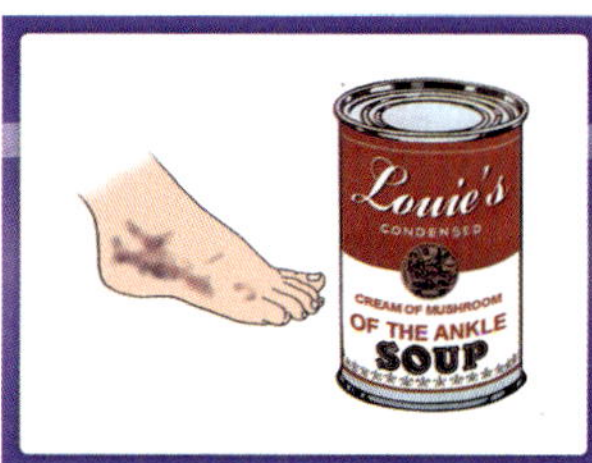

- Another way to think of this is...soup.
- When you sprain your ankle, tissues get injured.
- Tissues release chemicals that make the ankle swell and become hot and sensitive.
- In essence you develop a soup...an inflammatory soup.
- Can you imagine: Cream of mushroom of the ankle?
- This is normal and part of the process that starts the healing.

- The soup contains a lot of ingredients, including spices.
- One of the spices is pepper.
- Pepper makes the soup spicier.
- For an ankle sprain, a spicier soup means more sensitivity.
- In essence, the soup becomes angry.

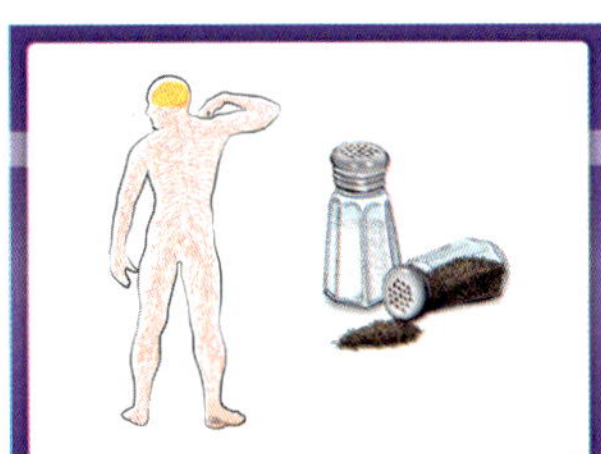

- What's important to know is that scientists have shown that when our nerves are more active, they dump more pepper into the soup.
- This would mean pain and swelling can last longer, resulting in angry soup.

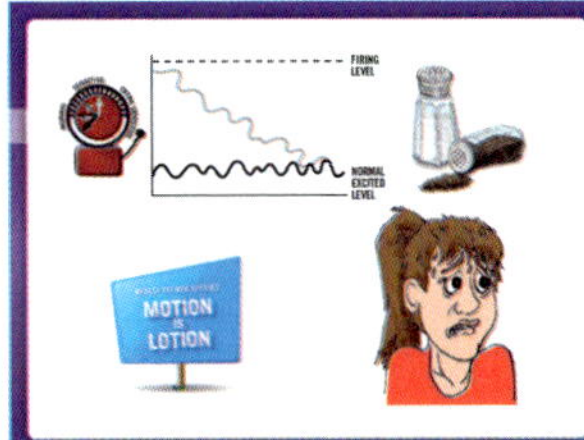

- How do we make the soup less spicy?
- By getting our nerves to calm down, the amount of pepper produced is decreased, the soup becomes less spicy, and recovery can start.
- How do we calm nerves?
  - Thoughts are nerve impulses and decreasing fear and anxiety can help.
  - Scientists have shown when we pump blood and oxygen around nerves, they calm down. Motion is lotion.

4.4.11: The Brain's Body Maps

On the cutting-edge of our understanding of pain via graded motor imagery is the primary somatosensory cortex. Neuroplasticity is alive! Body maps depend on movement and use. In people with pain, decreased use of body parts and various complex biological processes (neglect, blood-brain barrier changes, etc.) change the body maps. This has far-reaching implications for people, often on the severe end of the pain spectrum, such as complex regional pain syndrome (CRPS), phantom limb pain and more.

This story covers issues regarding:
- Neuroplasticity
- Homunculus
- Sensory cortex
- Phantom limb pain
- Complex regional pain syndrome
- Use it or lose it
- Spreading pain
- Neglect
- Laterality
- Smudging
- Graded motor imagery

Many of the concepts built into stories are well established in the scientific literature. For example, central sensitization, peripheral sensitization, etc. The neuroplastic changes including "smudging" are new, but given the increased evidence for altered mapping in people with low back pain, CRPS, etc., the need to explain this to patients increases. This prompted the idea of explaining this phenomenon to patients. A recent fMRI study on CRPS used the following stories and showed a significant positive change in brain activity on various processing levels of the pain neuromatrix.[51] Similarly, when used to explain the use of manual therapy for chronic low back pain, it yielded positive results,[41] thus indicating this advanced science is understood by patients and yields positive therapeutic results. We offer a few examples:

- Smudging 101
- Charcoal drawings
- Coffee spills

4.4.11.A: **The brain's body maps – smudging 101**

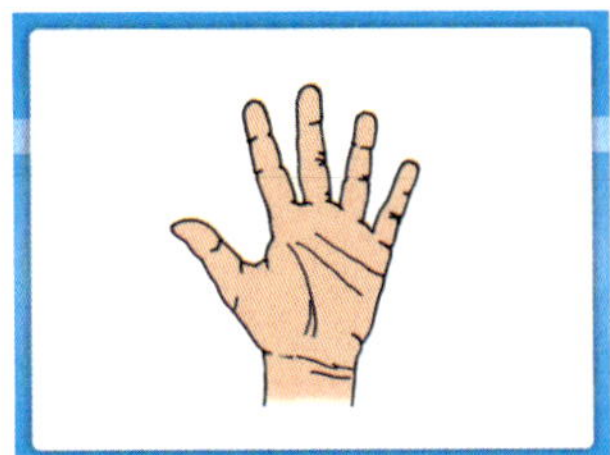

- Is this a left hand or a right hand?

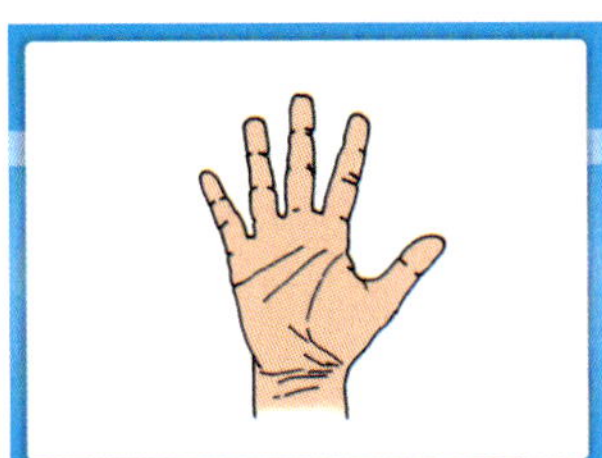

- How about this one? Left or right?
- Ever wondered how you know what left or right is?

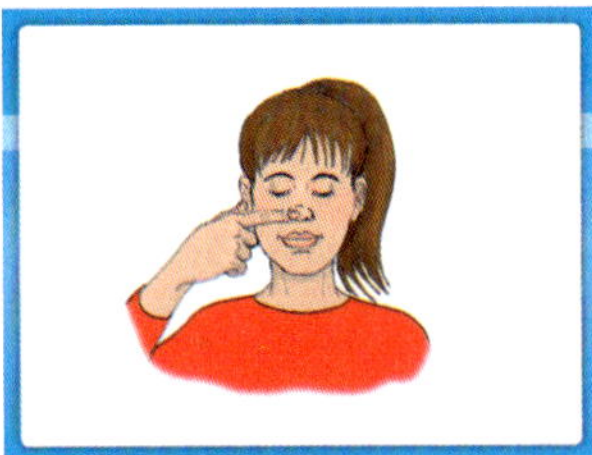

- OK – yes, you can see it.
- Let's try this: Close your eyes – keep them closed.
- Take your right index finger and touch your nose.
- Open your eyes.
- Why didn't you put your left thumb on your ear?
- You did not see your hand, yet you knew:
  - Right from left.
  - Hand versus elbow.
  - Index finger from thumb.
  - Nose from ear.
  - Spatial awareness to move the thumb to the nose.

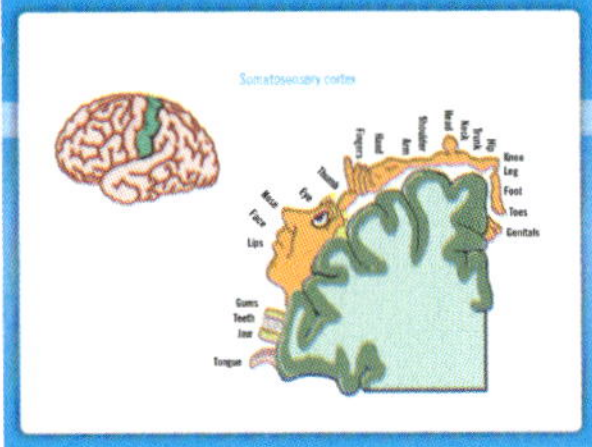

- Scientists have now shown us that there are areas in your brain that contain maps of the body.
- If you look close, the map has all the parts of the body.
- Some areas are larger than others.

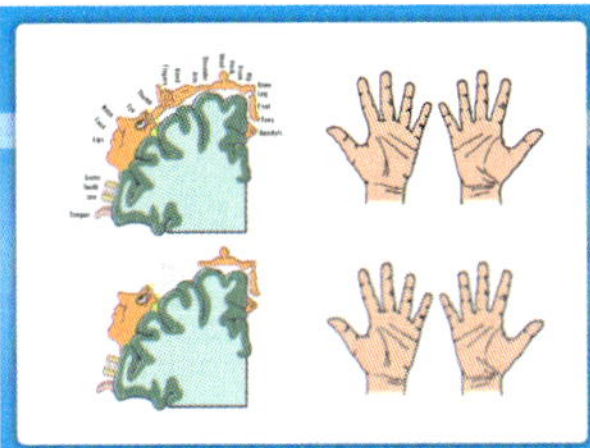

- When you regularly use a body part, for example, when you have little to no pain, the map is exercised and the body parts stay healthy, crisp and in focus.
- Because of this exercise and focus, it is easy to use the body parts as well as determine left from right.
- When pain prevents someone from moving, and thus exercising these body maps, the body parts become a little blurred.
- Body parts that have become "blurry" due to pain, a cast, surgery, etc. are difficult to use.
- This can happen in a matter of minutes.
- In other words, use it or lose it.

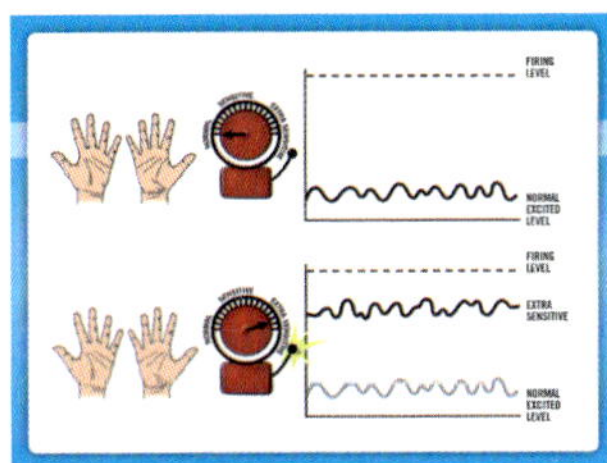

- If a body part is "blurry," the brain becomes confused and concerned, and it will produce pain to protect you.
- The body's alarm system – the nervous system – will increase its sensitivity from a normal resting level to extra sensitive to protect you.

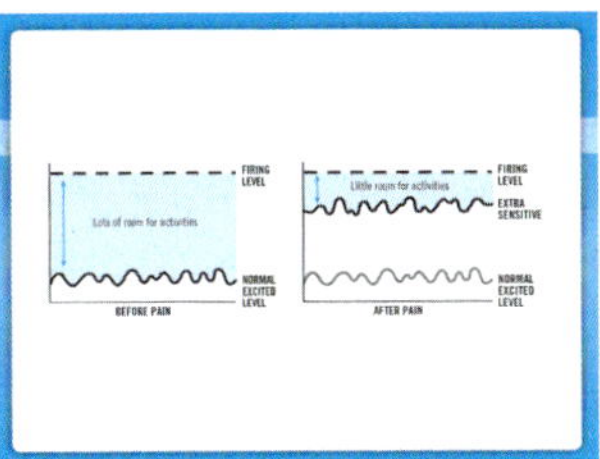

- When the alarm system increases its sensitivity, it impacts your life a lot.
- Before you experienced pain, you had lots of room to do many activities.
- With the alarm set at extra sensitive, there is little room to do activities before the alarm goes off.
- This might make you think there is something seriously wrong, but that is not the case.
- Your nervous system has become extra sensitive to protect you, but this does not necessarily mean something is wrong.

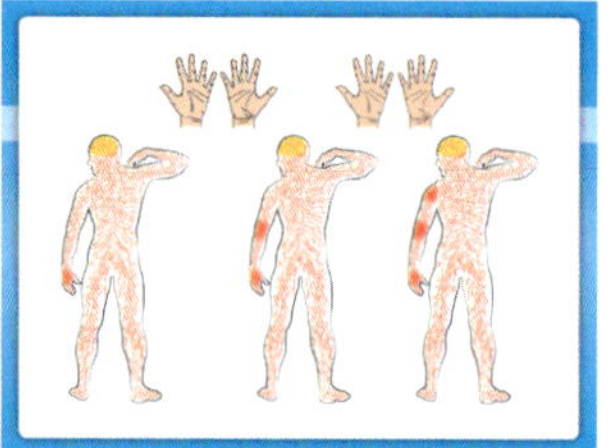

- Since you are struggling to identify body parts, another interesting phenomenon occurs.
- In an attempt to "find" a specific body part (a hand, for example), the brain starts knocking on many neighbors' doors, asking if they have seen the hand.
- The neighbor to the hand is the wrist, and the neighbor to the wrist is the elbow and so forth.
- The end result is the whole neighborhood is alerted and woken up.
- What started as hand pain has now spread up your arm because you are more aware of the neighboring areas.
- This is completely normal. It does not mean you have increased injury.

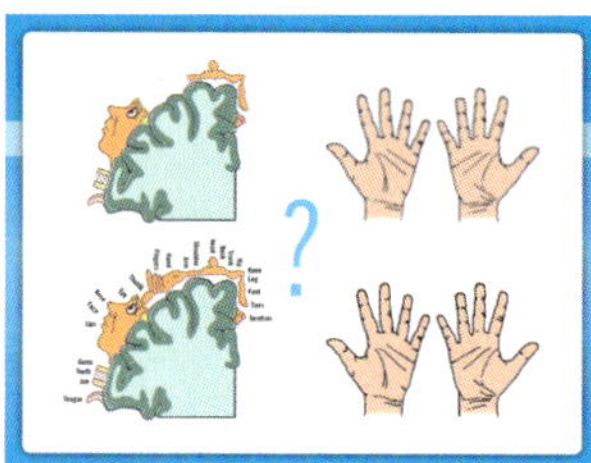

- Now your question should be: How do I get these "blurry body parts" back into focus?
- Glad you asked.

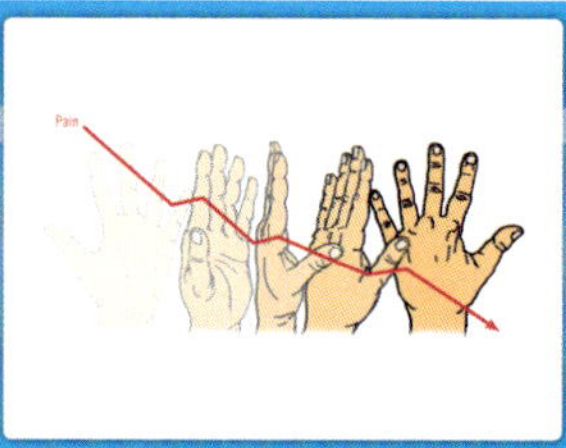

- Movement!
- When body parts are used and exercised frequently, the body maps gain focus and become well defined.
- As you move the body part, you are exercising the body map.
- You are doing brain exercises!
- As the maps get sharper and sharper, pain decreases.
- Movement and exercise are essential for recovery. Therapy exercises might sometimes seem boring or silly, but it is crucial that you keep doing them to help remap the brain.

- If moving the body part (your hand, for example) is too painful or you are too afraid to move the body part, we have another exercise for you.
- Close your eyes and "see" your hand, palm down. Do this for a few seconds – keep breathing, and then open your eyes.
- Now, do the same with your hand in different positions.
- If these stationary movement images are OK, move to the next step; visualizing your hand moving.
- You can also visualize your hand performing specific tasks, like using a screwdriver or clicking a computer mouse.
- These visualizations also exercise the body maps, but require less work for the brain. Once the maps have become more defined and pain has eased a bit, you can start performing actual movements and tasks as you progress and recover.

- Another non-threatening way to exercise your body maps is by using a magazine.
- Page through the magazine, and every time you see a body part similar to the one in which you are having pain, circle it with a marker. Make sure to only circle a left or right body part.
- Identifying body parts (foot versus hand) and determining left versus right will exercise the maps as well.
- Remember: As the maps get sharper and crisper, the pain will ease.

- In therapy we can also use mirrors to help your brain.
- By moving the unaffected or less affected body part but watching it in a mirror, the brain can also get more practice and restore the map and…the affected body part is not moved.
- As you do this again and again, the nerves calm in the affected body part and pain is eased.

4.4.11.B: **The brain's body maps – charcoal drawings (Jerry Bouslog, PT, STS, CEAS, CSMT, TPS)**

- Artists use many different ways to draw images.
- This might include specific paints, watercolors, pencils, markers, etc.
- One way is charcoal drawings.
- When an artist draws, he or she has to be careful not to smear the image.
- If the image gets smeared it becomes distorted and might even make it hard to recognize.
- With a charcoal drawing, the original image is thus constantly under threat of being smudged.

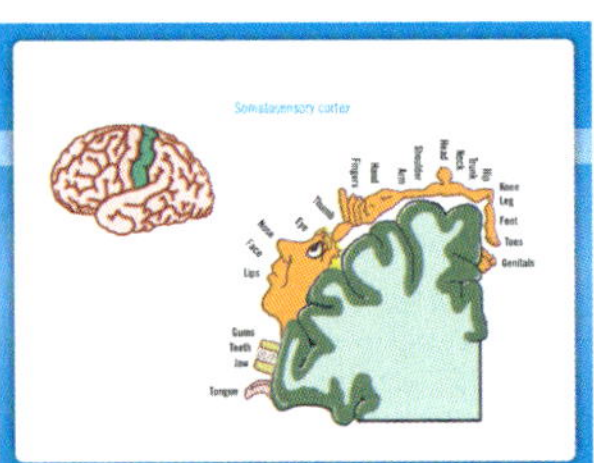

- What's interesting is that this smudging process also occurs with people in pain.
- Scientists have now shown us that there are areas in your brain that contain maps of the body.
- If you look closely, the map has all the parts of the body.
- Some areas are larger than others.
- These maps, however, constantly change.
- When we use our body parts a lot, the map is sharp and crisp; when you see a foot, you know it is a foot, etc.

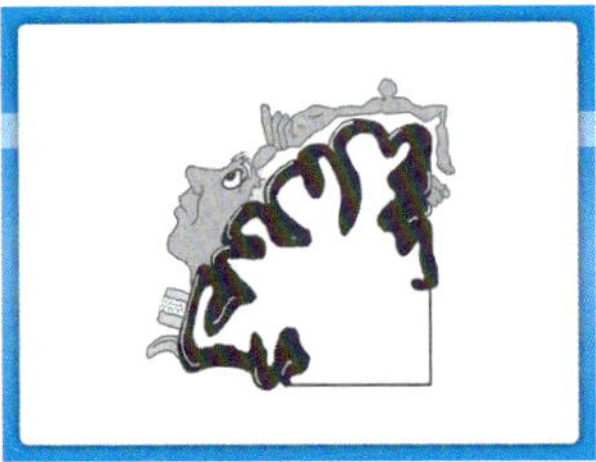

- These maps, however, constantly change and are part of being a human.
- We were born with these maps, but we need movement to keep them healthy.
- So in essence, the map is drawn in charcoal and can thus easily be smudged.

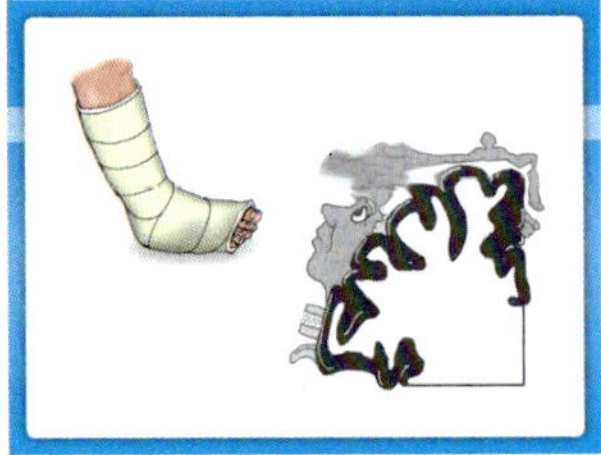

- When we don't move, the map smudges.
- People move less when they:
  - Are in casts or braces.
  - Have pain.
  - Are afraid to move, etc.

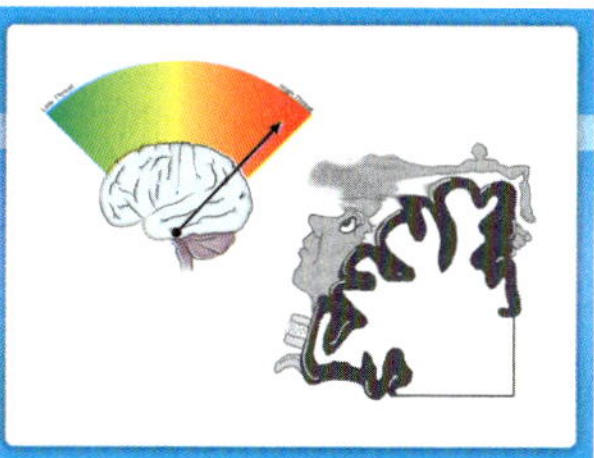

- When maps blur, the brain gets very worried.
- The brain gets your attention by producing pain in the affected body part or region.
- Obviously, the more pain you now have, the less inclined you become to move. A vicious cycle starts.

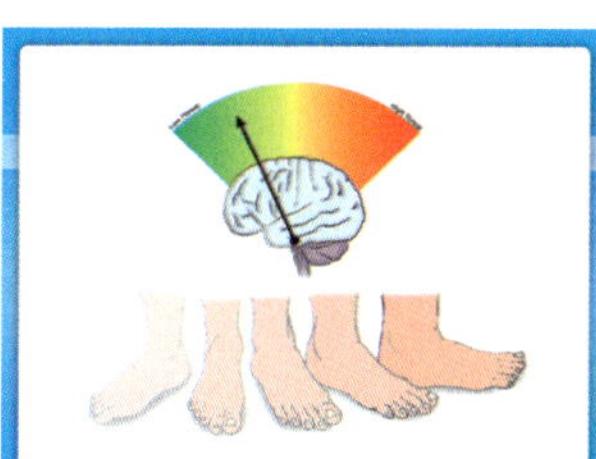

- How do we turn smudged maps sharp again?
- Movement!
- When body parts are used and exercised frequently, the body maps gain focus and become well defined.
- As you move the body part, you are exercising the body map.
- You are doing brain exercises!
- As the maps get sharper and sharper, pain decreases.

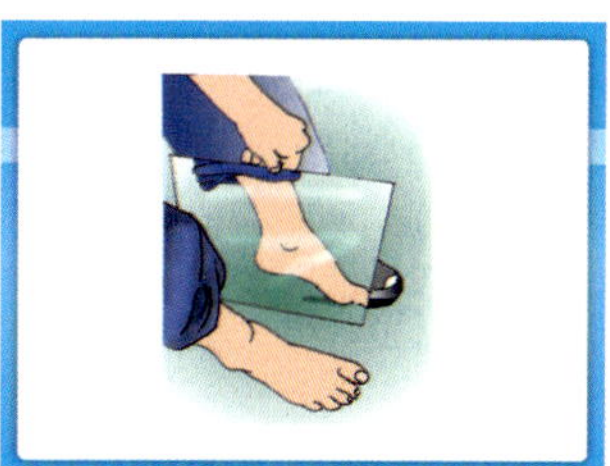

- If movement of the actual body part is too sensitive, therapists might use other strategies to sharpen the map, without actually moving the painful body part.
- One example is mirror therapy.
- By moving the unaffected or less affected body part but watching it in a mirror, the brain can also get more practice and restore the map without moving the affected body part.
- As you do this again and again, the map is sharpened and pain is eased.

4.4.11.C: The brain's body maps – coffee spills (Jen DeLorenzo, PT, CFMT, MCWC, TPS)

- Imagine you're on vacation in a foreign country, let's say Paris, France.
- This is a life-long dream but you're also a little nervous.
- You haven't traveled internationally, and you're not familiar with Paris and do not have any personal contacts there.
- To make things even worse, you rented a car and now have to face driving in Paris traffic on the opposite side of the road while navigating old, narrow streets in irregular patterns.

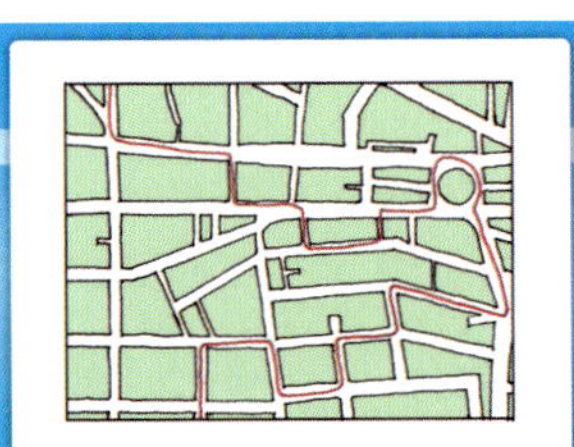

- To make things even worse (especially for the younger people), your smartphone does not work there and there's no way to download maps.
- The solution?
- An actual, physical (old-time) paper map!
- You find the location of the museum you want to visit, look at all the one-way roads and mark the best route from your hotel to the museum.

- You are super excited and might be a little more at ease knowing your path for the day.
- Then it happens – disaster!
- As you stand up from the table to go get dressed, you spill coffee all over your one and only map.

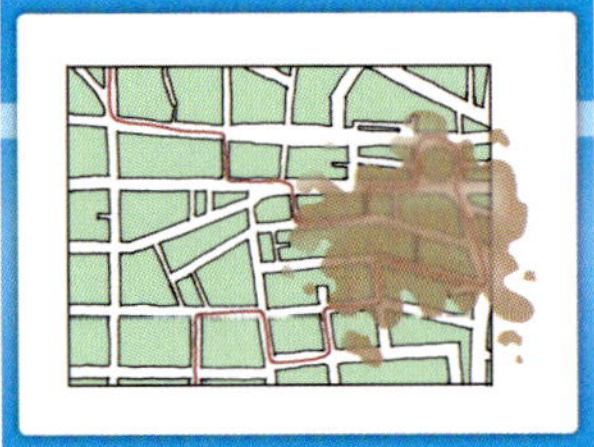

- As the coffee mixes with the map, it blurs the map more and more.
- Right before your eyes the map becomes more and more difficult to read.

- As the map fades, what happens to your stress level?
- Obviously it increases, right?
- The same process occurs when we experience pain.

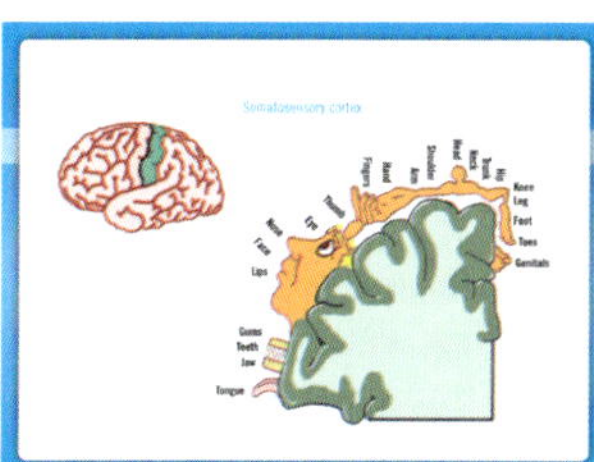

- Scientists have now shown us that there are areas in your brain that contain maps of the body.
- If you look closely, the map has all the parts of the body.
- Some areas are larger than others.

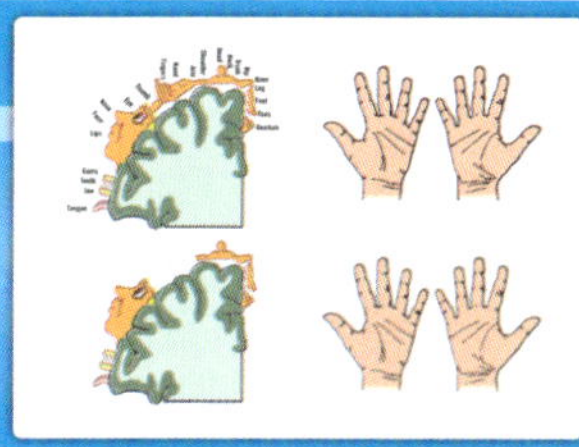

- When you regularly use a body part, for example, when you have little to no pain, the map is exercised and the body parts stay healthy, crisp and in focus.
- Because of this exercise and focus, it is easy to use the body parts as well as determine left from right.
- When pain prevents someone from moving, and thus exercising these body maps, the body parts become a little blurred.
- Body parts that have become "blurry" due to pain, a cast, surgery, etc. are difficult to use.
- This can happen in a matter of minutes.
- In other words, use it or lose it.

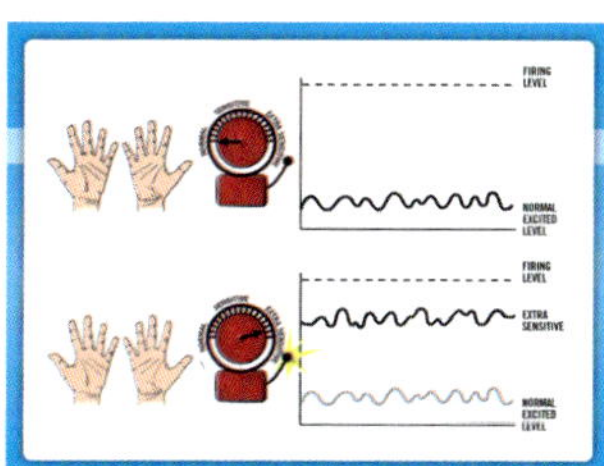

- If a body part is "blurry," the brain becomes confused and concerned, and it will produce pain to protect you.
- The body's alarm system – the nervous system – will increase its sensitivity from a normal resting level to extra sensitive to protect you.

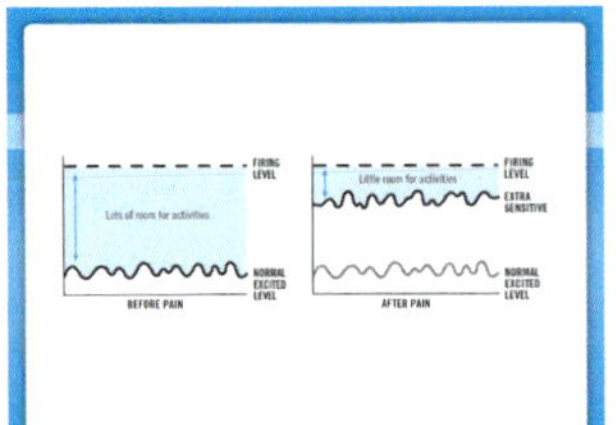

- When the alarm system increases its sensitivity, it impacts your life a lot.
- Before you experienced pain, you had lots of room to do many activities.
- With the alarm set at extra sensitive, there is little room to do activities before the alarm goes off.
- This might make you think there is something seriously wrong, but that is not the case.
- Your nervous system has become extra sensitive to protect you, but this does not necessarily mean something is wrong.

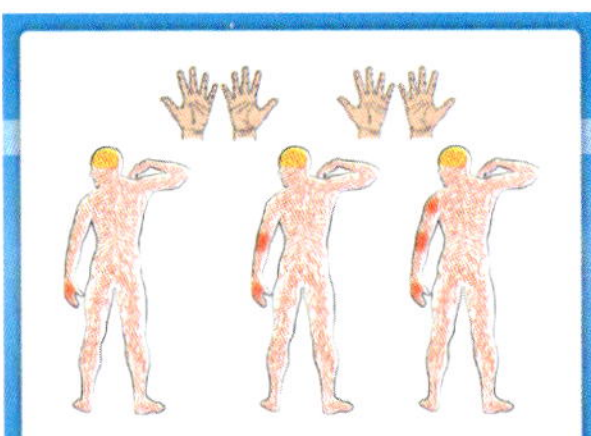

- Since you are struggling to identify body parts, another interesting phenomenon occurs.
- In an attempt to "find" a specific body part (a hand, for example), the brain starts knocking on many neighbors' doors, asking if they have seen the hand.
- The neighbor to the hand is the wrist, and the neighbor to the wrist is the elbow and so forth.
- The end result is the whole neighborhood is alerted and woken up.
- What started as hand pain has now spread up your arm because you are more aware of the neighboring areas.
- This is completely normal. It does not mean you have increased injury.

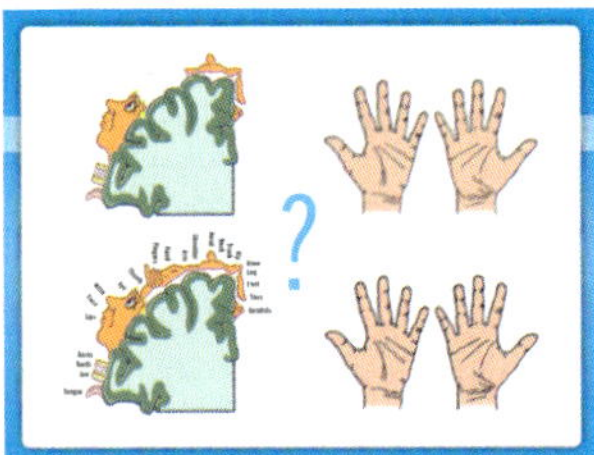

- Now your question should be: How do I get these "blurry body parts" back into focus?
- Glad you asked.

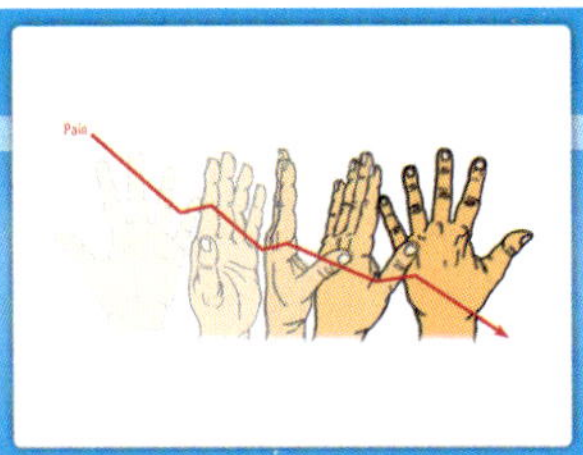

- Movement!
- When body parts are used and exercised frequently, the body maps gain focus and become well defined.
- As you move the body part, you are exercising the body map.
- You are doing brain exercises!
- As the maps get sharper and sharper, pain decreases.
- Movement and exercise are essential for recovery. Therapy exercises might sometimes seem boring or silly, but it is crucial that you keep doing them to help remap the brain.

- If moving the body part (your hand, for example) is too painful or you are too afraid to move the body part, we have another exercise for you.
- Close your eyes and "see" your hand, palm down. Do this for a few seconds – keep breathing, and then open your eyes.
- Now, do the same with your hand in different positions.
- If these stationary movement images are OK, move to the next step – visualizing your hand moving.
- You can also visualize your hand performing specific tasks, like using a screwdriver or clicking a computer mouse.
- These visualizations also exercise the body maps, but require less work for the brain. Once the maps have become more defined and pain has eased a bit, you can start performing actual movements and tasks as you progress and recover.

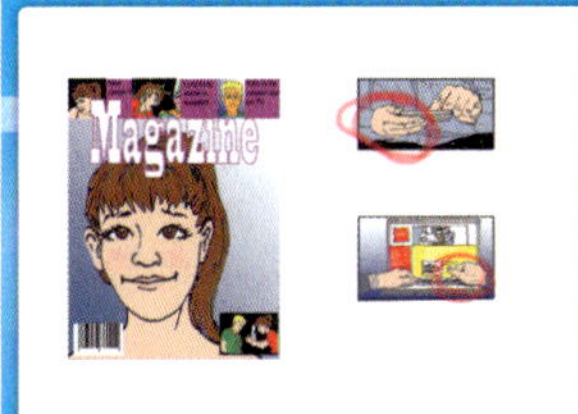

- Another non-threatening way to exercise your body maps is by using a magazine.
- Page through the magazine, and every time you see a body part similar to the one in which you are having pain, circle it with a marker. Make sure to only circle a left or right body part.
- Identifying body parts (foot versus hand) and determining left versus right will exercise the maps as well.
- Remember: As the maps get sharper and crisper, the pain will ease.

- In therapy we can also use mirrors to help your brain.
- By moving the unaffected or less affected body part but watching it in a mirror, the brain can also get more practice and restore the map without moving the affected body.
- As you do this again and again, the nerves calm in the affected body part and pain is eased.

4.4.12: Emotions and Pain

It is estimated that up to one in four people experience pain but have not had an injury. Injury and pain are not synonymous. In fact, such thoughts are outdated and follow the Cartesian model. Emotional overload due to various stressors can also result in pain. This series of stories illustrates how various emotional stressors can activate the alarm system and result in pain.

This story covers issues regarding:

- Emotional overload
- Fear
- Catastrophization
- Nociception
- Threat
- Homunculus

- Ever noticed a bruise on your body and had no idea where it came from?
- In this case you had a real tissue injury that caused a bruise, but no pain.
- If you had pain, you would remember the incident and be able to tell people all about it.
- Pain is produced by the brain. If the brain receives information from tissues, such as danger messages, it might produce pain to grab your attention and get you to take care of the threat.
- In some cases, the brain does not produce pain.

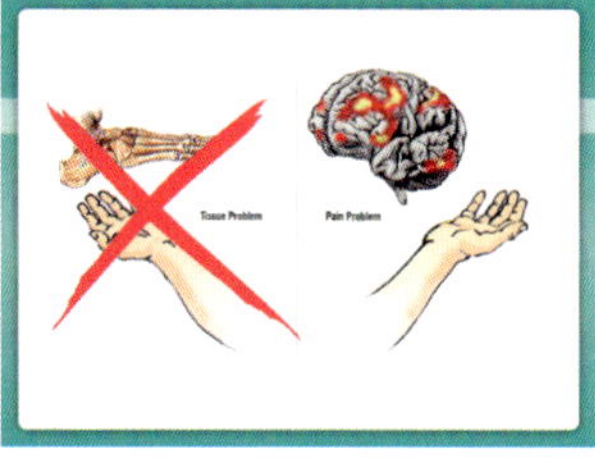

- On the other hand, some people never experienced an injury or surgery, but suffer a lot of pain.
- This is true in approximately one in four people:
  - No injury, accident or surgery, but a lot of pain.
  - How do we explain someone having pain without an injury, accident or surgery?

- Let's start here, with a measuring cup.

- Obviously, if we pour water into the cup, the cup will eventually reach its limit.
- If we continue past that point, it will overflow.

- If we place a hot flame under the cup, it will cause the water to boil.
- This might accelerate the overflow of the cup.

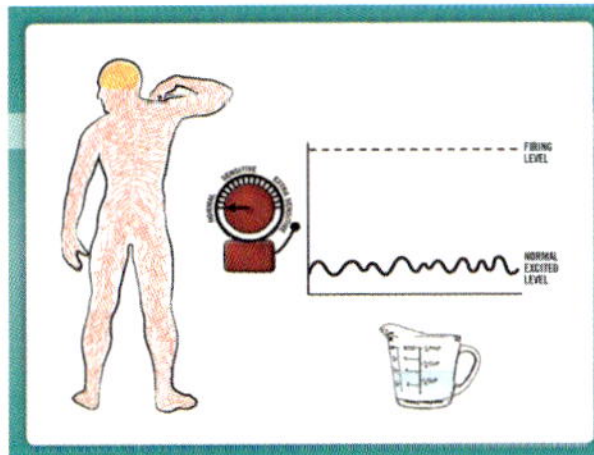

- The human body contains over 400 nerves, totaling 45 miles.
- All nerves have a little bit of electricity in them at all times.
- This is normal; it shows you are alive.
- Nerves, however, are influenced a lot by emotions.
- Emotions (good or bad), will get the nerves to increase or decrease their levels of sensitivity.

- People in pain have many stressors they have to deal with.
  - Ongoing pain: Pain might be normal, but living in pain all the time is not. Pain is very stressful.
  - Failed treatments: The more treatments to ease your pain fail, the more worried you will become. This is normal and expected.
  - Job/money: Doctor's visits, pain, tests and limited movement make work difficult and might in turn add more stress about job and money issues.
  - Different explanations: Not having an understanding of why you hurt adds stress. The more opinions you get, the worse off you are!
- All these stressors act as an open flame heating your measuring cup.

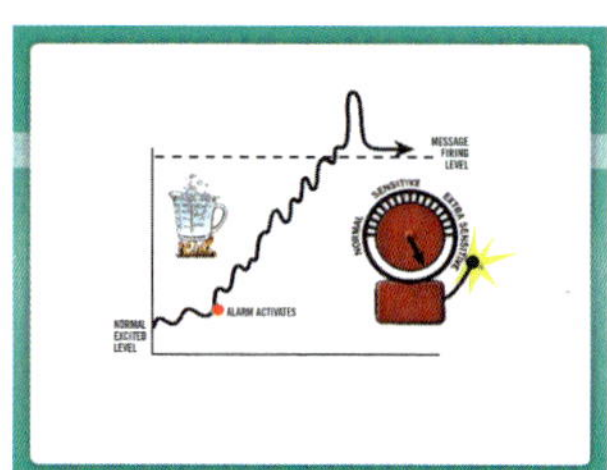

- The increased emotion, fueled by all the stressors in your life as a result of your pain, activates the alarm system.
- Since nerves are barometers for stress and anxiety, the alarm system can be set off by emotions.
- Adding all the other worries, the alarm system is set off much more easily.

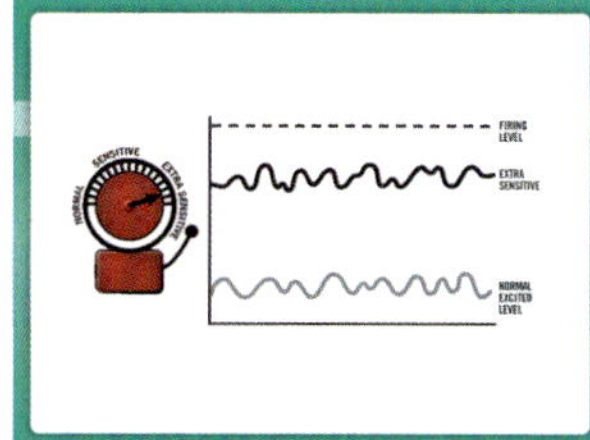

- In approximately one in four people, the alarm does not go down and stays extra sensitive.
- This is usually the case when pain extends beyond the normal healing time.
- Your pain, limited movement and sensitivity might be due to an extra-sensitive alarm system.

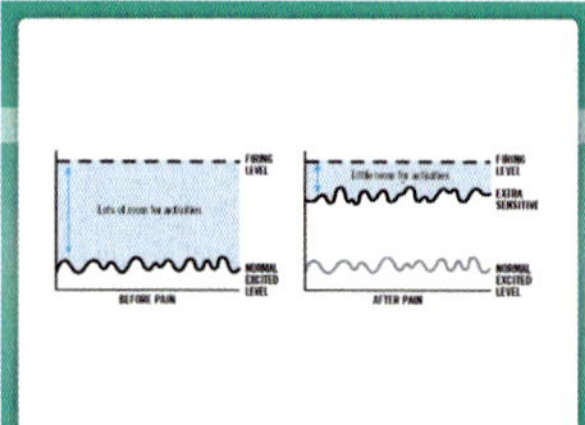

- When your alarm is set to extra sensitive, it impacts your life considerably.
- In the days before pain you had lots of room to do "stuff."
- Since you developed pain, there is little room to perform tasks.
- The limited activity and movement is not necessarily due to injury or tissue, but an extra-sensitive alarm system.

Two powerful teaching tools

In sections 4.4.1 to 4.4.12, we used various examples, metaphors, stories and pictures to educate patients about the neuroscience of pain. These sections cover the most important aspects of pain, as described in the literature and ranked highest by clinicians using PNE.[54] There are, however, two powerful teaching tools we want to share that do not specifically fit into one of these categories, but are truly helpful in the clinic. The tools pertain to:

- Fear-Avoidance
- Yellow Flags

Fear-avoidance and roundabouts (Jessie Podolak, PT, DPT, TPS)

Have you ever seen someone drive into a roundabout and struggle to exit? They simply drive around and around, looking confused and frustrated. While roundabouts have been a mainstay of traffic control in many countries for decades, they are just coming into fashion in many parts of the U.S., and many Americans struggle with them! Roundabouts are designed to enhance safety and efficiency at intersections, slowing drivers down, yet maintaining the flow of traffic. Exits to the desired streets are there, but sometimes the signage is tricky to see, and drivers just cannot seem to find the proper off ramp.

Similarly, one in four people struggle with ongoing pain, long after the pain has done its job. Like a roundabout, pain has a purpose. When we have an injury or other overload to the system, pain slows us down and asks us to pay close attention to what is going on. It protects us for a time while tissues heal, and fortunately for us, tissues do heal! Under normal circumstances, when a pain experience occurs and is addressed without fear, pain can be confronted and overcome, leading to recovery. This looks much like a driver passing through a roundabout and finding his or her desired exit on the first try. The system works!

Unfortunately, some individuals struggle to find the exit out of the "pain roundabout." They enter it through a painful experience, and things like threatening information about their problem, or other negative thoughts, cause catastrophic, or worst-case-scenario thinking. Catastrophization distracts them from seeing the exits. People in this scenario go on to develop pain-related fear, and because of that fear, they avoid movement and activities, becoming hypervigilant. This avoidance of movement and normal activity causes them to lose hope, as disuse leads to depression and disability. Disuse can lead to an overall decrease in resilience, making someone even more vulnerable to remain stuck in the roundabout. A strong association exists between depression and pain, with one often driving another, so the pain experience grows. Increasing pain leads a person to further search for answers and find more threatening information about possible ailments. Thinking worst-case-scenario leads to more fear, and fear to more avoidance, and avoidance to further withdrawal from activities, and then, more depression. The cycle becomes a perpetual roundabout, with the person in pain having no clear vision of the exits. Can you see yourself in this endless roundabout?

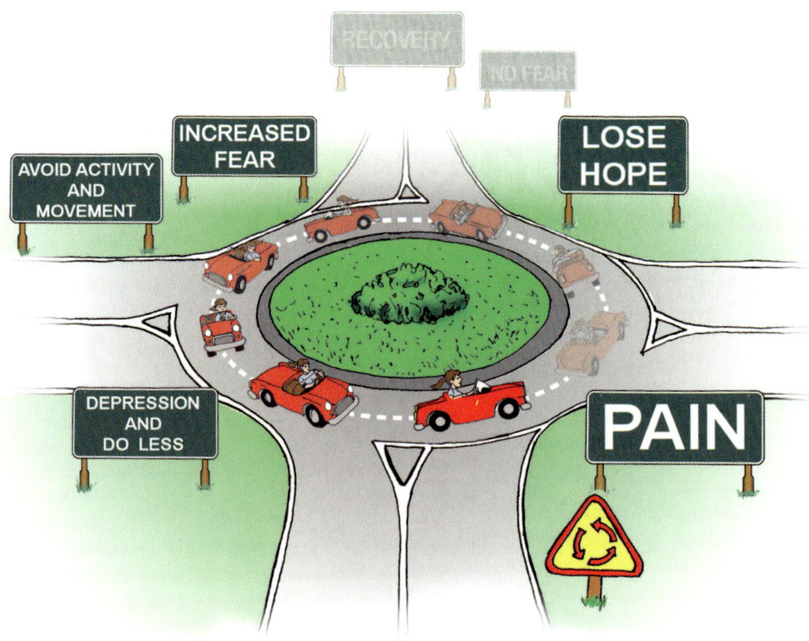

Thankfully, at each of the difficult landmarks in the roundabout, exits do exist. The exit from "Pain Experience" involves addressing pain promptly, with treatments that promote pain reduction and tissue healing. Catastrophic thinking has an exit sign that says PNE, pain neuroscience education, which is what we are going through right now. Having good information on how pain works helps calm fear and gets us out of the roundabout quickly. If fear has taken hold, there are many options for off ramps to calm the system, including relaxation training, breathing exercises, and prayer/meditation. Avoidance has an exit marked "Engage:" stay connected or re-connect to things that are important to you; go outside, help others, etc. Depression and disability have off ramps such as talking to someone, walking your dog, maintaining purpose and nurturing creativity.

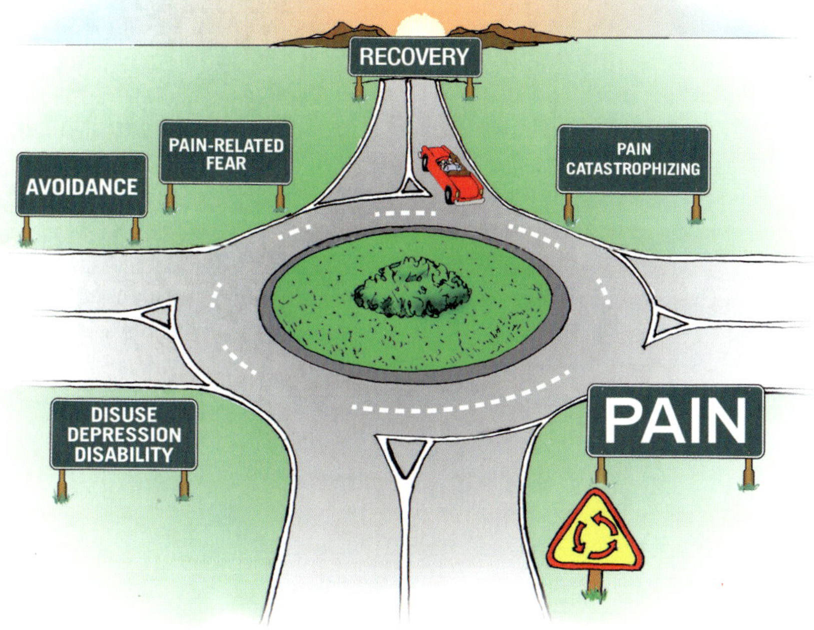

There are so many things that one can do to get out of the pain roundabout, and the exits vary from one individual to another. It makes sense to look closely at what might be holding you in the vicious cycle, and to confront those things with the help of your healthcare team. The off ramps might be hard to see right now, but do not lose hope. More and more providers are understanding how the pain roundabout works and are making those off ramps easier to navigate. And remember, YOU are in the driver's seat. You have the power to get out of that roundabout and onto the road to recovery!

Yellow flags and green paint (adapted from Louis Gifford, FCSP, Chartered Physiotherapist)

In Chapter 1 we showcased yellow flags, biopsychosocial risk factors for chronicity. Yellow flags can be seen as "caution" flags, while the familiar red flags indicate medical etiologies we need to screen for and refer to appropriate medical attention. It is proposed that patients be screened accordingly for biopsychosocial yellow flags as it drives the decision for treatment.[55,56] Examples include fear-avoidance, pain catastrophization, kinesiophobia, etc.[57] In line with this, it is established that patients who tend to see the cup more as "half empty" have an extremely difficult time shifting toward the positive.[58] At the heart of this is hope. Many people in pain have lost hope and it is imperative that clinicians aim to create a positive vantage point. One way is painting yellow flags green – green for go. In Gifford's writings he called them "pink" flags, or positives.[53] In order to stick to the traditional traffic light, we will keep to green flags. Therefore, clinically it is important to have patients develop a working knowledge of yellow flags and see their importance. But, more importantly, they also need to develop skills of "painting yellow flags green." For example, a patient's job situation might be a significant contribution to the patient's persistent pain and, unless that situation is also dealt with, limited progress can be seen. In this case, we could identify issues at work (relationship with the boss, beliefs about work and pain, compensation issues, etc.) and have the patient realize how this might impact their pain. On the flipside, we should also focus on the "what's good" about your job. So much of therapy is focused on what people cannot do and not on what they can do. Maybe recognizing (a) you have a job with pay and benefits is a positive and (b) you work in a climate-controlled environment with air conditioning and not outside in the elements, might help a patient shift ever so slightly. By doing this over and over and extending it to several yellow flags, the patient's perspective might change, and it has been well established that this can impact their pain experience.[55]

PNE 101

In recent years, there has been significant interest in developing an abbreviated PNE story that can readily be used in clinical practice, taking into consideration the ever-increasing time crunch for clinicians.[12,54] Additionally, academic calendars are also filled with ever-increasing demands, yet there is a need to teach students about PNE.[59] Even though pain is complex, individualized and comprises numerous different aspects, what follows is the most abbreviated PNE version we have developed, taking into consideration the overarching theme of central sensitization, tissue health versus sensitization, effect of movement and function, psychosocial factors and treatment plans.[12] This story combines all of the stories that have been ranked highest by clinicians using PNE[54] and by patients (Louw – unpublished data).

- The body has a living, breathing alarm system that's always buzzing along, checking for threats.
- When the alarm is tripped, it ramps up, hitting a threshold and firing a danger message to the brain.
- Once action is taken, the alarm is designed to steadily calm down and life returns to normal.
- Unfortunately, for one in four people the alarm is activated, calls for help, and never calms down, leaving an extra sensitive alarm system.
- Before pain your alarm system allowed you to do lots of "stuff," but since developing pain, the extra sensitive alarm system severely limits your ability to do "stuff."

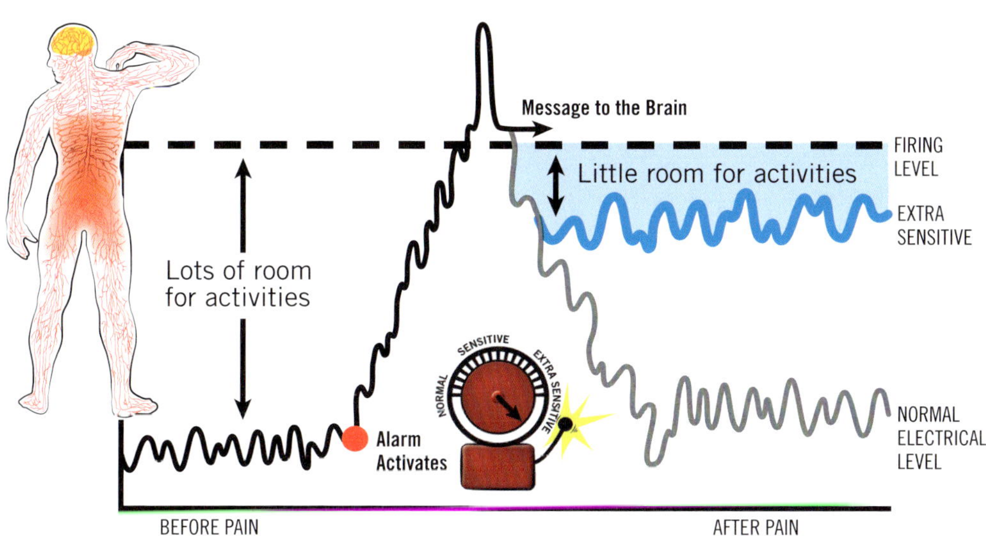

In all the years we have used this story, patients have really only asked us three questions:

1. How do you know this?
2. Why did the alarm not calm down?
3. How do we turn the alarm down?

1. How do you know this?

Of the three questions, this is least asked, but still happens quite a bit. The essence of the question pertains to proof. In an era of scans, tests and evidence you might need to find a way to prove to the patient you know this. For clinicians lower on the hierarchy of medicine this might be more of an issue, since the surgeon said something else. The same might be the case for younger clinicians. The answer simply pertains to your ability to convince the patient they have central sensitization. Answers might include:

- You told us. Here we use information from the subjective examination and tie it to signs and symptoms of central sensitization (Chapter 5), including widespread pain, sensitivity to light touch, decreased ability to move and function – here is where the "before" and "after" picture of the alarm is critical.

- Your doctor told us. No, your doctor did not call us, but if we look at your medicine, your doctor is indirectly telling us he or she wants to calm the nervous system. Medications such as membrane stabilizers, anti-depressants and muscle relaxers are often used for this purpose and can thus be used to further explain a sensitive nervous system

- Your examination told us. Here we tie the physical examination to our discussion. In patients with pain we typically see limited ROM, decreased neurodynamic tests, and sensitivity to palpation, both locally and in remote sites, etc.

2. **Why did the alarm not calm down?**
   This answer pertains to yellow flags. When we hurt ourselves, have surgery or experience an emotional time in life, there are many other issues that might keep the alarm elevated. For example, failed treatments. If we see many different providers and pain is not getting better, will the alarm calm down? Obviously not. What if, since developing pain, there has been increased stress on your relationships at home? (By the way, have the Kleenex ready; this is real and very emotional). The skilled clinician will identify and now bring back information from the subjective examination, tying yellow flags to a hypervigilant nervous system. This is where we typically personalize the story, which is critical in any form of cognitive therapy.

3. **How do we turn the alarm down?**
   This is by far the most common question, and we believe if a patient asks this one first, it is a great indication they likely have accepted the PNE message. Instead of trying to challenge the clinician's knowledge or approach, they are interested in seeking a way to get help. This is the fun part, since the clinician can now go through the various non-pharmacological ways pain can be eased, focusing on the PNE+ program (Chapter 6).

Clinicians should not kid themselves. This is complex, clinically challenging, and not as simple as 1-2-3. Inevitably, you will get the "you think it's in my head" comment, or the "you don't understand, I have a bulging disc" comment. This is the iceberg – you need to be more clever than your patient and therefore, when they veer in these directions, you need to have the proper answers. Think of this as an onion and peeling its layers. In some people a simple story such as PNE 101 can work, while in others you need all the stories and even have to repeat several. Cognitive therapy is challenging, but the evidence shows it can be done very successfully. Furthermore, what is the alternative? More drugs? More surgery? Chapter 4 had one main goal – take the advanced neuroscience from Chapter 3 and put it into stories for patients to grasp the concepts. In Chapter 5 we will delve into the various clinical application issues.

Chapter 4 References

1. Waddell G, Newton M, Henderson I, Somerville D, Main CJ. A Fear-Avoidance Beliefs Questionnaire (FABQ) and the role of fear-avoidance beliefs in chronic low back pain and disability. *Pain.* Feb 1993;52(2):157-168.
2. Kovacs FM, Seco J, Royuela A, Pena A, Muriel A. The correlation between pain, catastrophizing, and disability in subacute and chronic low back pain: a study in the routine clinical practice of the Spanish National Health Service. *Spine.* Feb 15 2011;36(4):339-345.
3. McRae M, Hancock MJ. Adults attending private physiotherapy practices seek diagnosis, pain relief, improved function, education and prevention: a survey. *J Physiother.* Oct 2017;63(4):250-256.
4. Greene DL, Appel AJ, Reinert SE, Palumbo MA. Lumbar disc herniation: evaluation of information on the internet. *Spine* (Phila Pa 1976). Apr 1 2005;30(7):826-829.
5. Sloan TJ, Gupta R, Zhang W, Walsh DA. Beliefs about the causes and consequences of pain in patients with chronic inflammatory or noninflammatory low back pain and in pain-free individuals. *Spine.* Apr 20 2008;33(9):966-972.
6. Sloan TJ, Walsh DA. Explanatory and diagnostic labels and perceived prognosis in chronic low back pain. *Spine* (Phila Pa 1976). Oct 1;35(21):E1120-1125.
7. Louw A, Louw Q, Crous LCC. Preoperative Education for Lumbar Surgery for Radiculopathy. *South African Journal of Physiotherapy.* July 2009 2009;65(2):3-8.
8. Verbeek J, Sengers MJ, Riemens L, Haafkens J. Patient expectations of treatment for back pain: a systematic review of qualitative and quantitative studies. *Spine.* Oct 15 2004;29(20): 2309-2318.
9. Gifford L, Muncey H. *Explaining Pain to Patients.* Paper presented at: International Association on the Study of Pain1999; Vienna, Austria.
10. Moseley L. Combined physiotherapy and education is efficacious for chronic low back pain. *The Australian journal of physiotherapy.* 2002;48(4):297-302.
11. Louw A, Puentedura EJ, Zimney K, Schmidt S. Know Pain, Know Gain? A Perspective on Pain Neuroscience Education in Physical Therapy. *J Orthop Sports Phys Ther.* Mar 2016;46(3): 131-134.
12. Louw A, Zimney K, O'l lotto C, Hilton S. The clinical application of teaching people about pain. *Physiother Theory Pract.* Jul 2016;32(5):385-395.
13. Nijs J, Paul van Wilgen C, Van Oosterwijck J, van Ittersum M, Meeus M. How to explain central sensitization to patients with 'unexplained' chronic musculoskeletal pain: Practice guidelines. *Manual therapy.* Oct 2011;16(5):413-418.
14. Moseley GL. A pain neuromatrix approach to patients with chronic pain. *Manual therapy.* Aug 2003;8(3):130-140.
15. Global Burden of Disease Study C. Global, regional, and national incidence, prevalence, and years lived with disability for 301 acute and chronic diseases and injuries in 188 countries, 1990-2013: a systematic analysis for the Global Burden of Disease Study 2013. *Lancet.* Aug 22 2015;386(9995):743-800.
16. Woolf AD, Pfleger B. Burden of major musculoskeletal conditions. *Bull World Health Organ.* 2003;81(9):646-656.
17. Moseley GL, Butler DS. Fifteen Years of Explaining Pain: The Past, Present, and Future. *The journal of pain: official journal of the American Pain Society.* Jun 5 2015.
18. Louw A, Butler DS, Diener I, Puentedura EJ. Development of a preoperative neuroscience educational program for patients with lumbar radiculopathy. *American journal of physical medicine & rehabilitation/Association of Academic Physiatrists.* Might 2013;92(5):446-452.
19. Berl MM, Duke ES, Mighto J, et al. Functional anatomy of listening and reading comprehension during development. *Brain Lang.* Aug 2010;114(2): 115-125.
20. Jolles DD, Crone EA. Training the developing brain: a neurocognitive perspective. *Front Hum Neurosci.* 2012; 6:76.
21. Louw A, Podolak J, Zimney K, Schmidt S, Puentedura E. Can Pain Beliefs Change in Middle School Students? A Study of the Effectiveness of Pain Neuroscience Education. *Physiother Theory Pract.* 2017 - Accepted for publication.
22. Moseley GL. Unravelling the barriers to reconceptualisation of the problem in chronic pain: the actual and perceived ability of patients and health professionals to understand the neurophysiology. *The journal of pain: official journal of the American Pain Society.* 2003;4(4): 184-189.

23. Louw A, Diener I, Butler DS, Puentedura EJ. The effect of neuroscience education on pain, disability, anxiety, and stress in chronic musculoskeletal pain. *Archives of physical medicine and rehabilitation.* Dec 2011;92(12):2041-2056.
24. Louw A, Zimney K, Puentedura EJ, Diener I. The Efficacy of Therapeutic Neuroscience Education on Musculoskeletal Pain – A Systematic Review of the Literature. *Physiother Theory Pract.* 2016;32(5): 332-355.
25. Catley MJ, O'Connell NE, Moseley GL. How good is the neurophysiology of pain questionnaire? A Rasch analysis of psychometric properties. *The journal of pain: official journal of the American Pain Society.* Aug 2013;14(8):818-827.
26. Moseley G. Combined physiotherapy and education is efficacious for chronic low back pain. *Aust J Physio.* 2002;48: 297-302.
27. Moseley GL. Joining Forces - Combining Cognition - Targeted Motor Control Training with Group or Individual Pain Physiology Education: A Successful Tretment For Chronic Low Back Pain. *Journal of Manual & Manipulative Therapy.* 2003;11(2): 88-94.
28. Moseley GL, Nicholas MK, Hodges PW. A randomized controlled trial of intensive neurophysiology education in chronic low back pain. *The Clinical journal of pain.* 2004;20(5):324-330.
29. Ryan CG, Gray HG, Newton M, Granat MH. Pain biology education and exercise classes compared to pain biology education alone for individuals with chronic low back pain: a pilot randomised controlled trial. *Manual therapy.* 2010;15(4):382-387.
30. Meeus M, Nijs J, Van Oosterwijck J, Van Alsenoy V, Truijen S. Pain physiology education improves pain beliefs in patients with chronic fatigue syndrome compared with pacing and self-management education: a double-blind randomized controlled trial. *Archives of physical medicine and rehabilitation.* 2010;91(8):1153-1159.
31. Vibe Fersum K, O'Sullivan P, Skouen J, Smith A, Kvåle A. Efficacy of classification-based cognitive functional therapy in patients with non-specific chronic low back pain: A randomized controlled trial. *European Journal of Pain.* 2013;17(6):916-928.
32. Gallagher L, McAuley JH, Moseley GL. A Randomized-controlled Trial of Using a Book of Metaphors to Reconceptualize pain and Decreass Catastrophizing in people with Chronic Pain. *The Clinical journal of pain.* 2013;29:20-25.
33. Van Oosterwijck J, Meeus M, Paul L, et al. Pain physiology education improves health status and endogenous pain inhibition in fibromyalgia: a double-blind randomized controlled trial. *The Clinical journal of pain.* 2013;29(10):873-882.
34. Ittersum MW, Wilgen CP, Schans CP, Lambrecht L, Groothoff JW, Nijs J. Written pain neuroscience education in fibromyalgia: a multicenter randomized controlled trial. *Pain practice.* 2014;14(8):689-700.
35. Louw A, Diener I, Landers MR, Puentedura EJ. Preoperative Pain Neuroscience Education for Lumbar Radiculopathy: A Multicenter Randomized Controlled Trial With 1-Year Follow-up. *Spine.* Aug 15 2014;39(18):1449-1457.
36. Téllez-García M, de-la-Llave-Rincón AI, Salom-Moreno J, Palacios-Ceña M, Ortega-Santiago R, Fernández-de-las-Peñas C. Neuroscience education in addition to trigger point dry needling for the management of patients with mechanical chronic low back pain: A preliminary clinical trial. *J Bodyw Mov Ther.* 2014;19(3):464-472.
37. Beltran-Alacreu H, López-de-Uralde-Villanueva I, Fernández-Carnero J, La Touche R. Manual Therapy, Therapeutic Patient Education, and Therapeutic Exercise, an Effective Multimodal Treatment of Nonspecific Chronic Neck Pain: A Randomized Controlled Trial. *American journal of physical medicine & rehabilitation/Association of Academic Physiatrists.* 2015.
38. Pires D, Cruz EB, Caeiro C. Aquatic exercise and pain neurophysiology education versus aquatic exercise alone for patients with chronic low back pain: a randomized controlled trial. *Clinical rehabilitation.* 2015;29(6):538-547.
39. Louw A, Zimney K, Johnson EA, Kraemer C, Fesler J, Burcham T. De-educate to re-educate: aging and low back pain. *Aging Clin Exp Res.* Mar 09 2017.
40. Louw A, Puentedura E, Nijs J. A Clinical Perspective on a Pain Neuroscience Education Approach to Manual Therapy. *Journal of Manual & Manipulative Therapy.* 2017.

41. Louw A, Farrell K, Landers M, et al. The effect of manual therapy and neuroplasticity education on chronic low back pain: a randomized clinical trial. *Journal of Manual & Manipulative Therapy.* 2016:1-8.
42. Ross MD, Boissonnault WG. Red flags: to screen or not to screen? *J Orthop Sports Phys Ther.* Nov 2010;40(11):682-684.
43. Sizer PS, Jr., Brismee JM, Cook C. Medical screening for red flags in the diagnosis and management of musculoskeletal spine pain. *Pain practice: the official journal of World Institute of Pain.* Mar 2007;7(1): 53-71.
44. Maitland GD. *Vertebral Manipulation.* 6th ed. London: Butterworths; 1986.
45. Jones MA. Clinical reasoning: the foundation of clinical practice. Part 1. *Australian Journal of Physiotherapy.* 1997;43:167-170.
46. Nijs J, Van Houdenhove B, Oostendorp RA. Recognition of central sensitization in patients with musculoskeletal pain: Application of pain neurophysiology in manual therapy practice. *Manual therapy.* Apr 2010;15(2):135-141.
47. Diener I, Kargela M, Louw A. Listening is therapy: Patient interviewing from a pain science perspective. *Physiother Theory Pract.* Jul 2016;32(5):356-367.
48. Louw A. *Why You Hurt Therapeutic Neuroscience Education System.* Minneapolis, MN: OPTP; 2014.
49. Louw A, Reed J, Zimney K, Puentedura E, Grimm D, Landers M. *A Randomized Clinical Trial of Preoperative Pain Neuroscience Education for Total Knee Arthroplasty.* 2018; Submitted for publication.
50. Louw A, Benz P, Podolak J, Zimney K, Wassinger CA. *Pain Neuroscience Education for Middle School Kids and Fear of Physical Activity.* Physiotherapy 2017 - Submitted for Publication.
51. Fercho KA, Baugh LA, Louw A, Zimney K. Pain Neuroscience Education Effect on Pain Matrix Processing in an Individual with Complex Regional Pain Syndrome: A Single Subject Research Design. *European Pain Journal.* 2017 - Submitted for publication.
52. GL M, DS B. *Explain Pain Supercharged.* Adelaide: NOI Group; 2017.
53. Gifford L. *Aches and Pains.* Cornwall: Wordpress; 2014.
54. Louw A, Puentedura EJ, Zimney K, Cox T, Rico D. The clinical implementation of pain neuroscience education: A survey study. *Physiother Theory Pract.* Nov 2017;33(11):869-879.
55. Kendall N, Watson P. *Identifying psychosocial yellow flags and modifying management.* In: Gifford LS, ed. Topical Issues in Pain 2. Falmouth: CNS Press; 2000.
56. Watson P, Kendall N. *Assessing psychosocial yellow flags.* In: Gifford LS, ed. Topical Issues in Pain 2. Falmouth: CNS Press; 2000.
57. Vlaeyen JW, Linton SJ. Fear-avoidance and its consequences in chronic musculoskeletal pain: a state of the art. *Pain.* Apr 2000;85(3):317-332.
58. Ledgerwood A, Boydstun AE. Sticky prospects: loss frames are cognitively stickier than gain frames. *Journal of experimental psychology.* General. Feb 2014;143(1):376-385.
59. Cox T, Puentedura E, Louw A. An Abbreviated Therapeutic Neuroscience Education Session Improves Pain Knowledge in First Year Physical Therapy Students But Does Not Change Attitudes or Beliefs *Journal of Manual & Manipulative Therapy.* 2017;25(1):11-21.

Notes

Chapter 5

Clinical Implementation of PNE

5.1: Introduction

In the preceding chapters, we outlined the importance of patient cognitions, beliefs and their relationship to pain. This was followed by a review of educational strategies which can be employed to address faulty cognitions in order to alter their pain experience. We introduced PNE as a means to help patients reconceptualize their pain according to the updated neuroscience model of pain. Improving knowledge and understanding about pain has been correlated to patients experiencing less pain, improving function, decreasing catastrophization, improving physical movements and reducing healthcare utilization.[1,2] A systematic method of bringing about this reconceptualization of pain was introduced by utilizing the M.O.M,[3] NPQ[4] and the rNPQ.[5] In Chapter 4 we used a variety of examples, metaphors, stories and images to teach patients more about the neuroscience of pain.[6,7] However, none of this matters unless it can be implemented into clinical practice, taking into consideration the increased efficiency and productivity demands. In a recent survey of clinicians utilizing PNE, the single biggest perceived barrier to implementation of PNE was reported to be time constraint.[8] Given that some of the original research pertaining to PNE cited sessions lasting an hour, two and a half hours and even four hours,[9-11] it is easy to see some skepticism among clinicians working in "the real world" of clinical practice. It should be stated that the original "lengthy" PNE sessions resulted in significant improvements but were designed to test the theoretical premise of PNE before "abbreviated" PNE studies could be undertaken.

This chapter will discuss various aspects regarding the clinical application of PNE. In the first edition of this textbook, much of the information pertaining to clinical application was developed through trial and error, and years of testing various aspects of PNE application.[12] In this second edition, we still utilize various clinical experiences, but also draw from growing research evidence in this field.[7,8] Please note that every clinician's unique scenarios and practice environment will involve requirements that can be different on so many levels pertaining to scheduling, documentation, billing, etc. Additionally, given that PNE developed out of orthopedic manual therapy practice (Chapters 1 and 2), the vast amount of clinical application processes therefore apply to outpatient orthopedic and private practice environments. PNE is permeating into other therapeutic realms and this is briefly addressed at the end of this chapter, i.e., emergency medicine, acute care, neurological rehabilitation, sports medicine, etc. We encourage all clinicians to read through this chapter and pick the various aspects that might be beneficial to your daily practice, but also to adapt to your situation – remember, you are the expert in your domain. Our message to you is that you should review the suggestions and apply them where appropriate. Not all of the strategies will work for you. Not all of the strategies can be absorbed by the healthcare systems, and every clinician will likely have their own unique clinical environment.

5.2: The Clinical Picture of PNE

Before we delve into specific details regarding time constraints, billing and documentation, etc., it is imperative to set the clinical scene. This will allow for a deeper understanding of what follows and also provide insight into various, often assumed issues in the delivery of PNE in clinical practice.

5.2.1: Safety screening

In a perfect clinical environment, a clinician will already know that the next new patient on his or her schedule is an ideal candidate for PNE, will be receptive to PNE, and know which of the various metaphors would be best for this patient in order to have the necessary educational tools ready to go. This is far from what happens in the real clinical setting. Additionally, many people believe that the experts in PNE "only" sit people down and explain to their patients the nuances of pain neuroscience. This once again is not the case. Any new patients should be screened for the presence of red flags indicating medical etiologies needing a referral to a physician. It is estimated that approximately two percent of patients attending outpatient PT present with a red flag needing referral to a medical provider.[13-16] This stresses the need for a thorough interview, medical intake forms and a review of systems. Current best-evidence supports a PT's ability to screen for red flags.[13-16] This first screening should be seen as a screening to determine if the patient is a candidate for therapy, not PNE (Figure 5.1).

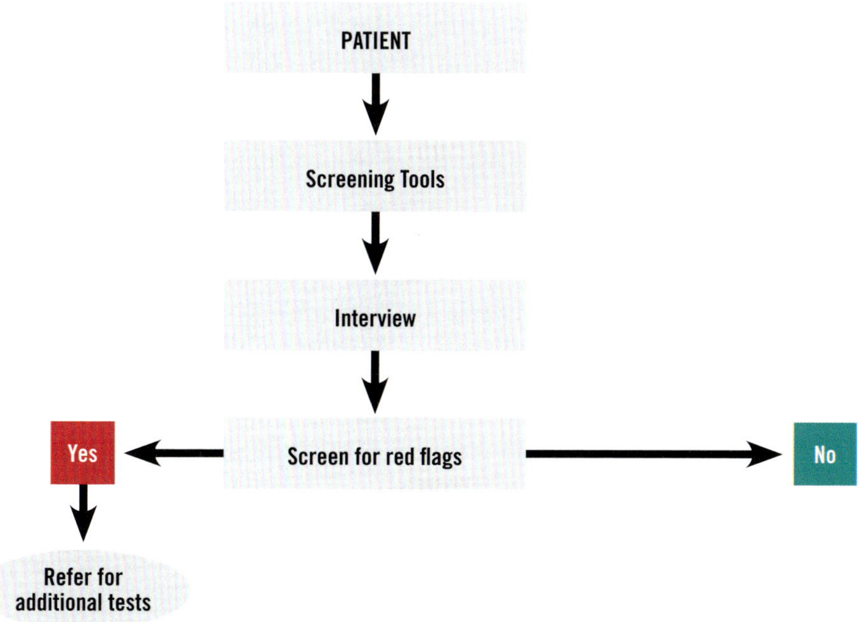

Figure 5.1: Screening for red flags (Adapted from Diener, et. al).[17]

5.2.2: Intake forms and screening

It is now commonplace for all clinics to ask patients to complete demographic information as well as a series of intake forms before even seeing the clinician. It could be argued that the influx of intake forms and outcome measures can be tied to third party payer concerns over increased healthcare cost and a means to obtain objective data, measure a functional baseline and quantify subsequent progress (or not) with treatment. In the infancy of this process, the vast majority of questionnaires pertained to pain and function. With the advent of the yellow flags research and recognition that a small percentage of patients with pain and disability account for a large proportion of healthcare expenditures, screening tools have shifted from outcome measures toward screening tools to stratify care. Clinical tools to identify various psychosocial issues include the Fear Avoidance Beliefs Questionnaire (FABQ), Tampa Scale of Kinesiophobia (TSK), Pain Catastrophization Scale (PCS), the Keele STarT Back screening tool (SBST), Orebro questionnaire, etc. Additionally, with the growing interest in central sensitization and its impact on the pending physical examination and plan of care, questionnaires such as the Central Sensitization Inventory (CSI) have been suggested to further screen patients for proper care. In research, many questionnaires and screening inventories have been used and each has its strengths and weaknesses, which is well-described in the literature. What about usefulness in the clinic? In clinical practice, there has to be a balance between collecting pertinent information and not overburdening the patient. Section 5.9 will specifically address outcome measures that might be better suited for PNE. However, in this section we need to discuss the various screening tools that drive the physical examination and plan of care, including a potential PNE candidate.[17] The body of literature surrounding which patients might be better suited for PNE is growing and current best-evidence surrounds three main characteristics:[7,8,18,19]

- High fear-avoidance
- High pain catastrophization
- Presence of central sensitization

Given the global burden of LBP, especially chronic LBP, a lot of attention has focused specifically on stratifying care with various screening tools. The Keele SBST has gained considerable interest, thus warranting its inclusion as an additional screening tool.[20,21] The Keele SBST is a simple prognostic questionnaire that helps clinicians identify modifiable risk factors (biomedical, psychological and social) for back pain disability. The resulting score stratifies patients into low, medium or high risk categories (Figure 5.2).[20]

- Presence of biomedical, psychological and social risk factors for disability.

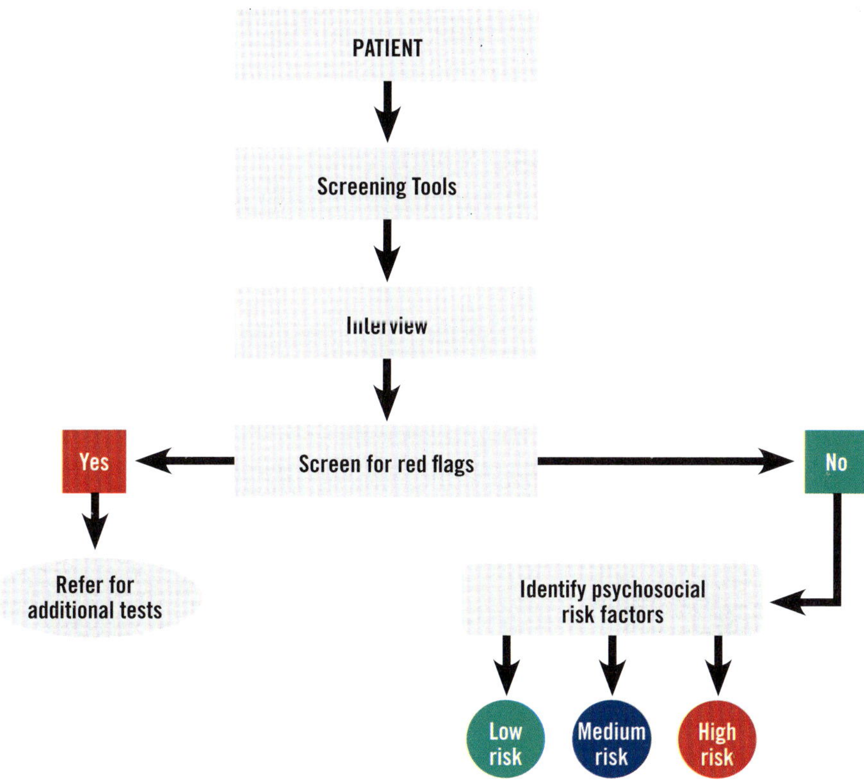

Figure 5.2: Risk stratification using psychosocial questionnaires (Adapted from Diener, et. al).[17]

In Chapter 1 we discussed the FABQ and TSK to measure fear-avoidance and kinesiophobia (section 1.4). Additionally, Chapter 1 also describes the PCS (section 1.5). The important part for this discussion is to recognize how the FABQ, TSK and PCS scores can be used to stratify categories:

- **FABQ:** The FABQ is often used to screen patients with LBP to assess their potential risk for prolonged disability. It has been suggested that a FABQ-Physical Activity sub-scale score > 15 and a FABQ-Work sub-scale score > 34 are associated with a high risk for prolonged disability from LBP.[22,23] In line with these elevated scores, it is then proposed that these patients be treated with a more comprehensive biopsychosocial or multi-disciplinary approach containing PNE and PNE+ principles.[22]

- **TSK:** Kinesiophobia is often measured with the TSK.[24] Each of the 17 items is scored on a four-point Likert-type scale that ranges from strongly disagree [1] to strongly agree [4]. Total scores range from 17 to 68, and higher scores indicate more fear of movement and/or (re)injury.[24] The TSK does not have a cut-off score, but it's implied that higher scores might be more suited for cognitive interventions including PNE.

- **PCS:** The PCS utilizes a 13-item, five-point Likert scale with higher scores indicating elevated levels of catastrophizing. Previous studies utilizing the PCS have shown a median score of 18 for healthy individuals and in patients with pain, the PCS is generally higher.[25] The PCS, as with the FABQ, has been shown to have a definite cut-off for risk stratification with a score > 30 indicating a clinically relevant level of catastrophization.[25]

Various studies have explored the clinical aspects of central sensitization. For example, Smart et. al., used a mechanism-based classification to determine the presence of central sensitization in patients with LBP with and without radiculopathy, whereby three symptoms and one sign became predictive of central sensitization.[26] Nijs and colleagues described information obtained from the medical diagnosis, combined with the medical history of the patient, as well as the clinical examination and the analysis of the treatment response in order to recognize central sensitization.[27]

CSI: More recently, there has been a greater focus on the use of the CSI as a means to quantify the potential presence of central sensitization. The 25-question survey scores answers for each question ranging from zero to four points, with the CSI potential score ranging from zero to 100 points.[28] The CSI has been found to have high reliability and validity, and it is proposed that a score of 40 or above is indicative of central sensitization.[18] It might thus be implied that a CSI score > 40 could be used as a potential threshold for the use of more extensive PNE sessions.

Keele SBST: The Keele SBST is a nine-item questionnaire that contains questions that are established predictors for disabling low back pain (Figure 5.3). Each item is responded to as "agree" or "disagree," except for the bothersomeness item which uses a Likert scale of "not at all" to "extremely." The overall score is used to separate into low and medium risk subgroups. The distress subscale is used to separate medium risk subgroup into medium and high risk. It is used to identify potential "at-risk" patients for potential long-term chronic problems. These patients need careful assessment and intervention with suitable cognitive and behavioral strategies.[20]

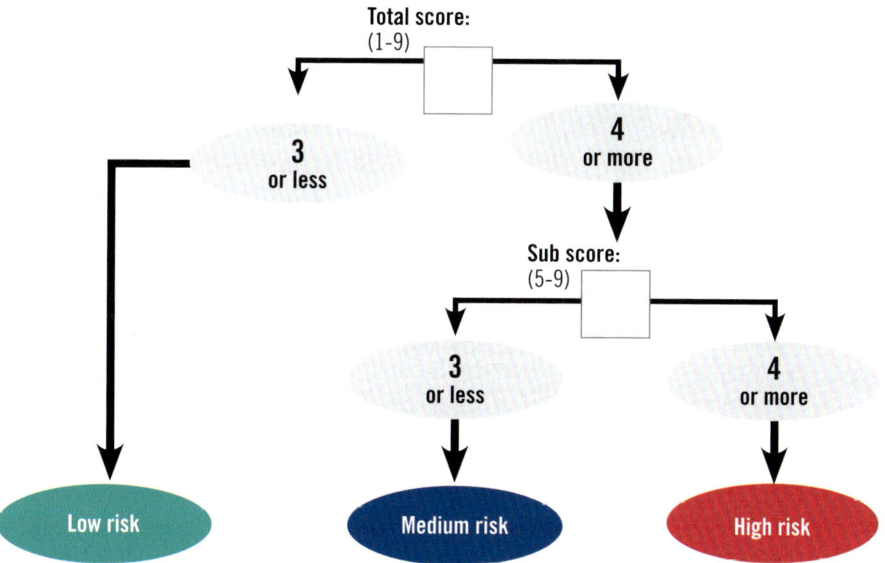

Figure 5.3: The Keele SBST risk questionnaire stratification.

Following a review of the FABQ, TSK, PCS, CSI and Keele SBST, clinicians should be able to develop a working knowledge of patients suited for more extensive PNE, based on the current literature. Section 5.3 will delve further into other potential candidates for PNE, including the concept that PNE should become an overall language and not just another treatment technique. The aim of this section was to showcase a deliberate, scientifically-validated process of screening patients for potential appropriate care.

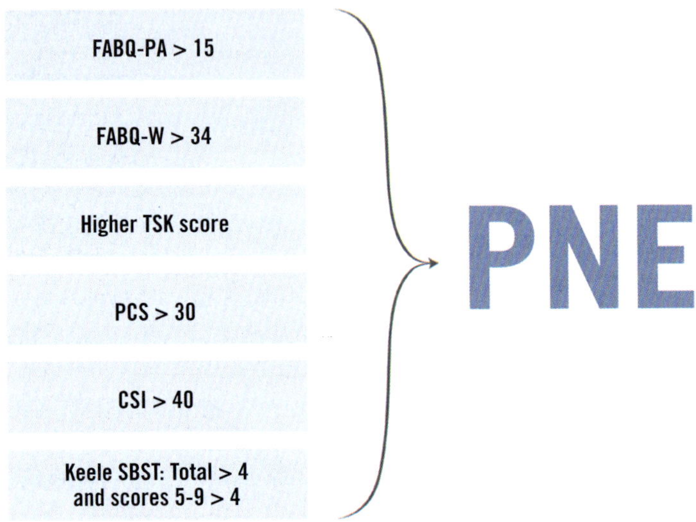

For the sake of being thorough, we need to mention the notion that patients typically are also asked to fill in a "pain rating." Most governing agencies require it as well as third-party payers. In section 5.9 we will discuss pain ratings specifically from a perspective of measuring progress. However, it is interesting to note that few studies on risk stratification have focused on pain ratings. This is interesting given the information covered on C fiber barrage into the CNS resulting in significant, potentially-irreversible changes.[29,30] Furthermore, Moseley has shown that patients who report a pain score of five or more (out of 10) in the first week after a wrist fracture have a significantly higher chance of developing complex regional pain syndrome.[31]

5.2.3: Subjective

Upon completion of the initial screening processes (red flags and risk stratification), new patients embark on the subjective interview and the physical examination.[32] A skilled interview that embraces the biopsychosocial approach is most likely a key first step of a successful PNE treatment.[7] The patient interview is far more than just collecting information, but rather a critical part in establishing a therapeutic alliance with a patient and a fundamental first step in PNE.[17]

The alliance between the clinician and the patient can have a positive effect on treatment outcome.[33,34] A biopsychosocial approach implies a patient-centered approach, which holds the key to personal, responsive and fulfilling communication between patients and clinicians.[35] The clinician therefore, must determine how the problem impacts their patient's life and how their patient's lifestyle impacts their problem.[36,37] If this is not established, there could easily be a mismatch between patient and clinician beliefs, values and expectations, making it very difficult to form a therapeutic alliance.[34,38] A therapeutic alliance cannot happen without certain conditions existing to foster engagement between clinician and patient. Both clinician and patient need to be present, receptive, genuine, and committed during the initial and subsequent encounters to build an effective therapeutic alliance. In Chapter 6, when we discuss developing a safe, healing and welcoming clinical environment, we will delve further into the therapeutic alliance. However, it is imperative for clinicians to understand the subjective interview is not merely a series of questions, but rather the process of trust building and relationship development, which are critical to the success of PNE.[8] The aim of this section is to showcase how an interview can be used to further screen patients for the possible appropriate use of PNE.

Traditionally, questioning during the subjective interview has focused on biomedical, biomechanical and patho-anatomical factors.[17,39] While this is helpful, it limits the clinician's understanding of the patient's unique pain experience and shows disregard for cognitive and lifestyle factors that contribute to an individual's pain experience. The clinical question that arises is how to best collect needed information without using language that might negatively affect the patient. Traditional questions designed to identify medical red flags might increase anxiety in the patient, yet are critical screening elements and are fundamental to clinical reasoning.[32,37] The solution might be a blending of both worlds – biomedical and biopsychosocial. Clinicians should utilize traditional questions but purposefully aim to soften the words, use less provocative language, and limit use of the word "pain."[40-42] Geoff Maitland, when describing the interview process, was adamant that clinicians should use patient words as a means to reiterate they were listening to the patient to foster a therapeutic alliance.[36] In that approach, a clinician was encouraged to use the patient's own words when describing their pain experience. When a patient described their pain as a "deep ache," the clinician should ask follow-up questions, but continue to use the "deep ache" wording when referring to their pain. For example, asking, "Is the deep ache there all the time or does it come and go?" versus turning the "ache" into "pain." It is argued the softer word "ache" might be less provocative than the word "pain."[43] In Table 5.1 on the following page a proposed series of more "in-depth" questions are proposed to move beyond traditional manual therapy questions in order to gain a better understanding of pain beliefs, expectations and fears.[17]

Table 5.1: Proposed "in-depth" questions for clinical use (from Diener, et. al).[17]

• What do you think is going on with your [fill in area they are seeking help for]?
• What do you think should be done for your [fill in area they are seeking help for]?
• Why do you think you still hurt?
• What would it take for you to get better?
• Where do you see yourself in three years in regard to [fill in area they are seeking help for]?
• What have you found to be most helpful for your [fill in area they are seeking help for]?
• You have obviously seen many people seeking help. What are your thoughts on this?
• What gives you hope?
• What is your expectation of PT/OT?
• If I could flip a switch and remove all your pain, what things that you have given up on would you do again?
• How has your pain impacted your family and friends?
• Are you angry at anyone about your [fill in area they are seeking help for]? Tell me about it.
• Has anyone made you feel like you're "just making it up" or "it's in your head?" Tell me about it.

During the interview, various subjective clues can be gathered to further help screening and once again, risk stratification. In Chapter 3, we used the M.O.M. from Louis Gifford (Figure 5.4).[3] The interesting part is that the M.O.M. is now also being used for risk stratification and directing physical examination and treatment.[26,44,45]

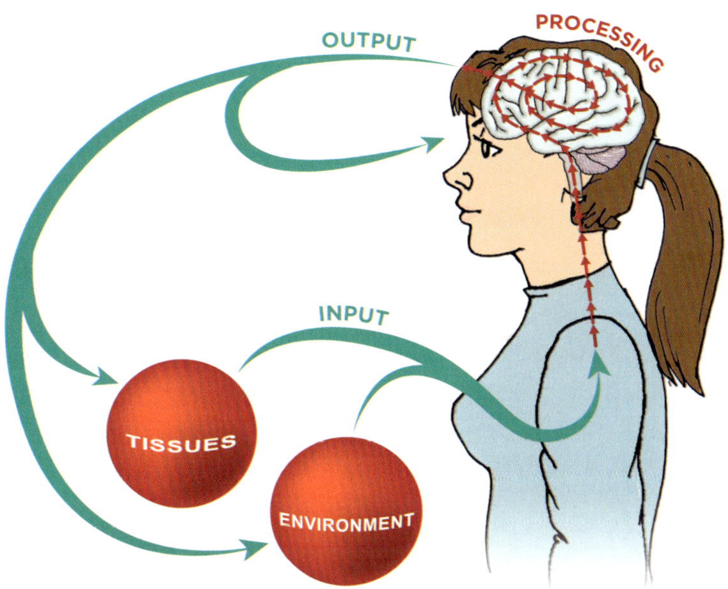

Figure 5.4: The Mature Organism Model – Adapted from Gifford.[3]

Even though all of the components of the M.O.M. are present in all pain states, it is also apparent that various biological processes might be more dominant during various different pain experiences. For example, following an acute ankle sprain, it could be reasoned that the nociceptive (tissue) component will be far more dominant, even though there are definite environmental, input, processing and output mechanisms involved in the pain experience. On the flipside, in someone struggling with chronic LBP, the nociception will still likely be a part of the pain experience, but modern pain science would imply that input (peripheral neurogenic), processing (CNS and pain neuromatrix) and even output (sympathetic, linguistic, motor, etc.) play a more dominant role.[46] There is thus a "shift" in mechanisms over time. Now the important part: Depending on which part of the M.O.M. is dominant, it powerfully drives treatments, including the choice of delivering PNE. In recent years, Keith Smart and his colleagues have examined the various subjective (and some objective) clues to determine which pain mechanism is dominant.[26,39,4046,47] In Table 5.2 on the following page we showcase the three main categories; nociceptive, peripheral neurogenic and central sensitization.[26,44,45]

Table 5.2: Common signs and symptoms associated with different pain mechanisms.[26,44,45]

PAIN MECHANISMS		
Nociceptive	**Peripheral Neurogenic**	**Central Sensitization**
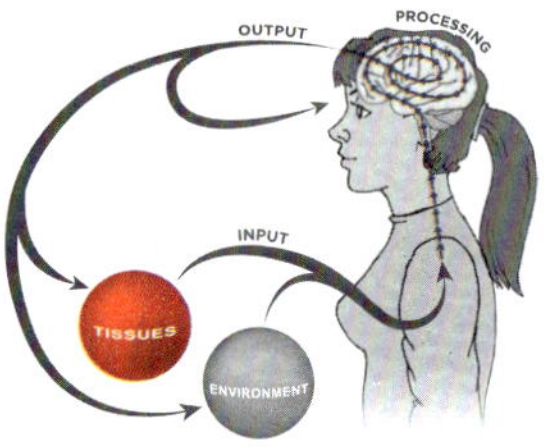	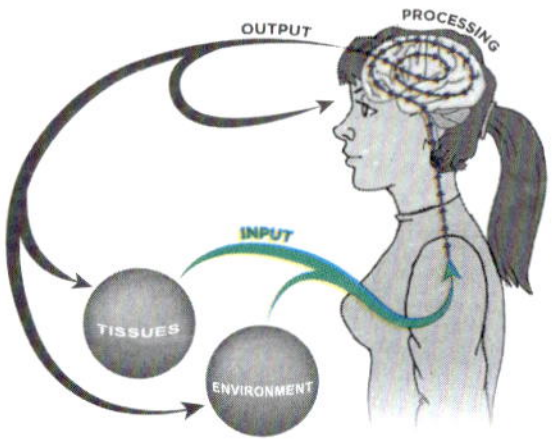	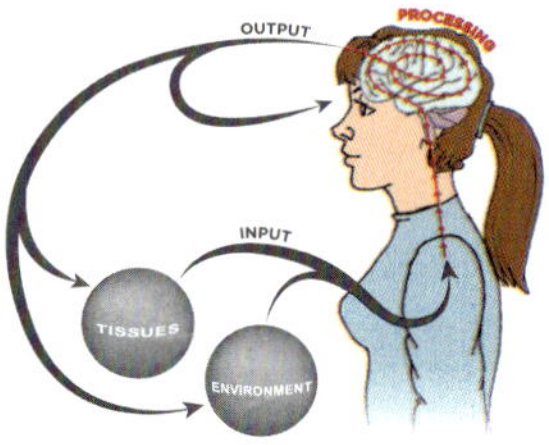
Nociceptive symptom and examination clusters indicate individuals that have these features are 100 times more likely to accurately predict a clinical classification nociceptive pain in patients classified with this type of pain:[45] • Proportionate pain • Aggravating and easing factors • Pain that is intermittent sharp, dull ache or throb at rest • No night pain, dysesthesia, burning, shooting or electric symptoms	Peripheral neurogenic symptoms and sign clusters identified indicating patients are 150 times more likely to have peripheral neurogenic pain states:[44] • Pain in dermatomal or cutaneous distribution • Positive neurodynamic tests and palpation (mechanical tests) • History of nerve pathology or compromise	Central sensitization symptoms and sign clusters identified indicating patients are 486 times more likely to have a central sensitization pain state:[26] • Disproportionate pain • Disproportionate aggravating and easing factors • Diffuse palpation tenderness • Psychosocial issues, i.e., fear-avoidance and pain catastrophization

This classification system by Smart, et. al., will further help clinicians in their plan of care (Figure 5.5). Given the growing evidence for central sensitization as being a prime target for PNE, with the combination of this classification system along with the CSI, clinicians should be able to identify central sensitization clinically.

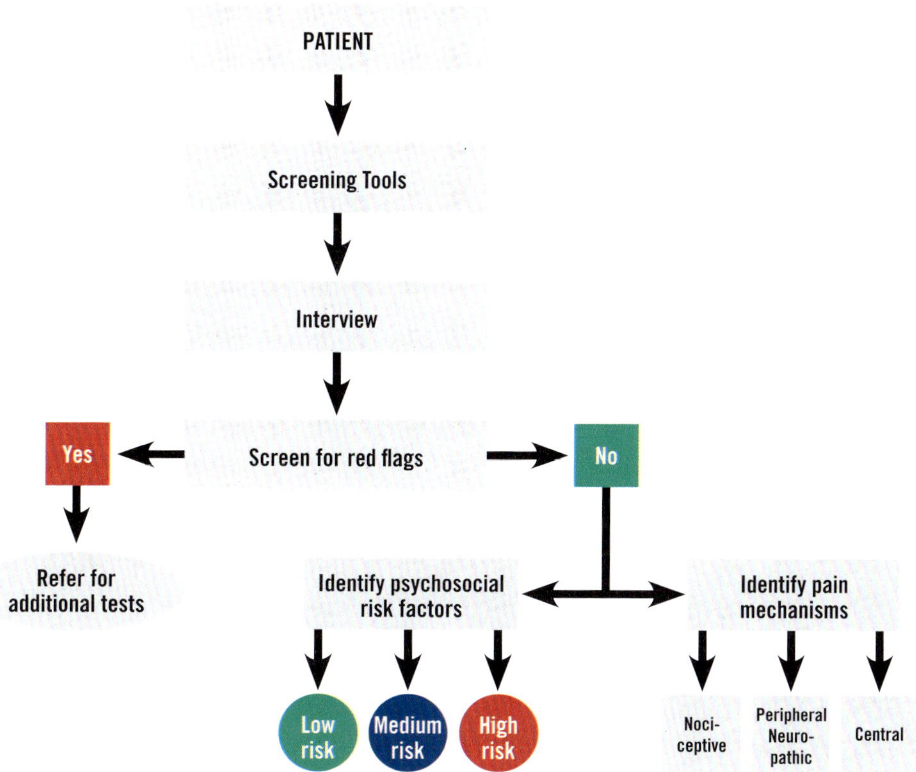

Figure 5.5: Addition of the various pain mechanisms to aid in clinical decision making (Adapted from Diener, et. al).[17]

5.2.4: Objective

In the big scheme of things, all the aforementioned strategies aim to direct the physical examination and treatment. Sections 5.2.2 and 5.2.3 provided ample strategies to screen patients as potential candidates for PNE, and in section 5.4 we will provide additional details on this topic. With the interview process completed, clinicians embark on their physical examination. The physical examination is a significant part of the overall diagnostic process and further enhances the therapeutic alliance.[34] In fact, given that studies have shown that the average physician consultation ranges around 15 minutes,[48-50] it might underscore why professions such as PT and OT might be ideally situated to use PNE. The physical examination is important for a variety of reasons:

- It provides another layer of medical screening for red flags, i.e., Babinski, clonus, ataxic gait, etc.
- It helps further the clinical reasoning and diagnostic accuracy gained from the subjective interview.
- If movement strategies are considered as part of the treatment, movement must be assessed.
- It's part of evidence-based medicine.
- Patients want it. Several qualitative studies on patients attending medical visits highlight an expectation by patients to be physically examined.[51-53]

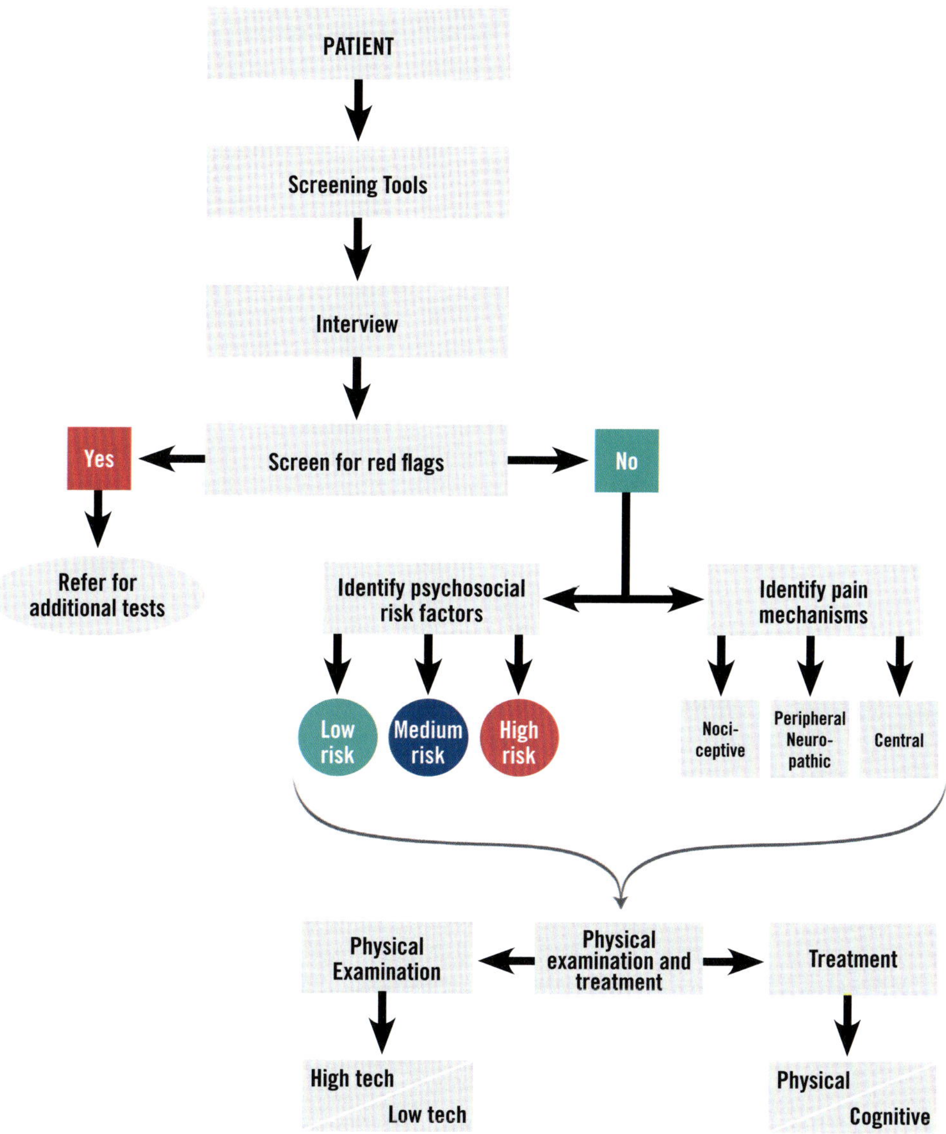

Figure 5.6: Algorithm driving the choice of treatment (Adapted from Diener, et. al).[17]

In regard to screening for the use of PNE, the physical examination should assist to confirm or refute a hypothesis of central sensitization (CS). In Smart's classification, physical tests including disproportionate pain with palpation at the site of symptoms and remote areas are two features which might support the presence of central sensitization. With the growing interest in CS, various physical tests have been described as a means to validate the presence of CS (Table 5.3).[18]

Table 5.3: Clinical tests proposed in the examination of patients with suspected central sensitization.[18]

• Assessment of pressure pain thresholds at sites remote from the symptomatic site
• Assessment of sensitivity to touch during manual palpation at sites remote from the symptomatic site
• Assessment of sensitivity to vibration at sites remote from the symptomatic site
• Assessment of sensitivity to heat at sites remote from the symptomatic site
• Assessment of sensitivity to cold at sites remote from the symptomatic site
• Assessment of pressure pain thresholds during and following exercise
• Assessment of joint end feel
• Brachial plexus provocation test

In the algorithm, it is recommended that in more complex pain presentations such as central sensitization, examinations become less "high tech" so as to not focus on small minutia that might not be all that relevant (Figure 5.6 on page 309).[54] It is recommended that the examination focus on larger, physiological movements of various body parts looking at global movement. Neurodynamic tests are widely described as a screening mechanism for central sensitization and in line with a "low tech" approach and high probability for the presence of allodynia and/or hyperalgesia.[55] A sound neurological screening exam is important for various reasons. First, it is a key part of additional screening to help clear any potentially missed red flags during the patient interview. Second, many patients have concerns regarding a worsening of their condition and having a neurological screening performed by a skilled clinician might help alleviate fears and, in essence, help "paint yellow flags green." Third, is that PNE by its nature will discuss the nervous system – peripheral, spinal and brain. A thorough neurologic screening, together with other components of the physical exam, provide valuable insight into the patient's pain experience, improves the diagnostic reasoning process and collects information that will be critical to a PNE approach. Together, a well-performed patient interview and physical exam are essential for clinician credibility and contribute significantly to strengthening the therapeutic alliance. It is noteworthy that in clinical practice, we often find a significant amount of patients become very emotional after the physical examination. The reason? Many quiver and state: "That might have been the most thorough medical examination I've had in 10 years." We feel this is critical in building a relationship and trust, which in turn is critical in the potential success of PNE. Once again remember, the physical examination should be "low tech" but thorough. The physical examination should convey to the patient that you care and are deeply interested in examining them thoroughly in order to help.

As we complete the physical examination, reflect on this: A recent survey of clinicians using PNE asked what they thought were the biggest factors predicting success. The top five factors identified in the survey are neatly intertwined with material we have already discussed: Listening to the patient, spending time with the patient, patient developing trust in the clinician, thorough interview, and thorough physical examination.[8]

5.2.5: Starting the pain talk

Once the decision is made that a patient might be appropriate for PNE, there should be a bridge between the examination and performing PNE.[7] For PT and OT especially, this is critical as patients typically expect some form of physical intervention, not a cognitive behavioral session. Education, however, is a typical normal process regardless of the approach taken. If the approach is biomedical, a manual therapist might spend some time explaining the findings of the examination, answer questions and discuss the plan of care. PNE should be no different, but it is often viewed as a separate cognitive intervention. Furthermore, patients might get the false impression that the only treatment to be provided will be education. Or they might jump to the conclusion, "Oh, you think it's in my head." So, how do we bridge this gap?

There are several potential options and it's primarily driven by information obtained during the patient's interview. By listening carefully and asking specific questions, you can often determine a potential avenue to begin. For example, "What about your ongoing pain bothers you the most?" Simple questions about the nature of the pain experience and the patient's pain beliefs can provide tremendous insight for a PNE approach. Notice how the following questions drive toward the various PNE metaphors:

- Would you like to know why you hurt?
- Would you like to know why you still hurt?
- Would you like to know why your pain is spreading?
- Would you like to know why stress (or cold) increases your pain?
- Would you like to know why you're having trouble with focus and concentration since the accident?
- Would you like to know why you are "wiped out" at two o' clock every day?
- Would you like to know why you're having trouble sleeping?

This list can go on and on, and the skilled clinician, likely through trial and error, will develop a favorite strategy. One specific strategy that might be of interest for movement-based professions such as PT and OT is: Before we go to the gym and review the stretches and exercises, can I explain to you ________________ [fill in the topic you'd like to focus on]? This strategy basically lets the patient know there will be some type of physical treatment and not just a cognitive/educational "counseling" session. For the seasoned clinician experienced in various educational strategies, it's easy to see that this style of education is opposite to a technique often employed in more complicated behavioral issues, called motivational interviewing (MI). In section 5.11 we will showcase MI as a means to motivate patients who appear ambivalent to change when confronted with PNE.

5.3: Who Needs PNE?

In section 5.2 we discussed the various well-described categories that might respond well to PNE, including central sensitization, high fear-avoidance, high kinesiophobia and high pain catastrophization scores. A recent clinical implementation study of PNE surveyed PTs as to their daily use and experiences related to PNE, showing agreement with high fear-avoidance, pain catastrophization and central sensitization as primary targets for PNE.[8] The surveyed clinicians also identified chronic and acute pain.

The interesting finding was that acute pain was ranked as an important clinical scenario to address with PNE. Historically, PNE was designed for chronic pain, but recent research has taken PNE to the acute environment (Chapter 7) as a means to decrease potential disability.[21,56,57] Acute pain might often present with high fear-avoidance and pain catastrophization,[58,59] so it should not be a surprise that it was highly ranked. Additionally, it can be argued that a subgroup of patients with acute pain might have elements of central sensitization and, therefore, it is not confined to chronic pain. For example, it has been shown that a subgroup of patients following a motor vehicle collision begin to develop generalized sensory hypersensitivity suggestive of central sensitivity soon after the collision.[60]

Apart from the clinical predictors, we need to consider the business perspective. As more clinicians get exposed to PNE and it becomes more interprofessional, there might be an increased need to deliver PNE. The simple business reality is that if a referring physician has been exposed to PNE and sends a patient to a therapist specifically for PNE, it would (from a business perspective) be inconceivable not to consider PNE as part of the plan of care.

For the more casual user of PNE, it has been advised that PNE be considered for E-flags.[61] E-flags, or educate/explain pain flags, refer to the process whereby an astute clinician will listen for specific problems that need education during the patient interview. As they mention issues that need explanation, a list is made and, via PNE, explained to them at appropriate points during the episode of care. For example, a patient might be describing how his pain increases in cold weather. A clinician will note this on the E-flag list (and others) and, once the interview is done, return to these and explain them to the patient as part of the plan of care.

There are a few final issues pertaining to PNE and "who needs it." PNE as described above can be seen as just another technique, similar to other treatments, i.e., spinal manipulation, spinal stabilization exercises, etc. If a patient meets certain criteria (as discussed), PNE should be added to the plan of care and delivered to the patient. Another viewpoint is that PNE is more than just a treatment technique, but an approach that should permeate all facets of care and thus be used with all patients. This is a philosophical discussion and arguments can be made in both directions. There is an argument to be made that pain science can and should become an overarching theme for clinics from the front desk to the treatment room, treating patients with both acute and chronic pain states. PNE is, by definition, an educational intervention and all patients should receive education. However, PNE is a specific type of education, and does not preclude the use of traditional treatments. In fact, the PNE+ concept, underscored by current evidence, suggests PNE will be more successful when combined with other physical treatments.[1]

5.4: PNE and Time Management

Original PNE research and recent clinical implementation studies support PNE's efficacy tied to increased time spent with the patient.[8-10] For any cognitive treatment to work; that is, truly work, there should be ample time for the patient and clinician to engage in the discussion without any outside distractions, i.e., overhead announcements or a knock on the door stating "the next patient is here." The more complex the case, the more time will be needed. Considering the balance between "more time" and ensuring productivity standards are met, there are some strategies that can be trialed. What follows are examples of how PNE was implemented by various practices, clinics and hospitals. Review each, and once again, determine which ones might be possible for your practice setting. The good news is the first two are already in place, making it easier to implement PNE:

- **Initial evaluation:** PNE is usually started as soon as the evaluation is completed on the first visit, which commonly allows for extra time.[7,62] If a clinician, for example, spends 30 minutes to complete the interview and physical examination during a 60-minute initial evaluation, it leaves ample time for a PNE metaphor, instruction in some PNE-related homework, and physical treatment.

- **Paced education:** With exercise, we expose patients and their body tissues to a progressive increase in resistance, duration and frequency. We should do the same with education. However, prior to refining an optimal method of applying PNE concepts, eager clinicians would often provide patients with a large bolus of PNE during the first session, covering any/all aspects of pain. In many ways this was the equivalent of taking a drink from a fire hydrant. After being flooded with information, which might have challenged deeply rooted pain beliefs, many patients would feel emotionally overloaded. As PNE developed and became more refined, it became clear that the education should also be paced. Chapter 4 showcased a series of short, simple and easy-to-use metaphors and examples. These metaphors have been used in a variety of studies demonstrating that abbreviated PNE can be effective, efficient and easily integrated into a busy practice.[7,21,57,62] Ideally, in clinical practice following the initial evaluation, subsequent sessions will use a combination of these abbreviated PNE metaphors and physical treatments, allowing for a gradual exposure to PNE, opportunity for patients to absorb and reflect on the content, and build a working knowledge of the pain neuroscience associated with their pain experience.

- **Be deliberate with scheduling:** In section 5.2, a comprehensive overview is provided on how to screen patients who might benefit from PNE. In this section, it has already been stated that PNE does better when there is more time available to present concepts at a pace that patients are able to comprehend. It would therefore seem logical to screen patients ahead of time and allocate patients to longer appointments as appropriate. In current clinical practice, it is common to send patients their intake forms ahead of time for completion. Ideally, patients should complete their necessary paperwork prior to attending their first visit; paperwork can be reviewed and screened against set criteria and then time for appointments can be allotted based on the clinical presentation. This is far removed from the current model. In a typical outpatient clinic, time slots are set in place in the scheduling software and patients, regardless if they need that much time or more, are slotted into the system (i.e. clinic-centered vs patient-centered). This style of scheduling is stressful for the healthcare provider and might lead to a potentially limited efficacy of PNE. To reduce provider stress, improve efficacy and optimize productivity, other scheduling methods might be more effective. For example, a certain number of shorter time slots could be allocated to more nociceptive, clinically treatable patients, and a certain number of longer slots assigned for more complex patients, as well as a number of new evaluations. Color coding in scheduling software can help (Figure 5.7).

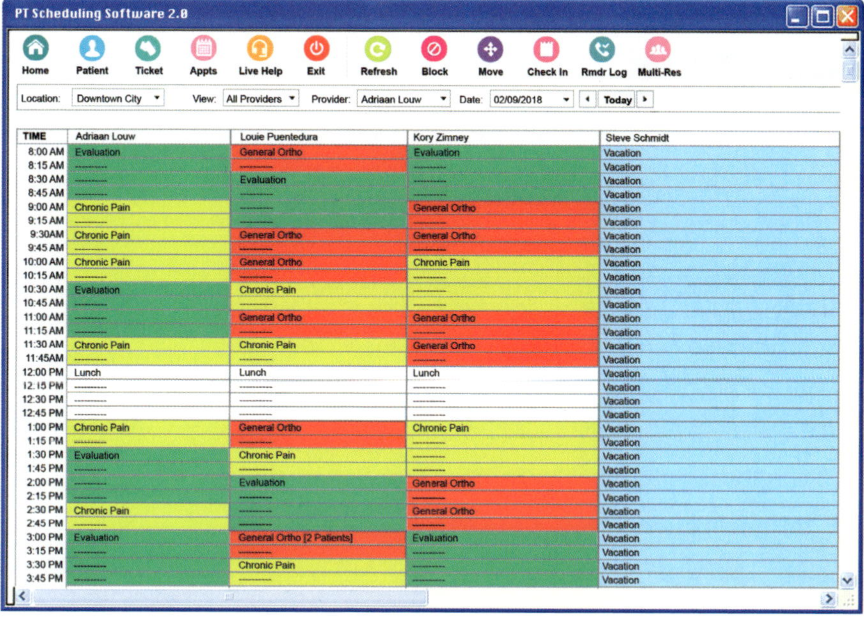

TIME	Adriaan Louw	Louie Puentedura	Kory Zimney	Steve Schmidt
8:00 AM	Evaluation	General Ortho	Evaluation	Vacation
8:15 AM	----------	----------	----------	Vacation
8:30 AM	----------	Evaluation	----------	Vacation
8:45 AM	----------	----------	----------	Vacation
9:00 AM	Chronic Pain	----------	General Ortho	Vacation
9:15 AM	----------	----------	----------	Vacation
9:30AM	Chronic Pain	General Ortho	General Ortho	Vacation
9:45 AM	----------	----------	----------	Vacation
10:00 AM	Chronic Pain	General Ortho	Chronic Pain	Vacation
10:15 AM	----------	----------	----------	Vacation
10:30 AM	Evaluation	Chronic Pain	----------	Vacation
10:45 AM	----------	----------	----------	Vacation
11:00 AM	----------	General Ortho	General Ortho	Vacation
11:15 AM	----------	----------	----------	Vacation
11:30 AM	Chronic Pain	Chronic Pain	General Ortho	Vacation
11:45AM	----------	----------	----------	Vacation
12:00 PM	Lunch	Lunch	Lunch	Vacation
12:15 PM	----------	----------	----------	Vacation
12:30 PM	----------	----------	----------	Vacation
12:45 PM	----------	----------	----------	Vacation
1:00 PM	Chronic Pain	General Ortho	Chronic Pain	Vacation
1:15 PM	----------	----------	----------	Vacation
1:30 PM	Evaluation	Chronic Pain	----------	Vacation
1:45 PM	----------	----------	----------	Vacation
2:00 PM	----------	Evaluation	General Ortho	Vacation
2:15 PM	----------	----------	----------	Vacation
2:30 PM	Chronic Pain	----------	General Ortho	Vacation
2:45 PM	----------	----------	----------	Vacation
3:00 PM	Evaluation	General Ortho [2 Patients]	Evaluation	Vacation
3:15 PM	----------	----------	----------	Vacation
3:30 PM	----------	Chronic Pain	----------	Vacation
3:45 PM	----------	----------	----------	Vacation

Figure 5.7: Example of a daily clinical schedule with various scenarios.

Another consideration in being deliberate with scheduling should be the well-being of the clinician. There is growing evidence that treating chronic pain is tied to burnout.[63-65] It is interesting to note that in research of very productive people, be it business men and women, writers, academics, etc., have shown highest productivity when work is done in accordance with circadian rhythms.[66] Your circadian rhythm is basically a 24-hour internal clock that is running in the background of your brain and cycles between sleepiness and alertness at regular intervals. As it turns out, these cycles are roughly one-and-a-half to two hours long. This implies we can only work at optimal efficiency and effectiveness for one-and-a-half to two hours, and then we need a break.[67] By alternating between work and taking short breaks, productivity increases significantly.[66,67] The opposite is currently being done in clinical practice: Clinicians getting to the office and seeing patients all morning long with a busy and hectic schedule, only to get to lunch time. Lunch time consists of eating, checking emails, checking in with the family and writing charts (otherwise you need to stay late again), only to start up once more after lunch. This continues with patient care all afternoon, on to the end of the day, finishing with...more paperwork. Yes, the circadian clinical rhythm is just a theoretical model and research into the well-being of clinicians is sparse, but warrants a further look when it comes to treating chronic pain. It is suggested that by at least alternating more complex patients with less challenging patients, a rhythm can be developed to allow for a healthier clinical scenario for both patients and the clinician.

Another PNE scheduling consideration might be related to cortisol. Cortisol plays a big role in our daily energy and alertness by various processes, including increases in blood sugar, protein and carbohydrate metabolism.[68,69] However, cortisol is released on a diurnal cycle, peaking in the mornings toward the middle of the day and then decreases. Scientists have shown that in people with chronic pain, cortisol levels are altered and in conditions such as chronic fatigue syndrome, there is an overall blunting of the entire diurnal cortisol curve.[70] Clinically, this might imply patients are more biologically awake during the periods when cortisol levels peak (Figure 5.8).

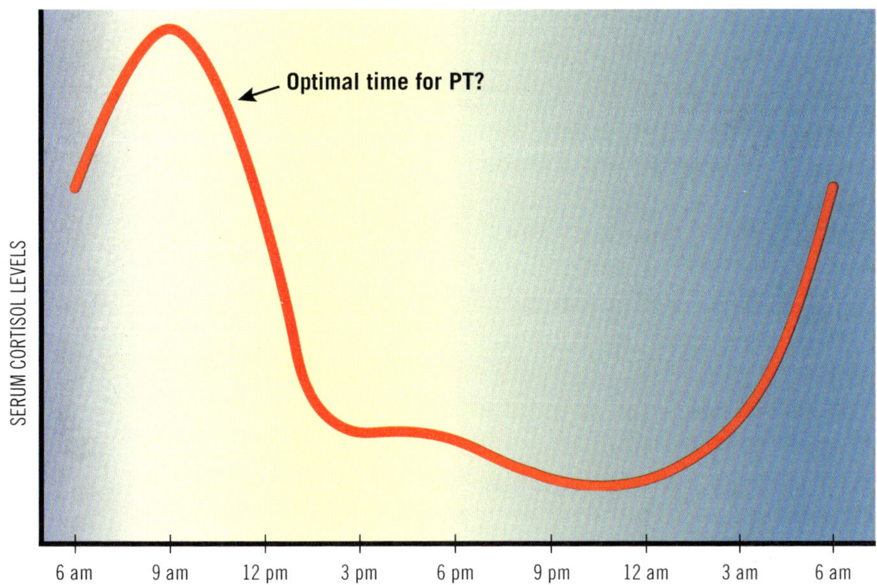

Figure 5.8: Diurnal cortisol curve.

If you wanted to make another potential neuroscience case for this consideration, consider the pain neuromatrix and especially the anterior cingulate. It is now well documented that the anterior cingulate is a key area of the brain activated during the pain neuromatrix.[71,72] One of the primary functions of the anterior cingulate is focus and concentration. This implies, and has been clinically verified, that people in chronic pain have difficulty with focus and concentration. What does this have to do with scheduling? In most outpatient and private practice settings, mornings and late afternoons are typically quite busy and even noisy, with many people trying to squeeze in their therapy before or after school or work. By considering mid-morning, late morning and early afternoon as a potential optimal time for patients with chronic pain, not only is the clinic relatively quieter but cortisol levels are also high (Figure 5.9).

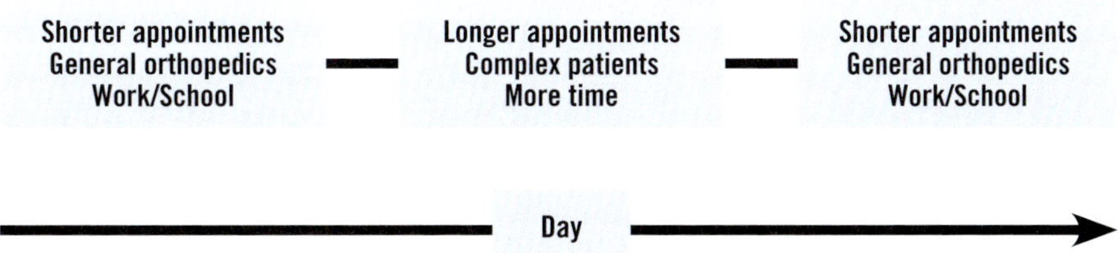

Figure 5.9: Scheduling option based on various biological processes.

The aforementioned idea of balancing patients with being alert but avoiding overstimulation refers to the Yerkes-Dodson law (Figure 5.10).[73] This law pertains to various situations and has been applied to students studying for examinations, optimal timing for preoperative education and even sports performance for elite athletes. If arousal is too low, performance suffers; if arousal is too high, performance also suffers. This discussion also includes a commonly asked question; is PNE best done in a private room versus in an open gym area. This question includes issues about privacy and a patient's willingness to share personal information in an open gym area or behind a curtain, versus an actual physical room. Yes, we propose that PNE must be combined with physical treatments (PNE+), but this often occurs as a trusting relationship that is developed over time. Based on the concept of arousal and how much the brain is being used by pain (pain neuromatrix), it might be advantageous to schedule more complex patients in a private room with the intent of aiming for optimal arousal and providing the best environment for attention.

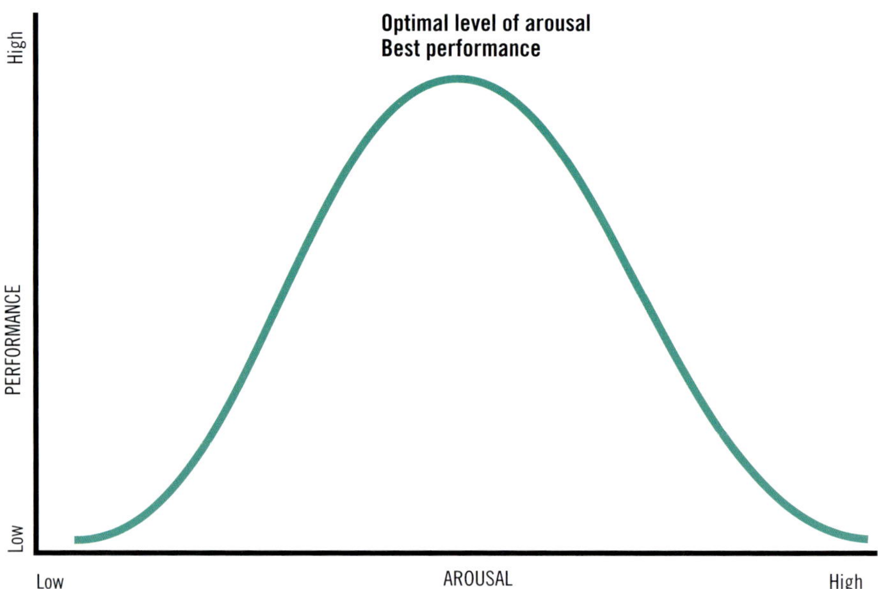

Figure 5.10: Yerkes-Dodson law of arousal and performance.

- **Pain clinic day:** Outpatient clinics and private practices have a natural ebb and flow. Some times of the day and days of the week are busier than others. Therefore, another potential strategy that has been used by PNE-trained clinicians is to designate slower days as a "pain clinic" day (Figure 5.11 from Galen Danielson, PT, DPT). This concept is not new to medicine. For example, in orthopedics it's not uncommon for an orthopedic surgeon to have a sports medicine clinic one day a week. On these pain clinic days, appointments are longer, which is beneficial to both patient and clinician. If these weekly sessions are lengthier and more comprehensive, a once a week schedule can suffice in providing significant benefit for patients experiencing chronic pain. The key element here, however, is screening. An optimal screening system must be in place to screen patients appropriate for allocation to this style of schedule. A potential bonus of this style of scheduling is marketing. A common issue that often arises during marketing calls to physicians is the notion that physical therapy is a commodity that "can be found on every corner."[74] By providing a specialized program, especially for chronic pain, it might create a significant marketing opportunity.

Figure 5.11: Designation of a pain clinic day once per week.

- **Collaborative clinical environment:** This approach encompasses various options:
  - In most clinic scenarios, clinicians are surrounded by peers. Each clinician has his or her individualized schedule comprising a variety of patients, ranging from relatively uncomplicated to more challenging, i.e., chronic pain. If a clinician knows he/she has a challenging patient, he/she might ask a colleague to start their next patient when they show up, allowing the clinician to complete the session with the more challenging patient. This "I help you and you help me" philosophy might allow for the extra few minutes needed to drive home a crucial PNE message.
  - In the US, PTs and OTs have assistants – physical therapist assistants (PTA) and certified occupational therapy assistants (COTA). PNE is not only readily taught to PTs and OTs, but also assistants. A clinical scenario might be where a therapist treats a patient for a set amount of time, and the additional treatment can then be completed by a PTA or COTA. A recent survey of PTs using PNE indicated that 97 percent of PTs believed PNE should be taught in PTA schools.[8] PTA textbooks now include PNE.[75]

- In section 5.5 we will discuss cognitive homework. For the sake of being thorough in this section, we need to mention that shifting cognitive restructuring to patients (homework) would be an additional way to increase clinic time with the patient.

5.5: PNE and Cost-Effectiveness

We can hear clinic owners and directors say, "This all sounds great, but there are increasing costs and pressures driving the necessity to see more patients." As long as the current payment system of fee-for-service remains, this will continue to be a challenge. Yes, there is the fantasy world we described in section 5.4 of allotting more time for chronic pain, but when taught in classes, working clinicians agree, the current way we are seeing patients is very demanding. Furthermore, for the business people, anecdotal evidence suggests increasing clinical demands, high productivity standards and impacted schedules as a significant reason for burnout in physical therapy. Why is this important? In the business world, replacement costs are typically around 30-50 percent of the salary of the person being replaced, depending on the market and skill set. To replace a therapist, there is a significant financial cost. The current US mean annual salary for a PT is estimated by the Department of Labor Statistics at around $84,000. If a therapist is working at full capacity and resigns, a new therapist has to be found, trained and brought up to speed. The replacement therapist's cost would therefore be around $25,000-$42,000.

If PNE demands more time, yet we have a fiscal requirement to remain productive, how do we go about solving this dilemma? There are some strategies that can be used:

- **Section 5.3:** Many of the strategies already discussed in section 5.3 should showcase how PNE can be delivered in the current model. This includes paced education, screening appropriately, using ancillary staff, scheduling deliberately, etc.

- **PNE+:** Research on PNE provides strong evidence for PNE improving pain ratings, pain knowledge, disability, pain catastrophization, fear-avoidance, attitudes and behaviors regarding pain, physical movement and healthcare utilization.[1] However, current PNE research demonstrated that PNE combined with other physical treatments yielded superior results (PNE+).[1] This provides support for clinicians to integrate PNE while doing other treatments. For example, a patient with a knee replacement needs passive and active-assisted range of motion and even scar massage to facilitate increased knee flexion.

However, during the initial evaluation this patient might have said he typically feels more knee pain when it's cold outside. An astute clinician can recall this information, recognize the need for education on the topic and pre-print materials related to "nerve sensors." During the next session, the clinician can use the printed materials to explain and discuss the neuroscience of ion channel expression while performing physical treatment (e.g. manual therapy). The utility of this clinical strategy is that two treatments are delivered at the same time. Another advantage of this "backdoor" approach is that a patient might not see this as a formal, cognitive session and therefore, be more open to "talking about pain."

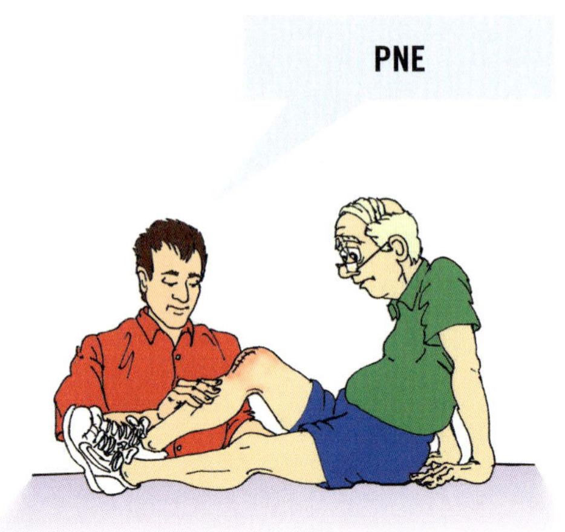

- **Group PNE:** The current best evidence for PNE and all educational models show that one-on-one verbal education is superior to other forms of education.[1] One-on-one education, however, is relatively expensive from a time efficiency and personnel utilization perspective. If you consider the Institute of Medicine estimating that more than 100 million Americans suffer from chronic pain in some way[76] and all pain education is to be done one-on-one, the war on pain will be lost. Yes, on a larger societal scale this calls for mass education with significant funding and government support,[77,78] but what can be done within individual clinics or departments? The answer might be group PNE. While the evidence suggests one-on-one education is better, group PNE has been tested and shown to be quite effective as well for decreasing pain and disability. In the latest systematic review, two studies utilized group sessions[79,80] and several other non-randomized clinical trials have been performed in a group format.[4,81-84]

Unfortunately, to date, only one PNE group study has measured group PNE in terms of healthcare cost.[9] Moseley showed that even though one-on-one PNE was superior to group, it yielded a cost savings (decreased number of PT visits), which would be very important to consider as the world grapples with the increased financial demands of chronic pain. Considering the positive impact of providing PNE in groups, a simple cost-benefit analysis suggests it is favorable to shift at least some PNE to group settings. Group therapy has been used extensively in psychology and specifically in cognitive behavioral therapy (CBT).[85,86]

A huge clinical barrier to the implementation of group therapy in the US has been reimbursement and "how to bill for it." It is argued that, as the US healthcare system shifts towards bundled payments, group therapy's allure will increase.[87,88] The ability to have 10-12 people meet once or twice a week for three to four weeks and learn more about their pain will allow a clinician to influence far more people. If several groups meet each week, the numbers can steadily increase. Please realize there are many different potential formats for group PNE:

- The simplest way might just be for a hospital, healthcare system or clinic to have a monthly or bi-monthly pain lecture open to anyone interested in pain. This could be the same lecture every time, or even a potential revolving series of topics. This educational format has been done before, demonstrating increased knowledge of pain,[4] retention of pain knowledge over time[82] and a positive shift in the view of PT by patients with chronic pain.[81]

- A small group of patients attending therapy once or twice a week for a lecture on PNE. This might be twice a week for four weeks with eight popular PNE stories related to a specific condition, i.e., fibromyalgia or chronic LBP.

- A formal, intensive pain management program. Various large systems offer comprehensive inpatient or outpatient pain programs combining a full day of various activities, including education. PNE has found its way into various national, regional and local PNE group sessions. Here, patients are extensively screened to be admitted to the programs, and these are truly multidisciplinary. The key element here would be that all concerned in the program "speak the same language" when it comes to pain.

Given the increasing interest in group PNE, Table 5.4 on the following page provides a comprehensive PNE group program. This program, provided to the authors by Dana Scott PT, DPT – a fellow faculty member – utilizes PNE extensively throughout and allows the reader to see what such a program looks like. Depending on your clinical setting, you might find the program or parts of the program helpful in the potential development of a group PNE approach. Table 5.4 also provides significant insight into clinical issues with billing, scheduling, etc. This program has been running successfully for more than eight years.

Table 5.4: Example and layout of an existing group PNE program. (Special thanks to Dana Scott, PT, DPT.)

• The options for setting up PNE groups are limitless. Configurations depend on the time, flexibility and staff available to assist with these groups. Preoperative groups for patients in the acute phase exhibiting yellow flags could easily be one-session groups.
• The more complex pain issues or the more diverse the group, the more sessions will likely be needed. Adding other disciplines to the group program will also add to the variety of information that can be delivered in these groups. Examples might include health psychologists, dietitians, and yoga instructors.
• **Diagnosis:** The patients that are involved in this group are diverse in their diagnosis but all have some type of ongoing pain problem. On average, they have a pain history of 10 years and the majority are on disability or seeking disability.
• **Age:** The group is open to any age. The age range is 20 to 80 years old with the average in the 40-50 year-old range. It is recommended that you keep patients grouped together in similar age ranges, however, we experience times when the generation gap is beneficial.
• **Gender:** These groups are primarily female, often having only one male in each group. This does not seem to pose a problem, however, having two to three men in a group of mostly females frequently leads to the men vying to establish dominance in the group. This at times would nearly sabotage the group environment with the females, and sometimes make the less dominant men feel unsafe. There were several times when we had to pull a male out of the group to "save" the group dynamic. This could be an argument for limiting groups to all male or all female, especially with complex, longstanding pain issues where abuse might be a factor.
• **Length:** One of the biggest changes we made was lengthening the program from four weeks to six. This change was made because it seemed that most patients were just starting to click with the information at four weeks. Adding the two additional weeks allowed us more time to progress them further, once they had their "ah-ha" moment.

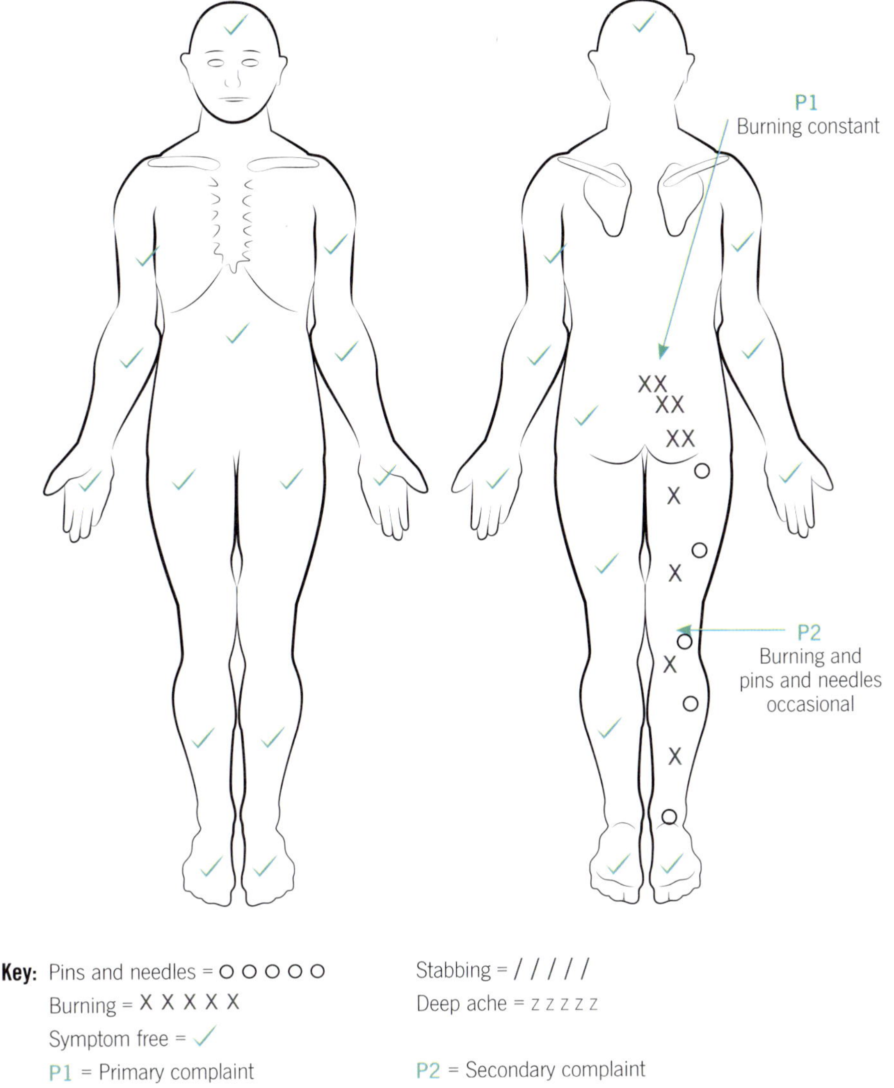

Figure 7.7: Patient presentation with acute LBP and leg pain. Image from Zimney, et. al.[37]

Four days later, the patient returned to the occupational medicine provider's office for follow-up:

- No change in symptoms.
- Constant pain of 3/10 with increased pain of 7/10 with activity.
- Burning sensation in her right low back region with occasional pain radiating down the right leg into her heel.
- She was now referred for PT.

- In PT she presented with:
    - Pain with standing and walking > 20-30 minutes
    - ODI 36 percent – indicating moderate disability
    - $FABQ^{PA}$ 23 – indicating high probability not to returning to work[38,39]
    - $FABQ^{W}$ 30 – indicating moderate risk for not returning back to work
    - Acute LBP Screening (ALBPS) Questionnaire and SBST – medium risk for prolonged disability (examples of patient ratings on questions)
        - > Is your work heavy or monotonous?
            - Patient answer = 10 (10 = extremely)
        - > How would you rate the pain that you have had during the past week?
            - Patient answer = 7 (10 = pain as bad as it could be)
        - > How tense or anxious have you felt in the past week?
            - Patient answer = 7 (10 = As tense and anxious as I've ever felt)
        - > In your view, low large is the risk that your current pain may become persistent?
            - Patient answer = 4 (10 = very large risk)
        - > An increase in pain is an indication that I should stop what I am doing until the pain decreases
            - Patient answer = 10 (10 = completely agree)

This clinical presentation showcases a typical patient with LBP presenting with various yellow flags which, if not dealt with, could result in prolonged disability and chronic pain. The various patient-reported outcome measure scores suggest that treatment should include cognitive restructuring aimed at decreasing fear-avoidance, i.e., PNE. Even though this was a single case study, it highlights the screening process, the reasoning process, PNE application for an acute LBP condition, as well as merger of movement strategies (exercise and manual therapy) with PNE (PNE+). Table 7.2 shows the initial and discharge data of this case.

Table 7.2: Initial and discharge scores after PNE implementation for acute LBP.

Measurements	Initial	1 week	2 weeks (discharge)
Lumbar ROM: Flexion	15º	30º	60º
Lumbar ROM: Extension	5º	15º	25º
Standing tolerance	20-30 minutes	1-2 hours	unlimited
Lifting tolerance	10 pounds	15 pounds	50 pounds

Outcome measures	Initial	Discharge
ODI	18/50	0/50
NPRS	3/10	0/10
$FABQ^{PA}$	23	0
$FABQ^{W}$	30	0
Keele SBT	4/9	0/9
ALBPS Questionnaire	101	0
PSFS	4/10	10/10

7.7: Middle School Children

Considering the global epidemic of chronic pain, a strategy of taking this education (PNE) to the masses would seem to be very beneficial. This means that PNE would be taught to the general population. One section of the population getting some attention for PNE is the education of children. This can be seen as a means to inoculate children against chronic pain. By teaching children about pain, the premise is that if and when they experience pain, they will understand pain better, have less fear and keep moving. This theory forms part of a series of studies:

- **Study 1:** 147 middle school children in the fifth, sixth, seventh, and eighth grades were taught a 30-minute PNE lecture in groups of approximately 20-25 students.[40] Prior to and immediately after, the rNPQ and various beliefs regarding pain were measured. The results were encouraging:
  - Significant improvement in knowledge was found with a mean score on the rNPQ test scores improving from 29.5 percent pre-PNE to 60.8 percent post-PNE. This shift is one of the largest recorded shifts in PNE. Furthermore, fifth-grade students outscored their older counterparts in the sixth, seventh, and eighth grades.
  - Significant shifts in beliefs were also found in all but one of the pain beliefs questions, with a medium effect size for "*you can control how much pain you feel*" ($p<.001$; $r=.354$) and large effect size for "*your brain decides if you feel pain, not your tissues*" ($p<.001$; $r=.545$).
    - The study clearly showed that middle school children can understand PNE.
- **Study 2:** Around the same time, the same research group conducted a similar 30-minute PNE study on 94 eighth grade students, studying its effect on the rNPQ as well as the ability of the PNE lecture to shift fear of physical activity ($FABQ^{PA}$) (Louw, et al. – unpublished data). The study showed a similar increase in rNPQ scores and also a positive shift in less fear of physical activity despite having pain.
- **Study 3:** The third study (ongoing at this time) is an RCT whereby 578 middle school children either receive the 30-minute PNE program or a standard sports medicine presentation (sprains and strains). Then, differences are assessed between the two groups during the school year in regard to pain experiences, medical visits, medicine use, days absent at school, missing sports and missing physical education.

7.8: Conclusions

We might have written this book for clinicians but, ultimately, we believe it is also very much for, and about, the patient. The patient comes first. We truly believe that a patient-centered approach is what PNE is all about. Pain is personal, and a personalized biological explanation of the pain experience, applied to the individual situation and needs, is vital. The evidence for PNE is compelling and should provide hope for even the most impacted patients; those suffering with chronic pain. PNE helps patients reconceptualize their pain, take charge of their life and steadily progress back to reclaiming their lives. PNE is not merely about helping patients manage their pain. PNE should be seen as an effective treatment for pain.

As we stated earlier, we wrote this book for clinicians, especially the clinicians we encounter week after week at seminars and conferences. Those therapists who say they are tired, frustrated and worn out. Chronic pain takes a toll on clinicians and they continue to struggle with the treatment of patients with chronic pain conditions. Dr. Patrick Wall believed that PT and OT were the ideal professions to treat pain. PNE is at the core of this belief and is a product of Wall's belief in the profession. Clinicians should be energized and see the numerous opportunities to help their patients with chronic pain, including changes in beliefs and cognitions, as well as a more movement-based approach that includes exercise, manual therapy and more (PNE+). The reality is that therapy has much to offer the patient with chronic pain. Clinicians should be energized and empowered by the neuroscience of pain, which in turn changes their beliefs and attitudes about chronic pain.

PNE is here to stay. We encourage clinicians to take on the pain message. Take it to your patients. Patients are interested in pain and the evidence indicates they are much better for it on so many levels.

Education is therapy

Know pain, know gain

Chapter 7 References

1. Moseley L. Combined physiotherapy and education is efficacious for chronic low back pain. *The Australian journal of physiotherapy.* 2002;48(4):297-302.
2. Gema BP, Enrique LG, Nathalie AR, Tomas GI, Virginia JP, Daniel PM. Pain Neurophysiology Education and Therapeutic Exercise for Patients With Chronic Low Back Pain: A Single-Blind Randomized Controlled Trial. *Arch Phys Med Rehabil.* Nov 11 2017.
3. Vlaeyen JW, Linton SJ. Fear-avoidance and its consequences in chronic musculoskeletal pain: a state of the art. *Pain.* Apr 2000;85(3):317-332.
4. Moseley GL. Reconceptualising pain acording to modern pain sciences. *Physical Therapy Reviews.* 2007;12: 169-178.
5. Louw A, Puentedura EJ, Zimney K, Cox T, Rico D. The clinical implementation of pain neuroscience education: A survey study. *Physiother Theory Pract.* Nov 2017;33(11):869-879.
6. Moseley GL, Butler DS. Fifteen Years of Explaining Pain: The Past, Present, and Future. *The journal of pain: official journal of the American Pain Society.* Jun 5 2015.
7. Gifford L. *Aches and Pains.* Cornwall: Wordpress; 2014.
8. Louw A, Puentedura EJ, Zimney K. A clinical contrast: physical therapists with low back pain treating patients with low back pain. *Physiother Theory Pract.* Nov 2015;31(8):562-567.
9. Louw A, Louw Q, Crous LCC. Preoperative Education for Lumbar Surgery for Radiculopathy. *South African Journal of Physiotherapy.* July 2009 2009;65(2):3-8.
10. Louw A, Butler DS, Diener I, Puentedura EJ. Development of a Preoperative Neuroscience Educational Program for Patients with Lumbar Radiculopathy. *American journal of physical medicine & rehabilitation/Association of Academic Physiatrists.* Mar 8 2013.
11. Oosterhuis T, Costa LO, Maher CG, de Vet HC, van Tulder MW, Ostelo RW. Rehabilitation after lumbar disc surgery. *The Cochrane database of systematic reviews.* 2014;3:CD003007.
12. Loupasis GA, Stamos K, Katonis PG, Sapkas G, Korres DS, Hartofilakidis G. Seven- to 20-year outcome of lumbar discectomy. *Spine.* Nov 15 1999;24(22):2313-2317.
13. Gibson JN, Waddell G. Surgery for degenerative lumbar spondylosis: updated Cochrane Review. *Spine.* Oct 15 2005;30(20):2312-2320.
14. Baert IA, Lluch E, Mulder T, Nijs J, Noten S, Meeus M. Does pre-surgical central modulation of pain influence outcome after total knee replacement? A systematic review. *Osteoarthritis Cartilage.* Sep 14 2015.
15. Theunissen M, Peters ML, Bruce J, Gramke HF, Marcus MA. Preoperative anxiety and catastrophizing: a systematic review and meta-analysis of the association with chronic postsurgical pain. *The Clinical journal of pain.* Nov-Dec 2012;28(9):819-841.
16. McGregor AH, Dore CJ, Morris TP, Morris S, Jamrozik K. ISSLS prize winner: Function After Spinal Treatment, Exercise, and Rehabilitation (FASTER): a factorial randomized trial to determine whether the functional outcome of spinal surgery can be improved. *Spine.* Oct 1 2011;36(21):1711-1720.
17. Ronnberg K, Lind B, Zoega B, Halldin K, Gellerstedt M, Brisby H. Patients' satisfaction with provided care/information and expectations on clinical outcome after lumbar disc herniation surgery. *Spine.* Jan 15 2007;32(2):256-261.
18. Louw A, Butler DS, Diener I, Puentedura EJ. Preoperative education for lumbar radiculopathy: A Survey of US Spine Surgeons. *International Journal of Spine Surgery.* 2012;6:130-139.
19. Landers MR, Puentedura E, Louw A, McCauley A, Rasmussen Z, Bungum T. A population-based survey of lumbar surgery beliefs in the United States. *Orthopaedic nursing/National Association of Orthopaedic Nurses.* Jul-Aug 2014;33(4): 207-216.
20. Louw A, Diener I, Butler DS, Puentedura EJ. Preoperative education addressing postoperative pain in total joint arthroplasty: review of content and educational delivery methods. *Physiother Theory Pract.* Apr 2013;29(3):175-194.

21. Louw A, Diener I, Butler D, Puentedura E. The effect of neuroscience education on pain, disability, anxiety, and stress in chronic musculoskeletal pain. *Arch Phys Med Rehabil.* 2011;92:2041-2056.
22. Louw A, Diener I, Fernandez-de-Las-Penas C, Puentedura EJ. Sham Surgery in Orthopedics: A Systematic Review of the Literature. *Pain medicine.* Jul 11 2016.
23. Louw A. *Your Nerves Are Having Back Surgery.* Minneapolis: OPTP; 2012.
24. Louw A, Diener I, Puentedura EJ. The short term effects of preoperative neuroscience education for lumbar radiculopathy: A case series. *International Journal of Spine Surgery.* 2015;9:11.
25. Moseley GL. Widespread brain activity during an abdominal task markedly reduced after pain physiology education: fMRI evaluation of a single patient with chronic low back pain. *The Australian journal of physiotherapy.* 2005;51(1): 49-52.
26. Louw A, Puentedura EJ, Diener I, Peoples RR. Preoperative therapeutic neuroscience education for lumbar radiculopathy: a single-case fMRI report. *Physiother Theory Pract.* Oct 2015;31(7):496-508.
27. Louw A, Diener I, Landers MR, Puentedura EJ. Preoperative pain neuroscience education for lumbar radiculopathy: a multicenter randomized controlled trial with 1-year follow-up. *Spine.* Aug 15 2014;39(18):1449-1457.
28. Louw A, Zimney K, Puentedura EJ, Diener I. The Efficacy of Therapeutic Neuroscience Education on Musculoskeletal Pain – A Systematic Review of the Literature. *Physiother Theory Pract.* 2016;32(5): 332-355.
29. Louw A, Puentedura EJ, Zimney K, Schmidt S. Know Pain, Know Gain? A Perspective on Pain Neuroscience Education in Physical Therapy. *J Orthop Sports Phys Ther.* Mar 2016;46(3): 131-134.
30. Louw A, Diener I, Landers MR, Zimney K, Puentedura EJ. Three-year follow-up of a randomized controlled trial comparing preoperative neuroscience education for patients undergoing surgery for lumbar radiculopathy. *J Spine Surg.* Dec 2016;2(4):289-298.
31. Louw A, Puentedura EJ, Diener I. A descriptive study of the utilization of physical therapy for postoperative rehabilitation in patients undergoing surgery for lumbar radiculopathy. *Eur Spine J.* Nov 2016;25(11):3550-3559.
32. Lluch E, Torres R, Nijs J, Van Oosterwijck J. Evidence for central sensitization in patients with osteoarthritis pain: a systematic literature review. *European journal of pain.* Nov 2014;18(10): 1367-1375.
33. Louw A. *Your Nerves Are Having A Knee Replacement.* Minneapolis, MN: OPTP; 2015.
34. Louw A, Zimney K, Puentedura E, Reed J. Immediate Effects of Preoperative Pain Neuroscience Education for Patients Undergoing Total Knee Arthroplasty: A Case Series *Physiother Theory Pract.* 2017; Accepted for publication.
35. Louw A, Reed J, Zimney K, Puentedura E, Grimm D, Landers M. A Randomized Clinical Trial of Preoperative Pain Neuroscience Education for Total Knee Arthroplasty. 2018; Submitted for publication.
36. Louw A. *Your Nerves Are Having Shoulder Surgery.* Minneapolis, MN: OPTP; 2017.
37. Zimney K, Louw A, Puentedura EJ. Use of Therapeutic Neuroscience Education to address psychosocial factors associated with acute low back pain: a case report. *Physiother Theory Pract.* Apr 2014;30(3):202-209.
38. Fritz JM, George SZ. Identifying psychosocial variables in patients with acute work-related low back pain: the importance of fear-avoidance beliefs. *Physical therapy.* Oct 2002;82(10): 973-983.
39. Williamson E. Fear Avoidance Beliefs Questionnaire (FABQ). *The Australian journal of physiotherapy.* 2006;52(2):149.
40. Louw A, Podolak J, Zimney K, Schmidt S, Puentedura E. Can Pain Beliefs Change in Middle School Students? A Study of the Effectiveness of Pain Neuroscience Education. *Physiother Theory Pract.* 2017 – Accepted for publication.

Notes

Stage	Rationale	Potential criteria for progression
2. Laterality	Laterality must be intact to progress to other GMI treatments such as mirror therapy. If laterality is diminished, mirror therapy will further confuse the brain, potentially resulting in increased pain.	There are different thresholds for hands, feet, back and neck. Broadly stated, if a patient has achieved laterality accuracy of over 80 percent and under three seconds per image, progression to the motor imagery stage might be considered.[453-455]*
3. Motor Imagery	Solidifying brain maps and being able to run maps with little to no pain, without actual movement.[105] Hebbian theory: Nerves that fire apart, wire apart.	When a patient can rehearse and run through static, dynamic, functional and context rich imagery with little to no pain, they might be ready for the sensory discrimination training stage.*
4. Sensory Discrimination	This strategy is not common in some of the GMI descriptions, but there is compelling evidence that these techniques are able to sharpen maps and ease pain.[391,392,446,447]	Progression to the mirror therapy stage might be considered when patients are able to tolerate sensory discrimination techniques on or close to the affected area. Localization threshold of 80 percent accuracy[391,446] and two-point discrimination within normal thresholds.[436,456]*
5. Mirror Therapy	Mirrors are used to "trick" the brain, allowing for a visual cue that movement is occurring with little to no pain.	Mirror therapy is about exposure. The previous four stages allow for mirror therapy preparation.*

* Even when thresholds are met, i.e., laterality, it is not often clinically abandoned. Many of the treatments in various stages continue, even with the addition of a new stage, since one stage builds on another. This is especially true for laterality. The intent of this section is not to provide a thorough GMI description and choices of treatments are based on extensive testing including laterality, two-point discrimination, etc. Books specific to GMI have been developed and readers are encouraged to consult such resources.[452,457]

6.5.20: Neurodynamics

Apart from the neuroscience nuances of ion channel expression, myelination and demyelination, etc., the body's alarm system – the nervous system – also has physical properties closely tied to movement. The physical movement of the nervous system is referred to as neurodynamics[458] and includes three key elements that are physically required for a healthy nervous system: Space, movement, and blood.[459-461]

- **Space:** Delicate nerves, spinal cord and meninges all travel within containers or passage ways. For nerves to properly function, they need to have the ability to "slide" and "glide" unhindered through different areas of the body.[461-463] As nerves travel through the body, they encounter many surrounding tissues including muscle, bone, ligaments and fascia.[461,463-465] Numerous studies have shown that if the interface is altered (injury or disease), it might have repercussions for the adjacent neural tissues.[466-476]

- **Movement:** Closely linked to the above discussion on the space requirements of the nervous system is the nervous system's ability to perform complex signaling processes during physiological movement. Under normal conditions nerves move quite well.[462,463,469,477-479] From a cervical spine neutral position to cervical spine flexion, the spinal cord lengthens approximately 10 percent, while from cervical spine extension to cervical spine flexion, the cervical cord lengthens approximately 20 percent.[480] It has also been shown that the spinal canal (the "container") can lengthen approximately 30 percent from spinal extension to spinal flexion.[481] The peripheral nervous system must be able to accommodate increased movement as well, and research has shown that, from a position of wrist and elbow flexion to a position of wrist and elbow extension, the median nerve must adapt to a nerve bed that is almost 20 percent longer.[482] Updated research, utilizing fine-wire sensors[483] and diagnostic ultrasound[484-488] clearly show the movement properties of the nervous system.

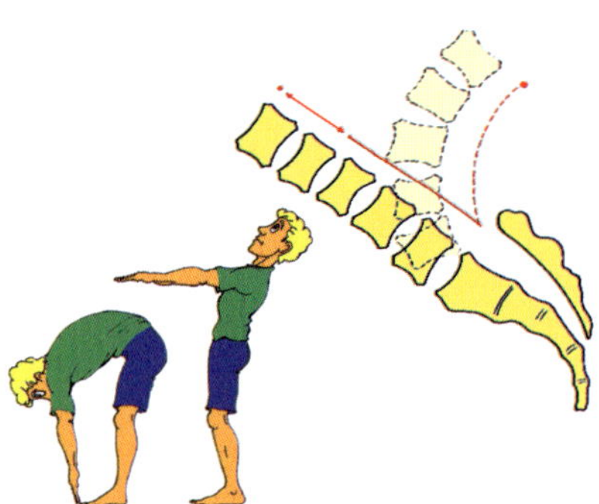

- **Blood:** Neural tissue is extremely "bloodthirsty." The brain and spinal cord are estimated to only account for two percent of the total body mass, yet they consume 20-25 percent of the available oxygen in the circulating blood.[489] Additionally, it has been shown that if a nerve is "lengthened" more than six to eight percent of its length, blood flow in the peripheral nerve will slow.[490,491] If the nerve is elongated approximately 15 percent, blood flow might be completely occluded.[491]

Again, books and book chapters have been written about neurodynamics[461,464,465,480] and the intent is not to discuss neurodynamics in detail, but rather have clinicians consider neurodynamics as a part of the PNE+ program. The inclusion of neurodynamics is justified, because:

- Altered neurodynamic tests have been proposed as a means to detect a sensitized nervous system. If a decreased neurodynamic test is associated with increased sensitization, it can be argued that normalizing neurodynamics can indicate a lessened sensitization.[492,493]
- There is evidence that neurodynamic tests increase various endogenous mechanisms.[114-116]
- Neurodynamic treatments have been shown to improve pressure pain thresholds, increase movements, decrease pain, etc.[494-496]
- Neurodynamics have been used in PNE+ studies.[497,498]

In terms of PNE+ and the various elements associated with creating independence, it's recommended that clinicians focus on active neurodynamic treatments versus passive to allow for independence. Furthermore, with a sensitized nervous system, gentler techniques ("sliders") would be more advantageous than stronger techniques ("tensioners") so as to not increase sensitivity or result in latent pain experiences.[483]

6.5.21: Yoga and Tai Chi

Even though Chapter 6 focuses specifically on specialized forms of movement, such as aerobic exercise, isometric exercises, neurodynamics and aquatic therapy, the astute reader should realize there is a growing body of evidence supporting generalized movement. For example, even just walking has been shown to have a significant positive effect on chronic LBP.[499] This would imply that, if we review exercise and movement in a broader perspective, we will find other types of movement also beneficial, such as yoga, Tai Chi, etc. For example, yoga has shown an ability to turn on the various endogenous mechanisms.[120-122] It can even be argued that yoga, if combined with strategies such as meditation, relaxation, mindfulness or breathing, might have an even larger effect size. A critical aspect of treatments such as yoga and Tai Chi is body awareness, which in itself has an endogenous effect.[153,154]

6.5.22: Breathing

Every clinician knows that people in pain often stop breathing in a normal pattern, especially when they exercise. How often do you have to remind a patient to breathe? Breathing, apart from the vital life function, also calms the nervous system.[99-101] Dedicated strategies to enhance slow, deep, cleansing breaths are needed and should be taught to patients. There are several different types of breathing exercises and, just as with other strategies, clinicians should explore these as part of their PNE+ approach. One example is the simple 4-7-8 breathing technique:[500]

- Exhale through your mouth.
- Close your mouth and inhale through your nose for a count of four.
- Hold your breath for seven counts.
- Exhale for eight counts.
- Repeat the sequence three times.
- Breathing slowly and deeply has been shown to calm the nervous system and help with relaxation and sleep.

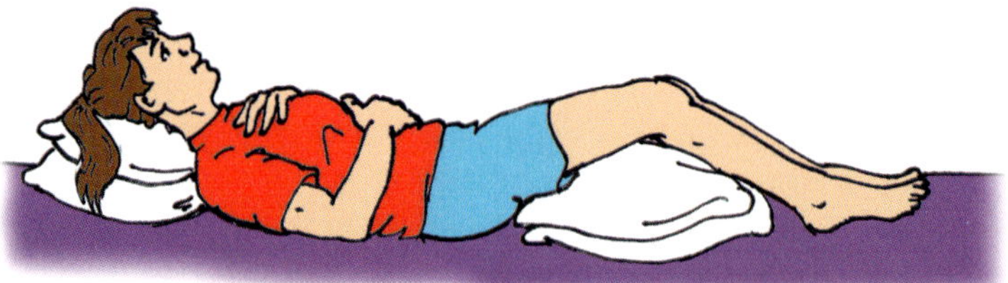

6.5.23: Counseling

In a small percentage of patients attending PNE, there might be a need for specialized counseling, i.e., psychologist, psychiatrist, social worker or counselors. Unfortunately, with the emergence of PNE, there is not much known about who needs counseling. It could be argued specialized counseling would be needed for patients presenting with:

- Concerns about them hurting themselves or someone around them.
- Abuse issues.
- Issues that the clinician is not equipped to handle.
- Scores on various outcome measures indicating specialized needs, i.e., high levels of depression or anxiety, etc.
- Multiple layers of psychosocial issues needing specialized care, i.e., serious family issues, etc.

Unfortunately, there are issues with counseling, especially in the US, pertaining to this discussion. First, there is a shortage of qualified mental health providers, making it hard to find help, especially in the private sector. In large hospital systems and federal systems, it is much easier to access these services. Second, various counsellors specialize in different areas, i.e., family counseling, etc., and to add to the first dilemma that pain psychologists are even harder to find. Third, and once again influenced by concepts from Rene Descartes, counseling is marred with stigma; "Oh, you think it's in my head." Presenting and proposing counseling is tricky and challenging. For PNE clinicians we have found it best to (i) develop a relationship with a patient before presenting this option (i.e., visit three or four) and (ii) continue PNE and PNE+ while undergoing counseling, as a means to not pass the patient off to someone else (counsellor) and work on the other issues that need help, i.e., movement, sleep, etc.

6.6: Conclusion

Clinicians should take a few minutes and view the extensive list and discussions of treatments. As we started this chapter, we commented that clinicians often express frustration because they don't know what to do for patients who are struggling with chronic pain. This chapter aimed to show clinicians the vast number of strategies that can be used for such patients. All of these suggested treatments should be "bathed" in neuroscience and ultimately in PNE. We do not make this statement lightly. It has been reported that the late Dr. Patrick Wall, one of the original authors of the pain gate theory, believed PTs to be the ideal profession to take on chronic pain. Why PTs? Therapists are in a unique position because they possess most of the qualities needed to treat chronic pain: Understanding of all of the biological systems involved with a pain experience (neuro, endocrine, immune, and others), knowledge and use of movement and exercise, cheaper treatments provided within the healthcare community, ability to motivate patients, the use of time to develop a therapeutic alliance, application of touch within a therapeutic visit, the sheer number of therapists available to help chronic pain, etc. There is so much we can offer these patients through the use of PNE and PNE+ interventions.

Chapter 6 References

1. Engers A, Jellema P, Wensing M, van der Windt DA, Grol R, van Tulder MW. Individual patient education for low back pain. *Cochrane Database Syst Rev.* 2008(1):CD004057.
2. Gross AR, Aker PD, Goldsmith CH, Peloso P. Patient education for mechanical neck disorders. *Cochrane Database Syst Rev.* 2000(2):CD000962.
3. Haines T, Gross A, Goldsmith CH, Perry L. Patient education for neck pain with or without radiculopathy. *Cochrane Database Syst Rev.* 2008(4):CD005106.
4. McDonald S, Hetrick SE, Green S. Pre-operative educatiin for hip or knee replacement. *Cochrane Database Syst Rev.* 2008(4).
5. Louw A, Zimney K, Puentedura EJ, Diener I. The Efficacy of Therapeutic Neuroscience Education on Musculoskeletal Pain – A Systematic Review of the Literature. *Physiother Theory Pract.* 2016;32(5): 332-355.
6. Gilpin EA, Pierce JP, Farkas AJ. Duration of smoking abstinence and success in quitting. *Journal of the National Cancer Institute.* Apr 16 1997;89(8):572-576.
7. Raherison C, Marjary A, Valpromy B, Prevot S, Fossoux H, Taytard A. Evaluation of smoking cessation success in adults. *Respiratory medicine.* Oct 2005;99(10):1303-1310.
8. Oztuna F, Can G, Ozlu T. Five-year outcomes for a smoking cessation clinic. *Respirology.* Nov 2007;12(6):911-915.
9. Fordyce WE, Fowler R, Lehman J, la I. Operant conditioning in the treatment of chronic pain. *Archives of Physical Medicine and Rehabilitation.* 1973;54:399-408.
10. Mayoux-Benhamou A, Giraudet-Le Quintrec JS, Ravaud P, et al. Influence of patient education on exercise compliance in rheumatoid arthritis: a prospective 12-month randomized controlled trial. *J Rheumatol.* Feb 2008;35(2):216-223.
11. Medina-Mirapeix F, Escolar-Reina P, Gascon-Canovas JJ, Montilla-Herrador J, Collins SM. Personal characteristics influencing patients' adherence to home exercise during chronic pain: a qualitative study. *Journal of rehabilitation medicine.* Apr 2009;41(5):347-352.
12. Mori DL, Sogg S, Guarino P, et al. Predictors of exercise compliance in individuals with Gulf War veterans illnesses: Department of Veterans Affairs Cooperative Study 470. *Mil Med.* Sep 2006;171(9):917-923.
13. Blickenstaff C, Pearson N. Reconciling movement and exercise with pain neuroscience education: A case for consistent education. *Physiother Theory Pract.* Jul 2016;32(5):396-407.
14. Louw A, Farrell K, Landers M, et al. The effect of manual therapy and neuroplasticity education on chronic low back pain: a randomized clinical trial. *Journal of Manual & Manipulative Therapy.* 2016:1-8.
15. Jones MD, Valenzuela T, Booth J, Taylor JL, Barry BK. Explicit Education About Exercise-Induced Hypoalgesia Influences Pain Responses to Acute Exercise in Healthy Adults: A Randomized Controlled Trial. *The journal of pain: official journal of the American Pain Society.* Nov 2017;18(11):1409-1416.
16. Sapolsky RM. *Why zebras don't get ulcers: an updated guide to stress, stress-related diseases, and coping.* New York: W.H. Freeman and Co; 1998.
17. Louw A. *Why You Hurt: A Neuroscience Approach to Pain.* Minneapolis: OPTP; 2013.
18. Harden RN, Duc TA, Williams TR, Coley D, Cate JC, Gracely RH. Norepinephrine and epinephrine levels in affected versus unaffected limbs in sympathetically maintained pain. *The Clinical journal of pain.* Dec 1994;10(4):324-330.
19. Chapman CR, Tuckett RP, Song CW. Pain and stress in a systems perspective: reciprocal neural, endocrine, and immune interactions. *The journal of pain : official journal of the American Pain Society.* Feb 2008;9(2):122-145.
20. Riva R, Mork PJ, Westgaard RH, Okkenhaug Johansen T, Lundberg U. Catecholamines and heart rate in female fibromyalgia patients. *Journal of psychosomatic research.* Jan 2012;72(1):51-57.
21. Riva R, Mork PJ, Westgaard RH, Lundberg U. Comparison of the cortisol awakening response in women with shoulder and neck pain and women with fibromyalgia. *Psychoneuroendocrinology.* Feb 2012;37(2):299-306.
22. Gifford LS. Pain, the tissues and the nervous system. *Physiotherapy.* 1998;84:27-33.
23. Baron R, Janig W. The role of the sympathetic nervous system in pain processing. In: Villanueva L, Dickenson A, Ollat H, eds. *The Pain System in Normal and Patological States: A Primer for Clinicians.* Seattle: IASP Press; 2004.

24. Yanagida H. Sympathetic nervous system and pain: introduction. *The Pain Clinic.* 1995;8(1):1-3.
25. Matalka KZ. Neuroendocrine and cytokines-induced responses to minutes, hours, and days of mental stress. *Neuro endocrinology letters.* Oct 2003;24(5):283-292.
26. Nippoldt T. Mayo Clinic office visit. *Adrenal fatigue.* An interview with Todd Nippoldt, M.D. Mayo Clinic women's healthsource. Mar 2010;14(3):6.
27. Baschetti R. Chronic fatigue syndrome, decreased exercise capacity, and adrenal insufficiency. *Archives of internal medicine.* Jun 25 2001;161(12): 1558-1559.
28. Tanriverdi F, Karaca Z, Unluhizarci K, Kelestimur F. The hypothalamo-pituitary-adrenal axis in chronic fatigue syndrome and fibromyalgia syndrome. *Stress.* Mar 2007;10(1):13-25.
29. Devor M. Sodium channels and mechanisms of neuropathic pain. *The journal of pain: official journal of the American Pain Society.* Jan 2006;7(1 Suppl 1):S3-S12.
30. Sarzi-Puttini P, Atzeni F, Diana A, Doria A, Furlan R. Increased neural sympathetic activation in fibromyalgia syndrome. *Annals of the New York Academy of Sciences.* Jun 2006;1069:109-117.
31. Bradley LA. Pathophysiologic mechanisms of fibromyalgia and its related disorders. *The Journal of clinical psychiatry.* 2008;69 Suppl 2:6-13.
32. Schweinhardt P, Sauro KM, Bushnell MC. Fibromyalgia: a disorder of the brain? *The Neuroscientist: a review journal bringing neurobiology, neurology and psychiatry.* Oct 2008;14(5):415-421.
33. Bennett RM, Goldenberg DL. Fibromyalgia, myofascial pain, tender points and trigger points: splitting or lumping? *Arthritis research & therapy.* 2011;13(3):117.
34. Moseley GL, Hodges PW. Are the changes in postural control associated with low back pain caused by pain interference? *The Clinical journal of pain.* Jul-Aug 2005;21(4):323-329.
35. Moseley GL, Hodges PW. Reduced variability of postural strategy prevents normalization of motor changes induced by back pain: a risk factor for chronic trouble? *Behavioral neuroscience.* Apr 2006;120(2):474-476.
36. Wakefield E, Holtermann A, Mork PJ. The effect of delayed onset of muscle soreness on habitual trapezius activity. *European journal of pain.* Jul 2011;15(6):577-583.
37. Edmondston SJ, Chan HY, Ngai GC, et al. Postural neck pain: an investigation of habitual sitting posture, perception of 'good' posture and cervicothoracic kinaesthesia. *Manual therapy.* Nov 2007;12(4):363-371.
38. Fernandez-de-las-Penas C, Alonso-Blanco C, Cuadrado ML, Gerwin RD, Pareja JA. Trigger points in the suboccipital muscles and forward head posture in tension-type headache. *Headache.* Mar 2006;46(3):454-460.
39. Larsson SE, Alund M, Cai H, Oberg PA. Chronic pain after soft-tissue injury of the cervical spine: trapezius muscle blood flow and electromyography at static loads and fatigue. *Pain.* May 1994;57(2): 173-180.
40. Moseley GL, Nicholas MK, Hodges PW. Does anticipation of back pain predispose to back trouble? *Brain: a journal of neurology.* Oct 2004;127(Pt 10): 2339-2347.
41. Moseley GL, Hodges PW. Are the changes in postural control associated with low back pain caused by pain interference? *The Clinical journal of pain.* Jul-Aug 2005;21(4):323-329.
42. Moseley GL, Hodges PW. Reduced variability of postural strategy prevents normalization of motor changes induced by back pain: a risk factor for chronic trouble? *Behav Neurosci.* Apr 2006;120(2):474-476.
43. Hodges PW, Richardson CA. Delayed postural contraction of transversus abdominis in low back pain associated with movement of the lower limb. *J Spinal Disord.* Feb 1998;11(1):46-56.
44. Hodges PW, Richardson CA. Altered trunk muscle recruitment in people with low back pain with upper limb movement at different speeds. *Arch Phys Med Rehabil.* Sep 1999;80(9):1005-1012.
45. Hodges PW. The role of the motor system in spinal pain: implications for rehabilitation of the athlete following lower back pain. *J Sci Med Sport.* Sep 2000;3(3):243-253.
46. Tsao H, Danneels LA, Hodges PW. ISSLS prize winner: Smudging the motor brain in young adults with recurrent low back pain. *Spine.* Oct 1 2011;36(21):1721-1727.
47. Tsao H, Galea MP, Hodges PW. Reorganization of the motor cortex is associated with postural control deficits in recurrent low back pain. *Brain: a journal of neurology.* Aug 2008;131(Pt 8): 2161-2171.
48. Tsao H, Hodges PW. Immediate changes in feedforward postural adjustments following voluntary motor training. *Exp Brain Res.* Aug 2007;181(4):537-546.

49. Jull G, Kristjansson E, Dall'Alba P. Impairment in the cervical flexors: a comparison of whiplash and insidious onset neck pain patients. *Manual therapy.* May 2004;9(2):89-94.
50. Jull GA, Falla D, Vicenzino B, Hodges PW. The effect of therapeutic exercise on activation of the deep cervical flexor muscles in people with chronic neck pain. *Manual therapy.* Dec 2009;14(6): 696-701.
51. Jones KD, Horak FB, Winters-Stone K, Irvine JM, Bennett RM. Fibromyalgia is associated with impaired balance and falls. *J Clin Rheumatol.* Feb 2009;15(1):16-21.
52. Van Houdenhove B, Van Den Eede F, Luyten P. Does hypothalamic-pituitary-adrenal axis hypofunction in chronic fatigue syndrome reflect a 'crash' in the stress system? *Medical hypotheses.* Jun 2009;72(6):701-705.
53. Pae CU, Luyten P, Marks DM, et al. The relationship between fibromyalgia and major depressive disorder: a comprehensive review. *Current medical research and opinion.* Aug 2008;24(8):2359-2371.
54. Jerjes WK, Peters TJ, Taylor NF, Wood PJ, Wessely S, Cleare AJ. Diurnal excretion of urinary cortisol, cortisone, and cortisol metabolites in chronic fatigue syndrome. *Journal of psychosomatic research.* Feb 2006;60(2):145-153.
55. Cardoso-Cruz H, Lima D, Galhardo V. Impaired spatial memory performance in a rat model of neuropathic pain is associated with reduced hippocampus-prefrontal cortex connectivity. *The Journal of neuroscience: the official journal of the Society for Neuroscience.* Feb 6 2013;33(6):2465-2480.
56. Thacker MA, Clark AK, Marchand F, McMahon SB. Pathophysiology of peripheral neuropathic pain: immune cells and molecules. *Anesth Analg.* Sep 2007;105(3):838-847.
57. Moseley GL. Reconceptualising pain acording to modern pain sciences. *Physical Therapy Reviews.* 2007;12: 169-178.
58. Dimsdale JE, Dantzer R. *A biological substrate for somatoform disorders: importance of pathophysiology. Psychosomatic medicine.* Dec 2007;69(9): 850-854.
59. Nijs J, Meeus M, Van Oosterwijck J, et al. In the mind or in the brain? Scientific evidence for central sensitisation in chronic fatigue syndrome. *European journal of clinical investigation.* Feb 2012;42(2):203-212.
60. Meeus M, Nijs J. Central sensitization: a biopsychosocial explanation for chronic widespread pain in patients with fibromyalgia and chronic fatigue syndrome. *Clinical rheumatology.* Apr 2007;26(4):465-473.
61. Woolf CJ. Central sensitization: implications for the diagnosis and treatment of pain. *Pain.* Mar 2011;152(3 Suppl):S2-15.
62. Fernandez-Carnero J, Fernandez-de-Las-Penas C, de la Llave-Rincon AI, Ge HY, Arendt-Nielsen L. Widespread mechanical pain hypersensitivity as sign of central sensitization in unilateral epicondylalgia: a blinded, controlled study. *The Clinical journal of pain.* Sep 2009;25(7):555-561.
63. Togo F, Natelson BH, Adler GK, et al. Plasma cytokine fluctuations over time in healthy controls and patients with fibromyalgia. *Experimental biology and medicine.* Feb 2009;234(2):232-240.
64. Miller GE, Cohen S, Ritchey AK. Chronic psychological stress and the regulation of pro-inflammatory cytokines: a glucocorticoid-resistance model. *Health psychology: official journal of the Division of Health Psychology, American Psychological Association.* Nov 2002;21(6):531-541.
65. Di Franco M, Iannuccelli C, Valesini G. Neuroendocrine immunology of fibromyalgia. *Annals of the New York Academy of Sciences.* Apr 2010;1193: 84-90.
66. Adler GK, Kinsley BT, Hurwitz S, Mossey CJ, Goldenberg DL. Reduced hypothalamic-pituitary and sympathoadrenal responses to hypoglycemia in women with fibromyalgia syndrome. *Am J Med.* May 1999;106(5):534-543.
67. Staud R. Peripheral pain mechanisms in chronic widespread pain. *Best Pract Res Clin Rheumatol.* Apr 2011;25(2): 155-164.
68. Bonifazi M, Suman AL, Cambiaggi C, et al. Changes in salivary cortisol and corticosteroid receptor-alpha mRNA expression following a 3-week multidisciplinary treatment program in patients with fibromyalgia. *Psychoneuroendocrinology.* Oct 2006;31(9):1076-1086.
69. Maizels M, McCarberg B. Antidepressants and antiepileptic drugs for chronic non-cancer pain. *American family physician.* Feb 1 2005;71(3):483-490.
70. Marinus J, Moseley GL, Birklein F, et al. Clinical features and pathophysiology of complex regional pain syndrome. *Lancet Neurol.* Jul 2011;10(7):637-648.

71. Beggs S, Liu XJ, Kwan C, Salter MW. Peripheral nerve injury and TRPV1-expressing primary afferent C-fibers cause opening of the blood-brain barrier. *Molecular pain.* 2010;6:74.
72. Echeverry S, Shi XQ, Rivest S, Zhang J. Peripheral nerve injury alters blood-spinal cord barrier functional and molecular integrity through a selective inflammatory pathway. *The Journal of neuroscience: the official journal of the Society for Neuroscience.* Jul 27 2011;31(30):10819-10828.
73. Louw A, Hilton S, Vandyken C. *Why Pelvic Pain Hurts.* Minneapolis, MN: OPTP; 2014.
74. Weissbecker I, Floyd A, Dedert E, Salmon P, Sephton S. Childhood trauma and diurnal cortisol disruption in fibromyalgia syndrome. *Psychoneuroendocrinology.* Apr 2006;31(3):312-324.
75. Stephens R, Atkins J, Kingston A. Swearing as a response to pain. *Neuroreport.* Aug 5 2009;20(12):1056-1060.
76. Stephens R, Umland C. Swearing as a response to pain-effect of daily swearing frequency. *The journal of pain: official journal of the American Pain Society.* Dec 2011;12(12):1274-1281.
77. Vlaeyen JW, Linton SJ. *Fear-avoidance and its consequences in chronic musculoskeletal pain: a state of the art.* Pain. Apr 2000;85(3):317-332.
78. Hamilton NA, Affleck G, Tennen H, et al. Fibromyalgia: the role of sleep in affect and in negative event reactivity and recovery. *Health psychology: official journal of the Division of Health Psychology, American Psychological Association.* Jul 2008;27(4):490-497.
79. Rusu AC, Pincus T, Morley S. Depressed pain patients differ from other depressed groups: examination of cognitive content in a sentence completion task. *Pain.* Sep 2012;153(9):1898-1904.
80. Tsatali M, Papaliagkas V, Damigos D, Mavreas V, Gouva M, Tsolaki M. Depression and anxiety levels increase chronic musculoskeletal pain in patients with Alzheimer's disease. *Current Alzheimer research.* 2014;11(6): 574-579.
81. Krause SJ, Wiener RL, Tait RC. Depression and pain behavior in patients with chronic pain. *The Clinical journal of pain.* Jun 1994;10(2):122-127.
82. Faucett JA. Depression in painful chronic disorders: the role of pain and conflict about pain. *Journal of pain and symptom management.* Nov 1994;9(8):520-526.
83. Theadom A, Cropley M, Smith HE, Feigin VL, McPherson K. Mind and body therapy for fibromyalgia. *The Cochrane database of systematic reviews.* 2015;4:CD001980.
84. Luerding R, Weigand T, Bogdahn U, Schmidt-Wilcke T. Working memory performance is correlated with local brain morphology in the medial frontal and anterior cingulate cortex in fibromyalgia patients: structural correlates of pain-cognition interaction. *Brain: a journal of neurology.* Dec 2008;131(Pt 12): 3222-3231.
85. Barbara G, Stanghellini V, De Giorgio R, et al. Activated mast cells in proximity to colonic nerves correlate with abdominal pain in irritable bowel syndrome. *Gastroenterology.* Mar 2004;126(3): 693-702.
86. Stasi C, Rosselli M, Bellini M, Laffi G, Milani S. Altered neuro-endocrine-immune pathways in the irritable bowel syndrome: the top-down and the bottom-up model. *Journal of gastroenterology.* Nov 2012;47(11):1177-1185.
87. Bonaz B. Inflammatory bowel diseases: a dysfunction of brain-gut interactions? *Minerva gastroenterologica e dietologica.* Sep 2013;59(3):241-259.
88. Kendall NAS, Linton SJ, Main CJ. *Guide to assessing psychosocial yellow flags in acute low back pain: risk factors for long term disability and work loss.* Wellington: Accident Rehabilitation & Compensation Insurance Corporation of New Zealand and the National Health Committee; 1997.
89. Gifford L. *Aches and Pains.* Cornwall: Wordpress; 2014.
90. Woby SR, Watson PJ, Roach NK, Urmston M. Are changes in fear-avoidance beliefs, catastrophizing, and appraisals of control, predictive of changes in chronic low back pain and disability? *European Journal of Pain.* Jun 2004;8(3):201-210.
91. Watson P. Psychosocial predictors of outcome from low back pain. In: Gifford LS, ed. *Topical Issues in Pain 2.* Falmouth: CNS Press; 2000.
92. Van Oosterwijck J, Meeus M, Paul L, et al. Pain physiology education improves health status and endogenous pain inhibition in fibromyalgia: a double-blind randomized controlled trial. *The Clinical journal of pain.* Oct 2013;29(10): 873-882.
93. Moseley GL. A pain neuromatrix approach to patients with chronic pain. *Manual therapy.* Aug 2003;8(3):130-140.

94. Jensen KB, Kosek E, Wicksell R, et al. Cognitive Behavioral Therapy increases pain-evoked activation of the prefrontal cortex in patients with fibromyalgia. *Pain.* Jul 2012;153(7):1495-1503.
95. Spencer JP. Flavonoids and brain health: multiple effects underpinned by common mechanisms. *Genes & nutrition.* Dec 2009;4(4):243-250.
96. Dufresne CJ, Farnworth ER. A review of latest research findings on the health promotion properties of tea. *The Journal of nutritional biochemistry.* Jul 2001;12(7):404-421.
97. Tauler P, Aguilo A, Gimeno I, Fuentespina E, Tur JA, Pons A. Influence of vitamin C diet supplementation on endogenous antioxidant defences during exhaustive exercise. *Pflugers Archiv: European journal of physiology.* Sep 2003;446(6):658-664.
98. Butterfield D, Castegna A, Pocernich C, Drake J, Scapagnini G, Calabrese V. Nutritional approaches to combat oxidative stress in Alzheimer's disease. *The Journal of nutritional biochemistry.* Aug 2002;13(8):444.
99. Singh V, Wisniewski A, Britton J, Tattersfield A. Effect of yoga breathing exercises (pranayama) on airway reactivity in subjects with asthma. *Lancet.* Jun 9 1990;335(8702):1381-1383.
100. Kim SH, Schneider SM, Bevans M, et al. PTSD symptom reduction with mindfulness-based stretching and deep breathing exercise: randomized controlled clinical trial of efficacy. *The Journal of clinical endocrinology and metabolism.* Jul 2013;98(7):2984-2992.
101. Vassilakopoulos T, Roussos C, Zakynthinos S. The immune response to resistive breathing. *The European respiratory journal.* Dec 2004;24(6):1033-1043.
102. Rokicki LA, Holroyd KA, France CR, Lipchik GL, France JL, Kvaal SA. Change mechanisms associated with combined relaxation/EMG biofeedback training for chronic tension headache. *Applied psychophysiology and biofeedback.* Mar 1997;22(1):21-41.
103. deCharms RC, Maeda F, Glover GH, et al. *Control over brain activation and pain learned by using real-time functional MRI.* Proceedings of the National Academy of Sciences of the United States of America. Dec 20 2005;102(51):18626-18631.
104. Ciancarelli I, Tozzi-Ciancarelli MG, Spacca G, Di Massimo C, Carolei A. Relationship between biofeedback and oxidative stress in patients with chronic migraine. *Cephalalgia: an international journal of headache.* Oct 2007;27(10):1136-1141.
105. Moseley GL, Zalucki N, Birklein F, Marinus J, van Hilten JJ, Luomajoki H. Thinking about movement hurts: the effect of motor imagery on pain and swelling in people with chronic arm pain. *Arthritis and rheumatism.* May 15 2008;59(5):623-631.
106. Bowering KJ, O'Connell NE, Tabor A, et al. The effects of graded motor imagery and its components on chronic pain: a systematic review and meta-analysis. *J Pain.* Jan 2013;14(1):3-13.
107. Michielsen ME, Smits M, Ribbers GM, et al. The neuronal correlates of mirror therapy: an fMRI study on mirror induced visual illusions in patients with stroke. *J Neurol Neurosurg Psychiatry.* Apr 2011;82(4):393-398.
108. Van Ree JM, Niesink RJ, Van Wolfswinkel L, et al. Endogenous opioids and reward. *European journal of pharmacology.* Sep 29 2000;405(1-3):89-101.
109. Benedetti F, Amanzio M. The neurobiology of placebo analgesia: from endogenous opioids to cholecystokinin. *Progress in neurobiology.* Jun 1997;52(2):109-125.
110. Fields HL. "A motivation-decision model of pain: the role of opioids." Paper presented at: 11th World Congress on Pain2006; Washington, USA.
111. Nijs J, Van Houdenhove B. From acute musculoskeletal pain to chronic widespread pain and fibromyalgia: application of pain neurophysiology in manual therapy practice. *Manual therapy.* Feb 2009;14(1):3-12.
112. Bialosky JE, Bishop MD, Price DD, Robinson ME, George SZ. The mechanisms of manual therapy in the treatment of musculoskeletal pain: a comprehensive model. *Manual therapy.* Oct 2009;14(5):531-538.
113. Bialosky JE, Bishop MD, Robinson ME, Zeppieri G, Jr., George SZ. Spinal manipulative therapy has an immediate effect on thermal pain sensitivity in people with low back pain: a randomized controlled trial. *Physical therapy.* Dec 2009;89(12):1292-1303.
114. Santos FM, Silva JT, Giardini AC, et al. Neural mobilization reverses behavioral and cellular changes that characterize neuropathic pain in rats. *Molecular pain.* 2012;8:57.

115. Santos FM, Grecco LH, Pereira MG, et al. The neural mobilization technique modulates the expression of endogenous opioids in the periaqueductal gray and improves muscle strength and mobility in rats with neuropathic pain. *Behavioral and brain functions: BBF.* May 13 2014;10:19.
116. Beneciuk JM, Bishop MD, George SZ. Effects of upper extremity neural mobilization on thermal pain sensitivity: a sham-controlled study in asymptomatic participants. *J Orthop Sports Phys Ther.* Jun 2009;39(6):428-438.
117. Bender T, Nagy G, Barna I, Tefner I, Kadas E, Geher P. The effect of physical therapy on beta-endorphin levels. *European journal of applied physiology.* Jul 2007;100(4):371-382.
118. Wright A, Sluka KA. Nonpharmacological treatments for musculoskeletal pain. *The Clinical journal of pain.* Mar 2001;17(1):33-46.
119. Sabino GS, Santos CM, Francischi JN, de Resende MA. Release of endogenous opioids following transcutaneous electric nerve stimulation in an experimental model of acute inflammatory pain. *The journal of pain: official journal of the American Pain Society.* Feb 2008;9(2):157-163.
120. Sengupta P. Health Impacts of Yoga and Pranayama: A State-of-the-Art Review. *International journal of preventive medicine.* Jul 2012;3(7):444-458.
121. Kulkarni DD, Bera TK. Yogic exercises and health--a psycho-neuro immunological approach. *Indian journal of physiology and pharmacology.* Jan-Mar 2009;53(1):3-15.
122. Sharma M, Lingam VC, Nahar VK. A systematic review of yoga interventions as integrative treatment in breast cancer. *Journal of cancer research and clinical oncology.* Dec 2016;142(12): 2523-2540.
123. Zeidan F, Emerson NM, Farris SR, et al. Mindfulness Meditation-Based Pain Relief Employs Different Neural Mechanisms Than Placebo and Sham Mindfulness Meditation-Induced Analgesia. *The Journal of neuroscience: the official journal of the Society for Neuroscience.* Nov 18 2015;35(46):15307-15325.
124. Sharon H, Maron-Katz A, Ben Simon E, et al. Mindfulness Meditation Modulates Pain Through Endogenous Opioids. *Am J Med.* Jul 2016;129(7):755-758.
125. Esch T, Stefano GB. Endogenous reward mechanisms and their importance in stress reduction, exercise and the brain. *Archives of medical science: AMS.* Jun 30 2010;6(3):447-455.
126. Koltyn KF. Analgesia following exercise: a review. *Sports Med.* Feb 2000;29(2): 85-98.
127. O'Connor PJ, Cook DB. Exercise and pain: the neurobiology, measurement, and laboratory study of pain in relation to exercise in humans. *Exerc Sport Sci Rev.* 1999;27:119-166.
128. Naugle KM, Fillingim RB, Riley JL, 3rd. A meta-analytic review of the hypoalgesic effects of exercise. *The journal of pain: official journal of the American Pain Society.* Dec 2012;13(12):1139-1150.
129. Martin RA. Humor, laughter, and physical health: methodological issues and research findings. *Psychological bulletin.* Jul 2001;127(4):504-519.
130. Berk LS, Felten DL, Tan SA, Bittman BB, Westengard J. Modulation of neuroimmune parameters during the eustress of humor-associated mirthful laughter. *Alternative therapies in health and medicine.* Mar 2001;7(2): 62-72, 74-66.
131. Finan PH, Garland EL. The role of positive affect in pain and its treatment. *The Clinical journal of pain.* Feb 2015;31(2):177-187.
132. Mazzardo-Martins L, Martins DF, Marcon R, et al. High-intensity extended swimming exercise reduces pain-related behavior in mice: involvement of endogenous opioids and the serotonergic system. *The journal of pain: official journal of the American Pain Society.* Dec 2010;11(12):1384-1393.
133. Becker BE. Aquatic therapy: scientific foundations and clinical rehabilitation applications. *PM & R: the journal of injury, function, and rehabilitation.* Sep 2009;1(9):859-872.
134. Karelina K, DeVries AC. Modeling social influences on human health. *Psychosomatic medicine.* Jan 2011;73(1): 67-74.
135. Lopez-Martinez AE, Esteve-Zarazaga R, Ramirez-Maestre C. Perceived social support and coping responses are independent variables explaining pain adjustment among chronic pain patients. *The journal of pain: official journal of the American Pain Society.* Apr 2008;9(4):373-379.
136. Krahe C, Springer A, Weinman JA, Fotopoulou A. The social modulation of pain: others as predictive signals of salience - a systematic review. *Frontiers in human neuroscience.* 2013;7:386.
137. Bandura A, Cioffi D, Taylor CB, Brouillard ME. Perceived self-efficacy in coping with cognitive stressors and opioid activation. *Journal of personality and social psychology.* Sep 1988;55(3):479-488.

138. Hebb AL, Poulin JF, Roach SP, Zacharko RM, Drolet G. Cholecystokinin and endogenous opioid peptides: interactive influence on pain, cognition, and emotion. *Progress in neuro-psychopharmacology & biological psychiatry.* Dec 2005;29(8):1225-1238.
139. Goodin BR, McGuire L, Allshouse M, et al. Associations between catastrophizing and endogenous pain-inhibitory processes: sex differences. *The journal of pain : official journal of the American Pain Society.* Feb 2009;10(2):180-190.
140. Smith MT, Quartana PJ, Okonkwo RM, Nasir A. Mechanisms by which sleep disturbance contributes to osteoarthritis pain: a conceptual model. *Current pain and headache reports.* Dec 2009;13(6):447-454.
141. Menefee LA, Cohen MJ, Anderson WR, Doghramji K, Frank ED, Lee H. Sleep disturbance and nonmalignant chronic pain: a comprehensive review of the literature. *Pain medicine.* Jun 2000;1(2):156-172.
142. Edwards RR, Grace E, Peterson S, Klick B, Haythornthwaite JA, Smith MT. Sleep continuity and architecture: associations with pain-inhibitory processes in patients with temporomandibular joint disorder. *European journal of pain* (London, England). Nov 2009;13(10):1043-1047.
143. Goats GC, Keir KA. Connective tissue massage. *British journal of sports medicine.* Sep 1991;25(3):131-133.
144. Frey Law LA, Evans S, Knudtson J, Nus S, Scholl K, Sluka KA. Massage reduces pain perception and hyperalgesia in experimental muscle pain: a randomized, controlled trial. *The journal of pain : official journal of the American Pain Society.* Aug 2008;9(8):714-721.
145. Ireland M, Olson M. Massage therapy and therapeutic touch in children: state of the science. *Alternative therapies in health and medicine.* Sep 2000;6(5): 54-63.
146. Kraemer WJ, Ratamess NA, French DN. Resistance training for health and performance. *Curr Sports Med Rep.* Jun 2002;1(3):165-171.
147. Kraemer WJ, Aguilera BA, Terada M, et al. Responses of IGF-I to endogenous increases in growth hormone after heavy-resistance exercise. *J Appl Physiol* (1985). Oct 1995;79(4):1310-1315.
148. Fuentes CJ, Armijo-Olivo S, Magee DJ, Gross DP. Effects of exercise therapy on endogenous pain-relieving peptides in musculoskeletal pain: a systematic review. *The Clinical journal of pain.* May 2011;27(4):365-374.
149. Ambrose KR, Golightly YM. Physical exercise as non-pharmacological treatment of chronic pain: Why and when. *Best Pract Res Clin Rheumatol.* Feb 2015;29(1):120-130.
150. Bruehl S, Chung OY, Burns JW. Anger expression and pain: an overview of findings and possible mechanisms. *Journal of behavioral medicine.* Dec 2006;29(6):593-606.
151. Wright JG, Chung OY. Mastery or mystery? Therapeutic writing: A Review of the Literature. *British Journal of Guidance and Counseling.* 2001;29(3):277-291.
152. Baikie KA, Wilhelm K. Emotional and physical health benefits of expressive writing. *Advances in psychiatric treatment.* 2005;11(5):338-346.
153. da Costa BR, Vieira ER. Stretching to reduce work-related musculoskeletal disorders: a systematic review. *Journal of rehabilitation medicine.* May 2008;40(5):321-328.
154. Hodges PW, Smeets RJ. Interaction between pain, movement, and physical activity: short-term benefits, long-term consequences, and targets for treatment. *The Clinical journal of pain.* Feb 2015;31(2):97-107.
155. Bohns VK, Wiltermuth SS. It hurts when I do this (or you do that): Posture and pain tolerance. *Journal of Experimental Social Psychology.* 2012;48(1):341-345.
156. Carney DR, Cuddy AJ, Yap AJ. Power posing: brief nonverbal displays affect neuroendocrine levels and risk tolerance. *Psychological science.* Oct 2010;21(10):1363-1368.
157. Arnold LM, Crofford LJ, Martin SA, Young JP, Sharma U. The effect of anxiety and depression on improvements in pain in a randomized, controlled trial of pregabalin for treatment of fibromyalgia. *Pain medicine.* Nov-Dec 2007;8(8):633-638.
158. Goldenberg DL. Pharmacological treatment of fibromyalgia and other chronic musculoskeletal pain. *Best Pract Res Clin Rheumatol.* Jun 2007;21(3):499-511.
159. Hauser W, Bernardy K, Uceyler N, Sommer C. Treatment of fibromyalgia syndrome with antidepressants: a meta-analysis. *JAMA: the journal of the American Medical Association.* Jan 14 2009;301(2):198-209.
160. Rezende LF, Sa TH, Mielke GI, Viscondi JY, Rey-Lopez JP, Garcia LM. All-Cause Mortality Attributable to Sitting Time: Analysis of 54 Countries Worldwide. *Am J Prev Med.* Aug 2016;51(2):253-263.

161. McGavock JM, Hastings JL, Snell PG, et al. A forty-year follow-up of the Dallas Bed Rest and Training study: the effect of age on the cardiovascular response to exercise in men. *The journals of gerontology. Series A, Biological sciences and medical sciences.* Feb 2009;64(2):293-299.
162. McGuire DK, Levine BD, Williamson JW, et al. A 30-year follow-up of the Dallas Bedrest and Training Study: I. Effect of age on the cardiovascular response to exercise. *Circulation.* Sep 18 2001;104(12):1350-1357.
163. Carville SF, Arendt-Nielsen S, Bliddal H, et al. EULAR evidence-based recommendations for the management of fibromyalgia syndrome. *Ann Rheum Dis.* Apr 2008;67(4):536-541.
164. Brosseau L, Wells GA, Tugwell P, et al. Ottawa Panel evidence-based clinical practice guidelines for aerobic fitness exercises in the management of fibromyalgia: part 1. *Phys Ther.* Jul 2008;88(7):857-871.
165. Goldenberg DL, Burckhardt C, Crofford L. Management of fibromyalgia syndrome. *JAMA.* Nov 17 2004;292(19): 2388-2395.
166. Sim J, Adams N. Systematic review of randomized controlled trials of nonpharmacological interventions for fibromyalgia. *Clin J Pain.* Sep-Oct 2002;18(5):324-336.
167. Busch AJ, Barber KA, Overend TJ, Peloso PM, Schachter CL. Exercise for treating fibromyalgia syndrome. *Cochrane Database Syst Rev.* 2007(4):CD003786.
168. Rooks DS, Gautam S, Romeling M, et al. Group exercise, education, and combination self-management in women with fibromyalgia: a randomized trial. *Arch Intern Med.* Nov 12 2007;167(20): 2192-2200.
169. Gowans SE, deHueck A, Voss S, Silaj A, Abbey SE, Reynolds WJ. Effect of a randomized, controlled trial of exercise on mood and physical function in individuals with fibromyalgia. *Arthritis Rheum.* Dec 2001;45(6):519-529.
170. Voet NB, van der Kooi EL, Riphagen, II, Lindeman E, van Engelen BG, Geurts A. Strength training and aerobic exercise training for muscle disease. *Cochrane Database Syst Rev.* 2010(1):CD003907.
171. Smith PJ, Blumenthal JA, Hoffman BM, et al. Aerobic exercise and neurocognitive performance: a meta-analytic review of randomized controlled trials. *Psychosom Med.* Apr 2010;72(3):239-252.
172. van Uffelen JG, Chin APMJ, Hopman-Rock M, van Mechelen W. The effects of exercise on cognition in older adults with and without cognitive decline: a systematic review. *Clin J Sport Med.* Nov 2008;18(6):486-500.
173. Pontifex MB, Hillman CH. Neuroelectric measurement of cognition during aerobic exercise. *Methods.* Aug 2008;45(4): 271-278.
174. Uysal N, Tugyan K, Kayatekin BM, et al. The effects of regular aerobic exercise in adolescent period on hippocampal neuron density, apoptosis and spatial memory. *Neurosci Lett.* Aug 5 2005;383(3):241-245.
175. Sharma NK, Ryals JM, Gajewski BJ, Wright DE. Aerobic exercise alters analgesia and neurotrophin-3 synthesis in an animal model of chronic widespread pain. *Phys Ther.* May 2010;90(5): 714-725.
176. Hurkmans E, van der Giesen FJ, Vliet Vlieland TP, Schoones J, Van den Ende EC. Dynamic exercise programs (aerobic capacity and/or muscle strength training) in patients with rheumatoid arthritis. *Cochrane Database Syst Rev.* 2009(4):CD006853.
177. Hoffman MD, Hoffman DR. Does aerobic exercise improve pain perception and mood? A review of the evidence related to healthy and chronic pain subjects. *Curr Pain Headache Rep.* Apr 2007;11(2): 93-97.
178. Chatzitheodorou D, Kabitsis C, Malliou P, Mougios V. A pilot study of the effects of high-intensity aerobic exercise versus passive interventions on pain, disability, psychological strain, and serum cortisol concentrations in people with chronic low back pain. *Phys Ther.* Mar 2007;87(3):304-312.
179. Hoffman MD, Shepanski MA, Mackenzie SP, Clifford PS. Experimentally induced pain perception is acutely reduced by aerobic exercise in people with chronic low back pain. *Journal of rehabilitation research and development.* Mar-Apr 2005;42(2):183-190.
180. Bruce B, Fries JF, Lubeck DP. Aerobic exercise and its impact on musculoskeletal pain in older adults: a 14 year prospective, longitudinal study. *Arthritis Res Ther.* 2005;7(6): R1263-1270.
181. Hoffman MD, Shepanski MA, Ruble SB, Valic Z, Buckwalter JB, Clifford PS. Intensity and duration threshold for aerobic exercise-induced analgesia to pressure pain. *Arch Phys Med Rehabil.* Jul 2004;85(7):1183-1187.

182. Koltyn KF, Garvin AW, Gardiner RL, Nelson TF. Perception of pain following aerobic exercise. *Med Sci Sports Exerc.* Nov 1996;28(11):1418-1421.
183. Reid KJ, Baron KG, Lu B, Naylor E, Wolfe L, Zee PC. Aerobic exercise improves self-reported sleep and quality of life in older adults with insomnia. *Sleep Med.* Aug 31 2010.
184. Ucok K, Aycicek A, Sezer M, et al. Aerobic and anaerobic exercise capacities in obstructive sleep apnea and associations with subcutaneous fat distributions. *Lung.* Jan-Feb 2009;187(1):29-36.
185. Yamamoto U, Mohri M, Shimada K, et al. Six-month aerobic exercise training ameliorates central sleep apnea in patients with chronic heart failure. *J Card Fail.* Dec 2007;13(10):825-829.
186. Catai AM, Chacon-Mikahil MP, Martinelli FS, et al. Effects of aerobic exercise training on heart rate variability during wakefulness and sleep and cardiorespiratory responses of young and middle-aged healthy men. *Braz J Med Biol Res.* Jun 2002;35(6):741-752.
187. Gondoh Y, Sensui H, Kinomura S, et al. Effects of aerobic exercise training on brain structure and psychological well-being in young adults. *J Sports Med Phys Fitness.* Jun 2009;49(2):129-135.
188. Dittrich SM, Gunther V, Franz G, Burtscher M, Holzner B, Kopp M. Aerobic exercise with relaxation: influence on pain and psychological well-being in female migraine patients. *Clin J Sport Med.* Jul 2008;18(4):363-365.
189. Stringer WW, Berezovskaya M, O'Brien WA, Beck CK, Casaburi R. The effect of exercise training on aerobic fitness, immune indices, and quality of life in HIV+ patients. *Medicine and science in sports and exercise.* Jan 1998;30(1): 11-16.
190. O'Brien K, Nixon S, Tynan AM, Glazier R. Aerobic exercise interventions for adults living with HIV/AIDS. *Cochrane Database Syst Rev.* 2010;8:CD001796.
191. Kramer MS, McDonald SW. Aerobic exercise for women during pregnancy. *Cochrane Database Syst Rev.* 2006;3:CD000180.
192. Bollo RJ, Williams SC, Peskin CS, Samadani U. When the air hits your brain: cerebral autoregulation of brain oxygenation during aerobic exercise allows transient hyperoxygenation: case report. *Neurosurgery.* Aug 2010;67(2):E507-509.
193. Caglar E, Sabuncuoglu H, Keskin T, Isikli S, Keskil S, Korkusuz F. In vivo human brain biochemistry after aerobic exercise: preliminary report on functional magnetic resonance spectroscopy. *Surg Neurol.* 2005;64 Suppl 2:S53-56; discussion S56-57.
194. Quaney BM, Boyd LA, McDowd JM, et al. Aerobic exercise improves cognition and motor function poststroke. *Neurorehabil Neural Repair.* Nov 2009;23(9):879-885.
195. Pontifex MB, Hillman CH, Fernhall B, Thompson KM, Valentini TA. The effect of acute aerobic and resistance exercise on working memory. *Med Sci Sports Exerc.* Apr 2009;41(4):927-934.
196. Miles C, Hardman E. State-dependent memory produced by aerobic exercise. *Ergonomics.* Jan 1998;41(1):20-28.
197. Exercise may slow or reverse brain decline. Aerobic exercise benefits executive-control brain function, and may enable the brain to continue to grow and develop. *Duke Med Health News.* Mar 2009;15(3):3.
198. Wedekind D, Sprute A, Broocks A, et al. Nocturnal urinary cortisol excretion over a randomized controlled trial with paroxetine vs. placebo combined with relaxation training or aerobic exercise in panic disorder. *Curr Pharm Des.* 2008;14(33):3518-3524.
199. Haaland DA, Sabljic TF, Baribeau DA, Mukovozov IM, Hart LE. Is regular exercise a friend or foe of the aging immune system? A systematic review. *Clinical journal of sport medicine: official journal of the Canadian Academy of Sport Medicine.* Nov 2008;18(6):539-548.
200. Castellano V, White LJ. Serum brain-derived neurotrophic factor response to aerobic exercise in multiple sclerosis. *J Neurol Sci.* Jun 15 2008;269(1-2): 85-91.
201. Bauer T, Weisser B. [Effect of aerobic endurance exercise on immune function in elderly athletes]. *Praxis (Bern 1994).* Jan 30 2002;91(5):153-158.
202. Boas SR, Danduran MJ, McColley SA, Beaman K, O'Gorman MR. Immune modulation following aerobic exercise in children with cystic fibrosis. *Int J Sports Med.* May 2000;21(4):294-301.
203. Woods JA, Ceddia MA, Wolters BW, Evans JK, Lu Q, McAuley E. Effects of 6 months of moderate aerobic exercise training on immune function in the elderly. *Mech Ageing Dev.* Jun 1 1999;109(1):1-19.
204. Newman CL, Motta RW. The effects of aerobic exercise on childhood PTSD, anxiety, and depression. *Int J Emerg Ment Health.* Spring 2007;9(2):133-158.

205. Blumenthal JA, Babyak MA, Doraiswamy PM, et al. Exercise and pharmacotherapy in the treatment of major depressive disorder. *Psychosomatic medicine.* Sep-Oct 2007;69(7):587-596.
206. Oman RF, Oman KK. A case-control study of psychosocial and aerobic exercise factors in women with symptoms of depression. *J Psychol.* Jul 2003;137(4):338-350.
207. Dimeo F, Bauer M, Varahram I, Proest G, Halter U. Benefits from aerobic exercise in patients with major depression: a pilot study. *Br J Sports Med.* Apr 2001;35(2):114-117.
208. Sculco AD, Paup DC, Fernhall B, Sculco MJ. Effects of aerobic exercise on low back pain patients in treatment. *The spine journal: official journal of the North American Spine Society.* Mar-Apr 2001;1(2):95-101.
209. Petruzzello SJ, Tate AK. Brain activation, affect, and aerobic exercise: an examination of both state-independent and state-dependent relationships. *Psychophysiology.* Sep 1997;34(5): 527-533.
210. Clinic M. *Aerobic exercise increases size of aging brain.* Mayo Clin Health Lett. May 2007;25(5):4.
211. Colcombe SJ, Erickson KI, Scalf PE, et al. Aerobic exercise training increases brain volume in aging humans. *J Gerontol A Biol Sci Med Sci.* Nov 2006;61(11): 1166-1170.
212. Rossi M, Santoro G, Ricco R, Pentimone F, Carpi A. Effect of chronic aerobic exercise on cutaneous microcirculatory flow response to insulin iontophoresis and to ischemia in elderly males. *Int J Sports Med.* Sep 2005;26(7):558-562.
213. Nathan PA, Wilcox A, Emerick PS, al. e. Effects of an aerobic exercise program on median nerve conduction and symptoms associated with carpal tunnel syndrome. *Journal of Occupational and Environmental Medicine.* 2001;43(10): 840-843.
214. Hart LE, Haaland DA, Baribeau DA, Mukovozov IM, Sabljic TF. The relationship between exercise and osteoarthritis in the elderly. *Clin J Sport Med.* Nov 2008;18(6):508-521.
215. Roos E. [Physical activity can influence the course of early arthritis. Both strength training and aerobic exercise provide pain relief and functional improvement]. *Lakartidningen.* Nov 7 2002;99(45):4484-4489.
216. Zhang KR, Liu HT, Zhang HF, et al. Long-term aerobic exercise protects the heart against ischemia/reperfusion injury via PI3 kinase-dependent and Akt-mediated mechanism. *Apoptosis.* Sep 2007;12(9):1579-1588.
217. Deley G, Kervio G, Verges B, et al. Comparison of low-frequency electrical myostimulation and conventional aerobic exercise training in patients with chronic heart failure. *Eur J Cardiovasc Prev Rehabil.* Jun 2005;12(3):226-233.
218. Ferreira ML, Ferreira PH, Latimer J, et al. Comparison of general exercise, motor control exercise and spinal manipulative therapy for chronic low back pain: A randomized trial. *Pain.* Sep 2007;131(1-2):31-37.
219. Tritilanunt T, Wajanavisit W. The efficacy of an aerobic exercise and health education program for treatment of chronic low back pain. *J Med Assoc Thai.* Oct 2001;84 Suppl 2:S528-533.
220. Dobkin PL, Da Costa D, Abrahamowicz M, et al. Adherence during an individualized home based 12-week exercise program in women with fibromyalgia. *J Rheumatol.* Feb 2006;33(2):333-341.
221. Jentoft ES, Kvalvik AG, Mengshoel AM. Effects of pool-based and land-based aerobic exercise on women with fibromyalgia/chronic widespread muscle pain. *Arthritis Rheum.* Feb 2001;45(1):42-47.
222. Wigers SH, Stiles TC, Vogel PA. Effects of aerobic exercise versus stress management treatment in fibromyalgia. *Scandinavian Journal of Rheumatology.* 1996;25:77-86.
223. Jackson D, Turner-Stokes L, Culpan J, et al. Can brain-injured patients participate in an aerobic exercise programme during early inpatient rehabilitation? *Clin Rehabil.* Oct 2001;15(5):535-544.
224. Fulcher KY, White PD. Randomised controlled trial of graded exercise in patients with the chronic fatigue syndrome. *Bmj.* Jun 7 1997;314(7095):1647-1652.
225. Janal MN, Colt EW, Clark WC, Glusman M. Pain sensitivity, mood and plasma endocrine levels in man following long-distance running: effects of naloxone. *Pain.* May 1984;19(1):13-25.
226. Cox KL, Burke V, Gorely TJ, Beilin LJ, Puddey IB. Controlled comparison of retention and adherence in home- vs center-initiated exercise interventions in women ages 40-65 years: The S.W.E.A.T. Study (Sedentary Women Exercise Adherence Trial). *Preventive medicine.* Jan 2003;36(1):17-29.

227. Mailloux J, Finno M, Rainville J. Long-term exercise adherence in the elderly with chronic low back pain. *Am J Phys Med Rehabil.* Feb 2006;85(2):120-126.
228. Moseley GL. Do training diaries affect and reflect adherence to home programs? *Arthritis and rheumatism.* Aug 15 2006;55(4):662-664.
229. Hurling R, Catt M, Boni MD, et al. Using internet and mobile phone technology to deliver an automated physical activity program: randomized controlled trial. *J Med Internet Res.* 2007;9(2):e7.
230. Duncan KA, Pozehl B. Staying on course: the effects of an adherence facilitation intervention on home exercise participation. *Progress in cardiovascular nursing.* Spring 2002;17(2):59-65, 71.
231. Friedrich M, Gittler G, Halberstadt Y, Cermak T, Heiller I. Combined exercise and motivation program: effect on the compliance and level of disability of patients with chronic low back pain: a randomized controlled trial. *Arch Phys Med Rehabil.* May 1998;79(5):475-487.
232. Friedrich M, Gittler G, Arendasy M, Friedrich KM. Long-term effect of a combined exercise and motivational program on the level of disability of patients with chronic low back pain. *Spine.* May 1 2005;30(9):995-1000.
233. Scales R, Miller JH. Motivational techniques for improving compliance with an exercise program: skills for primary care clinicians. *Curr Sports Med Rep.* Jun 2003;2(3):166-172.
234. Asenlof P, Denison E, Lindberg P. Individually tailored treatment targeting motor behavior, cognition, and disability: 2 experimental single-case studies of patients with recurrent and persistent musculoskeletal pain in primary health care. *Physical therapy.* Oct 2005;85(10):1061-1077.
235. Engstrom LO, Oberg B. Patient adherence in an individualized rehabilitation programme: a clinical follow-up. *Scand J Public Health.* 2005;33(1):11-18.
236. Dobkin PL, Sita A, Sewitch MJ. Predictors of adherence to treatment in women with fibromyalgia. *The Clinical journal of pain.* Mar-Apr 2006;22(3):286-294.
237. Lysack C, Dama M, Neufeld S, Andreassi E. A compliance and satisfaction with home exercise: a comparison of computer-assisted video instruction and routine rehabilitation practice. *Journal of allied health.* Summer 2005;34(2):76-82.
238. Ainsworth KD, Hagino CC. A survey of Ontario chiropractors: their views on maximizing patient compliance to prescribed home exercise. *J Can Chiropr Assoc.* Jun 2006;50(2):140-155.
239. Louw A. Therapeutic neuroscience education via e-mail: a case report. *Physiother Theory Pract.* Nov 2014;30(8):588-596.
240. Reis FJJ, Bengaly AGC, Valentim JCP, et al. An E-Pain intervention to spread modern pain education in Brazil. *Braz J Phys Ther.* Sep - Oct 2017;21(5):305-306.
241. Gollwitzer PM, Brandstatter V. Implementation Interventions and Effective Goal Pursuit. *Journal of personality and social psychology.* 1997;73:186-199.
242. Gollwitzer PM. Implementation Intensions: Strong Effects of Simple Plans. *American psychologist.* 1999;54(7):496-503.
243. Capomolla S, Ceresa M, Civardi A, et al. [Home exercise therapy in chronic congestive heart failure: observational study of factors affecting adherence to the program]. *Italian heart journal. Supplement: official journal of the Italian Federation of Cardiology.* Nov 2002;3(11):1098-1105.
244. Ronda G, Van Assema P, Brug J. Stages of change, psychological factors and awareness of physical activity levels in The Netherlands. *Health promotion international.* Dec 2001;16(4):305-314.
245. Rhodes RE, de Bruijn GJ. How big is the physical activity intention-behaviour gap? A meta-analysis using the action control framework. *British journal of health psychology.* May 2013;18(2):296-309.
246. Butler D, Moseley L. *Explain Pain.* Adelaide: Noigroup Publications; 2003.
247. Wilson D, Williams M, Butler D. Language and the pain experience. *Physiotherapy research international: the journal for researchers and clinicians in physical therapy.* Mar 2009;14(1):56-65.
248. Takacs J, Pollock CL, Guenther JR, Bahar M, Napier C, Hunt MA. Validation of the Fitbit One activity monitor device during treadmill walking. *J Sci Med Sport.* Sep 2014;17(5):496-500.
249. Cadmus-Bertram L, Marcus BH, Patterson RE, Parker BA, Morey BL. Use of the Fitbit to Measure Adherence to a Physical Activity Intervention Among Overweight or Obese, Postmenopausal Women: Self-Monitoring Trajectory During 16 Weeks. *JMIR mHealth and uHealth.* Nov 19 2015;3(4):e96.

250. Adam Noah J, Spierer DK, Gu J, Bronner S. Comparison of steps and energy expenditure assessment in adults of Fitbit Tracker and Ultra to the Actical and indirect calorimetry. *Journal of medical engineering & technology.* Oct 2013;37(7):456-462.
251. Valkeinen H, Hakkinen A, Alen M, Hannonen P, Kukkonen-Harjula K, Hakkinen K. Physical Fitness in Postmenopausal Women with Fibromyalgia. *Int J Sports Med.* Oct 24 2007.
252. Brosseau L, Wells GA, Tugwell P, et al. Ottawa Panel Evidence-Based Clinical Practice Guidelines for Aerobic Fitness Exercises in the Management of Fibromyalgia: Part 1. *Physical therapy.* 2008/07/01/ 2008;88(7):857-871.
253. Lederman E. The Myth of Core Stability. *CPDO Online Journal.* June 2007:1-17.
254. Marcell TJ. Sarcopenia: causes, consequences, and preventions. The journals of gerontology. *Series A, Biological sciences and medical sciences.* Oct 2003;58(10):M911-916.
255. Narici MV, Maganaris CN. Adaptability of elderly human muscles and tendons to increased loading. *J Anat.* Apr 2006;208(4):433-443.
256. Busch AJ, Barber KA, Overend TJ, Peloso PM, Schachter CL. Exercise for treating fibromyalgia syndrome. *The Cochrane database of systematic reviews.* 2007(4):CD003786.
257. Busch AJ, Webber SC, Richards RS, et al. Resistance exercise training for fibromyalgia. *The Cochrane database of systematic reviews.* 2013;12:CD010884.
258. Thacker M. Physiotherapy management of whiplash injuries: a review. In: Gifford L, ed. *Topical Issues in Pain. Vol 1.* Cornwall: NOI Press; 1998.
259. Staud R, Robinson ME, Price DD. Isometric exercise has opposite effects on central pain mechanisms in fibromyalgia patients compared to normal controls. *Pain.* Nov 2005;118(1-2):176-184.
260. Naugle KM, Naugle KE, Riley JL, 3rd. Reduced Modulation of Pain in Older Adults After Isometric and Aerobic Exercise. *The journal of pain: official journal of the American Pain Society.* Jun 2016;17(6):719-728.
261. Ring C, Edwards L, Kavussanu M. Effects of isometric exercise on pain are mediated by blood pressure. *Biological psychology.* Apr 2008;78(1):123-128.
262. Koltyn KF, Brellenthin AG, Cook DB, Sehgal N, Hillard C. Mechanisms of exercise-induced hypoalgesia. *The journal of pain: official journal of the American Pain Society.* Dec 2014;15(12):1294-1304.
263. Smith A, Ritchie C, Pedler A, McCamley K, Roberts K, Sterling M. Exercise induced hypoalgesia is elicited by isometric, but not aerobic exercise in individuals with chronic whiplash associated disorders. *Scand J Pain.* Apr 2017;15:14-21.
264. Jull G, Sterling M, Falla D, O'Leary SP, Treleaven J. *Whiplash, Headache, and Neck Pain: Research-Based Directions for Physical Therapies.* Philidelphia, PA: Churchill Livingston; 2008.
265. Richardson C, Jull GA, Hodges P, Hides J. *Therapeutic Exercise For Spinal Segmental Stabilization in Low Back Pain.* London: Churchill Livingstone; 1999.
266. Richardson C, Hodges P, Hides J. *Therapeutic Exercise For Lumbopelvic Stabilization.* Second ed. London: Churchill Livingstone; 2004.
267. Hides JA, Richardson CA, Jull GA. Magnetic resonance imaging and ultrasonography of the lumbar multifidus muscle. Comparison of two different modalities. *Spine.* Jan 1 1995;20(1): 54-58.
268. Hides JA, Richardson CA, Jull G. Multifidus muscle recovery is not automatic after resolution of acute first-episode low back pain. *Spine.* 1996;21:2763-2769.
269. Hodges PW, Richardson CA. Relationship between limb movement speed and associated contraction of the trunk muscles. *Ergonomics.* Nov 1997;40(11):1220-1230.
270. Hodges PW, Richardson CA. Feedforward contraction of transversus abdominis is not influenced by the direction of arm movement. *Exp Brain Res.* Apr 1997;114(2):362-370.
271. Hodges PW, Richardson CA. Contraction of the abdominal muscles associated with movement of the lower limb. *Physical therapy.* Feb 1997;77(2):132-142; discussion 142-134.
272. Hodges PW. Changes in motor planning of feedforward postural responses of the trunk muscles in low back pain. *Exp Brain Res.* Nov 2001;141(2):261-266.
273. Hodges PW, Cresswell AG, Daggfeldt K, Thorstensson A. In vivo measurement of the effect of intra-abdominal pressure on the human spine. *J Biomech.* Mar 2001;34(3):347-353.

274. Hodges PW, Cresswell AG, Thorstensson A. Perturbed upper limb movements cause short-latency postural responses in trunk muscles. *Exp Brain Res.* May 2001;138(2):243-250.
275. Jull G, Barrett C, Magee R, Ho P. Further clinical clarification of the muscle dysfunction in cervical headache. *Cephalalgia: an international journal of headache.* Apr 1999;19(3):179-185.
276. Jull GA, O'Leary SP, Falla DL. Clinical assessment of the deep cervical flexor muscles: the craniocervical flexion test. *Journal of manipulative and physiological therapeutics.* Sep 2008;31(7):525-533.
277. Falla D, Jull G, Hodges PW. Feedforward activity of the cervical flexor muscles during voluntary arm movements is delayed in chronic neck pain. *Exp Brain Res.* Jul 2004;157(1):43-48.
278. Falla D, Jull G, Hodges P, Vicenzino B. An endurance-strength training regime is effective in reducing myoelectric manifestations of cervical flexor muscle fatigue in females with chronic neck pain. *Clinical neurophysiology: official journal of the International Federation of Clinical Neurophysiology.* Apr 2006;117(4):828-837.
279. Falla D, Jull G, O'Leary S, Dall'Alba P. Further evaluation of an EMG technique for assessment of the deep cervical flexor muscles. *J Electromyogr Kinesiol.* Dec 2006;16(6):621-628.
280. Hodges PW. Core stability exercises for chronic low back pain. *Orthopedic Clinics of North America.* 2003;34:245-254.
281. Cairns MC, Foster NE, Wright C. Randomized controlled trial of specific spinal stabilization exercises and conventional physiotherapy for recurrent low back pain. *Spine.* Sep 1 2006;31(19):E670-681.
282. Goldby LJ, Moore AP, Doust J, Trew ME. A randomized controlled trial investigating the efficiency of musculoskeletal physiotherapy on chronic low back disorder. *Spine.* May 1 2006;31(10):1083-1093.
283. Critchley DJ, Ratcliffe J, Noonan S, Jones RH, Hurley MV. Effectiveness and cost-effectiveness of three types of physiotherapy used to reduce chronic low back pain disability: a pragmatic randomized trial with economic evaluation. *Spine.* Jun 15 2007;32(14):1474-1481.
284. Fritz JM, Whitman JM, Childs JD. Lumbar spine segmental mobility assessment: an examination of validity for determining intervention strategies in patients with low back pain. *Arch Phys Med Rehabil.* Sep 2005;86(9):1745-1752.
285. Koumantakis GA, Watson PJ, Oldham JA. Trunk muscle stabilization training plus general exercise versus general exercise only: randomized controlled trial of patients with recurrent low back pain. *Physical therapy.* Mar 2005;85(3):209-225.
286. Vera-Garcia FJ, Brown SH, Gray JR, McGill SM. Effects of different levels of torso coactivation on trunk muscular and kinematic responses to posteriorly applied sudden loads. *Clin Biomech (Bristol, Avon).* Jun 2006;21(5):443-455.
287. Fenwick CM, Brown SH, McGill SM. Comparison of different rowing exercises: trunk muscle activation and lumbar spine motion, load, and stiffness. *Journal of strength and conditioning research/ National Strength & Conditioning Association.* Mar 2009;23(2):350-358.
288. Niemisto L, Rissanen P, Sarna S, Lahtinen-Suopanki T, Lindgren KA, Hurri H. Cost-effectiveness of combined manipulation, stabilizing exercises, and physician consultation compared to physician consultation alone for chronic low back pain: a prospective randomized trial with 2-year follow-up. *Spine.* May 15 2005;30(10):1109-1115.
289. Nilsson-Wikmar L, Holm K, Oijerstedt R, Harms-Ringdahl K. Effect of three different physical therapy treatments on pain and activity in pregnant women with pelvic girdle pain: a randomized clinical trial with 3, 6, and 12 months follow-up postpartum. *Spine.* Apr 15 2005;30(8):850-856.
290. Moseley GL, Flor H. Targeting cortical representations in the treatment of chronic pain: a review. *Neurorehabil Neural Repair.* Jul 2012;26(6):646-652.
291. Luomajoki H, Moseley GL. Tactile acuity and lumbopelvic motor control in patients with back pain and healthy controls. *British journal of sports medicine.* Apr 2011;45(5):437-440.
292. O'Sullivan K, McCarthy R, White A, O'Sullivan L, Dankaerts W. Can we reduce the effort of maintaining a neutral sitting posture? A pilot study. *Manual therapy.* Dec 2012;17(6):566-571.
293. Roffey DM, Wai EK, Bishop P, Kwon BK, Dagenais S. Causal assessment of occupational sitting and low back pain: results of a systematic review. *The spine journal: official journal of the North American Spine Society.* Mar 2010;10(3):252-261.
294. Poitras S, Blais R, Swaine B, Rossignol M. Management of work-related low back pain: a population-based survey of physical therapists. *Physical therapy.* Nov 2005;85(11):1168-1181.

295. Dankaerts W, O'Sullivan P, Burnett A, Straker L. Differences in sitting postures are associated with nonspecific chronic low back pain disorders when patients are subclassified. *Spine*. Mar 15 2006;31(6):698-704.
296. Womersley L, May S. Sitting posture of subjects with postural backache. *Journal of manipulative and physiological therapeutics*. Mar-Apr 2006;29(3): 213-218.
297. Karahan A, Kav S, Abbasoglu A, Dogan N. Low back pain: prevalence and associated risk factors among hospital staff. *Journal of advanced nursing*. Mar 2009;65(3):516-524.
298. Szeto GP, Straker LM, O'Sullivan PB. A comparison of symptomatic and asymptomatic office workers performing monotonous keyboard work--2: neck and shoulder kinematics. *Manual therapy*. Nov 2005;10(4):281-291.
299. Childs JD, Whitman JM, Sizer PS, Pugia ML, Flynn TW, Delitto A. A description of physical therapists' knowledge in managing musculoskeletal conditions. *BMC musculoskeletal disorders*. 2005;6:32.
300. Claus AP, Hides JA, Moseley GL, Hodges PW. Different ways to balance the spine: subtle changes in sagittal spinal curves affect regional muscle activity. *Spine*. Mar 15 2009;34(6):E208-214.
301. Claus AP, Hides JA, Moseley GL, Hodges PW. Is 'ideal' sitting posture real? Measurement of spinal curves in four sitting postures. *Manual therapy*. Aug 2009;14(4):404-408.
302. Grimmer K. An investigation of poor cervical resting posture. *The Australian journal of physiotherapy*. 1997;43(1): 7-16.
303. Raine S, Twomey LT. Head and shoulder posture variations in 160 asymptomatic women and men. *Arch Phys Med Rehabil*. Nov 1997;78(11):1215-1223.
304. O'Sullivan K, O'Sullivan P, O'Sullivan L, Dankaerts W. What do physiotherapists consider to be the best sitting spinal posture? *Manual therapy*. Oct 2012;17(5):432-437.
305. Lis AM, Black KM, Korn H, Nordin M. Association between sitting and occupational LBP. *Eur Spine J*. Feb 2007;16(2):283-298.
306. Roffey DM, Wai EK, Bishop P, Kwon BK, Dagenais S. Causal assessment of workplace manual handling or assisting patients and low back pain: results of a systematic review. *The spine journal: official journal of the North American Spine Society*. Jul 2010;10(7):639-651.
307. Hartvigsen J, Leboeuf-Yde C, Lings S, Corder EH. Is sitting-while-at-work associated with low back pain? A systematic, critical literature review. *Scandinavian journal of public health*. Sep 2000;28(3):230-239.
308. Darlow LA, Pesco J, Greenberg MS. The relationship of posture to myofascial pain dysfunction syndrome. *Journal of the American Dental Association*. Jan 1987;114(1):73-75.
309. Lewis JS, Green A, Wright C. Subacromial impingement syndrome: the role of posture and muscle imbalance. *Journal of shoulder and elbow surgery/American Shoulder and Elbow Surgeons* ... [et al.]. Jul-Aug 2005;14(4):385-392.
310. Louw A, Zimney K, Landers M. Assessing posture in the individual with fibromyalgia, what's the value? *Pain and Rehabilitation*. 2017;Winter (42):13-21.
311. Larsson SE, Cai H, Zhang Q, Larsson R, Oberg PA. Microcirculation in the upper trapezius muscle during sustained shoulder load in healthy women – an endurance study using percutaneous laser-Doppler flowmetry and surface electromyography. *Eur J Appl Physiol Occup Physiol*. 1995;70(5):451-456.
312. Chau JY, Sukala W, Fedel K, et al. More standing and just as productive: Effects of a sit-stand desk intervention on call center workers' sitting, standing, and productivity at work in the Opt to Stand pilot study. *Preventive medicine reports*. Jun 2016;3:68-74.
313. Hassett AL, Gevirtz RN. Nonpharmacologic treatment for fibromyalgia: patient education, cognitive-behavioral therapy, relaxation techniques, and complementary and alternative medicine. *Rheumatic diseases clinics of North America*. May 2009;35(2):393-407.
314. Goldstein KM, Shepherd-Banigan M, Coeytaux RR, et al. Use of mindfulness, meditation and relaxation to treat vasomotor symptoms. *Climacteric: the journal of the International Menopause Society*. Apr 2017;20(2):178-182.
315. Meeus M, Nijs J, Vanderheiden T, Baert I, Descheemaeker F, Struyf F. The effect of relaxation therapy on autonomic functioning, symptoms and daily functioning, in patients with chronic fatigue syndrome or fibromyalgia: a systematic review. *Clin Rehabil*. Mar 2015;29(3):221-233.

316. Meeus M, Nijs J, Vanderheiden T, Baert I, Descheemaeker F, Struyf F. The effect of relaxation therapy on autonomic functioning, symptoms and daily functioning, in patients with chronic fatigue syndrome or fibromyalgia: a systematic review. *Clin Rehabil.* 2014/09/08/ 2014:0269215514542635.
317. Aas RW, Tuntland H, Holte KA, et al. Workplace interventions for neck pain in workers. *The Cochrane database of systematic reviews.* 2011(4):CD008160.
318. Harris M, Richards KC. The physiological and psychological effects of slow-stroke back massage and hand massage on relaxation in older people. *J Clin Nurs.* Apr 2010;19(7-8):917-926.
319. Charalambous A, Giannakopoulou M, Bozas E, Paikousis L. A Randomized Controlled Trial for the Effectiveness of Progressive Muscle Relaxation and Guided Imagery as Anxiety Reducing Interventions in Breast and Prostate Cancer Patients Undergoing Chemotherapy. *Evidence-based complementary and alternative medicine: eCAM.* 2015;2015:270876.
320. Charalambous A, Giannakopoulou M, Bozas E, Paikousis L. A Randomized Controlled Trial for the Effectiveness of Progressive Muscle Relaxation and Guided Imagery as Anxiety Reducing Interventions in Breast and Prostate Cancer Patients Undergoing Chemotherapy. *Evid Based Complement Alternat Med.* 2015;2015:270876.
321. Kaplan KH, Goldenberg DL, Galvin-Nadeau M. The impact of a meditation-based stress reduction program on fibromyalgia. *General hospital psychiatry.* Sep 1993;15(5):284-289.
322. Huntley A, White AR, Ernst E. Relaxation therapies for asthma: a systematic review. *Thorax.* Feb 2002;57(2):127-131.
323. Manzoni GM, Pagnini F, Castelnuovo G, Molinari E. Relaxation training for anxiety: a ten-years systematic review with meta-analysis. *BMC psychiatry.* Jun 2 2008;8:41.
324. Williams AM, Cano A. Spousal mindfulness and social support in couples with chronic pain. *The Clinical journal of pain.* Jun 2014;30(6): 528-535.
325. Million M, Larauche M. Stress, sex, and the enteric nervous system. *Neurogastroenterology and motility: the official journal of the European Gastrointestinal Motility Society.* Sep 2016;28(9):1283-1289.
326. Husby S, Murray J. Non-celiac gluten hypersensitivity: What is all the fuss about? *F1000prime reports.* 2015;7:54.
327. Fardet A. Wheat-based foods and non celiac gluten/wheat sensitivity: Is drastic processing the main key issue? *Medical hypotheses.* Sep 6 2015.
328. Shahbazkhani B, Sadeghi A, Malekzadeh R, et al. Non-Celiac Gluten Sensitivity Has Narrowed the Spectrum of Irritable Bowel Syndrome: A Double-Blind Randomized Placebo-Controlled Trial. *Nutrients.* Jun 2015;7(6):4542-4554.
329. Losowsky MS. A history of coeliac disease. *Digestive diseases.* 2008;26(2):112-120.
330. Mansueto P, Seidita A, D'Alcamo A, Carroccio A. Non-celiac gluten sensitivity: literature review. *Journal of the American College of Nutrition.* 2014;33(1):39-54.
331. Stevens L, Rashid M. Gluten-free and regular foods: a cost comparison. *Canadian journal of dietetic practice and research: a publication of Dietitians of Canada = Revue canadienne de la pratique et de la recherche en dietetique: une publication des Dietetistes du Canada.* Fall 2008;69(3):147-150.
332. Lebwohl B, Cao Y, Zong G, et al. Long term gluten consumption in adults without celiac disease and risk of coronary heart disease: prospective cohort study. *Bmj.* May 02 2017;357:j1892.
333. Alrabadi NI. The effect of lifestyle food on chronic diseases: a comparison between vegetarians and non-vegetarians in Jordan. *Global journal of health science.* Nov 4 2012;5(1):65-69.
334. Bunner AE, Wells CL, Gonzales J, Agarwal U, Bayat E, Barnard ND. A dietary intervention for chronic diabetic neuropathy pain: a randomized controlled pilot study. *Nutrition & diabetes.* May 26 2015;5:e158.
335. Barnard ND, Katcher HI, Jenkins DJ, Cohen J, Turner-McGrievy G. Vegetarian and vegan diets in type 2 diabetes management. *Nutrition reviews.* May 2009;67(5):255-263.
336. Barnard ND, Cohen J, Jenkins DJ, et al. A low-fat vegan diet and a conventional diabetes diet in the treatment of type 2 diabetes: a randomized, controlled, 74-wk clinical trial. *The American journal of clinical nutrition.* May 2009;89(5):1588S-1596S.
337. Barnard ND, Bunner AE, Agarwal U. Saturated and trans fats and dementia: a systematic review. *Neurobiology of aging.* Sep 2014;35 Suppl 2:S65-73.

338. Barnard ND. The physician's role in nutrition-related disorders: from bystander to leader. *The virtual mentor: VM.* Apr 1 2013;15(4):367-372.
339. Barnard ND. The lipid-lowering effect of lean meat diets falls far short of that of vegetarian diets. *Arch Intern Med.* Feb 14 2000;160(3):395-396.
340. Katz DL, Meller S. Can we say what diet is best for health? *Annual review of public health.* 2014;35:83-103.
341. Wolfe F. Sleep problems and risk of fibromyalgia – untenable conclusions: comment on the article by Mork et al. *Arthritis and rheumatism.* May 2012;64(5):1692-1693; author reply 1693-1694.
342. Mork PJ, Nilsen TI. Sleep problems and risk of fibromyalgia: longitudinal data on an adult female population in Norway. *Arthritis and rheumatism.* Jan 2012;64(1):281-284.
343. Schaefer C, Chandran A, Hufstader M, et al. The comparative burden of mild, moderate and severe fibromyalgia: results from a cross-sectional survey in the United States. *Health Qual Life Outcomes.* 2011;9:71.
344. Shah MA, Feinberg S, Krishnan E. Sleep-disordered breathing among women with fibromyalgia syndrome. *J Clin Rheumatol.* Dec 2006;12(6):277-281.
345. Lauderdale DS, Knutson KL, Rathouz PJ, Yan LL, Hulley SB, Liu K. Cross-sectional and longitudinal associations between objectively measured sleep duration and body mass index: the CARDIA Sleep Study. *American journal of epidemiology.* Oct 1 2009;170(7):805-813.
346. Schwartz T. *The Way We're Working Isn't working.* First ed. New York, NY: Free Press; 2010.
347. Wolfson AR, Harkins E, Johnson M, Marco C. Effects of the Young Adolescent Sleep Smart Program on sleep hygiene practices, sleep health efficacy, and behavioral well-being. *Sleep health.* Sep 2015;1(3):197-204.
348. Saeedi M, Shamsikhani S, Varvani Farahani P, Haghverdi F. Sleep hygiene training program for patients on hemodialysis. *Iranian journal of kidney diseases.* Jan 2014;8(1):65-69.
349. Rodham K, McCabe C, Pilkington M, Regan L. Coping with chronic complex regional pain syndrome: advice from patients for patients. *Chronic illness.* Mar 2013;9(1):29-42.
350. Miro E, Lupianez J, Martinez MP, et al. Cognitive-behavioral therapy for insomnia improves attentional function in fibromyalgia syndrome: a pilot, randomized controlled trial. *Journal of health psychology.* Jul 2011;16(5): 770-782.
351. Kloss JD, Nash CO, Walsh CM, Culnan E, Horsey S, Sexton-Radek K. A "Sleep 101" Program for College Students Improves Sleep Hygiene Knowledge and Reduces Maladaptive Beliefs about Sleep. *Behavioral medicine.* 2016;42(1):48-56.
352. Kaku A, Nishinoue N, Takano T, et al. Randomized controlled trial on the effects of a combined sleep hygiene education and behavioral approach program on sleep quality in workers with insomnia. *Industrial health.* 2012;50(1):52-59.
353. De La Rue-Evans L, Nesbitt K, Oka RK. Sleep hygiene program implementation in patients with traumatic brain injury. *Rehabilitation nursing: the official journal of the Association of Rehabilitation Nurses.* Jan-Feb 2013;38(1):2-10.
354. Arora VM, Georgitis E, Woodruff JN, Humphrey HJ, Meltzer D. Improving sleep hygiene of medical interns: can the sleep, alertness, and fatigue education in residency program help? *Arch Intern Med.* Sep 10 2007;167(16):1738-1744.
355. Hayashi M, Motoyoshi N, Hori T. Recuperative power of a short daytime nap with or without stage 2 sleep. *Sleep.* Jul 2005;28(7):829-836.
356. Moore CE. The power nap. *The Journal of the Florida Medical Association.* Nov 1990;77(11):955-956.
357. Davidhizar R, Poole V, Giger JN. Power nap rejuvenates body, mind. *The Pennsylvania nurse.* Mar 1996;51(3): 6-7.
358. Currie SR, Wilson KG, Gauthier ST. Caffeine and chronic low back pain. *The Clinical journal of pain.* Sep 1995;11(3):214-219.
359. Fernandez-De-Las-Penaz C, Arendt-Nielsen L, Gerwin R. *Tension-Type and Cervicogenci Headache: Pathology, Diagnosis, and Management.* Sudbury: Jones and Bartlett; 2010.
360. Klerman EB, Goldenberg DL, Brown EN, Maliszewski AM, Adler GK. Circadian rhythms of women with fibromyalgia. *The Journal of clinical endocrinology and metabolism.* Mar 2001;86(3): 1034-1039.
361. Roehrs T, Roth T. Sleep, sleepiness, sleep disorders and alcohol use and abuse. *Sleep medicine reviews.* Aug 2001;5(4):287-297.

362. Sandberg J, Barnard Y. Deep learning is difficult. *Instruc Sci.* 1997;25(1):15-36.
363. Gifford LS. Tissue and input related mechanisms. In: Gifford LS, ed. *Topical Issues in Pain.* Falmouth: NOI Press; 1998.
364. Rabin BS. *Stress, Immune Function and Health.* New York: Wiley-Liss; 1999.
365. Vlaeyen JW, Crombez G, Linton SJ. The fear-avoidance model of pain. *Pain.* Aug 2016;157(8):1588-1589.
366. Sternberg WF, Bokat C, Kass L, Alboyadjian A, Gracely RH. Sex-dependent components of the analgesia produced by athletic competition. *The journal of pain: official journal of the American Pain Society.* Feb 2001;2(1):65-74.
367. Stabell A, Eide H, Solheim GA, Solberg KN, Rustoen T. Nursing home residents' dependence and independence. *Journal of clinical nursing.* Sep 2004;13(6): 677-686.
368. Taylor SS, Davis MC, Zautra AJ. Relationship status and quality moderate daily pain-related changes in physical disability, affect, and cognitions in women with chronic pain. *Pain.* Jan 2013;154(1):147-153.
369. Reese JB, Somers TJ, Keefe FJ, Mosley-Williams A, Lumley MA. Pain and functioning of rheumatoid arthritis patients based on marital status: is a distressed marriage preferable to no marriage? *The journal of pain: official journal of the American Pain Society.* Oct 2010;11(10):958-964.
370. Yacoub YI, Amine B, Laatiris A, Hajjaj-Hassouni N. Spinsterhood and its impact on disease features in women with rheumatoid arthritis. *Health Qual Life Outcomes.* 2011;9:58.
371. Teasell RW, Bombardier C. Employment-related factors in chronic pain and chronic pain disability. *The Clinical journal of pain.* Dec 2001;17(4 Suppl):S39-45.
372. Murrell SA, Meeks S. Psychological, economic, and social mediators of the education-health relationship in older adults. *Journal of aging and health.* Nov 2002;14(4):527-550.
373. Eisenberger NI, Lieberman MD, Williams KD. Does rejection hurt? An FMRI study of social exclusion. *Science.* Oct 10 2003;302(5643):290-292.
374. Singer T, Seymour B, O'Doherty JP, Stephan KE, Dolan RJ, Frith CD. Empathic neurall responses are modulated by the perceived fairness of others. *Nature* 2006;439:466-469.
375. Singer T, Seymour B, O'Doherty J, Kaube H, Dolan RJ, Frith CD. Empathy for pain imvolves the affective but not sensory components of pain. *Science.* 2004;303:1157-1162.
376. Alexander BK, Coambs RB, Hadaway PF. The effect of housing and gender on morphine self-administration in rats. *Psychopharmacology.* Jul 6 1978;58(2):175-179.
377. Robins LN. The sixth Thomas James Okey Memorial Lecture. Vietnam veterans' rapid recovery from heroin addiction: a fluke or normal expectation? *Addiction.* Aug 1993;88(8):1041-1054.
378. Bozikas VP, Kosmidis MH, Giannakou M, et al. Humor appreciation of captionless cartoons in obsessive-compulsive disorder. *Annals of general psychiatry.* Nov 21 2011;10(1):31.
379. Bokarius A, Ha K, Poland R, Bokarius V, Rapaport MH, Ishak WW. Attitude toward humor in patients experiencing depressive symptoms. *Innovations in clinical neuroscience.* Sep 2011;8(9): 20-23.
380. Falkenberg I, Jarmuzek J, Bartels M, Wild B. Do depressed patients lose their sense of humor? *Psychopathology.* 2011;44(2):98-105.
381. Puentedura EJ, Landers MR, Hurt K, Meissner M, Mills J, Young D. Immediate effects of lumbar spine manipulation on the resting and contraction thickness of transversus abdominis in asymptomatic individuals. *J Orthop Sports Phys Ther.* Jan 2011;41(1):13-21.
382. Maitland GD. *Vertebral Manipulation.* 6th ed. London: Butterworths; 1986.
383. Grieve GP. *Common Vertebral Joint Problems.* Edinburgh: Churchill Livingstone; 1981.
384. Linton SJ. The socioeconomic impact of chronic back pain: is anyone benefiting? *Pain.* Apr 1998;75(2-3):163-168.
385. Nijs J, Roussel N, Paul van Wilgen C, Koke A, Smeets R. Thinking beyond muscles and joints: Therapists' and patients' attitudes and beliefs regarding chronic musculoskeletal pain are key to applying effective treatment. *Manual therapy.* Dec 28 2012.
386. McKenzie R. *The Lumbar Spine.* Waikanae: Spinal Publications; 1981.
387. McRae M, Hancock MJ. Adults attending private physiotherapy practices seek diagnosis, pain relief, improved function, education and prevention: a survey. *J Physiother.* Oct 2017;63(4):250-256.

388. Verbeek J, Sengers MJ, Riemens L, Haafkens J. Patient expectations of treatment for back pain: a systematic review of qualitative and quantitative studies. *Spine*. Oct 15 2004;29(20): 2309-2318.
389. Hopayian K, Notley C. A systematic review of low back pain and sciatica patients' expectations and experiences of health care. *The spine journal : official journal of the North American Spine Society*. Aug 1 2014;14(8):1769-1780.
390. Louw A, Farrell K, Wettach L, Uhl J, Majkowski K, Welding M. Immediate effects of sensory discrimination for chronic low back pain: a case series. *New Zealand Journal of Physiotherapy*. 2015:60-65.
391. Louw A, Farrell K, Zimney K, et al. Pain and Decreased Range of Motion in Knees and Shoulders: A Brief Sensory Remapping Intervention. *Pain and Rehabilitation*. 2017;Summer(43):20-30.
392. Moseley GL, Zalucki NM, Wiech K. Tactile discrimination, but not tactile stimulation alone, reduces chronic limb pain. *Pain*. Jul 31 2008;137(3):600-608.
393. Louw A, Puentedura E, Nijs J. A Clinical Perspective on a Pain Neuroscience Education Approach to Manual Therapy. *Journal of Manual & Manipulative Therapy*. 2017.
394. Lluch Girbes E, Meeus M, Baert I, Nijs J. Balancing "hands-on" with "hands-off" physical therapy interventions for the treatment of central sensitization pain in osteoarthritis. *Manual therapy*. Apr 2015;20(2):349-352.
395. Coppieters MW, Stappaerts KH, Wouters LL, Janssens K. The immediate effects of a cervical lateral glide treatment technique in patients with neurogenic cervicobrachial pain. *J Orthop Sports Phys Ther*. Jul 2003;33(7):369-378.
396. Brochwicz P, von Piekartz H, Zalpour C. Sonography assessment of the median nerve during cervical lateral glide and lateral flexion. Is there a difference in neurodynamics of asymptomatic people? *Manual therapy*. Jun 2013;18(3): 216-219.
397. George SZ, Bishop MD, Bialosky JE, Zeppieri G, Jr., Robinson ME. Immediate effects of spinal manipulation on thermal pain sensitivity: an experimental study. *BMC musculoskeletal disorders*. 2006;7:68.
398. Melzack R. From the gate to the neuromatrix. *Pain*. Aug 1999;Suppl 6:S121-126.
399. Karason AB, Drysdale IP. Somatovisceral response following osteopathic HVLAT: a pilot study on the effect of unilateral lumbosacral high-velocity low-amplitude thrust technique on the cutaneous blood flow in the lower limb. *Journal of manipulative and physiological therapeutics*. May 2003;26(4):220-225.
400. Win NN, Jorgensen AM, Chen YS, Haneline MT. Effects of Upper and Lower Cervical Spinal Manipulative Therapy on Blood Pressure and Heart Rate Variability in Volunteers and Patients With Neck Pain: A Randomized Controlled, Cross-Over, Preliminary Study. *J Chiropr Med*. Mar 2015;14(1):1-9.
401. Bakhtadze MA, Vernon H, Karalkin AV, Pasha SP, Tomashevskiy IO, Soave D. Cerebral perfusion in patients with chronic neck and upper back pain: preliminary observations. *Journal of manipulative and physiological therapeutics*. Feb 2012;35(2):76-85.
402. de Araujo FX, Macagnan FE, Della Mea Plentz R, Silva MF. Autonomic effects after anterior-to-posterior cervical mobilization. *J Orthop Sports Phys Ther*. Jan 2015;45(1):46-47.
403. McGuiness J, Vicenzino B, Wright A. Influence of a cervical mobilization technique on respiratory and cardiovascular function. *Manual therapy*. Nov 1997;2(4):216-220.
404. Jowsey P, Perry J. Sympathetic nervous system effects in the hands following a grade III postero-anterior rotatory mobilisation technique applied to T4: a randomised, placebo-controlled trial. *Manual therapy*. Jun 2010;15(3): 248-253.
405. McGlone F, Cerritelli F, Walker S, Esteves J. The role of gentle touch in perinatal osteopathic manual therapy. *Neuroscience and biobehavioral reviews*. Jan 2017;72:1-9.
406. Twomey LT. A rationale for the treatment of back pain and joint pain by manual therapy. *Physical therapy*. Dec 1992;72(12):885-892.
407. Sato K, Kikuchi S, Yonezawa T. In vivo intradiscal pressure measurement in healthy individuals and in patients with ongoing back problems. *Spine*. Dec 1 1999;24(23):2468-2474.
408. McNair PJ, Portero P, Chiquet C, Mawston G, Lavaste F. Acute neck pain: cervical spine range of motion and position sense prior to and after joint mobilization. *Manual therapy*. Nov 2007;12(4): 390-394.

409. Puentedura EJ, Cleland JA, Landers MR, Mintken PE, Louw A, Fernandez-de-Las-Penas C. Development of a clinical prediction rule to identify patients with neck pain likely to benefit from thrust joint manipulation to the cervical spine. *J Orthop Sports Phys Ther.* 2012;42(7):577-592.
410. Raney NH, Teyhen DS, Childs JD. Observed changes in lateral abdominal muscle thickness after spinal manipulation: a case series using rehabilitative ultrasound imaging. *J Orthop Sports Phys Ther.* Aug 2007;37(8):472-479.
411. McClatchie L, Laprade J, Martin S, Jaglal SB, Richardson D, Agur A. Mobilizations of the asymptomatic cervical spine can reduce signs of shoulder dysfunction in adults. *Manual therapy.* Aug 2009;14(4):369-374.
412. Dunning J, Rushton A. The effects of cervical high-velocity low-amplitude thrust manipulation on resting electromyographic activity of the biceps brachii muscle. *Manual therapy.* Oct 2009;14(5):508-513.
413. Boyles RE, Ritland BM, Miracle BM, et al. The short-term effects of thoracic spine thrust manipulation on patients with shoulder impingement syndrome. *Manual therapy.* Aug 2009;14(4): 375-380.
414. Grindstaff TL, Hertel J, Beazell JR, Magrum EM, Ingersoll CD. Effects of lumbopelvic joint manipulation on quadriceps activation and strength in healthy individuals. *Manual therapy.* Aug 2009;14(4):415-420.
415. Hoving JL, de Vet HC, Koes BW, et al. Manual therapy, physical therapy, or continued care by the general practitioner for patients with neck pain: long-term results from a pragmatic randomized clinical trial. *The Clinical journal of pain.* May 2006;22(4):370-377.
416. United Kingdom back pain exercise and manipulation (UK BEAM) randomised trial: cost effectiveness of physical treatments for back pain in primary care. *Bmj.* Dec 11 2004;329(7479):1381.
417. Childs JD, Fritz JM, Flynn TW, et al. A clinical prediction rule to identify patients with low back pain most likely to benefit from spinal manipulation: a validation study. *Ann Intern Med.* Dec 21 2004;141(12):920-928.
418. Flynn TW, Smith B, Chou R. Appropriate use of diagnostic imaging in low back pain: a reminder that unnecessary imaging may do as much harm as good. *J Orthop Sports Phys Ther.* Nov 2011;41(11):838-846.
419. Iversen MD, Chhabriya RK, Shadick N. Predictors of the use of physical therapy services among patients with rheumatoid arthritis. *Physical therapy.* Jan 2011;91(1):65-76.
420. Bayer TL, Baer PE, Early C. Situational and psychophysiological factors in psychologically induced pain. *Pain.* 1991;44(1):45-50.
421. Louw A, Zimney K, Landers M, Luttrell M, Clair B, Mills J. A randomised controlled trial of "clockwise" ultrasound for low back pain. *South African Journal of Physiotherapy.* 2016;72(1).
422. Khadilkar A, Milne S, Brosseau L, et al. Transcutaneous electrical nerve stimulation for the treatment of chronic low back pain: a systematic review. *Spine.* Dec 1 2005;30(23):2657-2666.
423. Evcik D, Yigit I, Pusak H, Kavuncu V. Effectiveness of aquatic therapy in the treatment of fibromyalgia syndrome: a randomized controlled open study. *Rheumatol Int.* Jul 2008;28(9):885-890.
424. Louw A, Puentedura EL, Mintken P. Use of an abbreviated neuroscience education approach in the treatment of chronic low back pain: A case report. *Physiother Theory Pract.* Jul 3 2011.
425. Louw A, Puentedura EL, Mintken P. Use of an abbreviated neuroscience education approach in the treatment of chronic low back pain: a case report. *Physiother Theory Pract.* Jan 2012;28(1):50-62.
426. Pires D, Cruz EB, Caeiro C. Aquatic exercise and pain neurophysiology education versus aquatic exercise alone for patients with chronic low back pain: a randomized controlled trial. *Clin Rehabil.* Jun 2015;29(6):538-547.
427. Fuentes J, Armijo-Olivo S, Funabashi M, et al. Enhanced therapeutic alliance modulates pain intensity and muscle pain sensitivity in patients with chronic low back pain: an experimental controlled study. *Physical therapy.* Apr 2014;94(4):477-489.
428. Schmidt SG. Recognizing potential barriers to setting and achieving effective rehabilitation goals for patients with persistent pain. *Physiother Theory Pract.* Jul 2016;32(5):415-426.
429. de Jong JR, Vlaeyen JW, Onghena P, Cuypers C, den Hollander M, Ruijgrok J. Reduction of pain-related fear in complex regional pain syndrome type I: the application of graded exposure in vivo. *Pain.* Aug 2005;116(3):264-275.

430. de Jong JR, Vangronsveld K, Peters ML, et al. Reduction of pain-related fear and disability in post-traumatic neck pain: a replicated single-case experimental study of exposure in vivo. *The journal of pain: official journal of the American Pain Society.* Dec 2008;9(12):1123-1134.
431. George SZ, Zeppieri G. Physical therapy utilization of graded exposure for patients with low back pain. *J Orthop Sports Phys Ther.* Jul 2009;39(7):496-505.
432. Goudsmit EM, Nijs J, Jason LA, Wallman KE. Pacing as a strategy to improve energy management in myalgic encephalomyelitis/chronic fatigue syndrome: a consensus document. *Disabil Rehabil.* 2012;34(13): 1140-1147.
433. Gladwell P. A practical guide to goalsetting. In: Gifford LS, ed. *Topical Issues in Pain 5.* Falmouth: CNS Press; 2006.
434. Flor H, Braun C, Elbert T, Birmbaumer N. Extensive reorganisation of primary somatosensory cortex in chronic back pain patients. *Neuroscience letters.* 1997;244:5-8.
435. Maihofner C, Handwerker HO, Neundorfer B, Birklein F. Patterns of cortical reorganization in complex regional pain syndrome. *Neurology.* Dec 23 2003;61(12):1707-1715.
436. Moseley GL. I can't find it! Distorted body image and tactile dysfunction in patients with chronic back pain. *Pain.* Nov 15 2008;140(1):239-243.
437. Lotze M, Moseley GL. Role of distorted body image in pain. *Curr Rheumatol Rep.* Dec 2007;9(6):488-496.
438. Moseley GL. Distorted body image in complex regional pain syndrome. *Neurology.* Sep 13 2005;65(5):773.
439. Flor H, Elbert T, Muhnickel W, Pantev C. Cortical reorganisation and phantom phenomena in congenital and traumatic upper-extremity amputees. *Experimental Brain Research.* 1998;119:205-212.
440. Lloyd D, Findlay G, Roberts N, Nurmikko T. Differences in low back pain behavior are reflected in the cerebral response to tactile stimulation of the lower back. *Spine.* May 20 2008;33(12):1372-1377.
441. Flor H, Braun C, Elbert T, Birbaumer N. Extensive reorganization of primary somatosensory cortex in chronic back pain patients. *Neuroscience letters.* 1997;224(1):5-8.
442. Moseley GL. Graded motor imagery is effective for long-standing complex regional pain syndrome: a randomised controlled trial. *Pain.* Mar 2004;108(1-2):192-198.
443. Moseley GL. Graded motor imagery for pathologic pain: a randomized controlled trial. *Neurology.* Dec 26 2006;67(12):2129-2134.
444. Daly AE, Bialocerkowski AE. Does evidence support physiotherapy management of adult Complex Regional Pain Syndrome Type One? A systematic review. *European journal of pain* (London, England). Apr 2009;13(4):339-353.
445. Bowering KJ, O'Connell NE, Tabor A, et al. The effects of graded motor imagery and its components on chronic pain: a systematic review and meta-analysis. *The Journal of Pain.* 2013;14(1):3-13.
446. Louw A, Farrell K, Wettach L, Uhl J, Majkowski K, Wedling M. Immediate effects of sensory discrimination for chronic low back pain: a case series. *New Zealand Journal of Physiotherapy.* 2015;43(2):58-63.
447. Louw A, Schmidt SG, Louw C, Puentedura EJ. Moving without moving: immediate management following lumbar spine surgery using a graded motor imagery approach: a case report. *Physiother Theory Pract.* Oct 2015;31(7):509-517.
448. Wand BM, Tulloch VM, George PJ, et al. Seeing It Helps: Movement-related Back Pain Is Reduced by Visualization of the Back During Movement. *The Clinical journal of pain.* Sep 2012;28(7): 602-608.
449. Moseley GL. Using visual illusion to reduce at-level neuropathic pain in paraplegia. *Pain.* Aug 2007;130(3): 294-298.
450. Louw A, Puentedura EJ, Reese D, Parker P, Miller T, Mintken PE. Immediate Effects of Mirror Therapy in Patients With Shoulder Pain and Decreased Range of Motion. *Arch Phys Med Rehabil.* May 05 2017.
451. Fercho KA, Baugh LA, Louw A, Zimney K. Pain Neuroscience Education Effect on Pain Matrix Processing in an Individual with Complex Regional Pain Syndrome: A Single Subject Research Design. *European Pain Journal.* 2017 - Submitted for publication.
452. Louw A, Louw C, Zimney K. *Why Are My Nerves So Sensitive?* Minneapolis, MN: OPTP; 2014.
453. Moseley GL. Why do people with complex regional pain syndrome take longer to recognize their affected hand? *Neurology.* Jun 22 2004;62(12):2182-2186.

454. Moseley GL, Sim DF, Henry ML, Souvlis T. Experimental hand pain delays recognition of the contralateral hand – evidence that acute and chronic pain have opposite effects on information processing? Brain research. *Cognitive brain research.* Sep 2005;25(1): 188-194.

455. Bray H, Moseley GL. Disrupted working body schema of the trunk in people with back pain. *British journal of sports medicine.* Mar 2011;45(3):168-173.

456. Catley MJ, Tabor A, Wand BM, Moseley GL. Assessing tactile acuity in rheumatology and musculoskeletal medicine – how reliable are two-point discrimination tests at the neck, hand, back and foot? *Rheumatology.* Aug 2013;52(8):1454-1461.

457. Moseley GL, Butler DS, Beames TB, Giles TJ. *The Graded Motor Imagery Handbook.* Adelaide Noigroup Publications; 2012.

458. Shacklock M. Neurodynamics. *Physiotherapy.* 1995;81:9-16.

459. Louw A, Mintken P, Puentedura L. Neuophysiologic Effects of Neural Mobilization Maneuvers. In: Fernandez-De_Las_Penas C, Arendt-Nielsen L, Gerwin RD, eds. *Tension-type and Cervicogenic Headache.* Boston: Jones and Bartlett; 2009:231-245.

460. Nee RJ, Butler D, S. Management of peripheral neuropathic pain: integrating neurobiology, neurodynamics and clinical evidence. *Physical Therapy in Sport.* 2006;7:36-49.

461. Butler DS. *The Sensitive Nervous System.* Adelaide: Noigroup Publications; 2000.

462. Coppieters MW, Butler DS. Do 'sliders' slide and 'tensioners' tension? An analysis of neurodynamic techniques and considerations regarding their application. *Manual Ther.* 2007;doi:10.1016/j.math.2006.12.008.

463. Shacklock M. *Clinical Neurodynamics.* Edinburgh: Elsevier; 2005.

464. Butler DS. *Mobilization of the Nervous System.* London: Churchill Livingstone; 1991.

465. Breig A. *Adverse Mechanical Tension in the Central Nervous System.* Stockholm: Almqvist and Wiksell; 1978.

466. Coppieters MW, Bartholomeeusen KE, Stappaerts KH. Incorporating nerve-gliding techniques in the conservative treatment of cubital tunnel syndrome. *J Manipulative Physiol Ther.* Nov-Dec 2004;27(9):560-568.

467. Byl NN, Melnick M. The neural consequences of repetition: clinical implications of a learning hypothesis. *J Hand Ther.* Apr-Jun 1997;10(2): 160-174.

468. Coveney B, Trott P, Grimmer K. "The upper limb tension test in a group of subjects with a clinical presentation of carpal tunnel syndrome." Paper presented at: Tenth Biennial Conference: Manipulative Physiotherapists Association of Australia1997; Melbourne.

469. Greening J, Smart S, Leary R, Hall-Craggs M, O'Higgins P, Lynn B. Reduced movement of median nerve in carpal tunnel during wrist flexion in patients with non-specific arm pain.[see comment]. *Lancet.* Jul 17 1999;354(9174): 217-218.

470. Mackinnon SE. Double and multiple "crush" syndromes. Double and multiple entrapment neuropathies. *Hand Clin.* May 1992;8(2):369-390.

471. Nakamichi K, Tachibana S. Restricted motion of the median nerve in carpal tunnel syndrome. *J Hand Surg [Br].* Aug 1995;20(4):460-464.

472. Rozmaryn LM, Dovelle S, Rothman ER, Gorman K, Olvey KM, Bartko JJ. Nerve and tendon gliding exercises and the conservative management of carpal tunnel syndrome. *J Hand Ther.* Jul-Sep 1998;11(3):171-179.

473. Siddiqui M, Karadimas E, Nicol M, Smith FW, Wardlaw D. Influence of X Stop on neural foramina and spinal canal area in spinal stenosis. *Spine.* Dec 1 2006;31(25):2958-2962.

474. Fritz JM, Delitto A, Welch WC, Erhard RE. Lumbar spinal stenosis: a review of current concepts in evaluation, management, and outcome measurements. *Archives of Physical Medicine & Rehabilitation.* Jun 1998;79(6):700-708.

475. Chang S-B, Lee S-H, Ahn Y, Kim J-M. Risk factor for unsatisfactory outcome after lumbar foraminal and far lateral microdecompression. *Spine.* May 1 2006;31(10):1163-1167.

476. de Peretti F, Micalef JP, Bourgeon A, Argenson C, Rabischong P. Biomechanics of the lumbar spinal nerve roots and the first sacral root within the intervertebral foramina. *Surg Radiol Anat.* 1989;11(3):221-225.

477. Wright TW, Glowczewskie F, Jr., Cowin D, Wheeler DL. Ulnar nerve excursion and strain at the elbow and wrist associated with upper extremity motion. *J Hand Surg [Am].* Jul 2001;26(4):655-662.

478. Beith ID, Robins, E J and Richards, P R An assessment of the adaptive mechanisms within and surrounding the peripheral nervous system, during changes in nerve bed length resulting from underlying joint movement. In: Shacklock MO, ed. *Moving in on Pain.* Australia: Butterworth-Heinemann; 1995.

479. Dilley A, Lynn B, Greening J, DeLeon N. Quantitative in vivo studies of median nerve sliding in response to wrist, elbow, shoulder and neck movements. *Clin Biomech.* Dec 2003;18(10):899-907.
480. Breig A. *Biomechanics of the central nervous system.* Stockholm: Almqvist and Wiksell; 1960.
481. Troup JDG. Biomechanics of the lumbar spinal canal. *Clin Biomech (Bristol, Avon).* 1986;1:31-43.
482. Millesi H, Zoch G, Reihsner R. Mechanical properties of peripheral nerves. *Clin Orthop.* May 1995(314):76-83.
483. Coppieters MW, Butler DS. Do 'sliders' slide and 'tensioners' tension? An analysis of neurodynamic techniques and considerations regarding their application. *Manual therapy.* Mar 29 2007.
484. Greening J, Dilley A, Lynn B. In vivo study of nerve movement and mechanosensitivity of the median nerve in whiplash and non-specific arm pain patients. *Pain.* Jun 2005;115(3): 248-253.
485. Erel E, Dilley A, Greening J, Morris V, Lynn B. Longitudinal sliding of the median nerve in the forearm during fin ger movements in n ormal subjects and in patietns with carpal tunnel syndrome. *Journal of Hand Surgery (Br).* 2003;28:439-444.
486. Dilley A, Lynn B, Greening J, al. E. Quantitative in vivo studies of median nerve sliding in response to wrist, elbow, shoulder and neck movements. *Clin Biomech* (Bristol, Avon). 2003;18: 899-907.
487. Greening J, Lynn B, Leary R, Warren L, O'Higgins P, Hall-Craggs M. The use of ultrasound imaging to demonstrate reduced movement of the median nerve during wrist flexion in patients with non-specific arm pain. *J Hand Surg [Br].* Oct 2001;26(5):401-406; discussion 407-408.
488. Greening J, Smart S, Leary R, Hall-Craggs M, O'Higgins P, Lynn B. Reduced movement of median nerve in carpal tunnel during wrist flexion in patients with non-specific arm pain. *Lancet.* Jul 17 1999;354(9174):217-218.
489. Dommisse GF. The blood supply of the spinal cord and the consequences of failure. In: Boyling J, Palastanga N, eds. *Grieve's Modern Manual Therapy.* 2nd ed. Edinburgh: Churchill Livingstone; 1994.
490. Lundborg G, Rydevik B. Effects of stretching the tibial nerve of the rabbit. A preliminary study of the intraneural circulation and the barrier function of the perineurium. *J Bone Joint Surg Br.* May 1973;55(2):390-401.
491. Ogata K, Naito M. Blood flow of peripheral nerve: effects of dissection, stretching and compression. *J Hand Surg [Am].* 1986;11B(1):10-14.
492. Nijs J, Van Houdenhove B, Oostendorp RA. Recognition of central sensitization in patients with musculoskeletal pain: Application of pain neurophysiology in manual therapy practice. *Manual therapy.* Apr 2010;15(2):135-141.
493. Smart KM, Blake C, Staines A, Thacker M, Doody C. Mechanisms-based classifications of musculoskeletal pain: Part 2 of 3: Symptoms and signs of peripheral neuropathic pain in patients with low back (+/-leg) pain. *Manual therapy.* Aug 2012;17(4):345-351.
494. Nee RJ, Vicenzino B, Jull GA, Cleland JA, Coppieters MW. Neural tissue management provides immediate clinically relevant benefits without harmful effects for patients with nerve-related neck and arm pain: a randomised trial. *J Physiother.* 2012;58(1):23-31.
495. Ellis RF, Hing WA. Neural mobilization: a systematic review of randomized controlled trials with an analysis of therapeutic efficacy. *The Journal of manual & manipulative therapy.* 2008;16(1):8-22.
496. Shacklock M. Neural mobilization: a systematic review of randomized controlled trials with an analysis of therapeutic efficacy. *The Journal of manual & manipulative therapy.* 2008;16(1):23-24.
497. Moseley G. Combined physiotherapy and education is efficacious for chronic low back pain. *Aust J Physio.* 2002;48: 297-302.
498. Beltran-Alacreu H, López-de-Uralde-Villanueva I, Fernández-Carnero J, La Touche R. Manual Therapy, Therapeutic Patient Education, and Therapeutic Exercise, an Effective Multimodal Treatment of Nonspecific Chronic Neck Pain: A Randomized Controlled Trial. *American journal of physical medicine & rehabilitation/Association of Academic Physiatrists.* 2015.
499. Vanti C, Andreatta S, Borghi S, Guccione AA, Pillastrini P, Bertozzi L. The effectiveness of walking versus exercise on pain and function in chronic low back pain: a systematic review and meta-analysis of randomized trials. *Disabil Rehabil.* Dec 5 2017:1-11.
500. Louw A, Flynn TW, Puentedura E. *Everyone Has Back Pain.* Minneapolis, MN: OPTP; 2015.

Chapter 7

PNE and Beyond...

7.5: Shoulder Surgery

Following the development and testing of the LS and TKA PNE programs, attention shifted to shoulder surgery. The LS and TKA material has been adapted for shoulder surgery,[36] and is being trialed at this time. Look for results in journal articles sometime in the future.

7.6: Acute and Sub-Acute LBP

The majority of the preemptive PNE has focused on surgery. In line with the proposed screening processes for LBP, i.e., Keele STarT Back Screening Tool (SBST), it could be argued that patients presenting with acute or sub-acute LBP, meeting certain criteria, may in fact also be primed for PNE. As an example of this, we published a case study involving a nursing aide presenting with acute LBP after an injury lifting a patient:[37]

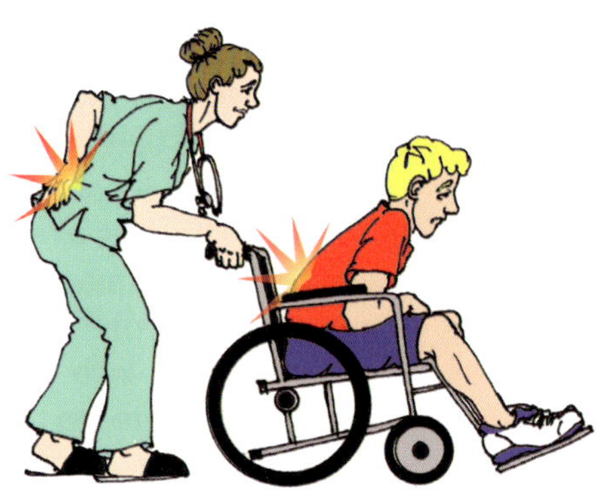

- Immediate onset of pain in her right low back region with some pain spreading into the right leg (Figure 7.7).
- The occupational medicine physician evaluated her and diagnosed her with a "lumbar strain" and right lower extremity radicular pain.
- She was provided with 800 milligrams of Ibuprofen, to be taken four times a day.
- She continued at her work with restrictions of no lifting more than 10 pounds, and no bending or twisting.

When contemplating group PNE, some practical guidelines are as follows:

- Two studies incorporating PNE group sessions consisted of 20 and 30 patients, respectively.[79,80] Given the individual nature of pain, it is argued that smaller group sizes are more likely to be successful. As to what the optimal group size is, psychology research suggests the maximum group size as 10-12 people. If a group is too large, patients might not be engaged. The ideal size would allow the maximum number of patients to successfully participate, and also keep the content personally relevant for each attendee.

- It is recommended patients be "like-minded." Biologically, problems with pain in different body regions might share a common representation within the pain neuromatrix. There are likely some nuances between someone struggling with chronic LBP, fibromyalgia, failed back surgery syndrome or chronic fatigue syndrome. If all these types of patients attend a single "pain group" there might be a disconnect and thus some patients might not engage. If, however, the group session is geared to only people with chronic low back pain, there would likely be enough overlap to allow for a common discussion and application of PNE.

- There are obviously many unknowns regarding group PNE. Given the extensive screening process we covered in section 5.2, it could even be argued that the more complicated cases (high risk – i.e., Keele SBST) should be considered for individualized PNE, while the moderate and lower risk patients be treated with group PNE.

- **PNE Homework:** The future of healthcare is to teach people how to help themselves, and this includes people with chronic pain. There are so many reasons for this approach. First, the concept of "fixing" pain might be a biologic fallacy, especially when it comes to the complex problem of chronic pain. Pain can get better (Chapter 2), but it takes work, lots of work.

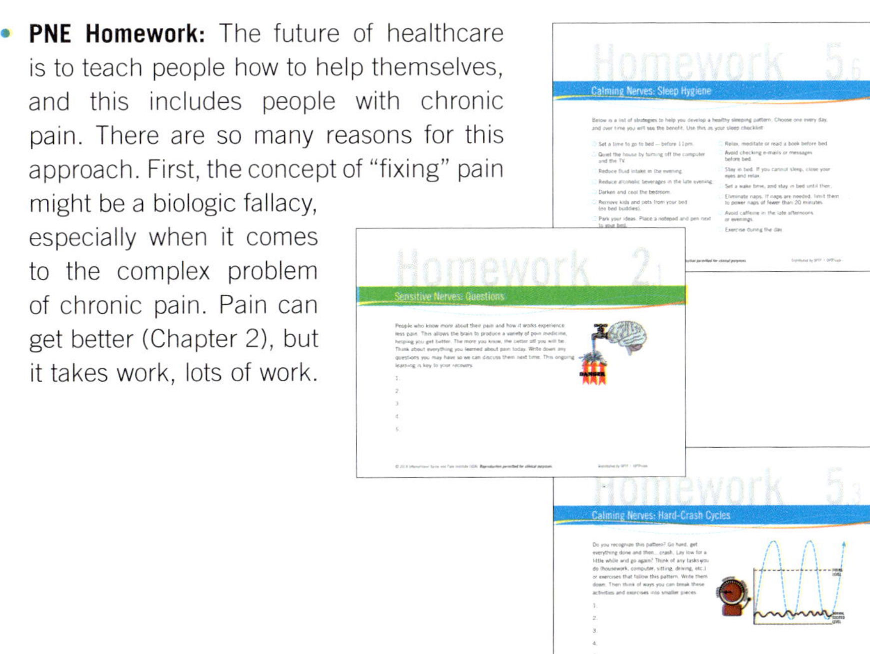

Pros	Cons
• Deliver PNE efficiently to large groups of patients. • Less push back and resistance from individual patients who might otherwise be resistant to the information. • Group dynamic can add to the learning process.	• In order to bill, an evaluation is need for each patient. • Coordinating the scheduling of each group class. • Appropriately capturing charges for the time spent with patients.

The Intensive Pain Management Class

- Six weeks, meeting two days a week, five hours a day.
- Class size is limited to 12 and includes both females and males.
- The class consists of three hours of treatment with health psychology and two hours with physical therapy. Health psychology treatment is from 9am to 12pm, and physical therapy treatment is from 1pm to 3pm.
- The overall goals for the physical therapy portion are to improve understanding of pain physiology, improve functional level of activity, decrease pain symptoms, decrease kinesiophobia, and improve mobility.
- To accomplish this, the class includes a lecture portion, cardiovascular activity, education and performance of therapeutic exercises, and education and performance of fundamental concepts.
- During the first and eleventh treatment session, pre and post tests are performed. This testing includes the Roland Morris Disability Questionnaire (RMDQ) and TSK, Timed Up and Go (TUG) test, video analysis of standing trunk active range of motion, and filling in a body diagram of pain.
- Pre and post-testing results are discussed with the patients as a group and/or individually in order to provide feedback regarding improvements.
- In regard to PNE, the class focuses on key pain science education concepts.
- Each patient begins week two with five minutes of cardiovascular activity (treadmill, bicycle, recumbent bike, Nu Step™ or arm ergometer) and uses graded exposure to progress to 20 minutes on the final day of the group.
- Treatment intensity and heart rate are recorded each time, and this information is used for feedback to encourage patients to gradually increase their intensity and assist with their understanding of perceived exertion.

Second, with the ever-increasing cost of healthcare, there is a strong mandate to empower patients to help themselves. The basic premise is that the world's economic resources are getting stretched more and more for healthcare, thus signaling a huge philosophical shift. Third, if we contemplate the idea that chronic pain problems are also large scale behavioral problems[89] and behavior change needs to come "from within," the patient must play a crucial role in their own recovery. This all implies a significant shift from the patient not being "fixed" to being part of the solution. In a PNE approach, this involves the use of PNE homework to reinforce learned concepts. Once the patient has been exposed to PNE, it is best to follow up on the PNE session by having the patient complete and return with cognitive homework. The various PNE stories lend themselves to a variety of homework tasks. Figure 5.12 showcases some examples, as well as Table 5.5.[90]

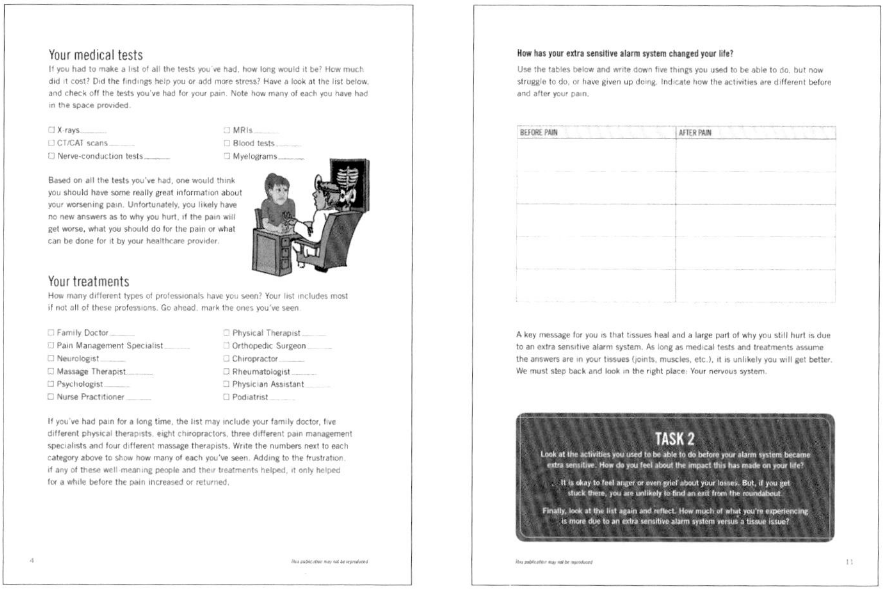

Your medical tests

If you had to make a list of all the tests you've had, how long would it be? How much did it cost? Did the findings help you or add more stress? Have a look at the list below, and check off the tests you've had for your pain. Note how many of each you have had in the space provided.

- ☐ X-rays____
- ☐ CT/CAT scans____
- ☐ Nerve-conduction tests____
- ☐ MRIs____
- ☐ Blood tests____
- ☐ Myelograms____

Based on all the tests you've had, one would think you should have some really great information about your worsening pain. Unfortunately, you likely have no new answers as to why you hurt, if the pain will get worse, what you should do for the pain or what can be done for it by your healthcare provider.

Your treatments

How many different types of professionals have you seen? Your list includes most if not all of these professions. Go ahead, mark the ones you've seen.

- ☐ Family Doctor____
- ☐ Pain Management Specialist____
- ☐ Neurologist____
- ☐ Massage Therapist____
- ☐ Psychologist____
- ☐ Nurse Practitioner____
- ☐ Physical Therapist____
- ☐ Orthopedic Surgeon____
- ☐ Chiropractor____
- ☐ Rheumatologist____
- ☐ Physician Assistant____
- ☐ Podiatrist____

If you've had pain for a long time, the list may include your family doctor, five different physical therapists, eight chiropractors, three different pain management specialists and four different massage therapists. Write the numbers next to each category above to show how many of each you've seen. Adding to the frustration, if any of these well-meaning people and their treatments helped, it only helped for a while before the pain increased or returned.

4 This publication may not be reproduced

How has your extra sensitive alarm system changed your life?

Use the tables below and write down five things you used to be able to do, but now struggle to do, or have given up doing. Indicate how the activities are different before and after your pain.

BEFORE PAIN	AFTER PAIN

A key message for you is that tissues heal and a large part of why you still hurt is due to an extra sensitive alarm system. As long as medical tests and treatments assume the answers are in your tissues (joints, muscles, etc.), it is unlikely you will get better. We must step back and look in the right place: Your nervous system.

TASK 2

Look at the activities you used to be able to do before your alarm system became extra sensitive. How do you feel about the impact this has made on your life?

It is okay to feel anger or even grief about your losses. But, if you get stuck there, you are unlikely to find an exit from the roundabout.

Finally, look at the list again and reflect. How much of what you're experiencing is more due to an extra sensitive alarm system versus a tissue issue?

This publication may not be reproduced 11

Figure 5.12: Examples of deliberate PNE homework. From Louw.[90]

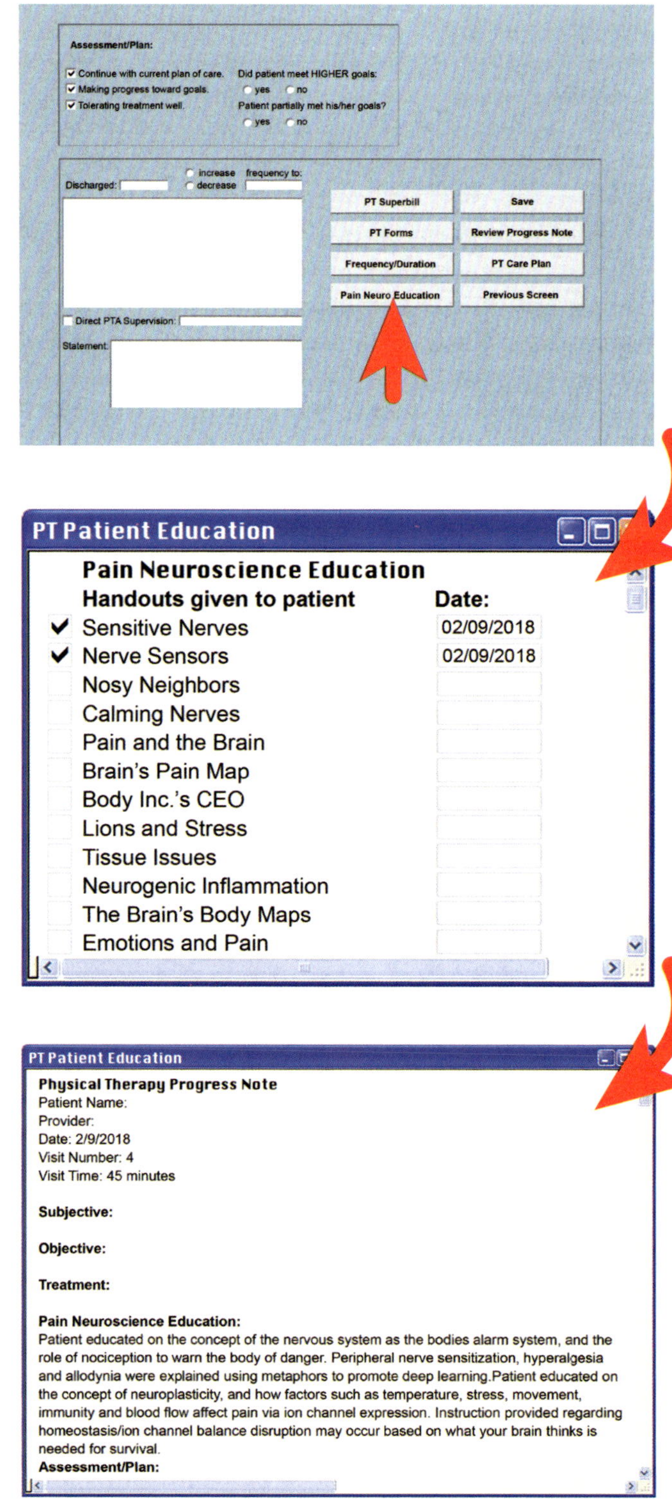

Figure 5.14: PNE in an EMR showcasing how PNE stories are selected and posted into the patient notes.

5.7: Training Clinic Staff

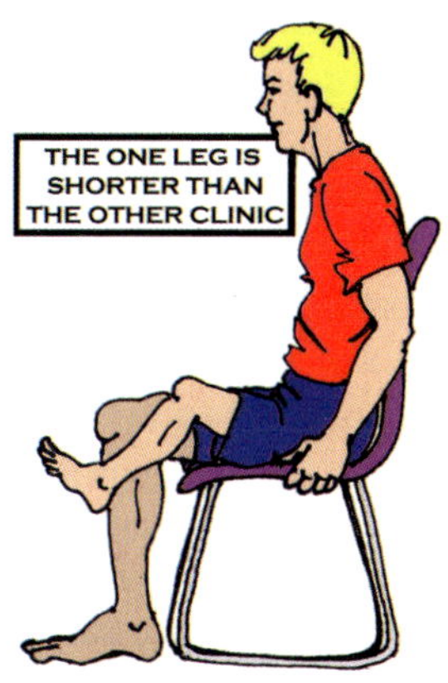

Clinicians should not underestimate the Cartesian and biomedical model's influence on how patients view pain. Utilizing PNE as a treatment is a relatively new concept and support is needed to help engrain the PNE conceptual change message. This also pertains to training clinic staff. If there is only one therapist in a clinic performing PNE and the rest of the clinicians follow a stringent biomedical model, it will no doubt be an uphill battle for the PNE-trained clinician. Imagine spending considerable time trying to reconceptualize a patient's thoughts and beliefs about pain. You take a few days off for vacation and your colleague covering for you turns to your patient and says, "*The reason you hurt all over your body is that one leg is shorter than the other.*" Upon return, surely the job will be even harder trying to reengage the patient into the PNE message. In a perfect world, everyone in the clinic should be trained in PNE at some level. This should span from the front desk (administrative staff), to ancillary support personnel all the way to the pain specialist. A proposed ideal situation would be a pyramid approach:

- **Pain specialist:** As clinicians are exposed to PNE, some might find the new pain science material a life-changing experience and even a calling. In any approach, i.e., manual therapy, there is a need for specialists. Examples include fellows, residents or clinical specialists. This clinician is truly a specialist with significant higher levels of training, beyond PNE. For a pain specialist this might include PNE, advanced PNE, neurodynamics, graded motor imagery, motivational interviewing, cognitive behavioral therapy, etc. These clinicians will become the "designated hitters" and thus be involved in:
    - Assessing and treating the more complicated cases
    - Training other staff

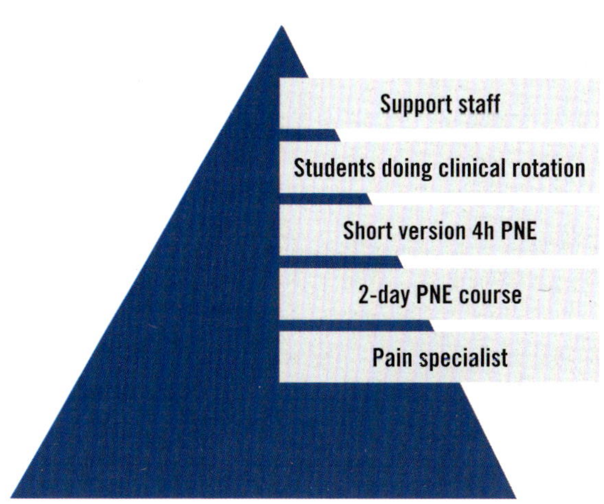

5.8: PNE Clinical Tools

The evidence for PNE calls for the use of pictures, metaphors and examples that maximize effectiveness.[1,2] A quick glance at Chapter 4 should make you realize you need some images to help convey the PNE message. Humans are very visually orientated, therefore having access to compelling visual aids can greatly enhance the comprehension, retention and usefulness of PNE.[106] The good news is that as PNE develops and grows, more clinical tools are being developed. This includes textbooks,[12,55,61,107,108] patient-focused books,[109-113] PNE educational flash cards,[96] posters, workbooks,[90,114] etc. Apart from the commercially available products, clinicians might also consider developing their own clinical tools. For example, for years, prior to the development of these resources, students were encouraged to find images of various PNE-related concepts, print them in color and put them in a binder as a PNE resource. For example, showing a patient a picture of an ankle sprain and then a speeding bus can help facilitate the discussion of pain as an output of the brain. The binder might include pictures of:

- ☐ Ankle sprain
- ☐ NPQ and rNPQ
- ☐ Whole body nervous system
- ☐ Aging versus low back pain
- ☐ Brain with flags
- ☐ Car alarm
- ☐ Alarm thresholds
- ☐ Airport security levels
- ☐ Neighborhood
- ☐ Pain versus function
- ☐ Car with flat tire
- ☐ Airline map
- ☐ Pain versus tissue healing
- ☐ Cup
- ☐ Speeding bus
- ☐ Action potential
- ☐ Christmas tree
- ☐ Lion
- ☐ Homunculus
- ☐ Car dashboard
- ☐ Sunburn
- ☐ Military base
- ☐ Boom bust cycle
- ☐ Pain acknowledgement scale
- ☐ Four pillars of recovery
- ☐ Organizational chart
- ☐ Bowl of soup and pepper
- ☐ Roundabout
- ☐ fMRI of the brain in pain
- ☐ Rusted nail
- ☐ Amazing X-rays
- ☐ Lion cub
- ☐ Visual illusions
- ☐ House alarm
- ☐ Radar screen
- ☐ Apartment building
- ☐ Spider picture
- ☐ Toblerone®
- ☐ Pain neuromatrix
- ☐ M.O.M. (Gifford)[3]
- ☐ Mirror box

Given the importance of visual feedback and the individualized nature of pain, it is highly recommended clinics have available dry-erase boards or flip charts for clinicians to draw various aspects of PNE (i.e., sensitive alarm). As clinicians become more and more adept at performing PNE in clinical settings, they will move away from commercially designed educational tools versus personalization of the information, i.e., drawings. For homework, it is not uncommon to take a picture of the drawing, print it out and ask a patient to take it and reflect on it at home prior to the next session. It is also not uncommon to store a similar picture of the drawing in a chart as a means to have a reference point at the next visit for the attending clinician.

An added clinical tool would be the use of PNE-specific posters. Even though it is a passive tool, clinicians might utilize the posters as a teaching tool as well. A second, more subliminal result of clinical PNE posters is that it might stimulate conversation with a patient. For example, while doing exercises with a patient, a clinical poster showcasing a "sensitive alarm system" might have the patient ask the clinician what the poster is about. This would then open the opportunity to discuss the various aspects of a sensitized nervous system including central sensitization, allodynia and hyperalgesia, with the conversation being initiated by the patient. Finally, in line with staff training and the power of the biomedical model, it is also imperative to consider "dethreatening" the current outpatient PT clinic by removing provocative posters, anatomical charts and scary joint models with patho-anatomical messages. Instead of displaying plastic anatomical models with "red" areas indicating swelling and bleeding, it might be best to have these available for the correct patient, but stored in a cabinet versus prominently displayed.

As mentioned in pain ratings, it has been shown that focusing on function versus pain results in superior outcomes.[118] Figure 5.15 highlights a very significant way to show patients their projected recovery.[7] The long-term studies on PNE showcase pain easing steadily over time.[10,57,119] The fact that pain is so closely linked to emotions would furthermore imply a normal daily and weekly "up and down" oscillation (Toblerone®), but overall a downward trend. Similarly, the long-term PNE studies demonstrate improvements in function over time.[10,57,119] The important aspect is that function would, over time, override pain and allow a patient to move on with life "despite the pain." This shift toward a focus on function is considered the holy grail of PNE and describes a true behavioral shift.[120,121] In any chronic condition the ultimate success is a true behavioral shift. The smoker should stop smoking. The overweight person needs to eat differently and exercise more. Given that chronic pain is a biologic state that cannot instantly be ceased, the true change is to get moving and functioning at a higher level despite pain. Clinically, a very helpful strategy is to use a visual representation of a predicted recovery pathway (such as Figure 5.15) as a teaching tool to reinforce the treatment plan objectives. The clinician can quickly draw this during the patient session, and then provide them with a printed version to place around their daily life as a reminder (e.g. office, refrigerator at home, etc.). This will allow patients to keep an eye on the goal of better function and have a broader perspective of the problem. If they become discouraged by their ongoing challenges with pain, the graph can help them refocus on the overall goal.

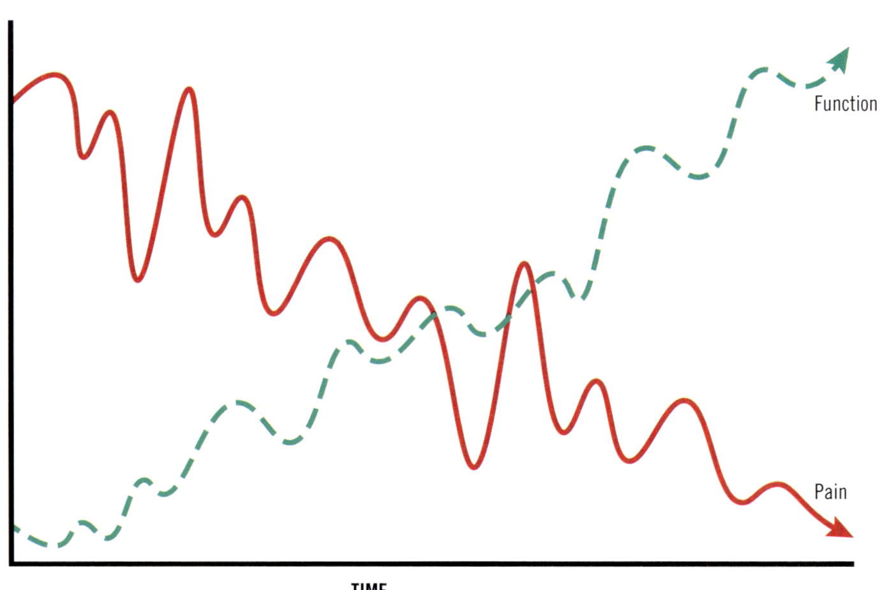

Figure 5.15: The proposed path of recovery in chronic pain.[7]

As discussed previously, many different outcome measures are available. Each has its strengths and weaknesses. From a clinical perspective, the various screening tools mentioned in section 5.2 (Keele SBST, FABQ and TSK) were used at the initial evaluation to identify modifiable risk factors and fear-avoidance beliefs. However, it might be helpful to reassess these measures again at a later point during the episode of care to monitor progress and reappraise risk stratification.

An additional measurement that has been complementary to pain science is the assessment of pressure pain thresholds (PPT). To evaluate PPT, a clinician uses a device known as a pressure algometer to quantify the amount of pressure a patient can tolerate before the pressure becomes painful. In its simplest form, PPT measures the sensitivity of the nervous system to pressure, and various standardized protocols have been described in the literature.[122,123] The PPT is often assessed at sites local to the area of pain, but also at remote sites in the body to identify features suggesting central sensitivity. Research has shown that a reduction of 15 percent on PPT is clinically meaningful (able to push 15 percent harder prior to the pain threshold).[122,123] In clinical practice the advantage of pressure algometry is that it's an objective number that doesn't correlate with the normal daily fluctuations in pain levels that many patients report. For example, a recent patient with CRPS was getting very depressed about her pain. When asked how she thinks she was progressing, she said, "I'm not sure; I still hurt." Figure 5.16 showcases her PPT over the course of her treatments. The graph shows the results of her pressure algometry testing, showcasing over time the clinician could push harder and harder around the painful area, indicating the nervous system progressively calming. This resulted in a significant shift in her outlook of the therapy and played a role in her recovery.

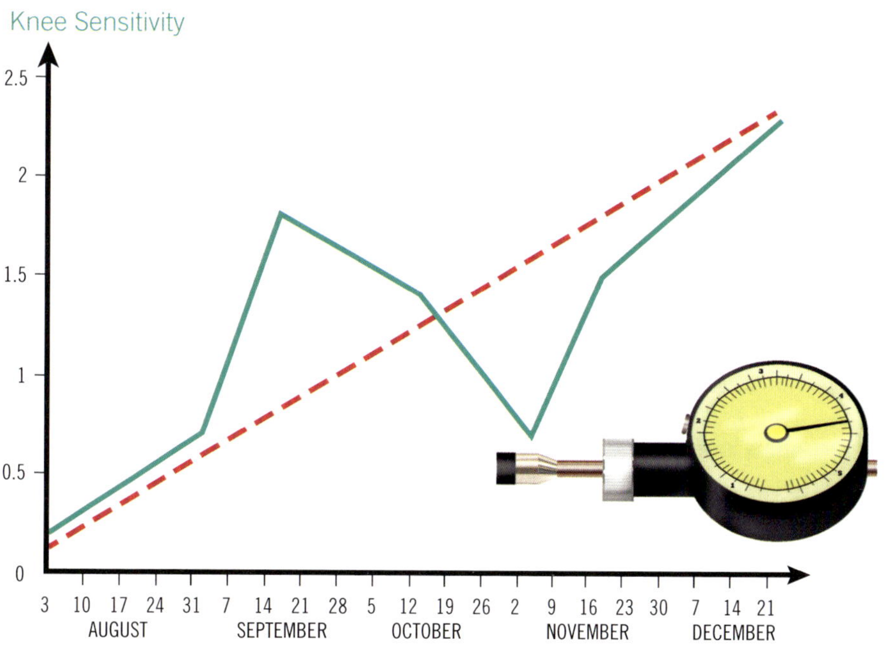

Figure 5.16: Pressure algometry over time in a patient with CRPS.

Why are they in this stage?

Books have been written on this topic. Why people don't want to change habits like smoking, drug use, etc.? In regards to pain, the question likely has several complex answers:

- Entrenched neurological pathways (nerves that fire together wire together).
- Potential secondary gain issues including disability ratings, compensation, social acceptance, etc.
- Loss of identity. After being in pain so long with so many opinions, failed treatments, labeling, etc., they might be so entrenched it is hard to shift.
- The patient has very deep-rooted biomedical beliefs driven by the clinicians, tests, family, etc.
- The complexity of the pain problem is like onion skins with layer upon layers of deeper underlying issues (these might include abuse, abandonment, loss of self-worth, etc.).
- Timing: PNE might be the right message but at the wrong time. In recent years, PNE research has shifted to determine who needs PNE. Invariably the answers (as previously discussed) include central sensitization, high fear-avoidance, pain catastrophization, etc. An additional factor that is gaining interest is the Prochaska and DiClemente's stages of change model[128,129] (Figure 5.20). This model is well known in programs for smoking cessation and weight management and can easily be applied to PNE. For PNE specifically, it is important to consider where in the cycle of behavioral change you are meeting your patient. The all-to-familiar "I am here because my doctor sent me here (and I don't really want to be here)" fits beautifully in stage one of precontemplation characterized with no recognition of need or interest in change. Table 5.6 showcases the various stages, including characteristics of each stage.

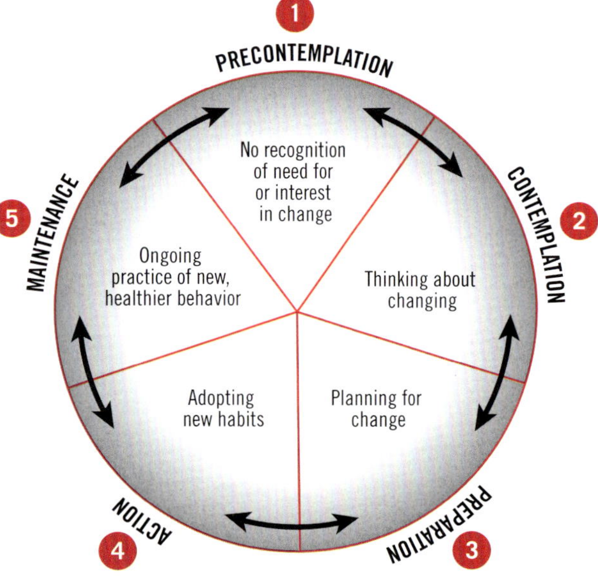

Figure 5.20: Stages of change model.

Table 5.6: Stages of change with various characteristics.

Stage of change	Characteristics
Precontemplation	• Not currently considering change • "Ignorance is bliss"
Contemplation	• Ambivalent about change • "Sitting on the fence" • Not considering change within the next month
Preparation	• Some experience with change and are trying to change • "Testing the waters" • Planning to act within one month
Action	• Practicing new behavior for three to six months
Maintenance	• Continued commitment to sustaining new behavior • Post-six months to five years
Relapse	• Resumption of old behaviors • "Fall from grace"

Based on Figure 5.20 and Table 5.6 it could thus be argued that a patient might have received the perfect PNE message, but if they're in phase one or two, it will likely have a limited effect.

What do we do with patients in this stage?

When a patient rejects your message, it hurts. This is normal, expected and not uncommon, but realizing that it is not up to you to change them will sometimes help. Remember, all we can do is plant the seeds; water them with compassion and empathy and see what happens. It's imperative for clinicians to NOT "take patients home with them." PNE is a proven strategy with outcomes in line with the best treatment approaches on the planet with little to no serious side-effects. What's the alternative? More medicine? More surgery? When a patient rejects the message, the response will vary depending on the nature of the rejection. Below are some clinical guidelines for patients in this phase:

- Regardless of the situation and outcome, there is no excuse not to treat the person in front of you with compassion, empathy and respect. This includes respecting their decision to not listen to your message.

- Keep in mind pain is complex and many factors determine recovery. All pain is real.

- Do not force yourself or your approach on them.

- If you recognize resistance early on, consider using the back door. By defusing the situation and addressing issues the patient wants to address, albeit biomedical, it might allow the patient to become more open to receiving the PNE message during future visits.

- If resistance builds, consider additional strategies such as motivational interviewing where the patient comes up with the solutions (internal driver), versus you telling them (external driver).

- What about the patient that leaves upset and storms out of your clinic? We strongly recommend giving these patients some "space." It is believed the reason they reject the message is that they were not ready for change or PNE touched on various emotional aspects, which they might need to come to grips with before coming back. We do, however, recommend you consider contacting these patients at a later stage to check in with them, or send a form letter…as a potential means for them to reestablish contact. It could likely be that after "getting it," they might feel overwhelmed or embarrassed and not call for a follow-up appointment. Always keep an open-door policy.

- Don't make it personal. A key element we encounter is when the clinician takes it personally and feels the patient's behavior is "not fair to them." This might be a reflection of the "find it-fix it" model often learned during previous therapy encounters.

- There is still suffering. Don't forget the person "inside" the condition.
- A percentage of patients you see have truly been wronged or possibly abused.
- "Play the game." Within secondary gain, workman's compensation, litigation, etc., there is a process to follow and no single person can likely "undo" it. Once again, focus on the person in front of you.

One final thought regarding the approach to patients in this phase comes from the behavioral medicine realm. Figure 5.21 highlights powerful research that is worth considering in the delivery on PNE.[130] The research shows that if a patient enters care in the precontemplation phase and, one month later they are still in the precontemplation phase, they have a mere three percent chance of success, which is defined as a true behavioral shift that is maintained for at least six months. If a patient enters care in the precontemplation phase and, one month later ends up in the contemplation phase, the chance of success shifts to seven percent. If a patient enters care in the contemplation phase and one month later still find themselves in the contemplation phase, the chance of success shifts to 20 percent. This research implies the stages of change be used as yet another potential stratification tool. Given the limited potential success of patients entering into treatment in the precontemplation phase, a clinical question might be asked as to how much skilled care should be delivered in this phase. Should these patients receive a comprehensive PNE session or might it be best to give these patients a very abbreviated PNE session mixed into other more traditional therapeutic treatments and monitor their response as they shift in order to increase their PNE exposure.

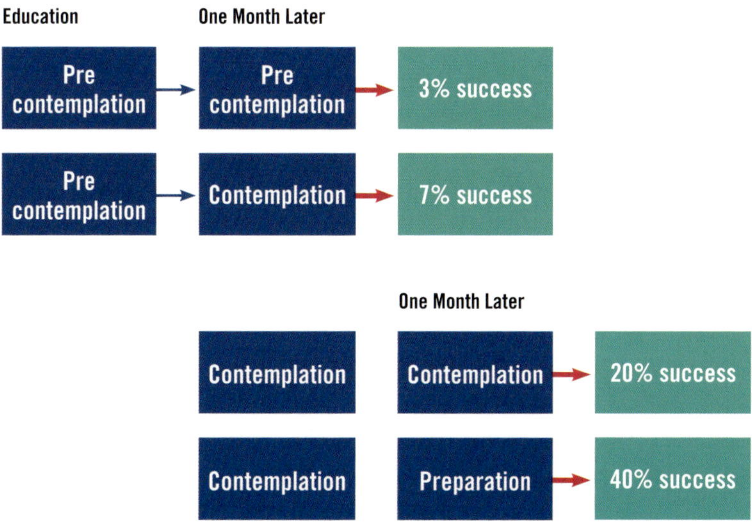

Figure 5.21: Success probability based in the stages of change presentation.

There are various models that can be used to facilitate patients along the behavioral path. Figure 5.22 shows the Kubler-Ross change curve, more commonly known as the five stages of grief. It can be argued that many of the patient responses detailed in the Kubler-Ross change curve might apply to a patient being exposed to PNE. Similarly, the various approaches listed as what to do in each phase align very well with the current ideas of creating trust, therapeutic alliance, etc.

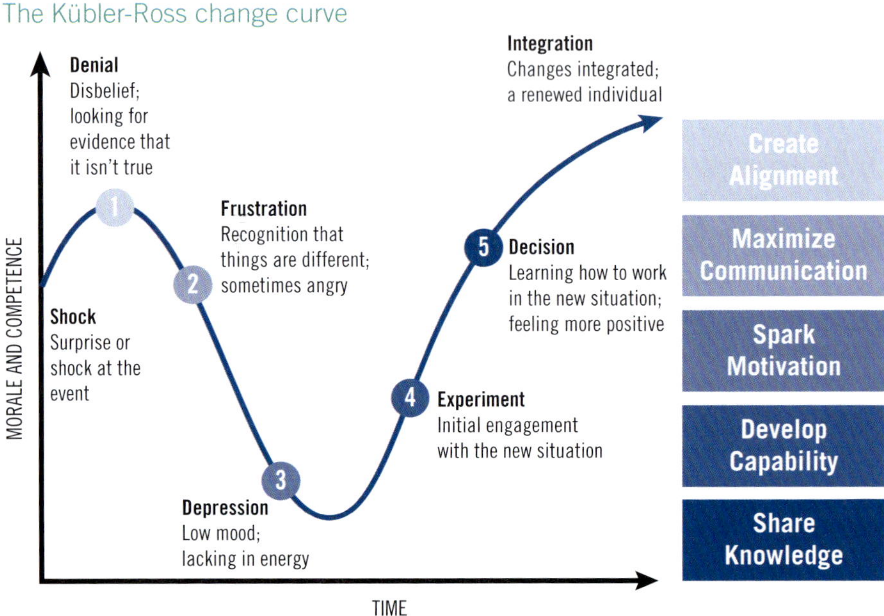

Figure 5.22: The Kubler-Ross change curve.

5.12.2: They take on the message superficially, but never really make any change

The majority of patients end up in this category and likely pose some of the biggest challenges for clinicians since they were given "the message" and just "go through the motions." In PT, for example, they come in twice per week for months, if not years, and never really make any progress. Clinicians become increasingly frustrated and the situation tends to take a toll on the clinician. Typically, the clinician moves to a new clinic location or town, rotates to another department or the patient is passed off to the new therapist that starts next week or to a student. Unfortunately, these patients also take a vast number of resources and this might additionally add clinical stress, especially in lieu of healthcare reform changes.

How do we identify these patients?

- They tell you they "get it" but their actions show they don't.
- Patients in this phase often "understand it all," but when questioned display significant gaps in their knowledge and understanding. It is recommended that if a patient says, "yes, yes, I get it all" and they do not display the associated behaviors, you need to ask them to explain concepts of PNE back to you to assess their true understanding. Also, be careful here. A patient might factually know a concept of PNE, but it's imperative the PNE be applied to their situation. So, if they explain a PNE concept, you could further ask them to explain how they see this applying to their pain experience.
- They develop "clinical routines" (watch out – they will clean, water plants and even do laundry in some cases!).
- They continually attend treatments, yet make little to no progress.

- When confronted, they do one of three things:
  - They get mad and try harder for a while, only to fall back to the original pattern.
  - They promise to try harder, but don't and continue the original pattern.
  - They ask to see someone else.
- These patients "draw energy out of the attending clinicians."
- They have seen all the providers in the clinic and have been passed from clinician to clinician.

Why are they in this stage?

The answer to this question is likely a combination of all the information we're covering on behavioral changes:

- Timing.
- Not ready for change.
- PNE was not delivered adequately.
- Patient getting both PNE and biomedical messages.
- Various opinions by different providers.

Table 5.7 provides a summary for the various factors associated with the challenges of applying PNE into clinical practice. Upon review, it is easy to understand and determine why patients are in this stage of superficial learning.

Table 5.7

Which patients do worst with PNE?	What factors predict failure?	Most challenging clinical issues with PNE application
1. Patient with strong beliefs about treatments	1. Belief something is definitely wrong in the tissues	1. Time constraints
2. Seen multiple providers	2. Physician's influence on the patient's pain	2. Non-compliance by patients
3. Multiple treatment failures	3. Belief pain is due to injury or disease	3. Physicians (especially if biomedically oriented)
4. High catastrophization	4. Not having enough time	4. Don't know the material well enough
5. Chronic pain	5. Duration of the pain	5. Fellow therapists' influences on the patient

What do we do with them?

As stated in section 5.11.1, caring and empathizing with them is a key component. We recommend:

- Always look at YOURSELF first – did you explain everything well enough?
- Did your words match your body language, showing you care?
- Give them the benefit of the doubt.
- Remember, you're planting seeds and watering them with compassion and empathy.
- Keep at it. They might have to hear it again and again until, at visit 42, they say "I got it!"

An important aspect of patients in this phase is the fact that we are trying to "change them" once again. Behavioral change has to come from within to be successful. In recent years there has been growing interest in ways to help patients drive these changes and interest in change from within. One emerging and powerful strategy is motivational interviewing (MI). The intent of this PNE textbook is not to become an authoritative text regarding MI, but have clinicians realize MI is a potential strategy to consider when aiming to have patients shift from precontemplation to contemplation, or contemplation to preparation and beyond. In regards to MI, for this textbook, we offer some guidance:

- If MI interests you, we highly recommend you add this to your "want to attend" list of continuing education.
- MI is not necessarily a "technique" but rather an approach, similar to PNE.
- Many of the aspects and key components of MI are intertwined in PNE and the material is already covered.[131,132]
- MI focuses on exploring and resolving ambivalence and centers on motivational processes within the individual that facilitate change. The method differs from more "coercive" or externally-driven methods for motivating change as it does not impose change (that might be inconsistent with the person's own values, beliefs or wishes), but rather supports change in a manner congruent with the person's own values and concerns.

- Motivational Interviewing includes three essential elements:
  - MI is a particular kind of conversation about change (counseling, therapy, consultation, method of communication).
  - MI is collaborative (person-centered, partnership, honors autonomy, not expert-recipient).
  - MI is evocative (seeks to call forth the person's own motivation and commitment).

- The Principles of Motivational Interviewing:
  - Express Empathy: Empathy involves seeing the world through the client's eyes, thinking about things as the client thinks about them, feeling things as the client feels them, sharing in the client's experiences. This approach provides the basis for clients to be heard and understood, and, in turn, clients are more likely to honestly share their experiences in depth.

  - Support Self-Efficacy: MI is a strengths-based approach that believes clients have within themselves the capabilities to change successfully. In MI, counselors support self-efficacy by focusing on previous successes and highlighting skills and strengths that the client already has.

  - Roll with Resistance: From an MI perspective, resistance in treatment occurs when the client experiences a conflict between their view of the "problem" or "solution" and that of the clinician's view, or when the client experiences their freedom or autonomy being impinged upon. These experiences are often based in the client's ambivalence about change. MI places value on having the client define the problem and develop their own solutions (which leaves little room for the client to resist).

  - Develop Discrepancy: Motivation for change occurs when people perceive a mismatch between "where they are and where they want to be," and a counselor practicing MI works to develop this by helping clients examine discrepancies between their current circumstances/behavior and their values and future goals.

- OARS: Often called microcounseling skills, OARS is a brief method for remembering the basic approach used in MI. Open Ended Questions, Affirmations, Reflections, and Summaries are core counselor behaviors employed to move the process forward by establishing a therapeutic alliance and eliciting discussion about change.

- Practical examples related to PNE:

  - Questions asking permission:

    "Do you mind if we talk about your pain?"

    "Can we talk a bit about your pain?"

  - Questions to evoke Change Talk:

    "What would you like to see different about your pain?"

    "What will happen if your pain doesn't change?"

    "What good things would happen if your pain became less?"

    "What would your life be like three years from now if your pain decreased?"

    "Why do you think others are concerned about your pain?"

    "What would need to occur to make your pain ease?"

    "Suppose your pain doesn't change, what is the WORST thing that might happen?"

    "What is the BEST thing you could imagine that could result from your pain easing?"

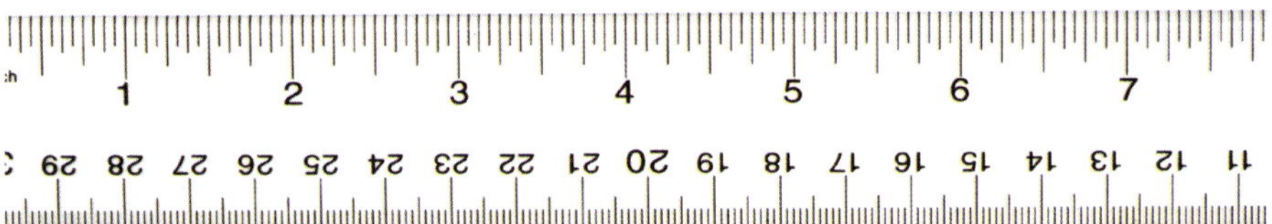

- Exploring importance and confidence: Another way to motivate and shift patients pertains to goals and using a ruler/scale. This allows both clinicians and patients to see that change can be obtained. Let's say, on a scale of zero to 10, 10 represents being pain-free; life is good, while zero indicates severe pain, limited movement, restriction in doing daily tasks and exercising. Where would you rate yourself right now? In our example, a patient says four.

- "Why did you select a score of four and not a two or one?" (why do they see themselves not as bad?)

- "What would need to happen to move the four to a six?" (small steps; pacing)

- An essential part of PNE is to have our patients understand pain is a normal human experience. This "normality" of pain is a key element and it is also imperative that patients realize their problem is not "unique." Many times patients present with statements such as "I have a very unique case of back pain." MI also "normalizes" experiences with the aim to make people understand they are not alone, which is also important in PNE. The current pain epidemic is staggering and most people "suffer in silence" and are unaware there are MANY who hurt and they are not alone. Examples of normalizing (be careful not to minimize their pain experience) might include:

    - *"A lot of people are concerned about changing their pain."*
    - *"Most people report both good and not-so-good things about their pain."*
    - *"Many people report feeling like you do. They want to change their pain, but find it difficult."*
    - *"That is not unusual, many people report having made several previous quit attempts."*

- A few key MI nuggets:
    - List the pros and cons of having pain… (we realize just mentioning the "pros" seem unrealistic, but it might help a patient think differently and ultimately shift the scale. Maybe a scale that is so heavily tilted one way might help people realize they need to change.)
    - Look back: What has worked in the past; what has not worked in the past? For people in despair, looking back to a time things went really well, might create a glimmer of hope.
    - Looking forward: What would happen if they don't change? Where would they be in three to five years? What if pain can steadily be turned down, where do they see themselves three to five years from now?

5.12.3: They internalize the message, "get it" and make meaningful change in their life and move on

The ultimate goal...success! This is the deep learner; the patient listens to the message, internalizes it and starts applying the information to their situation. This is referred to as deep learning.[133,134]

Clinically, you can observe the changes in the individual who truly "gets it" – they do more, they come to visits on time, they use the mantra "despite the pain," etc. These are also the patients who understand they are the key to recovery and can help themselves. In line with the "homework" associated with PNE, patients are asked to constantly bring any/all questions. The successful patient asks a lot of (good) questions. The clinician is excited because they can see the growth. What do we do here? Apart from the obvious celebration, it is well worth it (clinical reasoning) to take a little time and reflect on why this case was a success. An imperative part of clinical growth is reflection, even making a list, of successes.[47,135]

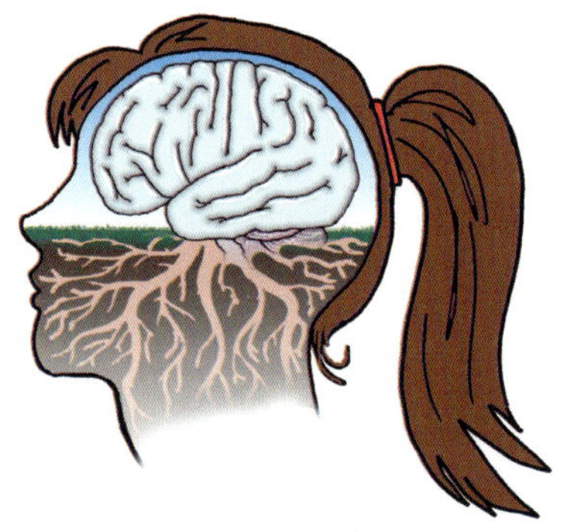

One recommendation pertains to the process of tethering,[89] which is extremely important in this stage as a means to create independence. When a patient is told they're doing well and could be "done," it often increases their stress level and the feeling of being alone and in a wide open ocean. This ties into a statement by renowned professor Johan Vlaeyen at a recent pain science conference:

> "Patients might not have fear as much as a lack of safety"

Over weeks of PNE, activities of daily living, exercise and movement, they have reached a certain level, and:

- Have a good understanding of their pain (PNE)
- Are sleeping better (sleep hygiene)
- Are on a walking program (aerobic exercise)
- Have pacing and graded exposure of daily activities
- Are meeting goals and progressing

Now visits can be spaced further and further apart with increased homework, but the patient is still "attached" to the clinic and thus has a safety net. We also need to be mindful of social attachments patients might have to you and the healthcare system. A person who has been in suffering through a pain experience for any length of time might have lost other social connections in their life. In some cases their only social connection might be with the medical providers. Discharging them from healthcare in this case is also disconnecting them from their primary social connection. Just as we have done in rehabilitation units, when a patient who has survived a stroke is preparing for discharge, increased emphasis is placed on community re-integration prior to discharging to the home environment. Likewise, we might need to assist the chronic pain patient with re-integration back into society and reconnection with other social outlets beyond the medical visits. As this process progresses, the patient develops increased confidence and self-efficacy and might actually propose to conclude formal therapy. If the discharge comes from the patient, it comes from a position of strength, independence and autonomy, which is ideal for recovery. In this model, patients might also do well for a while, but come in for a periodic "checkup" addressing relevant issues, questions and clarity for the continued path forward. In the US there is current talk about the notion of creating a dental model for PT. As with dentists, this model would imply a patient return periodically for a "checkup" which might be a good fit for model tethering (Figure 5.23).

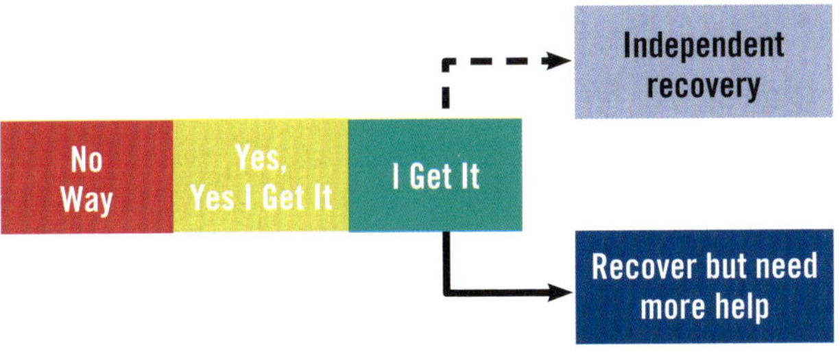

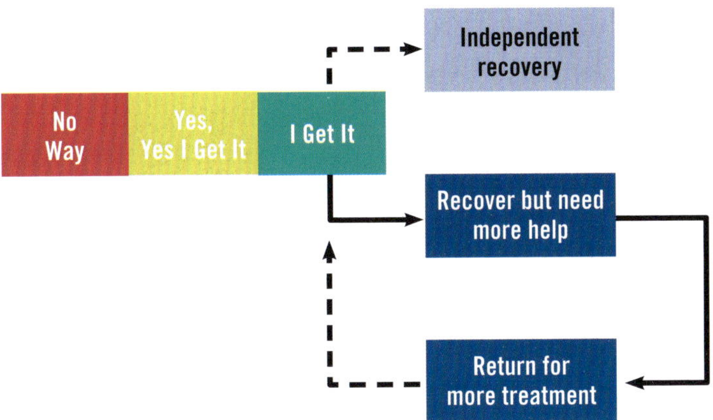

Figure 5.23: Tethering following deep learning.

At the completion of this section, we have covered as extensively as possible the various aspects of clinical implementation of PNE. The remaining sections (5.12 – 5.14) pertain to larger scale clinical issues such as marketing, developing multi- and interdisciplinary programs and expanding PNE beyond outpatient orthopedics. At this point, a clinician should have a step-by-step guide as to how PNE can be utilized on a daily basis. Figure 5.24 provides a visual description of this process, ensuring clinicians recognize PNE is only one part of a comprehensive process of facilitating recovery.

Between the four authors there is more than 100 years of clinical experience (yes, we're old), much of it in the PNE environment. Collectively, knowing what we know about PNE, our take-home top 10 clinical pearls include:

1.	You have to be smarter than your patient (you need to know pain science well)
2.	Education should be paced, similar to exercise
3.	All you can do is plant the PNE seeds, water them with compassion and empathy and see what happens
4.	Sometimes the best way "in" is the back door
5.	Focus on function and tether over time
6.	Set boundaries because you care
7.	Your patients are smarter than you think
8.	All pain is real
9.	Movement is the biggest pain killer in the world
10.	Every patient has a brain; every brain is connected to a person

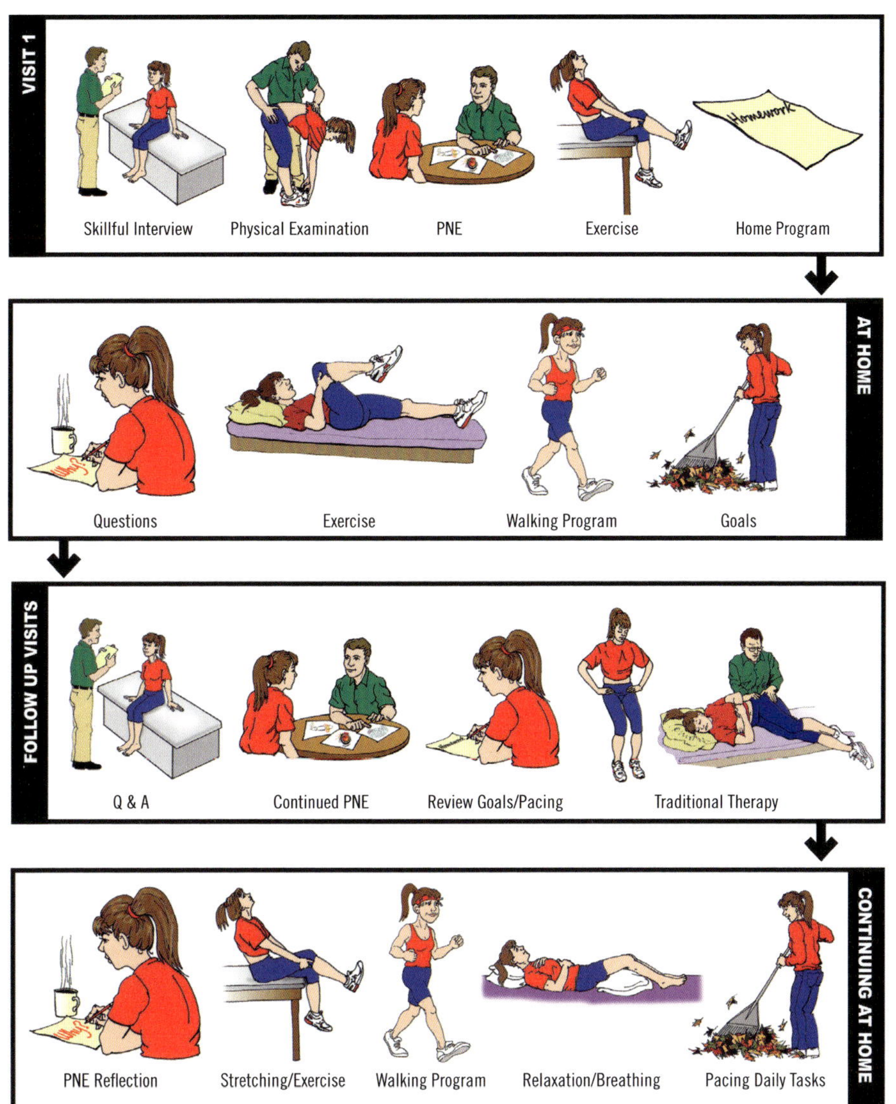

Figure 5.24: PNE, combined with various aspects of recovery in the clinic, as part of exercise, function and goals.[7]

5.13: Marketing PNE

The development and evidence for PNE provides an avenue for marketing. This might include marketing to patients, the general population, other healthcare providers, referral sources, third party payers, government agencies, etc. It could even be argued that, in lieu of the significant risk-benefit ratio in favor of PNE and the current opioid epidemic, PNE must be marketed. There are obviously numerous ways to market and sell the concept of PNE, depending on the target audience.

- **Physicians and referral sources:** In the US, direct access to PT is expanding[136] yet many therapists are in a position of having to market PNE to a referral source such as a physician. Since the inception of PNE and the subsequent research, PNE-related research has been published in dozens of different journals, spanning various healthcare disciplines. This implies physicians are getting more and more exposure to PNE. As for marketing PNE to physicians and referral sources, some practical ideas include:
    - Chronic pain is at epidemic levels[76] and it could be argued that all potential referral sources would be willing to listen to anyone able and willing to help them with their patients struggling with chronic pain.
    - Actions speak louder than words. Many physicians are likely tired of hearing, "*I'm from clinic ABC and we're the best...*" Not only does this mimic pharmaceutical sales, but there is likely little to no evidence to support an individual clinic's superiority. The best option? Show the physicians how good you are. When patients with chronic pain consistently return for follow-up visits and (i) are much improved or (ii) even if not improved, are very satisfied with their care, it often has a lasting effect. Treat the patient right and many of the marketing issues will fall into place.

- Patients as postcards. Over the years of treating people with chronic pain there is often the inevitable, "*I cannot thank you enough for helping me; if there's ever anything I can do for you, let me know.*" This might be a great opportunity to ask a patient to sign a thank you card that can be sent to the referring physician on their behalf. Physicians also have various daily clinical struggles, including chronic pain. Getting a thank you note and mentioning you and your exceptional (PNE) care might provide a lasting impression.

- Attend physician visits. In many cases physicians are open to you accompanying the patient to a follow-up visit, especially when it's a complex case. This might provide valuable time with the referring physician and an ability to share your perspective, thus developing a working professional relationship.

- Be smart but respectful. Physicians respect peers more than subordinates. The most fulfilling professional relationships we have encountered have been when the physician sees you as a peer – skilled, specialized and knowledgeable in your area – and values your opinion. Show what you know; know the material well and have scientific backup. On the flipside, be respectful and know your professional boundaries.

- Research: Share research if and when needed. The occasional research paper, especially as a follow-up of a specific patient, might be beneficial. If possible, attend and participate in journal clubs or any possible learning experience with the physicians.

- Be flexible and get them in: No clinician likes surprises to their work schedule. When you show up in the morning, have a set schedule, and you can mentally plan for the day, it's a good day in the clinic. What happens when an unexpected "add-on" is dropped onto your schedule or your number one referral source wants somebody in the clinic today? Even though on your end it makes for a more stressful day, it could be a very powerful marketing strategy. This willingness and ability to help out goes a long way and ultimately fosters the most important aspect of marketing; developing a relationship. Obviously if this happens frequently, a new system needs to be developed to accommodate for this and ensure the needs of the physicians, therapists, new patient and existing patients are being met.

- Treat physicians: Every clinician reading this book is nodding their head at this one. Sometimes your best referral source is a physician who was a patient. This is the ultimate "show and tell" showcasing your skills and ample time to discuss any and all topics you're passionate about, including PNE.

This list can go on and on, but a key element for physicians related to PNE is its relationship to CBT. Many physicians are aware of CBT and have likely seen value in CBT for the more complex patients. The ultimate question is if PNE is CBT. CBT in the US is often synonymous with comprehensive pain clinics and psychotherapy, thus rendering it often hard to access and more than often not within the reach of the average physician and his or her patient. The argument as to whether PNE is synonymous with CBT is ongoing[120] and, in its simplest form, the answer to the question would be yes, kind of. It is believed that PNE is the "C" of the CBT. In PNE we restructure cognitions and beliefs. The + part of the PNE+ program contains various "B" parts including goal setting, pacing, graded exposure, etc. In essence therefore, the PNE + program would be seen as a therapeutic version of CBT. CBT and the delivery of CBT is very political and these statements might anger some CBT purists. The question of if PNE is CBT was best answered by pain scientist professor Jo Nijs (personal communication). He is of the belief that a significant limitation of CBT is the "C" component and most behavioral psychologists spend the vast amount of their CBT sessions on the "B" part, in essence resulting in a cBT approach. His belief is that PNE adds significantly to the "C" part, thus bolstering the overall CBT program. What is the marketing version of this answer? PNE is a form of CBT, but delivered in daily clinical practice by an army of physical therapists, occupational therapists, assistants, etc. PNE thus in essence allows a form a CBT to be accessible and affordable to the masses, which has a significant appeal to physicians needing help with their patients.

- **Third party payers and government agencies:** A small percentage of clinicians have access to, or are asked to, present to third party payers and/or government agencies. Even though clinicians consider pain and function often as the "gold standard" outcome measures, one must ask what matters to the people who have to pay for treatment. Two outcome measures are incredibly important: Healthcare utilization (money) and patient satisfaction. Both of these have been shown to be significantly impacted by PNE.[57,119,137] Furthermore, data such as the NNT and its comparison to various "gold standards" (i.e., often medicine) might also be of importance for such agencies.[10]

As a side note and worthy of reflection here is a thought related to what would be the ideal professions to treat chronic pain. In the early days of PNE, Louis Gifford spent time with Dr. Patrick Wall, the co-author of Gate Control, sharing ideas about pain.[108] In these early conversations, Dr. Wall commented that professions such as PT might be the ideal profession to treat chronic pain. The reason for this (listed below), might be well worth a mention in the marketing to third party payers and government agencies. PT (and surely OT) is ideally suited to treat chronic pain due to its:

1. Biological knowledge
2. Use of and specialization in movement and exercise
3. Hands-on professions
4. Time with patients
5. Large workforce
6. Low cost
7. Various aspects of psychology integrated throughout therapy
8. Being a direct-access profession, in many cases
9. Growing knowledge of pain sciences (only recently added)

This list is important. As healthcare faces the increased financial burdens associated with it, a solution is needed. If, for a second, you consider the US and this plight, consider the following:

- In the US alone, there are over 210,000 licensed PTs. This is a huge and growing workforce. Add to the PT workforce approximately 85,000 PT assistants and the workforce is now around 300,000. If we add OTs (105,000) and COTAs (45,000), it nears a half million clinicians.

- PT education in the US is now at a doctorate level with OT recently deciding to also award a doctorate. The result is not only a large workforce but a highly trained workforce at low cost that is easily accessible.

- **Fellow clinicians:** As stated in section 5.7, in an ideal clinical setting, all clinicians have been exposed to PNE in some way, but this is not always the case. In some unfortunate circumstances a PNE-trained therapist might find himself/herself surrounded by biomedicalists who have little or no knowledge of PNE, but openly question and criticize PNE. An obvious "marketing" strategy in this scenario would be to influence fellow clinicians with clinical results and provide assistance in helping with difficult cases. Over time this might evolve to providing in-house training to fellow clinicians and encouragement to do formal education in PNE. The reality is that the old models are not working and a noteworthy quote for fellow clinicians stuck in the biomedical model comes from Dr. Patrick Wall:

> "If we were so good; then why are our patients so bad?"

- **Patients:** A point should be made that various aspects of the PNE approach (trust, listening, compassion, empathy, decreased use of provocative words, etc.) will impact any and all patients, even non-PNE patients. The reality is that your current patient has many friends and family members who might, in time, be in need of PT. By turning your approach and the clinic's approach toward PNE you can use this as a powerful marketing tool to existing patients. Providing informational handouts, using posters, etc. might be a great opportunity for existing patients to be exposed to your PNE program. Additionally, community talks in your clinic might help spread the word.

- **General public:** The ultimate mandate is to teach all of society the new pain science view of pain. If the current state of affairs continue, this strategy will need to be implemented. Anytime a population is faced with an epidemic (i.e., AIDS, West Nile Virus, etc.), there is a need for mass education. Chronic pain is listed as one of the biggest epidemics and challenges the WHO will face and thus requires mass education. As a marketing tool, community lectures are very powerful ways to expose people to your clinic and program. Speaking at community events might be very helpful. Taking PNE and various aspects of pain science to schools for career day or building it into the curricula is also a must. Recent PNE studies have shown that middle school kids can learn PNE, resulting in significant improvements in pain knowledge as well as attitudes and beliefs regarding pain.

5.14: Multi and Interdisciplinary Care

In the mid and late 1990s, as biopsychosocial approaches in PT emerged mainly due to yellow flags research, a "best-evidence" approach to chronic pain was developed.[54,108,138-140] Even though the original references are dated, modern pain science underscores and validates this list. Simply stated, the following list describes the current best-evidence approach to chronic pain and might in some ways be considered a curriculum:

- Identify patients with "red flags"
- Educate the patient about the nature of the problem
- Provide prognostication
- Promote self-care
- Get patients active and moving as early as possible and appropriately after injury
- Decrease unnecessary fear related to movement, leisure and work activities
- Help the patient experience success
- Perform a skilled physical examination and communicate results to the patient
- Make any treatment strategy as closely linked to evidence of the biological nature of the problem rather than a particular syndrome or anatomical geography
- Use any measures possible to reduce pain
- Minimize the number of treatments and contacts with medical personnel
- Consider multidisciplinary management
- Manage identified and relevant physical dysfunctions
- Assess and assist recovery of general physical fitness
- Assess the effects on the patient's creative outlets

One of the aims of this textbook is to validate and expand on the various aspects of this "best of" list. If you review the list, you'll notice various aspects already covered. In Chapter 6 we aim to complete a few of the aspects not covered. For example, exercise, goal setting, etc. One key element, however, fits into this chapter and warrants some discussion…multidisciplinary care.

One of the fundamental underpinnings associated with pain, especially due to the complexity of pain, is the interest in developing a multidisciplinary treatment program. First, we must distinguish between multidisciplinary and interdisciplinary programs (Table 5.8).

Table 5.8: Comparison of multidisciplinary and interdisciplinary programs.

Multidisciplinary	Interdisciplinary
• Utilizes the skills and experience of individuals from different disciplines, with each discipline approaching the patient from their own perspective. • Involves separate individual consultations. • Common for team to meet regularly, in the absence of the patient, to "case conference" findings and discuss future directions for the patient's care.	• Integrates separate discipline approaches into a single consultation. • The patient history, assessment, diagnosis, intervention and short- and long-term management goals are conducted by the team, together with the patient, at the one time. • The patient is intimately involved in any discussions regarding their condition or prognosis and the plans about their care.

The most common approach for chronic pain is multidisciplinary and it is associated with the more complex issues such as chronic LBP, CRPS, FM, etc.[141-156] In Europe multidisciplinary care is well established but in the US multidisciplinary care is associated with long waiting lists, difficulty gaining access and often associated with expense – the exact opposite of what is needed.[148,151,157-162] As for evidence, there seems to be (i) a definite need for more research, (ii) some evidence and (iii) various opinions that it "should point" toward the use of multidisciplinary care.[163-166]

In line with Chapter 5, it is argued that, following risk stratification, patients on the high-risk side be more aligned to receiving multidisciplinary care. When building, or contemplating on building, a multidisciplinary program, it can be done under one roof or a little wider in the community under an "umbrella of care" (Figure 5.25).

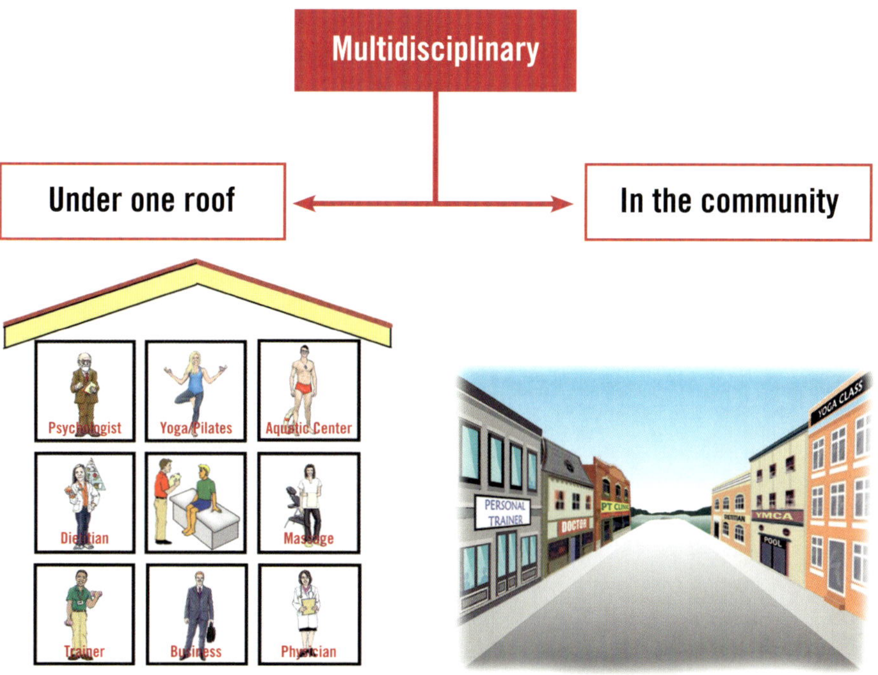

Figure 5.25: Opportunities for building a multidisciplinary program.

What should such a team look like? The answer probably depends on who you ask, who's in control of it, various professional biases, and financial interests. The list below is supported by current literature,[160,166] and is likely controversial and definitely open to discussion. The multidisciplinary program needs someone to handle:

- Medication use
- Medical tests
- Exercise, movement and hands-on treatment
- Education
- Mental health
- Other relevant wellness issues, i.e., nutrition, sleep, etc.

A critical aspect of this process is that the program should aim to be cost-effective and easily accessible. All clinicians should use a similar and supportive model (i.e., PNE) and thus not contradict each other, allowing team members autonomous practice versus being subordinate to others on the team. One final "PT" consideration would be to build a truly biopsychosocial multidisciplinary program under your PT clinic's roof. In an ideal situation, in order of potential importance, a clinic owner might build such a program over time:

1. Physical Therapist
2. Physical Therapist Assistant
3. Occupational Therapist
4. Psychologist
5. Aquatic Therapist
6. Dietician
7. Personal Trainer
8. Etc.

Another option might be consultation or subleasing space:

On staff:

- Physical Therapist
- Physical Therapist Assistant
- Occupational Therapist
- Therapist specializing in:
    - Aquatic
    - Yoga
    - Pilates

Consultants:

- Psychologist
- Dietician
- Massage Therapist
- Personal Trainer
- Etc.

5.15: PNE Beyond Outpatient Orthopedics

As stated in the introduction to this chapter, the clinical implementation described here is very outpatient or private practice focused, especially orthopedics. The evolution of PNE from manual therapy and thus its presence in this domain likely has a large part to do with this. In this final section, considering all the material covered to this point, we briefly showcase potential opportunities for pain science, including PNE, to be spread to other realms of PT (Figure 5.26). Orthopedics is the largest section of PT, but many other avenues might benefit significantly from pain science.

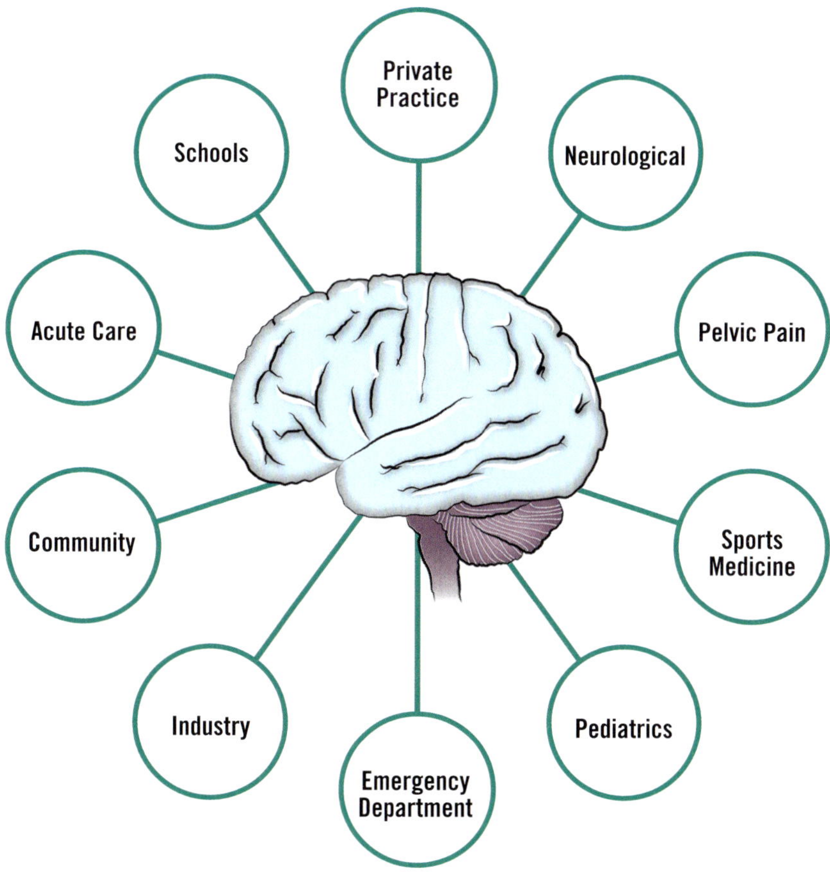

Figure 5.26: Various physical therapy opportunities for pain science and PNE.

Neurological rehabilitation

Many pain science students ask about the use of various aspects of pain science in patients with neurological conditions. It seems logical, but various issues come to mind, including specific areas of the brain being insulted, cognitive abilities, etc. An easy way to start is the concept of neuroplasticity[167] which, neurologically, has been showcased in treatments such as constraint therapy.[168,169] In regard to research, there have been investigations into the use of treatments such as mirror therapy and motor imagery, which is encouraging and definitely shows some potential efficacy for the neurological patient population, including stroke.[170,171] One specific area we need to consider (since it's been neglected) is pain in this population. So much of the attention is given to function, but patients with neurological deficits struggle a lot with pain.[172-178] Consider the following data on the reported percentage of patients experiencing pain with a neurological condition:[172-178]

- Spinal cord injury: 26-96%
- Stroke: 21-47%
- Brain injury: 43-58%
- Multiple Sclerosis: 64-92%
- Amputee: 50-78%
- Guillain-Barre: 50-75%
- Parkinson's: 30-50%

Given the limitations of information about the treatment approach, it is suggested we borrow from other realms of pain science, including analyzing patients with neurological conditions from Smart's classification perspective (Table 5.2).[179] Emerging pain science research is also showing overlaps between different conditions such as stroke, CRPS and phantom limb pain when it comes from a neuroplasticity perspective.[180] Finally, pertaining to PNE for neurological conditions, it likely depends on the extent of the insult to the brain, i.e., stroke. It could be argued that a subgroup of patients with neurological conditions might be able to take on PNE. The delivery might have to be adapted to be slower, repeated more, increased in font sizes for reading, etc. An additional PNE consideration is training and teaching PNE to caregivers as well.

Pelvic Health and Pelvic Pain

One area of PT that has migrated significantly toward PNE is the pelvic health/pain specialists.[112] It would make sense, given the immense suffering, complexity of pelvic pain and the various emotional and psychological issues associated with pelvic pain. From a scientific perspective, it is important to realize this population might be ideal for PNE and any other pain treatments including graded motor imagery, given its association with pain catastrophization, central sensitization, fear-avoidance, disability, pain, etc.[181-186] One area specific to pelvic pain is the fact that pain is not the only issue – hence the concerns about the name "pelvic pain," since we need to contemplate bowel and bladder function, intercourse, etc. Humanly speaking, we need to realize that these functions are critical issues associated with "being human" and are at the core of being human. If they go unfulfilled or are an issue, they create significant stress. Even one level up, safety, freedom, etc., can be tied to pelvic health.[112]

Sports Medicine

As we discuss pain, you can likely already see how various "pain" issues can be used to assist recovery from injury, or even optimize sports performance.[187] We need to realize that sports performance, just like pain, is an output of the brain – a result of synergistic working of the various brain areas. This concept of the brain being in charge of sports performance is not new and referred to as the central governor, whereby the brain simultaneously analyzes all biological information (CO_2, oxygen, glucose, etc.) and will "allow" the athlete to push to a safe level, so as not to harm the organism. When the threat is altered (only 100m left in the race), it takes away the limits and allows a final sprint at a higher capacity. [188,189] It is believed what separates the novice from expert is this ability to synergize the brain for optimal performance.[190] What is remarkable is that this coordination needs to occur at lightning speed. It would thus seem logical that a brain that is "busy with pain" will not allow for optimal sports performance. Additionally, it is also important that the brain performs "the right activity" at "the right time." For example, in golf, quieting the brain seems to be key, with a novice golfer and professional activating different brain areas despite performing the same task.[190-194] It would thus seem imperative to include the brain and various neuroscience-related issues into sports medicine to help with a top-down and bottom-up approach.

Pediatrics

It would also seem logical that there might be some intriguing avenues to consider from a pediatric perspective. Neuroplastic issues associated with various developmental concerns, early onset of CRPS, sensory processing disorders, etc., might respond well to various PNE+ treatments. It is also imperative that caregivers, including parents, be educated along the way – be it teaching them about pain, decreasing catastrophization[195] or giving hope via neuroplasticity. The recent middle school studies on PNE showcase how kids can be taught pain science. As with neurological rehabilitation, it might be just as powerful to also train the parents of kids, since they play a huge role in the pain experience of the child. For example, it has been shown that a parent's catastrophization after surgery might be one of the biggest predictors of the child developing chronic pain.[195]

Emergency Department

An area ripe for pain science is the emergency department. Given the issues associated with predicting chronic pain (acute pain, fear, catastrophization, etc.), it would seem logical that early access to pain science approaches can be of huge benefit to patients. The overall inclusion of more PT in the emergency department is already a topic of discussion.[196-198] One area of particular interest should be motor vehicle collisions (MVC). We know MVCs produce significant levels of stress, which is predictive of pain.[199,200] It is well established that there is an immediate upregulation of the nervous system following an MVC, indicating a potential acute onset of central sensitization.[60] Apart from MVC, and in line of acute pain predicting chronic pain, it has been shown that a high level of acute pain 48 hours after wrist fracture is a strong predictor of CRPS.[31] It would seem an early intervention aimed at pain, education and behaviors might in fact potentially help defuse the potential for chronicity. Given these fractures are typically immobilized, which might alter

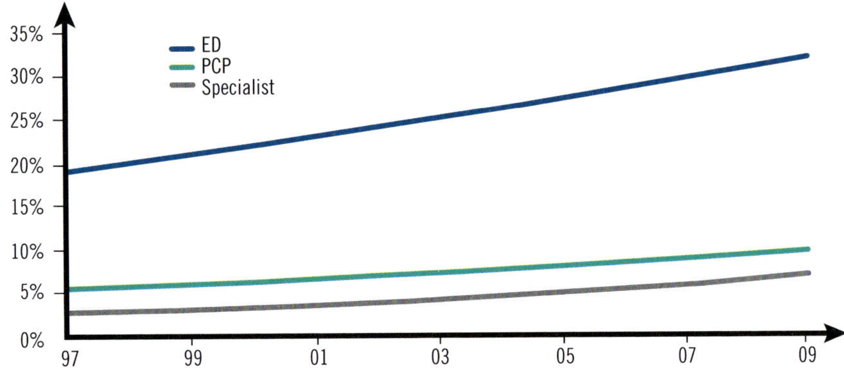

Figure 5.27: Prescription of opioids (overall).

body representation maps, it can be argued an early graded motor imagery might be potentially advantageous. A current and progressive concern faced in the emergency department is opioid dependence and opioid-seeking behaviors. There is growing evidence that the emergency room might be a significant instigator of the opioid issues in the US. Figure 5.27 showcases the abnormal volume of opioid use in the emergency department compared to primary care and specialists overall, specific to LBP.[201]

Industry

In the US alone, billions of dollars are spent on pain and disability in industry. As industrial environments and workplace injuries are prone to be associated with yellow flags, it would follow that early interventions incorporating biopsychosocial approaches would be ideal.[140,202] In regard to LBP, there is increased interest in the early access model for PT (Figure 5.28).[203]

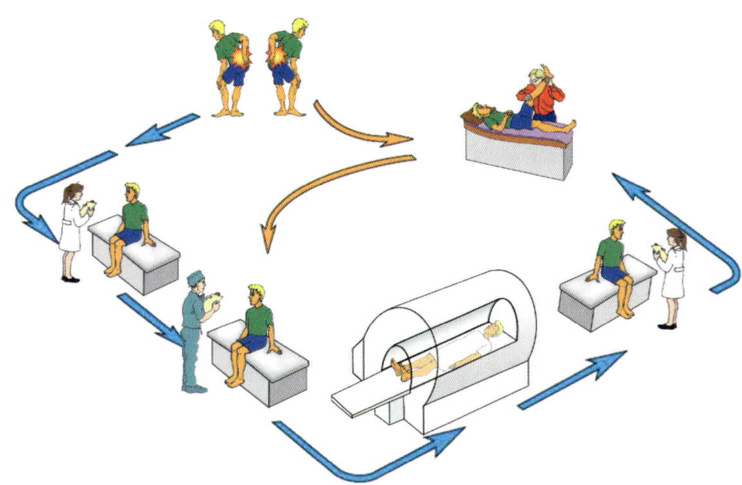

Figure 5.28: Early access to PT. Adapted from Aetna; Virginia Mason Medical Center.

In line with current beliefs that pain is normal,[108,115] we need to consider changing industrial medicine to reflect this idea. We now know pain is normal, but what people do about it (coping) is likely far more important than the actual pain experience.[111] An important aspect associated with industry is ensuring we don't "scare" patients. It seems various messages used in industry might in fact set people up for failure, for example, "If you don't sit/stand this way, you will get pain."[204] It would thus also seem early access providers should be familiar with PNE, often to help defuse the issues (i.e., anger), associated with pain.[205]

Community

The ultimate mandate is to take pain to the masses; the community (section 5.13). Community PNE talks have been done and show that pain can the understood by patients, and healthcare providers often underestimate a patient's ability to take it on.[4,82]

Acute Care

Various issues pertaining to acute care and pain indicate the necessity to take pain science to acute care (acute pain, duration of pain, fear, coping strategies).[30,206-208] Additionally, immobilization such as immediate postoperative can be viewed from a neuroplastic perspective of brain map changes.[209,210]

Schools

Pain is biology and...biology is taught in school. It is now well established that kids experience pain[211] and another "mandate" is taking pain science to schools. Recent research has done this exact work, demonstrating that, after a 30-minute PNE lecture, middle school kids:[56]

- Increase their knowledge of pain
- Develop healthier beliefs regarding chronic pain
- Are less afraid to move in the presence of pain

Chapter 7 will showcase the various preemptive PNE approaches, including the middle school programs.

Chapter 5 References

1. Louw A, Zimney K, Puentedura EJ, Diener I. The Efficacy of Therapeutic Neuroscience Education on Musculoskeletal Pain – A Systematic Review of the Literature. *Physiother Theory Pract.* 2016;32(5):332-355.
2. Louw A, Diener I, Butler DS, Puentedura EJ. The effect of neuroscience education on pain, disability, anxiety, and stress in chronic musculoskeletal pain. *Archives of physical medicine and rehabilitation.* Dec 2011;92(12):2041-2056.
3. Gifford LS. Pain, the tissues and the nervous system. *Physiotherapy.* 1998;84:27-33.
4. Moseley GL. Unravelling the barriers to reconceptualisation of the problem in chronic pain: the actual and perceived ability of patients and health professionals to understand the neurophysiology. *The journal of pain: official journal of the American Pain Society.* 2003;4(4):184-189.
5. Catley MJ, O'Connell NE, Moseley GL. How good is the neurophysiology of pain questionnaire? A Rasch analysis of psychometric properties. *The journal of pain: official journal of the American Pain Society.* Aug 2013;14(8):818-827.
6. Louw A, Butler DS, Diener I, Puentedura EJ. Development of a preoperative neuroscience educational program for patients with lumbar radiculopathy. *American journal of physical medicine & rehabilitation/Association of Academic Physiatrists.* May 2013;92(5):446-452.
7. Louw A, Zimney K, O'Hotto C, Hilton S. The clinical application of teaching people about pain. *Physiother Theory Pract.* Jul 2016;32(5):385-395.
8. Louw A, Puentedura EJ, Zimney K, Cox T, Rico D. The clinical implementation of pain neuroscience education: A survey study. *Physiother Theory Pract.* Nov 2017;33(11):869-879.
9. Moseley GL. Joining forces – combining cognition-targeted motor control training with group or individual pain physiology education: a successful treatment for chronic low back pain. *J Man Manip Therap.* 2003;11(2):88-94.
10. Moseley L. Combined physiotherapy and education is efficacious for chronic low back pain. *The Australian journal of physiotherapy.* 2002;48(4):297-302.
11. Moseley GL. Widespread brain activity during an abdominal task markedly reduced after pain physiology education: fMRI evaluation of a single patient with chronic low back pain. *The Australian journal of physiotherapy.* 2005;51(1):49-52.
12. Louw A, Puentedura E. *Therapeutic Neuroscience Education: Teaching patients about pain.* Minneapolis, MN: OPTP; 2013.
13. Downie A, Williams CM, Henschke N, et al. Red flags to screen for malignancy and fracture in patients with low back pain: systematic review. *Bmj.* 2013;347:f7095.
14. Leerar PJ, Boissonnault W, Domholdt E, Roddey T. Documentation of red flags by physical therapists for patients with low back pain. *The Journal of manual & manipulative therapy.* 2007;15(1):42-49.
15. Ross MD, Boissonnault WG. Red flags: to screen or not to screen? *J Orthop Sports Phys Ther.* Nov 2010;40(11):682-684.
16. Sizer PS, Jr., Brismee JM, Cook C. Medical screening for red flags in the diagnosis and management of musculoskeletal spine pain. *Pain practice: the official journal of World Institute of Pain.* Mar 2007;7(1):53-71.
17. Diener I, Kargela M, Louw A. Listening is therapy: Patient interviewing from a pain science perspective. *Physiother Theory Pract.* Jul 2016;32(5):356-367.
18. Nijs J, Van Houdenhove B, Oostendorp RA. Recognition of central sensitization in patients with musculoskeletal pain: Application of pain neurophysiology in manual therapy practice. *Manual therapy.* Apr 2010;15(2):135-141.
19. Nijs J, Paul van Wilgen C, Van Oosterwijck J, van Ittersum M, Meeus M. How to explain central sensitization to patients with 'unexplained' chronic musculoskeletal pain: Practice guidelines. *Manual therapy.* Oct 2011;16(5):413-418.
20. Hill JC, Dunn KM, Lewis M, et al. A primary care back pain screening tool: identifying patient subgroups for initial treatment. *Arthritis and rheumatism.* May 15 2008;59(5):632-641.
21. Zimney K, Louw A, Puentedura EJ. Use of Therapeutic Neuroscience Education to address psychosocial factors associated with acute low back pain: a case report. *Physiother Theory Pract.* Apr 2014;30(3):202-209.

22. Fritz JM, George SZ. Identifying psychosocial variables in patients with acute work-related low back pain: the importance of fear-avoidance beliefs. *Physical therapy.* Oct 2002;82(10):973-983.
23. Williamson E. Fear Avoidance Beliefs Questionnaire (FABQ). *The Australian journal of physiotherapy.* 2006;52(2):149.
24. Hapidou EG, O'Brien MA, Pierrynowski MR, de Las Heras E, Patel M, Patla T. Fear and Avoidance of Movement in People with Chronic Pain: Psychometric Properties of the 11-Item Tampa Scale for Kinesiophobia (TSK-11). *Physiother Can.* Summer 2012;64(3):235-241.
25. Sullivan MJL, Bishop SR, Pivik J. The Pain Catastrophizing Scale: Development and validation. *Psychological Assessment.* 1995;7(4):524-532.
26. Smart KM, Blake C, Staines A, Thacker M, Doody C. Mechanisms-based classifications of musculoskeletal pain: Part 1 of 3: Symptoms and signs of central sensitisation in patients with low back (+/-leg) pain. *Manual therapy.* Aug 2012;17(4):336-344.
27. Nijs J, Van Houdenhove B, Oostendorp RA. Recognition of central sensitization in patients with musculoskeletal pain: Application of pain neurophysiology in manual therapy practice. *Manual therapy.* Apr 2010;15(2):135-141.
28. Mayer TG, Neblett R, Cohen H, et al. The development and psychometric validation of the central sensitization inventory. *Pain practice: the official journal of World Institute of Pain.* Apr 2012;12(4):276-285.
29. Woolf CJ, Salter MW. Neuronal plasticity: increasing the gain in pain. *Science.* Jun 9 2000;288(5472):1765-1769.
30. Woolf CJ. Central sensitization: uncovering the relation between pain and plasticity. *Anesthesiology.* Apr 2007;106(4):864-867.
31. Moseley GL, Herbert RD, Parsons T, Lucas S, Van Hilten JJ, Marinus J. Intense pain soon after wrist fracture strongly predicts who will develop complex regional pain syndrome: prospective cohort study. *The journal of pain: official journal of the American Pain Society.* Jan 2014;15(1):16-23.
32. Jones MA. Clinical reasoning in manual therapy. *Physical therapy.* 1992;72: 875-883.
33. Hall AM, Ferreira PH, Maher CG, Latimer J, Ferreira ML. The influence of the therapist-patient relationship on treatment outcome in physical rehabilitation: a systematic review. *Physical therapy.* Aug 2010;90(8):1099-1110.
34. Ferreira PH, Ferreira ML, Maher CG, Refshauge KM, Latimer J, Adams RD. The therapeutic alliance between clinicians and patients predicts outcome in chronic low back pain. *Physical therapy.* Apr 2013;93(4):470-478.
35. Roter D. The medical visit context of treatment decision-making and the therapeutic relationship. *Health expectations : an international journal of public participation in health care and health policy.* Mar 2000;3(1):17-25.
36. Maitland GD. *Vertebral Manipulation.* 6th ed. London: Butterworths; 1986.
37. Jones MA, Rivett DA. *Clinical Reasoning for Manual Therapists.* Edinburgh: Butterworth Heinemann; 2004.
38. Schmidt SG. Recognizing potential barriers to setting and achieving effective rehabilitation goals for patients with persistent pain. *Physiother Theory Pract.* Jul 2016;32(5):415-426.
39. Nijs J, Roussel N, Paul van Wilgen C, Koke A, Smeets R. Thinking beyond muscles and joints: Therapists' and patients' attitudes and beliefs regarding chronic musculoskeletal pain are key to applying effective treatment. *Manual therapy.* Dec 28 2012.
40. Wilson D, Williams M, Butler D. Language and the pain experience. *Physiotherapy research international: the journal for researchers and clinicians in physical therapy.* Mar 2009;14(1):56-65.
41. Ploghaus A, Narain C, Beckmann CF, et al. Exacerbation of pain by anxiety is associated with activity in a hippocampal network. *The Journal of neuroscience: the official journal of the Society for Neuroscience.* Dec 15 2001;21(24):9896-9903.
42. Louw A, Diener I, Puentedura E. Comparison of Terminology in Patient Education Booklets for Lumbar Surgery. *International Journal of Health Sciences.* 2014;2(3):47-56.
43. Ballantyne JC, Sullivan MD. Intensity of Chronic Pain--The Wrong Metric? *N Engl J Med.* Nov 26 2015;373(22):2098-2099.
44. Smart KM, Blake C, Staines A, Thacker M, Doody C. Mechanisms-based classifications of musculoskeletal pain: Part 2 of 3: Symptoms and signs of peripheral neuropathic pain in patients with low back (+/-leg) pain. *Manual therapy.* Aug 2012;17(4):345-351.

45. Smart KM, Blake C, Staines A, Thacker M, Doody C. Mechanisms-based classifications of musculoskeletal pain: Part 3 of 3: Symptoms and signs of nociceptive pain in patients with low back (+/-leg) pain. *Manual therapy.* Aug 2012;17(4):352-357.
46. Smart KM, Blake C, Staines A, Doody C. Clinical indicators of 'nociceptive', 'peripheral neuropathic' and 'central' mechanisms of musculoskeletal pain. A Delphi survey of expert clinicians. *Manual therapy.* Feb 2009;15(1):80-87.
47. Smart K, Doody C. The clinical reasoning of pain by experienced musculoskleletal physiothrepists. *Manual therapy.* 2007; 12:40-49.
48. Mechanic D, McAlpine DD, Rosenthal M. Are patients' office visits with physicians getting shorter? *N Engl J Med.* Jan 18 2001;344(3):198-204.
49. Tai-Seale M, McGuire TG, Zhang W. Time allocation in primary care office visits. *Health Serv Res.* Oct 2007;42(5):1871-1894.
50. Shaw MK, Davis SA, Fleischer AB, Feldman SR. The duration of office visits in the United States, 1993 to 2010. *The American journal of managed care.* Oct 2014;20(10):820-826.
51. Verbeek J, Sengers MJ, Riemens L, Haafkens J. Patient expectations of treatment for back pain: a systematic review of qualitative and quantitative studies. *Spine.* Oct 15 2004;29(20): 2309-2318.
52. Hopayian K, Notley C. A systematic review of low back pain and sciatica patients' expectations and experiences of health care. *The spine journal: official journal of the North American Spine Society.* Aug 1 2014;14(8):1769-1780.
53. McRae M, Hancock MJ. Adults attending private physiotherapy practices seek diagnosis, pain relief, improved function, education and prevention: a survey. *J Physiother.* Oct 2017;63(4):250-256.
54. Linton SJ. The socioeconomic impact of chronic back pain: is anyone benefiting? *Pain.* Apr 1998;75(2-3):163-168.
55. Butler DS. *The Sensitive Nervous System.* Adelaide: Noigroup; 2000.
56. Louw A, Podolak J, Zimney K, Schmidt S, Puentedura E. Can Pain Beliefs Change in Middle School Students? A Study of the Effectiveness of Pain Neuroscience Education. *Physiother Theory Pract.* 2017 - Accepted for publication.
57. Louw A, Diener I, Landers MR, Puentedura EJ. Preoperative pain neuroscience education for lumbar radiculopathy: a multicenter randomized controlled trial with 1-year follow-up. *Spine.* Aug 15 2014;39(18):1449-1457.
58. Cleland JA, Fritz JM, Childs JD. Psychometric Properties of the Fear-Avoidance Beliefs Questionnaire and Tampa Scale of Kinesiophobia in Patients with Neck Pain. *Am J Phys Med Rehabil.* Feb 2008;87(2):109-117.
59. George SZ, Bialosky JE, Fritz JM. Physical therapist management of a patient with acute low back pain and elevated fear-avoidance beliefs. *Physical therapy.* Jun 2004;84(6):538-549.
60. Sterling M, Jull G, Vicenzino B, Kenardy J. Sensory hypersensitivity occurs soon after whiplash injury and is associated with poor recovery. *Pain.* Aug 2003;104(3):509-517.
61. GL M, DS B. *Explain Pain Supercharged.* Adelaide: NOI Group; 2017.
62. Louw A, Puentedura EL, Mintken P. Use of an abbreviated neuroscience education approach in the treatment of chronic low back pain: A case report. *Physiother Theory Pract.* Jan 2012;28(1):50-62.
63. Wolff MS, Hoskins Michel T, Krebs DE, Watts NT. Chronic pain- assessment of orthopedic physical therapist's knowledge and attitudes. *Physical therapy.* 1991;71:207-214.
64. Latimer J, Maher C, Refshauge K. The attitudes and beliefs of physiotherapy studetns to chronic back pain. *Clinical Journal of Pain.* 2004;20:45-50.
65. Louw A, Louw Q, Crous LCC. Preoperative Education for Lumbar Surgery for Radiculopathy. *South African Journal of Physiotherapy.* July 2009 2009;65(2):3-8.
66. Schwartz T. *The Way We're Working Isn't working.* First ed. New York, NY: Free Press; 2010.
67. Dijk DJ, von Schantz M. Timing and consolidation of human sleep, wakefulness, and performance by a symphony of oscillators. *Journal of biological rhythms.* Aug 2005;20(4): 279-290.
68. Segal TY, Hindmarsh PC, Viner RM. Disturbed adrenal function in adolescents with chronic fatigue syndrome. *Journal of pediatric endocrinology & metabolism: JPEM.* Mar 2005;18(3):295-301.
69. Riva R, Mork PJ, Westgaard RH, Okkenhaug Johansen T, Lundberg U. Catecholamines and heart rate in female fibromyalgia patients. *Journal of psychosomatic research.* Jan 2012;72(1):51-57.

70. Jerjes WK, Peters TJ, Taylor NF, Wood PJ, Wessely S, Cleare AJ. Diurnal excretion of urinary cortisol, cortisone, and cortisol metabolites in chronic fatigue syndrome. *Journal of psychosomatic research*. Feb 2006;60(2):145-153.
71. Melzack R. Pain and the neuromatrix in the brain *Journal of Dental Education*. 2001;65:1378-1382.
72. Kregel J, Meeus M, Malfliet A, et al. Structural and functional brain abnormalities in chronic low back pain: A systematic review(). *Seminars in arthritis and rheumatism*. Oct 2015;45(2): 229-237.
73. Mair RG, Onos KD, Hembrook JR. Cognitive activation by central thalamic stimulation: the yerkes-dodson law revisited. *Dose-response: a publication of International Hormesis Society*. 2011;9(3):313-331.
74. Jull G, Moore A. Specialization in musculoskeletal physiotherapy – the Australian model. *Manual therapy*. Jun 2008;13(3):181-182.
75. Louw A, Cox T. Pain. In: Manske R, ed. *Fundamental Orthopedic Management for the PTA*. 4th ed: Elsevier; 2015.
76. Institute of Medicine . Committee on Advancing Pain Research C, Education. *Relieving pain in America: A blueprint for transforming prevention, care, education, and research*. National Academies Press; 2011.
77. Buchbinder R, Jolley D. Effects of a media campaign on back beliefs is sustained 3 years after its cessation. *Spine*. Jun 1 2005;30(11):1323-1330.
78. Buchbinder R, Jolley D, Wyatt M. 2001 Volvo Award Winner in Clinical Studies: Effects of a media campaign on back pain beliefs and its potential influence on management of low back pain in general practice. *Spine*. Dec 1 2001;26(23):2535-2542.
79. Pires D, Cruz EB, Caeiro C. Aquatic exercise and pain neurophysiology education versus aquatic exercise alone for patients with chronic low back pain: a randomized controlled trial. *Clinical rehabilitation*. 2015;29(6):538-547.
80. Moseley GL. Joining Forces – Combining Cognitiion – Targeted Motor Control Training with Group or Individual PainPhysiology Education: A Successful Tretment For Chronic Low Back Pain. *Journal of Manual & Manipulative Therapy*. 2003;11(2):88-94.
81. Louw A, Puentedura E. Therapeutic Neuroscience Education, Pain, Physiotherapy and the Pain Neuromatrix. *International Journal of Health Sciences*. 2014;2(3):33-45.
82. Louw A, Zimney K, Puentedura E. Retention of pain neuroscience knowledge: a multi-centre trial. *New Zealand Journal of Physiotherapy*. 2016;44(2):91-96.
83. Louw A, Zimney K, Puentedura E, Reed J. Immediate Effects of Preoperative Pain Neuroscience Education for Patients Undergoing Total Knee Arthroplasty: A Case Series *Physiother Theory Pract*. 2017;Accepted for publication.
84. Cox T, Puentedura E, Louw A. An Abbreviated Therapeutic Neuroscience Education Session Improves Pain Knowledge in First Year Physical Therapy Students But Does Not Change Attitudes or Beliefs *Journal of Manual & Manipulative Therapy*. 2015;Accepted for Publication - Nov 2015.
85. Sim J, Adams N. Systematic review of randomized controlled trials of nonpharmacological interventions for fibromyalgia. *The Clinical journal of pain*. Sep-Oct 2002;18(5):324-336.
86. Vranceanu AM, Safren S. Cognitive-behavioral therapy for hand and arm pain. *Journal of hand therapy: official journal of the American Society of Hand Therapists*. Apr-Jun 2011;24(2):124-130; quiz 131.
87. Curtin BM, Russell RD, Odum SM. Bundled Payments for Care Improvement: Boom or Bust? *J Arthroplasty*. Oct 2017;32(10):2931-2934.
88. Scalise J, Jacofsky D. Payor Reform Opportunities for Spine Surgery: Part I: Background and Stimulus for Bundled Payments. *Clinical spine surgery*. Jun 2017;30(5):229-231.
89. Vlaeyen JW. "It's all about behavior." Paper presented at: Pain In Motion2015; Brussels, Belgium.
90. Louw A. *Why Do I Hurt Workbook*. Minneapolis, MN: OPTP; 2016.
91. Gregory P, Alexander J, Satinsky J. Clinical telerehabilitation: applications for physiatrists. *PM & R: the journal of injury, function, and rehabilitation*. Jul;3(7):647-656; quiz 656.
92. Tousignant M, Boissy P, Moffet H, et al. Patients' satisfaction of healthcare services and perception with in-home telerehabilitation and physiotherapists' satisfaction toward technology for post-knee arthroplasty: an embedded study in a randomized trial. *Telemed J E Health*. Jun;17(5):376-382.

93. Thomas K, Burton D, Withrow L, Adkisson B. Impact of a preoperative education program via interactive telehealth network for rural patients having total joint replacement. *Orthop Nurs.* Jan-Feb 2004;23(1):39-44.
94. Louw A. Therapeutic neuroscience education via e-mail: a case report. *Physiother Theory Pract.* Nov 2014;30(8):588-596.
95. Reis FJJ, Bengaly AGC, Valentim JCP, et al. An E-Pain intervention to spread modern pain education in Brazil. *Braz J Phys Ther.* Sep - Oct 2017;21(5): 305-306.
96. Louw A. *Why You Hurt Therapeutic Neuroscience Education System.* Minneapolis, MN: OPTP; 2014.
97. Latimer J, Maher C, Refshauge K. The attitudes and beliefs of physiotherapy students to chronic back pain. *The Clinical journal of pain.* Jan-Feb 2004;20(1):45-50.
98. Louw A, Vogsland R, Marth L, Marshall P, Landers M, Cox T. *Pain Neuroscience Education across Healthcare Disciplines.* Submitted for publication. 2017.
99. Boissonnault W, Bryan JM. Thrust joint manipulation clinical education opportunities for professional degree physical therapy students. *J Orthop Sports Phys Ther.* Jul 2005;35(7):416-423.
100. Zheng P, Kao MC, Karayannis NV, Smuck M. Stagnant Physical Therapy Referral Rates Alongside Rising Opioid Prescription Rates in Patients With Low Back Pain in the United States 1997-2010. *Spine* (Phila Pa 1976). May 1 2017;42(9):670-674.
101. Solimeo SL, Ono SS, Stewart KR, Lampman MA, Rosenthal GE, Stewart GL. Gatekeepers as Care Providers: The Care Work of Patient-centered Medical Home Clerical Staff. *Medical anthropology quarterly.* Mar 2017;31(1):97-114.
102. Solimeo SL, Stewart GL, Rosenthal GE. The Critical Role of Clerks in the Patient-Centered Medical Home. *Annals of family medicine.* Jul 2016;14(4):377-379.
103. Keith RA. Patient satisfaction and rehabilitation services. *Arch Phys Med Rehabil.* Sep 1998;79(9):1122-1128.
104. Brathwaite H. First impressions count. Initial contact--receptionist. *Dentessence.* Summer 1990;1(3):4-6.
105. Miles LL. Defining duties in the business arena. "When the front desk hums, the back office sings". *Dental assistant.* Jan-Feb 2007;76(1):22, 24.
106. Moseley GL, Olthof N, Venema A, et al. *Psychologically induced cooling of a specific body part caused by the illusory ownership of an artificial counterpart.* Proceedings of the National Academy of Sciences of the United States of America. Sep 2 2008;105(35):13169-13173.
107. Butler D, Moseley L. *Explain Pain.* Adelaide: Noigroup Publications; 2003.
108. Gifford L. *Aches and Pain.* Cornwall: Wordpress; 2014.
109. Moseley L. *Painful Yarns.* Minneapolis: OPTP; 2007.
110. Louw A. *Why Do I Hurt? A Neuroscience Approach to Pain.* Minneapolis: OPTP; 2013.
111. Louw A, Flynn TW, Puentedura E. *Everyone Has Back Pain.* Minneapolis, MN: OPTP; 2015.
112. Louw A, Hilton S, Vandyken C. *Why Pelvic Pain Hurts.* Minneapolis, MN: OPTP; 2014.
113. Louw A, Louw C, Zimney K. *Why Are My Nerves So Sensitive?* Minneapolis, MN: OPTP; 2014.
114. Louw A. *Your Fibromyalgia Workbook: A Neuroscience Approach.* Minneapolis, MN: OPTP; 2013.
115. Moseley GL. Reconceptualising pain acording to modern pain sciences. *Physical Therapy Reviews.* 2007;12:169-178.
116. Network PN. AMA Drops Pain as Vital Sign. 2016; https://www.painnewsnetwork.org/stories/2016/6/16/ama-drops-pain-as-vital-sign.
117. Commission J. Joint Commission Statement on Pain Management. 2016; https://www.jointcommission.org/joint_commission_statement_on_pain_management/.
118. Stenstrom CH. Home exercise in rheumatoid arthritis functional class II: goal setting versus pain attention. *J Rheumatol.* Apr 1994;21(4):627-634.
119. Louw A, Diener I, Landers MR, Zimney K, Puentedura EJ. Three-year follow-up of a randomized controlled trial comparing preoperative neuroscience education for patients undergoing surgery for lumbar radiculopathy. *J Spine Surg.* Dec 2016;2(4):289-298.
120. Louw A, Puentedura EJ, Zimney K, Schmidt S. Know Pain, Know Gain? A Perspective on Pain Neuroscience Education in Physical Therapy. *J Orthop Sports Phys Ther.* Mar 2016;46(3):131-134.
121. Louw A. If we're so good, then why are our patients so bad? *Pain and Rehabilitation.* 2016;Summer 2016(41):4-5.

122. Fernandez-de-Las-Penas C, Madeleine P, Caminero A, Cuadrado M, Arendt-Nielsen L, Pareja J. Generalized neck-shoulder hyperalgesia in chronic tension-type headache and unilateral migraine assessed by pressure pain sensitivity topographical maps of the trapezius muscle. *Cephalalgia.* Jun 8 2009.
123. Fernandez-de-las-Penas C, de la Llave-Rincon AI, Fernandez-Carnero J, Cuadrado ML, Arendt-Nielsen L, Pareja JA. Bilateral widespread mechanical pain sensitivity in carpal tunnel syndrome: evidence of central processing in unilateral neuropathy. *Brain: a journal of neurology.* Jun 2009;132(Pt 6): 1472-1479.
124. Fordyce WE. Operant conditioning as a treatment method in management of selected chronic pain problems. *Northwest Med.* Aug 1970;69(8): 580-581.
125. Moseley GL. Do training diaries affect and reflect adherence to home programs? *Arthritis and rheumatism.* Aug 15 2006;55(4):662-664.
126. Hurling R, Catt M, Boni MD, et al. Using internet and mobile phone technology to deliver an automated physical activity program: randomized controlled trial. *J Med Internet Res.* 2007;9(2):e7.
127. Mailloux J, Finno M, Rainville J. Long-term exercise adherence in the elderly with chronic low back pain. *Am J Phys Med Rehabil.* Feb 2006;85(2):120-126.
128. Prochaska JO, Velicer WF. Behavior Change: The transtheoretical model of health behaviour change. *American Journal of Health Promotion.* 1998; 12:38-48.
129. Prochaska JO, Velicer WF. Then transtheoretical model of health behaviour change. *American Journal of Health Promotion.* 1997;12:38-48.
130. Prochaska JO, Norcross JC. Stages of Change. *Psychotherapy* 2001;38(4):443-448.
131. Amrhein PC, Miller WR, Yahne CE, Palmer M, Fulcher L. Client commitment language during motivational interviewing predicts drug use outcomes. *Journal of consulting and clinical psychology.* Oct 2003;71(5):862-878.
132. Miller WR, Rollnick S. Ten things that motivational interviewing is not. *Behavioural and cognitive psychotherapy.* Mar 2009;37(2):129-140.
133. Sandberg J, Barnard Y. Deep learning is difficult. *Instruc Sci.* 1997;25(1):15-36.
134. Crabtree JL, Royeen CB, Mu K. The effects of learning through discussion in a course in occupational therapy: a search for deep learning. *J Allied Health.* Winter 2001;30(4):243-247.
135. Jones M. Clinical reasoning and pain. *Manual therapy.* 1995;1:17-24.
136. Flynn TW. Direct access: the time has come for action. *J Orthop Sports Phys Ther.* Mar 2003;33(3):102-103.
137. Louw A, Reed J, Zimney K, Puentedura E, Grimm D, Landers M. *A Randomized Clinical Trial of Preoperative Pain Neuroscience Education for Total Knee Arthroplasty.* 2018;Submitted for publication.
138. Louw A, Butler DS. Chronic Pain. In: S.B. B, Manske R, eds. *Clinical Orthopaedic Rehabilitation.* 3rd Edition ed. Philadelphia, PA: Elsevier; 2011.
139. Linton SJ. Behavioural remediation of chronic pain: a status report. *Pain.* 1986;24:125-141.
140. Kendall NAS, Linton SJ, Main CJ. *Guide to assessing psychosocial yellow flags in acute low back pain: risk factors for long term disability and work loss.* Wellington: Accident Rehabilitation & Compensation Insurance Corporation of New Zealand and the National Health Committee; 1997.
141. Campello MA, Weiser SR, Nordin M, Hiebert R. Work retention and nonspecific low back pain. *Spine.* Jul 15 2006;31(16):1850-1857.
142. Anema JR, Steenstra IA, Bongers PM, et al. Multidisciplinary rehabilitation for subacute low back pain: graded activity or workplace intervention or both? A randomized controlled trial. *Spine.* Feb 1 2007;32(3):291-298; discussion 299-300.
143. Hildebrandt J, Pfingsten M, Saur P, Jansen J. Prediction of success from a multidisciplinary treatment program for chronic low back pain. *Spine.* 1997;22:990-1001.
144. Bogduk N. Management of chronic low back pain. *The Medical journal of Australia.* Jan 19 2004;180(2):79-83.
145. Kaapa EH, Frantsi K, Sarna S, Malmivaara A. Multidisciplinary group rehabilitation versus individual physiotherapy for chronic nonspecific low back pain: a randomized trial. *Spine.* Feb 15 2006;31(4):371-376.

146. Chou R, Loeser JD, Owens DK, et al. Interventional therapies, surgery, and interdisciplinary rehabilitation for low back pain: an evidence-based clinical practice guideline from the American Pain Society. *Spine*. May 1 2009;34(10):1066-1077.
147. Garcia AN, Saragiotto BT. Multidisciplinary biopsychosocial rehabilitation for chronic low back pain (PEDro synthesis). *British journal of sports medicine*. Sep 23 2015.
148. Kamper SJ, Apeldoorn AT, Chiarotto A, et al. Multidisciplinary biopsychosocial rehabilitation for chronic low back pain: Cochrane systematic review and meta-analysis. *Bmj*. 2015;350:h444.
149. Bono CM, Ghiselli G, Gilbert TJ, et al. An evidence-based clinical guideline for the diagnosis and treatment of cervical radiculopathy from degenerative disorders. *The spine journal: official journal of the North American Spine Society*. Jan 2011;11(1):64-72.
150. Bennett RM. Multidisciplinary group programs to treat fibromyalgia patients. *Rheumatic Disease Clinics of North America*. 1996;22(2, May):351-367.
151. Bonifazi M, Suman AL, Cambiaggi C, et al. Changes in salivary cortisol and corticosteroid receptor-alpha mRNA expression following a 3-week multidisciplinary treatment program in patients with fibromyalgia. *Psychoneuroendocrinology*. Oct 2006;31(9):1076-1086.
152. Arnold LM, Bradley LA, Clauw DJ, Glass JM, Goldenberg DL. Multidisciplinary care and stepwise treatment for fibromyalgia. *The Journal of clinical psychiatry*. Dec 2008;69(12):e35.
153. Carville SF, Arendt-Nielsen L, Bliddal H, et al. EULAR evidence-based recommendations for the management of fibromyalgia syndrome. *Annals of the rheumatic diseases*. Apr 2008;67(4): 536-541.
154. Goldenberg DL. Multidisciplinary modalities in the treatment of fibromyalgia. *The Journal of clinical psychiatry*. 2008;69 Suppl 2:30-34.
155. Goldenberg DL. Using multidisciplinary care to treat fibromyalgia. *The Journal of clinical psychiatry*. May 2009;70(5):e13.
156. Bruehl S. Complex regional pain syndrome. *Bmj*. 2015;351:h2730.
157. Becker N, Bondegaard Thomsen A, Olsen AK, Sjogren P, Bech P, Eriksen J. Pain epidemiology and health related quality of life in chronic non-malignant pain patients referred to a Danish multidisciplinary pain center. *Pain*. Dec 1997;73(3):393-400.
158. Eriksen J, Jensen MK, Sjogren P, Ekholm O, Rasmussen NK. Epidemiology of chronic non-malignant pain in Denmark. *Pain*. Dec 2003;106(3):221-228.
159. Coudeyre E, Jardin C, Givron P, Ribinik P, Revel M, Rannou F. Could preoperative rehabilitation modify postoperative outcomes after total hip and knee arthroplasty? Elaboration of French clinical practice guidelines. *Ann Readapt Med Phys*. Apr 2007;50(3):189-197.
160. Castel LD, Freburger JK, Holmes GM, Scheinman RP, Jackman AM, Carey TS. Spine and pain clinics serving North Carolina patients with back and neck pain: what do they do, and are they multidisciplinary? *Spine*. Mar 15 2009;34(6):615-622.
161. Choiniere M, Dion D, Peng P, et al. The Canadian STOP-PAIN project – Part 1: Who are the patients on the waitlists of multidisciplinary pain treatment facilities? *Canadian journal of anaesthesia = Journal canadien d'anesthesie*. Jun 2010;57(6):539-548.
162. Guerriere DN, Choiniere M, Dion D, et al. The Canadian STOP-PAIN project – Part 2: What is the cost of pain for patients on waitlists of multidisciplinary pain treatment facilities? *Canadian journal of anaesthesia = Journal canadien d'anesthesie*. Jun 2010;57(6):549-558.
163. Kamper SJ, Apeldoorn AT, Chiarotto A, et al. Multidisciplinary biopsychosocial rehabilitation for chronic low back pain. *The Cochrane database of systematic reviews*. 2014;9:CD000963.
164. Karjalainen K, Malmivaara A, van Tulder M, et al. Multidisciplinary biopsychosocial rehabilitation for subacute low back pain among working age adults. *The Cochrane database of systematic reviews*. 2003(2):CD002193.
165. Karjalainen K, Malmivaara A, van Tulder M, et al. Multidisciplinary rehabilitation for fibromyalgia and musculoskeletal pain in working age adults. *The Cochrane database of systematic reviews*. 2000(2):CD001984.
166. Nijs J, Mannerkorpi K, Descheemaeker F, Van Houdenhove B. Primary care physical therapy in people with fibromyalgia: opportunities and boundaries within a monodisciplinary setting. *Physical therapy*. Dec 2010;90(12):1815-1822.
167. Doidge N. *The Brain That Changes Itself*. New York: Penguin Books; 2007.

168. Medee B, Bellaiche S, Revol P, et al. Constraint therapy versus intensive training: implications for motor control and brain plasticity after stroke. *Neuropsychological rehabilitation.* Dec 2010;20(6):854-868.
169. Candia V, Elbert T, Altenmuller E, Rau H. Constraint-induced movement therapy for focial dystonia in musicians. *Lancet.* 1999;353:42.
170. Thieme H, Mehrholz J, Pohl M, Behrens J, Dohle C. Mirror therapy for improving motor function after stroke. *The Cochrane database of systematic reviews.* 2012;3:CD008449.
171. Kho AY, Liu KP, Chung RC. Meta-analysis on the effect of mental imagery on motor recovery of the hemiplegic upper extremity function. *Australian occupational therapy journal.* Apr 2014;61(2):38-48.
172. Bryce TN, Biering-Sorensen F, Finnerup NB, et al. International Spinal Cord Injury Pain (ISCIP) Classification: Part 2. Initial validation using vignettes. *Spinal cord.* Jun 2012;50(6):404-412.
173. Seifert CL, Mallar Chakravarty M, Sprenger T. The complexities of pain after stroke – a review with a focus on central post-stroke pain. *Panminerva medica.* Mar 2013;55(1):1-10.
174. Nampiaparampil DE. Prevalence of chronic pain after traumatic brain injury: a systematic review. *JAMA.* Aug 13 2008;300(6):711-719.
175. Foley PL, Vesterinen HM, Laird BJ, et al. Prevalence and natural history of pain in adults with multiple sclerosis: systematic review and meta-analysis. *Pain.* May 2013;154(5):632-642.
176. Hsu E, Cohen SP. Postamputation pain: epidemiology, mechanisms, and treatment. *Journal of pain research.* 2013;6:121-136.
177. Ruts L, Drenthen J, Jongen JL, et al. Pain in Guillain-Barre syndrome: a long-term follow-up study. *Neurology.* Oct 19 2010;75(16):1439-1447.
178. Fil A, Cano-de-la-Cuerda R, Munoz-Hellin E, Vela L, Ramiro-Gonzalez M, Fernandez-de-Las-Penas C. Pain in Parkinson disease: a review of the literature. *Parkinsonism & related disorders.* Mar 2013;19(3):285-294; discussion 285.
179. Smart KM, Blake C, Staines A, Doody C. The Discriminative validity of "nociceptive," "peripheral neuropathic," and "central sensitization" as mechanisms-based classifications of musculoskeletal pain. *The Clinical journal of pain.* Oct 2011;27(8):655-663.
180. Acerra NE, Souvlis T, Moseley GL. Stroke, complex regional pain syndrome and phantom limb pain: can commonalities direct future management? *Journal of rehabilitation medicine: official journal of the UEMS European Board of Physical and Rehabilitation Medicine.* Mar 2007;39(2):109-114.
181. Pinto PR, McIntyre T, Almeida A, Araujo-Soares V. The mediating role of pain catastrophizing in the relationship between presurgical anxiety and acute postsurgical pain after hysterectomy. *Pain.* Jan 2012;153(1):218-226.
182. McGowan L, Luker K, Creed F, Chew-Graham CA. How do you explain a pain that can't be seen?: the narratives of women with chronic pelvic pain and their disengagement with the diagnostic cycle. *British journal of health psychology.* May 2007;12(Pt 2):261-274.
183. Sutton KS, Pukall CF, Chamberlain S. Pain ratings, sensory thresholds, and psychosocial functioning in women with provoked vestibulodynia. *Journal of sex & marital therapy.* 2009;35(4):262-281.
184. Pukall CF, Young RA, Roberts MJ, Sutton KS, Smith KB. The vulvalgesiometer as a device to measure genital pressure-pain threshold. *Physiological measurement.* Dec 2007;28(12):1543-1550.
185. Pukall CF, Smith KB, Chamberlain SM. Provoked vestibulodynia. *Women's health.* Sep 2007;3(5):583-592.
186. Pukall CF, Baron M, Amsel R, Khalife S, Binik YM. Tender point examination in women with vulvar vestibulitis syndrome. *The Clinical journal of pain.* Sep 2006;22(7):601-609.
187. Puentedura EJ, Louw A. A neuroscience approach to managing athletes with low back pain. *Physical therapy in sport: official journal of the Association of Chartered Physiotherapists in Sports Medicine.* Aug 2012;13(3):123-133.
188. Hill AV, Long CN, Lupton H. The effect of fatigue on the relation between work and speed, in contraction of human arm muscles. *The Journal of physiology.* Mar 14 1924;58(4-5):334-337.
189. Kayser B. Exercise starts and ends in the brain. *European journal of applied physiology.* Oct 2003;90(3-4):411-419.
190. Milton J, Solodkin A, Hlustik P, Small SL. The mind of expert motor performance is cool and focused. *NeuroImage.* Apr 1 2007;35(2):804-813.

191. Witt JK, Linkenauger SA, Bakdash JZ, Proffitt DR. Putting to a bigger hole: golf performance relates to perceived size. *Psychonomic bulletin & review.* Jun 2008;15(3):581-585.
192. Crews DJ, Landers DM. Electroencephalographic measures of attentional patterns prior to the golf putt. *Medicine and science in sports and exercise.* Jan 1993;25(1):116-126.
193. Milton JG, Small SS, Solodkin A. On the road to automatic: dynamic aspects in the development of expertise. *Journal of clinical neurophysiology: official publication of the American Electroencephalographic Society.* May-Jun 2004;21(3):134-143.
194. Deecke L, Scheid P, Kornhuber HH. Distribution of readiness potential, pre-motion positivity, and motor potential of the human cerebral cortex preceding voluntary finger movements. *Experimental brain research.* 1969;7(2):158-168.
195. Page MG, Campbell F, Isaac L, Stinson J, Katz J. Parental risk factors for the development of pediatric acute and chronic postsurgical pain: a longitudinal study. *Journal of pain research.* 2013;6:727-741.
196. Fleming-McDonnell D, Czuppon S, Deusinger SS, Deusinger RH. Physical therapy in the emergency department: development of a novel practice venue. *Physical therapy.* Mar 2010;90(3): 420-426.
197. Lebec MT, Jogodka CE. The physical therapist as a musculoskeletal specialist in the emergency department. *J Orthop Sports Phys Ther.* Mar 2009;39(3): 221-229.
198. de Gruchy A, Granger C, Gorelik A. Physical Therapists as Primary Practitioners in the Emergency Department: Six-Month Prospective Practice Analysis. *Physical therapy.* Sep 2015;95(9):1207-1216.
199. Oliveira A, Gevirtz R, Hubbard D. A psycho-educational video used in the emergency department provides effective treatment for whiplash injuries. *Spine.* Jul 1 2006;31(15):1652-1657.
200. Hellsing A, Linton SJ, Kalvemark M. A prospective study of patients with acute back and neck pain in Sweden. *Physical therapy.* 1994;74:116-128.
201. Jeffrey Kao MC, Minh LC, Huang GY, Mitra R, Smuck M. Trends in ambulatory physician opioid prescription in the United States, 1997-2009. *PM & R: the journal of injury, function, and rehabilitation.* Jul 2014;6(7):575-582 e574.
202. Bigos SJ, Battie MC, Spengler DM, al. e. A longitudinal, prospective study of industrial back injury reporting. *Clinical Orthopedics and Related Research.* 1992;279:21-34.
203. Fritz JM, Magel JS, McFadden M, et al. Early Physical Therapy vs Usual Care in Patients With Recent-Onset Low Back Pain: A Randomized Clinical Trial. *JAMA.* Oct 13 2015;314(14):1459-1467.
204. Lederman E. The fall of the postural-structural-biomechanical model in manual and physical therapies: Exemplified in lower back pain. *CPDO Online Journal.* March 2010 2010:1-14.
205. Fernandez E, Turk DC. The scope and significance of anger in the experience of chronic pain. *Pain.* May 1995;61(2):165-175.
206. Crombez G, Vlaeyen JWS, Heuts PHTG, Lysens R. Fear of pain is more disabling than pain itself. Evidence on the role of pain related fear in chronic back pain disability. *Pain.* 1999;80:329-340.
207. de Vries HJ, Reneman MF, Groothoff JW, Geertzen JH, Brouwer S. Factors promoting staying at work in people with chronic nonspecific musculoskeletal pain: a systematic review. *Disabil Rehabil.* 2012;34(6):443-458.
208. Mortimer M, Ahlberg G. To seek or not to seek? Care-seeking behaviour among people with low-back pain. *Scand J Public Health.* 2003;31(3):194-203.
209. Fortuna M, Teixeira S, Machado S, et al. Cortical reorganization after hand immobilization: the beta qEEG spectral coherence evidences. *PLoS One.* 2013;8(11):e79912.
210. Langer N, Hanggi J, Muller NA, Simmen HP, Jancke L. Effects of limb immobilization on brain plasticity. *Neurology.* Jan 17 2012;78(3):182-188.
211. King S, Chambers CT, Huguet A, et al. The epidemiology of chronic pain in children and adolescents revisited: a systematic review. *Pain.* Dec 2011;152(12): 2729-2738.

6.1: Introduction

In Chapter 2, education as a treatment strategy was discussed. In general, there is a lack of convincing evidence for the usefulness of education in musculoskeletal conditions as a standalone intervention.[1-4] This also applies to PNE. The latest systematic review of PNE clearly shows that education, by itself, is not as powerful as when it is combined with physical treatments, especially movement-based treatments such as exercise (Figure 6.1).[5] This phenomenon is part of the rationale as to why CBT might have shifted powerfully to focus more on the behavioral component of the approach (Chapter 5). The limited efficacy of education alone can be clearly appreciated when you consider the evidence regarding education for smoke cessation, weight loss, etc., yet current smoke cessation studies show an efficacy around 20 percent.[6-8] In a famous quote on the limited efficacy of education alone, William Fordyce, the father of CBT, stated it best:[9]

"Education to behavior change is like throwing wet spaghetti at a brick"

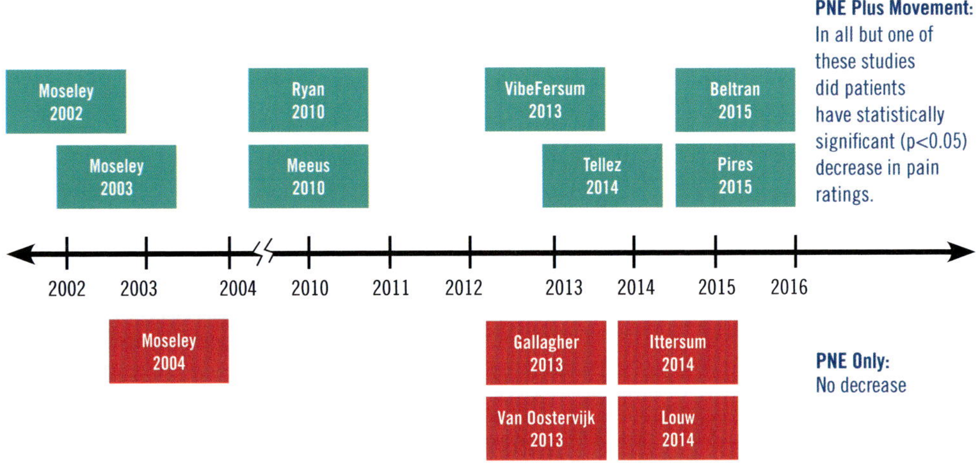

Figure 6.1: Efficacy of PNE with and without movement.[5]

The evidence seems quite clear: PNE needs additional strategies to facilitate true behavior change, hence the PNE+ program.

6.2: Biological Support for PNE+

One way to develop an appropriate PNE+ program might be to review the current literature or perform a Delphi-study to ascertain what should be added to PNE. We would not endorse such an approach, as we believe it would be telling patients what to do without providing a biological justification.[10-12] PNE by its nature uses the latest pain neuroscience information to explain to patients the biological and physiological processes associated with their pain experience. Similarly, we believe that the various treatments associated with PNE require an in-depth biological understanding. This way the explanation of pain (i.e., sensitive nervous system), can be (biologically) tied to the proposed treatment, thus helping a patient to understand why a certain treatment might help. Both PNE and PNE+ components need to be seamlessly linked together from the same explanatory understanding. For example, knowledge that increased blood flow and oxygen are an effective way to "calm the sensitive nervous system" and ease pain over time, might be far more motivational than just telling a patient to "go exercise." It is proposed that, by marrying PNE with a biological explanation for the various treatments, there might be an increased probability of compliance and follow-through,[13] as well as potential increased efficacy.[14] For example, it has been shown that explicit education about exercise-induced hypoalgesia is more advantageous than education about exercise alone.[15] The education about the nature of a treatment, especially the rationale, might powerfully impact the outcome of the proposed treatment.

In Chapters 3 and 4, we outlined the various biological systems that are engaged to protect during a pain experience in response to threat (Figure 6.2).[16] These systems include immune, sympathetic, parasympathetic, endocrine, linguistic, motor and more. These systems are activated in response to a threat, which we can metaphorically describe as a lion entering the room.[17] The activation and regulation of the various bodily systems are complex and driven primarily by changes in catecholamines, such as adrenaline and cortisol. The stress response alters the catecholamines, resulting in body-wide systems altering the physical and mental health of the patient. With prolonged alteration in these catecholamines, there are various long-lasting changes that might occur in patients with chronic pain (Figure 6.3).[18-21]

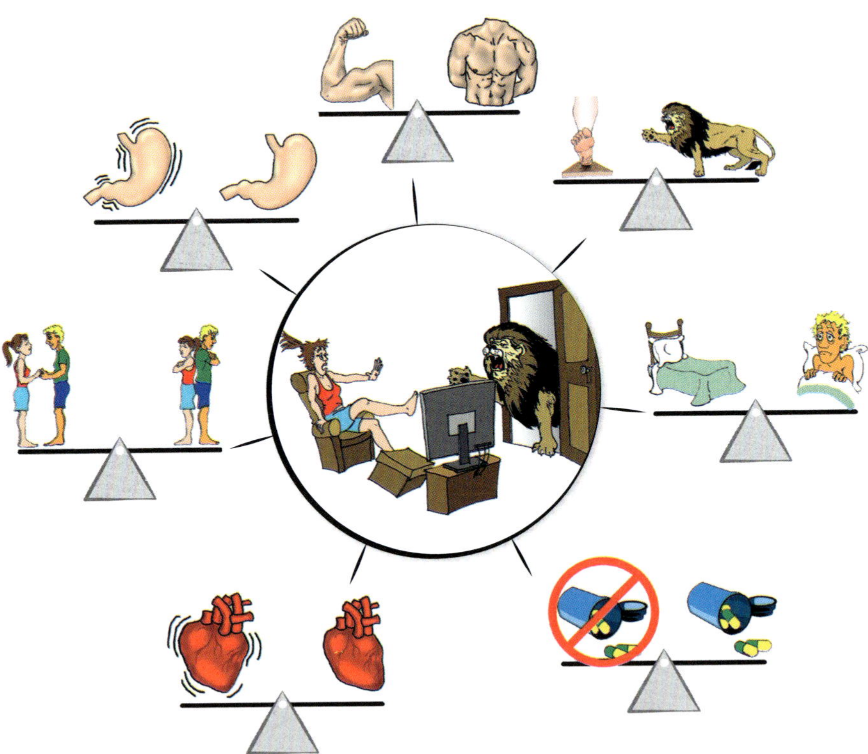

Figure 6.2: The various biological systems engaged to protect during a pain experience in response to threat.

A practical and simple way to "biologize" treatments is through the utilization of the M.O.M.[22] In the following sections, we will systematically explore each output system. The columns of each table will indicate the immediate response of the system during an acute stress response, e.g., lion jumping in the room. The second column will describe the changes to the system if the stressor remains, e.g., lion following you around for weeks, months or years. In the final column, treatment options are described, and are specifically directed at the signs and symptoms associated with the long-term changes in each system. Not only will this allow clinicians to develop a working biological knowledge of why certain treatments might work, but it might increase their PNE knowledge and ability to educate patients further.

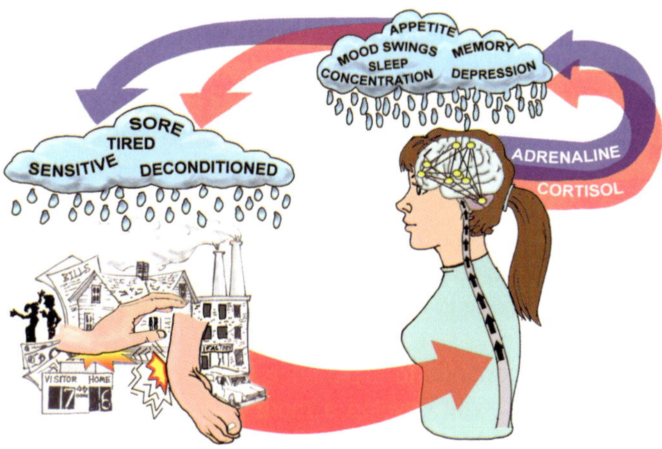

Figure 6.3: With prolonged alteration of catecholamines, long-lasting changes might occur in patients with chronic pain. Adapted from Gifford.[22]

6.2.2: Muscle/motor[34,35]

In the acute stress response, blood is diverted via catecholamine activation to areas in need of immediate protection or action, i.e., larger muscle groups.[19] In the acute phase, larger leg muscles, such as the gluteal muscles, gastrocnemius and soleus as well as quadriceps, might be needed to run away (flight response to stress). Larger muscles in the upper body might be activated, such as the deltoids, biceps and triceps, to defend. In the acute phase, smaller, less important muscles often pay the price and become inhibited. Blood, energy and oxygen is diverted away from postural muscles.[36] Over time, lack of activity of these postural muscles might lead to the development of postural disorders or muscle imbalances (Table 6.2).[37] Overactive muscles shorten and become more prone to trigger points and lengthened muscles weaken.[38] Postural muscles also become ischemic as blood and oxygen is diverted from the muscle, which might additionally contribute to the pain experience.[39]

When faced with a threat, stabilizing muscles such as transversus abdominis and lumbar multifidus have been shown to experience delays in contraction.[40-42] With an impending threat, such as a lion bursting into the room (Figure 6.2), the immediate need for joint protection via spinal stabilization would likely rank as a lower priority than muscles required to fight or flee. In cases like this, the brain and central nervous system would likely disengage the stabilizing system in favor of a flight response (avoidance of threat). Numerous studies have shown that pain changes motor control related to spinal stabilization.[43-45] Furthermore, clinicians need to remember that the motor cortex will be engaged in the pain neuromatrix, and this will likely impact motor control as well.[46-48] Similar research has demonstrated that pain affects the deep cervical spine flexors, which are designed to provide stabilization and protection in the cervical spine.[49,50] Another interesting finding is that muscles rich in proprioceptive innervation are affected in persistent pain states. With persistent pain states, such as fibromyalgia, it is well established that balance and coordination are affected over time, which might be a reflection of the various biological shifts including proprioceptive function in muscles.[51]

Table 6.2: Effects of acute and prolonged stress on activity in the muscle/motor system.

Acute response to threat	Long-term changes	Potential treatment options
• Larger muscles activate in the legs to run away, i.e., glutes, hamstrings and quadriceps • Larger upper extremity muscles activate to protect, i.e., hit, push, etc. • Smaller postural muscles deactivate (posture is not important right now) • Stabilizing muscles deactivate; transversus abdominus, multifidus and deep neck flexors (stabilization is not important right now). • Although likely a larger proprioceptive issue, it should be noted that smaller muscles containing a high number of proprioceptive fibers likely deactivate, influencing balance and proprioception	• Muscle imbalances • Fatigue • Trigger points • Balance and proprioception issues • Loss of joint protection	• PNE to explain symptoms and reduce threat • Stabilization exercise • Aerobic exercise • Isometric exercise • Posture re-education • Stretches • Range of motion exercise • Relaxation • Balance, proprioceptive and sensorimotor retraining • Trigger point therapy • Soft tissue treatment • Hydration • Biofeedback • Yoga • Tai Chi

6.2.3: Endocrine system[21,52,53]

It is now well established that pain is a neuro-endocrine-immune response.[19] The main culprit responsible for the endocrine changes is the catecholamine cortisol. Cortisol is more formally known as hydrocortisone and is a glucocorticoid steroid hormone produced by the adrenal gland. Cortisol is produced in response to stress and low levels of blood glucocorticosteroids.[54] The primary function of cortisol is to increase blood sugar, suppress the immune system and aid in fat, protein and carbohydrate metabolism. The release of cortisol from the adrenal gland is controlled by the hypothalamus. The secretion of corticotropin-releasing hormone (CRH) by the hypothalamus triggers anterior pituitary secretion of adrenocorticotropic hormone (ACTH).[19] ACTH is carried by the cells to the vascular cortex where it triggers blood secretion. Cortisol also prevents the release of substances in the body that cause inflammation. This is why cortisol is used to treat conditions resulting from over activity of the B-cell mediated antibody response such as allergies, inflammatory processes and rheumatoid diseases.[20,21,52] Cortisol also has a diurnal pattern. Levels peak in the early and late mornings, after which they decrease and bottom out between midnight and 4am or three to five hours after sleep initiation (Figure 5.8 on page 319).

Cortisol is affected by changes in ACTH, depression, psychological stress, and physiological stressors such as illness, surgery, fear, injury and pain.[20,21,25,52] Over time, cortisol dysregulation is associated with proteolysis, resulting in muscle wasting as well as reduction in bone formation (e.g., stress dwarfism in children under extreme stress such as in war zones). Furthermore, cortisol works along with adrenaline to create short-term memories. Long-term exposure to cortisol damages cells in the hippocampus, limiting learning and altering memory.[55] Systemically, cortisol changes lead to increased blood pressure, increases in the vascular system's sensitivity to adrenaline, inhibition of the reproductive system leading to low libido and temporary infertility, weight gain, appetite changes and obesity (Table 6.3).[16,20,21,25,52] Over time, the endocrine system significantly alters the immune system as well (section 6.2.5).[19,56]

Table 6.3: Effects of acute and prolonged stress on activity in the endocrine system.

Acute response to threat	Long-term changes	Potential treatment options
• Very similar to adrenaline • Shunts blood • Mobilize energy • Increase vigilance	• Changes in tissues: o Fatigue o Sensitivity o "Sore, tired, sluggish" o Deconditioned o Potential failure • Changes in the brain: o Short-term memory loss o Weight gain o Mood swings o Problems with focus and concentration o Sleep disturbance o Changes in appetite	• PNE to explain symptoms and reduce threat • Skillful delivery of medication • Aerobic exercise • Relaxation, meditation, mindfulness • Sleep hygiene • Nutrition • Aerobic exercise • Yoga • Breathing exercises • Biofeedback • Pacing

6.2.4: Pain[57]

Pain is an output by the brain based on the perception of threat.[57] A primary "system" involved with pain is the brain and central nervous system. Using the previous example of a lion in the room, an immediate stress response such as this might significantly alter the pain system. As an example, if a person was to run from the room to escape the lion and they happen to step on a nail or thumbtack, it would not likely produce pain because the lion is the greater threat to survival. Pain felt from the nail or thumbtack injury while trying to escape a bigger threat (lion) would not be advantageous for overall survival.

Once the immediate threat has dissipated (lion chase concluded), pain might be produced by the brain to make you aware of the nail or thumbtack in the foot, which will no doubt require attention. This concept is highlighted by individuals who arrive at hospital emergency departments impaled by sharp objects and with significant tissue damage, yet experience little to no pain.[58] Over time though, pain will most likely be experienced. With persistent threat, failed treatments, different explanations for pain, etc., the "pain system" will alter its state of alertness and patients will develop an extra-sensitive nervous system.[59,60] The clinical picture is dominated by central sensitization,[60,61] decreased pressure pain thresholds,[62] sensitivity to movement and decreased activity and function. Terminology that applies here includes hyperalgesia and allodynia (Table 6.4). Allodynia is pain provoked from a non-noxious stimulus such as a light brushing with a cotton swab. Hyperalgesia refers to an increased response from a stimulus that is normally painful.

Table 6.4: Effects of acute and prolonged stress on activity in the pain system.

Acute response to threat	Long-term changes	Potential treatment options
• Down regulated	• Overactive • Hypersensitive • Hyperalgesia • Allodynia	• PNE to explain symptoms and reduce threat • Skillful delivery of medication • Select modalities – ice, TENS, etc. • Aerobic exercise • Aquatic therapy • Nociceptive unloading, i.e., tape, brace, orthotic, cane, etc. • Manual therapy • Graded motor imagery

6.2.5: Immune system[63,64]

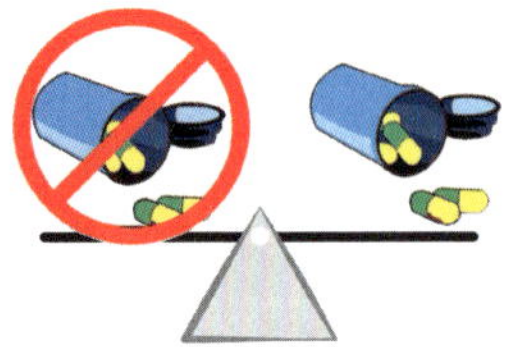

There is increasing evidence that the immune system is a key player in a human's pain experience. The immune system is very complex and, from a therapy point of view, represents a new frontier. There is strong evidence that the immune system plays a significant role in persistent pain states, widespread pain, body part recognition and inflammation.[19,56,63-65] The immune system is slow to respond and changes occur over time. In an acute stress state, spending time and energy on a sore throat is not a survival priority, and the workings of the immune system are likely to be put on hold. This might lead to a heightened vulnerability to pathogens as immune system function is suppressed.

Over time, however, immune molecules are altered by the workings of catecholamines, especially cortisol.[19,56,63-68] Altered cortisol levels cause pro-inflammatory immune molecules such as interleukin-1 (IL-1), interleukin 6 (IL-6) and tumor necrosis factor alpha (TNF-α), to proliferate, and might contribute to increased pain states. It is now well established that these immune molecules are implicated in increased neuropathic pain via ion channel activation[29,69] as well as neurogenic inflammation.[56,70] During infections, trauma or injury, cytokines such as interleukin 6 (IL-6) increase 1000-fold, thus allowing more cytokine-specific ion channels to open up, potentially resulting in increased sensitivity. This is the process that occurs in the flu.

Adding to the complexity of pain, it is also now understood that the immune system is likely to change the blood-brain and blood-spinal cord barriers, which has been implicated in increasing nervous system sensitivity and neuroplastic changes within the brain and spinal cord.[71,72] These changes are thought to be one of the mechanisms involved in the spreading of pain, receptor field changes, and problems with laterality construction of the somatosensory homunculus. With poorer representation of the body part in brain maps, pain will likely be increased to help defend. With persistent threat, clinicians might see patients develop immune deficiency over time; they seem to get the flu or infections more easily and take longer to recover. Memory changes, a sensitive nervous system, spreading pain, alterations to body schema, problems with body part recognition and increased pain are all thought to be tied to changes in the immune system response associated with persistent threat (pain) (Table 6.5).

Table 6.5: Effects of acute and prolonged stress on activity in the immune system.

Acute response to threat	Long-term changes	Potential treatment options
• Initially nothing • Start slowing down	• Immune system slows and shuts down • Immune deficiency • More prone to infection, sore throats, flu, etc. • Prolonged swelling and inflammation of tissues • Hypersensitive nerves • Tender to palpation • Memory changes • Problems with laterality • Altered body maps • Neglect • Spreading pain • Old injury sites and surgery sites increase sensitivity • Health issues	• PNE to explain symptoms and reduce threat • Skillful delivery of medication • Exercise • Sleep hygiene • Nutrition • Meditation, relaxation and mindfulness • Goal setting • Coping skills • Spirituality • Humor • Social interaction • Graded motor imagery • Sensory retraining

6.2.6: Reproductive system

Most people would agree that if they were faced with an imminent threat to their survival (e.g. a lion entering the room), their last thought would be about engaging in reproductive activities. In the immediate stress response, sexual function and sexual desire is suppressed or put on hold.[73] This is partly due to hormones but might also be due to the pain neuromatrix utilizing the brain's areas associated with emotions and arousal. Prolonged stress will lead to lower sex drive and infertility (Table 6.6). This biological mechanism of sexual down-regulation can also be affected by weight gain, lower self-esteem and even abuse, which has been shown to be prevalent in chronic pain patients.[74] Furthermore, a sensitive nervous system might also cause painful intercourse, which might contribute to the pain experience and further reduce interest in sexual activity.

Table 6.6: Effects of acute and prolonged stress on activity in the reproductive system.

Acute response to threat	Long-term changes	Potential treatment options
• Inhibited sexual interest and function	• Low libido • Self-confidence issues • Hyperalgesia • Infertility • Pain • Depression	• PNE to explain symptoms and reduce threat • Skillful delivery of medication • Pelvic health specialist • Counseling • Biofeedback • Relaxation, meditation and mindfulness • Breathing • Exercise • Graded motor imagery • Safe, healing and welcoming clinical environment

6.2.7: Language

When confronted by sudden stressful situations, people often respond linguistically in an uncharacteristic, and perhaps disinhibited manner. Should a lion jump into the room, there's likely to be a very colorful linguistic response. This is typically loud and might involve swearing.[75,76] Over time, continued stress and pain might cause a linguistic change. Patients with persistent pain become less expressive, softer spoken and withdrawn (Table 6.7). Even if patients tend to "talk a lot," clinicians will recognize that it is primarily focused on the pain they are experiencing. Patients might also describe the process of struggling to find words. Language is also likely impacted by social withdrawal, which is part of the fear avoidance model and associated with persistent pain.[77]

Table 6.7: Effects of acute and prolonged stress on language.

Acute response to threat	Long-term changes	Potential treatment options
• Short • Sharp • Abrasive • Expressive • Loud	• Softer • Less expressive • Difficulty finding words	• PNE to explain symptoms and reduce threat • PNE as new language – "alarm, soup, lion, etc." • Skilled and thorough interview • Motivational interviewing • Safe, healing and welcoming clinical environment • Therapeutic alliance • Counseling • Art and recreational therapy, i.e., coloring books • Journaling

6.2.10: Sleep

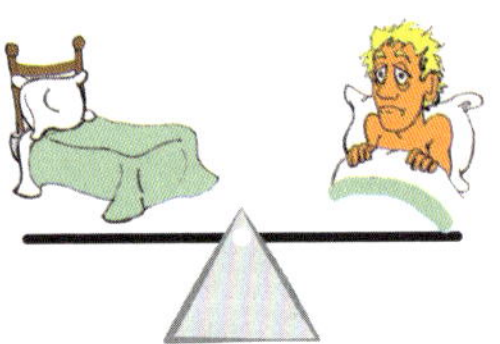

When faced with immediate danger, such as a roaring African lion, it is not time for sleep. With the adrenal system activated, a hypervigilant state is present.[23,24] Pupils dilate, hair stands up on the back of the neck and hearing increases to an acute level. Over time, cortisol causes similar changes in the adrenal system and causes significant interference with sleep (Table 6.10). Patients with chronic pain have significant problems with sleep, especially falling asleep, accessing the deeper restorative phases of sleep or staying asleep.[30,78,83] Overall, the sleep disturbance has a significant effect on fatigue.[30,78,83] Furthermore, sleep deprivation is associated with memory changes, which is prevalent in patients with chronic pain.[84] A system often associated with sleep issues is the parasympathetic nervous system (PNS). The PNS might be altered, causing changes in sleep, the nourishing of cells and the healing of tissues.

Table 6.10: Effects of acute and prolonged stress on sleep.

Acute response to threat	Long-term changes	Potential treatment options
• No sleep • Vigilance • Adrenaline	• Difficulty falling asleep • Fatigue • No deep phases of sleep • Sensitivity • Irritability • Decreased memory	• PNE to explain symptoms and reduce threat • Skillful delivery of medication • Sleep hygiene • Sleep study evaluation • Nutrition • Exercise • Relaxation, meditation and mindfulness • Breathing • Journaling • Biofeedback

6.2.11: The gastrointestinal (GI) system

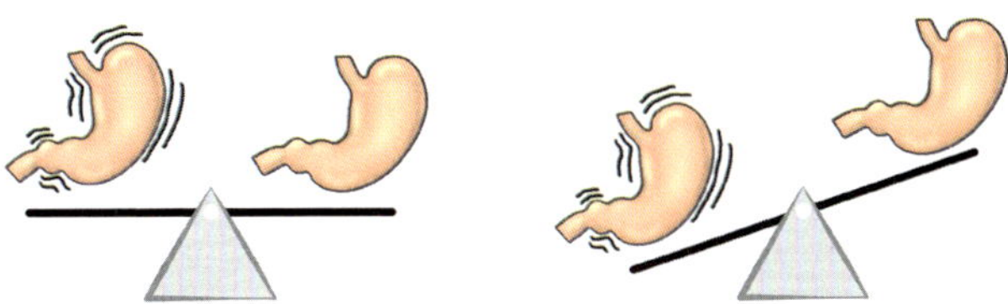

As previously stated, pain is a neuro-endocrine-immune response[19] and section 6.2.3 discusses this in detail. Section 6.2.3 delves somewhat into the GI system, but it's definitely worth a discussion as it pertains to the stress response. The increased interest in immune function and pain has recently improved our understanding of some of the mechanisms associated with irritable bowel syndrome (IBS). For example, when mast cells secrete cytokines in the proximity to mucosal innervation there is a significant increase in abdominal pain due to primary afferent neuron excitability.[85] The central nervous system affects all features of the GI tract, such as bowel movements, the perception of intestinal pain and illness behavior. Over time, prolonged stress might lead to some of the clinical manifestations seen with IBS (Table 6.11).[86,87]

Table 6.11: Effects of acute and prolonged stress on activity in the gastrointestinal system.

Acute response to threat	Long-term changes	Potential treatment options
• Slows down • Decreased activity	• Constipation • Diarrhea • Sensitive GI system • Altered eating behaviors • Abdominal pain • Malnourishment	• PNE to explain symptoms and reduce threat • Nutrition • Exercise • Relaxation, meditation and mindfulness • Biofeedback

6.3: Layout of the PNE+ Program

The various tables in section 6.2 pertaining to the suggested treatment approaches are not designed to be a comprehensive approach to intervention, but rather provide clinicians with an understanding that there is a lot that can be done for people suffering from chronic pain. Inevitably, at a weekend seminar, a course participant might say, "I have no idea what to do with a patient with chronic pain." A quick review of the various treatment options should negate that thought, especially when you consider PNE is only one of the strategies discussed. Additionally, the "plus" part of PNE+ would include a series of different strategies, which can be individualized for the patient's needs and the training of the attending clinician.

- ✔ Medication
- ✔ Meditation
- ✔ Yoga
- ✔ Isometric exercises
- ✔ Soft tissue
- ✔ Tai Chi
- ✔ Manual therapy
- ✔ Humor
- ✔ Neurodynamics
- ✔ Journaling
- ✔ Safe, welcome environment
- ✔ Balance and proprioception
- ✔ Aerobic exercise
- ✔ Mindfulness
- ✔ Nutrition
- ✔ Posture re-education
- ✔ Hydration
- ✔ Modalities
- ✔ Goal setting
- ✔ Social interaction
- ✔ Alliance/trust
- ✔ Soft tissue treatment
- ✔ Specialist consult (i.e., pelvic health)
- ✔ Range of motion exercises
- ✔ Relaxation
- ✔ Sleep hygiene
- ✔ Breathing exercise
- ✔ Stretches
- ✔ Biofeedback
- ✔ Pacing
- ✔ Spirituality
- ✔ Counseling
- ✔ Art therapy
- ✔ Graded motor imagery
- ✔ Stabilization exercises
- ✔ Trigger point therapy

The list contains 36 different potential treatments. The astute clinician will need to use his or her clinical reasoning skills, experience and intuition, along with the patient's beliefs, expectations, clinical presentation, etc., to build an individualized PNE+ program. Although other treatment strategies could certainly be added, the above list contains interventions used in conjunction with PNE in the current literature.[5] Given the best-evidence approaches for treating patients with chronic pain and current pain science knowledge, there are four key elements that must be part of the PNE+ program. The four pillars are PNE, aerobic exercise, sleep hygiene, and goal setting (Figure 6.4).

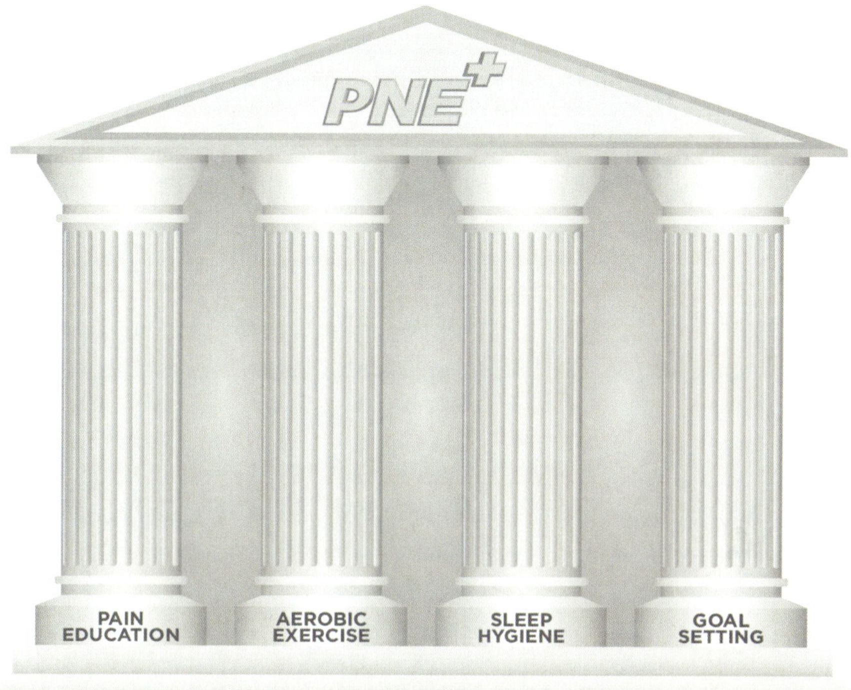

Figure 6.4: Four pillars of the PNE+ program.

The four pillars are key to recovery and it's proposed that if any of these are not in place, there might be a limitation in the recovery potential. Think of this as a vehicle with four wheels. All four are needed for travel and if one of them is flat, the vehicle cannot move. For example:

1. **PNE:** A patient might be sleeping well, exercising regularly and have goals, but have little to no idea why they hurt. If pain is produced by the brain based on perception of threat, it could be argued one of the most dangerous scenarios would be the many unknowns involved in an ongoing pain problem. Uncertainty in various forms (failed treatments, different explanations for pain, etc.) are key yellow flags and will perpetuate pain, and likely exacerbate the problem.[88] A deep, fundamental understanding of why you hurt (Gifford – *What's Wrong with Me*) is a key element in treating patients with persistent pain and, if missing, will likely result in a poor prognosis.[89]

2. **Aerobic Exercise:** A patient might have a deep biological understanding of his or her pain, sleep well and have goals, but engage in no exercise. Again, there will likely be recovery to some extent, but limited overall potential for maximum results. The overwhelming body of evidence for movement, specifically aerobic exercise, warrants its inclusion as a second pillar. If a patient such as this does little to no physical activity, the various negative effects will undoubtedly increase pain and disability. An example is Watson's disability model whereby pain leads to guarded movement, reduced activity, social and work withdrawal and physical deconditioning, which further fuels pain (Figure 6.5).[90,91] Intertwined in this process would also be concepts of fear avoidance.

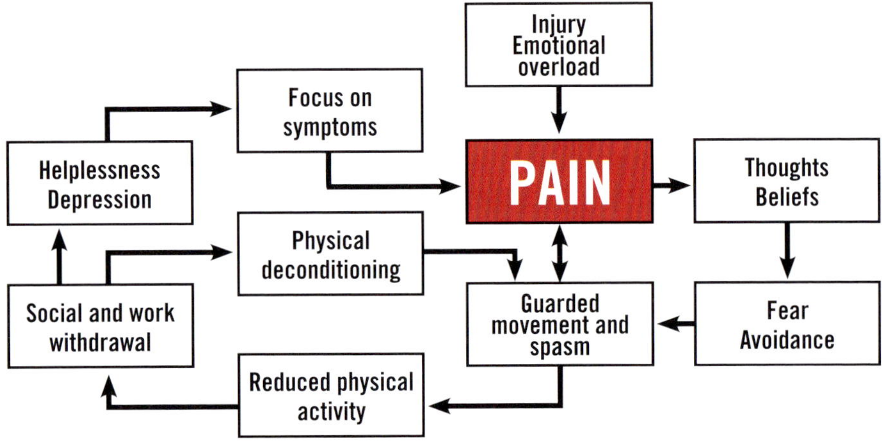

Figure 6.5: Disability model. Adapted from Watson.

3. **Sleep Hygiene:** A patient might have a deep biological understanding of their pain, exercise regularly and have goals, but might not be sleeping well, or has not slept well for a long time. Given the increased evidence for sleep affecting various biological processes including immune function, memory, tissue health, neurotransmitters, etc., it is hard to believe that having only the other elements in place will provide an optimal recovery plan. In fact, given the immense importance of sleep, it is often anecdotally stated that if a clinician can get a patient with chronic pain to experience deep, restorative and ample sleep, half the battle is won.

4. **Goal Setting:** Again, if PNE, aerobic exercise and sleep are in place but there's no internal or external motivation to change, the recovery will once again be severely limited. Many patients with chronic pain have poorly defined or no goals in place, yet it's a key element in recovery. There must be a reason to get out of bed or off the couch. Yes, the "system" might not drive this, but an internal goal (i.e., example being set for kids), might be enough to encourage patients to move forward.

6.4: Opioid Epidemic and the PNE+ Program

Before we describe strategies for the clinical application of PNE+ treatment, we need to discuss the significance of the concept of the PNE+ program to address the opioid epidemic. The current opioid epidemic prompts both the public and healthcare providers to ask, "What do we do?" As you read through the various components of the PNE+ approach, we want you to see it from the perspective of the opioid crisis. As a whole, the PNE+ program should be used as an alternative to the pharmaceutical delivery of opioids to treat pain. The various treatments we are describing have been studied extensively for their ability to turn on the non-pharmacological, naturally occurring endogenous systems, thus decreasing the need for medicine. The body of evidence in favor of the PNE+ approach versus the current use of opioids is staggering. Additionally, it can provide significant benefit with little to no side effects. It is proposed that the PNE+ program, as it's delivered and built into a patient's recovery, should coincide with the physician's tapering off the pain medication and thus be part of the anti-opioid initiative. Therapists need to study this following concept, know it well and propagate the idea:

The PNE+ program facilitates naturally occurring endogenous mechanisms, is far more powerful than the current pharmaceutical approach, and has little to no side effects. As the various aspects of the PNE+ program are applied, tapering of pharmaceuticals should occur per physician discretion.

The evidence? Below is a listing of various PNE+ components and evidence for engaging the various endogenous mechanisms. Collectively, this program demonstrates the relative efficacy of PNE+ over pharmaceutical opioids (Figure 6.6):

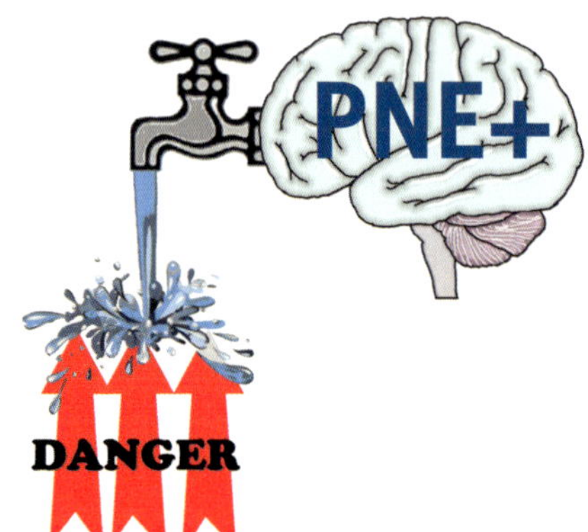

- PNE[92-94]
- Nutrition[95-98]
- Breathing[99-101]
- Biofeedback[102-104]
- Graded motor imagery[105-107]
- Safe, healing environment with compassion and empathy[108-110]
- Manual therapy[111-113]
- Neural mobilization[114-116]
- Modalities[117-119]
- Yoga[120-122]
- Relaxation and meditation[100,123,124]
- Aerobic exercise[125-128]
- Humor[129-131]
- Aquatic therapy[132,133]
- Social interaction[134-136]
- Coping skills[137-139]
- Sleep hygiene[140-142]
- Soft tissue/trigger point therapy[143-145]
- Stabilization and resistance training[146-149]
- Journaling[150-152]
- Stretches, movement and body awareness[153,154]
- Posture and position of power and confidence[155,156]

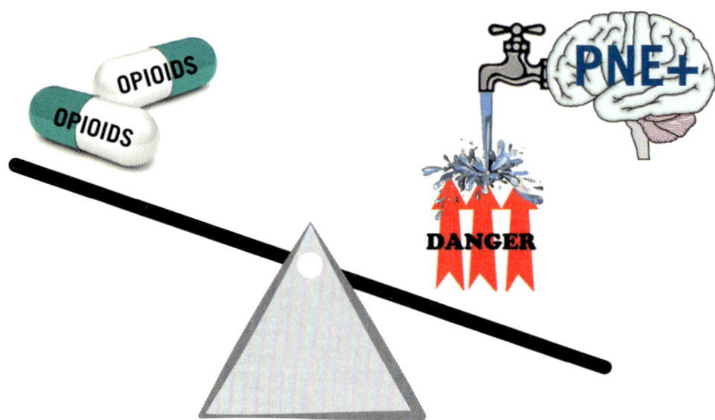

Figure 6.6: Relative efficacy of pharmaceutical opioids versus PNE+ endogenous mechanisms.

6.5: Clinical Guidelines for PNE+

For the remainder of this chapter, we provide some guidelines for the clinical application of PNE+ interventions. There are numerous books written on many of these individual topics (e.g. sleep, exercise, nutrition, etc.), therefore the intent of these guidelines is not to provide a comprehensive "how to" manual. Instead, they are based on the neuroscience theme and principles of this textbook, allowing for a more rounded biopsychosocial approach to treating patients in pain.

6.5.1: Skillful delivery of medication

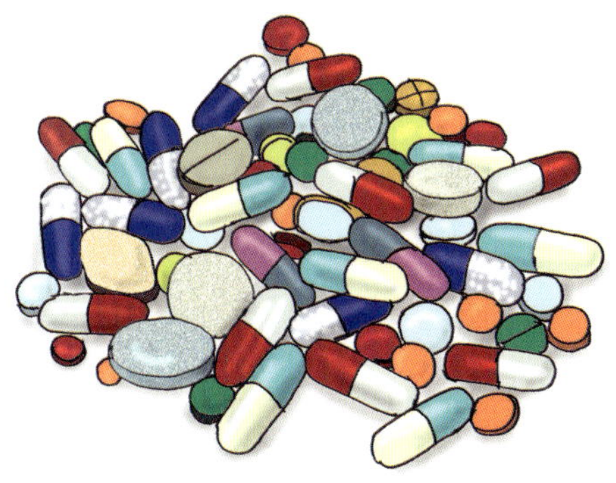

Even with the advent of the doctorate in physical therapy (DPT) and the inclusion of pharmacology into PT curricula, we would strongly advise that all pharmacological questions be directed to the patient's treating physician. However, a therapist should develop an understanding of medications used for pain management. This is important to help patients better understand the role of medication as a component of their pain intervention plan. It is well established that low dose antidepressants and membrane stabilizing medication might help patients in chronic pain.[157-159] Low dose antidepressants, such as selective serotonin reuptake inhibitors (SSRIs) or serotonin-norepinephrine reuptake inhibitors (SNRIs), likely help modulate pain by enhancing the endogenous mechanisms of the brain and balancing levels of various neurotransmitters.[159] It is believed that membrane-stabilizing medications deactivate ion channels, thus making the axon less reactive, resulting in a nerve that's less prone to fire. Patients who are too sensitive to move, exercise or be touched during therapy might have the ability to engage in movement-based therapy if medication is used to lower the sensitivity of their nervous system. Ideally, patients can be slowly tapered off the medication over time. It is important to realize that most of the membrane stabilizing medications take several weeks to have a clinical effect on pain and sensitivity. Additionally, there appear to be patient-specific characteristics or individuality to the current membrane stabilizing drugs. Patients might report that they have taken a certain membrane stabilizing drug and it did not help them, yet when switched to a different medication in the same drug class, they get much-needed relief.

6.5.2: PNE (make the threat smaller)

The theme of this textbook is PNE, an approach which has been already been described in detail. One of the primary mechanisms behind PNE is the ability to help patients reconceptualize their pain experience.[57] When patients understand more about the biology and physiology of their pain experience, the threat is lessened. We have represented these threats metaphorically as an African lion bursting into the room and the resultant stress system responses.

If a small African lion cub walked into a room, the systems need not engage. If adrenaline and cortisol do not activate, because the threat is perceived to be small, it is likely that almost none of the stress system responses cataloged in the previous sections will be required. Thus, PNE can have a significant biological effect on patients and should likely be the cornerstone of this approach.

6.5.3: Aerobic exercise

It is probably common sense that movement and exercise in general are tied to wellbeing on various levels. For example, it is now commonly stated that "sitting is the new smoking" and it's estimated that over 433,000 people die annually due to the effects of sitting too much.[160] There are many iconic studies on exercise, however, one which was particularly informative on the nature of exercise is the Dallas Bed Rest study. In this study, researchers recruited five college students to spend their summer in bed. After just three weeks in bed, the students experienced deterioration in cardiovascular fitness that was equivalent to 20 years of aging. Thirty years later, all five of the students were retested. Only two had continued to exercise with any regularity, and all had gained weight and body fat. Even so, the declines from 30 years of actual aging were less than the effects they had suffered during the original three weeks of bed rest. Immediately after being retested, the five men were put on an aerobic exercise program, which included regular walking, jogging and cycling. In just six months, the declines they had suffered over the previous 30 years were completely reversed.[161,162]

One specific exercise that is of critical value to individuals with persistent pain is aerobic exercise. Aerobic exercise is defined as activity of low to high intensity that depends primarily on the use of oxygen to adequately meet energy demands during exercise via aerobic metabolism. Aerobic exercise is important for chronic pain[68,163-169] and it has been shown to help a variety of health and pain-related issues (Table 6.12).

Table 6.12: Positive effects of aerobic exercise.

Issues	Diagnoses
• Helps with muscle disease[170] • Improves cognition[171-174] • Decreases pain/changes pain perception[175-182] • Improves sleep[183-186] • Improves quality of life[178,183,187-189] • Enhances cardiopulmonary fitness[190,191] • Improves muscle tone[190] • Oxygenates the brain[192,193] • Increases motor function[194] • Improves memory[174,195,196] • Inhibit gray matter loss[187,197] • Facilitate cortisol changes[198] • Aids the immune system[189,199-203] • Decreases chronic inflammation[199] • Decreases anxiety[204] • Lifts depression[204-207] • Improves mood[177,208,209] • Equally powerful as antidepressants[205] • Increase brain size[210,211] • Help with pregnancy, labor and delivery[191] • Helps diabetic patients with insulin function[212] • Decrease nerve sensitivity[213]	• HIV patients[189,190] • Stroke patients[194] • RA patients[176] • Panic disorder[198] • OA patients[214,215] • Migraines[188] • Helps heart disease[216,217] • PTSD[204] • LBP[179,208,218,219] • Fibromyalgia (gold-level evidence Cochrane)[167,220-222] • Brain injured patients[223] • Cystic fibroses[202] • Chronic fatigue syndrome[224]

In terms of the PNE+ approach, aerobic exercise should be seen as a very powerful tool to help patients in chronic pain. For example, aerobic exercise produces an immediate post-exercise hypoalgesia[125-128,179,225] which is just as effective as antidepressants in patients with chronic pain.[205]

Clinicians must have the necessary skills to effectively highlight the importance and benefit of an aerobic exercise program to their patient. Patients in chronic pain are often reluctant to engage in exercise because they experience pain with activity and movements. Additionally, they might believe the pain during exercise indicates they are causing harm to their tissues. PNE aims to help patients reconceptualize their pain.[57] Once PNE has changed how a patient understands their pain, the patient needs to be introduced to the benefit of aerobic exercise through a neuroscience approach. Benefits over time would include changes such as normalized adrenaline release, decreased activation of the ion channels, decreased firing of the nervous system, decreased upregulation of the central nervous system, improved respiration, improved sleep, decreased pain, improved immune function, regulation of cortisol, improved oxygenation of the brain, improved mood, improved cognitions, improved memory, improved appetite, lifting of depression, oxygenation and energizing of tissues, decreased sensitivity of tissues, and improved blood flow throughout the body.

Once a patient has been educated via PNE to reconceptualize their pain and persuaded as to the neurophysiological benefits of aerobic exercise, clinicians might consider various strategies to help patients remain compliant with their home exercise program (HEP). Strategies include the following:

- Keeping an exercise logbook[226-229]

- Providing no more than five exercises for the home exercise program (HEP)[11,230]
- Educating the patient more about the importance of exercise[12,231,232]
- Making the exercises personal to the patient rather than a generic approach[233,234]
- Treating pain before and even during the exercise program[11,235,236]
- Keeping instructions simple[237,238]
- Constantly motivating patients[233,238]
- Using low-cost equipment[238]

In addition to such strategies, clinicians might want to consider the use of electronic aids to help patients in the current and ever-evolving technical world, such as smartphones and their applications, fitness trackers, etc. In a recent study, a fully automated internet and mobile phone-based motivation and action support system was shown to significantly increase and maintain the level of physical activity in healthy adults.[229] The test group received tailored solutions for perceived barriers, a weekly schedule to plan their exercise sessions with mobile phone and email reminders, a message board to share their experiences with others, and feedback on their level of physical activity. We would strongly urge clinicians to begin looking at the use of similar technology to help remind and motivate patients about their exercise program.

While we are on the subject of using technology to enhance patient care, clinicians might consider the delivery of PNE via the use of these new technologies. Existing PNE research has demonstrated PNE can be effectively and efficiently delivered using digital media and electronic communication (Figure 6.7).[239,240] Using screening criteria (Chapter 5), it can be argued that, after risk stratification, patients might receive PNE only via telehealth (low risk) or a blended model of telehealth and personal visits (Figure 5.13; moderate risk). In the telehealth PNE case study, not only was PNE delivered but guidance on activities and exercises was also provided.[239] We propose that approaches such as this might be of significant benefit for patients in remote areas, and future research should aim to investigate such avenues.

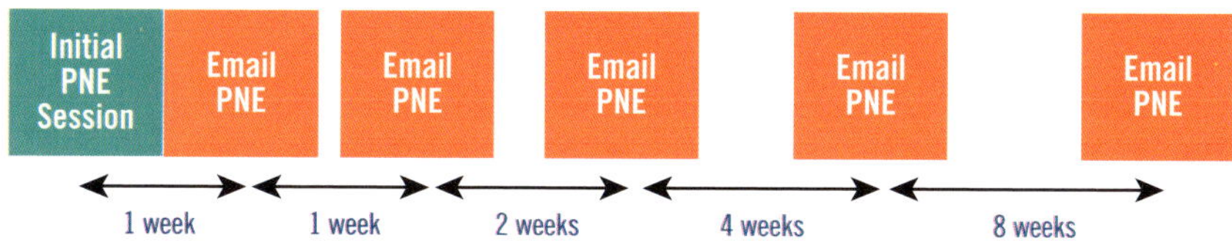

Figure 6.7: Delivery of PNE via telehealth. Image from Louw.[239]

Another strategy for increasing exercise compliance is borrowed from the body of evidence regarding procrastination.[241,242] Healthy college students were randomized into three groups to measure compliance with an exercise plan.

- **Group one:** Instructed to exercise at least once for 20 minutes during the following week with no further parameters provided.

- **Group two:** Given the same challenge, but this group was given a detailed education session about the importance of exercise in reducing the risk of heart disease, as further motivation.

- **Group three:** Asked to commit to exercising at a specific time, on a specific day, at a designated location and write down that commitment on pen and paper.

    - Results from this study showed that after a week, only 29 percent of the students in the first group reported having completed their exercise tasks.

    - Compliance rose modestly for the second group (to 39 percent) by the provision of educational motivation.

    - The third group reported greatest compliance (91 percent), and the researchers concluded that exercise, especially for personal health reasons, is a habit.

By having the students commit to the task and build it into their daily schedule, it became a routine and much easier to follow. Most people will realize that a major reason they struggle to exercise is through falling out of the habit or routine. Clinicians should endeavor to create or build a routine for their patients. Having weekly and monthly calendars available and instructing patients to write out their exercise plan by committing to specific days, times and places might increase compliance.

Two important considerations in aerobic exercise are dosage and frequency. To explore this, we should revisit the definition of aerobic exercise. Aerobic exercise is working out at an intensity of 60-70 percent of one's age-predicted maximum heart rate (HR). Commonly, age-predicted max HR is calculated as 220 minus a person's age. So, as an example, a 40-year-old patient would have a max HR of 180 (220 minus 40). In this example, 60 percent of max HR would be 108 (180 x 0.6) and 70 percent of max HR would be 126 (180 x 0.7). This means that our 40-year-old patient should be exercising at a target HR of between 108 and 126 beats per minute. The American College of Sports Medicine recently updated the method of calculating maximum HR: 211 minus 0.64 x patient's age. So, for a 40-year old patient it would be 211 – (0.64 x 40), which is 211 – 25.6, which comes to a maximum HR of 185, slightly more than the first method of calculation.

Aerobic exercise at >50% VO_2 max and for a duration >10 minutes is required to elicit exercise-induced hyperalgesia.[179]

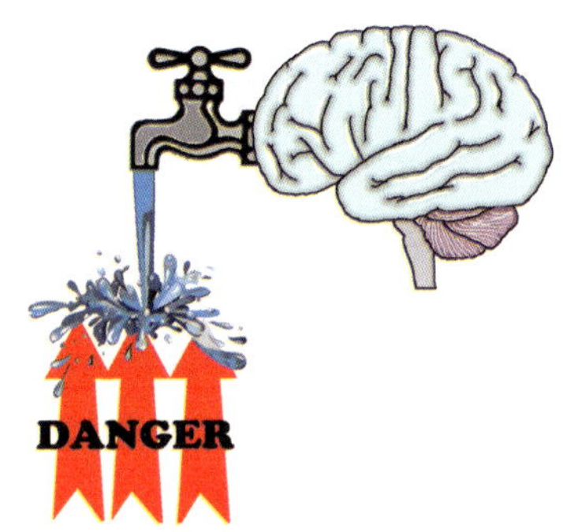

Without discussing the complexities of individualized max HR and VO_2 max, it is suggested that most patients in chronic pain should aim to raise their exercise HR to approximately 100–110 beats per minute. Clinicians should realize this is probably not that much elevated from the resting heart rate of most patients in chronic pain. A brisk walk might be all that is needed. Patients are often fearful that aerobic exercise will mean running a marathon or enduring boot camp-style vigorous exercises. This perception might cause undue stress and fear, which might in turn increase pain. Clinicians should seek to calm any fears and anxiety associated with aerobic exercise by reviewing the above information with their patient. A good example of this approach is a study on patients with chronic fatigue syndrome.[224] Patients with chronic fatigue syndrome started with five to 15 minutes of walking, five days per week, and tolerated it well. By adding one to two minutes per day, they worked their way up to 30 minutes. They had the choice to substitute walking with bicycling or swimming. After the 12-week study, more than half the patients reported feeling substantially better. After one year, 63 percent of the participants were still doing very well. In a second group of patients who were given stretches and relaxation exercises, only 25 percent reported improvement at the same follow-up point. Once again, the benefits of aerobic exercise cannot be overstated, even for chronic pain. Movement might well be one of the biggest pain killers on planet earth:[89]

A six-mile run stimulates endorphin release that is equivalent to 10 milligrams of morphine[225*]

*If you break your arm and go to the emergency room they'll likely give you between 2-3 milligrams of morphine

This section should not be taken lightly since the clinician will face a huge challenge ahead of them. We're asking people in pain, often severe pain, to exercise and move. Look at the data below:

- It has been shown in patients with chronic heart failure that only 22 percent adhere to their HEP. Further data shows that, following cardiac rehabilitation for patients who have had a heart attack, only one in seven continue their recommended exercise program.[243]

- Similarly, in the general population, up to 30 percent of individuals express no intent to exercise despite recommended activity guidelines."[244,245]

All of this information about movement and exercise is good news and plays a critical role in recovery. The evidence for exercise is compelling, but...the patient is in pain! They know exercise is good for them; they know it might even help, but you (the clinician) do not understand...they hurt! And the more they exercise, the more they hurt! It cannot be stressed enough that exercise should only be discussed once a patient has developed a better understanding of their pain. The key message of PNE is that tissues and injuries heal over time. Once they have healed, tissues can continue to be sore, sensitive and deconditioned; a significant proportion of the ongoing pain is more likely due to an oversensitive nervous system. The "alarm system" has become too sensitive in the patient with chronic pain. It only takes a few pulls on the resistance band for the alarm to go off. The important message the patient must understand is that their alarm is not signaling further injury but is more a reflection of increased sensitivity. It might be helpful to review or draw the extra-sensitive nerves for a patient as they embark on an exercise program (Figure 6.8). Patients can also be taught mantras or self-talk, a technique frequently used by athletes. For example, a marathon runner trying to qualify for the Olympic team will prepare himself, not only physically, but mentally. In this case, an experienced marathon runner will know the real race starts 20 miles into the race. He might mentally prepare through self-talk or mantras for that time of the race when the going will get tough. Patients in pain are really no different. Patients should learn, memorize and recite:

- Motion is lotion
- Hurt does not equal harm
- I am sore but I'm safe
- Movement is medicine

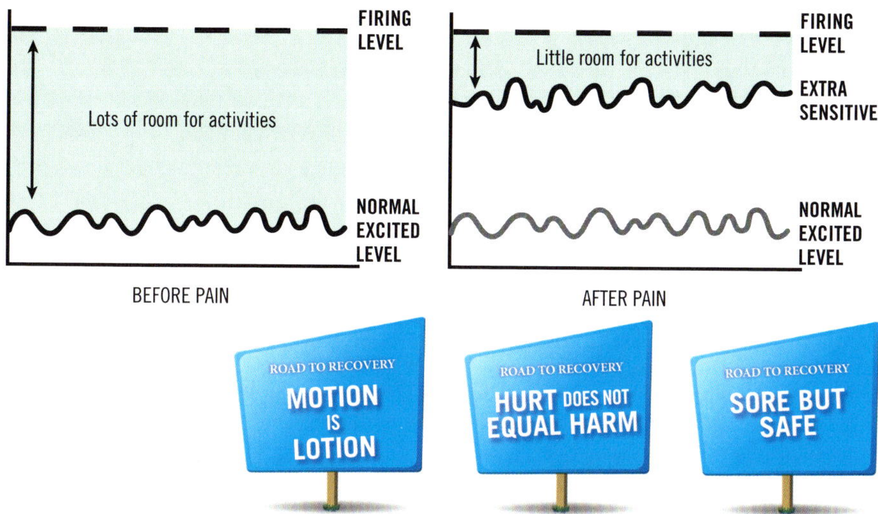

Figure 6.8: Explaining that the nervous system might be extra sensitive is an important part in helping a patient to understand why activity increases pain.

Now the really important part: The patient should be directed through a physical activity and coached through this experience. For example, once the patient has a basic understanding of the role of exercise in their pain experience, they can progress from the private treatment room to the gym area. In the gym, they might be provided a piece of resistance band and asked to perform a light task that challenges the sensitive system, possibly even provoking a pain response. The clinician should "talk them through it" making sure they understand that yes, they are feeling their pain, but it's "just sensitive" and not causing further injury. In other words, "you are sore, but you are safe." This is a critical part of the process and likely why physical and occupational therapy might be ideal to treat pain.

Conversely, there are other mantras that are likely to be detrimental to the patient in chronic pain. Two in particular are worthy of discussion; "no pain, no gain" (Figure 6.9) and "if it hurts, don't do it" (also known as – "let pain be your guide") (Figure 6.10). Or how about this one: "Pain is weakness leaving the body."

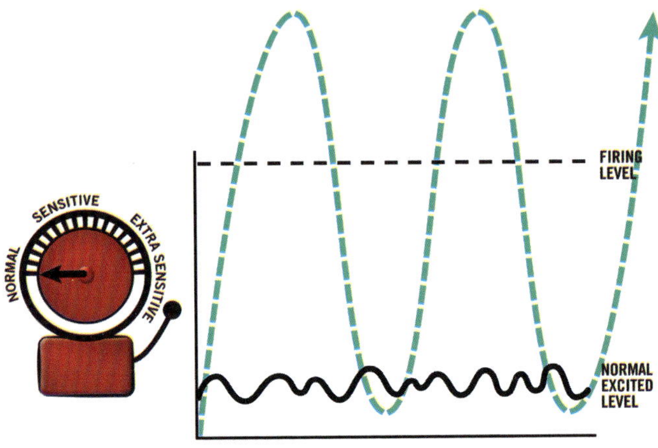

Figure 6.9: The detrimental consequences of following a "no pain, no gain" mantra when a patient has chronic pain.

In the "no pain, no gain" approach, patients might push themselves too hard, disregard their pain barrier and push too far. Pain protects, so the patient will crash and their symptoms will flare. He or she might valiantly try again, and the same will happen. This is the classic boom-bust cycle,[246] which will eventually overwhelm the patient as they will learn it does not help to push hard into pain. With failure, resentment, depression and even fear, pain is likely to be increased and will be produced earlier over time to protect. In an acute injury, such as an athlete rehabilitating from an ankle sprain, the "no pain, no gain" model might pose no particular problems, but it will likely not work in the patient with chronic pain. However, it is worth noting that an athlete who fights their way through the "no pain, no gain" scenario likely understands their pain. They expect pain, have a healthy view of pain, and likely, have very little fear of pain. Once again, knowledge is important in reducing fear. Pain that is understood does not induce fear and anxiety.

The second mantra, "if it hurts, don't do it," is probably much more common in patients with chronic pain. This approach is riddled with fear, anxiety and uncertainty. Another common phrase with a similar meaning is, "let pain be your guide." It could be argued that an approach such as this further increases the sensitivity of the alarm system by making patients focus on the exact moment he or she experiences pain. When patients focus on pain (i.e., pain ratings) it has been shown to increase their pain.[57,247] When the nervous system has become hypersensitive, a patient's ability to execute meaningful progressive tasks and exercises will be diminished considerably, and no progress will be made. In fact, given that fear and anxiety also increase nerve sensitivity, activity tolerances will continue to decrease over time, limiting exercise and movement more and more. This concept has been described in detail and is known as the classic Fear Avoidance Model.[77]

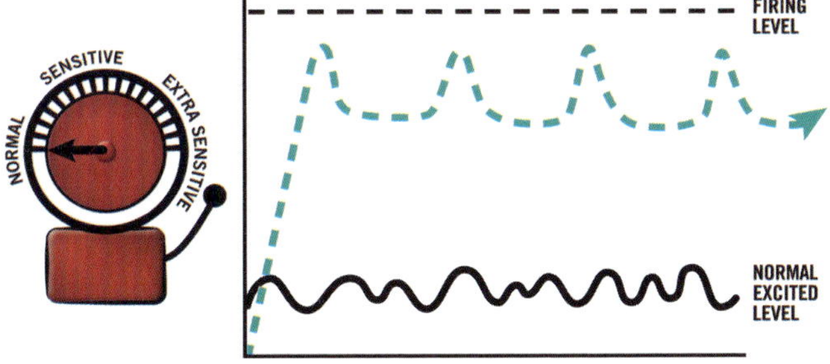

Figure 6.10: The detrimental consequences of following a "if it hurts, don't do it" mantra when a patient has chronic pain.

Because both of the previous approaches present significant limitations, clinicians might be left questioning what they can or should do for a patient with persistent pain. An alternative approach of "tease it, touch it, nudge it" (Figure 6.11) appears to lead to better outcomes over time for this patient population. In such an approach, patients are instructed to exercise or do a task slightly into some discomfort but not to charge well beyond the pain threshold or to stop short of pain. They need to operate within a "challenge it in order to change it" mindset.

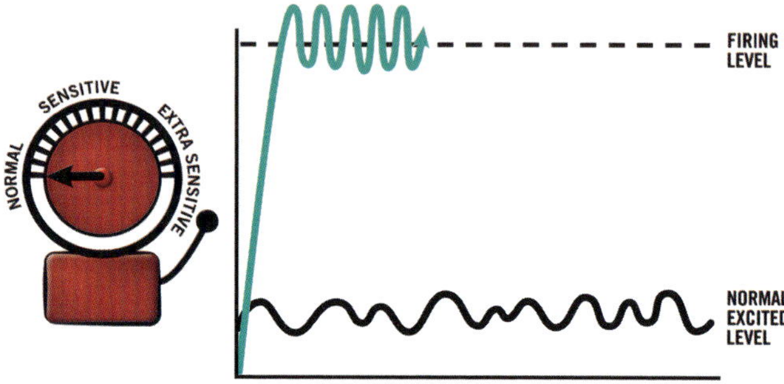

Figure 6.11: The concept of exercising and performing activities to the point of onset of discomfort or "tease it, touch it, nudge it," where 'it' represents pain.

Armed with improved knowledge about the neurobiology of pain, mantras, and coaching from the clinician, the patient will succeed. In this scenario (Chapter 4) it is important to be armed with, use and reiterate metaphors such as (Figure 6.12) (see Chapter 4):

- "It's OK to take pain out to dinner, but don't date it"
- "Don't burn the popcorn"
- "Don't burn the toast"

Figure 6.12: Powerful metaphors for graded exposure of exercise when experiencing discomfort.

Over time, the pain threshold will gradually increase as they reap the benefits of exercising, allowing them to push a little further with the exercise. Over time, the numbers, distance and time will increase: five minutes of walking becomes six, followed by seven, etc. (Figure 6.13).

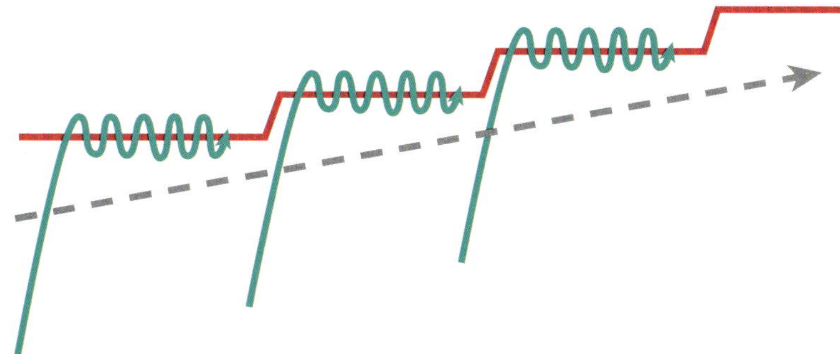

Figure 6.13: Over time, the patient will be able to perform more repetitions and longer sets over a longer time period as the pain threshold increases, allowing them to do more without experiencing their pain.

In line with the discussion of "teasing pain," a common clinical question is how much pain is acceptable during exercise and even various daily tasks. One example might be the pain acknowledgement scale (Figure 6.14). The beauty of the scale is in its name – "acknowledgement" – meaning pain is expected, acknowledged and yet, movement and function is still being performed.

Figure 6.14: Pain acknowledgement scale.

Even though we're focusing on aerobic exercise (Section 6.5.4 will focus on resistance training), it is imperative that clinicians consider all forms of exercise as a way to facilitate movement, wellbeing and activity. As appropriate, this could include swimming, Tai Chi, walking, step aerobics, cycling, etc. The goal is to have patients dedicate 20-30 minutes per day (at least five days a week) to do aerobic exercise. What about the other times during the day? It is proposed that patients be engaged in an overall strategy to improve movement on a regular basis or, as the commercials say, "Beat yesterday.™" The commercial outflow of this thought process is the FitBit™, Apple Watch™, fitness tracker devices, etc. Figure 6.15 highlights strategies to improve daily movement:

- **General physical activity:** During the course of the day and just by virtue of being alive, you perform general activity and expend energy. For example, getting up from a chair, walking, and going to the restroom.

- **Planned exercise:** This would fit into the aerobic category we have been discussing. These are preplanned, deliberate exercises. According to the American College of Sports Medicine, a weekly goal of 150 minutes, or at least three sets of 20 minutes of vigorous exercise per week is a target. This might include jogging, swimming, walking and weight training.

- **Health enhancing physical activity (HEPA):** HEPA is a deliberate attempt at performing activities toward your general health on a regular basis. Good examples include taking the stairs instead of the elevator, spending part of your lunch break doing a physical activity, standing at your desk and taking regular walking breaks versus sitting all the time, etc. This is deliberate but generalized activity performed throughout the day.

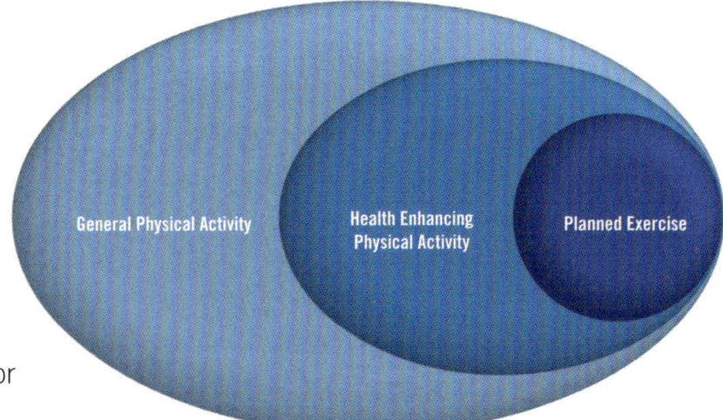

Figure 6.15: Strategies for human movement.

With the increased interest in wearable technology and evidence for its ability to positively influence activity levels,[248-250] patients can be encouraged to perform more HEPAs. This strategy can also be turned into a cognitive homework assignment whereby a patient can write down a typical day (maybe a weekday and weekend day) and then personally develop strategies to increase their activity purposefully.

6.5.4: Resistance training

In contrast to all the available research on aerobic exercise and pain, less is known about resistance training. Additionally, there does not appear to be compelling evidence that patients in chronic pain have become significantly weak.[251,252] In fact, evidence suggests that you have to lose 70 percent muscle mass to become structurally weak.[253-255] Bed rest, limited movement and generally decreased functioning might take a toll, but most of these patients will have become deconditioned rather than exhibiting true muscle weakness. The available evidence for strengthening in patients with chronic pain suggests the use of lighter weight and resistance exercise along with higher repetitions.[251,252,256,257] Clinically, it might be worth thinking of lighter-weight, higher-repetition exercises as conditioning exercises and another way to bring about increased heart rate, blood flow and oxygenation of tissues.

It should also be recognized that educating a patient that they need strengthening exercises might give them the impression of weakness, which in turn might produce fear and anxiety. Resistance exercises should therefore be described as conditioning exercises when communicating with the patient. As with aerobic exercise, conditioning exercises should be preempted with PNE and a reminder of the extra sensitivity of their nervous system. They should understand that the experience of some transient pain during exercise is normal and likely not signaling true tissue damage. Finally, conditioning exercises should not focus on pain. Patients should be encouraged to focus on a certain number of repetitions, duration or distance.[258] Not only will this help to de-focus pain, but reinforce the message that pain is not important in this case.

One area of resistance training that is getting more attention is the use of isometric exercises.[126] As with aerobic exercise, this naturally occurring hypoalgesic effect via isometric contractions occurs in normal healthy controls, but not in some patients with chronic pain, i.e., fibromyalgia.[259] Additionally, in line with other areas of research, the hypoalgesic effect of isometric exercises appears to be decreased in the elderly.[260] It is believed that a change in central processing mechanisms might be associated with the decreased effect in people with chronic pain. As to the mechanisms behind how isometric exercises reduce pain, several theories have been put forward. One theory proposes that the application of isometric exercises enhances hypoalgesia via a baroreceptor-related mechanism.[261] With increased force of isometric exercise, blood pressure is increased, resulting in a hypoalgesic effect. Additionally, recent work has shown that isometric exercises increase endogenous circulating chemicals, resulting in increased pressure pain thresholds and decreased pain ratings.[262]

An interesting clinical finding is that isometric exercises lead to hypoalgesia in both the local exercised areas as well as in more remote body regions. For example, in a study where nociceptive input was applied to the sural nerve (leg), pain inhibition was induced via isometric handgrip exercises at one, 10 and 15 percent of maximum voluntary contraction. This alone would be a huge consideration for people too painful to move. By contracting remote muscles, a modulating effect can be facilitated in the painful region. Another powerful example is where patients with chronic neck pain following a motor vehicle collision were given "wall squats" resulting in decreased neck pain.[263]

6.5.5: Spinal stabilization

The amount of research on spinal stabilization for LBP over the past two decades has been truly impressive.[264-266] Much of that research has focused on muscle properties, fine-wire needle electromyography findings in healthy and painful volunteers, muscle contractile properties, pain inhibition, effect of fear and catastrophization on motor control, imaging studies, physical tests associated with motor control, and more.[43,267-274] Additionally, similar research related to the cervical spine that focused on deep cervical spine flexors as a method to improve cervical spine stabilization has been conducted.[49,264,275,276]

The purpose of this section discussing spinal stabilization is not to review spinal stabilization theory but to discuss the clinical application of spinal stabilization in patients with chronic pain. Spinal stabilization has been proposed as a treatment for patients with chronic LBP.[280-283] Despite the popularity of spinal stabilization, controversy has ensued. The controversy has surrounded an approach whereby clinicians teach patients a very specific approach that focuses on specific muscles (e.g., transversus abdominis) using a specific sequence of retraining using biofeedback equipment or diagnostic ultrasound.[281,284,285] This is often referred to as "specific" spinal stabilization. This approach is summarized by Hodges as "firing the right muscles at the right time, in the right sequence for the right amount of time and then disengaging at the appropriate time."[266] This approach is attributed to researchers from Queensland University, including Hodges, Jull, Richardson and Hides.[264-266]

In contrast to the specific approach, it has also been postulated that stabilization can be retrained as a more generalized approach. The generalized approach to stability training is not overly concerned about specific muscles, sequences of contraction, or careful monitoring and quantification of contractions. This more generalized approach has been promoted mainly by McGill.[286,287] From a broad clinical perspective, most clinicians are likely to utilize one approach or the other, with the patient in the middle (Figure 6.16).

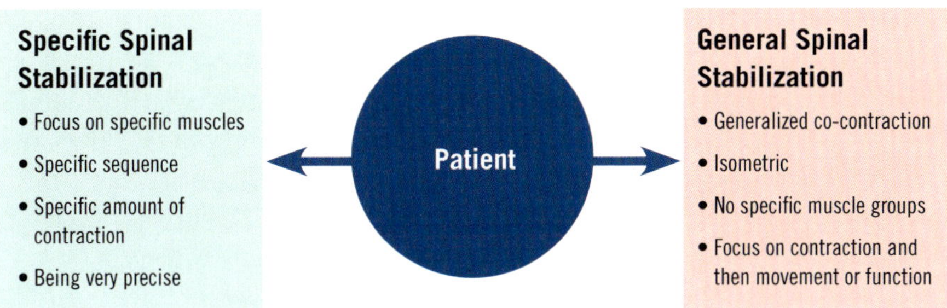

Figure 6.16: Spinal stabilization for low back pain can be approached from two differing points of view: A specific motor control approach, promoted by researchers from Queensland, versus a more general strengthening approach, advocated by researchers from Canada (McGill) and the US (Fritz).

The major contention surrounding the differing spinal stabilization approaches is the paucity of evidence for either approach. Current evidence, focusing on systematic reviews and high-quality randomized controlled trials, has failed to show that spinal stabilization exercises are superior to other forms of exercise and therapy for patients with LBP.[281,283,285,288,289] Once again, it is not our aim to describe spinal stabilization in detail but to offer useful strategies for patients with chronic pain. While it might be appropriate to focus on a specific motor control approach with some patients, we believe there is a stronger argument for a more generalized approach for patients with chronic pain. This is based on the realization that patients with persistent pain will struggle to perform small, well-coordinated tasks such as those required during the specific spinal stabilization approach. Various factors might contribute to this struggle, including:

- The motor cortex being utilized in the pain neuromatrix[93]
- Decreased importance in fine motor control when facing threat[16]
- Altered cortical representation of the low back, i.e., smudging[46-48,290]
- Psychological issues such as pain catastrophization and fear-avoidance affecting motor control[35]
- Spatial and body awareness[291]

The generalized approach we advocate for such patients would mean teaching patients a simple bracing exercise and then shifting focus quickly to more functional movements and tasks.[253] When considering spinal stabilization concepts from a PNE perspective, care should once again be directed to the language used when educating patients about their need for stabilization. Patients might assume stabilization means "instability" or weakness, which might induce fear. Additionally, if a clinician decides to opt for the specific spinal stabilization approach, with a stronger focus and emphasis on specific muscles and sequences of motor control retraining, the patient might become frustrated, as they will be unable to perform a simple abdominal drawing-in maneuver. The higher the fear, the more problems with motor control.[42]

6.5.6: Postural re-education

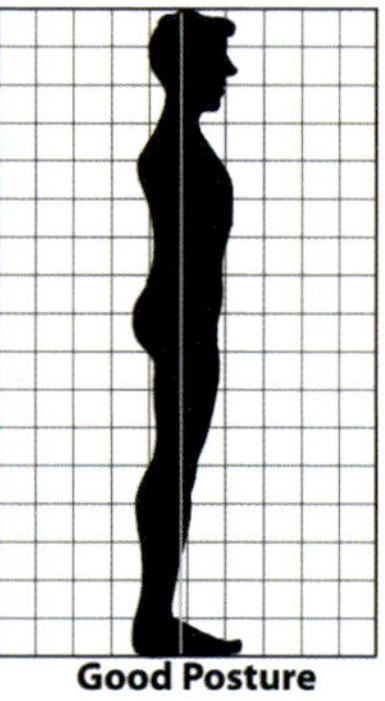
Good Posture

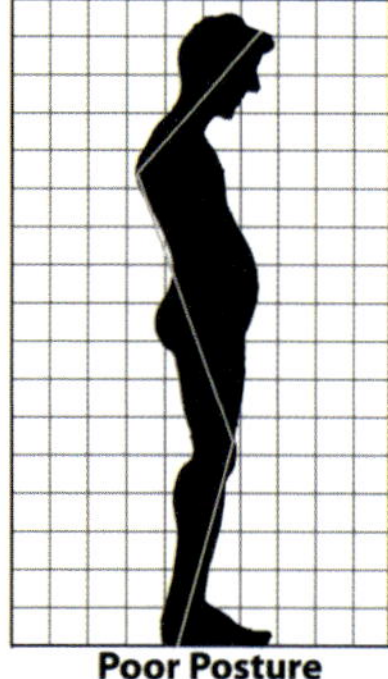
Poor Posture

One treatment commonly used in PT to address pain is analysis and correction of posture.[292,293] Various studies have shown the prevalence of postural strategies in PT to help aid patients suffering various levels of pain and dysfunction.[294-296] This includes analysis of sitting posture and pain, office workers, associations between posture and its predictive value in chronic pain, and more.[293,297,298] The main premise for these postural strategies is often based on the notion of "normal" posture, which is proposed to be associated with decreased current or future pain and disability. In contrast, any deviation from this "normal" posture is often cited as a potential reason for chronic pain.[299] This approach would thus necessitate the ability for a clinician to analyze a person's posture in order to establish if he/she displays a normal or abnormal posture, and if it is in need of treatment. To date, however, various studies have called into question the ability of clinicians to test for, or agree upon, what constitutes good posture.[300-303] For example, O'Sullivan, et. al[304] showed that 295 PTs spanning four countries who were asked to analyze nine different sitting postures had difficulty agreeing on the best sitting posture. Additionally, various studies question the correlation between posture and the prevalence of pain.[304-310] To add complexity, most studies to date have focused on healthy volunteers.[292,301,303,304,310]

If we recall the cascade of events that are likely to occur in the stress response, such as when a lion enters the room, there will be posture-related issues that develop over time. Patients will likely report pain associated with postural demands, but this might also be in part due to local tissue ischemia or altered sensitivity of the nervous system.[36] It is important that clinicians understand that even if posture is perceived to be poor, it might not correlate with pain and pathology.[304-310] A critical point to be made with respect to posture is that as long as there is the perception of threat (e.g., a lion in the room), there will be little chance for posture to be restored.

Given the neuroscience premise of constant threat and postural changes, clinicians are clinically challenged to teach patients self-correcting exercises, develop reminder strategies and focus on aerobic exercise to help oxygenate the sensitive postural muscles.[311] Some suggested strategies could include:

- Don't overemphasize posture as a source of persistent pain and thus induce increased fear
- Keep moving; it's stated that the best posture is in the next posture; therefore, keep moving
- Schedule reminders to move via notes, alarms, wearable technology (FitBit™, Apple Watch™, etc.) or even use a standing desk that can be easily altered between sitting and standing[312]
- Drink water. Not only is hydration good for you, but you need to visit the restroom frequently, thus keeping you out of prolonged postures and positions.

6.5.7: Relaxation, meditation and mindfulness[313]

Relaxation styles, approaches and schools of thought are varied. However, there is growing evidence for multiple forms of relaxation that produce positive changes in many individuals, including those with chronic conditions.[83,314-318] Clinicians might explore various strategies with their patients, but should make it as uncomplicated as possible.[313,319] Again, there are numerous ways of performing relaxation techniques, but a critical component to implementation is:

- Patients should be taught a longer, more relaxing version that might take 10-20 minutes in a designated space at home or some quiet area
- Patients should be taught a quick, 60-90 second version that can be done during stressful times such as traffic, meetings, etc.

Needless to say, relaxation is closely associated with breathing, meditation, mindfulness, therapeutic touch, etc. (see later). An example of a progressive muscle relaxation exercise can be found in Table 6.13.

Table 6.13: Example of progressive muscle relaxation.

Progressive muscle relaxation example[320]
• Begin by finding a comfortable position either sitting or lying down in a location where you will not be interrupted.
• Allow your attention to focus only on your body. If you begin to notice your mind wandering, bring it back to the muscle you are working on.
• Take a deep breath through your abdomen, hold for a few seconds, and exhale slowly.
• Again, as you breathe, notice your stomach rising and your lungs filling with air. As you exhale, imagine the tension in your body being released and flowing out of your body.
• Now let's begin. ○ Tighten the muscles in your forehead by raising your eyebrows as high as you can. Hold for about five seconds, then abruptly release feeling that tension fall away. Pause for about 10 seconds. ○ Now smile widely, feeling your mouth and cheeks tense. Hold for about five seconds and release, appreciating the softness in your face. Pause for about 10 seconds. ○ Next, tighten your eye muscles by squinting your eyelids tightly shut. Hold for about five seconds and release. Pause for about 10 seconds. ○ Gently pull your head back as if to look at the ceiling. Hold for about five seconds and release, feeling the tension melting away. Pause for about 10 seconds. ○ Now feel the weight of your relaxed head and neck sink. ○ Breathe in…and out. In…and out. Let go of all the stress. In…and out. ○ Now, tightly, but without straining, clench your fists and hold this position until I say stop. Hold for about five seconds and release. Pause for about 10 seconds.

Progressive muscle relaxation example[320]

- Now let's begin *(continued)*.
  - Now, flex your biceps. Feel that buildup of tension. You might even visualize that muscle tightening. Hold for about five seconds and release, enjoying that feeling of limpness. Breathe in...and out.
  - Now tighten your triceps by extending your arms out and locking your elbows. Hold for about five seconds and release. Pause for about 10 seconds.
  - Now lift your shoulders up as if they could touch your ears. Hold for about five seconds and quickly release, feeling their heaviness. Pause for about 10 seconds.
  - Tense your upper back by pulling your shoulders back trying to make your shoulder blades touch. Hold for about five seconds and release. Pause for about 10 seconds.
  - Tighten your chest by taking a deep breath in, then hold for about five seconds and exhale, blowing out all the tension.
  - Now tighten the muscles in your stomach by sucking in. Hold for about five seconds and release. Pause for about 10 seconds.
  - Gently arch your lower back. Hold for about five seconds, relax. Pause for about 10 seconds. Feel the limpness in your upper body letting go of the tension and stress, hold for about five seconds, and relax.
  - Tighten your buttocks. Hold for about five seconds and release, imagine your hips falling loose. Pause for about 10 seconds.
  - Tighten your thighs by pressing your knees together, as if you were holding a penny between them. Hold for about five seconds and release. Pause for about 10 seconds.
  - Now flex your feet, pulling your toes toward you and feeling the tension in your calves. Hold for about five seconds and relax, feeling the weight of your legs sinking down. Pause for about 10 seconds.
  - Curl your toes under, tensing your feet. Hold for about five seconds and release. Pause for about 10 seconds.
  - Now imagine a wave of relaxation slowly spreading through your body, beginning at your head and going all the way down to your feet. Feel the weight of your relaxed body.
  - Breathe in...and out...in...out....in...out.

Meditation is a practice where an individual operates or trains the mind or induces a mode of consciousness to allow the mind to engage in peaceful thoughts.[314,321] Meditation is often used to clear the mind, reduce stress, promote relaxation or train the mind.[124,321-323] In line with relaxation, mindfulness, yoga, Tai Chi, etc., there is growing interest in meditation. Once again, there are numerous different philosophies and approaches, and not only individual book titles, but aisles of books have been dedicated to these topics. It is highly recommended that clinicians reading this book consider making a wish list of techniques under the PNE+ program that might be of future interest when considering continuing education. In line with meditation is teaching patient strategies to declutter their life. This might be organization skills or even encouraging a patient to designate one night per week as a "TV-free" night dedicated to other helpful strategies such as reading, walking, stretching, yoga, etc.[321]

Often clumped together with relaxation and meditation is a technique referred to as mindfulness. Mindfulness is the psychological process of bringing one's attention to the internal and external experiences occurring in the present moment, which can be developed through the practice of meditation and other training.[83,100,123,324] The term "mindfulness" is a translation of the Pali term "sati," which is a significant element of some Buddhist traditions. There is an increasing interest in and evidence for the use of mindfulness for people with chronic pain.[83,324]

6.5.8: Nutrition

Any discussion of nutrition is a proverbial minefield. Few things in medicine, let alone society, polarize people and their various opinions in a way like the topic of nutrition and appropriate diet. If you think there are books or aisles in the bookstore dedicated to mindfulness and meditation, try nutrition! Once again, our aim is to alert clinicians that addressing nutrition or getting someone with chronic pain nutritional help can be a useful strategy to consider. In itself, as with any and all treatments discussed, nutrition is not the be-all and end-all. For example, a patient might be following the latest scientific diet (whatever that is), but not exercising at all, have poor sleep habits, and have limited knowledge of why they hurt. In this case, it's argued they will most likely still suffer significant pain and disability. Yes, we do agree that after the four pillars, nutrition should likely be one of the next key elements, but it is part of an overall program. None of the authors are authorities on nutrition and it is not the intent to provide nutritional advice, but rather to place nutrition into the overall PNE+ program. In regard to a clinician utilizing a PNE+ approach and nutrition, we recommend:

- Consider studying more about nutrition. As with many of the PNE+ approaches, nutrition might be something stimulating your professional interest. Going to classes on nutrition, reading and learning might be a future professional development direction. Again, it cannot be overemphasized that nutrition (just like PNE) is only one approach.

- Another clinical consideration might be consultation with a dietician. Clinicians working in large health systems have access to registered dieticians and can thus learn from them, or refer accordingly. In the private sector, clinicians might consider consulting with, hiring or sub-contracting with a dietician (Chapter 5). Most high-end grocery stores employ dieticians and patients could be directed to set up appointments with them to help their nutritional needs.

As the field of pain science expands, so will its reach into the nutritional world. Toward the end of Chapter 3, and even at the beginning of this chapter, we showcase how pain science and particularly immune activity, are gaining interest in the pain world.[85] Mast cells secrete histamine, serotonin, and cytokines. It is postulated that increased cytokine release via mast cells, along with already altered system-wide cytokine production due to long-term stress and cortisol, result in heightened sensitization of the central nervous system with increased primary afferent neuron excitability.[85,86] With increased sensitivity of the nervous system, it can be easily understood how patients develop sensitization to various foods, how distention of the tissues in the GI system might produce pain (hyperalgesia and allodynia) and affect bowel movements. This connection between the GI system through the enteric nervous system, central nervous system, and HPA axis is often referred to as the "gut-brain-axis," depicting the close relationship between the various systems once again.[85,86,325]

Every person and their circumstances are different, and it can be argued there is no magic one-size-fits-all diet, given so many different factors. This might be why there are different diets along with their followers including the anti-inflammatory diet, vegan diet, low-carb diet, low-fat diet, low-glycemic diet, Mediterranean diet, Paleolithic diet, ketogenic diet, etc.[333-339] Every now and then, consensus statements are given, only to be changed. Various meta-analyses have looked at dietary recommendations and many current best-evidence guidelines surround the notion that we should:[340]

Eat real food, not too much, mostly plants

6.5.9: Sleep hygiene[341-343]

Sleep disturbance is well documented in patients with chronic pain.[30,78,83,344] Of all the treatment strategies, restoring a healthy sleep pattern might be one of the most beneficial and provide long-lasting benefits.[341-343] The National Sleep Foundation recommends adults should sleep between seven and nine hours a day. Most people overestimate by approximately 20 percent how much sleep they get. In a Chicago study, 699 middle-aged adults reported that they slept 7.5 hours per day, but wrist monitors, worn to detect the true amount of sleep they got, reported an average of only 6.1 hours per day.[345] Many strategies have been proposed to assist patients to sleep better. From the clinical perspective, it is recommended that clinicians develop a checklist for their patient to systematically follow a set program. By having the patient add one additional strategy each night, the patient will steadily incorporate the strategies and develop a healthier sleeping pattern.[346-354] Such strategies include the following:

- **Turning the lights and television off.**[351] Lights and television stimulate the nervous system, and keeping them on until late night makes it more difficult to sleep. Ideally, have patients turn off all non-essential lights and turn the television, computers, smartphones and other electronics off one hour prior to bedtime. Patients should use this time for breathing, relaxation, reading and gentle stretches to prepare their body for sleep.

- **No napping during the day.**[347,351,352] Stating this to a patient might upset them. However, sleep cycles have been studied extensively, and if a person sleeps in the day for more than a 20-minute nap, it will have a negative effect on night sleep, which they need. This ties into the various sleep phases. It takes approximately 20 minutes to get to phase II sleep (Figure 6.17).[355,356] It is believed that once you enter phase II sleep during the day, it alters night patterns. Napping less than 20 minutes means that night sleep is not altered, so a short "powernap" can add more energy during a busy day.[355,357]

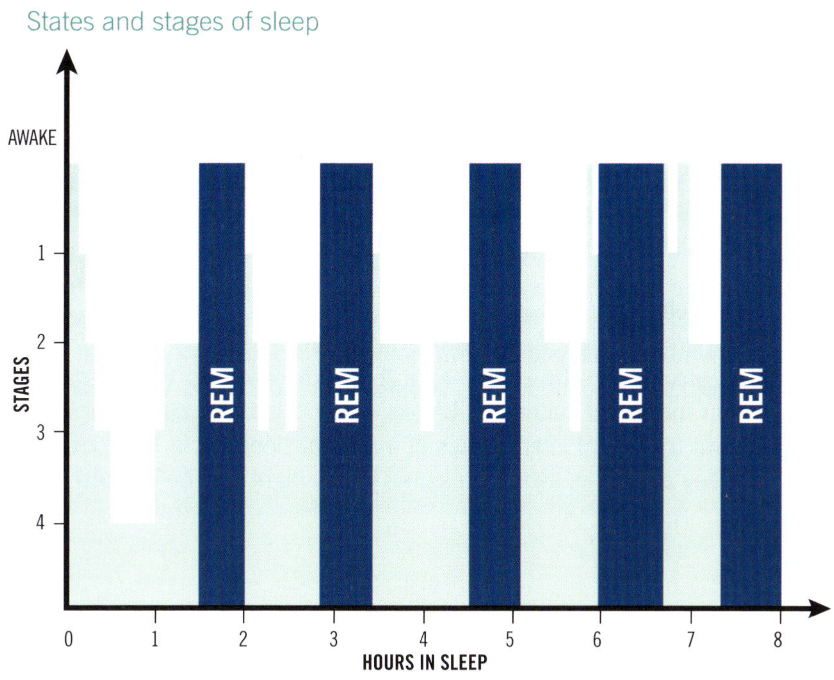

Figure 6.17: States and Stages of Sleep. From the National Sleep Foundation. REM = Rapid Eye Movement; dreams occur, accounts for 25% of the night.

6.5.11: Coping skills[363]

The ultimate goal of treatment should be independence. Patients should be taught ways to help themselves. This is a core strategy in recovery. Coping strategies are vital tools in helping a patient develop mastery over a problem in his or her life, and reduce fear and anxiety.[89] It has even been shown that coping strategies, such as the ability to take control of a situation like a flare up, have a positive effect on the immune system as well as various endogenous mechanisms.[137-139,364] Clinicians are encouraged to teach patients to engage in these coping tasks when they experience a bad day. Furthermore, clinicians might even place a reminder/sticker on the inside of a patient's HEP folder to remind them. Strategies include the following:

- **Problem solve:** Patients need to see the cause/relationship aspects of why they might experience more pain on a particular day or time. For example, they might have overdone a certain task, such as sitting too long in front of a computer or doing excessive loads of laundry, and this can be rectified in the future. Keeping true to the PNE message, specifically Chapter 1, the overload might not be only physical. There might also have been some emotional issue that caused a bad day in terms of pain. By recognizing an event and how it impacted pain, they can develop a deeper understanding of their pain.

- **Reduce nociception:** Any possible means to reduce nociception should be used, specifically the ones patients have found beneficial in the past. This might include application of ice, heat or a TENS unit.

- **Active approaches:** Patients should be encouraged to pursue active approaches to help their pain, particularly exercises like aerobic activities, such as a brisk walk, or specific stretches. Patients might even be asked to perform only a very special set of exercises on a bad day, e.g., ones marked with a red dot, or walk for five minutes only.

- **Get away:** Often a particular environment will impact pain considerably. Patients should be taught to escape the immediate "here and now" with some strategies. This might include getting up from a chair in a cubicle and going to the drinking fountain once every hour and, as they walk, taking in deep breaths and relaxing. Patients with private offices might close the door, lie on the floor and do a few breathing and relaxation exercises. A homemaker might step outside the house, walk down the sidewalk for a few minutes, turn around and return. Clocks, timers, applications or simple sticky notes can be used to remind patients to periodically "get away."

- **There is no on/off switch:** Patients should be discouraged from doing nothing. The tendency is for a patient experiencing a bad day to shut down, go home (or to the couch) and do nothing; this should be discouraged. Patients might indeed reschedule or reprioritize tasks on a bad day, but they should be encouraged to perform at least some of their scheduled tasks.

The end result of a coping strategy such as this is self-care. A patient finds ways to help him or herself and become less dependent upon the healthcare provider.

6.5.12: Social interaction

Social interaction is very important. It is well established that patients with chronic pain withdraw from life as they experience disuse, depression and disability.[365] Patients in pain limit their time out in the community, avoid family gatherings, do not go to the mall or movies, and often see their time out of the house as a time to gather supplies while living in a self-appointed confinement. It is interesting to note that social interaction plays a significant role in keeping the immune system healthy[364] and patients should be encouraged to get out of their comfort zone and experience life. Some interesting facts about social interaction:

- Social support buffers pain.[366]
- Risk factors for chronic musculoskeletal pain include poor social interaction, being widowed, separated or divorced.[367]
- Happily partnered patients in pain show less pain-related physical disability and more adaptive, affective and cognitive responses to daily pain changes than do unhappily partnered and un-partnered patients.[368,369]
- In rheumatoid arthritis, a well-adjusted or non-distressed marriage is linked with less pain and better functioning.[12,13]

- Spinsterhood in patients with rheumatoid arthritis:[370]
    - Associated with an altered quality of life even compared with distressed married women.
    - Associated with an early age at onset, severe joint pain, higher disease activity and altered functional ability.
- Social support is correlated to pain and educational level.[371,372]
- Social connection for humans is key for survival and humans have a fundamental need to belong.[373]
- Changes in activation of affective pain-related neural regions occur in response to social exclusion.[373]
- In 1992, Bill Clinton said to a protestor at a rally the now famous, "I feel your pain." Neuroscience has shown this is an actual biological phenomenon:
    - Knowledge that a loved person is in pain activates similar circuits in your own brain, especially more emotional (limbic/brainstem) parts of the circuitry.[374,375]
    - The activation for a loved person is higher than for an unfamiliar person.[374,375]

Given the opioid epidemic in the US, and the search for answers, sociologists have given us a lot to think about. Two landmark studies related to drug use surround social interaction (Table 6.15).

Table 6.15: Iconic social interaction programs showcasing their effect on heroin use.

Rat park[376]	Vietnam veterans[377]

• Original research showed that when a rat is placed by itself in an environment and given the option of drinking water or water laced with morphine, it migrates toward the morphine-laced water. This was the original work that proposed a "chemical hook" whereby once you're hooked to drugs you come back for more. • In the late 1970s, scientists repeated the experiment and created an idyllic environment whereby there were male and female rats, places to run, social environment, food, etc. Similarly, they placed the water and morphine-laced water in the enclosure and in this positive social environment, the rats migrated to the water-only side.	• When veterans returned from Vietnam, the US was bracing itself for many unknowns. • One unknown was related to the high heroin use during the Vietnam War. • With many veterans returning home and having used heroin, the concern was that many would end up with a drug problem. • Sociologists studied this phenomenon and showed that over 80 percent of the veterans stopped the heroin use when coming home. Analysis of the data showed that being able to re-engage in social life was one of the biggest factors in getting off heroin.

Table 6.15 powerfully showcases the positive influence of social interaction and, as part of the PNE+ program, clinicians should find ways to get patients re-engaging into social environments. Clinical examples:

- Exercise is good, but better when done outside or in a social environment versus on a treadmill in a lonely basement. Have patients commit to exercising outside, i.e., walking in the woods or a mall.
- Have them find an "accountability partner" that will walk with them and keep them compliant.
- Encourage going out to eat, or even going out to get a cup of coffee at least once a week.
- Encourage family gathering, going to the movies, art fairs, etc.

6.5.13: Humor[378,379]

Patients in pain don't laugh.[380] Patients with chronic pain laugh even less.[378,379] Apart from effects of pain, it is estimated that people, in general, laugh a lot less than they used to. When did you last experience a good old belly laugh? As with social interaction, it has been shown that humor correlates to a healthier immune system and various endogenous mechanisms.[129-131,364] Clinicians might use humor as a strategy to help with pain and lift depression.[380] Clinicians might consider joke books in the waiting room, a cartoon-of-the-day, joke telling, and even more importantly, not taking themselves too seriously in the clinic.

6.5.14: Manual therapy[381,382]

The application of manual therapy for chronic pain can also be a double-edged sword. Skillful delivery of manual therapy techniques has a significant potential to alter nociception, enhance the endogenous mechanisms and, ultimately, a pain experience.[111-113] Various concerns pertain to manual therapy:

1. **Models:** A significant concern is the model in which manual therapy tends to be presented to the patient. Manual therapy is often based on a single faulty structure phenomenon, i.e., a local joint. In the past, manual therapy dogma has implored clinicians to find the single faulty structure, possibly reproduce the patient's pain, and then set about "fixing" that pain.[382,383] Pain is more complex. Tissue problems and pain are poorly correlated. The patient's pain might well be elicited by a manual technique at a single level, but could that pain be experienced due to a sensitive nervous system, such as central sensitization, and fueled by high fear levels? To be fair, manual therapy has been breaching the pure biomedical realm, now including various other mechanisms behind manual therapy.[111-113]

2. **Creating dependence:** Another concern with a manual therapy approach to chronic pain is the creation of dependence. Manual therapy is a passive approach, making the patient dependent on the clinicians to manipulate/move the joint and "fix" the problem. This is a direct contrast to the ultimate goal of independence and self-help.[384] Once again, this "find it and fix it" model perpetuates the notion of a joint or a muscle as a single fault for the pain, fueling a biomedical approach.[385]

3. **Language:** Manual therapy is due for a major update in its language. First, it contains various provocative terms that fuel the biomedical model including, "instability," "derangement," "non-responder," "herniation," "disc," etc.[382,383,386] Additionally, manual therapy language focuses heavily on the use of the word "pain," including constant questions and assessments of pain.[382] As stated before, this might indeed increase the pain awareness and overall pain experience.

On the flipside, there is ample evidence that patients want to be physically touched, especially when attending PT.[387-389] Therapists should carefully consider the use of manual therapy in their patients with chronic pain states. Manual therapy, put into the right framework, can be very helpful. For example, if manual therapy is used to help gain some movement and increase blood flow, and is not proposed as fixing a structural issue, it might be a better model for a patient in chronic pain. Patients can be educated that the manual technique is being used to jumpstart some movement and help recovery, but the more active approach will help long-term. Manual therapy needs a paradigm shift. For too long, clinicians have viewed manual techniques through biomedical lenses. There are some pearls from neuroscience that can be considered for manual therapy:

1. **Plasticity:** The old biomechanical models imply that manual therapy aims at mechanical properties, i.e., a stiff spinal level or joint. Given the advances in neuroscience, specifically the structural and functional shifts in the brain, it can be argued that physical palpation (manual therapy), might also reestablish brain maps. Could it be that a gentle oscillation on spinal levels is a form of sensory integration? This concept was recently tested whereby patients with chronic LBP were given either a mechanical explanation for the ensuing manual treatment, or shown the homunculus and given a neuroplastic explanation, followed by the same manual techniques. Not only were patients able to understand the neuroplastic explanation of the ensuing manual therapy, but they experienced improved straight leg raise far superior to the mechanical explanation group.[14] Similarly, the same research group showed that just having patients with chronic LBP tell the attending clinician where they are being touched, resulted in a significant improvement in spinal movement and pain.[390] After only five minutes of random touch and the patient reporting where they are being touched, pain eased two points on a 10-point scale. Similar results have been shown for knees and shoulders.[391] This finding fits in with neuroscience research showing sensory discrimination (brain has to be involved) is superior to sensory desensitization (more passive stimulation).[392] This implies manual therapy needs to shift toward being more active, from a brain's perspective, instead of the patient having "things done to them." To engage the brain, the manual therapist can:

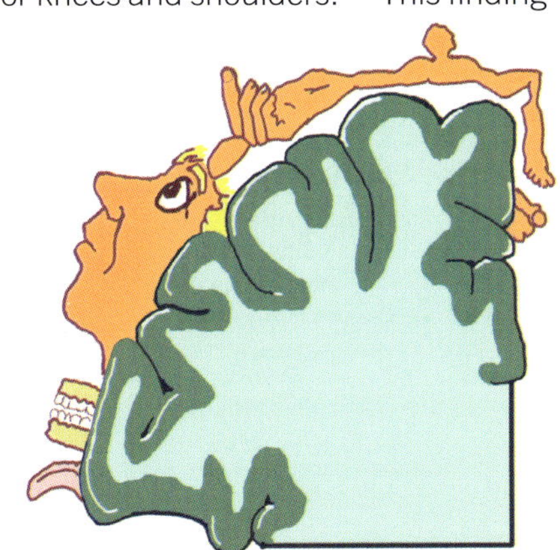

   a. Palpate and instruct on where you're palpating. For example, while palpating on L5 vertebral level, let the patient know – "this is L5." Then palpate and let the patient know another level or two, i.e., L3 and L1.

   b. As the clinician performs the manual technique, he or she can perform the oscillatory techniques but also ask the patient which level they're working on.

   c. Options to make manual therapy more brain active:

      i. Spinal levels
      ii. Sides of the spine
      iii. Light versus stronger techniques

2. **PNE is hands on:** Some individuals might perceive PNE and manual therapy to be polar opposites. Manual therapy has, by tradition, a clear focus on tissue sources of pain and dysfunction, while PNE does not.[382,393] These opposing strategies have led to a dichotomy for the modern manual therapist – is PNE a hands-on or hands-off approach?[394] Can PNE and manual therapy co-exist and, if so, how? We firmly believe that PNE and manual therapy can co-exist, but only if the aforementioned issues are considered in the rewording and reworking of the delivery of manual therapy. Clinically, a high percentage of patients presenting to therapy are often "too hot to handle," thus creating a dilemma for the manual therapist. Within the model of sensitization, it is argued that PNE can shift the sensitivity barrier positively, allowing for a space for manual therapy (Figures 6.18 and 6.19). Various studies have shown that PNE calms the nervous system (pressure pain thresholds, neurodynamics, and brain scans) which can then allow for graded exposure to palpation – mobilization.

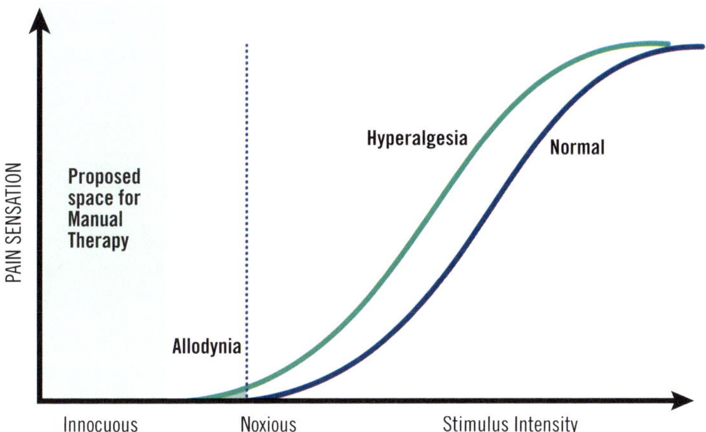

Figure 6.18: Proposed PNE-effect on sensitization, allowing for a manual therapy approach. Image from Louw, Puentedura and Nijs.[393]

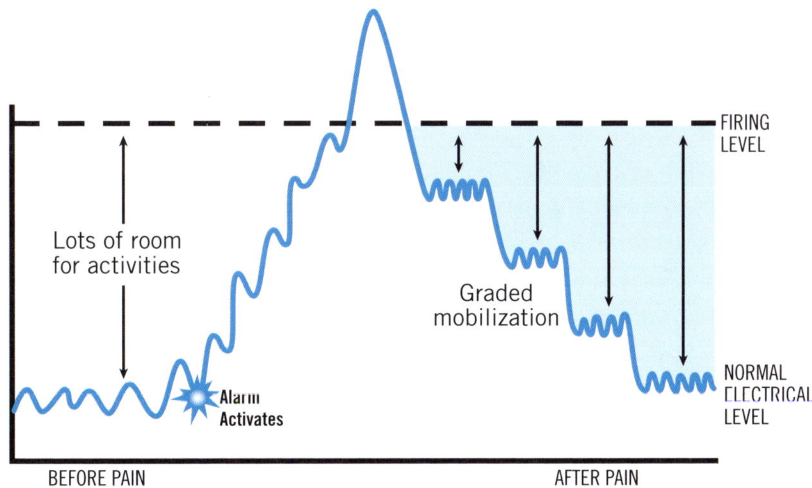

Figure 6.19: Graded mobilization using the alarm system analogy. Image from Louw, Puentedura and Nijs.[393]

In Chapter 1 we described the evolution of PNE out of the manual therapy world. In this section, we argue that manual therapy is in serious need of an "update." This might likely anger purists in the field of manual therapy, but it need not be so. The reality is that the field of pain science has provided so much information on the various mechanisms related to manual therapy, and that should be embraced. On the flipside, many clinicians learning PNE might think pain science is hands off and miss an opportunity to help people in pain. Table 6.16 should be viewed as a means to reconceptualize manual therapy from a pain science perspective. Given the collective information covered in this textbook up to this point, review the list and realize how many of the mechanisms have a neuroscience and biopsychosocial premise.

Table 6.16: Proposed pain science mechanisms for considering manual therapy.

Treatment effect
• Create space[395,396]
• Gate control[397,398]
• Activation of the endogenous mechanisms[111-113]
• Increased blood flow[399-403]
• Altered sympathethics[404]
• Changes in oxytocin[405]
• Decreased nociception[406-408]
• Plasticity[14,390,391]
• Patient beliefs and placebo[112,409]
• Neuromuscular effect[381,410-414]
• Graded exposure[393]
• Patient expectations[387-389]
• Decreased cost[415-418]

6.5.15: Modalities[419]

In this short discussion of modalities, we hope to highlight similar issues to those for manual therapy, discussed earlier. Skillful delivery of modalities such as electrical stimulation, transcutaneous electrical neuromuscular stimulation (TENS), etc., should be seen as valuable tools to help reduce nociception and might significantly impact a patient's pain experience.[419] Modality issues to consider:

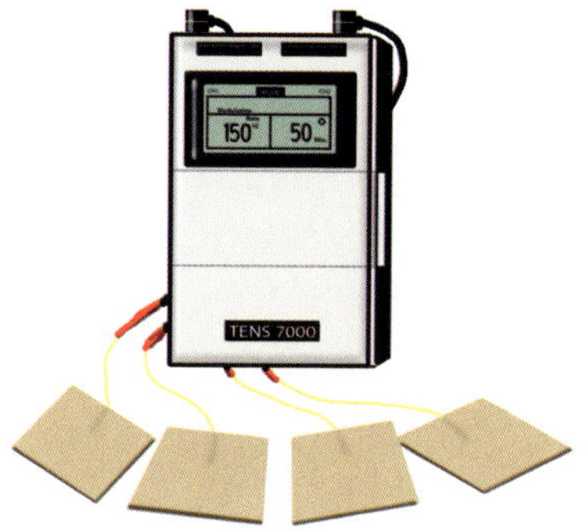

- There is evidence that various modalities increase endogenous mechanisms.[117-119]
- Gate control might be old, but not obsolete, and altering nociceptive information from the periphery (bottom up approach) has its place.
    - C fiber activity is closely linked to persistent pain by its persistent firing into the dorsal horn of the spinal cord as well as its increased release of pro-inflammatory chemicals, all associated with chronic pain. Cryotherapy has been shown to slow C fiber activity down, thus decreasing the nociception being sent into the dorsal horn and ultimately decreasing the threat appraisal of the brain.[8] Additionally, via its vasoactive properties, ice has been shown to decrease pro-inflammatory chemicals in injured and diseased tissues, which further decreases nociception.
    - Electrical stimulation, including TENS, has been shown to be effective in altering pain experiences via gate control.[9] By altering the amount and duration of peripheral input to the central nervous system it alters information passed onto the brain and the threat appraisal of the brain. Furthermore, TENS, apart from its "electrical" benefits, should be seen as a means to facilitate self-efficacy by providing a patient with the ability to help themselves with their pain and develop independence over time.
    - Recent work by Australian researchers has shown that electrical stimulation might in fact result in meaningful changes in cortical maps in the motor cortex, which in turn alter a pain experience, motor control and disability.[10]

- Numerous studies have shown that the "hot packs" might be as powerful or more powerful than most over-the-counter medications when it comes to low back pain.[11] However, neurobiologically, it's important to realize neuropathic pain increases with decreased blood flow and oxygen to the nervous system. Conversely, when blood and oxygen are increased around nerves, pain is often eased.[12] This might warrant a further investigation into modalities delivering superficial or deep heat to painful areas, including hot moist packs, diathermy, etc.

- Low-level laser therapy has been shown to stimulate various cellular responses, a process known as biophotomodulation, which promotes tissue healing, decreased inflammation and analgesia. Multiple mechanisms for analgesic effects are reported in the literature, with recent studies suggesting decreased nociception via modulation of the endogenous opioid system.[13]

- Topical analgesics, often delivered via therapeutic modalities such as ultrasound or by manual treatments, have shown considerable evidence for the treatment of acute and chronic pain, especially osteoarthritis.[14]

- Patient beliefs and modalities are intertwined and can be utilized to enhance treatments.[420,421]

- The biggest drawback for modalities is the tendency to become dependent upon their use. Modalities are inherently passive, and patients get a message of having to "go to therapy, lie on a table and receive the treatment." This goes against the current evidence for a more active, self-help approach. Clinicians might consider modalities whereby a patient can be taught and become self-reliant, e.g., TENS, to help them with their pain.[258,422] As with pharmacological approaches, patients might develop a tolerance and, over time, find less relief from such modalities. Clinicians are advised to teach patients not to use the devices all the time, and to use them specific to a task and not pain. Focusing on "when it hurts" is contrary to the PNE message. Patients should rather focus on using a TENS unit during a specific task with which they usually struggle, e.g., standing to cook a meal.

6.5.16: Aquatic therapy[423,424]

There is evidence for the use of aquatic therapy in patients with chronic pain such as fibromyalgia.[423,425] In recent PNE studies, PNE has been successfully combined with aquatic therapy.[426] Furthermore, aquatic therapy, just like most of the other movement-based approaches, has shown an ability to turn on the various endogenous mechanisms.[132,133] Unfortunately, aquatic therapy has seemingly become a dumping ground for patients with chronic pain and clinicians are encouraged to view aquatic therapy from a different perspective. The warmth of the water as well as the buoyancy will help patients move more than they might be able to on land. This freedom to move allows for increased blood flow and oxygen and, from a larger neuroscience perspective, allows healthy stimulation and mapping of body parts in the somatosensory and motor homunculi. Once again, the main concern will be dependence. Patients might become reluctant to leave the water and believe they cannot function or exercise outside the water. Clinicians should listen to their patients for evidence of poor cognitions, which will need addressing with PNE. Patients might say, "I will never be able to do without pool therapy." In such a scenario, clinicians should lay out the plan of care and explain to the patient that the aquatic environment should be but a first step, allowing them to get moving. Over time, they will be transitioning to more and more land-based therapy and exercises. This process can be compared to using a walker after a knee replacement. In the beginning it is important; it helps you get going. Over time, you transition to more independent activities.

Specific to the treatment followed during the aquatic therapy session, clinicians are encouraged to follow the exercise principles already discussed, including focusing on cardiovascular exercise, conditioning (resistance) exercise versus strength, and general stabilization. As with the land-based exercises, clinicians should be careful about the way they explain the approach, i.e., not doing "strengthening" exercises in the pool, which implies weakness. Finally, aquatic therapy should be performed under direct supervision by a clinician and this would, once again, be an ideal time to filter PNE to the patient, session-by-session.[425]

6.5.17: Welcoming, safe, healing environment

All of the treatment options discussed so far relate to this concept. We truly believe clinicians will often underestimate the ability to create a welcoming and safe healing environment. The therapeutic alliance that is developed in the clinic between a patient and clinicians has been found to be a significant variable with improving outcomes for people in pain.[427] Research projects are sterile and try to account for all outside factors, yet this phenomenon will creep into the study findings as well. Patients with chronic pain are often treated poorly, as if they have some kind of plague. Creating a welcoming clinical environment of warmth is a great start. Considering that the definition of pain is *an output of the brain based on perception of threat*, it should make sense that such a healing environment can alter a pain experience. How does this look, clinically? It starts at the front desk. As discussed in Chapter 5, front office staff should have pain science knowledge and thus start the process of educating and encouraging in the waiting room. Clinicians should listen to the patients and allow time for questions and answers. Another critical component is to keep a patient with a specific clinician. Too often, patients will be passed on from therapist to therapist, therapist to therapist assistant and, sometimes, therapist to technician. All of this impacts the patient's recovery significantly. In fact, we would challenge therapists to keep the patients all to themselves. "Own your patient."

6.5.18: Goal setting, pacing and graded exposure

Goal setting is one of the pillars of recovery. One of the biggest issues that patients with chronic pain struggle with is setting appropriate goals.[428] Patients often fall into one of two categories. One, a patient might not have any goals. Two, and more commonly, patients might have goals but they are poorly defined, non-specific, or so far out of reach that they might not see a need to try to achieve them. There are many components to goal setting and various descriptions of pacing, graded exposure, etc.[429-432] It is imperative that the patient and the therapist develop a therapeutic alliance and that goal setting be a mutual decision. Various patient factors and various clinician factors influence the ability to collaborate on goal setting (Figure 6.20).[428]

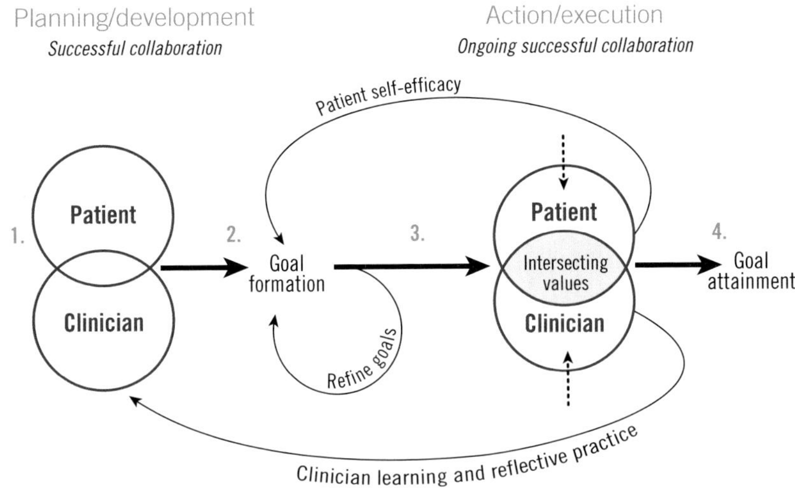

1. Both patient and clinician bring unique personal and environmental factors to the episode of care (e.g. pain beliefs, roles, experience, knowledge, social factors, etc.). A successful therapeutic alliance requires collaboration to identify shared values.

2. Continued collaboration to refine goals.

3. Successful intervention with ongoing collaboration further aligns patient/clinician values and perspective.

4. Successful goal attainment resulting in dynamic process for both patient and clinician.

Figure 6.20: Optimal clinical pathway: Collaborative goals to drive a successful plan. Image from Schmidt.[428]

In its simplest form, any task can be divided into smaller parts. Clinicians do it all the time. For example, a patient following knee replacement will go through weeks of therapy with the ultimate goals of walking, riding a bike, going up stairs, etc. Naturally, none of these activities can be performed one day after surgery. How do we set goals and help patients take small steps to accomplishing their therapy goals?[89,433] Here is an example:

- Ask your patient to write down some goals at home and bring them in. At first, don't be specific. Have them bring them in and then start molding them until they are measurable, broken down to small pieces and within reach. These first goals tend to be vague.

- See the example below that a recent patient emailed to the therapist:

Goals

1. Improve quality of life
2. Improve heart rate during cardio
3. Be happier and more positive
4. Reduce anxiety
5. Improve marriage
6. Have more energy
7. Know how it feels to be pain-free for a week

- As you can see, the goals at this early stage are very vague.

- These written goals might help with PNE. They can give you more information needed to address educational issues. Point four (reduce anxiety) is such an example. This can very easily be turned into a question: "What are you anxious about?" Maybe it's increased pain with therapy, which then allows for a small refresher education session about what pain actually means, covering sensitivity versus injury.

- We do recommend functional goals, i.e., tasks that can readily be measured and have meaning toward recovery.

- We also, however, require "deep desires." These might help patients give it another try. One clinically meaningful way we seek these would be as follows, "Suzy, if I could reach behind your back and magically switch off your pain and get rid of it all, what would you want to do again?" Patients often say things like take up dancing, play a round of golf, take a road trip or run a 5K race. The interesting thing is that there is likely no reason they cannot do any of these, given education, time and rehabilitation. This usually comes as a shock when you say, for instance, "There is nothing in your examination that shows me you are not able to do this. Sure, maybe not tomorrow, but it can be done." Maybe Suzy was a runner and her dream goal is to run a half-marathon. There is no reason she cannot run a half-marathon, just not next week. As she becomes healthier, stronger and able to push a little more, there is no reason why she could not do the local 5K race by a certain date. Sure, it will be slow, but she would have done it. After that, a few more and then a 10K, etc.

- Once goals are set, they need to be divided into smaller, more manageable pieces that will keep the patient motivated, on task, and not cause undue increased pain. Here is a good example of a patient with fibromyalgia:[425]
  - She brought her list. One main goal was to "clean her house."
  - Can you see how vague it is?
  - So, we asked her to make a list of tasks that constitute "clean the house."
  - After she brought the list (vacuuming, dusting, sweeping, mopping, etc.), we asked her which task she would choose if she could only do one. She chose vacuuming. Can you see we're now down to a specific task?
  - Then, how many rooms need vacuuming? She answered five.
  - We asked her next – if you could only vacuum one room, which one would it be? Living room. Then? Entryway and so forth. Soon the rooms were labeled A, B, C, D and E.
  - Then (the important part), we asked her – if she was to go home, take the vacuum out of the closet and vacuum a room today, how much of a room could she do before putting the vacuum away and still be OK...not wiped out on the couch? She answered a half of one room. Now, we changed the room labels to have her vacuum half a room at a time and gave her a vacuuming schedule:

Day	Room
1	A1
2	A2
3	B1
4	B2
5	C1

Day	Room
6	C2
7	D1
8	D2
9	E1
10	E2

  - Now we have a plan. In 10 days from now, this patient might actually have vacuumed her whole house! What a win.

In regard to pacing and graded exposure, clinicians might consider the following:

- Meals don't have to be cooked in one session.
- Dinner can gradually be prepared from AM to PM with rest periods between cutting vegetables for relaxation, stretches and exercise.
- All laundry does not have to be done in one day. One load per day is more than enough to keep a household going. Later, an AM load and a PM load can be done compared to doing all of it in one shot.
- All the floors do not need to be swept at the same time.
- Answering five emails at a time is progress instead of sitting in front of a computer for hours.
- Weeding a garden can be divided into manageable quadrants with neatly placed stakes.
- Walking exercise can be done in two or three small walks a day.

Everything can be paced. Take the large parts and break them down and start somewhere. Do not forget to get the patient involved. Let them come up with ideas on how to break it down; the level they think they can start at. This might include the use of motivational interviewing. Goal setting and pacing is best described by Louis Gifford:[89]

"Start easy, build slowly"

Set time-specific goals.[89,433] Patients who know they need to be ready for a task by a certain date will be more motivated. The goal might be to cook a complete meal. It might start in the AM or the day before to prepare some ingredients. As the patient gets better, stronger and accomplishes more, set a date (calendar) and have him/her invite someone for dinner. Another example might be walking. Walking should be steadily increasing, so look for a community event, e.g., a charity walk on a certain date.

6.5.19: Graded motor imagery

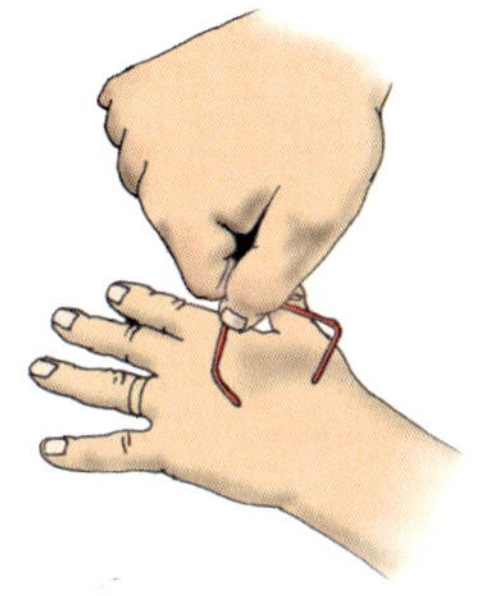

It has been shown that patients with pain display different primary somatosensory representations than people with no pain.[434-439] Growing evidence additionally supports the notion of these body maps expanding or contracting, thus essentially increasing or decreasing the body representation in the brain. The clinical importance is that these changes in shape and size of body maps seem to correlate to increased pain and disability.[434,440] Although various factors have been linked to the development of this altered cortical representation of body maps, it is believed that issues such as neglect and decreased use of the painful body part[70] might be a significant source of the altering of body maps.[71,441] One approach aimed at restoring altered body maps is graded motor imagery (GMI).[106,442-444] GMI is a collective term describing various "synaptic exercises" and include normalizing laterality (left/right discrimination of body parts), motor imagery (visualization), mirror therapy, sensory discrimination and more.[442-444] Various studies have shown GMI strategies might influence pain and movement,[106,442-444] but larger scale studies are needed to more clearly understand the effects of GMI on the wider persistent pain population.[445] Most research has focused on CRPS and LBP.[442-444,446,447] It has been proposed that GMI follows a sequential progression of treatments starting with laterality reconstruction, followed by motor imagery and then mirror therapy.[443] It has also been shown that individual remapping techniques such as mirror therapy, localization and sensory discrimination might yield clinical benefits without a sequential delivery of GMI.[391,446-450] Given there is emerging evidence for both approaches, the delivery of GMI is likely associated with the complexity of the clinical presentation (Figure 6.21).

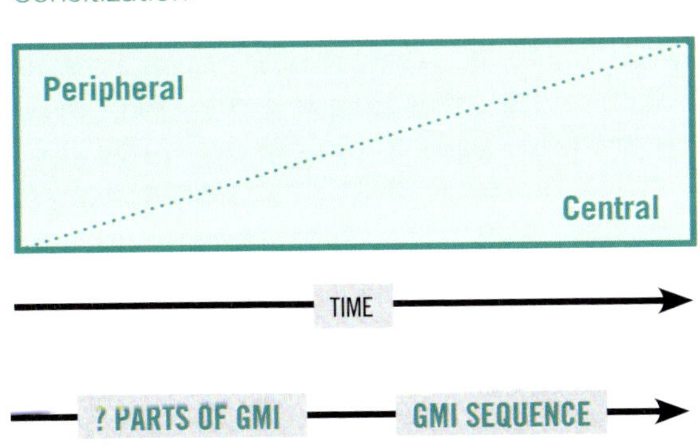

Figure 6.21: Proposed GMI clinical selection.

For example, in patients with central sensitization, hyperalgesia and allodynia, without advanced stages of neglect, a part of GMI can be used. It is also proposed that GMI be considered for the orthopedic patients with high fear-avoidance or in the postoperative period. In a recent case series, 69 patients with shoulder pain and limited range of motion, regardless of clinical presentation of central sensitization, fear-avoidance or type of pathology, raised the uninvolved arm ten times while watching it in a mirror with the affected arm behind the mirror. After only ten raises (< two minutes), there were significant differences in self-reported pain, pain catastrophization, and the Tampa Scale of Kinesiophobia, and there was also a significant increase (mean, 14.5 degrees) in affected shoulder flexion active range of motion immediately following mirror therapy (Figure 6.22).

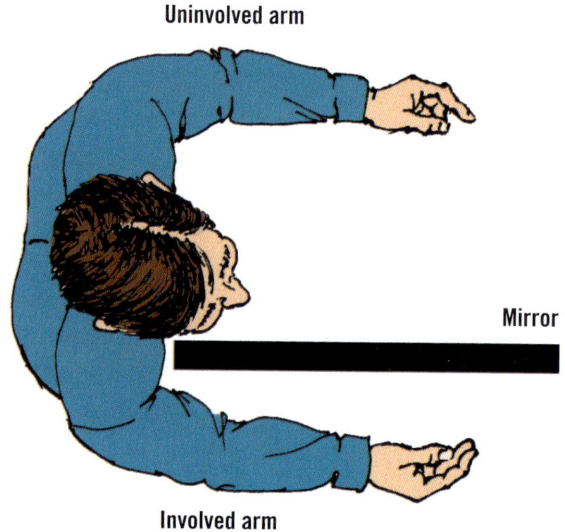

Figure 6.22: Mirror therapy for shoulder pain and limited range of motion. Image from Louw, et. al.[450]

Table 6.17 showcases the proposed GMI sequencing, with the rationale for each stage, as well as potential criteria for progression to the next stage.

Table 6.17: Proposed GMI stages.

Stage	Rationale	Potential criteria for progression
1. PNE	The patient has to have a deep understanding of their pain experience as well as why GMI is being used.[451,452]	Once the clinician believes the patient has a deep understanding of their pain and is able to verbalize and explain back to the clinician.*